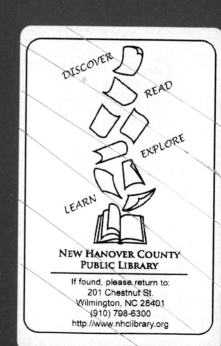

The Real History of the
COLD WAR
A New Look at the Past

Alan Axelrod

STERLING
New York / London
www.sterlingpublishing.com

Library of Congress Cataloging-in-Publication Data

Axelrod, Alan, 1952-
The real history of the Cold War : a new look at the past / Alan Axelrod.
p. cm.
Includes bibliographical references and index.
ISBN 978-1-4027-6302-1
1. Cold War. 2. World politics—1945-1989. 3. Soviet Union—Foreign relations—1945-1991. I. Title.
D843.A88 2009
909.82'5—dc22

2009012167

10 9 8 7 6 5 4 3 2 1

Published by Sterling Publishing Co., Inc.
387 Park Avenue South, New York, NY 10016

For photograph copyright information, please see
Picture Credits on page 452.
Distributed in Canada by Sterling Publishing
c/o Canadian Manda Group, 165 Dufferin Street
Toronto, Ontario, Canada M6K 3H6
Distributed in the United Kingdom by GMC Distribution Services
Castle Place, 166 High Street, Lewes, East Sussex, England BN7 1XU
Distributed in Australia by Capricorn Link (Australia) Pty. Ltd.
P.O. Box 704, Windsor, NSW 2756, Australia

Book design and layout: Oxygen Design / Sherry Williams, Tilman Reitzle

Printed in Singapore

Sterling ISBN-13: 978-1-4027-6302-1

For Anita, always

"Let us not be deceived—
we are today in the midst of a cold war."

Bernard Baruch, in a speech written by Herbert Bayard Swope, April 16, 1947

CONTENTS

THE REAL HISTORY OF THE COLD WAR

PART FOUR

CROSSING THE LINE

PART FIVE

COMBAT BY PROXY

PART SIX

DÉTENTE

Dramatis Personae

Acheson, Dean (1893–1971) U.S. secretary of state (1949–53) who played a key role in formulating early Cold War policy.

Adenauer, Konrad (1876–1967) First chancellor of the Federal Republic of Germany (West Germany), 1949 to 1963.

Allende, Salvador (1908–73) Marxist president of Chile (1970–73), who died in a U.S.-supported coup d'état led by Augusto Pinochet.

Amin, Hafizullah (1929–79) Pro-U.S. president of Afghanistan (1979) killed by Soviet KGB agents to make way for Babrak Kamal.

Andropov, Yuri (1914–84) General secretary of the Communist Party of the Soviet Union (1982–84).

Baruch, Bernard (1870–65) U.S. financier and presidential adviser, who popularized the term "Cold War."

Beria, Lavrenti Pavlovich (1899–1953) Chief of the Soviet secret police and espionage agencies under Stalin.

Brezhnev, Leonid (1906–82) General secretary of the Communist Party of the Soviet Union (1964–82).

Byrnes, James F. (1879–1972) FDR confidant, U.S. secretary of state (1945–47), and one of the architects of early Cold War policy.

Bush, George H. W. (1924–) 41st U.S. president (1989–93).

Bush, George W. (1946–) 43rd U.S. president (2001–9).

Carter, Jimmy (1924–) 39th U.S. president (1977–81).

Castro, Fidel (1926–) Cuban Marxist revolutionary who governed Cuba from 1959 to 2008, when, ailing, he turned over authority to his brother, Raoul.

Ceauşescu, Nicolae (1918–89) Dictator of Romania (1965–89) ousted in an anticommunist revolution and executed with his wife, Elena.

Chernenko, Konstantin (1911–85) General secretary of the Communist Party of the Soviet Union (1984–85).

Chiang Kai-shek (1887–1975) Anticommunist leader of the Nationalist Party and Nationalist government of China from 1928 to 1975.

Clinton, William J. (1946–) 42nd U.S. president (1993–2001).

Churchill, Winston (1874–1965) World War II prime minister of the United Kingdom, who, after the war, popularized the "iron curtain" phrase as well as the Cold War concept.

de Gaulle, Charles (1890–1970) President of the Fifth French Republic (1959–69), who developed a French nuclear arsenal and took France out of the NATO command structure.

Donovan, William Joseph "Wild Bill" (1883–1959) Head of the World War II–era U.S. Office of Strategic Services (OSS) and "father" (though never head) of the CIA.

Dubček, Alexander (1921–92) Communist reform leader of Czechoslovakia (1968–69) during the Prague Spring.

Dulles, Allen (1893–1969) American World War II spy master who directed the CIA from 1953 to 1961. Brother of John Foster Dulles.

Dulles, John Foster (1888–1959) U.S. secretary of state under Dwight Eisenhower (1953–59).

Eisenhower, Dwight D. (1890–1969) 34th U.S. president (1953–61); Supreme Allied Commander Europe (1951–52); Supreme Allied Commander of the Allied Expeditionary Force (1943–45).

Ellsberg, Daniel (1931–) Rand Corporation analyst who leaked the Pentagon Papers to the press in 1971, revealing the sordid history of U.S. involvement in the Vietnam War.

Farouk I (1920–65) King of Egypt (1936–52) overthrown by Gamal Abdel Nasser.

Ford, Gerald (1913–2006) 38th U.S. president (1974–77).

Forrestal, James (1892–1949) First U.S. secretary of defense (1947–49).

Franco, Francisco (1892–1975) Spain's longtime fascist dictator (1936–75).

Fuchs, Klaus (1911–88) German-born British physicist who revealed U.S. atomic and hydrogen bomb secrets to the Soviets.

Gold, Harry (1910–72) Manhattan Project chemist convicted of Soviet espionage.

Gomulka, Wladyslaw (1905–82) First secretary of the Polish United Workers' Party (effectively leader of communist Poland) from 1956 to 1970.

Gorbachev, Mikhail (1931–) Liberalizing final leader of the Soviet Union (1985–91).

Gottwald, Klement (1896–1953) Head of the Communist Party of Czechoslovakia, who was prime minister (1946–48) and president (1948–53) of that country.

Greenglass, David (1922–), and **Greenglass, Ruth** (1924–2008) Husband and wife atomic spies in the service of the Soviets; David Greenglass was the government's principal witness against Julius and Ethel Rosenberg.

Groves, Leslie (1896–1970) U.S. Army officer who was overall director of the Manhattan Project.

Havel, Václav (1936–) Czech anticommunist and playwright who became the president of Czechoslovakia (1989–92) and first president of the Czech Republic (1993–2003).

Hirohito (1901–89) Emperor of Japan during World War II, who continued to reign throughout the entire Cold War period.

Hiss, Alger (1904–96) State Department official accused in 1948 of being a Soviet spy; he was a cause célèbre for both the U.S. right wing and the left during the Red Scare.

Hitler, Adolf (1889–1945) Leader of Nazi Germany (1933–45) , instigator of World War II, and mass murderer.

Ho Chi Minh (1890–1969) Communist revolutionary leader of Vietnam.

Honecker, Erich (1912–94) Leader of the German Democratic Republic (East Germany) from 1971 to 1989.

Hoover, J. Edgar (1895–1972) Founding director of the Federal Bureau of Investigation and a leading figure in U.S. Cold War counterespionage.

Hoxha, Enver (1908–85) Communist ruler of the People's Republic of Albania, who isolated the nation from Stalin and the Soviet Union, loosely aligning it with Mao Zedong's China.

Hussein, Saddam (1937–2007) President of Iraq (1979–2003), deposed in the Iraq War (2003–) and executed in 2007.

John Paul II (1920–2005) Polish-born pope (1978–2005), whose pastoral visits to Poland were instrumental in inspiring the anticommunist movement there.

Johnson, Lyndon B. (1908–73) 36th U.S. president (1963–69).

Kamal, Babrak (1929–96) Soviet puppet president of Afghanistan (1979–86)

Kennan, George F. (1904–2005) U.S. diplomat whose insights into Stalin and the postwar Soviet policies laid the foundation for President Truman's policy of containment and the related Truman Doctrine.

Kennedy, John F. (1917–63) 35th U.S. president (1961–63).

Khomeini, Ayatollah Ruholla (1902–89) First "Supreme Leader of Iran" (1979–89), replacing the deposed Shah.

Khrushchev, Nikita (1894–1971) Leader of the Soviet Union (1953–64).

Kim Il Sung (1912–94) Leader of the Democratic People's Republic of Korea (North Korea) from 1948 to 1994.

Kissinger, Henry (1923–) U.S. national security adviser (1969–75) and secretary of state (1973–77) under Richard Nixon.

Krenz, Egon (1937–) Last leader of the German Democratic Republic (East Germany), 1989.

Lenin, Vladimir (1870–1924) Principal leader of the Bolshevik Revolution of 1917 and first de facto leader of the Soviet Union (1922–24).

LeMay, Curtis E. (1906–90) U.S. Air Force general who created and headed the Strategic Air Command (SAC), the principal American nuclear force.

MacArthur, Douglas (1880–1964) U.S. general who commanded U.S. and UN forces (1950–51) in the Korean War until he was relieved of command by President Truman for insubordination.

McCarthy, Joseph (1908–57) Junior U.S. senator from Wisconsin notorious for his communist "witch hunts."

McNamara, Robert S. (1916–) U.S. secretary of defense under John F. Kennedy and Lyndon Johnson; active during the Cuban Missile Crisis and the early escalation phase of the Vietnam War.

Mao Zedong (1893–1976) Leader of the communist revolution in China, radical communist theorist, and first leader of the People's Republic of China, from 1949 to 1976.

Marshall, George C. (1880–1959) Chief of staff of the U.S. Army during World War II, Marshall served as secretary of state (1947–49) and secretary of defense (1950–51) and was the principal promoter of the postwar European recovery program known as the Marshall Plan.

Marx, Karl (1818–83) Philosophical father of communism; radical communist leaders in the twentieth century often turned to Marxism as a "pure" (that is, non-Soviet) form of communism.

Masaryk, Jan (1886–1948) Czech foreign minister (1940–48), who unsuccessfully attempted to maintain independence from the Soviet Union.

McNamara, Robert (1916–) As secretary of defense under presidents Kennedy and Johnson, advocated expanded U.S. involvement in the Vietnam War and expanded the American strategic arsenal.

Molotov, Vyacheslav (1890–1986) Soviet foreign minister (1939–56) during World War II and the early Cold War period.

Morgenthau, Henry, Jr. (1891–1967) Longest-serving U.S. secretary of the treasury (under Roosevelt and, briefly, Truman), who advocated the deindustrialization of Germany after World War II.

Mussolini, Benito (1883–1945) Fascist dictator of Italy during World War II and key Hitler ally.

Nagy, Imre (1896–1958) Hungarian prime minister (1953–55, 1956), who withdrew Hungary from the Warsaw Pact, briefly led Hungary during the anti-Soviet uprising of 1956, and suffered execution for treason after the Soviets crushed the uprising.

Nasser, Gamal Abdel (1918–70) Soviet-oriented president of Egypt from 1956 to 1970 who was a leading figure in the Non-Aligned Movement.

Nehru, Jawaharlal (1889–1964) Prime minister of India (1947–64) and prime architect of the Non-Aligned Movement.

Ngo Dinh Diem (1901–63) First president of South Vietnam (1955–63); assassinated during a CIA-backed coup d'état.

Nixon, Richard M. (1913–94) 37th U.S. president (1969–74).

Oppenheimer, J. Robert (1904–67) American physicist who was scientific director of the Manhattan Project and is considered the "father of the atomic bomb."

Pahlavi, Mohammad Reza (1919–80) Pro-U.S. Shah of Iran (1941–79) deposed in the Iranian Revolution of 1979.

Philby, Kim (1912–88) Highly placed British intelligence officer who was an NKVD and KGB double agent during the Cold War.

Pinochet, Augusto (1915–2006) U.S.-supported leader of the coup d'état that toppled Salvador Allende in Chile; Pinochet led a brutal right-wing regime from 1973 to 1990.

Pol Pot (1925–98) Radical Maoist leader of the Khmer Rouge in Cambodia, whose regime (1975–79) was genocidal.

Powers, Francis Gary (1920–77) CIA pilot whose U-2 spy plane was shot down over the Soviet Union on May 1, 1960, precipitating an international incident.

Reagan, Ronald (1911–2004) 40th U.S. president (1981–89).

Reza Shah Pahlavi (1878–1944) Shah of Iran from 1925 to 1941; father of Mohammad Reza Pahlavi, Shah of Iran from 1941 to 1979

Rhee, Syngman (1875–1965) President of South Korea (1948–60) during the Korean War.

Ridgway, Matthew B. (1895–1993) U.S. general who replaced Douglas MacArthur as supreme commander of United Nations forces in Korea during the Korean War.

Roosevelt, Franklin D. (1882–1945) 32nd U.S. president (1933–45).

Rosenberg, Julius (1918–53), and **Rosenberg, Ethel** (1915–53) Brooklyn couple tried and executed for conspiracy to commit espionage in connection with the leaking of U.S. nuclear weapons secrets to the Soviets.

Stalin, Joseph (1878–1953) Absolute leader of the Soviet Union (1922–53).

Stimson, Henry (1867–1950) U.S. secretary of war (1940–45) during World War II.

Taraki, Nur Mohammed (1913–79) Communist president and prime minister of Afghanistan (1978–79) overthrown by Hafizullah Amin.

Teller, Edward (1908–2003) Hungarian-born U.S. scientist who is considered the "father of the hydrogen bomb."

Tito (Josip Broz) (1892–1980) Communist leader of Yugoslavia (1943–80), whose independence defied Stalin.

Truman, Harry S. (1884–1972) 33rd U.S president (1945–53).

Ulbricht, Walter (1893–1973) Communist politician instrumental in the creation of the German Democratic Republic (East Germany).

Von Braun, Wernher (1912–77) German scientist who developed the V-2 rocket weapon during World War II and, after the war, was a principal architect of the U.S. space program.

Wałesa, Lech (1943–) Cofounder of Solidarity, spearhead of Polish liberation from Soviet communist domination; served as Poland's president from 1990 to 1995.

Wisner, Frank (1909–65) World War II OSS officer who headed the CIA's covert Office of Policy Coordination (OPC) during the early Cold War period.

Yeltsin, Boris (1931–2007) Russian reform leader who successfully resisted the hard-line communist coup of 1991 and became the first president of Russia (1991–99) after the collapse of the Soviet Union.

Zhou Enlai (1898–1976) First premier of the People's Republic of China (1949–76).

Author's Note

THE STORY OF THE TWO WORLD WARS and the global depression, which scarred the first half of the twentieth century, is more easily told than that of the Cold War that blighted the second half. The Cold War was a bright and blurry constellation of beliefs, doctrines, principles, faiths, delusions, actions, errors, and actual wars—a long list of phenomena that no two historians perfectly agree on. It was not an orderly succession of sharply defined events. What all authorities do agree on is that the engine driving the Cold War was nuclear powered. Without the atomic bomb, there would have been no Cold War—World War III, perhaps, and maybe IV and V and more. Who knows? The point is that a world in which war did not entail the universal thermonuclear annihilation of "mutual assured destruction" would have had no need for a "cold" war. The old-fashioned hot ones—all-out combat with conventional weapons—would have met the needs of the planet's leaders, just as they had in 1914–18 and 1939–45.

The Cold War is unique in the entire history of human conflict because it was the only war fought as an alternative to fighting a war, *a* war that would have been *the* war, the end, almost certainly, of just about everything and everyone. It is this uniqueness that gives the telling of the Cold War a center, a core, a heart, that makes what would otherwise be a daunting half-century welter of details urgently compelling and endlessly fascinating.

In *The Real History of the Cold War*, I have tried to explain the details without ever losing sight of the heart that gave them life. I have tried to create a convincing portrait of some fifty years of political aspiration, manipulation, hope, and fear; of oppression and liberation; of threatened war and actual war, and of thermonuclear war both threatened and avoided. Just as no painted portrait actually duplicates reality, no written history is truly objective, and in writing recent history especially, objectivity becomes an even more elusive and ultimately illusory goal. If the portrait I present here is therefore sometimes impressionistic, colored by my perceptions of a reality my parents and I actually lived through, I trust it is never outright caricature.

This book would not be possible without the work of my editor, Barbara Berger, and that of Sterling's editorial director, Michael Fragnito.

— Alan Axelrod
Atlanta, Georgia

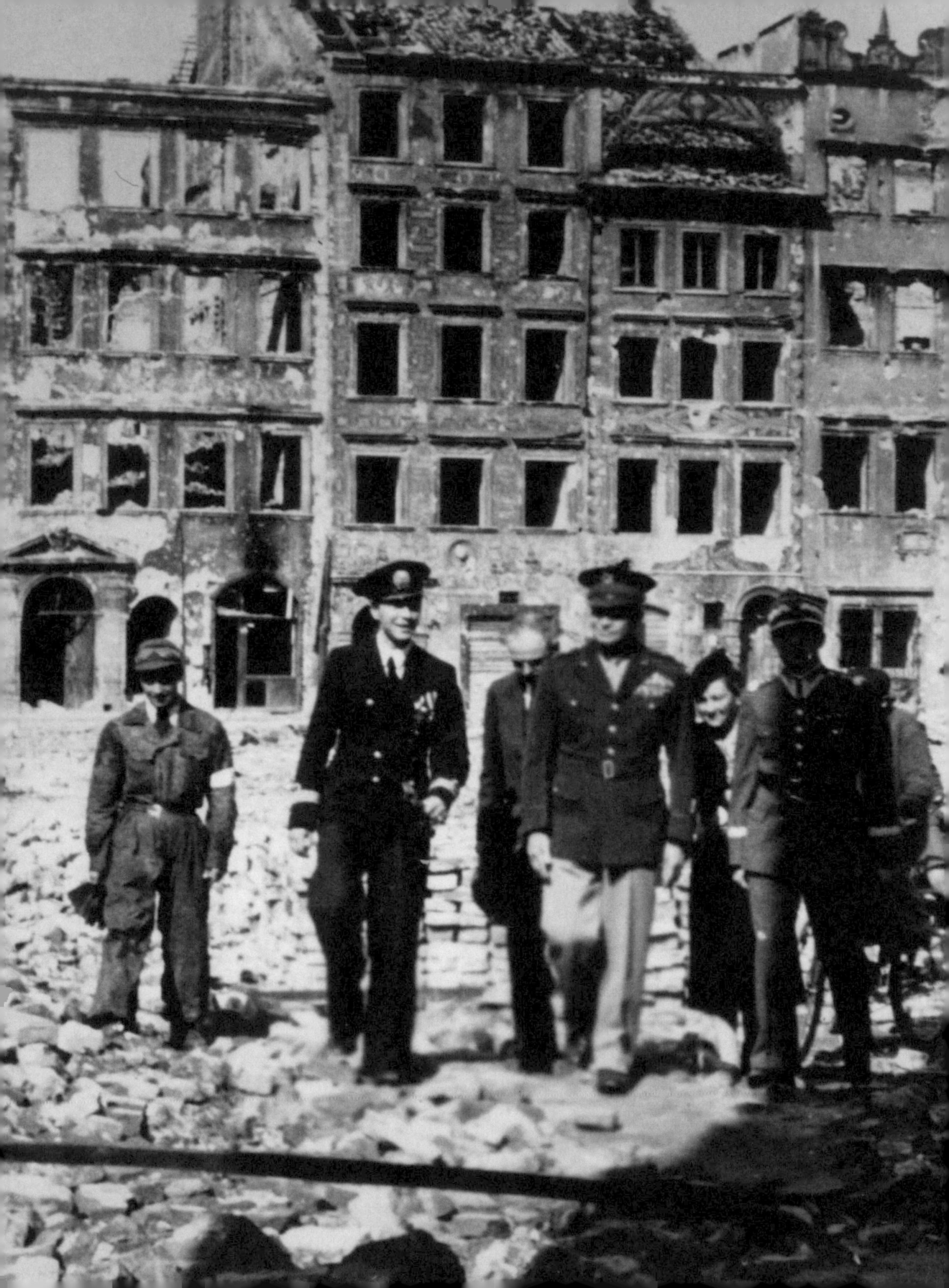

PART ONE

ASHES AND IDEOLOGY

CHAPTER 1

ALLIES AND ENEMIES

The World Takes Sides

POLITICS, THE OLD SAYING GOES, makes strange bedfellows. War makes even stranger ones. Put politics and war together, and you get the strangest of all. Just look at any one of the famous photographs of the "Big Three" at the last great Allied conference of World War II. There they are—Britain's prime minister Winston Churchill is tucked into an unadorned double-breasted greatcoat, Russian fur cap in his hands, trademark cigar between his fingers, that familiar round, nearly cherubic face, lips set in the merest hint of a smile, his eyes taking in both President Franklin Delano Roosevelt, whom he called "that great man whom destiny has marked for this climax of human fortune," and Joseph Stalin, "a hard-boiled egg of a man . . . a callous, a crafty and an ill-formed man." Seated between Churchill and Stalin, is Roosevelt, bareheaded like Churchill, an old-fashioned boat cape over his shoulders, cigarette between his fingers. Despite his broad, open-mouthed smile, he looks like what he was in February of 1945, a dying man. And then there is Stalin, smiling, too, beneath his Red Army cap and sinister mustache, jackboots prominent beneath the hem of his long uniform coat. A most unlikely group portrait of most unlikely allies.

As World War II enters its closing act, the "Big Three"—from left, British prime minister Winston Churchill, U.S. president Franklin Delano Roosevelt, and Soviet premier Joseph Stalin—meet in the Black Sea resort of Yalta to plan the postwar world; February 12, 1945.

Lines Drawn Sharp and Straight

There had been a time, not very long before the group photo was snapped, when these men—or men like them—would have had little to do with one another. Relations between the Americans and the British had long been cordial enough, but if, in 1917, President Woodrow Wilson had asked his countrymen to go to war to save the British Empire, he would have had few takers—far fewer, certainly, than proved willing to fight to "make the world safe for democracy" in 1917. At the time of World War I, it seemed possible to see the planet as divided between "democratic" nations—even imperial Britain counted itself one of these—and "autocratic" nations, of which Kaiser Wilhelm II's Germany was the prime example. No one on the Allied side (as the nations opposed to Germany and Austria-Hungary called themselves) seemed much bothered that the biggest of the Allied nations was Russia, which, under Czar Nicholas II, could hardly be considered a democracy by any contortion of the imagination. Then, early in 1917, a revolution deposed the czar, and Russia seemed to be on the verge of becoming a democracy after all—that is, until November 1917, when the communist Bolsheviks ousted the democratic Mensheviks. Up to this point the war had been a disaster for Russia, and the Bolsheviks

Previous Spread: *General Dwight D. Eisenhower, former supreme allied commander in Europe, tours the rubble of Warsaw as military governor of the U.S. Occupation Zone, February 1946.*

NUMBERS

Doomed Army

Almost half of the twelve million men who had served in the army of Russia's Czar Nicholas II had been killed, wounded, or captured by the time of the Bolshevik Revolution in November 1917.

were determined to withdraw from the war by making a "separate peace" with Germany. Bad enough that the Bolsheviks were communists—the ideological enemies of democratic capitalism—but their abandonment of the Western Allies was seen as both a terrible blow to the war effort and a treacherous betrayal.

Suddenly, new lines were drawn. It was the democracies versus the autocrats *and* the communists. When, in November 1918, the Allies defeated Germany and Austria-Hungary and dismembered both of these empires, the lines were made both straighter and bolder. Now it was the democracies—both the established ones and those newly created by the Treaty of Versailles—against the communists, who, after all, were not content to confine their form of government within the borders of Russia. Marxist doctrine sought to replace nationalism with class solidarity, thereby uniting the workers of the world, regardless of nationality. For communism to survive and prosper, Marxism dictated that it had to be spread worldwide. Thus the world's capitalist democracies had a good reason to join forces in opposition to international communism.

Karl Marx, who, with Friedrich Engels, created the theoretical foundation of communism.

Resistance to the spread of communism soon spawned a new alternative to both communism and democracy. First in Italy and then in Germany, a far right-wing ideology formed and began to take hold. Called "fascism" in Italy and "Nazism" in Germany, both systems were based on an alliance between capital—the major industrialists and financiers—and a strongly centralized government ruled by an absolute dictator. In effect, these new totalitarian governments embraced capitalism without democracy, and they acquired, maintained, and increased their power by strong-arm tactics ranging from street-level thuggery to the use of police, paramilitary, and military force against their own internal populations.

The March of Fascism

In World War I, although the Allies prevailed, in truth, there really were no victors. In the United States, a brief period of economic depression was succeeded by a boom that lasted (for many people, but not for all) through the 1920s. In Europe, however, most national economies were hard hit. Among the Allied nations, the Italian economy disintegrated into chaos, and the government therefore

Vladimir Ilyich Lenin, founder of Soviet communism.

become ripe for hijacking—by socialists, by communists, by whoever came on sufficiently strong.

Benito Mussolini was born on July 29, 1883, into the family of a full-time blacksmith and part-time socialist. Doted on by a mother who told him he was destined for greatness, young Benito devoured the works of such philosophers as Machiavelli and Friedrich Nietzsche, who wrote about leaders who made their own morality. Although he was a delinquent and a bully in school—he was expelled for stabbing a classmate—Mussolini trained as a schoolteacher, taught for a while, soon tired of it, and became a socialist journalist. With the outbreak of World War I, he wrote pacifist articles, arguing passionately against Italy's entry into the war, only to do a sudden about-face, urging the nation's entry on the side of the Allies. For this and other offenses, the Italian Socialist Party expelled Mussolini, who retaliated by starting his own newspaper, in which he advocated a political movement that would soon be called "fascism."

Mussolini enlisted as a private during World War I and rose no higher than corporal before he was seriously wounded in an explosion of an artillery weapon he was helping to test fire. After the war, he joined other early fascists in founding the Fasci di Combattimento, the core around which the Italian

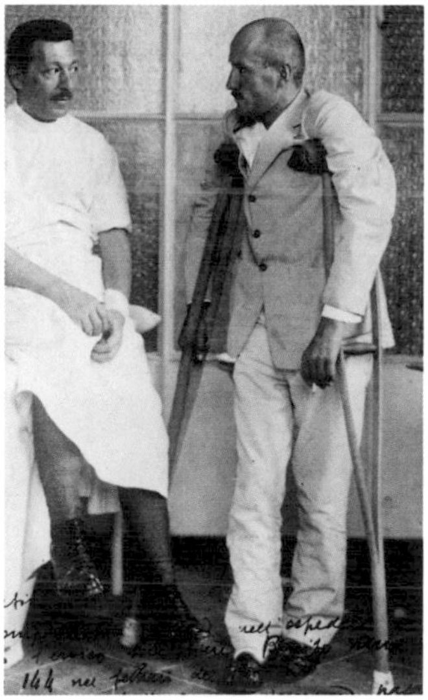

Benito Mussolini convalesces in 1917 from a shrapnel wound suffered when an artillery piece he was test firing exploded. In 1922, he would become Italy's premier and introduce to the world fascism, a political system intended to oppose communism and to remodel Italy as a modern Roman Empire.

REALITY CHECK

Sowing the Seeds

The Bolsheviks were so intent on spreading communism globally that in March 1919 they established the Comintern (Communist International), dedicated to employing "all available means, including armed force, for the overthrow of the international bourgeoisie and for the creation of an international Soviet republic as a transition stage to the complete abolition of the State." Marx and Lenin may have wanted to abolish the state—replacing it with a nationless class solidarity—but Stalin was wedded to the concept of an all-powerful state and abolished the Comintern in 1935. Stalin had not abandoned Soviet expansion, but rather changed the motive: he wanted to extend the power of the Soviet *state* in order to protect it against invasion and, most of all, to secure himself in a position of unassailable power.

Fascist Party would form. The name derived from the Italian word *fascio*, "bundle," and from *fasces*, a Latin word specifically denoting a bundle of rods bound together around an ax with the blade protruding—the ancient Roman symbol of power. As Mussolini promoted it, fascism was a form of government that, defining the state in terms of racial identity, put the state at the center of everyday life. In turn, at the center of the state was the absolute authority of a single leader who would reward the unquestioning loyalty of his people by leading them to national greatness and international preeminence. Mussolini promised nothing less than the transformation of a battered and beleaguered Italy into a state rivaling the imperial grandeur of ancient Rome.

Through a combination of street brawling, physical intimidation, political murder, and brilliant journalistic proselytizing, Mussolini recruited enough followers to make an impressive march on Rome on October 28, 1922, with the object of ousting sitting prime minister Luigi Facta. By this quasi-revolutionary gesture he extorted a mandate from Italy's king Vittore Emanuelle III to form a coalition government in which he obtained for himself "temporary" dictatorial powers and from which his rival, Facta, was excluded. Mussolini used this authority to radically refashion the Italian economy, forging cozy relations with

Long before the fasces, *symbol of state power in republican Rome, was appropriated as the emblem of Italian fascism, it was used to convey the ancient inspiration behind American democracy, as this image from 1861, the earliest known photograph of the House of Representatives, shows.*

LINK

A Fascist Symbol of Democracy

Mussolini was not the only national leader who harbored visions of a return to Roman grandeur. From the very beginning of the American republic, the founding fathers looked to ancient Rome for models of popular government. Most federal buildings, well into the twentieth century, have imitated Roman temples in architectural style, aiming to symbolize the republican ideals on which the government was founded. Another Roman symbol featured prominently in U.S. government is the fasces, the same ancient Roman symbol of rule that Mussolini appropriated. A pair of fasces flanks the American flag behind the Speaker's chair in the U.S. House of Representatives (see photograph at the right), and the great seal of the U.S. Senate includes a pair of crossed fasces. The "Mercury" dime (in circulation from 1916–45) includes a fasces around which an olive branch twines.

The Fascist march on Rome in 1922 catapulted Benito Mussolini to the head of Italian government—although, instead of joining the marchers, Mussolini rode into the Eternal City in the first-class comfort of a railway sleeper car.

leading industrialists and cutting taxes on industry to encourage production. Against opposition from socialists, communists, and would-be democrats, Mussolini wielded a paramilitary force of party loyalists—called "Blackshirts," after their uniforms—and a secret police force, the OVRA (translated from Italian, Organization for Vigilance and Repression of Anti-Fascism). Imprisonments, beatings, and assassinations became routine.

There were those both inside and outside of Italy who deplored the totalitarian brutality of fascism, but there were many more who admired Mussolini's resurrection of what had seemed a moribund nation. For years, the notoriously unreliable Italian rail system had been emblematic of the aimlessness of Italian industry and politics. Those who praised Mussolini commonly remarked that he "made the trains run on time."

In 1924, Mussolini relinquished his dictatorial powers and called for new elections. It was an act of pure political theater; he had guaranteed the outcome of the elections by obtaining legislation that gave his party a two-thirds parliamentary majority regardless of the popular vote. Even with the elections rigged, however, socialism persisted as a powerful force in Italian politics, and the leading socialist, Giacomo Matteotti, was a compelling opponent of fascism. His assassination in 1924 brought a tidal wave of antifascist attacks in the opposition press, to which Mussolini responded by outlawing all parties except for the fascists, abolishing trade unions, and imposing strict censorship. With socialism thus neutralized, there remained to be dealt with one more potent force in Italian life, the Catholic Church. Instead of trying to suppress this institution, Mussolini co-opted it by means of the Lateran Treaty of 1929, which established the Vatican as a city-state within the city of Rome under the absolute

REALITY CHECK

Mussolini Takes the Train

Approximately twenty-six thousand fascists marched on Rome, but Mussolini, a master of exaggeration, made King Vittore Emanuelle III believe that a hundred thousand Blackshirts were on the march. He therefore offered no real resistance. As for Mussolini, he waited out most of the march on Rome with his wife and children in Milan, then rode to Rome in the luxury of a railroad sleeper car bedroom. Immediately after the march established him as dictator, however, Italy was flooded with various depictions of Mussolini, on horseback, arm raised in the fascist salute, implying that this is how he had led his blackshirted columns of conquest.

REALITY CHECK

Did Mussolini Really Make the Trains Run on Time?

The glib claim that Mussolini made the trains run on time—meaning that he transformed Italy from a lazy, inefficient backwater into a modern industrial-military powerhouse—has been repeated so often that very little thought is ever given to its accuracy. During World War I, the Italian railway system had fallen into severe disrepair and was under reconstruction *before* Mussolini came to power in 1922. By that time, Italian trains were at least running—but rarely on time. Like most Italian industries, the railroads were plagued by strikes. Fascism outlawed labor demonstrations, which meant that there were fewer interruptions in rail service. But those who lived through the Mussolini era reported (after World War II) that the trains were still reliably late.

sovereignty of the pope. Thus, by the beginning of the 1930s, Mussolini and fascism were firmly ensconced in Italy, admired by some, hated by others, forces to be reckoned with by all.

Hitler Rises

One of those reckoning the man Italians now called "Il Duce" (the Leader) was another former World War I corporal—Adolf Hitler. Born in Austria, the son of a minor customs functionary, Hitler was brutalized by his father and doted on by his mother. A mediocre student, he took refuge in the dream of becoming a great artist, but after being twice rejected for enrollment at the Academy of Fine Arts in Vienna, Hitler became a drifter, barely eking out a living by painting postcards for tourists.

Depressed and shiftless, Hitler was a man without direction, let alone destiny—until the end of July 1914, when World War I broke upon Europe. Suddenly energized by the prospect of combat, Hitler rushed to enlist. Initially rejected as unfit for military service, he was finally inducted into the 16th Bavarian Reserve Infantry Regiment. In combat, he was a runner, assigned to hazardous front-line messenger duty. Wounded and gassed, he was decorated for valor with the Iron Cross, Second Class, in 1914, and, in 1918, with the Iron Cross, First Class—a medal rarely awarded to corporals.

> "To me those hours seemed like a release from the painful feelings of my youth. Even today I am not ashamed to say that, overpowered by stormy enthusiasm, I fell down on my knees and thanked Heaven from an overflowing heart for granting me the good fortune of being permitted to live at this time."
>
> *Adolf Hitler, in* Mein Kampf, 1925, *recalling his reaction to the news that World War I had started*

Hitler remained in the army after the war as a political agent, tasked with keeping tabs on the welter of popular political movements spawned by the armistice. He soon found himself drawn to one of these fledgling organizations, the German Workers Party, which he joined in Munich in 1919. Hitler was a slight, unprepossessing man, his jet-black hair and mustache—during the war it had been thick and full, but now he trimmed it into an abbreviated "cookie duster"—setting off the unhealthy pallor of his skin—yet he now discovered in himself a remarkable oratorical power. On the podium, he was transformed into a charismatic, even a hypnotic figure. He quickly rose to prominence in the new party, which in 1920 was renamed the Nationalsozialistische Deutsche Arbeiterpartei, the "Nazi Party" for short.

As in postwar Italy, economic and political chaos reigned in postwar Germany. The terms of the Treaty of Versailles had removed the kaiser (emperor) and installed a republican government—the Weimar Republic—that was particularly unpopular in conservative Bavaria, where Hitler and the Nazis were most active. As was also the case in Italy, Germany appeared ripe to fall into the hands of whatever party or faction made the most noise or bashed the most heads. Munich, the capital of Bavaria, was headquarters for disaffected veterans, many of whom had joined the Freikorps, an unofficial (and illegal) army organized from units of the German army that had refused to demobilize after the armistice. The Freikorps and its hangers on despised the Weimar Republic, believing its very existence a national betrayal. Hitler's Nazis recruited members from among the Freikorps, including former army lieutenant Ernst Röhm, who helped Hitler organize the Nazi paramilitary unit known as the Sturmabteilung—the stormtroopers—or SA. Modeled on Mussolini's Blackshirts—but, clad in brown, called "Brownshirts"—the SA engaged political opponents, mainly socialists and communists, in brutal street brawls, the violence sometimes escalating to murder.

Adolf Hitler, about 1920, at the start of his rise to power in Germany within the National Socialist—Nazi—movement.

On November 8, 1923, impatient to make a major move, Hitler led his men into a right-wing political meeting under way in a Munich beer hall and persuaded those attending to join a mass march on Berlin, patterned on Mussolini's dramatically successful march on Rome the year before. The next day, however, the column of some three thousand marchers was intercepted by police, who opened fire, killing sixteen Nazis. With this, Hitler's revolution died aborning, and he was arrested, tried, and convicted of treason—though his sentence was the minimum possible, five years' imprisonment.

Imprisoned for treason after the collapse of the abortive Beer Hall Putsch of 1923, Adolf Hitler gazes contemplatively through the window of the Landsberg Prison cell in which he drafted his autobiographical political manifesto, Mein Kampf.

The last thing Weimar authorities wanted was to make a martyr of Adolf Hitler. They assigned him comfortable quarters at Landsberg Prison, which he used as a study in which to write the first volume of a political memoir titled *Mein Kampf* ("My Struggle"). In this rambling and verbose book, Hitler chewed over his own version of fascism. Far more than Mussolini, he emphasized the role of race, drawing on then-current ideas of national racial destiny to develop a mythology of Germany's racial heritage as an "Aryan people," a naturally race destined to hold sway over the world as the "master race." It was, Hitler wrote, this momentous birthright that the Treaty of Versailles and the Weimar Republic sought to suppress and deny. Hitler further argued that democracy—the political philosophy of the Weimar Republic—lacked the strength and the will to realize the German destiny and to vanquish the great enemy of that destiny, Marxism, for which the Jews were generally responsible. The theme of anti-Semitism—endemic in German society at the time—was elaborately developed in *Mein Kampf*, which portrayed the Jews as the incarnation of everything evil and anti-Aryan. Only the destruction of the democratic Weimar Republic and its replacement by absolute rule under a single great Aryan leader could restore to the German people their birthright as members of the master race.

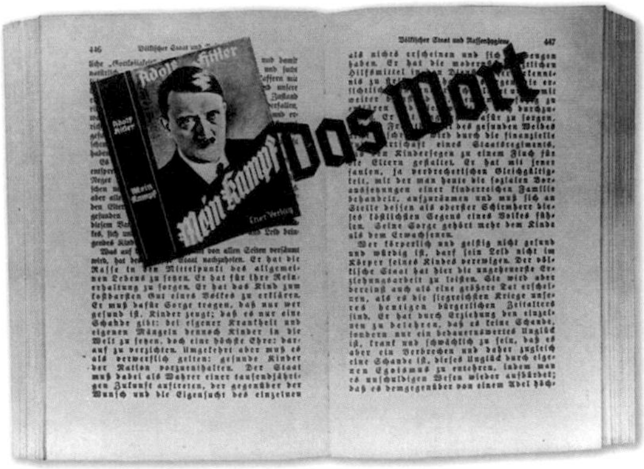

In Nazi Germany, Hitler's Mein Kampf *was treated as holy writ. The open book is pictured here, superimposed with an image of its dust jacket and the quasi-biblical inscription* Das Wort—*"The Word."*

"I set the Aryan and the Jew over against each other; and if I call one of them a human being, I must call the other something else. The two are as widely separated as man and beast. Not that I would call the Jew a beast. . . . He is a creature outside nature and alien to nature."

Adolf Hitler, Mein Kampf, *1925*

Sentenced to five years, Hitler was released after only nine months, but that had been long enough for the Nazi Party to have largely disintegrated. Worse for Hitler, German life under the Weimar Republic had actually improved. Unemployment was on the decline, and the economy was on the mend. Weimar officials felt sufficiently emboldened to bar Hitler from speaking, under pain of reimprisonment. Still, he spoke, reorganized the party, and nursed it back to health. It was, however, the sudden onset of worldwide depression following the crash of the American stock market in October 1929 that gave Hitler his great moment in which to resurrect Nazism. He recognized that the economic depression could accomplish what no political ideology could—make common cause between the suffering working class and the battered capitalists. Now Hitler appealed to both, promising a system of government that would reindustrialize Germany on a massive scale, thereby providing employment as well as wealth. In the 1930 elections, the Nazi Party polled more than six million votes, moving up to become the second largest party in the country. Two years later, Hitler ran for the presidency of the republic against Paul von Hindenburg, the superannuated and ailing hero of World War I. Although he lost to Hindenburg, Hitler captured more than a third of the votes, a demonstration of popularity that compelled Hindenburg (who personally despised him) to appoint Hitler chancellor, the second most powerful position in the government.

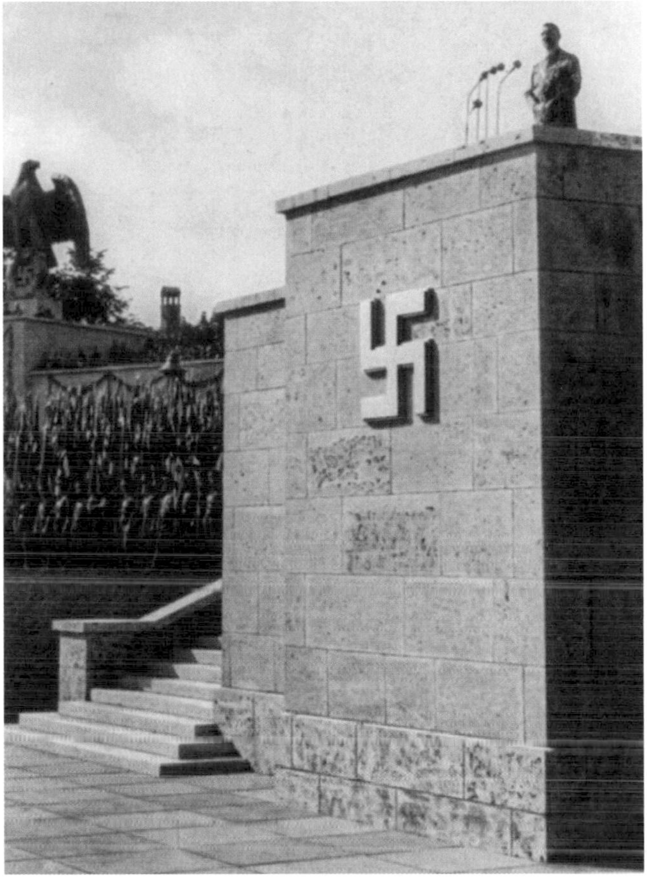

Hitler speaks at the Nuremberg rally of 1933, which extolled the Nazi Party's victory over the short-lived democracy of the post–World War I "Weimar Republic." Note the monumental rostrum adorned with the swastika. The Nazis developed and embraced a range of highly effective symbols.

ENTER THE "MAN OF STEEL"

AS ITALY EMBRACED MUSSOLINI and while Germany seethed on the brink of revolution, Lenin, the founder of Soviet communism, succumbed in 1924 to a long illness and the lingering effects of wounds suffered in an assassination attempt some six years earlier. Control of the nation's government and Communist Party passed to Joseph Stalin.

He had been born in 1879 Iosif Vissarionovich Dzhugashvili in czarist Georgia. His parents wanted him to study for the Orthodox

LINK

The Democratic Problem

By definition, democracy permits popular dissent. Such liberalism works well once a democratic government is firmly established—dissent keeps a democracy responsive and fresh—but it can be lethal to a newly founded democracy. Such was the case with the Weimar Republic, the tolerant policies of which were perceived and exploited by the Nazis as well as the communists and other dissident groups as weakness. After World War I, the Western Allies sought to impose democracy on Germany. But democracy tends to endure only when it is an outgrowth of the popular will, not an imposition from the outside. Forced on a people, democracy must compete with whatever genuinely popular movements arise. The problem of the Weimar Republic is similar to the problem of the recent American attempt to impose democracy on Iraq. History records the demise of Weimar. The world waits to see whether the form of government grafted onto Iraq will "take"—or wither and fall away, to be replaced by who knows what.

From the files of the czar's secret police: a mug shot of Iosif Vissarionovich Dzhugashvili—also known as Joseph Stalin—taken sometime between his first arrest in 1902 and 1910 during his early rise as a Marxist revolutionary.

priesthood, but his unruly behavior earned him two distinctions in his teen years: expulsion from the Tiflis Theological Seminary and the nickname "Koba," after a celebrated Georgian bandit rebel. Koba then immersed himself in covert anticzarist activity, eventually coming into the orbit of Vladimir Lenin. Arrested repeatedly, he always managed to escape, and in 1912 Lenin elevated him to membership on the Bolshevik Central Committee and assigned him to edit the Communist Party newspaper, *Pravda* ("Truth"). For this public role, he wanted a public name. He chose to be called Stalin, meaning "man of steel."

Stalin's luck ran out in 1913, and he was exiled by czarist authorities to Siberia. Although he was conscripted for army service in 1916, he was judged unfit and remained in exile until March 1917, when the overthrow of the czar won his release. During the period of the Bolshevik Revolution and afterward, Stalin continued his rise, ultimately coming to occupy the vacuum left by Lenin's death. From this position, he methodically eliminated all opposition. He attacked Communist Party leftists first, and, once they were out of the way—deposed, imprisoned, exiled, or killed—he turned on the rightists, ignoring both loyalty and ideology to ensure his own unchallenged preeminence, which was attained by 1930.

LAST WISHES, FINAL WARNING

Time magazine featured in its October 25, 1926, issue an article titled "Humble Pie," which reported the existence of a deathbed memorandum "by the great Lenin, warning Russian Communists against Joseph Stalin." _Time_ quoted the document, excerpted here:

> Comrade Stalin, having become general secretary [of the Communist Party] has concentrated an enormous power in his hands; and I am not sure that he always knows how to use that power with sufficient caution . . .
>
> On the other hand, Comrade Trotzky [sic], is distinguished not only by his exceptional abilities—personally he is, to be sure, the most able man in the present central committee; but also by his too far-reaching self-confidence and a disposition to be too much attracted by the purely administrative side of affairs. . . .
>
> Stalin is too rough, and this fault, entirely supportable in relations among us communists, becomes insupportable in the office of general secretary. Therefore, I propose to the comrades to find a way to remove Stalin from that position and appoint to it another man, who in all regards differs from Stalin, namely, more patient, more loyal, more polite, and more attentive to comrades, less capricious.

Reportedly, Stalin had managed to suppress the document long enough to establish himself on the path to absolute power. What if Lenin's deathbed warning had been published at the time of his death? Would Leon Trotsky have risen to the top position in the Soviet government? And, if so, would he have been more conciliatory to the Western democracies? That is likely, and the twentieth century would almost certainly have unfolded very differently. It is hardly likely that Trotsky, a Jew, would have made a pact with Hitler, as Stalin did, and so World War II might—*might*—never have broken out, at least not on a global scale. Moreover, the great divide between Soviet communism and the Western democracies might not have been sufficiently deep to create a Cold War or any other quasi-military conflict. Trotsky would almost certainly have been a far less brutal leader than Stalin—but that very fact might have led to his ouster by some other figure, quite possibly a resurgent Stalin himself.

Lev Davidovich Bronstein, better known as Leon Trotsky, was second only to Lenin during the Bolshevik Revolution and became a rival of Stalin, suffering, in consequence, expulsion from the Communist Party of the Soviet Union and, ultimately, assassination—a blow to the head with an ice axe wielded by an agent of the NKVD (Narodny Komissariat Vnutrennikh Del, or "Peoples Commissariat for Internal Affairs," the forerunner of the KGB)—on August 20, 1940. He is pictured here at the height of his early fame, administering "party discipline."

This Soviet poster from 1930 promotes the collectivization of Russian agriculture by seizing the farms of kulaks (peasant farmers) and converting them into state-controlled agricultural communes. The caption reads "We will annihilate kulaks as a class," but Stalin's policy of forced collectivization brought food shortages that annihilated millions of Russians, kulaks, city dwellers, and good communists included.

The Soviet Union was hardly immune to the worldwide economic depression of the 1930s, but because the Soviet economy was under his direct control, Stalin set about forcibly transforming his overwhelmingly agricultural nation into an industrial power. He expropriated the property of the kulaks, the middle-class farmers, killing any who resisted, and consolidated the nationalized farms into large "collectives," so that their production could be centrally controlled and distributed. With the nation in the grip of a devastating famine, the Russian people were in urgent need of efficient food production and distribution, but Stalin was intent on financing massive industrialization and therefore ordered most of the precious crop sold for export. When millions, on the verge of starvation, resisted this policy, he had them killed or sent into Siberian exile, a fate that was, more often than not, the eventual equivalent of a death sentence. Many of those who escaped execution or exile starved to death.

Common sense would suggest that the people would inevitably rise up against a mass murderer. But through propaganda, terror, and control of the army as well as a secret police force, Stalin created about himself a cult of personality that made it seem as if any act of opposition was neither more nor less than an act of insanity. Stalin became an object of veneration, even worship. He was the omniscient leader who would bring Russia to greatness and communism to the world.

In many ways, Stalin was a modern czar. Like the czars of old, he used the vastness of Siberia as a means of taking rivals, perceived rivals, and potential rivals out of circulation. Siberia also accommodated common criminals, such as the hard-labor convicts shown in this Stalin-era photograph.

A NIGHT OF LONG KNIVES

BY THE BEGINNING OF THE 1930S, Adolf Hitler had come a long way, but was not quite an absolute dictator—yet. President Hindenburg, however, could do nothing to stop him from building a power base. On February 27, 1933, a fire—almost certainly set by Nazi agitators—consumed the Reichstag, the German parliament building. Hitler responded by blaming the communists and, on the strength of this charge, secured authority to abolish the Communist Party and arrest the party's leaders. Having eliminated the Nazis' most formidable competition, Hitler next gained passage of the Enabling Act, which gave him dictatorial authority for four years, rendering Hindenburg both superfluous and irrelevant.

Hitler put his new power to work immediately, extending the ban against the Communist Party to all German political parties, save the Nazis. Now free to act on his anti-Semitic agenda, he purged all Jews and other "undesirables" from government as well as from such government-controlled institutions as universities. With the opposing parties disposed of, Hitler turned on his own party. Ernst Röhm's SA, whose brutal tactics had been essential to Hitler's rise, now loomed as a threat because the first allegiance of the stormtroopers was to Röhm rather than to Hitler. Accordingly, on June 30, 1934, Hitler led a violent purge of Röhm and the

POP CULTURE

How Do You Spell "Oblivion"?

By the nineteenth century "Siberia" had entered the popular lexicon as a synonym for oblivion. The czars came to their thrones with the understanding that they possessed a mighty weapon: the vastness of the realm they ruled. Russia swallowed up the greatest of invaders—such as Napoleon in 1812—and it also consumed internal dissidents. There was no need for firing squads, nooses, or guillotines when the czars had at their disposal Siberia, an immense territory from which there was, more often than not, no return. It was simultaneously a way of punishing dissent and of quarantining it. Stalin exploited Siberia more than all the czars put together. He made exile to a Siberian gulag—concentration camp—a fixture of twentieth century popular and political culture.

Hermann Göring, one of Adolf Hitler's top lieutenants, speaks at Munich's Königsplatz during the 1934 "people's elections" that elevated Hitler to Führer—*"absolute dictator"—of Germany. A Hitler Youth troop of young drummer boys is seen in the foreground.*

rest of the SA leadership in an operation that became known as the "Night of the Long Knives." Röhm and hundreds of highly placed stormtroopers were murdered or executed, and the SA was replaced by the Schutzstaffel, the SS, a kind of palace guard who had pledged personal loyalty to Hitler.

Under the command of Heinrich Himmler, a fanatical Hitler loyalist, the SS worked in collaboration with a secret police force, the Gestapo, to begin the roundup and "deportation" (that is, imprisonment in concentration camps) of Jews and political adversaries. In concert with this operation, Hitler's minister of propaganda, Joseph Goebbels, deployed a massive campaign of indoctrination to ensure that the German people would support a program of German economic recovery based on immediate and total rearmament in defiance of the Treaty of Versailles. By the time Paul von Hindenburg died on August 2, 1934, there was no one to oppose Adolf Hitler's permanent installation as *Führer*—absolute dictator of Germany.

"That's my trade. Hatred.
It takes you a long way further
than any other emotion."

Joseph Goebbels,
diary entry from 1929

Choosing Sides in a Civil War

By 1934, then, three of the most powerful nations in Europe, Germany, Italy, and the Soviet Union, were under absolute dictators. Sharing similar ideologies, Mussolini and Hitler emerged as natural allies in apparently absolute opposition to Stalin.

The leaders of the world's major democracies, the United States, Great Britain, and France, reeling under the heavy burden of the Great Depression, looked upon the dictatorships with a mixture of fear and loathing—and perhaps a dash of envy. The depression was causing some to doubt the viability of democratic capitalism. As for the ordinary people in the democracies, the more politically sophisticated among them chose sides. Some favored the partnership of government

The Spanish Civil War pitted a bewildering range of political factions against one another, occupying a spectrum ranging from extreme right-wing fascists to extreme left-wing communists and even more radical anarchists. This 1936 poster depicts soldiers firing from the cover of the letters C.N.T.–F.A.I., which stands for Confederación Nacional del Trabajo–Federación Anarquista Ibérica (National Confederation of Labor–Iberian Anarchist Federation), an "Anarcho-Syndicalist" militant organization.

This aggressively patriotic poster (c. 1936–39) for the Spanish fascist Falange Party is captioned "The blood of the fallen does not tolerate oblivion, barrenness, or treason."

and capital demonstrated in Italy and Germany and accepted the brutal tyranny that went along with it as a necessary evil, whereas others supported the Soviet government as a great experiment in social equality—the ultimate liberation of the vast working class—and did not so much accept Stalin's own tyrannical brutality as they simply decided to ignore its existence. As the decade ground on, taking sides increasingly became the pressing moral issue of the era. On the lips of most young, politically engaged people was the question, *What side are you on?* Pressing though it was, this question was largely academic—conversational fodder for the political salon—until the explosion of the Spanish Civil War in 1936.

The war had been brewing for years. Spain was deeply divided. On one side was the Roman Catholic Church, the military, the landowners, and the prosperous business interests; on the other, urban blue-collar workers, agricultural workers, and many of the educated middle class. Each of these sides had its own range of factions, the most extreme of which on the far right were the fascist-inspired and fascist-aligned Falange, and, on the far left, the anarchists. Between these poles were arrayed a spectrum of political parties, including those that embraced monarchism, liberalism, socialism, and communism. By the early 1930s, assassinations and sporadic acts of terrorist violence were common. Crippling mass strikes were called in Valencia and Zaragoza in 1934, and there was fighting on the streets of Madrid and Barcelona. That year, too, the miners in Asturias rose up in a rebellion that was crushed by soldiers under the command of General Francisco Franco, who instantly earned admiration from the Spanish Right and hatred from the Left.

Spain's Republican government did its best to weather the storms, but the elections of February 16, 1936, brought the situation to a crisis as the far-leftist Popular Front assumed a majority following, drawing fire from all of the parties of the Right as well as the handful of centrist parties. Among the first acts of the Popular Front was to send Franco into exile in the Canary Islands. Intended to keep him far from the centers of power, this action actually left Franco free to organize opposition to the leftists without being observed by them. He cobbled together a coalition of the military and right-wing conservative parties, and on July 18, 1936, launched attacks from military garrisons all across Spain, the soldiers taking over the towns adjacent to their garrisons. With this, the Spanish Civil War was under way.

In a matter of days, the right-wing rebels had gained control of Spanish Morocco, the Canary Islands, and the Balearic Islands (except Minorca), as well as parts of the Spanish mainland. Republican forces responded by crushing uprisings wherever and whenever they could. The result was the division of Spain, north from south, in a war that consisted not only of bloody military battles but also of wholesale political murders and executions.

Franco assumed overall command of the right-wing, "Nationalist," forces and was proclaimed head of a Nationalist government set up in Burgos. The Republican (or Loyalist) government was headed by a succession of socialists. Neither the Nationalists nor the Republicans possessed sufficient strength to win outright victory; therefore, both sides deliberately transformed a civil war into an international conflict. The Spanish Civil War was effectively "marketed" to the world as an ideological showdown between fascism and communism.

Franco called on Nazi Germany and fascist Italy to aid his Nationalists. Mussolini and Hitler responded by sending troops, tanks, and planes. The Republicans turned principally to the Soviet Union, but also appealed to France and Mexico,

«NO QUEREMOS ESPAÑA DOMINADA POR UN SOLO GRUPO, SEA ESTE O EL OTRO, NI DE LOS CAPITALISTAS, NI DE LOS PROLETARIOS. ESPAÑA ES PARA TODOS LOS ESPAÑOLES QUE LA QUIERAN Y LA SIRVAN CON LA DISCIPLINA POLITICA DEL ESTADO.»
FRANCO

This 1939 poster, featuring a photograph of General Francisco Franco, tries hard to portray the leader of the fascist Falange as a moderate, quoting his speech: "We do not want Spain dominated by only one group, whether it's this one or another, neither by capitalists nor proletariats."

POP CULTURE

Papa Goes to Spain

Hemingway went to Spain not to fight but to report on the war for the North American Newspaper Alliance. Already famous as a novelist committed to telling the unvarnished truth, Hemingway ended his friendship with another reporter, the novelist John Dos Passos, because Dos Passos refused to toe the Loyalist party line. He exposed atrocities committed by the fascists as well as by the Republicans. In an effort to discredit his former friend, Hemingway circulated a tale that Dos Passos fled Spain because he had grown afraid of combat. If Hemingway's reporting was biased, the great novel his experience in Spain inspired, *For Whom the Bell Tolls* (1940), was an unflinching account of the war and the fate of idealism in war.

whose governments had strong leftist elements. The United States government declared neutrality in the conflict, but many young American leftists put their political ideals on the line by enlisting in the Abraham Lincoln Brigade, one of many International Brigades formed by the Republicans to accept foreign troops. Some forty thousand non-Spaniards served in Republican military units, about half in noncombat roles, including driving ambulances and managing supply and support operations.

The Spanish Civil War was the century's first "proxy war," pitting the political ideology embraced by Italy and Germany on the one hand against that of the Soviet Union on the other—without, however, involving these countries in a direct conflict with one another. For individual volunteers, it was a moral quest—less a contest between fascism and communism than between tyranny and justice. Ideology and morality aside, by the end of 1936, the struggle was a grinding war of attrition for the Spanish. Italian and German commanders, however, saw it as an opportunity to rehearse for the next great European war they were already planning.

The war did not end until early 1939, when, on March 5, the Republican government fled to exile in France. Two days later, fighting broke out in Madrid between communist and anticommunist factions, but by March 28, all Republican armies had either disbanded or surrendered. In Spain, fascism had won, and Francisco Franco was installed as the nation's military dictator.

DETAILS, DETAILS

Rehearsal for Blitzkrieg

The pilots of the German Luftwaffe relished assignment in Spain because it gave them a matchless opportunity to practice and hone dive-bombing techniques against soldiers as well as civilians. The most infamous Luftwaffe mission was against Guernica, a northern Basque village, which was attacked on April 26, 1937—market day—killing from 250 to more than 1,000 villagers. The attack moved Pablo Picasso to create his mural masterpiece, *Guernica*, an evocation of the sheer, indiscriminate horror of a war waged (as Picasso saw it) against life itself.

A Succession of Betrayals

For the Spanish people, the Spanish Civil War was horror, heartbreak, and misery. For the rest of the world, it was a titanic drama that demonstrated the absolute opposition of fascism and communism. Although the outcome was deeply disappointing for communists as well as left-leaning democrats, those who had joined the foreign brigades at least came away feeling they had fought the good fight. Even though their side had lost, it was the right side to have been on.

Certainly, many deeply believed, the choice to volunteer for Republican Spain had been more honorable than what the Western democracies had done in the case of Czechoslovakia. When Adolf Hitler demanded the annexation of the Czech Sudetenland—the German-speaking portion of Czechoslovakia—in 1938, Britain and France simply

Stalin (second from left) looks on as his foreign minister, Vyacheslav Molotov (seated), signs the 1939 German-Soviet Non-Aggression Pact (also known as the Hitler-Stalin Pact) in Moscow. German foreign minister Joachim von Ribbentrop stands to Stalin's right.

folded, concluding the Munich Agreement on September 30, 1938, giving Hitler what he wanted in return for his promise that he would demand no more. As for the United States, its government again remained neutral. Many were surprised and disappointed that Stalin had not weighed in on the Sudetenland issue, but his apologists in the United States, Britain, and France felt confident that, if and when a major war with Italy and Germany erupted, the Soviet Union would unquestionably join—even lead—the fight against fascism and Nazism.

It did not take long for the folly of appeasement to become apparent. No sooner was the ink dry on the Munich Agreement than, on March 16, 1939, Hitler marched his army into Prague and seized all of Czechoslovakia. Even now, neither the Western democracies nor Stalin did anything.

As the leader not only of the Soviet Union but also of world communism, Joseph Stalin surely had no choice but to position himself as the absolute foe of Adolf Hitler, who had by 1939 totally eclipsed Mussolini as the leader of world fascism. But even as the shadow of Nazi Germany crawled across more and more of Europe, Stalin proposed to Hitler a so-called Non-Aggression Pact. The German dictator jumped at the offer, the agreement was signed on August 23, 1939, and it was announced to the world the following day.

The pact stunned communists and leftists everywhere, as well as everyone else who had faith in Stalin's unshakeable opposition to Hitler and who regarded the Soviet Union as the world's great bulwark against fascism. The public portion of the Non-Aggression Pact was just that, not a military alliance, but a mutual pledge of nonaggression, although there was also a separate trade agreement associated with it. Had the planet been privy to the *secret* portion of the agreement, the general response would have been far more extreme. Secretly, Stalin and Hitler agreed to partition Poland between one another, Stalin effectively giving Hitler leave to invade the country in return for yielding to the Soviet Union control of a portion of Poland. Hitler also secretly agreed not to interfere with Stalin's plan to invade the Baltic nations, especially Finland. Many onlookers feared that the Hitler-Stalin pact set the stage for a new world war. Had they known the contents of the full agreement, it would have been apparent that the pact did not merely invite a war, it virtually mandated one.

The Non-Aggression Pact demonstrated that, at bottom, neither Hitler nor Stalin were idealists committed to their respective and opposing political ideologies. They were, in fact, ruthless pragmatists, willing to say or do anything to advance their positions. In Hitler's case, his personal ambition was intimately bound to the spread of Nazism. Stalin's motives, in contrast, were rather different. Theoretically, as a communist, he was supposed to promote the spread of communism worldwide. In practice, however, Stalin was less interested in creating global communism than he was in protecting Soviet Russia. This certainly meant extending the Soviet sphere of influence and outright control beyond Russian borders, but the motive for such aggression was not ideological. It was defensive. Stalin wanted to insulate Russia with a broad buffer zone so that, if war broke out, it would be fought in the nations of Eastern Europe rather than on Soviet soil.

Stalin was pleased with the Non-Aggression Pact, feeling that he had purchased with it long-term security. He was quite certain there would be a war, and he thought it likely that Germany would win. But who won and who lost didn't matter to him now. Whatever happened, the West would be weakened, which meant that the Soviet Union—and Joseph Stalin—would be stronger.

What the man of steel had failed to take into account was the boundless treachery of which Adolf Hitler was capable. His armies invaded Poland on September 1, 1939, thereby commencing World War II. Warsaw fell on the twenty-seventh, and by mid-October the last vestiges of Polish resistance had been crushed. That Stalin had sold out to

REALITY CHECK

A Motive for Aggression

One might argue that Stalin's motive for concluding the Non-Aggression Pact with Hitler was patriotic: the protection of his homeland. Yet peel away the brittle layers of the hard onion that was Joseph Stalin, and you reach the bitter core of his motivation. It was not the propagation of communism, nor even the protection of Mother Russia. Everything he did was aimed at nothing more or less than keeping himself in power. This was his chief motive from the very beginning, and it would continue throughout World War II, and into the postwar period. Had the leaders of the Western democracies understood this, and not mistakenly attributed ideological motives to Stalin's aggressive policies, the intensity and duration of the Cold War might have been very different.

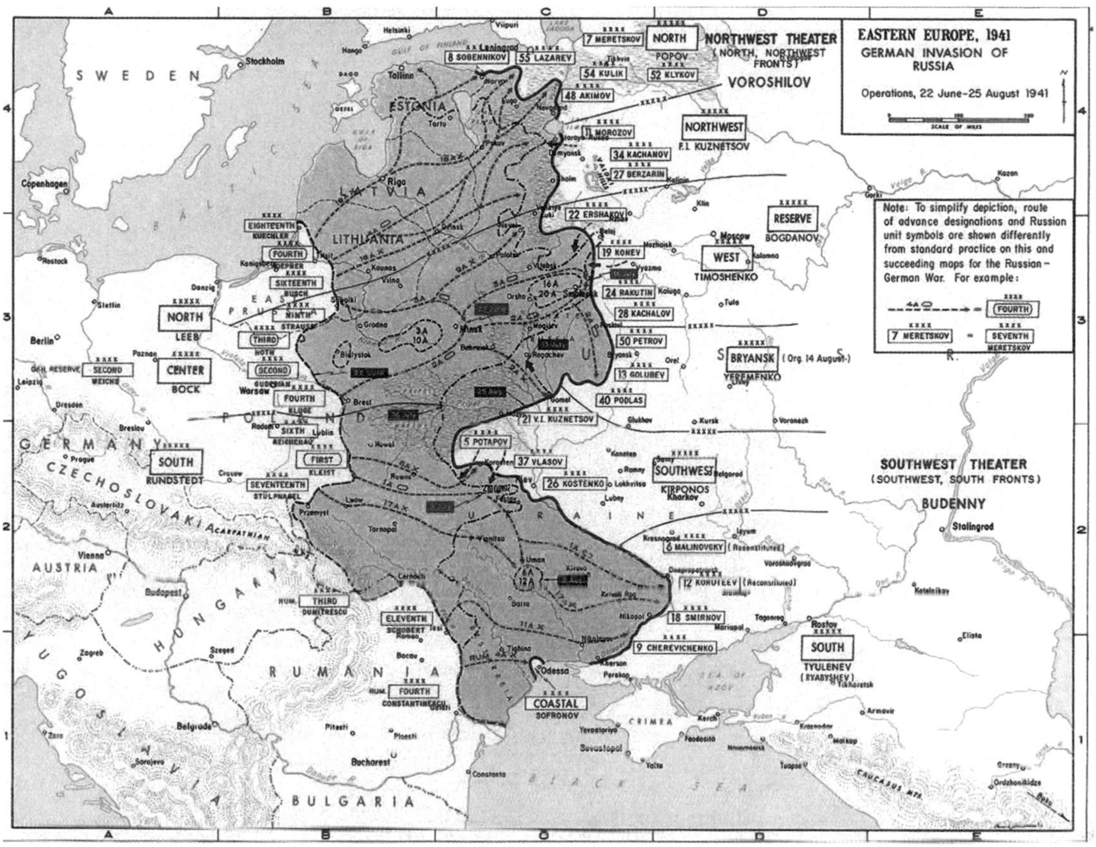

Hitler was made unmistakably clear by the Red Army's simultaneous invasion of Poland. In the end, the Soviet leader had to settle for a smaller slice of the conquered country than he had originally counted on, but he decided to take what he could get. In the meantime, his forces were locked in a brutal war of invasion in Finland. Meeting titanic resistance there, the Red Army suffered heavy casualties in the so-called Winter War, but ultimately prevailed by dint of sheer numbers. Stalin annexed Finland on March 12, 1940, but he did not have a very long time to relish his conquest. On June 22, 1941, Hitler showed him and the rest of the world just how much he valued the Non-Aggression Pact. Without warning, he sent the greatest land invasion force the world had ever seen storming across the Soviet border.

Operation Barbarossa: the German invasion of the Soviet Union, June 22–August 25, 1941. Breaking his Non-Aggression Pact with Stalin, Hitler penetrated deep into Russia and Ukraine before the tide began to turn against the Germans at the Battle of Stalingrad (July 17, 1942–February 2, 1943).

Joseph Stalin was nothing if not paranoid. Yet somehow his paranoia had failed him in the case of Adolf Hitler, who, of all people, he decided to trust. Stalin had given free rein to his paranoia earlier, however, during the Soviet show trials and political purges of 1936–38, when he eviscerated the Red Army by executing most of its senior officer corps. In large measure leaderless, that army was rolled over and routed in June 1941. Stalin was paralyzed by the events, unable to bring himself to rally effective resistance, and the German hordes penetrated deeply into the Soviet land.

Then, just as suddenly and as thoroughly as he had been stricken, Stalin shook off his stupor, took personal command of the Red Army, broadcast personal appeals to the Soviet people, and even enlisted the aid of the Orthodox Church (officially banned by Soviet law) to mount a credible defense. The cost was staggering. Red Army soldiers were at first mowed down like sheaves of Russian wheat. As for the land, what the Germans did not destroy, Stalin ordered burned, enforcing a scorched-earth policy intended to deny the invaders any succor. Slowly, agonizingly, the Soviet defense proved increasingly effective. Increasingly, it became the Germans' turn to die.

Like politics, war makes strange bedfellows. The capitalist democracies of Great Britain and the United States joined in alliance with the communist Soviet Union to defeat Nazi Germany and fascist Italy. This 1942 Soviet propaganda poster—captioned "We will cut off all roads to the evil enemy, he will not escape from this noose!"—depicts Adolf Hitler being strangled with a cloth pulled by British, Soviet, and American hands.

A New Enemy, a New Ally

On June 22, 1941, the Soviet Union had a new enemy, and the Western democracies—or more accurately, Great Britain—had a new, highly unlikely ally. Since the fall of France to the German blitzkrieg in June 1940, and with the United States still neutral, the island nation stood alone against the Nazi conquerors. Fiercely anticommunist though he was, Britain's prime minister Winston Churchill nevertheless now embraced Stalin. What choice did he have?

On September 27, 1940, Adolf Hitler had hosted in Berlin Italy's foreign minister, Count Galeazzo Ciano, and Saburo Kurusu, Japanese ambassador to Germany. The three signed the Tripartite Pact, creating the Rome-Berlin-Tokyo Axis, the military alliance that created the "Axis Powers" of World War II. It was not, however, until December 7, 1941, that the Asian partner in this alliance entered the war with a surprise attack on the United States naval and army bases in and around Pearl Harbor, Hawaii. Thrust into the war, the United States embraced not only Great Britain as an ally but also the Soviet Union. It is true that President Franklin Delano Roosevelt had been, in the years before the war, less vehement in his opposition to communist Russia than Churchill was. His administration extended diplomatic recognition to the Soviet Union at the start of his first term as president, back in 1933. Nevertheless, prewar relations were hardly cordial. Except for a small but vociferous left wing in American politics, the overwhelming popular and official sentiment in the United States held that communism was the implacable enemy of democratic capitalism, and it was assumed that this ideological enmity was fully reciprocated on the Soviet side.

Now, both in Britain and the United States, official policy and popular sentiment underwent a revolution. The Soviet people and their leader were nothing less than gallant allies. Moscow, London, and Washington were irrevocably linked together to oppose Tokyo, Berlin, and Rome. The leaders, armies, and peoples of Russia, Britain, and America were united in righteous might against a common enemy who represented absolute evil. All the old familiar national, political, moral, and ideological lines had been erased and redrawn—in an instant and, as almost everyone seemed willing to believe, indelibly.

TAKEAWAY

A World Redivided

Before World War II, the world appeared to be neatly divided into nations and peoples governed by democratic principles, by fascist (or Nazi) principles, and by communist principles. Just before World War II, this neat division was upset by a pact concluded between Adolf Hitler and Joseph Stalin, avatars of Nazism on the one hand and communism on the other. But Hitler's betrayal of Stalin early in the war forced a new alliance between the Western capitalist democracies and the Soviet communists against their common enemies, Nazi Germany, fascist Italy, and quasi-fascist Japan. The alliance was powerful, but also artificial—a product of temporary necessity—and therefore, in the long run, doomed.

CHAPTER 2

SPOILS OF WAR

The Geopolitics of Misery

THROUGH MUCH OF WORLD WAR II, the alliance between the United States and the Soviet Union and between Great Britain and the Soviet Union proceeded more smoothly than that between the two English-speaking democracies. This seems to defy common sense—until you take into account the vast geography of the war. America and England had to work out ways to fight effectively together, literally side by side, whereas the Red Army fought its war on battlefields far removed from those of the Anglo-American forces. True, Stalin grew impatient with Churchill's insistence on confronting the German and Italian armies in North Africa and Sicily before invading continental Europe via France. Desperately engaged on the war's Eastern Front, Stalin clamored for the Western Allies to open what he called a "second front" in the West, which would force Hitler to transfer troops out of Russia and thereby relieve some of the pressure on the Red Army. Both Churchill and Roosevelt did their best to persuade Stalin that the fighting in the south was indeed forcing Hitler to commit troops that would otherwise be thrown against the Russians, and Stalin was mollified if not satisfied. Nevertheless, he was greatly relieved when the Anglo-American invasion of Normandy finally commenced on D-Day, June 6, 1944. This was the high-water mark of the camaraderie between the Western Allies and the Soviets. The closer the three nations approached victory over Hitler, the more relations between the Anglo-American allies and the Soviets eroded.

BOUGHT WITH BLOOD

AS NAPOLEON HAD DISCOVERED some one hundred thirty years before the Nazis, it was one thing to invade Russia and quite another to conquer it. The scorched-earth landscape Stalin had created, followed by the Russian winter, swallowed up Hitler's hordes, stalling the German offensive. With the spring thaw of 1942, the offensive was resumed, aimed squarely at the Caucasus, rich in oil. To conquer this region required taking a city formerly called Volgograd but recently renamed Stalingrad. Stalin and the millions who, despite everything, still worshipped him were willing to sacrifice all rather than see the city named in honor of the nation's leader fall to the Germans.

In truth, once the ground combat got under way, there was little left of Stalingrad. The Luftwaffe had bombed it to dust. Nevertheless, the Red Army fought from ruined house to rubble heap, holding the Germans in the city while Stalin ordered virtually all that remained of the Red Army in the region to advance on Stalingrad from the north and south. These advancing columns linked up *behind* the German lines, sealing off every avenue of escape. The invaders were besieged, and, after horrifically bloody attempts to break out, they surrendered on February 2, 1943.

It was the turning point of the war on the Soviet Front. Following Stalingrad, the Red Army took the offensive and never gave it up, driving the Nazis out of Russia and back into Eastern Europe. That process, however, was hardly a rout. The retreating invaders burned a swath of devastation and slaughter as they marched to the western borders. Still, by early 1944, the German armies were out of Russia, and Red Army troops now controlled the

NUMBERS

The Price of a City

The Stalingrad campaign began on July 17, 1942, and did not end until February 2, 1943. Initially, the Germans attacked with 270,000 men, but by the time of the Soviet counteroffensive, they had poured in a staggering total of 1,011,000. Red Army strength at the beginning of the engagement was 187,000 men, but the Soviets finally mustered 1,103,000 for the counteroffensive. By the end of the campaign, 150,000 German troops had been killed or wounded and another 91,000 captured. Soviet losses were 130,000 killed, wounded, or captured, and civilian deaths exceeded 40,000.

Three German soldiers patrol a desolate street through the ruins of Stalingrad, September 1942.

Victory! The Soviet Sixty-second Army marches in victory down an Odessa street in April 1944. The battle marked the turning point on the Eastern Front—the beginning of the Red Army's counteroffensive against Hitler.

Baltic states, as well as eastern Poland, Ukraine, Romania, Bulgaria, and Finland. It was territory bought with Russian blood—and, as the Western Allies soon discovered, Stalin was not eager to relinquish it.

"A single death is a tragedy,
a million deaths is a statistic."

Attributed to Joseph Stalin

Spheres of Influence

Combined with the D-Day landings on the Western Front, the collapse of the Russian Front doomed the German cause. Seizing the initiative, the Soviets pushed from the east while the Americans and British advanced from the west and, more slowly, from the south, up the Italian peninsula.

Hitler's world grew smaller day by day, but the Führer was not the only war leader concerned over Stalin's increasingly fast-paced westward advance through Eastern Europe. Roosevelt and Churchill looked on as Poland, Hungary, Czechoslovakia, Yugoslavia, Romania, and other nations were "liberated" by the Red Army only to be occupied by the same.

Churchill, who had stood up against Hitler, did not scare easily, but he was scared now. To his foreign secretary, Anthony Eden, he wrote that the "Russians are drunk with victory and there is no length to which they may not go." Anxious to get into Germany—and to capture Berlin—before the Red Army, Churchill backed his top field commander, Bernard Law Montgomery, in launching Operation Market-Garden in September 1944. An attempt by combined British and U.S. paratroopers to force a Rhine crossing at Arnhem, Holland, the plan was strategically and logistically premature and plagued by poor coordination. Operation Market-Garden ended in retreat.

Having failed in his bid to check Stalin's advance by military means, Churchill, in October, made the perilous journey from London to Moscow in the hope of reaching a diplomatic agreement with Stalin that would at the very least confine Soviet control to a limited portion of Eastern Europe, thus preserving Central Europe for the Western powers. He met with the Soviet leader in his Kremlin office at ten o'clock on the night of October 9 and, exercising all the off-handed charm he could muster—and that was considerable—the prime minister asked the dictator: "How would it do for you to have ninety per cent predominance in Romania, for us to have ninety per cent of the say in Greece, and go fifty-fifty about Yugoslavia?"

In just this way, Churchill sought to divvy up the initial spoils of war. Meeting with no immediate objection from the man of steel, he took a sheet of paper and jotted down additional proportions that would define what he called the respective "spheres of influence" of the West and the Soviets in postwar Europe. In addition to what he had suggested about Romania, Greece, and Yugoslavia, he wrote down a 50-50 split for Hungary and a 25-75 division (in Stalin's favor) for Bulgaria. Silently, Stalin reached for the paper, seized a blue pencil, made a large check mark on the sheet, and slid it back to Churchill. Verbally, he also agreed to concede to Great Britain the postwar status of "leading Mediterranean power."

Conspicuously missing from Churchill's sheet were apportionments of Germany, Czechoslovakia, and Poland. Poland—together

The Eighth U.S. Air Force drops paratroops in an airborne attack on Arnhem, Netherlands, in the first phase of the Allies' ill-fated Operation Market-Garden, September 17, 1944.

POP CULTURE

A Bridge Too Far

One of the perks of victory is writing history from your own point of view. The Allies wanted heroes, and Bernard Law Montgomery was among those drafted for the role. Operation Market-Garden, a tragic failure, was generally depicted, both during the war and after, as at least a partial triumph. Some histories suppressed it altogether. In 1974 the popular historian Cornelius Ryan published *A Bridge Too Far,* which revealed for the first time the titanic failure of Market-Garden and laid the blame at Montgomery's feet. A bestseller, the book was made into a film in 1977 starring Michael Caine, Sean Connery, Anthony Hopkins, and Robert Redford. The title of both the book and the movie comes from one of Montgomery's subordinate commanders, Lieutenant General Frederick Browning, who expressed to the field marshal his fear that the planned operation was overreaching in attempting to force a Rhine crossing at the Arnhem bridge: "I think we may be going a bridge too far."

with the Balkans, except for Greece—Churchill already deemed a lost cause. Poland would lie wholly within the Soviet sphere of influence, and there was nothing, short of going to war against Russia, that could be done about it. As for Czechoslovakia and Germany, the Anglo-American as well as the Soviet armies were still advancing, and Churchill was willing to let the situation play itself out militarily.

From Grand Alliance to Mutual Suspicion

For the Western Allies, it was Soviet treatment of Poland that transformed the perception of Stalin from gallant comrade to ruthlessly opportunistic conqueror. Although its official armed forces were quickly crushed, the Polish Workers' Party organized active underground resistance by 1942 and in 1943 created a small military force known as the People's Army. Also in 1942, another underground resistance group, the Union for Armed Struggle, spun off the Home Army, which, in the course of the war, eclipsed the People's Army as the principal Polish vehicle of armed resistance to German occupation.

Polish Home Army and other resistance fighters go into action in the Warsaw Uprising, August 1944. Stalin purposely held back Red Army support, allowing a German counteroffensive to take a heavy toll on what he knew to be the mostly anticommunist Home Army, thereby paving the way for Soviet occupation and the installation of a communist puppet government.

For most of the war, the People's Army and the Home Army could do little more than carry out acts of sabotage and ambush, but as the Red Army advanced toward Warsaw in the summer of 1944, the Home Army, confident of imminent support from the Soviets, mounted a major uprising against German garrisons in the capital city. To the astonishment and disgust of Churchill as well as the American high command, with the Home Army's operations under way, the Red Army suddenly halted its advance outside of Warsaw. Unaided, the resistance fighters held out for two months before they were finally crushed by the Germans. Only then did the Red Army resume its advance, prompting the Germans to begin their westward retreat—but not before, out of sheer vengeance, they razed some 90 percent of the Polish capital.

To the Western leaders, the failure of the Red Army to aid the Polish Home Army hardly seemed accidental. They knew that Polish communists had created the Polish Committee of National Liberation (later called the Lublin Committee) to serve as the official authority in liberated Polish territory. The Western leaders were also aware that the Home Army included a large number of noncommunist resistance leaders. It seemed clear that Stalin had purposely held back the Red Army so that the Germans would crush the Home Army and, with it, eliminate most of the noncommunist contenders for authority in postwar Poland. Indeed, in January 1945, the Lublin Committee would become the nation's provisional government, and it was immediately recognized by the Soviets. Thus, even before the war in Europe was over, Poland had become a communist country—and a Soviet satellite. Stalin had purchased this outcome at what he must have deemed a bargain price, paying for it with Polish, not Russian, lives.

There was, then, ample reason for the British and Americans to be suspicious of Soviet motives and aims, but the Soviet leadership also had cause to doubt the commitment of the Western Allies. Stalin quite accurately suspected that the Anglo-American leaders were intent on blocking Soviet influence in Central Europe. He was mistaken, however, in his further suspicion that, in their desperation to bring about this end, they would betray the Soviet Union by concluding a separate peace with Germany.

As the European war made its transition from a struggle for the Allies' survival to a scramble for the spoils of war—or, at least, for

NUMBERS

The Biggest Loser

Stalin justified many of his postwar territorial ambitions by pointing to the magnitude of the sacrifice the Soviet people had made in combat. At peak strength, the Red Army fielded some 12.5 million troops. Total Soviet military deaths numbered at least 8,668,400. Civilian deaths directly resulting from the war are estimated at anywhere from seven to twelve million (though some authorizes believe these figures are too low). These losses beggar the imagination; nevertheless, in proportion to population, the devastation in Poland was even worse. Of a million regular Polish troops mobilized, nearly 600,000 were killed—mostly at the beginning of the war. Civilian deaths among Poles are estimated at 5,675,000. Over half of the civilian deaths were Polish Jews who were murdered in the Holocaust.

control of the ruins of war—the ability to subordinate divergent political agendas in a united effort against a common enemy rapidly diminished. The prospect of victory in war seemed to bring with it the equally strong prospect of losing the resulting peace. To avert this—to hold together what was, after all, an unnatural alliance and to forestall a new struggle for control of Europe, a struggle that might well mean World War III—the Allies agreed to meet in what was to be the penultimate grand conference of World War II.

From Malta to Yalta

Preparations for the conference began on twin notes of discord. President Roosevelt, recently elected to an unprecedented fourth term in office, was visibly exhausted and in ill health. Hoping to avoid a long and arduous journey and hoping, too, for a meeting in a salubrious climate, he suggested to Stalin that the conference be convened somewhere on the Mediterranean. Stalin responded by pleading his own health problems, claiming that his physicians vetoed his taking any long trips. He suggested a meeting in the Crimean Black Sea resort town of Yalta.

With much resignation, FDR agreed and set off almost immediately after his fourth inauguration. His first destination, however, was not Yalta, but the British-ruled Mediterranean island of Malta, where

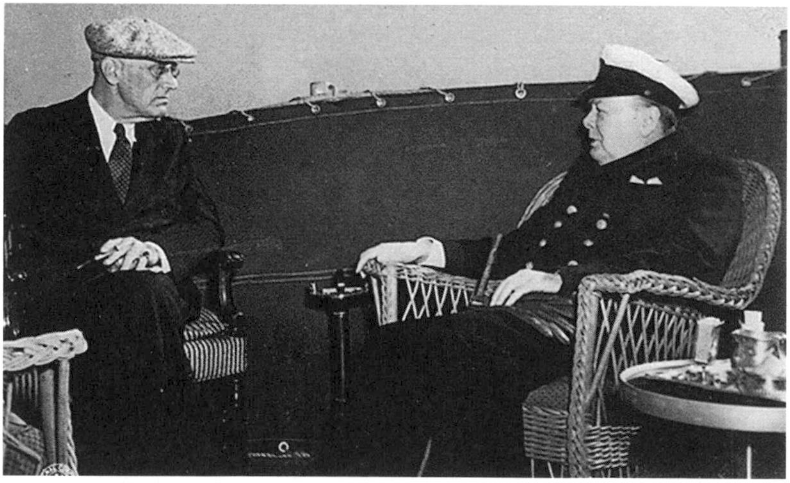

President Roosevelt and Prime Minister Churchill meet in Malta, February 2, 1945. Churchill called the meeting to prepare a united front in negotiations with Stalin at Yalta. He was disappointed by the American president's refusal to treat the preliminary meeting as much more than a social occasion.

Churchill wanted to confer with the president in order to better present a united front to Stalin. Clearly, Churchill expected a substantive meeting, but FDR kept it strictly social. The same was not the case with their respective military staffs. Throughout most of the war, British military planners tended to be methodical, cautious, even plodding—characteristics that often frustrated and galled the far more aggressive American commanders. Now, however, they were so alarmed by Soviet behavior in Eastern Europe that they proposed immediately launching a rapid armored advance on Berlin, with the object of taking and occupying it from the west before the Red Army could reach it from the east. Simultaneously, they wanted to mount a major assault from Italy against Vienna and Prague, again with the object of occupying these capitals in advance of the Red Army. To these proposals, the top American commander present, General George C. Marshall, U.S. Army chief of staff, protested vehemently. He dismissed all of these cities as "political" objectives without military value. The intention of the American army was not to throw away lives on "prestige" targets, but to end the war in the quickest way possible, which was not by capturing real estate, but by simply killing the enemy army.

President Roosevelt with his military advisers at Malta, February 2, 1945. Left to right: Fleet Admiral William D. Leahy (FDR's chief of staff), Fleet Admiral Ernest King (chief of naval operations), FDR, General George C. Marshall (U.S. Army chief of staff), Major General Laurence S. Kuter (substituting for Air Force head lieutenant General Henry "Hap" Arnold). As secretary of state and secretary of defense, Marshall would play a central role in the Cold War.

However the British point of view partook of a vision that looked beyond the present conflict. The British commanders probably did not know at the time that Stalin had remarked to members of a military mission from Yugoslavia who had recently visited him that "whoever occupies a territory also imposes on it his own social system. Everyone imposes his own system as far as his army has power to do so." This was not a matter of choice or policy, Stalin continued: "It cannot be otherwise." Although they may not have been aware of this statement, the British commanders held a view that was virtually identical to Stalin's. Wherever a nation's army stopped, whatever territory it occupied, that place would almost inevitably fall under the occupier's "social system." In the end, however, Marshall prevailed by issuing a threat. If the British plan were adopted, he would recommend to Dwight D. Eisenhower, the supreme allied commander in Europe, that he immediately resign. "Ike" Eisenhower was not only universally popular; it had been largely through the force of his personality—a beacon of goodwill—that the often-contentious Anglo-American alliance not only had survived but was also on the verge of winning the war. Nobody wanted to see him go—or to telegraph a crack in the alliance.

Marshall prevailed, but no one enjoys feeling that he has been blackmailed, and the Yalta Conference, which commenced on February 4, 1945, convened under a cloud of Anglo-American friction on the one hand and Anglo-American-Soviet mutual suspicion on the other. Each of the "Big Three" cherished his own separate agenda. FDR's aim was strictly military. His principal Pacific commander, General Douglas MacArthur, had drawn up a plan for the invasion of Japan that called

THE BERLIN QUESTION

Beginning immediately after the end of the war and continuing throughout the entire Cold War period, armchair generals and diplomats and historians debated what "might have been" had Eisenhower and Marshall agreed to target Berlin as an objective.

Some insist it would have kept the Soviets out of postwar Germany entirely, thereby precluding the division of the nation into East and West Germany. With Berlin and, indeed, all of Germany removed as flashpoints for wider conflict, some argue, the Cold War would have been less costly and perhaps of briefer duration. Others, however, have suggested that even an undivided Germany under the control of the Western Allies would still have required a large commitment of troops in the Cold War period and would still have been a flashpoint. They also suggest that, by dividing Germany, the Soviets had taken on as great a defensive responsibility as the Western nations. Furthermore, divided Germany—and divided Berlin—became an extraordinarily dramatic propaganda asset for the West. Whereas West Germany and West Berlin were economically successful and culturally vibrant in the postwar years, East Germany and East Berlin were places of grim economic struggle and drab existence, presided over by a repressive regime. Indeed, life under communism was so dreadful that East German authorities had to imprison the population behind the infamous Berlin Wall to keep them from defecting to the West. In any case, the military cost of capturing Berlin was staggering. American general Omar Bradley had counseled General Eisenhower that the cost of a Battle of Berlin would exceed 100,000 Allied killed and wounded. Ike was unwilling to spill this much blood for what he deemed a "prestige" or "political" objective. In fact, Bradley's estimate, high as it was, proved far too low. According to official Soviet records (which many historians believe undercount casualties), the Red Army lost 81,116 dead or missing (including 2,825 Polish troops) plus 280,251 sick or wounded, a total casualty roll of 361,367 men. (German losses in the Battle of Berlin were 458,080 killed and 479,298 captured.)

The Yalta Conference in progress, February 1945: President Roosevelt is seated second from right. To his right are Fleet Admiral William Leahy and General George C. Marshall. Stalin is seated second from left, and Churchill is seated at the lower left, his back to the camera and a cigar in smoking position.

for the Red Army to fight the Japanese forces on the Asian mainland, pinning them down while U.S. and British troops invaded the Japanese home islands. Churchill was already looking beyond the end of the war and wanted Stalin to assure him that there would be free elections and democratic governments in the nations of Eastern Europe. Stalin's agenda was also political, but what he wanted—what he demanded—was the assurance of a Soviet sphere of influence in the nations of Eastern Europe, arguing that such a buffer was vital to the national security of the Soviet Union. In addition, all three leaders agreed on the necessity of hammering out a plan to govern occupied Germany, but they differed as to the nature of the plan. Because the Red Army was a mere forty miles outside of Berlin at the time of the conference, Stalin believed he held the whip hand on this issue. FDR was more willing than Churchill to give him much of what he wanted in return for a pledge of Soviet participation in the invasion of Japan and a Soviet promise to join and to support the emerging United Nations.

The first item discussed was the fate of Poland. Stalin declared that this issue was bound up both with Soviet honor and Soviet security. He pointed out that, throughout history, invaders had used Poland as a corridor into Russia, and he insisted that a free and independent Poland, sufficiently strong to shut the corridor on would-be invaders, was in the Soviet interest. This said, he declared as nonnegotiable Soviet possession of all the territory it had already annexed in eastern Poland; however, the rest of Poland would be compensated for with territory annexed to it from the west at the expense of Germany. He promised free elections in Poland, and Churchill and Roosevelt took him at his word—which, when the elections actually took place in 1947, was revealed as worthless. Those blatantly rigged elections officially transformed Poland into a communist state and, two years later, new elections put into place what was essentially a Soviet puppet regime.

From the Polish question, FDR moved to address the role of the Soviet Union in the war against Japan. Stalin agreed to declare war on the empire within ninety days after the unconditional surrender of Germany, on condition that the United States recognize the independence of Mongolia from what was at the time noncommunist Nationalist China. Stalin wanted to ensure a buffer between Soviet territory and Chinese territory. Roosevelt and Churchill agreed—without bothering to consult China. Another high-handed agreement concerned the postwar repatriation of displaced citizens of the Soviet Union and Yugoslavia. They would be returned to their respective countries—regardless of their individual wishes.

Roosevelt, ailing, tired, and single-mindedly focused on obtaining a Soviet commitment to declare war on Japan and to join the UN, did not unite with Churchill to drive a hard bargain, but instead conceded much of what Stalin wanted. He did draw the line at Stalin's demand that each of the fifteen so-called Soviet Socialist Republics that formed the USSR be given separate United Nations membership—a move that would have multiplied the Soviet vote in the organization by fifteen. After protracted negotiation, separate membership for only two Soviet republics was allowed in addition to membership for the USSR itself; however, Stalin secured a secret understanding that each permanent member of the Security Council would have veto power, so that any country could block decisions it did not want.

TO DO IT RIGHT—THIS TIME

In retrospect, leaders such as FDR and Churchill believed that World War II might have been prevented had the League of Nations, established after World War I, been structured so as to be genuinely effective. Both Roosevelt and the British prime minister believed it essential to create a new international body to replace the discredited and largely defunct League. And, this time, they wanted to do it right.

The idea for the "United Nations," as the organization was to be called, flowed out of 1943 wartime Allied conferences in Moscow, Cairo, and Tehran. From August to October 1944, representatives of the Republic of China, Britain, the United States, and the Soviet Union convened at the Dumbarton Oaks estate in Washington, D.C., to hammer out plans for the organization, and on April 25, 1945, a United Nations Conference on International Organization commenced in San Francisco to draft a charter. Fifty nations as well as representatives from various non-governmental organizations participated, the Charter of the United Nations was signed on June 26, and United Nations officially came into being on October 24, 1945. The UN was destined to become a public forum in which the communist-dominated East and the democratically dominated West stated their positions and aired their grievances. Some onlookers believed the organization was just so much talk, whereas others insisted that was just the point. Better for nations to talk to one another than to shoot at one another.

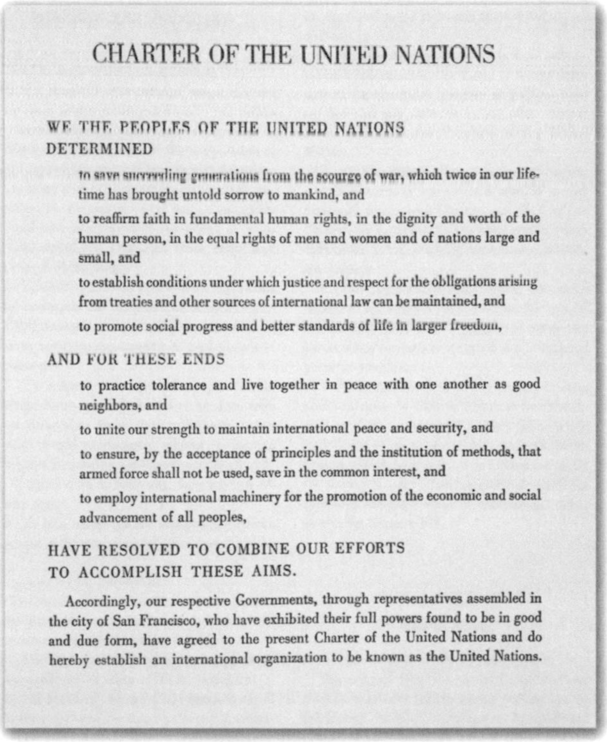

CHARTER OF THE UNITED NATIONS

WE THE PEOPLES OF THE UNITED NATIONS
DETERMINED

to save succeeding generations from the scourge of war, which twice in our lifetime has brought untold sorrow to mankind, and

to reaffirm faith in fundamental human rights, in the dignity and worth of the human person, in the equal rights of men and women and of nations large and small, and

to establish conditions under which justice and respect for the obligations arising from treaties and other sources of international law can be maintained, and

to promote social progress and better standards of life in larger freedom,

AND FOR THESE ENDS

to practice tolerance and live together in peace with one another as good neighbors, and

to unite our strength to maintain international peace and security, and

to ensure, by the acceptance of principles and the institution of methods, that armed force shall not be used, save in the common interest, and

to employ international machinery for the promotion of the economic and social advancement of all peoples,

HAVE RESOLVED TO COMBINE OUR EFFORTS
TO ACCOMPLISH THESE AIMS.

Accordingly, our respective Governments, through representatives assembled in the city of San Francisco, who have exhibited their full powers found to be in good and due form, have agreed to the present Charter of the United Nations and do hereby establish an international organization to be known as the United Nations.

This charter created the United Nations on June 26, 1945, an organization intended to provide what the League of Nations, established after World War I, had failed to provide: a peaceful alternative to war.

Turning to the occupation of Germany, the Big Three ratified a previously formulated plan for establishing three zones of occupation, an American Zone, a British Zone, and a Russian Zone. (Later, in response to French demands, the United States and Great Britain would cede portions of their zones to France, for the creation of a French Zone. Berlin was in the Russian Zone, but it was agreed that the city would be divided into three sectors, each controlled by one of the Allies.

Apparent agreement was reached on the restoration of original governments to all nations that had been invaded by the Axis. Exceptions to this were the Vichy French government, which had collaborated with the Nazis and was considered illegitimate, and the governments of Romania and Bulgaria, which the Soviets had simply liquidated. Stalin also insisted on excluding the Polish government-in-exile, requiring instead that an entirely new government be formed by "free" elections. All three leaders agreed that the form of each of the governments, whether restored or new, would be democratic insofar as all would hold free elections, subject to the stipulation that the "establishment of order in Europe, and the rebuilding of national economic life, must be achieved by processes which will enable the liberated peoples to destroy the last vestiges of Nazism and fascism and to create democratic institutions of their own choice."

"To jaw-jaw is better than to war-war."

Winston Churchill, speech,
Washington, D.C., June 26, 1954

As for Germany itself, beyond immediate issues of occupation, it was agreed that the nation would be both demilitarized and de-Nazified—all those with Nazi affiliations would be barred from government or other public service. Reparations would ultimately be determined by a reparation council, which, at Stalin's insistence, would be permanently located in the Soviet Union. It was immediately agreed, however, that some portion of reparations would consist of the forced labor of German soldiers, who would be employed in repairing war damage inflicted by their nation. There was also to be established a Committee on Dismemberment of Germany, which would issue recommendations on whether to divide Germany into several nations or to reconstitute it as a single nation.

At the end of the conference, the Big Three took pains to hide any evidence of discord and instead presented a strong united front to the world, embodied in a document called the "Declaration of Liberated Europe." Of the three participants at Yalta, Churchill came away most deeply dissatisfied. He had been forced to yield point after point to Stalin because FDR either compromised with the Soviet leader or acquiesced to him entirely. Churchill interpreted this as evidence that his friend and closest ally was simply too sick and too tired to fight or even to hold his ground.

Dying Hopes

When Franklin Roosevelt, back in Washington, delivered his report on the Yalta Conference to a joint session of Congress on March 1, 1945, he spoke as he had never before spoken in public: from a wheelchair. He also began the speech as he had never before begun a speech: with an apology. "I hope," he said, "that you will pardon me for this unusual posture of sitting down during the presentation of what I want to say, but I know that you will realize that it makes it a lot easier for me not to

An exhausted Franklin Roosevelt reports to Congress, March 1, 1945, on the Yalta Conference. He would die the next month.

have to carry about ten pounds of steel around on the bottom of my legs; and also because of the fact that I have just completed a fourteen-thousand-mile trip."

Those seated closest to the president were shaken by his appearance, which was gaunt, drawn, and ashen. He looked as if he had been used up, and his delivery, in the past always conversational but economical and energetic, was now rambling, a bit repetitious, its tone perhaps wistful. The greatness of Roosevelt's leadership had been founded on his ability to temper exuberant optimism with unflinching realism and vice versa. Now he seemed to struggle to bring optimism to the fore, even at the expense of realism. Uncharacteristically, the speech rang with a hint of hollowness, like a great bell harboring an unseen crack. The speech of March 1, 1945, would be Roosevelt's last, its words those of a dying man.

FDR managed to assure Congress that he came from the "Crimea Conference with a firm belief that we have made a good start on the road to a world of peace." He spoke of the "heroic advance of our troops in Germany, on German soil, toward a meeting with the gallant Red Army," a meeting (he omitted to note) that would take place *west* of Berlin. He spoke of the "tremendous stride" that had been made toward building "the foundation for an international accord that would bring order and security after the chaos of the war," and of the "enthusiastic effort" that had been made to reach agreement. "I have never for an instant wavered in my belief that an agreement to insure world peace and security can be reached." Thus the president verbally sparred without delivering the knockout punch of triumph. The speech was more a hope than an affirmation, and a dying hope at that.

FDR acknowledged the problem of what he called "queer ideas of . . . 'spheres of influence' that were incompatible with the basic principles of international collaboration. If allowed to go on unchecked, these developments might have had tragic results, in time." The conditional past tense—"might have had"—was strangely unconvincing. The president reported that "We met in the Crimea, determined to settle this matter of liberated areas," and he went on to say that he was "happy to confirm to the Congress that we did arrive at a settlement—and, incidentally, a unanimous settlement," yet—almost gratuitously—he hedged his bet by observing in the sentence prior to this one that "Things that might happen that we cannot foresee at this moment might happen suddenly—unexpectedly—next week or next month."

FDR THE MAN

For a dozen of the most difficult and fateful years of American and world history, the weight of decision had rested on the shoulders of Franklin Delano Roosevelt. Stricken by a paralytic disease in 1921—it was long assumed to have been polio, but recent medical scholars believe it was a severe case of Guillain-Barré syndrome—he was left a paraplegic, but, through sheer will and the support of his remarkable wife, Eleanor Roosevelt, he returned to public and political life.

His smile was both irresistible and inspirational, conveying a calm yet exuberant optimism, and the American people came to depend on him so thoroughly that he was elected to four terms as president in an era before the Twenty-second Amendment restricted presidents to two. The combination of ceaseless toil, heavy responsibility, and the chronic effects of his paralysis, high blood pressure, atherosclerosis, heart disease, and chain smoking eroded his health. By January 1944, FDR began suffering from chronic headaches and extreme fatigue, which even caused him at times to lose consciousness. He was diagnosed with hypertensive heart disease, a diagnosis that rapidly escalated to congestive heart failure, for which digitalis was prescribed. On April 28, 1944, he was stricken with acute inflammation of the gall bladder and was dosed with codeine. In August 1944, while campaigning for his fourth term, FDR suffered a severe bout of chest pain. His physicians feared that he had been stricken by a heart attack, but they found no evidence of one. In the meantime, he lost weight, becoming gaunt. In April 1945, he retreated to the "Little White House" at Warm Springs, Georgia, for a rest. While sitting for an artist's sketch on April 12, 1945, he remarked, "I have a terrific pain in the back of my head." Those were his last words. He fell into a coma, and then died. The cause of death was a massive cerebral hemorrhage. The morticians who prepared the president's body found his arteries so hardened that they could not insert a needle to inject embalming fluid.

FDR: The buoyant presence Americans had grown accustomed to—evident here in a speech during the 1930s—was a haggard memory in 1945, after four years of war. The March 1, 1945, report to Congress on Yalta was not only the president's final speech, it also was the only one he gave seated.

In all, it was the performance of a worn-out leader struggling to be affirmative and never quite succeeding in overcoming doubt—his or the nation's. He tried, valiantly, to work himself up to an uplifting and believably hopeful peroration: "The Crimea Conference was a successful effort by the three leading nations to find a common ground for peace. It ought to spell the end of the system of unilateral action, the exclusive alliances, the spheres of influence, the balances of power, and all the other expedients that have been tried for centuries and have always failed."

How tragic his use of the phrase *ought to* instead the simple verb *will*! In the course of the half-century that followed this speech, the world would be locked in a twilight war, a shadow war, a "cold war"—albeit one violently marked by hot spasms of violence and even prolonged shooting wars—a conflict that grew directly out of "exclusive alliances," "spheres of influence," and "balances of power."

Victory and Disillusionment

On April 9, 1945, while the armies of the Western Allies held back, as they had been ordered by their military and political leaders, Soviet forces captured Vienna and Königsberg (present-day Kaliningrad), then encircled Berlin on the twenty-fifth. During this period, Adolf Hitler, refusing to surrender, pressed children and old men into an army that barely existed anymore. Leaving his people to the indifferent mercy of air raids, artillery bombardments, and street fighting, he burrowed into a hardened command bunker beneath the streets of Berlin. About midnight of April 28/29, while Red Army soldiers were taking Berlin block by bloody block, he married his mistress, Eva Braun, in a Nazi civil ceremony, then appointed Admiral Karl Dönitz to succeed him as head of state with Joseph Goebbels as chancellor. The next day, April 30, he said his good-byes to Goebbels and the handful of others who remained

By April 1945, Adolf Hitler's vaunted "Thousand-Year Reich" had contracted to the space of his bunker beneath the ruined streets of Berlin. A boyish Red Army soldier stands in the Führer's private quarters, where Hitler and his bride of one day, Eva Braun, committed suicide on April 30.

American G.I. William Robertson embraces Red Army lieutenant Alexander Sylvashko as U.S. and Soviet forces link up for the first time in the war, at Torgau, Germany, April 25, 1945. The good feelings would not last.

with him in the bunker. Retiring to his austere suite with his bride, he committed suicide with her. Eva Braun took poison—biting down on a thin glass ampoule of cyanide—and Adolf Hitler either poisoned or shot himself or did both. No one knows for sure, because, when the Soviets at last overran the bunker, they found only the charred remains of a man and a woman, which they identified as Hitler and Braun, but with just enough uncertainty that rumors of Hitler's escape persisted for years, as if he were a monster that could not be killed.

Dönitz immediately opened negotiations with the Western powers, hoping to save as many troops and refugees as possible from the awful reprisals he knew the Soviets would rain down upon them. True to the agreement reached at Casablanca earlier in the war, the Allies refused to negotiate but insisted on nothing less than unconditional surrender. At 2:41 on the morning of May 7 in General Eisenhower's headquarters at Reims, France, General Alfred Jodl, chief military adviser to Adolf Hitler, signed a document stipulating just such a surrender. Days earlier, on April 25, in Torgau, an eastern German city on the River Elbe, soldiers of the United States Army and the Red Army met for the first time in World War II. Soldiers' letters and diaries on both sides report that the opposing columns approached each other hesitantly, cautiously at first before coming together in eager handshakes, slaps on the back, and even exuberant hugs. The photographs show only the handshakes and hugs, not the wariness.

EXTRA THE STARS AND STRIPES EXTRA

VICTORY

Nazis Reveal Surrender To Western Allies, Russia

The unconditional surrender of Germany to the Western Allies and Soviet Russia was announced by the German high command yesterday morning.

The official announcements from the Allied governments are expected to come simultaneously from Washington, London and Moscow today.

The British Ministry of Information, proclaiming that today would be 'Victory in Europe Day,' said Prime Minister Churchill would make 'an official announcement' at 3 PM.

President Truman said he had agreed with the British and Russian governments that no surrender proclamation would be made 'until simultaneous announcements could be made by the three governments.'

King George VI of England sent Gen. Eisenhower a cablegram last night congratulating him and his armies on the 'complete and crushing victory' in Europe.

Nazis Still Fight Reds At Prague

Prayer, Tears, Laughter —The World Celebrates

The Stars and Stripes, *official newspaper of the U.S. armed forces in World War II, trumpets the Allied victory in Europe, May 8, 1945. The second headline seems to unite the "Western Allies" and "Russia" even as it distinguishes between them.*

Stalin remained guarded. He refused to accept the May 7 surrender in the Western European headquarters of the supreme commander of the Western Allies, and insisted on a second surrender ceremony in Berlin, occupied by the Red Army, in Eastern Europe, on May 8.

> "I guess we didn't know what to expect from the Russians, but when you looked at them and examined them, you couldn't tell whether, you know? If you put an American uniform on them, they could have been American!"
>
> *Al Aronson, 69th Infantry Division, U.S. Army, commenting on the meeting of U.S. and Soviet troops at Torgau, Germany.*

Elsewhere among the people of the victorious nations there was jubilation at the announcement of V-E Day—Victory in Europe Day—a joy, in the United States, tempered only by the fact that Franklin Roosevelt was not alive to witness the victory. His successor, Harry S. Truman, lacked FDR's charismatic optimism, but made up for it with his blunt, frank, and firm realism. He took time to rejoice in the victory in Europe, but he knew that a hard and bloody road remained to be traveled in Japan, and he was far more wary of Stalin and the Soviets than FDR had been or, at least, had let on in public.

The truth was that Harry Truman probably understood Stalin better than Roosevelt had. Both he and the Soviet leader were, at bottom, pragmatists rather than idealists. One week after Hitler invaded the Soviet Union in June 1941, then-Senator Truman remarked, "If we see that Germany is winning we ought to help Russia, and if Russia is winning we ought to help Germany, and that way let them kill as many as possible although I don't want to see Hitler victorious under any circumstances." Four years later, on V-E Day, Truman could not help but recognize that Stalin's armies occupied Poland, Germany to the Elbe, half of Czechoslovakia, all of Hungary, Austria to the west of Vienna, and much of the Balkans. A keen student of history, the new president was convinced that Stalin would emulate the Russian czars of old and fiercely resist relinquishing any territory he now held. He understood that Stalin had in hand what the czars had always wanted, a buffer zone between Russia and the West. He also understood—or thought he understood—that Stalin had an even deeper motive for conquest: to spread communism on an international scale. Truman knew enough about Marx and Lenin to understand that both had believed the planet was too small to contain both capitalism and communism, and, as far as he knew, Stalin, pragmatist though he was, subscribed to this doctrine.

It is unclear what weight the moribund Roosevelt had given to the March 21, 1945, report of his ambassador to the Soviet Union, Averell Harriman, who was appalled by Red Army brutality in Poland. "Unless we wish to accept the 20th century barbarian invasion of Europe, with repercussions extending further and further East as well," he cabled the White House, "we must find ways to arrest the Soviet domineering policy. . . . If we don't face these issues squarely now, history will record the period of the next generation as the Soviet age." What is clear is that Truman took such assessments very seriously; however, he was not one

Harry S. Truman, having become president upon the death of FDR just four days earlier, addresses a special joint session of Congress, April 16, 1945.

ALTERNATE TAKE

If FDR Had Lived

To most observers, the difference between Roosevelt's attitude toward Stalin and Truman's approach to him was striking. Whereas FDR repeatedly made concessions to Stalin in an effort to maintain—or create—cordial relations, Truman regarded him with outright suspicion. This has led some historians to speculate that U.S.-Soviet relations under a continued Roosevelt administration would have been different from what developed under Truman. Some have suggested that the Cold War might have been delayed, lessened in intensity, or avoided altogether, whereas others have speculated that the nation and the free world were better off for Truman's blunt display of firmness. Neither of these views takes into consideration evidence that, in the days before his death, FDR was losing patience with Stalin. While at Warm Springs, he studied one of Ambassador Averell Harriman's telegrams warning of Soviet treachery. Slamming both fists on his wheelchair, he exclaimed, "Averell is right. We can't do business with Stalin."

to panic. When Harriman returned to Washington and presented the dire situation of Soviet "domineering" to the new president, Truman told him that he believed it was unrealistic to expect the Russians to yield to American wishes 100 percent, but he intended to get "85 percent" from them on the "big issues," including Poland. Anticipating a showdown with the Soviet Union's foreign minister Vyacheslav Molotov, he remarked, "I intend to tell Molotov that in words of one syllable."

On the morning of April 23, before his scheduled Oval Office meeting that afternoon with Molotov and representatives from China and Britain, Truman gathered his cabinet and Russian experts for a briefing. Secretary of War Henry Stimson counseled Truman to tread softly, lest relations with the Soviets break down just as they were needed to finish the fight against Japan. General George C. Marshall agreed, suggesting that the president not press the Soviets until Japan had been defeated. Secretary of the Navy James Forrestal sharply disagreed, warning Truman that the Soviets were violating the Yalta Agreement in their treatment of Poland and they clearly intended to grab Bulgaria and Romania as well. Ambassador Harriman took the hardest line of all, insisting that failure to be firm with the Russians now would only encourage Stalin to take more and more in the future. Truman announced that he would follow the recommendations of the consensus in dealing with Molotov. In other words, unlike FDR, he intended to take a hard line, even if this risked losing Soviet participation against Japan.

Some future key Cold War figures pose briefly together as the end of World War II approaches (likely shortly before or after the April 23 meeting with Truman): Averell Harriman, U.S. ambassador to the Soviet Union (1943–46) is fourth from left, and to his left is Soviet foreign minister Vyacheslav Molotov. U.S. Secretary of State (1944–45) and U.N. ambassador (1945–46) Edward Stettinius is seventh from left, and Alger Hiss, who would later be accused of being a Soviet mole in the Department of State, is at the far right in the photograph.

Molotov was accompanied at the meeting by Andrei Gromyko, the Soviet ambassador to the United States. As he had promised, Truman did not mince words. He told Molotov that he felt "deep disappointment" over the Soviet failure to honor the terms of the Yalta Agreement in Poland. He bluntly warned Molotov—and instructed him to convey the warning directly to Marshal Stalin—that continued failure to honor the Yalta Agreement "would seriously shake confidence in the unity of the three governments."

Molotov attempted a lengthy filibuster by way of reply, but Truman repeatedly broke in, interrupting him four times, each time speaking more bluntly than before until he finally said simply that there "was only one thing to do . . . Marshal Stalin [had] to carry out that agreement in accordance with his word."

At this, according to Truman's interpreter, Molotov's complexion turned "ashy." "I have never been talked to like that in my life," he sputtered.

"Carry out your agreements," Truman shot back, "and you won't get talked to like that." With this, the president rose from behind his desk to signal that the meeting was at an end.

The harsh words and the abrupt gesture signaled much more than the end of a meeting. It signaled the beginning of a new era in relations between the United States (and its Western allies) and the Soviet Union. The Russians, the "gallant comrades" of World War II, had become a pack of liars, and the goodwill born of struggle against a common menace dissolved in mutual suspicion verging on outright enmity. Even Harriman, who advocated a hard line against the Soviets, confessed himself "a little taken aback." As for Stimson, who had counseled forbearance, he was suddenly very, very worried and dashed off a note to the president: "I think it is very important that I should have a talk with you as soon as possible on a highly secret matter." Two days later, Stimson met with Truman in the Oval Office. With him was Major General Leslie R. Groves, head of something that only a handful of government officials knew about. It was called the "Manhattan Project," though Stimson referred to it simply as "S-1." Stimson withdrew from his briefcase a letter he had written that morning. "Within four months," it began, "we shall in all probability have completed the most terrible weapon ever known in human history, one bomb of which could destroy a whole city." Two weeks in office, and it was the first Harry Truman had heard of the atomic bomb.

TAKEAWAY

An Alliance Crumbles

As victory against their common enemy approached, the uneasy—indeed, unnatural—alliance between the Western democracies and Stalin's Soviet Union unraveled. The Soviet Red Army advanced rapidly to occupy much of Eastern Europe, not just in an effort to drive the Germans out, but to establish a Soviet "sphere of influence." President Roosevelt, anxious to secure Soviet aid in the imminent invasion of Japan, tended to give Stalin much of what he wanted in Eastern Europe, whereas Prime Minister Churchill—and later, President Truman—sought to hold a harder line or at least firmly negotiate the containment of Stalin's expansionist ambitions.

CHAPTER 3

NEW SUN RISING

Atomic Warfare, Nuclear Diplomacy

SECRETARY OF WAR HENRY STIMSON AND MAJOR GENERAL LESLIE R. GROVES, military head of the Manhattan Project, did not brief Truman on the existence and nature of the atomic bomb until two weeks after he was sworn into office. But the news didn't come as a complete surprise. James F. Byrnes, soon to become Truman's secretary of state, had already told the president that a new weapon, perhaps sufficiently powerful to wipe out entire cities, was about to be added to the U.S. arsenal. It would, he said, kill "people on an unprecedented scale," which, to Byrnes, meant that it was a war-ending, war-winning weapon that would put America in a position to dictate whatever surrender terms it wanted. Stimson's detailed briefing showed Truman that Byrnes had not been exaggerating, but Stimson had a different take on the significance of the atomic bomb. Yes, it might end the war, but the more enduring issue was how the bomb would shape the future after the war, the fate of humankind itself.

The day after he became president following the sudden death of Franklin Roosevelt, Truman confessed to reporters that he felt as if "the moon, the stars, and all the planets" had fallen on him. The news Byrnes and Stimson brought should have hit him even harder. The former vice president, senator from Missouri, failed haberdasher, and high school graduate was offered a Faustian bargain of unprecedented magnitude: the opportunity to end the most destructive war in history by using the most destructive weapon the world had ever known, a weapon that put into the hands of humanity the means of humanity's annihilation.

"No 'Great Decision' "

For years after he left the White House to live out the rest of his long life quietly in Independence, Missouri, Harry Truman was repeatedly asked how he could possibly have steeled himself to make such an unimaginably difficult decision. And, repeatedly, the former president responded that the "atom bomb was no 'great decision.' . . . It was merely another powerful weapon in the arsenal of righteousness. The dropping of the bombs stopped the war, saved millions of lives. It was a purely military decision."

During the night of March 9/10, 1945, Tokyo was firebombed by B-29s of the U.S. Army Air Forces. Police in Tokyo put the death toll at 124,711, with 286,358 buildings destroyed. The most destructive air raid in history, the Tokyo firebombing wrought more death and devastation than the atomic bombing of Hiroshima (August 6) or Nagasaki (August 9).

REALITY CHECK

The Nuclear Mystique

To many, during World War II and after, the use of atomic weapons was unthinkable—the most extreme form of strategic and tactical taboo. Truman's willingness to regard the atomic bomb as just another military weapon was not as callous as it may at first seem. The fact was that dropping even two atomic bombs was not the most destructive action the United States had taken against Japan. Curtis LeMay, who commanded B-29 bombing operations against Japan, ordered massive incendiary attacks on sixty-four Japanese cities, including the horrific firebombing of Tokyo during March 9/10, 1945. In three hours, the American aircraft dropped 1,665 tons of incendiary bombs; raging and unstoppable firestorms incinerated more than 100,000 civilians and razed sixteen square miles of the city. Total civilian deaths from the entire firebombing campaign certainly exceeded 200,000—a deadlier toll than that of the atomic attacks against Hiroshima and Nagasaki combined.

A Purely Military Decision

Truman was neither obtuse, blind, nor amoral. Nor was he focused on the future; instead, he looked strictly at the present, which was filled with a single overwhelming fact: the war with Japan. It had fallen to him to win—and end—that war.

"There are no innocent civilians, so it doesn't bother me so much to be killing innocent bystanders."

U.S. Army Air Forces major general Curtis E. LeMay, 1945

The Manhattan Project—the epic American effort to transform atomic theory into an operational atomic weapon—had its origin in fears that Nazi scientists were hard at work on just such a weapon. By 1939, a group of American scientists, a number of them recent refugees from European fascist and Nazi regimes, had became greatly alarmed by German research under the leadership of the brilliant physicist Werner Heisenberg, who was known to be investigating nuclear fission. This was the process by which the energy of the binding force within the nucleus of the uranium or plutonium atom—the force that holds the constituents of the nucleus together—could be liberated so as to yield a release of energy in an explosion greater than any that human beings had ever before created on earth. In March 1939, G. B. Pegram, a Columbia University physicist, arranged a meeting between the eminent nuclear physicist Enrico Fermi—a refugee from Mussolini's Italy—and the U.S. Department of the Navy. Shortly after this, Leó Szilárd, an expatriate physicist from fascist Hungary, called on America's most famous scientific refugee, Albert Einstein, to write a personal letter to President Roosevelt, urging him to begin work on a military fission project in order to beat the Germans to the punch. Einstein wrote the letter on August 2, 1939, and the president authorized, in February 1940, a preliminary research project. When Pearl Harbor was bombed

Major General Leslie Groves (left), military chief of the Manhattan Project, made for a sharp political, intellectual, and even physical contrast with the project's scientific head, physicist J. Robert Oppenheimer (right), but the two developed an extraordinarily effective working relationship built on a grudging mutual respect.

on December 7, 1941, thrusting the United States into the war, fission research was catapulted to very high priority status. By the middle of 1942, those at work on the project concluded that a military application of fission was indeed feasible, although it would require research and manufacturing facilities on an unprecedented scale. Hearing this, the War Department reclassified the work from a research project to a massive engineering enterprise and therefore assigned it to the U.S. Army Corps of Engineers. Since a great deal of the early research was being conducted at Columbia University, in Manhattan, the project was given to the Corps' "Manhattan Engineer District" in June 1942, and from that point on it was referred to—when the ultra-secret undertaking was referred to at all—as the Manhattan Project.

Under Groves, who took over the project in September 1942, having just finished managing the design and construction of the Pentagon outside of Washington (the biggest office building in the world), and J. Robert Oppenheimer, who came on board as scientific director the next year, the Manhattan Project recruited an army of brilliant scientists and engineers. Working in profound secrecy (though, as it turned out, not in *perfect* secrecy), they successfully detonated a prototype bomb at 5:29 A.M. on July 16, 1945, in a remote test site near Alamogordo, New Mexico.

The Trinity test near Alamogordo, New Mexico, at 5:29 on the morning of July 16, 1945, was the first explosion of an atomic bomb. The plutonium core of the bomb—Manhattan Project scientists called it the "Gadget"—was assembled off-site, then transported via a U.S. Army staff car to the tower from which the bomb would be detonated.

Manhattan Project scientists and technicians prepare to hoist the "Gadget" into place at the top of the tower from which it would be detonated above ground level.

The Trinity test—the birth of a war-winning weapon and the central fact of the Cold War that was yet to come. Ken Bainbridge, director of the test, turned to chief Manhattan Project scientist J. Robert Oppenheimer, after the fireball was out. "Now we're all sons of bitches," he said.

At the culminating moment, President Truman was half a world away, in the Berlin suburb of Potsdam, attending what would be the final conference of World War II with Churchill and Stalin. Hours later, Stimson shared with the president a coyly coded message he had received from his Washington-based special assistant on atomic issues, George L. Harrison: "Operated on this morning. Diagnosis not yet complete but results seem satisfactory and already exceed expectations. . . . Dr. Groves pleased." Truman's overriding emotion was relief that the "gadget," which had eaten up two billion secretly appropriated 1940s dollars, had actually worked.

Stimson read the coded cable to Dwight Eisenhower, the supreme Allied commander in Europe. "Well, I listened," Ike later remarked, "and I didn't volunteer anything because, after all, my war was over in Europe and it wasn't up to me. But I was getting more and more depressed just thinking about it. Then he asked for my opinion, so I told him I was against it on two counts. First, the Japanese were ready to surrender and it wasn't necessary to hit them with that awful thing. Second, I hated to see our country be the first to use such a weapon." Despite—or perhaps because of—the misgivings he himself had already expressed to Truman, Stimson (Eisenhower recalled) "got furious" at this reply. Ike understood the source of Stimson's anger: "After all, it had been his responsibility to push for all the huge expenditure to develop the bomb. . . . Still, it was an awful problem."

POP CULTURE

Atomic Legend

Tall, gaunt, yet strikingly handsome, physicist J. Robert Oppenheimer exuded a charisma that clings to his memory even today. For many, he became a veritable icon of tortured genius, the great, sensitive man who agonized over the moral implications of the atomic age he had been instrumental in ushering in. Oppenheimer himself contributed to this pop culture image when he famously recalled his initial thoughts on witnessing the successful test detonation of the atomic bomb near Alamogordo, New Mexico, on July 16, 1945. He said that a passage from the Hindu Bhagavad Gita had come to mind: "I am become death, the destroyer of worlds." Maybe. According to Oppenheimer's brother, Frank, also present at the test, Robert said just two words: "It worked."

On July 20, Truman himself discussed the role of the bomb in the Pacific war with Eisenhower as well as with the second highest-ranking general in Europe, Omar Bradley. Ike repeated his opposition at that time. Bradley later recalled that Eisenhower was the only military man opposed to the use of the weapon, but he was hardly the only person of consequence who protested the use of the bomb. Even before the prototype was tested in New Mexico, many of the scientists who had worked on the device expressed their opposition to its use. On June 11, 1945, Professor James Franck passed up through government channels the confidential report of a committee of seven distinguished Manhattan Project scientists who urged that the bomb not be used in an unannounced attack against Japan, but instead called for a "demonstration in an appropriately selected uninhabited area." Among these seven scientists was Leó Szilárd, the very man who had induced Einstein to write the 1940 letter that triggered the atomic bomb effort—albeit when it was a question of getting the bomb before the Nazis did.

Clearly, the weapon caused intense moral agonizing in the scientific community. Another panel, which consisted of more of the top Manhattan Project scientists, including Oppenheimer and Enrico Fermi (leader of the team that had created the world's first sustained nuclear chain reaction—the proof-of-concept for the bomb), issued a report on June 16 concluding that there was "no acceptable alternative to military use" of the bomb. A few days later, on June 27, Undersecretary of the Navy Ralph A. Bard transmitted a memorandum expressing just the opposite: that deploying the weapon without advance warning would destroy "the position of the United States as a great humanitarian nation," especially now that Japan seemed so close to surrender.

On July 3, Szilárd drew up a petition condemning atomic bombs as "a means for the ruthless annihilation of cities" and appealed to Truman to issue an executive order barring their use. He obtained the signatures of fifty-nine Manhattan Project scientists, but then held the petition back so that he could circulate another, on July 17, to which sixty-nine scientists subscribed. Four days earlier, eighteen scientists at the Oak Ridge, Tennessee, atomic laboratory signed a similar petition, and, shortly after this, another sixty-seven Oak Ridge scientists signed yet another petition—this one calling for a description and demonstration of the bomb before it was actually used.

REALITY CHECK

Scientific Mutiny?

The antibomb petitions were never leaked to the American public. Had they been, the impression might have been created that the scientists of the Manhattan Project were engaged in a mutiny on moral grounds. In truth, though more than a few leading scientists signed protests and petitions, the Manhattan Project employed thousands of scientists, the vast majority of whom either expressed no opinion or said that they favored the immediate military use of the atomic bomb. By and large, those who worked on the bomb believed they had acted as patriots who contributed to the safety of the world. They were proud of what they had achieved.

~~SECRET~~

July 17, 1945

A PETITION TO THE PRESIDENT OF THE UNITED STATES

Discoveries of which the people of the United States are not aware may affect the welfare of this nation in the near future. The liberation of atomic power which has been achieved places atomic bombs in the hands of the Army. It places in your hands, as Commander-in-Chief, the fateful decision whether or not to sanction the use of such bombs in the present phase of the war against Japan.

We, the undersigned scientists, have been working in the field of atomic power. Until recently we have had to fear that the United States might be attacked by atomic bombs during this war and that her only defense might lie in a counterattack by the same means. Today, with the defeat of Germany, this danger is averted and we feel impelled to say what follows:

The war has to be brought speedily to a successful conclusion and attacks by atomic bombs may very well be an effective method of warfare. We feel, however, that such attacks on Japan could not be justified, at least not unless the terms which will be imposed after the war on Japan were made public in detail and Japan were given an opportunity to surrender.

If such public announcement gave assurance to the Japanese that they could look forward to a life devoted to peaceful pursuits in their homeland and if Japan still refused to surrender our nation might then, in certain circumstances, find itself forced to resort to the use of atomic bombs. Such a step, however, ought not to be made at any time without seriously considering the moral responsibilities which are involved.

The development of atomic power will provide the nations with new means of destruction. The atomic bombs at our disposal represent only the first step in this direction, and there is almost no limit to the destructive power which will become available in the course of their future development. Thus a nation which sets the precedent of using these newly liberated forces of nature for purposes of destruction may have to bear the responsibility of opening the door to an era of devastation on an unimaginable scale.

If after this war a situation is allowed to develop in the world which permits rival powers to be in uncontrolled possession of these new means of destruction, the cities of the United States as well as the cities of other nations will be in continuous danger of sudden annihilation. All the resources of the United States, moral and material, may have to be mobilized to prevent the advent of such a world situation. Its prevention is at present the solemn responsibility of the United States--singled out by virtue of her lead in the field of atomic power.

The added material strength which this lead gives to the United States brings with it the obligation of restraint and if we were to violate this obligation our moral position would be weakened in the eyes of the world and in our own eyes. It would then be more difficult for us to live up to our responsibility of bringing the unloosened forces of destruction under control.

In view of the foregoing, we, the undersigned, respectfully petition: first, that you exercise your power as Commander-in-Chief, to rule that the United States shall not resort to the use of atomic bombs in this war unless the terms which will be imposed upon Japan have been made public in detail and Japan knowing these terms has refused to surrender; second, that in such an event the question whether or not to use atomic bombs be decided by you in the light of the considerations presented in this petition as well as all the other moral responsibilities which are involved.

R E Lapp
R S Mulliken
E P Wigner
George S. Monk
Leo Szilard

J. J. Nickson
W. H. Zachariasen
Francis R. Shonka
John A. Simpson Jr.
Walter Bartky
John R. Howe

Frank Foote

DECLASSIFIED
NND 730039
By ______ NARS, Date ______

One of several petitions some Manhattan Project scientists submitted to President Truman after the successful Trinity test, asking that he not use atomic weapons.

President Truman may not have actually seen any of the petitions, but he knew about them, and he had certainly gotten an earful from Eisenhower. He listened thoughtfully to all proposals of alternatives to the bomb, but for him it finally came down to military reality. Ike and others might believe that the Japanese were close to surrender in the summer of 1945, and, certainly, in any meaningful military sense Japan had lost the war. The Imperial armies had been forced to withdraw from most captured territory, the Japanese air arm had been knocked out of the skies, the Imperial Navy was almost entirely on the Pacific floor. Moreover, Japanese cities had been so intensively bombed that it would require an effort to find a handful that were still sufficiently intact to make bombing with an atomic weapon worthwhile.

Despite all of this, the Japanese continued to fight, and even if it was a losing battle, its toll on American lives was horrific. Truman became president on April 12, 1945. The successful test in New Mexico occurred on July 16. During the three months between these events, the Japanese military—fighting for a defeated nation—managed to inflict battle casualties on the Americans that amounted nearly to half the total of three full *years* of the Pacific war.

By the summer of 1945, Japan was a defeated military power—yet the nation kept fighting, taking a terrible toll on American lives. A measure of Japanese desperation was the introduction of the suicide—kamikaze—attack. The aircraft carrier USS Bunker Hill *was hit by two kamikazes thirty seconds apart on May 11, 1945. The ship remained afloat, but 372 sailors were killed and 264 wounded. Kamikazes accounted for the sinking of 34 U.S. Navy ships, severely damaged 368 others, and killed nearly 5,000 sailors, wounding more than 4,800. Numbers like these persuaded President Truman to use "the bomb" against Japan.*

ALTERNATE TAKE

Victory without the Bomb?

Even today, a number of historians continue to believe that Japan was so badly beaten by the summer of 1945 that it would have surrendered without the United States having resorted to the use of nuclear weapons. Yet actual combat experience persuasively supported the assessment of those who favored using the atomic bomb. During the entire Pacific campaign, not a single Japanese military unit had ever surrendered. At Iwo Jima, for instance, of 21,000 troops in the Japanese garrison, only 212 were captured by the end of the battle. The rest were either killed in action or committed suicide. U.S. casualties numbered 24,733 killed or wounded. And Iwo Jima was a speck of volcanic rock. How much more fiercely would the Japanese defend their home islands? On balance, it seems unlikely that the war against Japan would have been definitively ended without the degree of devastation wrought by what Emperor Hirohito called "a cruel new bomb."

Without using the bomb, Truman had just two options. The first was to continue bombing Japan with conventional explosives while also blockading the country into starvation. This approach would continue to kill Japanese civilians, and American experts estimated that the war conducted this way would grind on for well over a year. Even worse, many believed that this strategy might put an end to Japanese aggression, but it would nevertheless fail to extort unconditional surrender. The Japanese government, many highly placed authorities were convinced, would sooner see all of the nation's cities in ruins and the people starved than surrender.

The nonnuclear alternative to continued bombing and blockade was an immediate invasion on a scale so massive that it would dwarf the D-Day landings at Normandy. Everyone agreed that this would likely end the war more quickly and more decisively, but nevertheless victory was not projected until June 1946—and the cost in American lives would be at least a quarter million. General Douglas MacArthur, who would lead the invasion, put the number much higher, predicting a million killed or wounded.

Without doubt, Truman deeply appreciated the moral, even apocalyptic implications of the atomic bomb. "We have discovered the most terrible bomb in the history of the world," he recorded in his diary on July 25, 1945. "It may be the fire of destruction prophesied in the Euphrates Valley Era, after Noah and his fabulous Ark." But, for him, the terrible figures of American dead outweighed any moral objections to the use of the bomb, even if it risked apocalypse. The point was that the possibility of an end to civilization was just that—a possibility. What was real, here and now, was the war. To his wife, Bess, Truman wrote of his belief that the new weapon would "end the war a year sooner . . . and think of the kids who won't be killed! That's the important thing."

A Purely Political Decision

The "kids who won't be killed" was a very real, very compelling motive for Harry Truman. Even now, however, when ending the Pacific war was practically all he thought about, the president saw one more thing. At Yalta nearly a half-year earlier, FDR had extracted from Stalin a pledge to declare war against Japan. The Soviet leader had agreed to do so within ninety days of Germany's surrender. That deadline had not yet been reached by the time of the Potsdam Conference, but both

The Potsdam Conference—July 16–August 2, 1945—brought together President Harry S. Truman, Prime Minister Winston Churchill, and Premier Joseph Stalin to determine the shape of the postwar world. Truman is seated just left of center, his back to the camera; Churchill, cigar in mouth, is seen at the left, and Stalin, in the uniform of a Red Army field marshal, is seen in profile on the right.

Truman and Churchill appealed to Stalin to make the declaration now. They did so in the full realization of what had happened—what was happening—in Eastern Europe. Once the Red Army occupied territory, it was loath to withdraw from it. A Soviet presence in Manchuria and Japan (even the northern part of it) might doom these territories to becoming Soviet satellites after the war. Both Western Allied leaders were willing to risk this eventuality when Soviet aid seemed necessary to the success of the invasion of the Japanese home islands, but now that the atomic bomb loomed as a viable weapon, Truman realized that if he could use it to end the war before the Soviets started to invade, he might preempt some of Stalin's territorial claims in Asia.

Thus, even before anyone outside of the inner circles of the American government knew about the atomic bomb, it had become a strategic weapon of the postwar world.

"A little bit of a squirt."

Harry S. Truman, first impression of Joseph Stalin (standing five-foot-five) at Potsdam

A MOLE AT LOS ALAMOS

TRUMAN HAD EVERY REASON TO BELIEVE that the atomic bomb was unknown to the wider world. After all, he had been president of the United States for two weeks before he knew much about it.

On July 24, Secretary of War Stimson sat down to lunch with the president to discuss the best way to tell Stalin about the bomb—without telling him very much. On the one hand, Truman was anxious to keep a military-technological secret from this ally that neither he nor Churchill trusted in the least, and, on the other hand, he was leery of the response the legendarily volcanic dictator would have when he learned that the Western Allies had been cobbling together a secret super-weapon behind his back. After having goaded and urged Stalin to enter the war against Japan, Truman now also feared that the announcement of the weapon would prompt him to invade immediately—and stake his claim on Japanese territory. But to leave Stalin entirely in the dark would be an affront that was possibly tantamount to breaking the alliance. "Uncle Joe," as Truman and Churchill jocularly referred to the Man of Steel, had to be told.

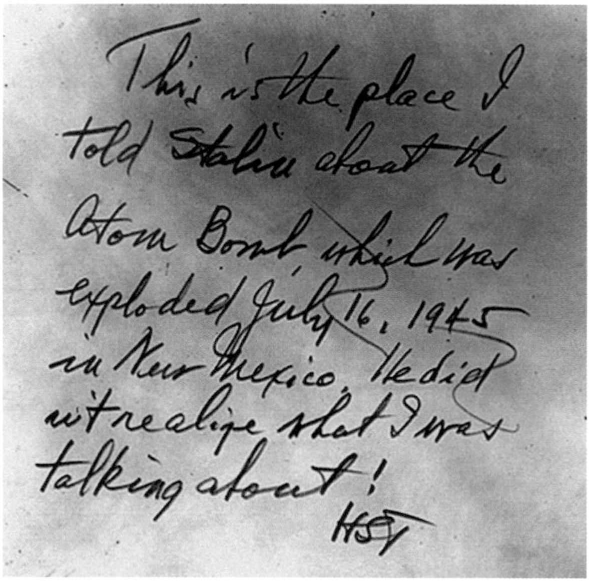

President Truman inscribed the back of a photo of the Potsdam Conference, "This is the place I told Stalin about the Atom Bomb, which was exploded July 16, 1945, in New Mexico. He didn't realize what I was talking about!" That was the way the president chose to explain the fact that Stalin barely reacted to the news of the bomb. In fact, thanks to moles in the Manhattan Project, the Soviets arrived at Potsdam very well informed about the U.S. atomic weapons program. For Stalin, Truman's news was yesterday's news.

Legendary among his friends, staff, and advisers as a consummately skilled poker player, Truman played it close to the vest. He knew he held the winning hand, but he was not about to lay his cards on the table. At the end of the July 24 plenary session of the Potsdam Conference, the president left his official translator behind and offhandedly approached Stalin. "I casually mentioned to Stalin that we had a new weapon of unusual destructive force." That was it. Stalin turned toward Truman his own perfect poker face. "The Russian Premier showed no special interest," Truman later reported. "All he said was that he was glad to hear it and hoped we would make 'good use of it against the Japanese.'"

Truman was puzzled and disturbed. The deadly games born of mutual distrust that would mark postwar relations between West and

East had, clearly, begun. That was bad enough. But was Stalin bluffing in his indifference to the news of the bomb? Or perhaps he simply failed to grasp its significance. Or did he already know about the bomb? And if so, how?

Those who had collaborated on the Manhattan Project confronted and solved staggering scientific and technological problems, but one problem they never satisfactorily solved was the basic opposition of the military need for absolute secrecy and the scientific need for absolute openness. Strategy proceeds by secrecy, whereas discovery proceeds by communication, discussion, and free exchange. In the end, compromises had to be reached, and Major General Leslie Groves reluctantly gave the scientists considerable freedom to meet, converse, and exchange information. He also was obliged to loosen restrictions on who was hired for the project. Ordinarily, anyone who worked on a project so secret that it was beyond top secret would have to pass the most stringent of background investigations. But, Groves well knew, many of the top atomic scientists were foreigners, not Americans, whose backgrounds were somewhat obscure. Furthermore, as intellectuals who opposed Nazism and fascism, many of the scientists, whether refugees, immigrants, or born Americans, had long-standing ties to communism and even to the International Communist Party. Ordinarily, such connections would have meant automatic disqualification for any high-level security clearance. But to apply such standards now would have meant disqualifying most of the only people capable of building the bomb—including the scientific director of the enterprise, J. Robert Oppenheimer, whose links to the Communist Party included close friends, his wife, and his former mistress. Groves knew all of this, but he also knew that he needed Oppenheimer, and he covered for him as well as for others.

As if these security compromises were not sufficiently risky, the Manhattan Project was a collaborative effort between the Americans and the British—who, after all, had already commenced atomic weapons research by the time the Manhattan Project got under way. Those scientists the British brought on board had not been vetted by U.S. security. It was assumed that British security specialists—who were, if anything, considerably more sophisticated than their U.S. counterparts—had thoroughly investigated everyone they sent to the research facility at Los Alamos, New Mexico.

REALITY CHECK

The Admirable General

Rotund, pompous, and full of bluster, Leslie Groves did not cut a very impressive military figure and, side by side with J. Robert Oppenheimer—slender, subtle, soft-spoken—he looked almost buffoonish. Yet this career military officer and hard-nosed engineer was precisely the ramrod the Manhattan Project required. He had come to the project having just completed managing the design and construction of the Pentagon in just eighteen months from first blueprints to finishing touches. He drove the atomic bomb effort with similar energy and efficiency and, what is more, possessed the sensitivity and sophistication to know just how much discipline he could force on freewheeling scientists without provoking them to rebellion. Physically, intellectually, emotionally, and even politically—Groves was a conservative Republican, Oppenheimer a left-leaning liberal Democrat—the general and the physicist could not have been less compatible, yet, thanks largely to the initiative of Groves, they forged a spectacularly successful working relationship built on mutual tolerance as well as respect.

Los Alamos Laboratory security badge photograph of Klaus Fuchs, the German-born British scientist who supplied the Soviets with a steady stream of top-secret information on the atomic bomb and the hydrogen bomb after it.

Klaus Fuchs was born in 1911 at Rüsselsheim, Germany, the son of a Lutheran pastor who became a professor of theology. He survived considerable emotional instability in his family—both his grandmother and mother as well as one of his sisters committed suicide, and his other sister was diagnosed as schizophrenic—to study at the universities of Leipzig and Kiel. Like many other young German intellectuals, Fuchs joined the Communist Party. Under threat from the Nazis in 1933, he fled to France and, from there, to England, where he took a PhD in physics at the University of Bristol in 1937 and, the same year, received a DSc degree from the University of Edinburgh. At Edinburgh he studied with another German expatriate, the great physicist Max Born, under whose tutelage he published an important paper on quantum mechanics, which earned him a teaching position at Edinburgh.

Despite Fuch's eminence as a scientist, he was still a German, and the British interned him as an enemy alien at the start of World War II. Max Born interceded on his behalf, and in early 1941 he was allowed to return to Edinburgh. There he was approached by another leading refugee scientist, Rudolf Peierls, who was teaching at the University of Birmingham. Peierls recruited him for work on what was called "Tube Alloys," the code name for Britain's atomic weapons project. Fuchs was considered so valuable for this work that he was summarily granted British citizenship in 1942 in return for signing the Official Secrets Act, by which he pledged to protect all the research and secret information to which he became privy.

He signed the act in bad faith.

"I joined the Communist Party because I felt I had to be in some organization."

Klaus Fuchs

When Hitler abrogated his non-aggression pact with Stalin by invading the Soviet Union in June 1941, Fuchs began covertly transmitting to Russia, through a Soviet embassy contact, military and scientific secrets. His belief, as he later explained at his trial for treason, was that the Soviets, as an ally, had a right to know what the British—and, later, the Americans—were developing. Late in 1943, while he was very much an active spy, Fuchs accompanied his mentor Peierls to Columbia University to work directly on the Manhattan Project.

He came to America armed with instructions from his Soviet embassy handler on precisely how he was to make contact with his "control" in New York. Fuchs was told to go to a certain spot at a certain time, carrying a book with a yellow cover. He was instructed to look for a man carrying a package in a brown paper wrapper, tied with string. Once they saw each other, they were to board different subway trains to another designated location and meet there. This first contact took place in 1944, just after New Year's.

While he was spying in England, Fuchs transmitted whatever information he thought valuable as he acquired it. In New York, however, his control, Harry Gold, relayed to Fuchs specific questions from Russian physicists. The Swiss-born son of Russian émigrés, Gold was a member of the Communist Party of the United States, worked as a chemist, and had been spying for the Soviets since 1934. Most of the questions he conveyed related in detail to the processing of fissionable material, something Soviet scientists had yet to figure out.

For the Soviets, the connection between Fuchs and Gold was highly productive for several months, but in August 1944, for the first time, Fuchs missed a rendezvous with Gold. Gold sought out Fuchs's sister, Kristel, who was living in Cambridge, Massachusetts. From her, he learned only that Fuchs had been transferred "somewhere in the Southwest" but would be returning to the East Coast for a visit during the winter holidays. Gold therefore bided his time, meeting with Fuchs in January 1945.

Since August 1944, Fuchs had been working in the Theoretical Physics Division of the Los Alamos laboratory under Hans Bethe, who had emigrated from Germany to the United States in 1935. Fuchs's work in Bethe's division was central to the development of the weapon's implosion trigger, the mechanism by which the bomb's fissile material was instantaneously compressed so as to create a critical mass that would result in a chain reaction sufficiently energetic to produce a tremendous explosion. Fuchs's work played an even more important role in the creation after the war of an implosion trigger for thermonuclear weapons: the hydrogen bomb.

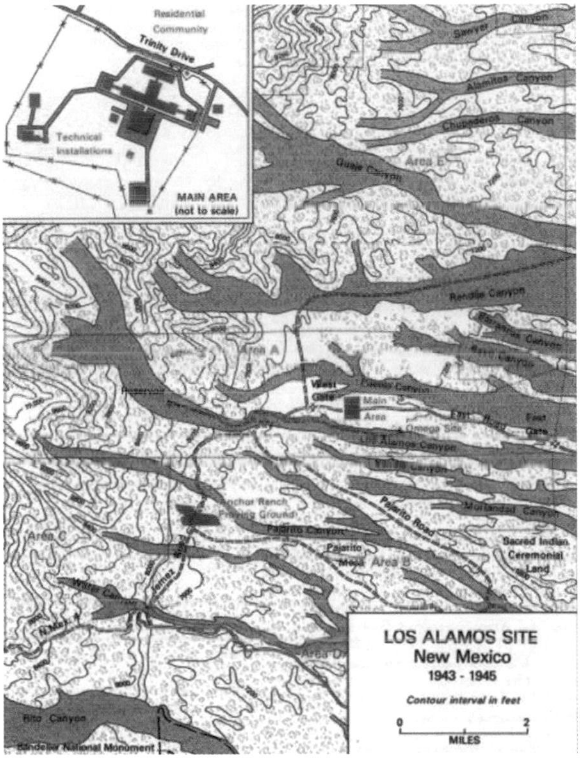

Map of the Los Alamos laboratory site as it existed during the war years.

Los Alamos mole David Greenglass and his handler Harry Gold were each given a torn half of a Jell-O box. By matching halves, they were to identify each other when they met in Santa Fe, New Mexico. At the 1951 trial of Julius and Ethel Rosenberg and Morton Sobell, prosecutor Roy Cohn (who also served as red-baiting Senator Joseph McCarthy's right-hand man) introduced a Jell-O box into evidence, explaining that Julius Rosenberg and his Soviet contact had likewise used the matching halves method to identify themselves to one another. The evidence box had actually been purchased by the prosecution at a grocery store.

The Web Widens

Gold's handler in the Soviet consulate in New York sent him to Santa Fe, New Mexico—the nearest city to Los Alamos—to meet with Fuchs as well as another Los Alamos spy, David Greenglass. Gold was supposedly given a torn half of a Jell-O box and told that Greenglass would have the other half. That is how they would identify each other.

Born in New York City in 1922, Greenglass married Ruth Printz in 1942, and the couple joined the Young Communist League shortly before Greenglass was drafted into the U.S. Army in 1943. A skilled machinist, he was quickly promoted to sergeant and sent to work at the gargantuan uranium enrichment plant at Oak Ridge, Tennessee. From there, he was transferred to the Los Alamos laboratory.

David Greenglass's sister Ethel and her husband Julius were New Yorkers who were also active in the Communist Party. Learning from Ruth that David had been assigned to work at a secret weapons laboratory, Julius—perhaps in concert with Ethel—prevailed on Ruth to recruit her husband as a spy. Thus, beginning in November 1944, Greenglass began passing nuclear secrets to the Soviets through Julius. In testimony given during his treason trial in 1951, Greenglass confessed to giving the Rosenbergs sketches and other information relating to the "implosion lenses" used for the bomb tested at Alamogordo and also for "Fat Man," the bomb used against Nagasaki on August 9, 1945.

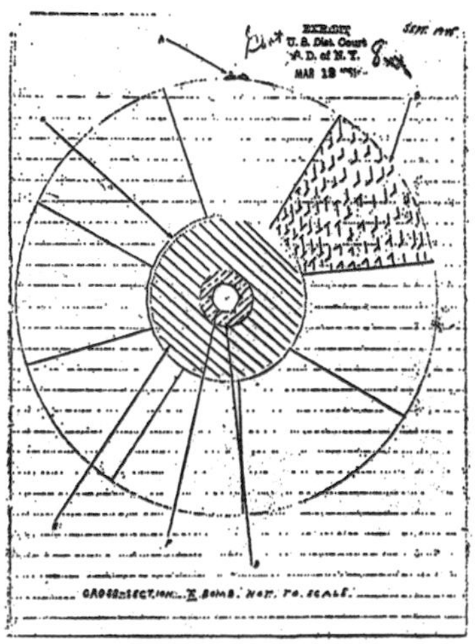

State's witness David Greenglass made this cross section sketch of the implosion-type atomic bomb in 1951, just before the start of United States v. Julius and Ethel Rosenberg and Morton Sobell, *to represent the drawing he gave to Julius Rosenberg to pass on to the Soviets. The sketch, marked Exhibit 8, was declassified by the Atomic Energy Commission but was nevertheless impounded immediately after the trial and not made public until 1966. Experts who examined it at that time judged it too crude to have been of any real value to Soviet scientists.*

We will return in detail to the subject of espionage in the Cold War in Chapter 11 and to the Rosenberg trial in Chapter 13; however, we should note here that while there has been much dispute over the value of what Greenglass gave the Soviets, everyone involved on the Soviet side has reported that Fuchs's intelligence was highly useful. Certainly we now know that it was valuable enough to make Truman's announcement of the weapon to Stalin come across to the dictator as yesterday's news.

Nuclear War

For the first and second times in history, atomic weapons were used in war on August 6, 1945, against the city of Hiroshima, and on August 9, against Nagasaki. At Hiroshima, 80,000 were killed by the blast, and an additional 50,000 to 60,000 died of injuries or radiation poisoning over the next several months. At Nagasaki, more than 70,000 died.

Official U.S. Army photo of Hiroshima, Japan, after the bomb.

This photograph of the detonation of the "Fat Man" bomb over Nagasaki, August 9, 1945, was taken by the reconnaissance B-29 shadowing Bock's Car, *the aircraft that dropped the weapon.*

President Truman broadcast a radio speech on the evening after the Nagasaki bomb was dropped. He explained:

> I realize the tragic significance of the atomic bomb. But we knew that our enemies were on the search for it. . . . We won the race of discovery against the Germans. . . . We have used it against those who attacked us without warning at Pearl Harbor, against those who have starved and beaten and executed American prisoners of war, against those who have abandoned all pretense of obeying international laws of warfare. We have used it to shorten the agony of war, in order to save the lives of thousands and thousands of young Americans. . . . We shall continue to use it until we completely destroy Japan's power to make war. Only a Japanese surrender will stop us.

The next day, August 10, the president received a message from the Japanese government, informing him that it would accept unconditional surrender—albeit, in effect, on one condition: that Emperor Hirohito be permitted to remain on the throne. This prompted some of the president's advisers to argue for outright rejection of the offer. Truman's executive order authorizing the use of atomic weapons against Japan had specified that the bombs could be dropped as they became available and at the discretion of the military commanders in charge. When the Hiroshima bomb did not elicit an immediate offer of surrender, it was decided to drop the next bomb as soon as possible in order to give the impression that the United States had a stockpile of them. But the fact was that America's nuclear arsenal on August 6 consisted of just two bombs, with a third on its way. It took time to manufacture an atomic weapon—especially to refine sufficient fissionable material—but the enemy did not know that, and thus the stratagem of bluff became a principal feature of nuclear warfare. Bluff—the impression that a nation commanded a bigger nuclear stockpile than it really did—would play a key role throughout the Cold War. Now, however, those who counseled rejecting the Japanese peace overture pointed out that a third bomb was indeed ready. Use it, and surely the Japanese would give up their emperor.

Oval Office, White House, August 14, 1945: President Truman announces the surrender of Japan. Note the absence of jubilation.

In contrast to Truman's somber Oval Office announcement of Japan's surrender, a crowd gathered outside of the White House cheers the arrival of V-J Day.

Truman, who in later years claimed never to have been troubled by his decision to bomb Hiroshima and Nagasaki, responded to his eager advisers by issuing a new executive order, specifying that no more atomic bombs were to be dropped without his explicit directive. He confessed to Secretary of Commerce Henry A. Wallace that he couldn't stand the thought of killing "all those kids," by which he meant—this time—*Japanese* kids.

The president had learned the first lesson of nuclear warfare: Everybody loses. It was a lesson that would resonate throughout the entire Cold War era, an era in which atomic weapons would proliferate, but would never be used.

Truman looked for a way to accommodate the single condition of Japan's "unconditional" surrender. He decided that he would allow the Japanese to keep Hirohito on the throne, but, as he noted in his diary, wholly "subject to the Supreme Commander of the Allied Powers." And though he balked at dropping a third atomic bomb, he did not hesitate to continue the use of conventional ordnance. He ordered air raids against Japan to recommence on August 13, using TNT-based and incendiary bombs. Japan, doubtless fearing more atomic weapons, accepted on the fourteenth.

DETAILS, DETAILS

The Shortest Presidential Press Conference Ever

Just past three o'clock on the afternoon of August 8, 1945, Harry S. Truman convened a press conference in the White House Press Room. He walked in smiling as usual, but, when he started to speak, nearly frowned: "I have only a simple announcement to make. I can't hold a regular press conference today, but this announcement is so important I thought I would call you in. Russia has declared war on Japan. That's all." The shortest press conference in White House history, it spoke volumes.

DETAILS, DETAILS

American Caesar

The Supreme Commander of the Allied Powers to whom Emperor Hirohito would be subject was General Douglas MacArthur. Already legendary for the immensity of his ego—he regarded himself as much a generalissimo as a general—MacArthur waged war against the Japanese with relentless skill and determination, fighting from island to island and then leading a massive invasion of the Philippines, which he had been forced to flee at the beginning of the war. A man of more conventional personality would likely have been driven, as victory approached, by a thirst for blood revenge against the enemy. Installed after the Japanese surrender as head of the government of occupied Japan, MacArthur administered the broken nation with extraordinary compassion and wisdom, ensuring the creation for the Japanese of a democratic government based on a constitution he himself wrote—a document still in force. In postwar Japan, General MacArthur was revered as a popular hero second only to the emperor.

General of the Army Douglas MacArthur, supreme Allied commander and head of the U.S. military occupation government of Japan, stands next to Emperor Hirohito, permitted, under the terms of the so-called unconditional surrender, to retain his throne. MacArthur's administration of postwar Japan was both brilliant and enlightened, elevating him to the status of popular hero among the Japanese, whom he had been instrumental in defeating.

NUCLEAR MONOPOLY

TWO ATOMIC BOMBS—AND THE THREAT OF MANY MORE—ended the war, extracting surrender from a people who, in thousands of years of history, had never before surrendered to anyone or any nation. That this bomb could prevail against such an enemy seemed to certify its status as the ultimate weapon, the Holy Grail of nations and their militaries. On the evening of August 6, President Truman had announced the atomic bombing of Hiroshima. "Before 1939," he said, "it was the accepted belief of scientists that it was theoretically possible to release atomic energy. But no one knew any practical method of doing it. By 1942, however, we knew that the Germans were working feverishly to find a way to add atomic energy to the other engines of war with which they hoped to enslave the world. But they failed. We may be grateful to Providence that the Germans got the V-1's and V-2's late and in limited quantities and even more grateful that they did not get the atomic bomb at all."

Truman was also "grateful to Providence" that the Soviets didn't have the bomb, either. Many politicians and diplomats believed that, with its nuclear weapons monopoly, the United States would be able to run the table on the postwar world. How long would this monopoly last? Most military experts and scientists predicted that it would be at least a decade before the Soviets would develop an atomic bomb.

Despite the Hiroshima bomb, the Soviet Union declared war on Japan on August 8, 1945, one day before the atomic raid on Nagasaki,

The Soviet Union declared war on Japan on August 8, 1945—two days after the atomic bombing of Hiroshima and one day before that of Nagasaki. Red Army soldiers collect rifles surrendered by Japanese troops, probably in Manchuria (Manchukuo), which the Red Army liberated from Japanese occupation.

and exactly ninety days after Germany's surrender. On August 9, a massive Soviet force invaded the Japanese puppet state of Manchukuo—Manchuria—and, over the next eleven days, expanded the invasion into neighboring Mengjiang, northern Korea, southern Sakhalin, and the Kuril Islands. Thus, Stalin established sovereignty over territory Russia had lost to Japan as a result of the Russo-Japanese War in 1905. The Red Army also occupied northern Korea—much as it occupied Eastern Europe. Nevertheless, the atomic bombs had ended the war before Stalin could invade the Japanese home islands, and thus Japan stayed out of Soviet hands.

Beyond thwarting Soviet expansion into Japan, the atomic bomb (optimistic Americans believed) would keep Stalin's ambitions in check elsewhere. Ten years was a long time, which the United States and the Western democracies could use to gain advantages against Soviet expansion. Yet it was also a finite period, and while some might be excused for thinking that the atomic bomb really was the ultimate weapon, some Los Alamos scientists were already looking to the future, to a weapon far more powerful. Ten years in the future, the Soviets might have an atomic bomb, but, if work started now, the United States would by then have what scientists called the thermonuclear bomb, the hydrogen bomb, the super bomb, or, more simply, the "super." As complex and demanding as atomic bomb technology was, that required for a "super" was even more daunting. Surely, it would take the Soviets many more years to acquire the required science and technology.

TAKEAWAY

Atomic Reality, Atomic Illusion

The compelling need to achieve total victory in World War II, regardless of the cost, drove the United States to create and then use the atomic bomb. Perceived as the "ultimate weapon," the atomic bomb (it was hoped) would give the Western democracies irresistible leverage to control and contain aggressive postwar Soviet expansion into Eastern Europe and Asia. The U.S. nuclear monopoly would prove short lived.

PART TWO

THE WORLD ACCORDING TO "X"

CHAPTER 4

THE IRON CURTAIN

Genesis of a Bipolar World

WRITING IN HIS DIARY ON JULY 16, 1945, OF HIS AUTOMOBILE RIDE through Berlin to the Potsdam Conference, Harry S. Truman recorded a scene of "absolute ruin . . . We saw old men, old women, young women, children from tots to teens carrying packs, pushing carts, pulling carts, evidently ejected by the conquerors and carrying what they could of their belongings to nowhere in particular." It brought to the president's mind a dreadful pageant of history's most awful devastations and devastators, "of Carthage, Baalbek, Jerusalem, Rome, Atlantis, Peking, Babylon, Ninevah, Scipio, Rameses II, Titus, Herman, Sherman, Jenghis Khan, Alexander, Darius the Great."

In 1948, Truman would win—against all odds—a second term in the White House, partly on the strength of an impromptu campaign slogan, "Give 'em hell, Harry!" It signified and celebrated the Missourian's reputation for cutting to the core of a situation and emerging with the truth, no matter how disagreeable. Riding through Berlin in 1945, Truman cut to the core of the world a world war had created. It was ruin, massive human displacement and utter ruin.

A MATTER OF PERCEPTION

IN THE FOG OF WAR, IT IS RUIN THAT STANDS OUT as the one indisputable truth. But even this was subject to interpretation in 1945. Truman looked around him and beheld great suffering, ample cause for pity, and the urgency of a crisis that cried out for relief and resolution. Joseph Stalin saw something very different. He saw opportunity.

A revolution requires a tearing down of the old order and a building up of the new. World War II had done the tearing down and then some. Governments destroyed, cities leveled, people without homes or homelands, this total devastation was fertile ground for the forcible planting of a new order, a communist order—better yet, from Stalin's perspective, a Stalinist order. A people living in the liberty and prosperity of democracy would not embrace classical Marxist communism, let alone Stalinist totalitarianism. A people displaced, without shelter, without money, without food, a people in abject misery and want were hardly in a position to shun the bargain Uncle Joe offered.

"We saw old men, old women, young women, children from tots to teens carrying packs, pushing carts, pulling carts, evidently ejected by the conquerors and carrying what they could of their belongings to nowhere in particular," Harry Truman wrote in his diary on July 16, 1945, reflecting on his automobile ride through Berlin to the Potsdam Conference. Postwar Europe was a continent of "displaced persons," as shown in this photograph of German refugees making their way through city ruins.

POP CULTURE

A Famous Slogan

"Give 'em hell, Harry!" was not the work of a campaign slogan writer—Truman would certainly have rejected it if it had been—but its precise source is harder to pin down. Truman claimed that he had first heard it from a crowd member at a whistle-stop in Harrisburg, Illinois, and it is a fact that the slogan quickly became a campaign catchphrase. Virtually everywhere he spoke, someone would yell "Give 'em hell, Harry!" and Truman would respond "That's just what I'm about to do!" or, on at least one occasion, "I don't give them hell, I just tell the truth and they think it's hell." Some have argued that the true source of the slogan was Truman's running mate, Alben Barkley, who exhorted at the start of the campaign, "Mow 'em down, Harry," to which Truman responded "I'm going to fight hard. I'm going to give 'em hell," and the two statements were conflated into "Give 'em hell, Harry."

PREVIOUS SPREAD: *On June 5, 1947, General George Catlett Marshall enters Harvard University, where he will deliver his momentous Marshall Plan speech.*

THE CALCULATING UNCLE JOE

Joseph Stalin saw devastation as an ally. In the closing months of the European war, Stalin aimed 2.5 million Red Army soldiers, 6,250 armored vehicles, and more than 7,500 aircraft at Berlin.

Yet when the Red Army's First Belorussian front (a "front" was the Russian equivalent of what the Western Allies called an "army group") reached the Oder River, within easy striking distance of Berlin, Stalin denied the request of the front commander, Marshal Georgi Zhukov, to make an immediate attack. Stalin's rationale was that he should await the arrival of the First Ukrainian front under Marshal Ivan Konev, so that the two could attack in their combined strength. It is, however, far more likely that, at this point, Stalin was not quite ready to end the war. He wanted more time to allow the effects of devastation on the civilian population of Eastern Europe to be fully felt. As he saw it, there was great political advantage in occupying territory hungry for food and desperate for shelter as well as order—the hungrier and more desperate the better. Nevertheless, the delay Stalin imposed on Zhukov proved costly. Had he been permitted to attack immediately, Zhukov would have faced in Berlin little more than the remnants of the severely depleted German Third Panzer Army and Ninth Army. Stalin's stalling gave the Germans time to shift resources, meager as they were, and mount a much deadlier defense, which made the conquest of Berlin a very bloody battle.

This May 1945 photograph of a Red Army soldier raising the Hammer and Sickle over the Reichstag (parliament building) in Berlin symbolizes the Soviet victory over Germany.

STALIN TAKES HOLD

OF ALL THE PRINCIPAL POWERS THAT HAD FOUGHT in World War II, only the United States emerged undamaged, a technological, industrial, and economic titan. Every other major combatant had been in varying degrees beaten. Moreover, the United States controlled the most destructive weapon in history, the atomic bomb. On the face of it, therefore, it would seem that America—and its Western democratic allies—held all the cards. Any postwar conflict with Russia or anyone else should have been a foregone conclusion.

But such was hardly the case. While it was true that large tracts of the civilian Soviet Union lay in ruin, the Red Army was very much intact, fully equipped, fully mobilized, and dug into advanced positions with regard to the armies of the West. Stalin claimed much of Eastern Europe as a buffer zone to protect Russia, but, the Western world saw this "buffer zone" as nothing less than a potential front line in the next war, maybe even the line of embarkation for an imminent invasion. Moreover, the Soviet Union was immense. Hitler's armies had penetrated the western expanses of the country, but they had failed to reach the even vaster east—the territory to which Stalin had, during the war, wisely evacuated his heavy industries. The Soviets had not only a viable military after World War II but also a formidable military-industrial complex. Powerful as the United States was, the Soviets commanded tremendous manpower, considerable industrial and technological capacity, and the advantage of strategic position, manning a long frontier that faced a devastated Western Europe. Moreover, they were secure in their occupation. Much of Europe, east and west, was on the move, homeless, and unable to resist an occupying force. Stalin had a weapon at least as powerful as the atomic bomb. It was human misery and human chaos on an unprecedented scale.

Human beings—these were Stalin's weapons and bargaining chips. Overwhelmed with the tragedy of immediate want, the Western Allies conceded to Stalin much of what he demanded. Better the Soviets should occupy Eastern Europe than that it should continue to languish in chaos and starvation. The apportionment of territory was not assigned to a grand peace conference like that which had produced the

These Hungarian Jews were liberated from a German concentration camp and taken to temporary shelter in the U.S. Army 121st Evacuation Hospital. But where would they go from here? The photograph is from May 1945.

DETAILS, DETAILS
Displaced Persons

Nobody could get an accurate count in 1945, but experts estimated that twenty-seven million persons had either fled the Nazis or had been forced out of their homelands by them. Another five million human beings had been enslaved by the Nazis. No one had any idea of the numbers who fled in the other direction, hoping to escape the wrath of the Red Army, but the best estimate anyone could come up with in 1945 was that sixty million men, women, and children from twenty-seven countries and fifty-five ethnic groups had been displaced by the war. Add to this the release or impending release of seven million POWs held by the Allies and eight million held by the former Axis, plus (according to some estimates) 670,000 survivors of the Holocaust that had killed six million Jews and some three million others Hitler had condemned as ethnic or political "undesirables."

Treaty of Versailles after World War I. In the first place, there was no fear that Germany and Austria, prostrate as they had not been at the end of World War I, would or even could suddenly rise up to pose a new threat. In the second place, there was simply no time for a grand conference. The crisis of Europe's humanity was far too pressing. Finally, there was the newly created United Nations. Truman and the other Western leaders took what comfort they could in the hope that this organization would, when the dust of war had settled and in the fullness of time, wrest from Stalin's grasp those Eastern European nations that truly wanted liberty and sovereignty. And, after all, Stalin had given his word at Yalta and again at Potsdam, that there would be free elections in all the territory currently under Red Army boots.

> "I hope for some sort of peace—but I fear that machines are ahead of morals by some centuries and when morals catch up perhaps there'll be no reason for any of it. I hope not. But we are only termites on a planet and maybe when we bore too deeply into the planet there'll [be] a reckoning—who knows?"
>
> *Harry S. Truman, recorded in his diary at Potsdam, July 16, 1945*

Uncle Joe Turns Ugly

In 1886, Robert Louis Stevenson published one of the iconic tales of modern literature. *The Strange Case of Dr. Jekyll and Mr. Hyde* tells the story of a London physician who concocts a potion that brings out humanity's dark side, one dose of which instantly transforms the decent and compassionate Dr. Jekyll into the rapacious and psychopathic Mr. Hyde. Under Western eyes, in 1945, much the same seemed to be happening to Joseph Stalin.

In reality, of course, the transformation was not *in* him but *about* him. During the war, the Western propaganda machine worked overtime to portray the Soviet dictator as a great and gallant leader, a trustworthy ally, and a fellow sufficiently amiable and generally down to earth to be called Uncle Joe. By the end of the war, in many democratic, capitalist nations, the leftist political wing freely established "fraternal" ties to the Soviets, and the Far Left became outright communists as well as an increasingly influential political force. During the war and in the war's

Since the Bolshevik Revolution in 1917, Americans had been told by their government that communism was a very bad thing. In World War II, with the Soviet Union a U.S. ally, they had to be persuaded that Joseph Stalin was a world leader who deserved to be Time *magazine's 1942 Man of the Year. "Uncle Joe" also captured the cover of* Life, *for a special March 29, 1943, issue celebrating the Soviet Union.*

REALITY CHECK

The Red Scare Was Real

In the immediate afternath of Word War II, communism was not confined to the Soviet Union or Eastern Europe. By the end of 1945, the Communist Party of France had nearly a million members, and that of Italy counted 1,771,000. In both countries, the Communist Party was the single biggest political party. In England the Communist Party was an inconsiderable force, but the Labour Party embraced many communists and others who saw in Stalin not an uncle, but a brother. In the United States, communism was always on the fringe, regarded largely as an academic affiliation for intellectuals and other dilettantes rather than a serious political force.

immediate aftermath, most of the American mass media was at pains to show Stalin in a favorable light and even to suggest that, under his leadership, the Soviet Union was veering away from Marxism (which it was) and toward capitalism (which it was not). While many in France and Italy enthusiastically embraced Stalin, openly declaring themselves communists, the effort among most in America was to portray him as something of an eccentric uncle, a man who held some strange beliefs, perhaps, but who, at bottom, was quite a decent fellow.

It was in this spirit of rationalization that many in the West interpreted the Soviet Union's late-war and early postwar moves in Eastern Europe. They portrayed the Soviet Union as just another great power, badly injured in war and therefore justifiably seeking to defend its interests and ensure its security. Apologists pointed out that this required exactly what Stalin was practicing, a mixture of diplomacy and military force. At the very top of the British and American governments, however, distrust of Stalin was escalating rapidly. Churchill, anticommunist to his core, had always been wary, and Truman carried to Potsdam far more misgivings about Stalin than FDR had entertained at Yalta. As 1945 drew to a close, the pro-Stalin propaganda in the West

Like his mortal enemies Hitler and Mussolini, Joseph Stalin maintained absolute rule by creating a cult of personality devoted to himself, whether in the Soviet Union or its postwar satellites. A poster of the dictator presides over the Oktogon plaza in Budapest, Hungary, 1946.

ground to an abrupt halt. Americans rapidly began to see him less as a leader and more as a dictator. Worse, he was a "godless" communist, and, even worse, he wanted the whole world to become godless communists. Uncle Joe was becoming Mr. Hyde—or Mr. Hyde-ski, a Russian monster.

Stalin Speaks . . .

On February 9, 1946, Stalin seemed to ratify the reversal of opinion of him under way in the West. He made a widely quoted speech that day in Moscow, in which he declared that communism and capitalism were fundamentally incompatible, drawing the conclusion that another war was therefore inevitable. Stalin used this as the springboard for his announcement of a new five-year plan, one designed (he said) to "guarantee" the Soviet people "against any eventuality." Weapons production would be tripled, whereas the consumer goods the average Soviet citizen had begun to clamor for would have to "wait on rearmament." He went on to get even more specific. The war with the West would come in the 1950s, by which time (he confidently assured his audience) the United States and other capitalist powers would be in the grip of a new Great Depression.

To call Stalin's speech provocative was a pale understatement. Supreme Court Associate Justice William O. Douglas, probably the most liberal voice in Washington at the time, pronounced it the "Declaration of World War III." Nor could it all be dismissed as saber rattling. After all, Stalin's armies were in Eastern Europe and facing the West. Having invaded Manchuria after declaring war on Japan (at the last possible minute), the Red Army remained there, as did a Red Army garrison in oil-rich Azerbaijan, Iran, a key gateway to the Middle East.

. . . and the Cold War Comes to Missouri

Dr. Franc L. McCluer was president of an institution few had ever heard of, tiny Westminster College, an all-male Presbyterian school in commensurately miniscule Fulton, Missouri. One day, having decided to put Westminster on the map, he invited Winston Churchill to speak at his school. It was not really such a long shot. For one thing Churchill was now a private citizen, having been defeated for reelection as prime minister in 1945 by Clement Attlee, and for another McCluer intended to enlist the support of the president of the United States. Through General Harry H. Vaughan, a Westminster alumnus who was a longtime friend and military aide to Harry Truman, McCluer secured an appointment with the president, who was sufficiently excited by the idea of the speech that he handwrote at the bottom of the invitation letter McCluer showed him an enthusiastic endorsement: "This is a wonderful school in my home state. Hope you can do it. I'll introduce you. Best regards." Churchill responded to the letter by assuring Truman that anything he said "under your auspices . . . will command some attention." With that, he flew from Florida, where he was vacationing, to Washington, carefully composed a speech, then, on Monday, March 4, boarded with President Truman the *Ferdinand Magellan*, a private railroad car President Roosevelt had ordered for himself, and made the long trip to Missouri.

Churchill and the president, together with his staff, passed much of the time playing poker. Churchill had already let on that his subject would be "the necessity for full military collaboration between Great Britain and the U.S. in order to preserve the peace of the world," and, in the wee hours of the morning of March 5, he briefly laid down his cards to remark that he would want to live in the United States, were he to be born again. As recounted in McCullough's biography, *Truman*, the former prime minister added that he did find a few American customs "deplorable." Somewhat taken aback, one of the party asked which ones he meant. "You stop drinking with your meals," Churchill replied.

McCullough describes how, after daybreak, Churchill made some last-minute alterations to the speech. He then handed it to a typist who prepared a mimeograph stencil so that the text could be distributed to all on board. To the president, Churchill—this man who had addressed Parliament and the imperiled free world during the darkest days of World War II, when the survival of civilization itself hung on his every word—casually remarked that the speech at little Westminster would be the most important in his career.

Truman, who had read his mimeographed copy, remarked that it would "do nothing but good," then added somewhat more ambiguously that it would be certain to "make a stir." A bit later, he felt compelled to direct Churchill's attention to the presidential seal on the wall of the *Ferdinand Magellan*. He pointed out that the eagle's head faced the olive branch. Churchill turned to the president and remarked that the head should be on a swivel.

When they alighted on the platform at Fulton, a throng was there to greet them. The president and the speaker lunched at Dr. McCluer's house, then walked, in solemn academic procession to the gymnasium, the largest indoor space on campus. True to his word, President Truman gave the introduction, praising the former prime minister as one of the "outstanding men of the ages" and remarking that he had first met him only very recently, at Potsdam, along with Marshal Stalin, adding, as if to avoid contributing to the demonization of the Soviet leader, that he had become fond of *both* men there.

President Harry Truman escorts Winston Churchill through the streets of Jefferson City, Missouri, en route to nearby Fulton, home of Westminster College, where, on March 5, 1946, the wartime British prime minister was to deliver his much-praised, much-criticized, and highly influential "iron curtain" speech.

"A shadow has fallen upon the scenes so lately lighted by the Allied victory," Churchill told his Westminster audience. He went on to express the anxious doubt that pervaded the early months of 1946: "Nobody knows what Soviet Russia and its Communist international organization intends to do . . . or what are the limits, if any, to their expansive and proselytizing tendencies." Like Truman, he voiced "strong admiration and regard for the valiant Russian people and for my wartime comrade, Marshal Stalin." He also conceded the "Russian need to be secure on her western frontiers by removal of all possibility of German aggression," but, he continued, it "is my duty . . . to place before you certain facts about the present position in Europe":

> From Stettin in the Baltic to Trieste in the Adriatic an iron curtain has descended across the Continent. Behind that line lie all the capitals of the ancient states of Central and Eastern Europe. Warsaw, Berlin, Prague, Vienna, Budapest, Belgrade, Bucharest and Sofia, all these famous cities and the populations around them lie in what I must call the Soviet sphere, and all are subject in one form or another, not only to Soviet influence but to a very high and, in some cases, increasing measure of control from Moscow. Athens alone—Greece with its immortal glories—is free to decide its future at an election under British, American and French observation. The Russian-dominated Polish Government has been encouraged to make enormous and wrongful inroads upon Germany, and mass expulsions of millions of Germans on a scale grievous and undreamed-of are now taking place. The Communist parties, which were very small in all these Eastern States of Europe, have been raised to pre-eminence and power far beyond their numbers and are seeking everywhere to obtain totalitarian control. Police governments are prevailing in nearly every case, and so far, except in Czechoslovakia, there is no true democracy.

Winston Churchill was a great writer, and he knew he was a great writer. He also knew that the image of the "iron curtain" descending across the Continent would make a tremendous impact. It was indeed a brilliant visualization. Had Churchill spoken of a wall, he would have conveyed the impression that the Soviets wanted nothing more than security in what they already possessed. If he had evoked the image of a trench, he would have sounded either hysterical or bellicose. But a curtain was his image, and a curtain implied a great deal. It suggested change, the ever-present possibility of farther advance, of deeper incursions into the West. It implied that the Soviets had many things to hide, and that they also wished to hide the promise of the West—a life of prosperous liberty—from the people of the East. Moreover, although the curtain was made of

> **REALITY CHECK**
> **Who Said It First?**
> Winston Churchill was not the first to use the term "iron curtain." In 1920, Ethel Snowden, in her travel memoir *Through Bolshevik Russia* tossed off the expression, comparing the border of Bolshevik Russia to the fireproof safety curtain used in theaters and popularly called an "iron curtain" because it was "an impenetrable barrier." Joseph Goebbels, Nazi propaganda minister, also used the phrase in his speeches. Churchill himself had used the phrase "iron curtain" in cables to President Truman on May 12, 1945, and on June 4 of that year. Others have cited even earlier uses of the term, as when Queen Elisabeth of Belgium compared in 1914 the hardening political situation between her nation and Germany to an *eiserner Vorhang*, another allusion to what was the familiar fireproof theatrical "iron curtain."

iron, it was still a curtain, which hinted at the possibility that it could be drawn back or even pulled down. The image suggested, simultaneously, vast, engulfing oppression and yet impermanence.

The Power of an Image

Impact? The image of the iron curtain electrified the West, and then refused to fade. To a very significant degree, it shaped Western policy throughout the Cold War period. The problem was that, like all compelling images, it conveyed more of the emotional crux of the Soviet threat than its full intellectual dimension. Churchill's speech elaborated on the Soviet threat wisely and in detail, but the iron curtain image was so powerful that much of the rest of what he said was lost in its glare.

After the Westminster speech, the public, especially in the United States and Britain, almost reflexively visualized a divided Europe. The

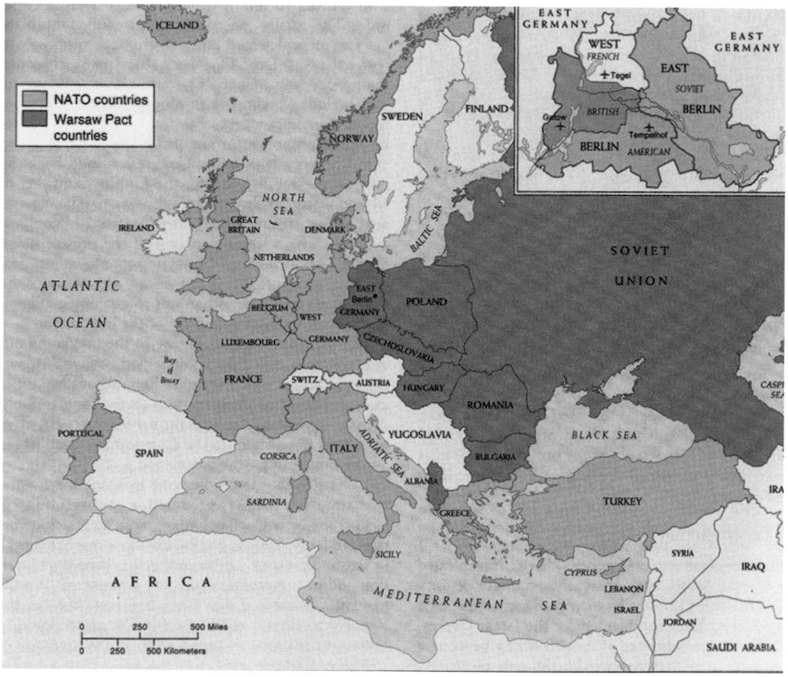

Cold War standoff: NATO countries (dark yellow) versus the Warsaw Pact (orange). Not shown here is the principal non-European NATO member, the United States. The inset depicts postwar Berlin. The West was divided into French, British, and American administrative zones, and the East was under the control of Soviet authorities.

iron curtain would come to include most of the countries of Eastern Europe and, in Central Europe, every nation except West Germany, Liechtenstein, Switzerland, and Austria. At the time Churchill used the phrase, most in the West thought of Eastern and much of Central Europe as effectively imprisoned by the Soviet Union. As the years went by, however, the region became known as the Soviet Bloc, and the nature of its relationship to the USSR was never quite certain. There was little doubt that most of the iron curtain countries were governed by Soviet puppet regimes, but the degree of popular allegiance to communism or the Soviet Union was always in doubt. Two nations that were geographically behind the iron curtain, Yugoslavia and Albania, for example, had very little to do with the Soviets. Under Josip Broz, called Tito, Yugoslavia was a communist state, but it was entirely independent of the Soviet Union—a circumstance many in the West found difficult to fathom. Tito's Yugoslavia maintained fairly cordial political and trade relations with the West; Albania, which, by the early 1960s, aligned itself with Communist China instead of the Soviet Union, was an insular entity, which had virtually nothing to do either with the West or with the Soviets or, for that matter, with any other nation.

THE RED MILL

This American newspaper cartoon from the early Cold War period is titled "The Red Mill" and depicts the Soviet economy as the product of slave labor ground up into the implements of war.

Despite these political ambiguities and variations, there seemed to be, quite simply, a sharp division on either side of the iron curtain. The people of those nations to the east of it operated under command economies and enjoyed few liberties if any. The populations living in Western Europe, Northern Europe, and Southern Europe (as well as in Austria, West Germany, Liechtenstein, and Switzerland) were capitalistic, enjoying the liberties of democratic government. The only exceptions were Spain,

REALITY CHECK

Churchill Stirs Controversy

While Churchill's "iron curtain" speech came to define the core of the Cold War, immediate response in the American press was often highly critical. The *Wall Street Journal* blasted Churchill for poisoning relations between Russia and the United States, and the *Nation* pronounced Truman "remarkably inept" for associating himself with the Westminster College speech. Walter Lippmann, probably the most respected political pundit of the era, pronounced the speech an "almost catastrophic blunder." Stalin—whose blatantly bellicose Moscow oration was scarcely a month old—said that Churchill's speech delivered in the United States was nothing less than a "call to war."

DETAILS, DETAILS

Kill Zone Kills

Between 1948 and 1981, shooting incidents along the border between West and East Germany were hardly routine, but they were not uncommon. Several hundred civilians—almost all of them East Germans attempting to cross into the West—were killed, as were twenty-eight East German border guards. In the midst of death, however, there was also life. The no-man's land that marked the border in some rural regions was both uninhabited and uncultivated for as much as fifty years. This resulted in an unintended wildlife preserve, running as a corridor over long stretches of Central and Eastern Europe.

governed under fascism from 1939 until the death of Franco in 1975, and Portugal, which had a fascist government from 1932 to 1974. Greece, threatened by communism, came under a U.S.-supported right-wing military dictatorship during the postwar years.

Within a few months of Churchill's speech, the "iron curtain" began a transition from metaphor to physical reality, as the Soviets and the Western powers militarized their frontiers. As we will see in Chapter 10, this was most visible in the border that came to separate West Germany from East Germany, and, within East Germany, the wall that divided West and East Berlin. *Die Grenze*, as the internal German border was called, featured double fences topped with razor wire (in rural areas) and concrete walls (near cities). This physical barrier was built by the East German government and was set back from the actual border, which was demarcated by posts and warning signs. The strip of land between the fence and the border proper was punctuated by East German watchtowers manned by armed guards. In some areas, the strip was marked as a "kill zone," meaning that anyone who wandered into it might be cut down in a hail of bullets.

Tapping Out the Long Telegram

Even with the physical fencing, walling, and militarization of the iron curtain, the image, compelling as it was, by no means fully explained the situation the world faced in the aftermath of World War II. The idea of the iron curtain focused the attention of most Americans exclusively on Eastern Europe, the "divided continent." Churchill knew this was a mistake. In his Westminster speech, he explained that "Turkey and Persia [Iran] are both profoundly alarmed and disturbed at the claims which are being made upon them and at the pressure being exerted by the Moscow Government," and he also warned of "other causes for anxiety" that existed "in front of the iron curtain." He warned of the ascendency of the Communist Party in Italy and in France and of "Communist fifth columns" that were being established "in a great number of countries, far from the Russian frontiers and throughout the world," cells that "work in complete unity and

The "Anglo-Russian Demarcation Line" separating the Western and Eastern administrative zones in Germany, September 1947. At this point, the border was not heavily fortified.

absolute obedience to the directions they receive from the Communist center." Churchill turned from Europe to "the Far East and especially in Manchuria," warning of the Red Army occupations that still endured in these places.

For most of the American public in 1946, warnings of the worldwide menace posed by Soviet aggression were somewhat obscured by the iron curtain image. At the higher levels of the American government, however, there was a growing awareness of the global dimension of postwar Soviet policies, together with an effort to understand them and to devise the means of dealing with them.

The man who would prove most influential in the effort to get control of this frightening situation had been born in Milwaukee, Wisconsin, in 1904. George F. Kennan prepped not far from his home, at St. John's Military Academy in Delafield, Wisconsin, then set out for the East Coast and Princeton University in 1921. As a Midwesterner of modest means, shy by nature, Kennan was acutely uncomfortable throughout his undergraduate career, and although his ambition was to study law, he decided that law school was both too expensive and the profession tuned at too high a key for him. He applied instead to the U.S. Foreign Service after graduation, was accepted, and served in Switzerland, Germany, Estonia, Latvia, and Lithuania. In the late 1920s, the State Department enrolled him in a program devoted to Russian history and language at the University of Berlin. Although far from Milwaukee, the experience seemed not unfamiliar. His grandfather's cousin, whom he was named after, had been an eminent American expert on czarist Russia. Kennan quickly became fluent not only in Russian but also in German, French, Polish, Czech, Portuguese, and Norwegian. An actual diplomatic posting in the Soviet Union was, however, out of the question until 1933, when the newly sworn president, Franklin D. Roosevelt, extended diplomatic recognition to the Soviet government. Kennan was immediately attached to the embassy staff of Ambassador William C. Bullitt and sent to Moscow.

As the American public saw it, President Roosevelt was open and receptive to Stalin and the Soviets, but the fact was that Kennan, together with two other Moscow embassy staffers, Charles E. Bohlen and Loy W. Henderson, quickly became convinced that productive, let alone cordial, U.S.-Soviet relations would never be possible. In much the same vein as Stalin's 1946 speech, they believed that the communist and

At 9 P.M. (local time) on February 22, 1946, George F. Kennan transmitted from the U.S. embassy in Moscow to Secretary of State James F. Byrnes in Washington, D.C., his celebrated "Long Telegram," in which he analyzed Soviet motives for postwar expansion and recommended a policy for "containment" of the Soviet sphere of influence.

capitalist systems were fundamentally incompatible. While Stalin's Western apologists scrambled to put the Kremlin political purges of the later 1930s in a positive political light, Kennan harbored no such illusions. Yet neither did he simply recoil from them. He observed the Moscow show trials closely. He watched Stalin's every move. He believed it his urgent duty to study a man and a nation bound, sooner or later, to be enemies of the United States.

The State Department transferred Kennan to the U.S. Embassy in Berlin in 1939 immediately after the outbreak of World War II. The Soviets might someday become an enemy, but the Germans were almost certain to become one—and sooner rather than later. Roosevelt's foreign experts wanted sharp eyes on this threat. The entry of the United States into the war as a result of the Japanese attack on Pearl Harbor on December 7, 1941, took the U.S. Embassy by surprise, and Kennan was interned by the Germans for half a year before he was repatriated. He served on the European Advisory Commission, which was instrumental in creating Allied policy in Europe, then was named deputy head of the U.S. mission in Moscow, where he served from July 1944 to April 1946.

As his term of service there drew to a close at the height of the first great U.S.-Soviet tension, Kennan drafted a cable to Truman's secretary of state, James Byrnes. At more than 5,300 words, it was appropriately dubbed the "Long Telegram," but it was actually very concise in its analysis of Soviet motives and its proposals for a comprehensive strategy to structure U.S.-Soviet diplomatic relations. In the Long Telegram, Kennan rejected the Marxist explanation of communist expansion—that the communist revolution would not be complete until all of the world's states had been replaced by a global union of the working class—and proposed instead that Stalin's aggressive expansionism was driven by his "neurotic view of world affairs," which was hardly unique to the nation's current leader, but, on the contrary, partook of "the traditional and instinctive Russian sense of insecurity." The Bolshevik Revolution, it is true, had catalyzed

STALIN'S SHOW TRIALS

During the "Great Purge" of the Soviet government and military during 1936–38, Joseph Stalin staged a series of public trials in Moscow. The defendants were opponents of Stalin—or individuals the paranoid dictator had decided were opponents.

There were three public trials and one secret military tribunal. The first was conducted in August 1936 and tried sixteen members of what Stalin condemned as the "Trotskyite-Zinovievite Terrorist Center." All were found guilty of the same crime, violation of Article 58 of the Russian Soviet Federative Socialist Republic (RSFSR) Penal Code, conspiring with Western powers to assassinate Stalin and other Soviet leaders, to destroy the Soviet Union, and to restore capitalism. All were executed, including prominent Communist Party leader Grigory Zinoviev. The second trial took place in January 1937. Of the seventeen defendants charged—again with having violated Article 58—all were found guilty, thirteen were shot, and four were consigned to labor camps. In March 1938, the third public trial was held. Twenty-one defendants were charged as having been members of the "Bloc of Rightists and Trotskyites." The most prominent defendant was Nikolai Bukharin, former head of the Communist International. The principal defendants, including Bukharin, were shot.

Perhaps the trial that had the most serious consequences was the 1937 secret military tribunal that tried General Mikhail Tukhachevsky and other senior military officers on blatantly bogus charges of anticommunist conspiracy. All those tried were executed, and their trials touched off Stalin's wider purge of the Red Army, which greatly reduced the senior officer corps and severely crippled the Soviet military on the eve of World War II.

Stunningly, at the time of the public trials, many Western observers who attended them believed they were fair (George Kennan was an exception), mainly because convictions rested heavily on confessions in open court. After Stalin's death in 1953, the trials were exposed as having been "show trials," entirely rigged, the verdicts decided in advance, the confessions having been coerced through torture, threats to family members, and other means.

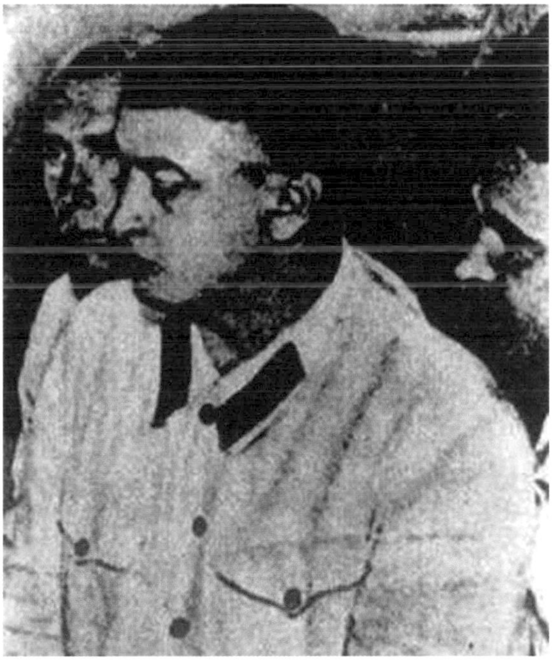

A grainy picture of General Mikhail Tukhachevsky taken during the 1937 secret military tribunal; he and seven other senior officers were executed on June 11, 1937.

this sense of insecurity, blending it with Marxist global ideology, but it was the more traditional Russian paranoia—what Kennan called an "Oriental secretiveness and conspiracy"—that most urgently drove Stalinist policy. Kennan argued that Stalin himself had internalized the traditional Russian world view—overlaid though it was with Marxist theory—and that he was motivated by a personal paranoia, which manifested itself above all in a need to preserve his own power. Ultimately, Soviet policy flowed from Stalin's twisted urge for self-preservation. Marx had theorized that capitalism and communism were fundamentally opposed and incompatible, that, in the end, the world was too small to contain both systems. Whether Stalin truly believed this or not, it was a most convenient theory, because, Kennan argued, he needed a hostile world—a world in which every non-communist country was an enemy—to legitimate and perpetuate his autocratic regime. For Stalin, Marxism-Leninism was a tool, a means of rationalizing and institutionalizing as national policy an "instinctive fear of the outside world." Out of this fear, the Soviet people would worship Stalin and make any sacrifice he called for.

Short of getting Stalin on a psychiatrist's couch, the only means Kennan saw of countering the effects of the dictator's paranoid policies was to endeavor to make Western policies and institutions so strong that they would successfully resist Soviet challenges and attacks, at least long enough for Stalin either to mellow (unlikely) or to die (certain—but when?). Kennan understood that Stalin's regime was based on a cult of personality, and his hope was that the paranoia would begin to fade when he left the stage. The mission of the West was to ride out the paranoia so as to outlast the regime.

X

Secretary of State Byrnes and Secretary of the Navy James Forrestal, both hard-line anticommunists, were greatly impressed by the Long Telegram and engineered Kennan's recall to Washington, where he was appointed to head up the newly created policy planning staff of the Department of State. In the meantime, Forrestal asked Kennan to use the Long Telegram as the basis for an article to be published in the highly influential journal *Foreign Affairs*. Titled "The Sources of Soviet Conduct," the article appeared anonymously—the author identified only as "X"—in the July 1947 issue. In contrast to the Long Telegram, the published

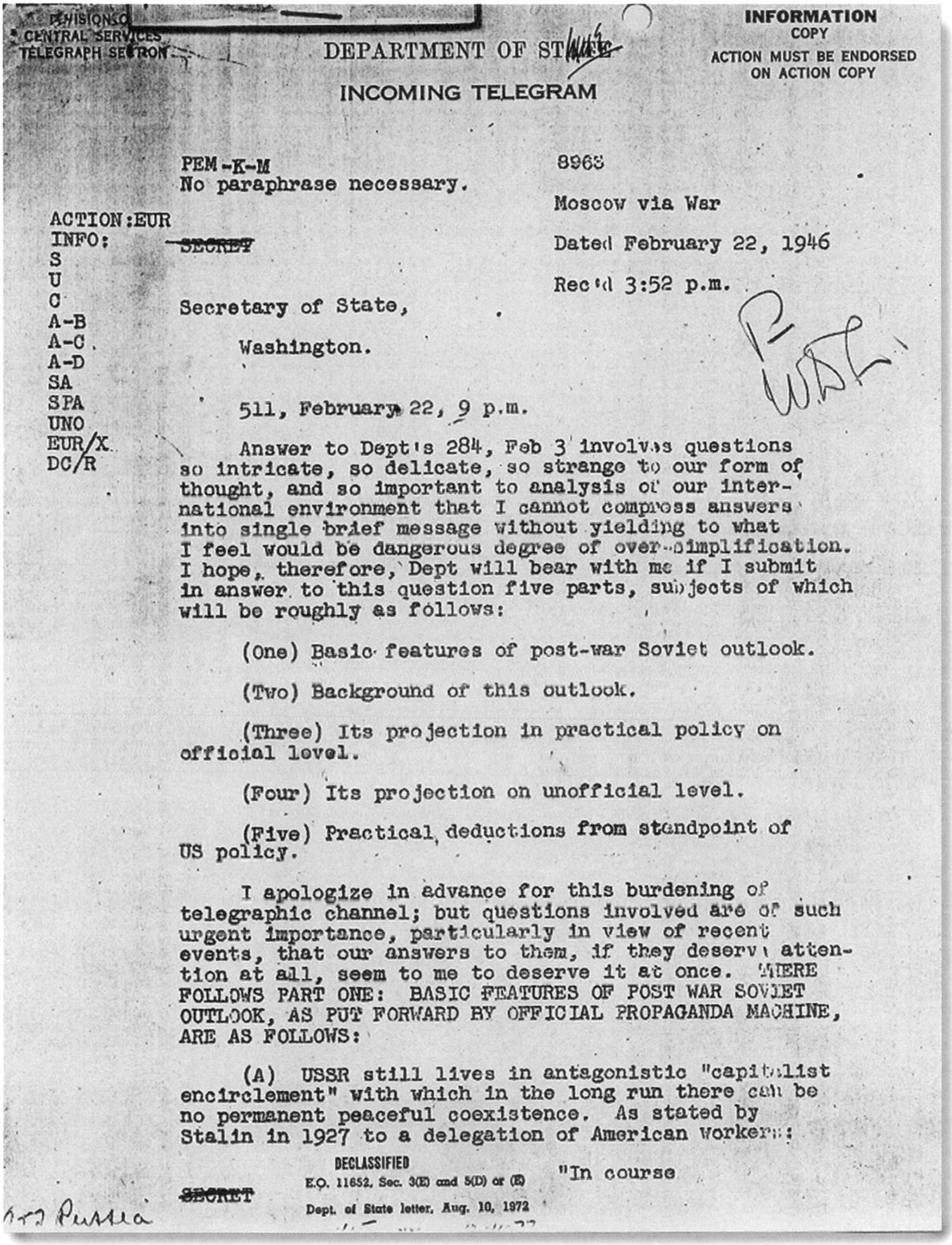

DIVISION OF CENTRAL SERVICES TELEGRAPH SECTION

DEPARTMENT OF STATE

INFORMATION COPY

ACTION MUST BE ENDORSED ON ACTION COPY

INCOMING TELEGRAM

PEM-K-M
No paraphrase necessary.

8963

Moscow via War

ACTION:EUR
INFO:
S
U
C
A-B
A-C
A-D
SA
SPA
UNO
EUR/X
DC/R

~~SECRET~~

Dated February 22, 1946

Rec'd 3:52 p.m.

Secretary of State,

Washington.

511, February 22, 9 p.m.

Answer to Dept's 284, Feb 3 involves questions so intricate, so delicate, so strange to our form of thought, and so important to analysis of our international environment that I cannot compress answers into single brief message without yielding to what I feel would be dangerous degree of over-simplification. I hope, therefore, Dept will bear with me if I submit in answer to this question five parts, subjects of which will be roughly as follows:

(One) Basic features of post-war Soviet outlook.

(Two) Background of this outlook.

(Three) Its projection in practical policy on official level.

(Four) Its projection on unofficial level.

(Five) Practical deductions from standpoint of US policy.

I apologize in advance for this burdening of telegraphic channel; but questions involved are of such urgent importance, particularly in view of recent events, that our answers to them, if they deserve attention at all, seem to me to deserve it at once. THERE FOLLOWS PART ONE: BASIC FEATURES OF POST WAR SOVIET OUTLOOK, AS PUT FORWARD BY OFFICIAL PROPAGANDA MACHINE, ARE AS FOLLOWS:

(A) USSR still lives in antagonistic "capitalist encirclement" with which in the long run there can be no permanent peaceful coexistence. As stated by Stalin in 1927 to a delegation of American workers:

"In course

~~SECRET~~

DECLASSIFIED
E.O. 11652, Sec. 3(E) and 5(D) or (E)
Dept. of State letter, Aug. 10, 1972

The opening page of Kennan's "Long Telegram."

article took the emphasis off traditional Russian insecurity and focused instead on Stalin's unremitting imperative to keep himself in power, regardless of cost. Kennan now argued that Stalin used Marxist-Leninist ideology, advocating global revolution to defeat capitalism worldwide, as a "fig leaf" to rationalize his imposition of harsh, repressive regimentation on Soviet society, the real purpose of which was nothing more or less than to maintain him in power.

Kennan believed that "Soviet pressure against the free institutions of the Western world . . . [could] be contained by the adroit and vigilant application of counterforce at a series of constantly shifting geographical and political points, corresponding to the shifts and manoeuvers of Soviet policy." The pressure of Soviet expansionism could be "contained," but not defeated outright or quickly; nor could it be "charmed or talked out of existence." Still, Kennan argued, there would be a victory at the end. If the United States could maintain containment, footing the bill for years of a globally demanding policy, the Soviet economy and the structure of the ruling Soviet Communist Party would be subjected to prolonged strain, which would yield one of two results: "either the break-up or the gradual mellowing of Soviet power."

LINK

John Adams on Power

In a letter to Connecticut's Roger Sherman on July 18, 1789, John Adams wrote, "Power naturally grows. Why? Because human passions are insatiable." Adams would have had no trouble understanding George F. Kennan's analysis of Stalin and the Soviets more than 150 years later. Driven by an insatiable passion for power, Stalin would never moderate his views on opposing, even overthrowing, the governments of the West. No amount of negotiation would avail. In his letter to Sherman, Adams had continued: "But that power alone can grow which is already too great; that which is unchecked; that which has no equal power to control it." Similarly, Kennan argued for a U.S. policy that would set up an "equal power," a controlling power, a "policy toward the Soviet Union [consisting of] a long-term, patient but firm and vigilant containment of Russian expansive tendencies."

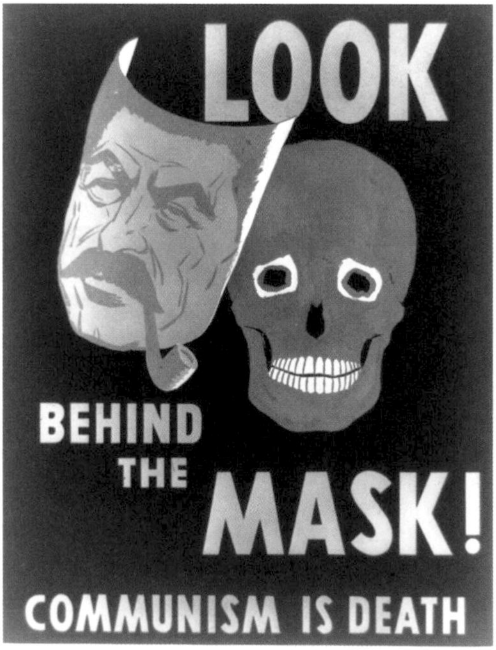

In the United States, early Cold War propaganda transformed Stalin, the gallant "Uncle Joe" of the war years, into the master of deception, who promised plenty but delivered death.

"COLD WAR"

THE "X" ARTICLE TOUCHED OFF AN INTENSE NATIONAL DEBATE. Some journalists and others believed that this call for what was effectively a long (but, it was hoped, bloodless) war of attrition would be recklessly dangerous—creating a climate of hostility in which World War III might readily erupt—and economically ruinous. Others argued virtually the opposite, that it was actually a policy of quasi-disengagement, an unspoken surrender to Soviet expansion, a refusal to face up to a military showdown. But many, including the inner circle of the Truman administration, enthusiastically embraced Kennan's analysis and proposals.

As we will see in Chapters 5 and 6, the ideas expressed in the "X" article became the basis of the "Truman Doctrine," the policy of "containment," which marked U.S. diplomatic, economic, and military strategy throughout the entire Cold War period. Kennan himself was fairly appalled by this fact throughout the remainder of his long life—he died in 2005, at the age of ninety-four—often complaining that the implications of his article had been pursued too literally, rigidly, and narrowly, that Truman and his successors had acted reflexively to each and every instance of Soviet expansionism or perceived expansionism. Moreover, Kennan expressed regret that he had failed to emphasize in his article the use of economic rather than military means to enforce containment. "My thoughts about containment," he wrote in his *Memoirs: 1925–1950*, "were . . . distorted by the people who understood it and pursued it exclusively as a military concept; and I think that that, as much as any other cause, led to 40 years of unnecessary, fearfully expensive and disoriented . . . Cold War."

"Cold War"—it was the perfect term for what Kennan's article—or perhaps the dominant interpretation of that article—had wrought. The phrase entered the world's popular lexicon after the Long Telegram had been written but just before the *Foreign Affairs* article was published. On April 16, 1947, the American financier and influential presidential adviser Bernard Baruch spoke in South Carolina, admonishing his audience not to "be deceived: we are today in the midst of a cold war." The phrase captured the imagination of public and politicians alike to describe the bewildering, terrifying, and frustrating state of international affairs. It was becoming clear that a warlike hostility was indeed developing between the United States (and its allies) and the Soviet Union, yet it was also clear—to most people—that the option of all-out warfare had been taken off the table by the presence of nuclear weapons. Few

REALITY CHECK
What's in a Name?

Most histories of the "Cold War" report that the phrase was coined by Bernard Baruch in a 1947 speech; however, it was not original with the famous financier and presidential adviser, but was furnished by his speechwriter, Herbert Bayard Swope, who had been using it—albeit not publicly—since 1940. The term received widespread circulation as a result of Baruch's 1947 speech and was codified later in the year by publication of *The Cold War*, the work of political pundit Walter Lippmann.

TAKEAWAY

Creating a "Cold War"

As the West struggled to fathom the intentions of Joseph Stalin, the Soviet dictator made a provocative speech in February 1946, asserting the eventual inevitability of war between the Soviet Union and the West, and Winston Churchill in effect responded on behalf of the West by defining and condemning the "iron curtain" the Soviets had stretched across Europe. This image immediately galvanized the West and endured as a powerful influence on relations with the Soviet Union; however, it was the analysis and recommendations of U.S. diplomat George F. Kennan that the Truman administration most extensively fashioned into the foreign relations policies that guided the nation's actions during the long Cold War.

people (least of all Harry Truman) wanted to start World War III. Thus the planet's two great military powers seemed doomed to perpetually verge on a war that would never quite break out. This said, the possibility that World War III would actually erupt continued to loom and did so with greater and greater terror as the nuclear and then thermonuclear arsenals of both nations grew. Thus the idea of a *Cold* War—as opposed to a "hot war"—provided what was literally cold comfort, the shivering hope that mutual annihilation would be postponed or avoided entirely, but at the cost of apparently interminable saber rattling, incessant hostility, and any number of "brushfire" conflicts. Although the Cold War period was an epoch of intense activity, there would be about it a sickly, anxious air of suspended animation, as if the world were frozen at the brink of Armageddon.

Newspaper cartoonist Rube Goldberg was best known for his exuberantly imaginative illustrations of hilariously complicated mechanical devices designed to perform ridiculously simple tasks; however, this political cartoon, titled "Cold War, 1949," earned Goldberg a Pulitzer Prize.

CHAPTER 5

Flashpoints: The Mediterranean and the Middle East

The Truman Doctrine in Action

If nothing else, World War II was a crash course in geography, acquainting Americans who had never ventured beyond Brooklyn or Bakersfield with places ranging from remote Pacific islands, to the capitals of North Africa, Asia, and Europe, and to sites in the Middle East that they had heard of only in tales of Sinbad and *One Thousand and One Nights*. Nevertheless, as soon as this latest world war was over, most Americans, focusing on the rapidly developing standoff between the West and the Soviet Union in Europe, forgot about places like Iran and Turkey. Yet it was in such countries along the Mediterranean and in the Middle East—far from Main Street—that the first open conflicts of the Cold War erupted.

Unfinished Business

At the outbreak of World War II, Iran declared itself neutral; however, the country's ruler, Reza Shah Pahlavi (reigned 1925–41), maintained friendly, even cozy, relations with Germany, which had long been a key trading partner and source of foreign investment. Iran offered nations at war two inestimable prizes. First, were its oil reserves and refineries.

DETAILS, DETAILS

Fateful Name

On March 21, 1935, Reza Shah Pahlavi issued a decree requesting that foreign delegates refer to the nation as "Iran" instead of "Persia." Although the Western world had called the country Persia for centuries, the Persians themselves had called it "Iran" since the Sassanid period (226–651 CE). Reza Shah justified his decree in nationalist terms, as an evocation of the country's ancient identity and heritage; however, critics of his decision denounced it as an overture to Nazi Germany. *Iran* translates as "land of the Aryans," and it was believed that Reza Shah was implying a racial connection with Hitler's German "Aryan race." Throughout World War II, Winston Churchill explicitly directed British diplomats and military officers to use Persia in all official documents.

Modern mechanized war ran on oil. On the land, sea, and air, petroleum drove all the engines of war and lubricated them as well. Second was the nation's location, adjacent to Turkey and Iraq—Turkey providing a direct overland route to the Mediterranean and the Black Sea, Iraq providing a route to Syria and the Mediterranean—and bordering the southern reaches of the Soviet Union, as well as offering ports on the Persian Gulf, the Caspian Sea, and the Indian Ocean. Possessing a highly developed rail system, Iran was also a vital overland link to the Soviet Union, the highway by which the Western Allies intended to convey urgently needed matériel to the Red Army.

With an eye on these prizes, the Allies, especially Great Britain, viewed with growing alarm the cordiality of the shah's policy toward the Germans. Accordingly, on August 21, 1941, Britain and the Soviet Union united in a request that the shah order the expulsion of the two- to three-thousand German nationals living in the country. When the shah refused, an Anglo-Soviet force invaded the country on August 25. Two Anglo-Indian divisions, the 8th and the 10th, entered from the south and west, while the Soviet Forty-seventh and Forty-fourth armies invaded from the north, and the Fifty-third entered from the east. The convergence of these forces rapidly overwhelmed Iranian resistance, forcing Reza Shah Pahlavi to flee to South Africa after abdicating in favor of his son, twenty-two-year-old Mohammad Reza Pahlavi (reigned 1941–79). The young man instantly reversed the course his father had taken, and, in exchange for a guarantee of territorial integrity and independence, he concluded a tripartite treaty of alliance with Great Britain and the Soviet Union at Tehran on January 29, 1942. Shortly after

Reza Shah Pahlavi, the Shah of Iran, is pictured here (in light-colored suit) with Turkish president Kemal Atatürk (left) and Turkish military officers, c. 1935.

this, he severed diplomatic relations with Germany, expelled all German nationals, and, on April 12, 1942, severed diplomatic relations with Japan as well. In September 1943, Iran formally declared war on Germany. For their part, the British and Russians pledged to evacuate their forces from Iran within six months after the end of hostilities with Germany, but they later extended this to six months after the end of hostilities with Japan. At the Tehran Conference of November 1943, the United States added its adherence to these terms as well. All three Allies promised to observe a strict policy of noninterference with the internal affairs of Iran during the war, but, in fact, they interfered extensively, asserting tight controls over roads, railways, waterways, ports, communications, and even food supplies and labor allotment, all with the object of ensuring an uninterrupted flow of oil to the Allies and the maintenance of a line of supply to the Soviet Union.

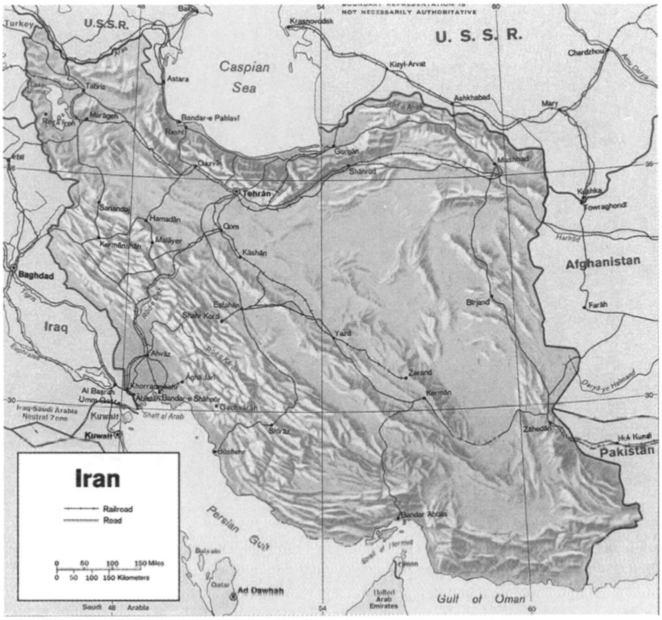

Iran—strategic prize during and after World War II.

The alliance Britain and the Soviet Union had extorted from Iran came at a substantial cost to the country. Supplies of food and other essentials grew scarce, and runaway currency inflation hammered the lower and middle classes even as black marketers made fortunes. Moreover, the presence of large numbers of foreign troops was a catalyst to rapid social change, of which many Iranians did not approve. The nation was swept by a combination of xenophobia and

Anglo-Indian forces seize control of the world's largest oil refinery on the Iranian Persian Gulf island of Abadan, October 13, 1941.

The Big Three—left to right, Joseph Stalin, Franklin Roosevelt, Winston Churchill—met in Tehran, Iran, from November 28 to December 1, 1943, to discuss the ongoing joint conduct of World War II. The photograph was taken on the steps of the Soviet embassy.

DETAILS, DETAILS

The "Bridge to Victory"

The United States delivered 4,159,117 tons of weapons, vehicles, aircraft, and other goods to the Soviet Union by way of Iran. This represented almost one-fourth of America's total wartime aid to the USSR. The Allies jointly dubbed Iran "the bridge to victory."

nationalism, creating widespread political unrest that was aggravated by a sudden influx of rural migrants in search of work in the cities. The upper classes, prospering in the wartime economy, showed little regard for the hard-pressed masses. This provided fertile ground for the rise of the communist Tudeh Party, which rushed to organize industrial workers and which agitated for sweeping economic and social reform.

Even with the war still raging, Lavrenty Beria—officially deputy chairman of the Council of People's Commissars but universally recognized as Stalin's right-hand man and head of the NKVD (Narodnyy Komissariat Vnutrennikh Del, People's Commissariat for Internal Affairs), the secret police and espionage apparatus—initiated Soviet collaboration with the Tudeh, hoping to undermine the government of the young pro-Western shah. When, in September 1944, U.S. oil companies began negotiating with Iran for oil concessions, the Soviets lodged competing requests in the country's five northern provinces. Seeking to avoid a conflict between two occupying forces, the Majlis—the Iranian parliament—quickly enacted legislation barring discussion of oil concessions until the end of the war. At this, the United States backed off, but the Soviets and the Tudeh launched an intense propaganda campaign pushing for an immediate Soviet oil concession.

The agitation continued throughout the war, culminating in rebellion when, in December 1945, Jafar Pishevari, leader of the Tudeh-allied Azerbaijan Democratic Party, proclaimed the creation of an autonomous Azerbaijan republic. This incited radicals in neighboring Kordestan to proclaim the Kurdish Republic of Mahabad. The Soviet Union wasted no time in announcing its support of these breakaway republics, and Red Army occupation forces remained in the north, barring the entrance of government forces into Azerbaijan and Kordestan. Indeed, the Soviets did even more than refuse to leave. On December 31, 1945, as promised in the wartime tripartite treaty, the United States withdrew its forces from Iran, and Britain, again in accordance with treaty promises, withdrew its troops on March 2, 1946. Two days later, fifteen additional Soviet armored brigades entered the northern Iranian province of Azerbaijan and deployed along the Turkish and Iraqi borders.

"One may fairly say that the Cold War began on March 4, 1946. On that day fifteen Soviet armored brigades began to pour into the northern Iranian province of Azerbaijan and to deploy along the Turkish and Iraqi frontiers and toward central Iran. Simultaneously, another Soviet army of comparable size and composition moved south across Bulgaria to deploy along the European frontier of Turkey."

Robert Rossow, U.S. vice-consul, Tabriz, Iran

At this juncture, Iranian prime minister Ahmad Qavam intervened. He secured a pledge from Stalin to withdraw his troops in exchange for his promise to endorse the oil concession bid the Soviets had submitted to the Majlis. He also agreed to open negotiations with the breakaway Pishevari government in order to resolve the Azerbaijan

In the Cold War as in World War II, Iran was a key source of oil. This portrait of an Iranian refinery was made in January 1945.

crisis. Stalin accepted these terms, but nevertheless maintained his troops in place even after the Iranian government granted an oil concession in April. The following month, under combined pressure from the United States, Britain, and the newly formed United Nations, the Red Army finally withdrew. For his part, Qavam formed a coalition with the communist Tudeh Party by taking three Tudeh members into his cabinet.

The Soviets Lose One

Stalin believed he had made a significant gain in Iran. He had obtained an oil concession—much needed in his postwar program of industrial expansion—and he had gotten a political foothold in the country, which he believed he could later expand and exploit in order to extend the iron curtain into the Middle East and secure a buffer zone for the Soviet Union's southern frontier.

Prime Minister Qavam, however, was about to demonstrate that Joseph Stalin was not the only master of ruthlessly pragmatic international politics. Popularly known as the "Old Fox," Qavam decided to label a tribal revolt in southern Iran as an anticommunist protest and "responded" to this by summarily dismissing the Tudeh cabinet officers, thereby removing potential Soviet puppets from the inner circles of the government. Next, declaring the necessity of securing civil order in preparation for the upcoming Majlis elections, Qavam sent an army into Azerbaijan. Now without Red Army support, the breakaway Pishevari government crumbled, and Pishevari fled to asylum in the Soviet Union. After this, another Iranian government force crossed into the Kurdish Republic of Mahabad, which also quickly folded. In the new political climate of Iran, politician Mohammad Mosaddeq led a powerful bloc of newly elected right-wing nationalist Majlis deputies, who voted down ratification of the Soviet oil concession agreement and enacted a law ending the practice of granting foreign oil concessions altogether. Henceforth, Iran would exploit its oil resources directly.

The "Old Fox," Iranian prime minister Ahmad Qavam os-Saltaneh.

Thanks to the Old Fox, Soviet influence faded in Iran. Worse for Stalin, in 1947, Iran signed an agreement with the United States to accept military equipment and to host a U.S. military advisory mission to help train the Iranian army. On February 4, 1949, Mohammad Reza Pahlavi was attending a ceremony commemorating the founding of Tehran University when one Fakhr-Arai suddenly fired five shots at him

President Truman confers with a young Mohammad Reza Pahlavi, the Shah of Iran, a staunch American ally. The photograph is from 1949.

from a range of no more than ten feet. Only a single round hit the shah, barely grazing his cheek, and Fakhr-Arai fell in a fusillade of bullets fired by nearby officers. The shah ordered an investigation, which duly concluded that Fakhr-Arai was a member of the Tudeh Party. On the strength of this, the party was banned, and Stalin lost his last foothold in Iran.

TURKEY UNDER THREAT

THE IRAN CRISIS MADE STALIN'S POSTWAR STRATEGY chillingly clear to the Western powers, but, even earlier, the Soviets had started making threatening moves in Turkey and Greece. The pressure on Turkey began in March 1945, when Stalin denounced a Turkish-Soviet treaty of friendship and non-aggression that had been in force since 1925. Two months after this, the Soviet Union demanded cession of Kars and Ardahan provinces, territories that had been annexed by czarist Russia from the old Ottoman Empire as a result of an 1877–78 war, then retaken by Turkey in 1920; in addition, the Soviets demanded possession of a military base on the Bosporus and Dardanelles, also called the Turkish Straits, connecting the Mediterranean with the Black Sea and serving as the strategic and commercial passage between Asia and Europe. Finally, Stalin called for a revision of the 1936 Montreux Convention, by which Turkey was given full control over the straits. The Soviet leader now demanded that his government share control with Turkey.

"I don't like our border right here!"

Attributed to Joseph Stalin, while pointing to the Caucasus region on a postwar map of the Soviet Union, 1945

REALITY CHECK

A Convenient Conclusion

The Truman administration breathed a sigh of relief on learning that the Shah of Iran, a staunch ally, had escaped death by assassination, and then was even more delighted when the upshot of the assassination attempt was the end of the Tudeh Party and the final purge of Soviet influence in an oil-rich nation perched strategically at the Soviets' back door. No one in the U.S. government cared to inquire very deeply into the Iranian government's investigation that had linked Fakhr-Arai to the Soviet-sponsored Tudeh Party. Good thing. The evidence supporting the connection was hardly conclusive, and it is far more likely that the would-be assassin was not a communist at all but a Muslim extremist. Since he was dead, however, the shah could affix to him whatever label worked best.

Stalin's troops threatened Turkey from Azerbaijan in the east and from Bulgaria in the west. Nevertheless, the Soviet leader's demands were so outrageous that his own foreign minister, the ruthlessly imperturbable Vyacheslav Molotov, warned him that the Western Allies would not allow any of it. Stalin cut him off. "Go ahead, press them for joint possession! Demand it!"

Molotov was right. When Turkey refused Stalin's demands and sought support from the United States, Harry Truman, on January 5, 1946, handwrote a letter to Secretary of State Byrnes and then called him into the Oval Office so that he could read the text to him aloud. He began by complaining that "At Potsdam we were faced with an accomplished fact and were by circumstances almost forced to agree to Russian occupation of Eastern Poland, and that part of Germany east of the Oder River by Poland. It was a high-handed outrage." Now, Truman continued, "There isn't a doubt in my mind that Russia intends an invasion of Turkey and seizure of the Black Sea Straits to the Mediterranean." He meant to stop them. "Unless Russia is faced with an iron fist," the president continued, "and strong language, another war is in the making. Only one language do they understand—'How many divisions have you?' I do not think we should play compromise any longer." Truman knew that both Romania and Bulgaria were solidly in the Soviet camp, well on their way to becoming Stalin's puppets. He told Byrnes that he wanted to "refuse to recognize Rumania and Bulgaria until they comply with our requirements." He also insisted on taking a firm stand in Iran and maintaining "complete control of Japan and the Pacific." More ambitiously, he declared that "We should rehabilitate China and create a strong central government there. We should do the same for Korea." He concluded: "I'm tired of babying the Soviets."

The next month, on February 9, Stalin made his speech asserting the incompatibility of communism and capitalism and proclaiming the inevitability of war between the Soviet Union and the West. Shortly after this, on February 22, George F. Kennan sent his "Long Telegram," and on March 5, Churchill delivered his iron curtain speech in Fulton, Missouri (see Chapter 4). Counterpointed to this rapidly escalating war of words, the Truman administration took the Soviet occupation of Iran to the United Nations Security Council—the first time this new international organization had been called on to handle an international crisis. He underscored the seriousness of his intentions by sending the mighty U.S. Sixth Fleet into the eastern Mediterranean.

"Mighty Mo," the U.S. battleship Missouri, *is shown here anchored off Piraeus, Greece, in April 1946. The ship was part of the U.S. Sixth Fleet, which President Truman sent to Greece to demonstrate the American resolve to support Greece and Turkey against a communist incursion or insurgency.*

Civil War in Democracy's Cradle

Rhetoric reverberated, armies awaited orders, and a great fleet sailed, but, so far, the Cold War had been just that. As yet, there had been no heat of battle. This was about to change.

During World War II, Greece had been invaded and occupied by Nazi forces, which were resisted chiefly by partisans belonging to the People's National Army of Liberation (ELAS), the military arm of the Communist National Liberation Front (EAM). In September 1944, the British army drove the Germans out of Greece and occupied the nation, bringing back the pre-invasion Greek government, which, however, now included members of the EAM. Not everyone in the ELAS was happy with a government supported by the capitalist Brits. When elements of this partisan group threatened armed insurrection, the British occupiers proposed that the entire ELAS be disarmed. This triggered a communist protest in the form of a general strike in Athens, beginning on December 2, 1944. The next day, government forces, including police and Greek and British troops, fought with ELAS members in the streets, prompting Prime Minister Churchill to make a personal visit, which he hoped would bring about a reconciliation. It did result in a truce and the withdrawal of ELAS guerrillas from the capital, and on February 12, 1945, a definitive agreement was concluded, calling for the ELAS to surrender its weapons within two weeks. Despite this, violence broke out anew, the Greek government became increasingly unstable, and, to complicate matters further, Yugoslavia and Albania, both communist powers, began territorial disputes with Greece.

It was just the scenario Joseph Stalin relished: confusion abounding and an indigenous communist movement ready to seize power. But, this time, it was not Stalin who stepped into the breach. Together with the

DETAILS, DETAILS

Uncle Joe's Wit

Truman's quip, that the Soviets understand only one language—"How many divisions have you?"—was an allusion to Stalin's retort to French premier Pierre Laval's question in 1935, "Can't you do something to encourage religion and the Catholics in Russia? It would help me so much with the Pope." "Oho," Stalin responded. "The Pope! How many divisions has he got?"

communist leaders of Albania and Bulgaria, Josip Broz (Tito), generalissimo of communist Yugoslavia, threw financial and military support behind the EAM and ELAS, thereby enabling the Greek communist guerrillas to withdraw in strength north into the mountains, where they were steadily supplied directly by Yugoslavia and Albania.

The British sought to counter this insurgency by sending forty thousand troops to Greece and extending a package of financial aid to the government, which very quickly became wholly dependent on both British finance and military support. Devastated by the war that had just ended, Great Britain could hardly afford to prop up the Greek government. Prime Minister Clement Attlee announced that Britain would be unable to continue its support beyond March 31, 1947, the day of the Greek elections. On February 21, 1947, the Attlee government appealed to the United States to aid not only Greece but also Turkey.

Having already resolved to support Turkey against Stalin, President Truman was eager to keep Tito out of Greece—though at this early point it is doubtful that anyone in the British or American governments recognized much difference between Stalin and Tito. There was already a tendency in the West to regard the so-called Soviet bloc as a monolithic structure in which every element, every individual answered directly to Stalin. In the case of Yugoslavia and Albania this was far from being true. Under the leadership of Enver Hoxha, Albania would eventually align itself with Communist China, but, even now, it kept aloof from the Soviet Union and avoided Stalin's broad thumb. In Yugoslavia, Tito continually played Soviet interests against those of the West, more often than not to the

A communist-led general strike erupts in Athens, Greece, on December 2, 1944. Note the British and American flags and military vehicles. With World War II still raging in Europe, Athens was occupied by the Allies.

benefit of the West—and at all times to further the interests of Yugoslavia. Despite his willingness to work with and to trade with capitalist powers, Tito was actually a more ideologically committed Marxist than Stalin was. Whereas Stalin's motives for Soviet expansion were ultimately rooted in a will to power and a need to preserve himself in office, Tito, while he did seek territory at the expense of Greece, was more genuinely interested in creating an ideologically like-minded neighbor. Tito wanted to propagate Marxism.

Josip Broz—Marshal Tito—of Yugoslavia.

THE TRUMAN DOCTRINE

TO PRESIDENT TRUMAN, COMMUNIST AGGRESSION was communist aggression, whatever its motivation, and he requested from Congress an appropriation of $400 million for the purpose of supporting the governments of Turkey and Greece against that aggression.

He justified his request with a speech to Congress on March 12, 1947, the most consequential of his presidency. It was founded on the principle George Kennan would publicly—albeit anonymously—articulate in his July 1947 "X" article for *Foreign Affairs*: "containment." The *containment* of the aggressive spread of communism, as Truman now explained to Congress, required a national policy dedicated to supporting "free peoples"—everywhere—against subversion, particularly Soviet-sponsored subversion. The press dubbed this the "Truman Doctrine," a phrase Truman himself never liked, but which stuck anyway.

Enver Hoxha, communist leader of Albania, addresses the Fourth Congress of Albanian Trade Unions, 1956. Like Yugoslavia's Tito, Hoxha was a communist who refused to submit to the authority of Stalin and the Soviet Communist Party. In contrast to Tito, who opened cordial relations with the capitalist West, Hoxha transformed Albania into an insular state, with ties to the People's Republic of China rather than to the Soviet Union or Western Europe.

> "It is hot and humid and lonely. Why in hell does anybody want to be a head of state? Damned if I know."
>
> *Harry S. Truman, diary, July 19, 1948*

In working with his writers to prepare the speech, Truman had been keenly aware of its great consequence. He rejected a first draft: "The writers had filled the speech with all sorts of background data and statistical figures about Greece and made the whole thing sound like an investment prospectus," he complained. He shot the draft back to Undersecretary of State Dean Acheson, asking him for more emphasis on general policy. He was anxious that Congress and the American people should understand that he was proposing not merely to help Greece and Turkey, but to take a precedent-setting ideological stand for

MONROE'S PROTOTYPE

The popular tag for Truman's foreign aid policy, the "Truman Doctrine," was a pointed reference to the "Monroe Doctrine," the policy articulated by President James Monroe in his 1823 message to Congress. The Napoleonic Wars had sparked widespread revolution in South America, and after Napoleon had been disposed of, Spain began making noises about reclaiming its lost colonies. President Monroe responded with the four principles collectively known as the Monroe Doctrine:

1. The Americas were no longer available for colonization by any power.
2. The political system of the Americas was essentially different from that of Europe.
3. The United States would consider any interference by European powers in the Americas a direct threat to U.S. security.
4. The United States would not interfere with existing colonies or with the internal affairs of European nations, nor would the United States participate in European wars.

Whereas the Monroe Doctrine was about protecting the integrity of the Western hemisphere—the neighborhood of the United States—the Truman Doctrine potentially staked out the entire world as its field of operations. Monroe sought to defend a geographical region. Truman pledged the United States to defend an ideology, democracy, wherever in the world it was threatened.

the very highest stakes. When the new draft was returned to him, Truman found it "half-hearted. The key sentence, for instance, read, 'I believe that it should be the policy of the United States. . .' I took my pencil, scratched out 'should' and wrote in 'must.'" He went on to make similar emendations throughout the manuscript. "I wanted," he wrote later, "no hedging in this speech. This was America's answer to the surge of expansion of Communist tyranny. It had to be clear and free of hesitation or double talk." He began:

> The gravity of the situation which confronts the world today necessitates my appearance before a joint session of the Congress. The foreign policy and the national security of this country are involved. One aspect of the present situation, which I present to you at this time for your consideration and decision, concerns Greece and Turkey. The United States has received from the Greek Government an urgent appeal for financial and economic assistance. Preliminary reports from

The president promulgates the "Truman Doctrine," March 12, 1947. It would constitute the core of U.S. Cold War policy for some fifty years.

> the American Economic Mission now in Greece and reports from the American Ambassador in Greece corroborate the statement of the Greek Government that assistance is imperative if Greece is to survive as a free nation. . . .

From the beginning, Truman made his appeal both with respect to aiding an individual country and to protecting U.S. national security by shaping a more general foreign policy. What he said next was a case study of how communist forces exploited postwar devastation and desperation:

> When forces of liberation entered Greece they found that the retreating Germans had destroyed virtually all the railways, roads, port facilities, communications, and merchant marine. More than a thousand villages had been burned. Eighty-five percent of the children were tubercular. Livestock, poultry, and draft animals had almost disappeared. Inflation had wiped out practically all savings. As a result of these tragic conditions, a militant minority, exploiting human want and misery, was able to create political chaos which, until now, has made economic recovery impossible.

> Greece is today without funds to finance the importation of those goods which are essential to bare subsistence. . . . Greece is in desperate need of financial and economic assistance to enable it to resume purchases of food, clothing, fuel, and seeds. These are indispensable for the subsistence of its people and are obtainable only from abroad. Greece must have help to import the goods necessary to restore internal order and security, so essential for economic and political recovery. . . .
>
> The very existence of the Greek state is today threatened by the terrorist activities of several thousand armed men, led by Communists, who defy the government's authority at a number of points, particularly along the northern boundaries. . . .

Desperation and want invited an insurgency by the communist minority. The restoration of economic stability was necessary to "restore internal order and security." Military assistance was also required:

> Meanwhile, the Greek Government is unable to cope with the situation. The Greek army is small and poorly equipped. . . . Greece must have assistance if it is to become a self-supporting and self-respecting democracy. The United States must supply this assistance. . . . There is no other country to which democratic Greece can turn. No other nation is willing and able to provide the necessary support for a democratic Greek government. . . .

The United States alone could save "democratic Greece." This theme would be reprised throughout the entire Cold War, only the countries needing rescue would be different. The "Truman Doctrine" was founded on an almost messianic vision of the United States, as the savior and redeemer of democracy in the world, a role "no other nation" was "willing and able" to play.

Truman sounded another theme, destined to be repeated over the Cold War Years:

> The Greek Government has been operating in an atmosphere of chaos and extremism. It has made mistakes. The extension of aid by this country does not mean that the United States

> condones everything that the Greek Government has done or will do. We have condemned in the past, and we condemn now, extremist measures of the right or the left. We have in the past advised tolerance, and we advise tolerance now.

United States economic and military assistance would prove to be a sturdy bulwark against the spread of communist aggression, yet it would, more often than not, bolster, sometimes entirely prop up, harsh, corrupt, quasi-fascist, right-wing regimes. These imperfect—or downright repugnant—as they were, were nevertheless judged preferable to a communist government that owed allegiance, even abject obedience, to Moscow.

Poverty and hunger were fertile ground for communism. The photograph shows a soup kitchen in Greece, 1946.

The case of Greece's neighbor, Turkey, was different, Truman went on to acknowledge. Neutral in World War II, it was

> spared the disasters that have beset Greece. . . . Nevertheless, Turkey now needs our support. Since the war, Turkey has sought additional financial assistance from Great Britain and the United States for the purpose of effecting that modernization necessary for the maintenance of its national integrity. That integrity is essential to the preservation of order in the Middle East. The British government has informed us that, owing to its own difficulties, it can no longer extend financial or economic aid to Turkey. As in the case of Greece, if Turkey is to have the assistance it needs, the United States must supply it. We are the only country able to provide that help.

With this acknowledgment that the threat facing Turkey was not a direct result of the war, Truman extended the policy of "containment"

WHAT IF TRUMAN HADN'T PUSHED HIS DOCTRINE?

Truman's foreign policy has often been compared to that of Woodrow Wilson. Both presidents saw the United States as the guardian of world democracy. In a letter to Ohio Congressman Michael J. Kirwan (August 13, 1962), Truman ranked Wilson third among the nation's five greatest presidents, behind Washington and Jefferson and ahead of Lincoln and Franklin D. Roosevelt.

But as much as he admired Wilson, he knew that his effort to "make the world safe for democracy" in World War I and his doomed struggle for the League of Nations had failed. Truman must have wondered what his own odds were. Yet he must have also realized that what the "Truman Doctrine" proposed was substantially different from Wilson's strategy. Whereas Wilson took an all-or-nothing stance—calling for imposition of democracy everywhere—Truman proposed merely to give democracy space to develop by holding back the communist forces that threatened it. Wilson was in a position wage all-out war to "make the world safe for democracy." Truman saw his only option as a combination of economic and military aid to threatened nations, a policy later augmented by limited military intervention by U.S. forces.

Had Truman taken Wilson's approach, it is quite possible that a new major war—perhaps a world war—would have erupted. On the other hand, had he decided to refrain from intervening, Soviet influence would almost certainly have been much greater in the world than it was, and the Cold War would have been lost before it fairly began.

beyond giving aid to the war-ravaged. *Any* democratic nation struggling to remain democratic would be eligible. Nevertheless, the president framed even this aspect of his policy in terms of the war just ended: "One of the primary objectives of the foreign policy of the United States is the creation of conditions in which we and other nations will be able to work out a way of life free from coercion. This was a fundamental issue in the war with Germany and Japan. Our victory was won over countries which sought to impose their will, and their way of life, upon other nations."

Like many other students of history, President Truman believed that the course of human events was shaped by specific decisions made at critical moments. As he saw it, the aftermath of World War II was a

> moment in world history [in which] nearly every nation must choose between alternative ways of life. The choice is too often not a free one. One way of life is based upon the will of the majority, and is distinguished by free institutions, representa-

> tive government, free elections, guarantees of individual liberty, freedom of speech and religion, and freedom from political oppression. The second way of life is based upon the will of a minority forcibly imposed upon the majority. It relies upon terror and oppression, a controlled press and radio, fixed elections, and the suppression of personal freedoms.

The role of the United States, he declared, was to facilitate the right choice by supporting "free peoples who are resisting attempted subjugation by armed minorities or by outside pressures. I believe," he continued, "that we must assist free peoples to work out their own destinies in their own way. I believe that our help should be primarily through economic and financial aid which is essential to economic stability and orderly political processes."

From these humanitarian and ideological principles, Truman proceeded to the subject of global military strategy, the world situation as it related immediately to the security of the United States and the rest of the free world:

> It is necessary only to glance at a map to realize that the survival and integrity of the Greek nation are of grave importance in a much wider situation. If Greece should fall under the control of an armed minority, the effect upon its neighbor, Turkey, would be immediate and serious. Confusion and disorder might well spread throughout the entire Middle East. Moreover, the disappearance of Greece as an independent state would have a profound effect upon those countries in Europe whose peoples are struggling against great difficulties to maintain their freedoms and their independence while they repair the damages of war.
>
> It would be an unspeakable tragedy if these countries, which have struggled so long against overwhelming odds, should lose that victory for which they sacrificed so much. Collapse of free institutions and loss of independence would be disastrous not only for them but for the world. Discouragement and possibly failure would quickly be the lot of neighboring peoples striving to maintain their freedom and independence.

LINK

Saving Democracy by Destroying Democracy?

As a result of the earliest episodes of the Cold War, United States aid fostered the regimes of Mohammad Reza Pahlavi as Shah of Iran, Ismet Inönü as president of Turkey, and a succession of right-wing strongmen and military dictators in Greece. As Truman proposed it, U.S. policy in the Cold War was intended to promote democracy. As actually implemented, the policy was more often directed at fighting communism, which often meant supporting, even installing, rightist regimes that were anything but democratic.

> Should we fail to aid Greece and Turkey in this fateful hour, the effect will be far reaching to the West as well as to the East.

Years later, Truman's successor in office, Dwight D. Eisenhower, would employ a homely metaphor to describe the effect of the "loss" of any single nation to communism. It would be, he said, as if the first domino in a row of dominoes had been toppled. Without doubt, the rest of the row would fall as well. This theory would also come to dominate the American world view throughout the Cold War.

Truman concluded by asking Congress to provide $400 million in aid to Greece and Turkey and "to authorize the detail of American civilian and military personnel to Greece and Turkey . . . to assist in the tasks of reconstruction, and for the purpose of supervising the use of such financial and material assistance as may be furnished. I recommend that authority also be provided for the instruction and training of selected Greek and Turkish personnel." He reminded Congress that the "United States [had] contributed $341 billion toward winning World War II." He called it "an investment in world freedom and world peace. The assistance that I am recommending for Greece and Turkey amounts to little more than 1 tenth of 1 percent of this investment. It is only common sense that we should safeguard this investment and make sure that it was not in vain."

NUMBERS

The Cost of Civil War

The conflict was lopsided. Peak strength of Greek government forces was 205,000, whereas the number of communist troops mustered at any one time did not exceed 28,000. Over the course of the war, 15,969 Greek government troops were killed, 38,557 wounded, and 2,001 went missing. Among communist combatants, probably 50,000 died—a number exceeding the peak strength of the force. Noncombatant and civilian deaths have been estimated at 158,000. There was nothing "cold" about the Greek Civil War.

Victory

Congress responded to the proclamation of "Truman Doctrine" by voting the funds and aid requested. In Greece, the ELAS responded by announcing the immediate formation of a communist government—the "Free Greek Government"—then advancing in a strength of twenty to thirty thousand guerrillas south, penetrating nearly to Athens. At this point U.S. military and financial aid began to reach government forces, and, from June 19 to August 20, 1948, forty thousand loyalist troops mounted a major campaign against the main communist base in the Grammos Mountains.

The biggest engagement of the war, the Battle of the Grammos Mountains proved decisive. Led by General "Markos" Vaphiades, the communists managed to break through an envelopment by three columns of government troops, but only at the devastating cost of

The cover of the May 22, 1948, issue of this British magazine featured one of the anticommunist Greek "commandos" the cash-strapped United Kingdom could no longer afford to aid.

more than three thousand killed and six thousand wounded. Against 12,500 badly mauled rebels who had withdrawn into the Vitsi Mountains, the government hurled fifty thousand U.S.-equipped troops. Although the communists were not dislodged, they were badly battered. As the winter of 1948–49 set in, government forces turned their attention to the Peloponnese, clearing it of rebels by the middle of March 1949. In Macedonia, the communists seized the initiative, taking a heavy toll on government forces but suffering, in turn, even heavier casualties.

Despite rapidly dwindling numbers, diehard rebels continued to fight until, in July 1949, their leaders made a fatal error. They proclaimed their allegiance to Joseph Stalin. Noting this, Yugoslavia's Tito, hitherto the main support of the Greek communists, summarily cut off aid. Within a month, the last of the communist guerrillas had been captured, and the country was declared secure on August 28, 1949. ELAS surrendered formally on October 16, 1949.

The victory taught Truman and other policy makers three lessons about fighting this Cold War. First, American aid—money and matériel, and lots of both—was effective, even essential. Second, the "Communist bloc" was not an unassailable monolith topped by Stalin; there were cracks in the structure—men like Tito—political fault lines to be exploited. And third, the first two hopeful lessons notwithstanding, final victory would be very hard and very costly.

TAKEAWAY

Initial Threats, First Victories

Early in the Cold War, most Americans focused on the iron curtain Stalin had drawn across Eastern and Central Europe. In reality, the Cold War first broke out in and near the Mediterranean region, as Stalin and (in Greece) Tito exploited circumstances and events created by World War II in attempts to gain control over Iran, Turkey, and Greece. Whereas the strategic exigencies of the final months of World War II had prompted the Western Allies to make extensive European concessions to Stalin, Britain and, to a larger extent, the United States, drew the line in the Middle East and Mediterranean. In this region, the West won its first Cold War victories.

CHAPTER 6

THE MARSHALL PLAN

Rescuing Europe and the Europeans

"IF YOU WANT A FRIEND IN WASHINGTON," Harry S. Truman once advised, "get a dog." While many hailed the "Truman Doctrine," everyone, it seemed, had different advice on how the president should act on it. Truman found himself under attack from some quarters as bellicose and reckless, while others criticized him for practicing what an earlier generation of American politicians condemned as "dollar diplomacy," trying to buy off enemies instead of confronting them forthrightly by military means. Few at either end of the political spectrum appreciated just how exquisite a balancing act the president was trying to pull off. The Cold War would last nearly half a century—not the longest war in world history, but certainly history's longest tightrope walk.

THE ARCHITECTURE OF "CONTAINMENT"

PRESIDENT TRUMAN THOUGHT IT ESSENTIAL TO CONFRONT Soviet expansion militarily by supplying threatened countries with military aid short of actual combat troops. During the early days of World War II—before Pearl Harbor, while the United States was still ostensibly neutral—Prime Minister Winston Churchill had appealed to President Roosevelt for the ships and weapons of war. "Give us the tools," he said, "and we will finish the job." This is what Truman wanted to do now for nations imperiled by communism—give them the tools and let *them* finish the job. As we will see in later chapters, however, Truman and his successors were not always able to limit aid to matériel, and the containment policy repeatedly involved the United States in a series of so-called proxy wars, of which the conflicts in Korea and Vietnam were the most intense. It would be in places like Korea's Pork Chop Hill and Vietnam's Khe Sanh, not Washington or Moscow, that the forces of capitalist democracy and the forces of communism would fight. It would not be the great cataclysmic World War III Joseph Stalin predicted as inevitable, but a succession of lesser yet nevertheless bloody and bitter wars. Containment spawned the strategic doctrine of limited warfare, averting Armageddon by means of a half century of violence and bloodshed, limited but chronic.

George F. Kennan, the intellectual father of containment, complained in later life that the concept had been hijacked by those who wanted to rationalize military confrontation with the Soviet Union. His intention, he said, had been that the United States would act to contain aggressive communist expansion chiefly by sending economic aid to threatened foreign governments, not military assistance, let alone American combat troops. In his March 12, 1947, address to Congress seeking aid for Greece and Turkey, Truman showed himself very much in step with Kennan's intentions. "I believe," the president said, "that our help should be primarily through economic and financial aid which is essential to economic stability and orderly political processes." That—not war—was the Holy Grail of the anti-communist, anti-Soviet crusade Harry Truman proposed to lead.

A 1947 U.S. political cartoon titled "Where To?" comments on the Truman Doctrine, which seemed to most Americans a scary venture into uncharted diplomatic, political, and financial territory.

PROXY WAR ROSTER

The term "cold war" was intended to denote the opposite of a "hot war"; that is, a cold war was conducted mainly through political, diplomatic, and economic means coupled with the *threat* of outright war while generally avoiding any shooting, whereas a hot war was strictly military.

As the Cold War actually unfolded, however, it spawned a series of proxy wars, in which the United States and the Soviet Union (and later, the People's Republic of China) avoided fighting each other directly by using third-party—usually Third World—nations as battlefields. The most important proxy wars of the Cold War period include:

Greek Civil War	(1946–49)	Bay of Pigs Invasion	(1961)
Arab-Israeli Conflict	(1948–)	Cuban Missile Crisis	(1962)
Korean War	(1950–53)	Angolan Civil War	(1974–2002)
Cuban Revolution	(1953–59)	Ogaden War	(1977–78)
Tibetan Uprising	(1959–73)	Afghan-Soviet War	(1979–89)
Vietnam War	(1957–75)	Iran Hostage Crisis	(1979)
Guatemalan Civil War	(1960–96)	Iran-Iraq War	(1980–88)
Congo Crisis	(1960–65)	U.S. Invasion of Grenada	(1983)

A CONTINENT UPROOTED

TO PONDER THE TOLL OF WORLD WAR II is to think of millions dead. But in the years immediately following the end of the war, the dead were not uppermost in the minds of victors and the vanquished. It was the living who created an unprecedented crisis.

Even today, no one knows for certain how many refugees World War II produced, but the most widely accepted estimate is approximately sixty million—far more than any other war in history. The refugee crisis was mostly a European phenomenon. In the years leading up to World War II and even during the early part of the war, before escape was completely cut off, tens of thousands of Jews and other ethnic and political refugees fled Germany and, later, German-occupied countries. During the war, invasion sent many more people into flight. Finally, the effects of total war—war waged against civilians as well as soldiers—especially the mass devastation created by Allied strategic bombing, left millions homeless, not only in Europe but also in Asia. Estimates of Japanese homeless reached some fifteen million and, for China, as high as sixty million.

Non-governmental aid organizations such as the American Red Cross began feeding European refugees even before World War II had ended.

The European refugee crisis evolved throughout the war. In the spring and summer of 1940, as the Germans stormed into Belgium and France, the people of Brussels, Lille, Paris, and other major metropolises fled southwest, some to new homes, some to a life of perpetual drift. On the Eastern Front, the German invasion of Poland created many more refugees, including Poles forcibly relocated to the east as Hitler sought to "Germanize" the western part of the country. Then, by the winter of 1944–45, it was the turn of the German people to flee their homes. A great many sought to escape the onslaught of the Red Army's counterinvasion of Germany by escaping to the west, throwing themselves on the mercy of the Western allies.

Even before the war in Europe ended, the U.S.-sponsored United Nations Relief and Rehabilitation Administration (UNRRA) sought to provide relief and resettlement for the refuges, officially designated "Displaced Persons," or DPs. UNRRA hurriedly established DP camps throughout Western and Central Europe, then worked tireless to piece together and reunite families torn apart by the war. It was a missing persons search on a mass scale. Only the Soviet Union resisted UNRRA's efforts. Red Army authorities purposely held out of UNNRA's reach those DPs unfortunate enough to find themselves within Soviet-controlled zones of occupation. Soviet-controlled refugees were lodged in camps, given a meager subsistence ration, and used as forced labor. Often, conditions were little better than in the Nazi concentration camps.

UNRRA

UNRRA was actually created before the UN, in the course of a conference of forty-four nations at the White House on November 9, 1943. These countries formed the wartime "United Nations"—that is, the allies united against Germany and its allies. That UNRRA was created even before the major Allied powers had invaded the European mainland is testament to concern over a refugee crisis that was bound to get worse with each day of the war. Although burdened by the staggering cost of world war, the U.S. government committed itself to funding about half of UNRRA's budget. It was not a military organization, but did operate under orders from the Supreme Headquarters of the Allied Expeditionary Forces (SHAEF) in Europe and was led by Americans: Herbert Lehman, former governor of New York, who was succeeded in March 1946 by former New York City mayor Fiorello La Guardia. He was followed by Major General Lowell Ward in early 1947.

The UNRRA mission included the repatriation of displaced persons; the management of displaced persons camps in Germany, Italy, and Austria, pending repatriation; relief and health care for displaced persons; and even vocational training as well as entertainment. UNRRA worked directly with refugees and also coordinated the efforts of twenty-three nongovernmental welfare agencies, the most important of which were the Joint Distribution Committee, the Organization for Rehabilitation through Training (ORT), and the Hebrew Immigrant Aid Society (HIAS). UNRRA itself was a major employer of displaced persons, who were hired to conduct much of the actual work of aid.

UNRRA burned through its funding by 1947, at which time it handed over its operations to the International Refugee Organization (IRO).

Battle of Winter

The Allied armies that swept through Europe in the spring of 1945 saw more than rubble where houses and great public buildings had been. They saw fallow fields and unplowed fields. They saw coal mines in ruins or shut down. Having already passed through a catalogue of horrors, most soldiers gave these sights little thought, but those who knew they would be responsible for administering the occupied territories regarded these scenes with anxiety and dread. They knew the coming winter would be hard, barren, and cold. Sickness, starvation, and exposure would be the new enemies, the new front, in World War II. In August 1945, General Eisenhower addressed the German people, warning them of the inevitable hardships of the coming months. To his own staff and occupation planners, Ike confessed his fear that great want and suffering would bring disorder, violence, even outright rebellion against the occupiers.

For many months after World War II, the typical German daily ration was not much more than 1,000 calories, much of that in potatoes. People did not immediately starve, but they were severely undernourished, such as this child being weighed by a relief worker c. 1945.

Did the Germans heed Eisenhower's warning? Probably not. Stunned and numbed by war, they were, even in the congenial sun of summer, already undergoing severe hardship. The daily food ration rarely rose above twelve hundred calories. With German paper currency, the reichsmark, virtually worthless in a runaway postwar inflation, farmers grew increasingly reluctant to part with their produce. Even if they had been willing, the transportation infrastructure throughout Europe, and especially in Germany, was hard pressed to distribute sufficient quantities of food. The same was true of coal. In the British, French, and American zones of occupation, coal production was impressive, especially given the ruinous state of many of the mines. Yet water and rail systems could transport no more than about 60 percent of what was mined. That meant that there were barely sufficient supplies to run the trains and power public utilities. As for heating residences, supplies were almost nonexistent, and each German child in the American zone was ordered to bring one piece of firewood to school for the purpose of heating the classrooms.

The devastation of World War II had reduced many European cities to medieval conditions. A woman looks for food on an unidentified European city street c. 1945.

Except for December 1945 and the first two months of 1946, the winter of 1945–46, like that of 1944–45, was especially harsh. The news U.S. administrators received in November 1945 did not make the winter any easier. Between December and July, some 2,250,000 Germans expelled from Eastern Europe would be flooding into the American-controlled zone of Germany—this out of a total of 6,650,000 who were scheduled to arrive in the Western zones at

Supreme Allied Commander Dwight D. Eisenhower (left) has just arrived in Berlin for the Potsdam Conference in July 1945. He is accompanied by Lieutenant General Lucius Clay, military governor of U.S.-occupied Germany, who faced the staggering task of sheltering and feeding the ruined nation's millions.

DETAILS, DETAILS

Hunger

General Clay's 1,500-calorie ration kept Germany alive but hungry; however, it did not provide adequate nutrition for the long term. The typical daily menu consisted of five and a half thin slices of bread, three medium-size potatoes, three tablespoons of oatmeal, one teaspoon of fat, and one teaspoon of sugar. This meant that, of the 1,500 allotted calories, 1,200 were in bread and potatoes.

the rate of a quarter million each month during December, January, and February, then in even greater numbers by the spring. (At the Potsdam Conference, the Western allies had acquiesced in a Soviet program of what must be termed the "ethnic cleansing" of both German nationals and ethnic Germans from Germany's former eastern territories, the former Sudetenland of Czechoslovakia, and some other regions. From the end of 1944 to 1950, an estimated fourteen million Germans were forced by Soviet or Soviet bloc action to evacuate these areas.) On top of this, prisoners of war were slated to be repatriated to Germany at the rate of 85,000 per month, beginning with 80,000 in December.

U.S. Army general Lucius D. Clay, America's man on the ground in the occupation and administration of Germany, was responsible for feeding and sheltering these millions. By early October 1945, it was clear to him that he would not have enough food to raise the daily per-person ration to 2,000 calories for the winter. He could barely reach 1,250—probably insufficient to sustain life in unheated dwellings in winter. He decided to bet on more food coming and set the short-term ration at 1,500 daily calories.

A stretch of unusually warm weather late in December 1945 and January–February 1946 gave Germany and the rest of ravaged Europe a respite from what had been a terrible winter, but from 1946 to 1947 the average German daily calorie intake increased to just 1,800 calories, moving one U.S. State Department official, William Clayton, to remark that "millions of people are slowly starving." Worse, the next winter, 1946–47, proved unremittingly brutal, and coal remained in critically short supply. People started to freeze in their homes—certainly by the hundreds, perhaps the thousands—and conditions in the DP camps were often only marginally better.

A Shattered Economy

Even before the war in Europe ended, Congress authorized massive amounts of humanitarian aid, a total of more than $9 billion by early 1947. The hope was that Britain and France would get on their feet quickly enough to support their own populations and even extend aid to others, but even the most conservative American predictions of when this might come about proved far too optimistic.

More than four years of total war had done more than destroy lives, buildings, and the visible infrastructure of the Continent. It had a less visible but ultimately more enduring effect on the dynamic systems of civilization, the basics of commerce, trade, the economy. The first evidence of this had been seen in the agricultural sector. There had been great fear that neglected and damaged farms and fields would produce an insufficient harvest. This was indeed a problem, but many farmers could still produce and harvest a crop. The urban dwellers to whom they would normally sell it, however, had no way to pay for it. With industrial plants in ruins, they were out of work. True, the factories could be put back together, but who would finance that? After all, neither city dwellers nor farmers could pay for manufactured goods. The economy of all Europe was like an enormous engine drained of oil. It had seized up. It could not move—certainly not without some massive impetus from outside of the frozen system.

Dueling Propositions

There was a growing understanding within the Truman administration that subsistence aid given directly to refugees and others was urgently needed, but this would not be enough to jump-start the broken engine that was the European economy. On September 6, 1946, Secretary of State James F. Byrnes proposed a sweeping economic aid plan in a speech he made at the Stuttgart Opera House. In the meantime,

Fruit trees blossom in spring 1945 beside the bombed-out ruins of a German industrial plant. Also visible in the picture are the houses of factory workers, most of them at least partially roofless, all with shattered windows like sightless eyes. The destruction of German industry crippled all of postwar Europe.

General Clay began putting together a plan to reindustrialize the country. It was at about this time that Undersecretary of State Dean Acheson and Vice President Alben W. Barkley each outlined his own relief proposal. Good hearts and fine minds applied themselves to problems staggering in scope as well as severity. But they all worked in opposition to a plan that had been introduced back in 1944 by Secretary of the Treasury Henry Morgenthau Jr. Morgenthau was a formidable man. One of the nation's premier financiers, he had served as treasury secretary through all four of Franklin Roosevelt's terms, raising and spending more money than all of his fifty-one predecessors in that office combined. He had managed the finances of the Depression-era New Deal and of World War II, and he had done so with extraordinary wisdom and efficiency. Not since Alexander Hamilton in the cabinet of George Washington had a treasury secretary played so important a role in American life and government. And when the Bretton Woods conference convened in July 1944 to hammer out a master plan for postwar worldwide economic cooperation under the aegis of the emerging United Nations, it was Morgenthau who took a leading role.

Morgenthau possessed the mind of a great economist and financial manager. But he was also a Jew, and it was with the Jewish people, six million of whom Hitler had murdered, that his heart lay. Morgenthau wanted to create a postwar world in which Germany would never pose a threat to Jews—or to any other people—again. Unlike the European leaders who had wanted to punish and humiliate Germany by imposing massive monetary reparations, Morgenthau advocated pastoralizing Germany, transforming it from an industrial country to

U.S. secretary of the treasury through the Great Depression and World War II, the formidable Henry Morgenthau (photographed here in 1942) wanted to reduce postwar Germany from an industrial titan to an agricultural country incapable of ever waging war again.

an agricultural one. He proposed stripping the nation of all territory it had acquired as a result of the war and then dividing the remainder into two states—not east and west, but north and south. Whatever industrial infrastructure remained intact—from heavy machinery to railroad rolling stock to vehicles to hand tools—would be appropriated and distributed to the Allied nations, the lion's share to go to the Soviet Union as "restitution." As for postwar relief, Morgenthau—at least originally—recommended against it. Germany and the German people would not be punished or humiliated, but they would be forced to live—and die—with the consequences of the war they had created.

In 1944, President Roosevelt greeted the "Morgenthau Plan" enthusiastically and authorized the secretary to present it at the second Quebec conference between FDR, Churchill, and their respective staffs. The British prime minister did not like it, but he needed Morgenthau's approval of additional wartime credit from the U.S. treasury, and so, reluctantly, he endorsed the plan along with Roosevelt. On both the British and American sides, there came objections from high-level staff and advisers, who argued that the Morgenthau Plan not only would cause untold human hardship but also would lay all of Germany open to communist takeover and, worst of all, it would repeat the tragic mistakes of the punitive Treaty of Versailles, which had beaten down a defeated Germany after World War I, making the rise of a vengeful dictatorship virtually inevitable. For the time being, therefore, the Morgenthau Plan was shelved, but by no means discarded. Indeed, when Byrnes and the others began proposing their ambitious relief and recovery plans, it reemerged with a vengeance.

President Truman, who, unlike the late FDR, had nothing invested either in Morgenthau or his plan, examined the proposal afresh. As was the case with every decision he made, Truman drew on his profound understanding of history. He had fought in World War I as a captain of artillery, and, a great admirer of Woodrow Wilson, he had judged the Treaty of Versailles a tragedy. The economic devastation and national humiliation the treaty had wrought created the climate in which the likes of Adolf Hitler and his Nazi regime could prosper. The attempt to reduce Germany to perpetual impotence after World War I did nothing less than ensure the outbreak of World War II.

"There is nothing new in the world
except the history you do not know."

Harry S. Truman,
quoted in William Hillman, Mr. President, *1952*

Truman, who had retained Morgenthau from Roosevelt's cabinet, pointedly excluded him from the Potsdam Conference in July 1945. Secretary of War Henry Stimson—another Roosevelt appointee—had counseled the president that he should punish German "war criminals in full measure. Deprive [Germany] permanently of her weapons. . . . Guard her governmental action until the Nazi-educated generation has passed from the stage. . . . But do not deprive her of the means of building up ultimately a contented Germany interested in nonmilitaristic methods of civilization." That made sense, good common sense, to the man from Missouri.

On July 5, 1945, Morgenthau confronted Truman in the Oval Office and issued an ultimatum. Either he would be permitted to accompany the president to Potsdam and play a part in the conference or he would resign. Truman replied coolly that, if this was the case, his resignation was accepted, and the president announced Morgenthau's resignation before the day was out.

"Morgenthau didn't know shit from apple butter."

Harry S. Truman, conversation with
Jonathan Daniels, November 12, 1949

Marshall: The Man and the Plan

The Potsdam Conference came and went without yielding any specific plan for European recovery and reconstruction. Despite U.S. financial aid, the years 1945 and 1946 brought great hardship to Germany and the rest of Europe. In January 1947, George Catlett Marshall, the man who, as U.S. Army chief of staff throughout World War II, had been instrumental in the Allied military victory, replaced James Byrnes as Truman's secretary of state. Like the president, Marshall understood the importance of avoiding a repetition of the errors of Versailles, but he also had a further insight. No one objected to aiding America's Allied partners in their recovery, but many Americans—and not just Morgenthau—objected to helping Germany get back on its feet. Marshall pointed out that one could argue the humanitarian merits of aiding a recent and terrible enemy, but there was no arguing about the economic importance of Germany. The fact was that the nation had been the most powerful industrial force in Europe between the two world wars. Why was the entire European economy stalled in a postwar depression? Marshall believed that the devastation of Germany, linchpin of the European economy—both the greatest producer and greatest consumer—was preventing the economic recovery of all Europe.

Like it or not, the welfare of Europe, this warlike and warring continent, flowed from the interdependence of all its nations. Vengeance against Germany was an understandable motive, but, if the continent was to recover, the leaders and people of Europe would have to act with a degree of concord and unity that was unprecedented. The consequences of failing to replace vengeance with a spirit of mutual cooperation were twofold. First, a prolonged depression would both lengthen and deepen the immediate postwar humanitarian crisis.

Former U.S. Army chief of staff George Catlett Marshall (hand raised, left) takes the oath of office as Harry Truman's secretary of state, January 21, 1947.

Second, an economically malfunctioning Europe would be an open invitation to the continued aggressive expansion of the Soviet Union. Like every other highly placed official in the Truman administration, Marshall had read George F. Kennan's analysis of Soviet expansion. He enthusiastically agreed with Kennan's recommendations for "containing" the spread of communism. But, unlike many of his civilian colleagues, this former military man grasped Kennan's notion that containment should be achieved mainly through economic rather than military means. Marshall concluded that a U.S.-financed plan of aid would serve the strategic purpose of containing the spreading stain of Soviet influence. Moreover, he even hoped that Stalin could be persuaded that cooperating with the plan would bring badly needed aid and relief to the iron curtain countries and to the Soviet Union itself, thereby increasing the prestige of the USSR in the world.

Money, which so often divided people and nations, might be the very means of bring them together. It was a wonderful thought, but the hope was shattered by the Foreign Ministers Conference held in Moscow from March 10 to April 24, 1947. The object of the conference was to arrive at a collaborative, all-encompassing plan for European recovery. From the beginning, however, it was apparent to the Western diplomats that their Soviet counterparts would never agree on the contours of such a plan and were, in fact, deliberately stalling all efforts at recovery and reconstruction. Soviet motives were the same that had been suspected in the closing months of the European war. Stalin actually wanted Europe to suffer. The worse off a region was, the riper it was for gathering into the Soviet fold. As Marshall explained in a 1952 interview, the Moscow conference "proved conclusively that the Soviet Union . . . could not be induced to cooperate in achieving European recovery." It was the disillusionment resulting from the conference that persuaded him and other American diplomats to forge ahead with a massive master plan for U.S.-funded European aid.

"The patient is sinking while
the doctors deliberate."

*George Catlett Marshall, April 28, 1947, on
the fruitless Foreign Ministers Conference*

As army chief of staff and now as secretary of state, Marshall was the executive who conceived the big picture, then assigned others to fill in the working details. It was to State Department staffers Kennan and William L. Clayton that Marshall gave the assignment to create a workable plan for European recovery, but he himself had a preliminary decision to make: What Allied nations would be involved in sponsoring the plan?

As it turned out, dire circumstance made this decision almost moot. The Soviets had opted out at the Foreign Ministers Conference, and the diplomatic principals of the only other likely partner, Great Britain, held very different views about war reparations. The British wanted Germany to pay, to pay sooner rather than later, and to pay in large amounts. They would not be inclined to fund German recovery. The only possible alternative, therefore, was for the United States to be the sole sponsor of the plan.

This presented a problem of its own. A *European* recovery plan that was wholly an *American* initiative would be a very hard sell, even to the desperate Europeans. However it was presented to them, it would appear as the worst kind of Yankee imperialism. This led Marshall to a second major preliminary decision: The plan would be sponsored and funded exclusively by the United States, but it would be entirely administered by Europe.

It was, in fact, a brilliant solution. Not only would self-administration preserve the European sense of self-

Whatever the weather
We only reach welfare
together

This promotional poster was intended as a graphic metaphor for the Marshall Plan, which required all European participant nations to work in harmonious agreement in order to receive U.S. money. Note that the American flag is represented as the vane that guides the windmill that is Europe.

determination, it also would force the fractious nations of Europe, friends and enemies alike, to come together and cooperate. If Europe was to be responsible for deciding how the American funds would be used, Marshall resolved to make the funds conditional on the nations of Europe—all those who wanted a share of the aid—getting together to formulate a single, unitary plan of distribution and use, a plan that all the participating nations endorsed. Not a penny would be released until such a plan was in hand.

The Campaign for a New Europe

Having cleared, at least in concept, the main obstacle to European acceptance of the American recovery plan, Marshall turned next to gaining approval of it from the American people and the United States Congress. He appreciated that the plan was unprecedented in scope and conditions. Essentially, he was proposing a massive gift to Europe with only one string attached: that Europeans, not Americans, decide how the *American* money was to be used. The best way to put such a proposition over, Marshall determined, was to do so suddenly, to "spring the plan with explosive force" so as to avoid prolonged political debate, which would certainly delay implementation, probably dilute the plan, and possibly even kill it. Nothing would be worse than a scenario in which the plan was announced, Congress and others debated, and the plan was reduced or killed. Such an outcome would destroy American credibility among Europeans, something that would give Stalin very high-powered propaganda ammunition.

For the very reason that the Midwest was overwhelmingly Republican and conservative, Marshall thought of "springing" it in a speech at the University of Michigan, "in the heartland of expected opposition," so that any negative response would arise and be knocked down quickly, before it could lead to a protracted debate. But Kennan and Clayton needed more time to hammer out the crucial details, so the secretary awaited the next convenient occasion. He was scheduled to give a speech accepting an honorary degree from Amherst College on June 16, 1947, and he decided to announce the plan then. Yet the humanitarian crisis reached such a desperate pitch that he changed his mind again and maneuvered instead for something sooner. Harvard University had earlier invited Marshall to accept an honorary degree. At the time, Marshall politely declined. Now he reversed that decision—

> **REALITY CHECK**
>
> **The Most Unsordid Act**
>
> Winston Churchill has been widely quoted as having praised the Marshall Plan as the "most unsordid act in history." Although Churchill was an enthusiastic supporter of the plan, the source of the phrase was his earlier description of the wartime lend-lease program, by which the United States supplied the British and other Allied nations with matériel even before Pearl Harbor. In a speech delivered on November 10, 1941, Churchill declared that the "Lease-Lend Bill must be regarded without question as the most unsordid act in the whole of recorded history." He reprised this description five years later, in the magnificent eulogy on Roosevelt he delivered in the House of Commons, citing "the extraordinary measure of assistance called Lend-Lease, which will stand forth as the most unselfish and unsordid financial act of any country in all history."

not for the purpose of collecting the degree, but to give the speech, which he did, in Cambridge, Massachusetts, on June 5, 1947.

By way of preparation, Marshall asked Kennan and Kennan's former colleague in the U.S. Embassy at Moscow, Charles Bohlen, to prepare separate and independent "memoranda concerning means of meeting the European crisis." In the meantime, Marshall wrote up his own analysis. He then evaluated the three memoranda and concluded that Kennan's was "the most succinct and useful." He handed it, together with his own memorandum, to Bohlen, who used the material to draft Marshall's Harvard address. Marshall also consulted with Kennan, insisting to him that the United States proposal would be "aimed at hunger, poverty, and chaos and not against any group" or ideology. Kennan protested this. He believed that the aid should be purposely exploited as an anti-Soviet weapon, and he certainly objected to providing funding to the Soviet Union and Soviet satellites. Marshall listened, but stood firm. The money could be associated with no overt ideological agenda. The very unbiased and disinterested nature of the American gift would carry in and of itself tremendous propaganda value.

In the end, the speech Marshall delivered at Harvard was as simple as it was momentous. It presented a funding plan unprecedented in the amount of dollars at stake, yet there was not a single sum, not one figure, mentioned in the entire speech. Marshall painted with the broadest possible strokes to create a canvas that was boldly affirmative. After explicitly disavowing any political or ideological purpose, he simply called on the leaders of Europe to convene in order to create their own plan for European recovery, which the United States would then fund. That was the essence of the speech, nothing more, nothing less. If Marshall had eschewed grandiosity in the speech, so he had taken pains to avoid any ballyhoo in Cambridge. In an effort to avoid *negative* press, Truman and Marshall decided to avoid just about *any* press at all. No press release was issued before the Harvard ceremony, and no reporters or journalists were contacted beforehand. President Truman even took the step of scheduling a White House press conference at the same time as the Harvard address in order to ensure that journalistic attention would be turned away from Cambridge.

This stratagem was used on members of the American press only. Truman and Marshall very much wanted the European press to report extensively on the speech and the aid plan. Marshall assigned Undersecretary of State Dean Acheson to contact the major European news organizations. The fuller the coverage in Europe, the better. The idea was to make a promise to the people of Europe, a promise so public that even the most conservative American politician would find it virtually impossible to vote for breaking the government's word.

As if balancing a news blackout in America with a news blitz in Europe did not call for a sufficiently difficult high-wire performance, Marshall and the president wanted to alert European journalists without revealing anything in advance to the European governments. The leaders of Europe, friends and former enemies alike, were given no warning of the plan or its announcement. Immediately following the Harvard speech, however, Marshall rushed to introduce the proposal directly to the American people. As if he were running for office, the secretary toured the nation, speaking out on the plan. Naturally taciturn, cool by nature, even somewhat aloof, Marshall nevertheless made an excellent salesman. He was widely respected. His judgment and his word were universally valued. He was, Truman understood, a certified brand name with the American public. If he endorsed something, people naturally believed it was worthwhile.

DETAILS, DETAILS

An Open Secret

Marshall and Truman were so sly about springing the Marshall Plan that even members of the U.S. diplomatic corps were kept in the dark. U.S. diplomat Ben T. Moore wrote to an associate on July 28, 1947, that the Marshall Plan "has been compared to a flying saucer—nobody knows what it looks like, how big it is, in what direction it is moving, or whether it really exists."

Political cartoonist D. R. Fitzpatrick titled this 1947 characterization of the Marshall Plan "The Way Back."

The Plan Is Sprung

As Truman and Marshall had intended, the American press was slow to pick up on the Harvard speech, but in Europe it was big news, and the BBC broadcast it in its entirety. One of those who heard it was British foreign secretary Ernest Bevin, who, like every other European government official, had not been given advance notification of the speech or the Marshall Plan. He immediately contacted his French counterpart, Georges Bidault, to get to work preparing Europe's acceptance of the proposal. Both ministers agreed that the Soviets would have to be invited to participate, but, after meeting with Bevin and Bidault, Soviet foreign minister Vyacheslav Molotov rejected the plan.

The English and French initiatives put the necessary machinery into motion, and representatives of almost every European nation were invited to a July 12 meeting in Paris. Only fascist Spain and the minor states (Andorra, San Marino, Monaco, and Liechtenstein) were excluded from the meeting. The Soviet Union was invited, but it was already understood that Stalin would send no representative. As for the nations under Soviet control, all were invited, but only Czechoslovakia and Poland accepted. Stalin, however, forbade either nation to send a delegation.

European financial ministers meet in the Grand Dining Room of the French Foreign Office during the July 1947 Conference for European Economic Cooperation.

ALTERNATE TAKE

The "Truman Plan"?

Clark Clifford, who would serve four presidents, including Lyndon Johnson (as secretary of defense), was a young aide to President Truman in 1947 when he suggested that it would be easier to "sell" the American people on what was officially called the European Recovery Plan if it had a catchier, more personal name. Perhaps eager to flatter his boss, he suggested calling it the "Truman Plan." Instead of smiling gratefully, the president exploded: "Are you crazy?" he demanded of Clifford. "If we sent it up to that Republican Congress with my name on it, they'd tear it apart. We're going to call it the Marshall Plan." Had President Truman, perpetually at war with conservative Republicans in Congress, possessed a sufficiently inflated ego to take up Clifford on his suggestion, it is quite probable that the "Truman Plan" would never have received the approval of Congress or the support of the American people.

The Soviet newspaper Izvestiya *(November 3, 1949) blasted the suggestion of Paul Hoffman, U.S. head of the Marshall Plan's Economic Cooperation Administration, that Europe band together in a European Economic Community. Hoffman is caricatured as a capitalist fat cat, his bludgeon turned into a dollar sign by the snake twisted around it. Having already demolished a picket fence labeled "Tariff Barriers," he knocks down a sign that says "Sovereignty of Western European Countries." The caption reads, "The American bludgeon in the solution of market problems."*

Stalin Counteroffers

Stalin understood that, whatever else it may have been, the Marshall Plan was an attempt to curb the expansion of the Soviet sphere of influence. He saw the danger of attaching any part of Eastern Europe to the Western economy—namely escape from his control. After he blocked Czech and Polish participation in the meeting, every other satellite nation followed suit. Although Finland had been liberated from Soviet domination, the Finnish government had no desire to antagonize the Soviets and so declined participation as well.

In a rare instance of offering both a carrot and a stick, Stalin created the Molotov Plan (also called the COMECON), which was a package of Soviet subsidies to its "bloc." In the meantime, in the United Nations, the Soviet deputy foreign minister, Andrei Vyshinsky, denounced the Marshall Plan as a violation of United Nations principles because it was a blatant attempt to impose the will of the United States on other nations by means of so-called humanitarian relief tied to a political agenda.

Nuts and Bolts

The Soviet attacks made little impression, and sixteen Western European nations proceeded to hammer out how they would distribute and use the aid. Bringing Europe into agreement was not easy—but the

ALTERNATE TAKE

If Stalin Had Said Yes

The leadership of the U.S. Department of State knew they had to invite the Soviet Union to participate in the Marshall Plan, but, at the same time, they were counting on Stalin's rejection of an offer of aid from the United States—and so were Bevin and Bidault. The Englishman and Frenchman invited Molotov to meet them in Paris, where they presented conditions Stalin couldn't possibly accept, including a full independent assessment of the economic situation of each participant (they knew Stalin would never agree to such transparency) and the establishment of a unified European economy (which represented a concession to capitalism Stalin could never make). Had the Marshall Plan somehow been made palatable to Stalin, it would surely have died aborning. The U.S. Congress would never have funded an aid program to Joseph Stalin's USSR.

participants knew that only by coming to an agreement would any of them receive Marshall Plan aid. The major points of dispute were these:

- France feared that aid to Germany would contribute to the resurgence of a military threat.
- Belgium, the Netherlands, and Luxembourg also had fears of a German military resurgence, but their economies had been traditionally linked to that of Germany—and so they were more interested in seeing the rebirth of a prosperous Germany.
- All of the Scandinavian nations, but most of all Sweden, were anxious to retain their trade relations with the nations of Eastern Europe, the nations now within the "Soviet bloc."
- Great Britain demanded special status; if aid were distributed in proportion to the degree of physical devastation incurred during the war, the British would not get what they believed was their fair share.

William Clayton, representing the U.S. Department of State, reiterated to the European delegates Secretary Marshall's promise that Europeans and Europeans alone would make all decisions concerning the plan and would be given a free hand to structure the aid package as they wished—but, he added, appropriations of funds for implementation of the plan were made not by the president but by Congress. Whatever plan they came up with, Clayton strongly implied, would have to pass muster with the legislators of the United States. This meant that the plan would need to incorporate two features. It would have to be structured, not explicitly but in practical effect, as a dam against the rising tide of European communism, and it could not call for a disproportionate sum assigned to Germany. A majority in Congress was certainly interested in rendering humanitarian aid, but many representatives also bristled at the idea of financing a former enemy.

In fact, when the sixteen participant nations finally agreed on a plan and sent it to Washington, it was the president who made the first significant change, reducing the European request for $22 billion to $17 billion before his staff drew up legislation to submit to Congress, where, predictably, Republican isolationists opposed it. Less expected was the opposition from left-leaning Democrats and others, who criticized the plan as a disguised subsidy for U.S. exporters and as an action sure to exacerbate the hostilities between the West and the Soviets.

The masters of the Marshall Plan meet on November 29, 1948. From left to right: President Harry S. Truman, Secretary of State George C. Marshall, Economic Cooperation Administration head Paul Hoffman, and Averell Harriman, formerly U.S. ambassador to the Soviet Union, who, in November 1948, had recently stepped down as U.S. secretary of commerce.

TIPPING POINT

DEBATE IN CONGRESS WAS RANCOROUS and created a deadlock that only a lightning bolt could loosen. That came, and it came quickly.

The Communist Party of Czechoslovakia had been influential in Czech politics as early as the 1920s. After World War II, the party emerged not only as a more powerful force but also as an attractive one. Czech communists had been valiant members of the resistance to Nazi oppression; they bore a fraternal and ideological connection to the Soviet Union, which had liberated the nation from Nazi occupation; and they were not aggressively doctrinaire. Like Tito's Yugoslav communists, those of the Czech Communist Party advocated aligning the nation with communism yet without spurning the West. At the end of the war, in 1945, the Czech Communist Party had perhaps forty thousand members. Three years later, 1,350,000 Czechs were communists—and they were determined to be communists without allowing their government to become a Soviet puppet. In sharp contrast to Stalin, for whom communism depended on totalitarian rule, the Czechs wanted to achieve a communist government through democratic means and without destroying democracy.

As a result of the 1946 elections, the communists won 38 percent of the vote, more than enough to persuade non-communist President Edvard Beneš to invite the Czech Communist Party leader, Klement Gottwald, to serve as prime minister. Yet, once the communists had attained a significant degree of power, it became apparent that communist doctrine and democracy were fundamentally incompatible, and much of the nation turned against the Communist Party, criticizing

Klement Gottwald, Czech Communist Party leader, prime minister (1946–48), and president (1948–53) of Czechoslovakia.

especially the oppressive tactics and policies of the communist-dominated national police, the prospect of the collectivization of agriculture, and the demands placed on industrial workers for increased production without commensurately higher wages. Most Czechs looked forward to the upcoming elections of 1948 as an opportunity to repudiate the communists.

When the Czech government accepted the U.S. invitation to participate in the Marshall Plan in July 1947, Stalin told Gottwald that he would take strong measures to prevent Czechoslovakia from being used by the West as an economic or political weapon against the Soviet Union. The implication was obvious to Gottwald: Czechoslovakia's liberation, hard won in World War II, was now on the line. Refuse to toe the mark, and the Czech state would become a Soviet satellite—without any semblance of parliamentary government or self-determination. In response to Stalin's warning, a plan took shape within the Czech Communist Party for a coup d'état. The communist-controlled Czech security forces would eliminate the party's opponents and carry out a general purge of dissidents. Early in February 1948, Václav Nosek, the communist minister of the interior, attempted to purge all non-communists from the National Police Force. This, combined with growing threats of force from the communists, prompted the twelve non-communist members of the cabinet to resign in protest on February 21, in the confident belief that President Beneš would refuse to accept their resignations, thereby forcing the communists to yield. Instead, Beneš, fearful of inciting a rebellion or outright revolution, declared his neutrality in the dispute. This gave the communists, supported and coached by Soviet ambassador Valerian Zorin, the opening they needed to stage a coup.

After the Czech communist coup: a portrait of Joseph Stalin in a Prague store window, 1948.

Communist militia and police took over the administration of Prague. Mass communist rallies and demonstrations were launched. Those government departments and ministries run by non-communists were physically occupied by communists. The army, which had a large communist element in its leadership, was confined to barracks and refused to intervene in the uprising. In the meantime, a general strike was threatened unless President Beneš immediately agreed to form a new government, dominated by communists.

> "The completion and reconstruction of the government was carried out *in a strictly constitutional, democratic and parliamentary manner. . . .* The agents of reaction must be *unconditionally* removed. . . . The purge of our public life is now going on."
>
> *Klement Gottwald, speech, March 10, 1948*

Beneš feared both the outbreak of civil war and an invasion by the Red Army in support of the coup. Therefore, on February 25, 1948, he installed a communist party–dominated government under the leadership of Klement Gottwald. Gottwald retained as foreign minister the much-loved Czech patriot Jan Masaryk, who was not a communist. By this, and the retention of a few other non-communists, he hoped to lend an air of complete legitimacy to the new government. Within two weeks, however, Masaryk was dead—the cause of death, officially, a suicide. Beneš resigned in June 1948, and Gottwald became president.

The Czech communist coup hit the West with catastrophic force. The only surviving democracy in Eastern Europe had been lost to the Soviet bloc. The governments and people of the West—especially the United States—now saw Czechoslovakia as a satellite of the Soviets, a political entity under the absolute control of Joseph Stalin. This nightmarish vision put an immediate end to opposition against the Marshall Plan. A shocked and shaken American public demanded that Congress act, and act it did, approving more than $5 billion in the inaugural year of what was officially called the European Recovery Program.

Into Action

President Truman signed the Marshall Plan into law on April 3, 1948. This created the Economic Cooperation Administration (ECA) to administer the program under former automobile industry executive Paul G. Hoffman. Shortly afterward, the Marshall Plan participating countries—Austria, Belgium, Denmark, France, West Germany, Great

REALITY CHECK
Death of a Patriot

On March 10, 1948, Jan Masaryk was found dead in the Foreign Ministry courtyard just below his bathroom window. He was clad in pajamas. An investigation by the communist-controlled Czech police ascribed his death to suicide. In 1968, during the brief period of Czech liberalization dubbed the "Prague Spring," a more impartial investigation was conducted. It also concluded that he had killed himself. Yet another investigation took place after the fall of the communist regime in the 1990s, and, yet again, the conclusion was death by suicide. Despite these three verdicts, many Czechs continue to believe that Masaryk was murdered. There can be little doubt that the Kremlin wanted him dead, but no one has ever come forward with evidence of homicide. All that is known for certain is that he either jumped or was pushed out of his bathroom window. The death of Masaryk remains an unsolved mystery of the Cold War.

REALITY CHECK

Cheesy Monolith

Americans saw the communist coup in Czechoslovakia as evidence of Stalin's absolute control over Eastern Europe. In fact, Gottwald had engineered the coup to create an independent communist government that would mollify Stalin and thereby prevent the Soviet Union from simply swallowing up Czechoslovakia. Although Czech autonomy was never fully achieved, Stalin's control over Czechoslovakia and the other so-called Soviet bloc nations was often tenuous at best. Most Americans—including government leaders—believed that the Soviet bloc was a monolith and that the satellite countries were nations in name only. In truth, the Eastern European "monolith" appeared solid, but was actually shot through with fault lines and often on the verge of crumbling. Throughout the entire postwar Soviet period, the Kremlin was perpetually hard-pressed to keep its client states in line.

A German poster promotes the "Marshall Plan New Life for Europe.*" "ERP" stands for European Recovery Program, the plan's official name.*

Britain, Greece, Iceland, Ireland, Italy, Luxembourg, the Netherlands, Norway, Sweden, Switzerland, Turkey, and the United States—together created the Organization for European Economic Cooperation (later called the Organization for Economic Cooperation and Development, OECD) to coordinate the plan in Europe.

The ECA opened its doors in July 1948. As Marshall Plan money was turned over to the governments of the European nations, ECA administered the funds jointly with the individual governments. The ECA was connected directly to the United States through a system of envoys—like Hoffman, prominent American businessmen—who were stationed in the capital cities of the participant countries. The envoys acted as advisers to the ECA and their host governments.

To many, the Marshall Plan seemed noble and selfless. It *was* noble, but not selfless. The overwhelming balance of money transferred to the Marshall Plan countries was used to buy goods from the United States. True, it could not have been any other way in 1948, since most of the world's manufactures came from America; nevertheless, it was a kind of government subsidy for American industry, and it helped to fuel the general American prosperity of the 1950s.

In the beginning, most imports were food and fuel, but as the months and years wore on, the countries were able to spend less on relief and more on genuine investment in infrastructure rebuilding. By the final two years of the program, 1950–51, the United States had pressured—or persuaded—an increase in expenditures to bolster the militaries of the Western European nations. At the height of the plan's operation, however, by the middle of 1951, approximately $13 billion had been transferred. Of this $3.4 billion was invested in importing raw

A MARSHALL PLAN RECEIPT

Nation	Funds Received
Austria	$468,000,000
Belgium and Luxembourg	$777,000,000
Denmark	$385,000,000
France	$2,296,000,000
Germany	$1,448,000,000
Greece	$366,000,000
Iceland	$43,000,000
Ireland	$133,000,000
Italy and Trieste	$1,204,000,000
Netherlands	$1,128,000,000
Norway	$372,000,000
Portugal	$70,000,000
Sweden	$347,000,000
Switzerland	$250,000,000
Turkey	$137,000,000
United Kingdom	$3,297,000,000
Total (1948–51)	$12,721,000,000

(Note: Data from Martin Schain, ed., *The Marshall Plan: Fifty Years After* (New York: Palgrave, 2001)

A smiling President Truman signs into law the Foreign Assistance Act of 1948, launching the Marshall Plan.

LINK

Seeds of the EU

The Marshall Plan fostered—indeed, forced—the integration of the nations of Europe at least to a high degree of economic cooperation. The plan created the precedent for the creation of the European Coal and Steel Community (ECSC), established by the 1952 Treaty of Paris, and the European Economic Community (EEC), more familiarly known as the Common Market, created in 1958 pursuant to a treaty signed in 1957 by Belgium, France, Italy, Luxembourg, the Netherlands, and West Germany. These organizations, in turn, gave rise to the European Union (EU), consisting of twenty-seven member states, and created by the Treaty of Maastricht in 1993. According to the highly respected company Global Vision Consulting Ltd., the EU is responsible for nearly one quarter of the world's gross domestic product.

The Marshall Plan was aimed at allies and former enemies alike. A cargo of industrial sulfur is unloaded into railcars at a dock in Manchester, England.

materials and semi-manufactured products; $3.2 billion was spent on food (plus feed and fertilizer); and $1.9 billion represented investment in machines, equipment, and vehicles. About $1.6 billion was spent on fuel.

In addition to administering money, the ECA created the Technical Assistance Program, which provided funding for European engineers, technicians, and industrialists to come to the United States to tour factories and mines so that they might emulate American industrial know-how. The program also sent U.S. engineers to Europe as technical advisers.

VICTORY WITHOUT BLOOD

THE YEARS OF THE MARSHALL PLAN, 1948 to 1951, overlapped the most rapid period of economic growth in the history of Europe. Even the plan's harshest critics agree that this was no coincidence. During these years, industrial production rose by more than one-third, and agricultural output easily outstripped prewar levels. During the last five years of the 1940s, Europe had the look of devastation, poverty, and even starvation. By the 1950s, these scars were rapidly fading—though much rebuilding had yet to be completed. In the two decades immediately following the Marshall Plan, Western Europe did not merely recover, it enjoyed

"It was like a life-line to a sinking man. It seemed to bring hope where there was none. The generosity of it was beyond our belief."

British foreign minister Ernest Bevin, speech, April 1, 1949

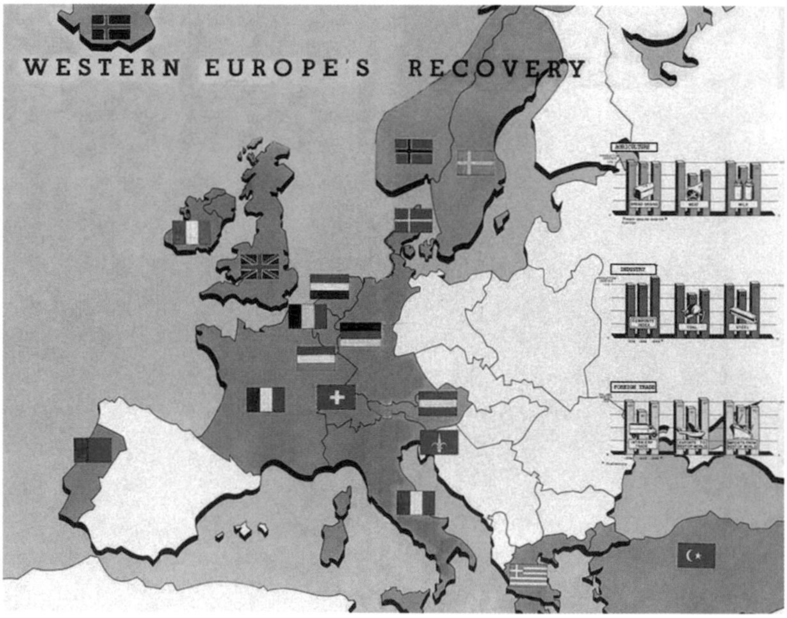

The countries of the Marshall Plan. Opting out: the iron curtain countries and fascist-ruled Spain.

an unparalleled increase in the standard of living. If the Marshall Plan did not create this, it surely facilitated and accelerated it.

Politically, the recovery stimulated by the Marshall Plan allowed the Western European democracies to reduce rationing and increase employment, thereby stabilizing governments and holding communist parties at arm's length. As the years passed, practically everyone could see that, for the ordinary person, life was better in the democratic, capitalist West than in the Soviet-dominated East. The influence of communist parties throughout Western Europe steadily diminished. What, after all, did communism have to offer generally prosperous people?

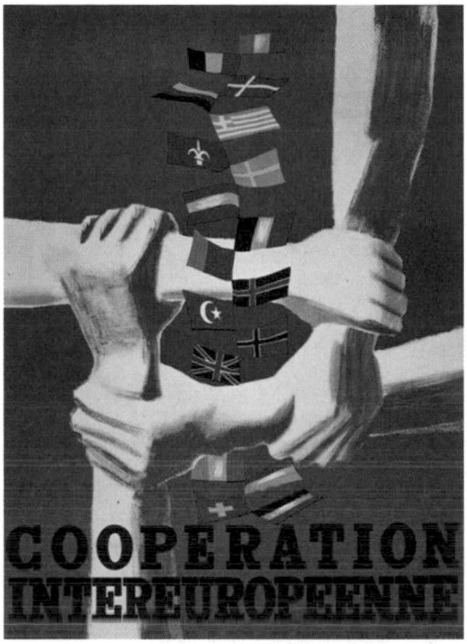

The French take on the Marshall Plan: "Inter-European Cooperation."

The Marshall Plan, linked into the Bretton Woods system of global monetary management that had been outlined by the forty-four Allied nations that had signed the Bretton Woods Agreements in July 1944, also mandated free trade throughout Europe. The trade relationships established under the Marshall Plan between the United States and Europe outlasted the plan, forming the basis for ongoing commerce as well as military alliances, the most important of which is the North Atlantic Treaty Organization (NATO; see Chapter 10). The plan and its enduring effects also deepened the division between that part of Europe under democratic capitalism and that part under Soviet-dominated communist command economies. The Marshall Plan inoculated the West against the spread of communism, partly through stimulating physical recovery and partly through creating a community of economic interest among the Western democracies, including the United States. Yet it also inevitably hardened the divisions that defined the adversaries in the Cold War, making the conflict both colder and harder, bringing to the world a diplomatic winter that, like any other bitterly cold, exceptionally hard winter, looked to be endless.

TAKEAWAY

An Inoculation against Communism

The Marshall Plan, 1948–51, transferred nearly $13 billion from the United States to most of the nations of Western Europe, plus Greece and Turkey, for the purposes of relief, reconstruction, and recovery. The bold plan attached few strings to the money, except that the participating European states were required to act in harmony and unity in creating a plan for the distribution and use of the funds. Although the plan was put forward without any explicit ideological agenda, it unquestionably had a political purpose, namely to restore stability to and popular confidence in the democratic governments of Europe in order to secure them against incursions by the Soviet Union and the proliferation of various national communist parties. As such, the Marshall Plan was the principle nonmilitary "weapon" the United States wielded in the Cold War—an economic means of containing the spread of Soviet-backed communism.

Военной Комендантуре Берлин Митте
Militär Kommandantur Berlin-Mitte
Fußgänger
BRITISH SECTOR
BRITISCHE SEKTOR
БРИТИСКИ СЕКТОР

Part Three

SUPERPOWERS

CHAPTER 7

A Monopoly Ends

The "Nuclear Club" Acquires New Members

THE TEST OF AMERICA'S FIRST ATOMIC BOMB took place on July 16, 1945, in New Mexico. At the time, President Harry Truman was wrestling with the Soviet Union's Joseph Stalin and Stalin's foreign minister, Vyacheslav Molotov, in Potsdam, a suburb of ruined Berlin (see "A Mole at Los Alamos" in Chapter 3). He knew when the test was scheduled, and just hours before the experimental bomb was set to detonate, the president remarked to his aides: "If it explodes—as I think it will—I will certainly have a hammer on these boys," by which he meant Stalin and Molotov. The coded cable announcing the successful results reached Truman just before one of the scheduled meetings with Churchill and Stalin. Churchill later remarked that the president "told the Russians just where they got off and generally bossed the meeting." Truman—the avid student of history surely knew Theodore Roosevelt's secret to successful negotiation embodied in a West African proverb: "Speak softly but carry a big stick." The cable Truman had just received told him that the United States now held the biggest stick of all, the biggest stick ever.

THE ARROGANCE OF IGNORANCE

AMERICANS, INCLUDING AMERICAN SCIENTISTS, American military men, and American political leaders, collectively thought very little of Russian science and technology. Never mind that, in the great world conflagration just ended, the Soviets had created a number of war-winning weapons, fielding what was generally considered the best tank in the world—the fabled T-34—and turning out at an amazing rate a series of highly innovative fighter aircraft. The arrogance of U.S. intelligence concerning the state of Soviet nuclear weapons development was matched only by its ignorance. In 1945, most U.S. experts confidently assured President Truman that the Soviets would not have a nuclear bomb for another five and more probably ten years. Five years after this prediction, the consensus remained exactly the same. As 1950 approached, U.S. Army intelligence estimated that the Soviets would not test fire a fission weapon before 1960. Naval intelligence pushed this back to 1965. The U.S. Air Force, a newly independent service branch, was the lone voice of pessimism, issuing a prediction that the Soviet bomb could come as early as 1952. Truman never hazarded a public prediction himself, but, in 1946, after Los Alamos scientific director J. Robert Oppenheimer confessed to him that he could not even guess when the Soviets would get the A-bomb, the president snapped back. "I know." "When?" an astonished Oppenheimer asked. "Never."

The Soviet nuclear physicist Andrei Sakharov, who had helped to build the Soviet atomic bomb, became a moral crusader against nuclear proliferation and suffered persecution by his government for these and other "dissident" efforts.

THE NATIONAL SECURITY ACT

DESPITE THE COMFORT HE TOOK IN WIELDING THE BIGGEST STICK, President Truman was thoroughly persuaded that the Soviet Union represented a grave threat to what American leaders called the "free world," and he acted accordingly. On February 26, 1947, the president transmitted to the House and Senate the draft of a bill that he would sign into law on July 26 as the National Security Act of 1947. The legislation authorized the establishment of a Central Intelligence Agency (CIA), the nation's first fully institutionalized espionage organization, which we will discuss in Chapter 11. The new law also conflated the separate departments of War and the Navy into a single cabinet-level Department of Defense, and, under this new department, created the United States Air Force, liberating it from the U.S. Army.

PREVIOUS SPREAD: *British military police erect a sign marking the division of the British and Russian sectors of Berlin, 1948.*

POP CULTURE

No Soviet Samsonite

During the late 1940s, the popular press stoked the American people's anxiety over atomic weapons by running stories about how Soviet agents might sneak atomic bombs into the United States in ordinary suitcases. This gave rise to a wisecrack that circulated in official government circles to the effect that there was absolutely no need to fear such an eventuality because Soviet scientists had yet to perfect the suitcase.

Unifying what were now three armed services under a single department was more than an administrative gesture. It was intended to transform the military into a thoroughly coordinated global force under the direct and immediate control of the president. The early nineteenth-century military theoretician Carl von Clausewitz famously described war as "the continuation of politics through other means." The Department of Defense was meant to bring this theoretical principle into actual practice. For one thing, the development and deployment of nuclear weapons was far too consequential a matter to be left to individual military commanders. Equally important was Truman's understanding that, pursuant to his "containment" policy, the U.S. military would have to be deftly used on a regular basis as a political instrument to help resolve any number of conflicts arising from communist expansive aggression anywhere in the world. Finally, the president wanted the nation's military arm to be closely integrated with its newly augmented intelligence-gathering apparatus, and both the CIA and the military tightly bound to the national policy-making authority—namely, the president himself.

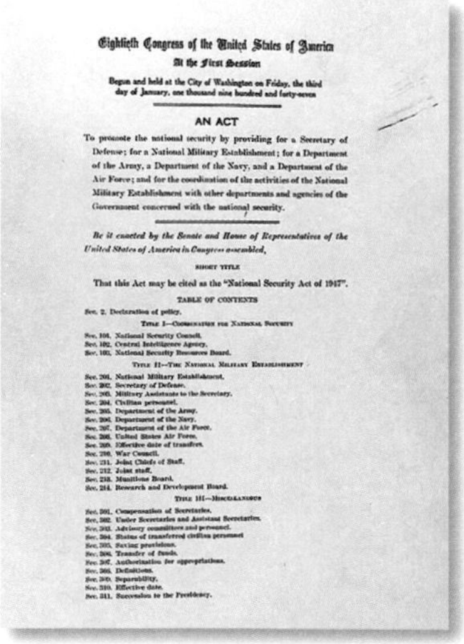

Eightieth Congress of the United States of America
At the First Session

Begun and held at the City of Washington on Friday, the third day of January, one thousand nine hundred and forty-seven

AN ACT

To promote the national security by providing for a Secretary of Defense; for a National Military Establishment; for a Department of the Army, a Department of the Navy, and a Department of the Air Force; and for the coordination of the activities of the National Military Establishment with other departments and agencies of the Government concerned with the national security.

Be it enacted by the Senate and House of Representatives of the United States of America in Congress assembled,

SHORT TITLE

That this Act may be cited as the "National Security Act of 1947".

TABLE OF CONTENTS

Sec. 2. Declaration of policy.

TITLE I—COORDINATION FOR NATIONAL SECURITY

Sec. 101. National Security Council.
Sec. 102. Central Intelligence Agency.
Sec. 103. National Security Resources Board.

TITLE II—THE NATIONAL MILITARY ESTABLISHMENT

Sec. 201. National Military Establishment.
Sec. 202. Secretary of Defense.
Sec. 203. Military Assistants to the Secretary.
Sec. 204. Civilian personnel.
Sec. 205. Department of the Army.
Sec. 206. Department of the Navy.
Sec. 207. Department of the Air Force.
Sec. 208. United States Air Force.
Sec. 209. Effective date of transfers.
Sec. 210. War Council.
Sec. 211. Joint Chiefs of Staff.
Sec. 212. Joint staff.
Sec. 213. Munitions Board.
Sec. 214. Research and Development Board.

TITLE III—MISCELLANEOUS

Sec. 301. Compensation of Secretaries.
Sec. 302. Under Secretaries and Assistant Secretaries.
Sec. 303. Advisory committees and personnel.
Sec. 304. Status of transferred civilian personnel
Sec. 305. Saving provisions.
Sec. 306. Transfer of funds.
Sec. 307. Authorization for appropriations.
Sec. 308. Definitions.
Sec. 309. Separability.
Sec. 310. Effective date.
Sec. 311. Succession to the Presidency.

The National Security Act of July 26, 1947, integrated the armed forces into a cabinet-level Department of Defense, created the United States Air Force, and established the CIA.

In writing of the significance of the National Security Act, most historians emphasize the establishment of the CIA and the Department of Defense, but equally important was the creation of an independent U.S. Air Force, effective as of September 18, 1947. Forty years earlier, on August 1, 1907, President Theodore Roosevelt, a prescient aviation enthusiast, had authorized creation of an "Aeronautical Division" under the aegis of the U.S. Army Signal Corps. This evolved into the Aviation Section in 1914, still under the Signal Corps, then became the U.S. Army Air Service in 1918. The Air Corps Act of 1926 created the U.S. Army Air Corps, making the air arm independent of the Signal Corps but still under army control. Just before the United States entered World War II, the Air Corps achieved semiautonomous status within the army as the U.S. Army Air Forces. Full independence, established by the National Security Act in 1947, was highly significant for three major reasons. First, it was an acknowledgment that the airplane had become a weapon of great importance, as essential to war as traditional ground and ocean forces. Indeed, political and military leaders began to think of the air arm as more

James Forrestal, secretary of the navy during World War II, became the nation's first secretary of defense in 1947. After suffering a nervous breakdown, he resigned on March 28, 1949, and while undergoing psychiatric treatment at Bethesda Naval Hospital, he leaped to his death on May 22 from the sixteenth-floor window of a kitchen across the hall from his room. Many believe his daunting job had killed him.

important than the other two and imagined fighting wars exclusively from the air. Second, the creation of a separate air force bowed to the extraordinary importance technology had assumed in modern warfare. The new service branch was intended to exploit the cutting edge of weapons technology. As it turned out, this emphasis would create controversy within the air force itself, as the USAF evolved from an *air* force into an *aerospace* force after the introduction of intercontinental ballistic missiles (ICBMs). America's air arm had always embodied the glamour of the extreme danger its dashing "flyboys" willingly engaged. The proliferation of technological weaponry threatened to bring on an era of what many called "pushbutton war," in which bold pilots would be replaced by cold military technicians closeted in air conditioned bunkers, their fingers poised indifferently above the buttons that launched the nuclear-tipped ICBMs. Not only would this development take the romance out of air combat, it also would remove from wars of mass destruction the human element altogether. In an extreme scenario, machines would fight wars on a planetary scale.

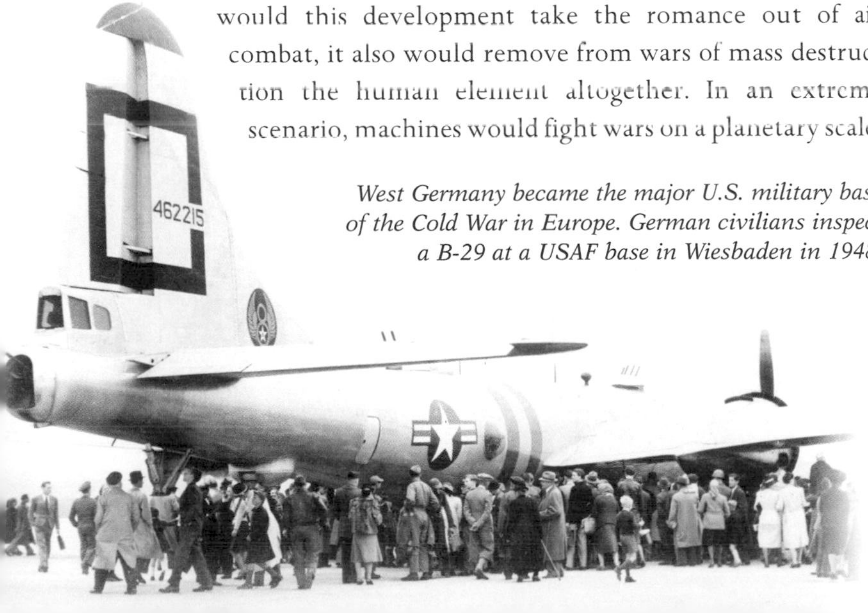

West Germany became the major U.S. military base of the Cold War in Europe. German civilians inspect a B-29 at a USAF base in Wiesbaden in 1948.

DETAILS, DETAILS

A Man-Killing Job

The first secretary of defense was James V. Forrestal. As secretary of the navy from 1944–47, he proved himself a tireless and innovative administrator, among whose achievements was putting the U.S. Navy in the forefront of racial integration during World War II, when the other services were strictly segregated. In 1947, Truman tapped him to lead—and virtually to create—the Department of Defense, a monumentally complex task that required the integration and coordination of the fractious service arms, plus the creation of an independent air force—all during a time of escalating tensions with the Soviets and drastically reduced military budgets. In late 1948, new U.S. Army chief of staff General Omar N. Bradley recalled meeting a haggard Forrestal, who looked, Bradley thought, like a doomed man. On May 22, 1949, while being treated for "nervous and physical exhaustion," Forrestal leaped to his death from the window of a kitchen directly across the hall from his room at Bethesda Naval Hospital, an early casualty of the Cold War.

THERMONUCLEAR CINEMA

In the 1964 film *Fail-Safe*, the president of the United States (played by Henry Fonda) is forced to drop a hydrogen bomb on New York City in order to avert World War III, after an American bomber—acting on orders from a malfunctioning Strategic Air Command (SAC) computer—annihilates Moscow.

Based on the 1962 novel of the same name by Eugene Burdick and Harvey Wheeler, *Fail-Safe* was shot in stark documentary black and white by director Sidney Lumet and brought to the screen one of the nightmares that haunted the Cold War period: the possibility that a faulty transistor or a button pressed in error would bring about the end of the world. Today considered a classic of Cold War culture, *Fail-Safe* was "big footed" at the box office by the nearly simultaneous release of a very different movie about the very same subject. Stanley Kubrick's *Dr. Strangelove or: How I Learned to Stop Worrying and Love the Bomb* (to give its full title) was the blackest of black comedies, portraying a thermonuclear attack against Russia launched by a deranged SAC base commander, General Jack D. Ripper, played by Sterling Hayden with a cigar clamped between his teeth precisely in the manner of real-life SAC chief General Curtis E. LeMay. Ripper launches the attack in order to preserve "our precious bodily fluids" from contamination by what he believes is a Soviet plot to fluoridate the American water supply. The film also includes hilariously dark depictions of a blustering Air Force chief of staff (General Buck Turgidson, played by George C. Scott) and an ineffectual U.S. president (Merkin Muffley), a well-meaning RAF exchange officer (Group Captain Lionel Mandrake), and a strategic and scientific adviser (Dr. Strangelove), all played by British comic genius Peter Sellers. Wheelchair-bound, speaking in a thick German accent, and struggling to control an arm that reflexively rises in a Nazi salute, Dr. Strangelove is a satiric combination of two German-born Americans, missile pioneer Dr. Wernher von Braun and high-level political adviser Dr. Henry Kissinger. Strangelove counsels the president to take advantage of the renegade attack to, in effect, restart the world—minus the Soviets. This plan is foiled when Russia's ambassador Alexei de Sadesky conveys the news that the Soviets have put in place a computer-controlled "doomsday machine," which will destroy all life on earth in automatic and unstoppable response to a nuclear attack.

In this scene from the 1964 film Dr. Strangelove, *Peter Sellers, as President Merkin Muffley, listens to Soviet ambassador Alexei de Sadesky (Peter Bull) in the U.S. War Room.*

Obsolescent before it was even built, the B-36 "Peacemaker" was a gawky, lumbering giant of a nuclear bomber intended to fill the gap until the more advanced, all-jet B-47 Stratojet and B-52 Stratofortress could come on line. The photograph shows a preproduction "XB" (eXperimental Bomber) version of the aircraft, powered by six pusher-type piston engines. As finally built for service, the piston engines were augmented by four turbojets, hung in two-jet pods near the outboard tips of each wing.

The third and perhaps most significant consequence of creating a separate air force was that this upstart was handed the keys to the nation's nuclear arsenal. The atomic bomb was, after all, meant to be dropped from the air. Unifying the armed forces under a single Department of Defense was intended to end the kind of interservice rivalries that resulted in waste, inefficiency, and strategic and tactical blunders. One of the lessons of Pearl Harbor was that lack of communication between navy and army commanders in Hawaii contributed to catastrophic vulnerability. Yet the inordinate shift of strategic priorities to the U.S. Air Force created great dissension within the postwar military. Army and navy leaders feared they were being marginalized, even rendered obsolete.

There was considerable justification for their fears. As it had done immediately after World War I, the government rushed to demobilize. Weapons contracts were canceled, and all manner of war matériel, from jeeps to ships, was mothballed or scrapped. Men were mustered out of the service faster than they had been drafted into it. Each of the services scrambled for a piece of a much-diminished pie. In 1949, one of many disputes between the navy and the air force erupted after the Department of Defense canceled funding for a planned U.S. Navy "supercarrier," the USS *United States*, and channeled the money instead to the air force to develop the B-36 bomber.

At this point, the air force had only one plane capable of carrying an atomic bomb, the B-29, the same aircraft that had dropped atomic bombs on Hiroshima and Nagasaki. Bigger aircraft, capable of carrying bigger bombs, including the forthcoming hydrogen bomb, were required. Ideally, the air force wanted to develop an all-jet bomber, but this would take time. The B-36 Peacemaker, an ungainly looking behemoth nicknamed the "flying cigar," was an intermediate step between the B-29 and the two planned jet bombers, the B-47 Stratojet and B-52 Stratofortress (see Chapter 8, "Jet Fuel"). The B-36 was a hybrid that combined four jet engines with six conventional piston engines that drove propellers. It could carry a heavy payload of bombs and could fly it across intercontinental distances; however, it was slow and vulnerable to attack.

Revolt of the Admirals

In 1949, air force generals argued for funding a large fleet of strategic bombers, starting with the B-36. Navy admirals countered that the experience of World War II in the Pacific had shown the dominant role of carrier-based aircraft and therefore asked Congress to fund a fleet of supercarriers, beginning with the USS *United States*. Secretary of Defense James Forrestal backed the navy and authorized construction of the *United States*, but when a nervous breakdown forced his resignation on March 28, 1949, his successor, Louis A. Johnson, threw his support behind the air force. The following month, without consulting Congress or the president, Johnson canceled construction (already under way) of the *United States*. This prompted John L. Sullivan, the secretary of the navy, to resign in protest. Several admirals followed suit. In the meantime, Captain (later Admiral) Arleigh Burke circulated an anonymous document criticizing the B-36 as a "billion-dollar blunder" and also accused Johnson of a conflict of interest, inasmuch as he had served on the board of directors of Convair, builder of the bomber. Another naval officer, Rear Admiral Daniel V. Gallery, wrote a series of articles for *The Saturday Evening Post*, including the sensational and inflammatory "Don't Let Them Scuttle the Navy!" Johnson called for Gallery's court-martial. The navy refused, but Gallery was eventually forced into resignation.

The navy brass was not finished, however. Before Congress, Admiral Louis E. Denfield, chief of naval operations, gave scathing testimony, claiming that strategic (nuclear) bombing would never be decisive in war and that the effectiveness of nuclear weapons had been generally overrated; moreover, Denfield protested, first use of nuclear weapons was inherently immoral. (Denfield and the other officers who gave testimony conveniently omitted to mention that the planned *United States* was specifically designed to accommodate aircraft big enough to carry nuclear weapons, and that it was to be the first of eight supercarriers, each of which could launch and land ten nuclear-capable bombers that could carry out a total of 640 nuclear weapons raids before

The air force and navy vied for scarce defense dollars during the early Cold War. Construction of the supercarrier United States *was halted—the unfinished keel plate is shown here in April 1949—and the project canceled to fund other things, especially the USAF's controversial B-36.*

requiring resupply of fuel and ammunition.) In retaliation for his testimony, Denfield was effectively removed from the navy—an act Congress subsequently condemned as retaliatory.

General Omar Nelson Bradley, who had commanded the U.S. 12th Army Group—the major American force in Europe—during World War II, had been appointed the American military's first chairman of the Joint Chiefs of Staff under the National Security Act. It fell to him to referee this and other interservice disputes. He testified to Congress that the Soviet surface fleet was negligible and, for that reason, funding elaborate naval projects was unnecessary. Because the U.S. Air Force had primary responsibility for atomic warfare, he argued, it was vital that the new service get its B-36, imperfect though it was. In the end, the cancellation of USS *United States* was upheld, and the air force was given its B-36 fleet.

" . . . our military forces are one team—in the game to win regardless who carries the ball. This is no time for 'fancy Dans' who won't hit the line with all they have on every play, unless they can call the signals. Each player on this team—whether he shines in the spotlight of the backfield or eats dirt in the line—must be all-American."

General Omar N. Bradley, criticizing the navy's position during the "admirals' revolt" of 1949

NUMBERS

To the Bone

By 1947, the armed forces of the United States had been slashed from a wartime high of 12 million men to 1.5 million. At the peak of World War II, the military budget had been $90.9 billion. For fiscal 1947, it was topped off at $10.3 billion.

REALITY CHECK

The Bottom Line

By the early 1960s, U.S. Air Force brass frequently presented requests for funding bigger and bigger nuclear weapons with the rationale that they offered (in the parlance of the era) "more damage per dollar." One anonymous American military analyst pointed out that this rationale, doubtless, was not exclusive to the United States and suggested that, in the Kremlin, some Red Air Force officer was justifying the purchase of new nukes with the phrase "more rubble per ruble."

Bradley's position revealed much about U.S. military doctrine and strategy during most of the Cold War. First, the chief assumption was that any major war would be fought against the Soviet Union. Second, any major war would use nuclear weapons. Thus, the lion's share of military spending throughout the 1950s went to the development and production of nuclear and thermonuclear weapons and delivery systems—at the expense of developing and even maintaining "conventional" (nonnuclear) forces. The American people were clamoring to reduce military spending, and, as Congress saw it, investing in nuclear weapons literally gave the nation the most bang for the buck. Yes, atomic weapons research and production were expensive, but they were a lot cheaper than maintaining a large conventional force. Militarily speaking, atomic bombs looked like bargains.

The all-nuclear orientation of the American military during the first two decades of the Cold War had two ominous consequences. First, the exclusive focus on preparing to fight an all-out atomic war left U.S. forces ill-prepared for the "limited" wars that were actually fought during the Cold War years. Second, if Congress was willing to finance only nuclear weapons, then all the services agitated to acquire them. The army and the navy looked for ways in which they, too, could join the nuclear club. The result was an interservice arms race that paralleled the arms race between the United States and the Soviet Union. This served to accelerate the stockpiling of nuclear weapons, which in turn heated up the international arms race.

JOE ONE

THE NUCLEAR ARMS RACE BEGAN LONG BEFORE almost anybody in the U.S. government, military, and scientific community anticipated. In addition to vastly underestimating Soviet scientific and technological sophistication, American experts labored under the mistaken belief that the United States enjoyed a monopoly not only on nuclear know-how but also on the principal raw ingredient of nuclear weapons, uranium. They thought it a great stroke of good fortune that the U.S. Southwest had major deposits of uranium ore, an element generally believed to be extremely rare. In fact, it proved to be relatively plentiful in several parts of the world, including Soviet Siberia.

Through a combination of espionage and original research—probably more of the latter than of the former—Soviet scientists pushed hard to build a bomb. Out of what U.S. intelligence leaders believed to be an abundance of caution, the air force had begun conducting long-range, high-altitude reconnaissance flights for the purpose of sampling radiation in the lower stratosphere. Few dreamed that the Soviets would detonate an atomic test any time soon, but the sampling flights were flown nevertheless. On September 3, 1949, a Geiger counter on one of the planes registered 85 counts per minute, 35 counts above the expected baseline reading. A second device on the aircraft measured 153 counts. Two days after this, another reconnaissance aircraft, flying from Guam to Japan, recorded readings in excess of a thousand counts per minute. Atmospheric sampling filters on this plane were brought back to a government laboratory in Washington for analysis. The high Geiger readings left no room for doubt that a radioactive release had taken place on Russian territory. The laboratory's finding of barium, cerium, and molybdenum isotopes, all products of nuclear fission, confirmed that the release had been the result of an explosive chain reaction. It was possible that this detonation had been accidental, but the radioactivity readings and results of the chemical analysis were so similar to findings from the U.S. Alamogordo test in 1945 that the conclusion seemed inescapable: The Soviets had successfully tested a nuclear device sometime between August 26 and 29. Joseph Stalin had "the bomb." With the combination of irreverence and gallows wit typical of the American defense community, intelligence officers dubbed the test weapon "Joe One."

This Soviet photo shows the mushroom cloud of the first Russian A-bomb, which U.S. intelligence dubbed "Joe One."

Harry Truman, not a man who typically dodged reality, nevertheless had a hard time accepting the news. He repeatedly grilled the Atomic Energy Commission scientists who reported to him on September 19, demanding of them, pleading with them: *"Are you sure?"* And when they told him that they were quite sure, the president speculated that the Soviet bomb had been the work of captured German scientists. So strong were American prejudices concerning the Russian intellect that Truman was reflexively prepared to credit the Soviet nuclear bomb to anyone but the Russians.

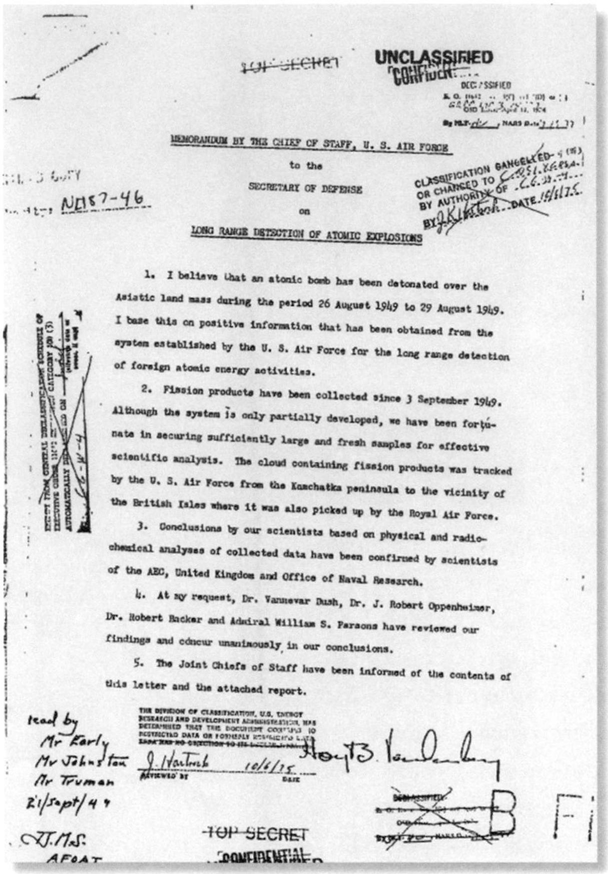

~~TOP SECRET~~ UNCLASSIFIED

MEMORANDUM BY THE CHIEF OF STAFF, U. S. AIR FORCE

to the

SECRETARY OF DEFENSE

on

LONG RANGE DETECTION OF ATOMIC EXPLOSIONS

1. I believe that an atomic bomb has been detonated over the Asiatic land mass during the period 26 August 1949 to 29 August 1949. I base this on positive information that has been obtained from the system established by the U. S. Air Force for the long range detection of foreign atomic energy activities.

2. Fission products have been collected since 3 September 1949. Although the system is only partially developed, we have been fortunate in securing sufficiently large and fresh samples for effective scientific analysis. The cloud containing fission products was tracked by the U. S. Air Force from the Kamchatka peninsula to the vicinity of the British Isles where it was also picked up by the Royal Air Force.

3. Conclusions by our scientists based on physical and radiochemical analyses of collected data have been confirmed by scientists of the AEC, United Kingdom and Office of Naval Research.

4. At my request, Dr. Vannevar Bush, Dr. J. Robert Oppenheimer, Dr. Robert Bacher and Admiral William S. Parsons have reviewed our findings and concur unanimously in our conclusions.

5. The Joint Chiefs of Staff have been informed of the contents of this letter and the attached report.

Hoyt S. Vandenberg

read by
Mr Early
Mr Johnston
Mr Truman
21/Sept/49

~~TOP SECRET~~

General Hoyt Vandenberg, U.S. Air Force chief of staff, sent this top-secret memo to the secretary of defense, reporting intelligence that revealed the detonation of "Joe One"—the Soviet Union's first atomic bomb.

The "Super"

President Truman broke the news to the nation personally, on September 23, 1949. He had delayed the announcement by nearly five days because he did not want it to hit the wires in the immediate aftermath of a stunning announcement from the British government that, gripped by postwar economic crisis, it was devaluing the pound. The Soviets wanted nothing more urgently than to undermine world capitalism, and Truman had no desire to help them by touching off a financial panic. And when he finally made the announcement, the man from Missouri, celebrated for his blunt plain speaking, expressed himself with uncharacteristic finesse. "Ever since atomic energy was first released by man, the eventual development of this new force by other nations was to be expected." Nowhere in this sentence did the word *bomb* appear. With similar disingenuousness, he added: "This probability has always been taken into account by us." The fact was that it had never really been taken into account.

It was not so much that the leaders of the United States feared a Soviet nuclear attack, but that they mourned the end of the big stick monopoly. Curtis LeMay defined the situation as the passing of "the era when we might have destroyed Russia completely and not even skinned our elbows doing it." From now on, the use of nuclear weapons by one side would surely trigger nuclear retaliation from the other.

Most American military planners advised that the next best thing to a monopoly on nuclear weapons was simply to have *more* bombs than anyone else. The race was to produce not only more bombs but also bombs with higher "yields"—more explosive power. There was still one atomic monopoly the United States could strive to acquire: exclusive possession of the so-called super, the hydrogen bomb.

Talk of a super had been in the air since before the prototype atomic bomb had been successfully exploded in the summer of 1945. During World War II, Enrico Fermi and a dark, passionate Hungarian expatriate named Edward Teller pursued the theoretical work on a thermonuclear device that had been sidelined to make way for the more immediately feasible development of a nuclear device. The difference between the two weapons was this:

- A nuclear bomb uses nuclear *fission*—the "splitting" of the atomic nucleus—to release a large amount of energy in a massively destructive explosion as the bomb's uranium or plutonium core is split into elements that, together, weigh less than the original atoms of the core. Matter can neither be created nor destroyed—only transformed. In this case, the remainder of the original mass is instantly transformed into energy.

- A hydrogen bomb uses nuclear *fusion*—the joining of hydrogen isotopes. Deuterium, a stable isotope of hydrogen, is fused with tritium, a radioactive hydrogen isotope, to create a reaction with an extremely high energy yield. Whereas the atomic bomb splits heavier elements into lighter ones, the fusion bomb joins lighter elements into a heavier element, which nevertheless has less mass than its components, the difference being realized as energy. If the energy liberated by fission is great, that produced by fusion is far greater. Tremendously high temperatures are required to initiate fusion—hence the term "thermonuclear." The required thermonuclear temperatures are achieved by a fission trigger, which provides the heat energy to initiate the much more energetic fusion explosion. Thus a hydrogen bomb is said to be "staged"; the first stage is a fission detonation, which initiates the second stage, a thermonuclear fusion reaction. A "simple" fission bomb may produce the explosive equivalent of anywhere from less than a ton of TNT to 500,000 tons—or 500 kilotons. In contrast, the "yield" of a fusion bomb is in the range of *millions* of tons of TNT and is therefore measured in megatons. If an atomic bomb could wipe out a city, a very big thermonuclear bomb could destroy a region. Use more than a few, and the weapon could annihilate civilization itself.

Edward Teller, an expatriate Hungarian, worked with Enrico Fermi on developing a thermonuclear bomb (the "super"), while the rest of the Manhattan Project group pursued the more immediately feasible, though far less powerful, atomic bomb. After the war, Teller became a passionate champion of pursuing development of the "H-bomb."

Teller, a scientific maverick who had devoted most of his wartime work on the Manhattan Project to attempting to transform the theory of a fusion bomb into a practical plan for one, was frustrated that most of his colleagues had clearly lost "their appetites for weapons work" after the atomic bomb had been successfully tested. In contrast to them, Teller—as vehemently anticommunist as he was anti-Nazi (both Stalin and Hitler had ravaged his native Hungary)—believed that while the atomic bomb might defeat the Japanese, it would not truly end the war, but just shift it to a new enemy: the Soviet Union. He judged that Stalin represented as serious a threat to the Western democracies as Hitler or Tojo had. Even as most of the Los Alamos scientists began returning to their prewar university jobs, Teller pushed for the full-out continuation of weapons work at the laboratory. He believed that the Russians would not be far behind in creating an atomic bomb, and he wanted the United States to have the super as soon as possible—in the knowledge that the Soviets would, eventually, develop that weapon as well.

For a long time, Teller's was a strident voice crying in the wilderness. On August 17, 1945, Los Alamos scientific director J. Robert Oppenheimer and other members of a high-level scientific panel charged with delivering a scientific opinion on the direction of postwar nuclear weapons policy issued their conclusions. They conceded that the "development, in the years to come, of more effective atomic weapons would appear to be a most natural element in any national policy of maintaining our military forces at great strength," but then went on to express "grave doubts that this further development can contribute essentially or permanently to the prevention of war." The scientists declared their belief that "the safety of this nation—as opposed to its ability to inflict damage on an enemy power—cannot lie wholly or even primarily in its scientific or technical prowess." Oppenheimer and the other scientists recommended that urgent steps be taken through diplomacy ("necessary international arrangements") to make "future wars impossible." This, they argued, was far more important to national security—indeed, to the security of humankind—than racing to develop more and more powerful weapons.

Late the next month, in September of 1945, the University of Chicago hosted a Conference on Atomic Energy Control at which Leó Szilárd—the godfather of the atomic bomb—painted a grim picture of a nuclear-armed future. He believed that the bombs would get bigger, reaching higher and higher into the megaton range, but he also believed that that the United States would lose its monopoly on nuclear as well as the projected super weapons not in a decade but in as little as two or three years. Indeed, he thought that a nuclear arms race was already under way. If both the United States and the Soviet Union possessed nuclear arsenals, the result would be an "armed peace," what he called a "durable peace," but not a "permanent peace." The latter would require "world government"—an unlikely eventuality in the near future, but (Szilárd thought) an eventual inevitability. Assuming the peoples of the world did not suddenly shift their national loyalties to voluntarily collaborate on the creation of a world government, nuclear weapons would enforce a "durable peace" built on deterrence. That is, neither the United States nor the Soviet Union would dare launch a nuclear war for fear of nuclear retaliation. The only good that could come of a peace built on deterrence was the creation of an interval of twenty or thirty years in which viable world government might become a reality. Szilárd also proposed an alternative to this scenario: a cataclysmic third world war. Yet the final result of that war, he believed, would be the same as that produced by thirty years of durable peace: world government—albeit one imposed by the victor at the cost of "25 million people dead."

This is the cover of the first issue of a serialized fictitious account of an atomic war between the United States and the Soviet Union. Published in 1952–53, the series exploited Americans' chronic terror of nuclear annihilation to sell—through accompanying ads—everything from U.S. Savings Bonds to men's girdles.

"Had we not pursued the hydrogen bomb, there is a very real threat that we would now all be speaking Russian. I have no regrets."

Edward Teller

On Your Mark . . .

With the notable exception of Teller, most scientists more or less shared Szilárd's view, but many political and most military leaders did not. Or, rather, they believed his vision of the future to be irrelevant. The Soviet Union was a gathering threat, just as Nazi Germany and Japan had been in the 1930s. It would be catastrophic, they held, to repeat the mistake the Western democracies had made in the decade leading up to World War II. Say what one might about war and peace and world government, all that really counted was military strength, which now meant nuclear strength. As Teller saw it, this meant developing the super.

President Truman took atomic energy out of military hands with the signing of the Atomic Energy Act of 1946. It established the U.S. Atomic Energy Commission, a civilian agency.

It was the detonation of Joe One that gave Teller what he wanted. Truman, always leery of military high command, had, on August 1, 1946, signed the McMahon/Atomic Energy Act, creating the civilian-run Atomic Energy Commission (AEC) to take atomic energy matters out of military hands. In the wake of Joe One, Truman consulted the AEC, whose director, David Lilienthal, had earlier counseled avoiding research on the hydrogen bomb during peacetime. Now AEC member Lewis Strauss became vocal in his criticism of Lilienthal's position and argued that embarking on a crash course to develop the super was the only way for the United States to regain its nuclear weapons superiority over the Soviets. Strauss's agitation threw the AEC into deadlock over the issue of the H-bomb, prompting Lilienthal to assign the AEC's General Advisory Committee (GAC) the task of formulating a recommendation.

A new emblem for a new agency.

Led by Oppenheimer, the GAC engaged in two days of rancorous debate, finally recommending stepped-up production of tactical atomic weapons, but calling for the abandonment of work on the super. Truman received the report in October 1949, but remained undecided about the H-bomb. He then brought in Secretary of State Dean Acheson and Secretary of Defense Louis Johnson to consult with Lilienthal and to formulate a more definitive recommendation. After these three men failed to arrive at a unanimous decision, Acheson and Johnson independently recommended, in January 1950, that work on the super proceed. Lilienthal remained adamantly opposed.

By now Truman worried that word of the internal debate over the H-bomb would leak to the public before a decision could be made. His concern was justified. At a January 19 press conference, he was stunned when a reporter, seemingly out of the blue, asked him about the super by name. With the thermonuclear cat apparently out of the bag, Truman acted quickly to forestall a public debate that would compromise national security at a critical juncture. He agreed with his two cabinet members that research and development of every possible type of atomic weapon, including thermonuclear devices, had to proceed, especially since current attempts to arrive at any kind of nuclear weapons agreement with the Soviets were proving fruitless.

Just two days after Truman announced his decision, Klaus Fuchs was arrested in Britain as a Soviet spy, a mole in the Manhattan Project (see Chapter 3, "A Mole at Los Alamos"). The president was now more determined than ever to gain a rapid and significant technological advantage over the Soviet Union. Accordingly, on March 10, he explicitly directed the AEC to develop an H-bomb program. Four days after this, the Kremlin announced that the USSR had begun designing a thermonuclear weapon of its own. The nuclear arms race—one of the defining activities of the Cold War—had begun.

"It's a Boy"

By this time, Teller had started working with the Polish-born American mathematician Stanisław Ulam to overcome the biggest stumbling block in the creation of a workable super: the mechanism for triggering the fusion reaction. Within a year, in 1951, Teller and Ulam arrived at a still officially classified solution, which (it is believed) places a fission bomb—an atomic bomb—"trigger" in proximity to a certain quantity of fusion material, probably a deuterium compound. The fission trigger (called the "primary") creates a radiation implosion that instantaneously compresses the fusion material (the "secondary") just before igniting it at a very high temperature. This process initiates a fusion reaction, resulting in an explosion at the megaton level.

REALITY CHECK

A Scientist's Agony, a President's Frustration

Of the Manhattan Project scientists, no one was more tortured by feelings of guilt than J. Robert Oppenheimer, the scientific director of the Los Alamos laboratory. President Truman had been looking forward to meeting Oppenheimer, who was brought to the Oval Office by then undersecretary of state Dean Acheson shortly after the war ended. In the course of their meeting, the scientist plaintively confessed, "Mr. President, I have blood on my hands." Reportedly, Truman responded, "Never mind. It will all come out in the wash." To Acheson, Truman later remarked, "Never bring that fucking cretin in here again. He didn't drop the bomb. I did. That kind of weepiness makes me sick."

"Ivy Mike," which the United States detonated on remote Eniwetok in the Pacific on October 31, 1952, was the first thermonuclear—hydrogen—bomb. The three-mile-wide fireball was followed by a mushroom cloud (first picture), which rose to 120,000 feet. The mushroom's "stem" (second picture) had a diameter of twenty miles. The last photograph shows servicemen watching the fireball from "Ivy King"—an all-fission (nuclear rather than thermonuclear) bomb with a yield of 500 kilotons—detonated on Eniwetok on November 16, 1952.

DETAILS, DETAILS

The "Progress" of "Civilization"

"Little Boy," the bomb dropped on Hiroshima, yielded an explosion equivalent to 13 to 16 kilotons of TNT, and "Fat Man," the Nagasaki bomb, was rated at 21 kilotons. The Ivy Mike H-bomb produced a 10.4-megaton blast, the explosive equivalent of more than five hundred Hiroshima bombs.

Once Teller and Ulam arrived at their breakthrough, construction of the super proceeded rapidly, and on November 1, 1952, at 7:15 in the morning, local time, the first fusion bomb was detonated on Eniwetok, an isolated atoll in the Pacific. Code-named "Ivy Mike," the test yielded a blast equivalent to 10.4 megatons of TNT. Ivy Mike sent into the sky a three-mile-wide fireball followed by a mushroom cloud rising to a maximum altitude of 120,000 feet with a diameter at the "stem" of twenty miles and, at the top, of one hundred miles. Ivy Mike blasted a crater 6,240 feet in diameter and 164 feet deep at its deepest, essentially obliterating the island of Elugelab and creating combined blast and water waves that tore all vegetation from the other tropical islands of the atoll. Deadly radioactive fallout was heavy, contaminating a wide area.

Working in a Berkeley, California, laboratory at the time of the test, Teller nevertheless knew immediately that Ivy Mike had been a success because he observed the distant effects of the shockwave on a local seismograph. He fired off a telegram to his Los Alamos colleagues. The message was intended to reveal everything while also preserving secrecy: "It's a boy."

The secrecy did not last long. Within a very short time, the government officially released censored film footage of the Eniwetok blast, and the fireball-mushroom cloud sequence was played and replayed in movie house newsreels and on television nationwide and across the globe. Doubtless, many Americans were terrified by Ivy Mike, but they were also relieved that the United States had beaten the Soviets to the H-bomb just as it had beaten the Nazis to the A-bomb.

A Race to What?

In the years immediately following World War II, American political leaders and military planners had regarded nuclear weapons as a cheap form of defense, a substitute for vast armies and large naval fleets. On average during the Cold War, the United States spent $600 billion on nuclear and thermonuclear weapons and the systems to support and deliver them. By the 1980s, each American household was contributing about $3,500 annually toward the nation's nuclear arsenal. The Soviet Union spent so much on the arms race that it ultimately destroyed its always precarious command economy, precipitating the total dissolution of the Soviet state in 1991. Such expenditures drew bitter criticism from moralists, who invited speculation about what the world would be like if even a fraction of this vast treasure were spent on feeding the hungry, clothing the naked, curing the sick, and educating the ignorant. AEC leaders endeavored to preempt some of this speculation by publicly promoting "atomic research" rather than "atomic weapons research." True, nuclear and thermonuclear energy could be released destructively in weapons, but, AEC scientists pointed out, it was still energy and, as such, could be "harnessed" for peaceful purposes, including the generation of cheap electricity and the powering of great ships and even aircraft.

Such was the fear created by the detonation of Joe One that all moral objections, up to and including the objection to creating a class of weapons capable of destroying life on planet earth, were swept aside. President Truman had sought advice from many quarters, including the GAC, but it was as if the decision had been preordained once the atomic genie was out of the bottle. AEC director David Lilienthal recorded in his diary, "We keep saying 'We have no other course'; what we should say is 'We are not bright enough to see any other course.'"

> "[Oppenheimer] is really a tragic figure; with all of his great attractiveness, brilliance of mind. As I left him he looked so sad: 'I am ready to go anywhere and do anything, but I am bankrupt of further ideas. And I find that physics and the teaching of physics, which is my life, now seems irrelevant.'"
>
> *AEC director David Lilienthal, on a meeting with J. Robert Oppenheimer, July 1946*

THE PLOWSHARE PROJECT

Designing and building large-scale reactors for the purposes of generating electricity takes time. In 1957, Edward Teller and other scientists proposed a way of realizing an almost instant "peaceful" use of atomic energy. Plowshare was a government project to finance nuclear explosions for the purpose of fast, cheap, big excavations.

One proposal was to detonate at least three hundred atomic bombs in Panama to excavate a new sea-level canal. Another idea was to detonate a nuclear device near Point Barrow, Alaska, to blast out a harbor. During the life of Project Plowshare, from 1957 to 1974, none of these excavations actually came to pass, but scientists did detonate a number of nuclear devices just below the surface of the Nevada desert by way of testing nuclear blasting techniques that might be applied to some fifty-four projected civil engineering projects in the United States and twenty-four other countries. As Teller explained, "If anyone wants a hole in the ground, nuclear explosives can make big holes." To the obvious objection that a nuclear blast would produce radioactive fallout and other debris contamination, Teller and other scientists responded that, done correctly, fallout could be both accurately predicted and minimized to the point of harmlessness. The many test craters, however, were highly radioactive, and the so-called Sedan crater—the result of a July 6, 1962, blast in Area 10 of Yucca Flat, Nevada—created a radioactive cloud carried east by prevailing winds and deposited a good deal of radioactive fallout in Iowa, Nebraska, South Dakota, and Illinois, exposing more than thirteen million Americans to potentially harmful levels of radiation. Today, the Sedan crater draws about ten thousand visitors a year, who are willing to brave the above-normal background radiation levels that linger still. Producing a predictable and "sanitary" nuclear excavation proved impossible, and Project Plowshare was finally scrapped.

The "Sedan Crater" was formed when a 100-kiloton nuclear explosive was detonated 635 feet beneath the surface of the Nevada desert on July 6, 1962. The blast displaced 12 million tons of earth, making a crater 320 feet deep and 1,280 feet in diameter. The blast was intended to demonstrate a peaceful use of atomic energy—instant excavation for big civil works projects. Big hole, but a big problem: high levels of radiation threatened to make any construction site lethal for years.

With the development of the super, the nuclear arms race accelerated alarmingly. The United States had detonated its first fission bomb in July 1945 and its first fusion bomb seven years later, in November 1952. The Soviet Union detonated its first fission device in August 1949. Its first hydrogen bomb came just four years after that, on August 12, 1953—less than a year after the first American super.

American intelligence officers dubbed it "Joe 4." Although it used deuterium, it was not a true fusion bomb. Instead of employing a focused fission explosion to initiate a much larger fusion detonation, as in the Ivy Mike "staged" thermonuclear device, Joe 4 used a deuterium compound known as heavy water (deuterium oxide, D_2O) to boost the yield of a conventional fission bomb. The explosion it produced was as powerful as the most advanced fission weapons of the time, but achieved nowhere near the yield of a true thermonuclear device. Doubtless, some Americans gathered a few crumbs of comfort from this, but, in any case, a genuine Soviet fusion bomb was not far behind. The weapon the Soviets called RDS-37 was tested on November 22, 1955, and did achieve megaton-range output.

Beginning in the 1950s, the Americans and the Soviets produced a staggering number of nuclear and thermonuclear weapons, mass-producing the means of mass destruction. By 1966, the United States had stockpiled 32,040 nuclear warheads of all kinds, some to be fitted to bombs, others to missiles. These included weapons ranging from small "tactical" nuclear devices intended for use on the battlefield to large "strategic" warheads meant to wipe out cities. In 1966, the major weapons in the American arsenal represented about fifty-six hundred megatons of TNT. This was the high point of the U.S. stockpile. The Soviets reached their maximum in 1986, with an inventory of some forty-five thousand weapons—again, ranging from tactical to strategic devices. Total megatonnage at this high point is estimated at about eight thousand. By the early 1960s, it was common to hear talk about the U.S. and Soviet capacity to destroy the world several times over. It was no exaggeration.

"We may be likened to two scorpions in a bottle, each capable of killing the other, but only at the risk of his own life."

J. Robert Oppenheimer,
quoted in Foreign Affairs, *July 1953*

THE CZAR OF ALL BOMBS

The Soviets hold the record for detonating the most powerful thermonuclear weapon ever built. The bomb, code-named by the West "Ivan" and nicknamed the "Tsar Bomba" (King of Bombs) by the Soviets, was tested on October 30, 1961, over the Arctic Sea island of Novaya Zemlya.

Its yield was an astounding 50 megatons—a leap in power beyond the largest previous detonation, a U.S. 15-megaton device. The weapon, which weighed 27 metric tons, was so big that the largest soviet bomber in 1961, the Tu-95, had to be specially modified to carry it. The aircraft's bomb-bay doors were removed, and the Tsar Bomba protruded precariously from under the aircraft's belly. A large parachute was rigged to the bomb to slow its descent, so that the Tu-95 would have sufficient time to veer and climb out of range of the blast.

As an operational weapon, the Tsar Bomba was highly impractical. It was too unwieldy to transport over intercontinental distances, and its use against most populated targets would have endangered areas either within or friendly to the Soviet Union. As it was, Soviet scientists had purposely reduced the yield of the bomb from an originally planned 100 megatons to half that amount because the blast of the larger bomb would have destroyed the aircraft, and the radioactive fallout would have been deadly over a vast area. The 50-megaton version produced a fireball flash visible at a distance of 1,000 kilometers. The sound pressure waves created by the detonation—3,800 times more powerful than the Hiroshima bomb—were also detectable at that incredible range. The fireball itself reached an altitude of 34,000 feet into the air. Anyone within 100 kilometers of ground zero would have suffered third-degree burns. The shockwave shattered windows as far away as Finland and was measurable virtually everywhere in the world. The blast ionized a large portion of the atmosphere, disrupting radio communications for nearly an hour.

The sole purpose of the Tsar Bomba was to demonstrate the superiority of the Soviet thermonuclear arsenal during a time in which Soviet aggression had escalated, East Germany having raised the infamous Berlin Wall just two months earlier.

The "Tsar Bomba" was the Soviet Union's fifty-megaton hydrogen bomb—the biggest and most powerful ever.

Duck and Cover

The U.S. government's Civil Defense Office issued a number of nuclear warfare survival manuals such as this one from 1950.

The evolution of military history has always been closely tied to the progress of military technology. This relationship was especially dramatic during the twentieth century. In World War I, the technology of defense was far in advance of the technology of attack. Two men operating a single machine gun from the defensive cover of a trench could wipe out hundreds of attackers. Twenty years later, the opening days of World War II, in which the German armies stormed through Poland, brushing aside defenders with a combination of armored vehicles and aircraft, demonstrated that the balance of technology had radically shifted in favor of the attacker. If it was difficult—almost impossible—to defend adequately against mass air raids during World War II, the situation in the postwar "atomic age" seemed utterly hopeless. What chance did ordinary people living in ordinary cities have against attacks by bombers and missiles armed with nuclear or even thermonuclear warheads? Even if a person managed to survive the initial blast, the radiation produced by the detonation of the highly radioactive bomb materials was both deadly and invisible. Worse yet was the nuclear fallout, the radioactive contamination of dust and debris that was insidious, pervasive, lethal, and long lasting. Death from radiation poisoning was slow and agonizing, beginning with nausea and uncontrollable vomiting, fever, loss of hair, infection throughout the body, and bleeding out through vomiting and bloody diarrhea. Those who somehow survived the acute stages of radiation poisoning could look forward to the early onset of cancer. Some types of radioactive contamination could last scores, hundreds, even thousands of years, rendering vast regions uninhabitable.

As the nuclear arms race accelerated, the governments of the United States, the Soviet Union, and other countries scrambled to put in place programs of civil defense. Throughout American cities and

The happy homemaker, c. 1962, U.S.A. The young lady displays the "must have" supplies for the family fallout shelter.

towns, the basements of public and commercial buildings were designated "Fallout Shelters" and marked with black and yellow signs bearing the international symbol for radiation hazard. A federal program instituted in the early 1960s, during the administration of John F. Kennedy, stocked these shelters with canned rations and sealed drums of drinking water. In 1950, a federal agency called the National Security Resources Board issued a 162-page "Blue Book" outlining civil defense procedures for local communities. It was a good start, but Congress never allocated much funding to civil defense, and even the "Blue Book" remained unrevised throughout the entire forty-plus years of the Cold War.

Although relatively little was done to create a civil defense infrastructure, the federal government issued a steady stream of booklets and short movies outlining the basics of surviving a nuclear attack. Generally, the instructions boiled down to elementary first aid and admonitions to eat only canned food and fruits and vegetables with skins that could be peeled to avoid ingesting radioactive fallout. Nothing the government published convincingly argued that the survivors were more fortunate than the dead.

There was a certain fatalism in the government's early civil defense efforts. It was assumed that big cities would be the primary targets of any attack, but federal authorities sought to discourage any attempts at evacuation. One short film from 1951, *Our Cities Must Fight*, delivered the explicit message that city dwellers had a patriotic duty to ride out an attack in place so that they could participate in rebuilding the city and be available to man vital services and industries. The municipal governments of a number of U.S. cities and towns defied the federal government by creating elaborate evacuation plans and even rehearsing them on a community-wide scale.

A more focused federal and local effort was made to create evacuation plans and elaborate shelters to ensure continuity of government. Many cities installed emergency command centers deep in the bowels of city halls or other municipal buildings, and, in 1959, at the suggestion of President Dwight Eisenhower, the federal government secretly began Project Greek Island. It was a vast underground bunker complex, occupying 112,000 square feet of floor space 64 feet beneath a wing of the luxurious Greenbrier resort hotel in West Virginia. The secrecy of the two-and-a-half-year, $86 million construction project beneath a popular upscale resort was maintained by a cover story that the Greenbrier was building a luxury medical clinic. The Project Greek Island plan was to evacuate to the Greenbrier bunker members of all three branches of the U.S. government in the event of war, about a thousand people, including all 535 members of the U.S. Senate and House of Representatives. From the bunker, they would continue to run the government.

The government kept the Greenbrier bunker top secret ostensibly to conceal its location from the Soviets. Perhaps another motive for the secrecy was to hide from the American public the fact that millions of dollars were being devoted to protect top federal officials even as very little was being done to shelter ordinary people. Those ordinary people, however, were quick to make up for what they perceived as the central government's inability to protect them. Just as the 1950s saw a sharp spike in home ownership, thanks to a combination of government loans under the postwar GI Bill, the proliferation of inexpensive suburban tract housing developments, and the general prosperity of the era, the decade also inspired many homeowners to excavate family fallout shelters in their brand-new backyards. Contractors grew wealthy supplying the demand for shelters, but many families, in a macabre resurgence of the fabled American pioneer spirit, made shelter construction the mother of all do-it-yourself projects. Most family shelters were variations on the old-fashioned storm

DETAILS, DETAILS

Home Sweet Bunker

The Government Relocation Center—the secret Greenbrier bunker—was designed to shelter a thousand people for up to sixty days, although its supply of "canned" fresh air would be exhausted after seventy-two hours. From that point on, those inside the bunker would have to breathe air brought in from the outside. Although filtered, it would still have a certain level of radioactive contamination. The secrecy of the installation ended in 1992 after the *Washington Post Magazine* published a story on the facility. The bunker was subsequently deactivated, and Greenbrier now maintains it as a paying tourist attraction.

The blast door leading to the bunker at Greenbriar weighs twenty-five tons but is so precisely engineered that only fifty pounds of pressure is required to open it.

IS FALLOUT FOREVER?

Most of the radiation hazard from nuclear bursts is short-lived and confined to areas downwind of the detonation point. The highly radioactive materials produced by the blast have half-lives ranging from seconds to a few months.

A one-megaton detonation would probably create a fallout pattern extending hundreds of miles downwind. About twenty to twenty-five miles from ground zero, people who failed to find shelter within twenty-five minutes of the onset of fallout would absorb a lethal dose of radiation. Forty to forty-five miles out, people would have about three hours to find cover. Assuming the United States were attacked by one hundred one-megaton weapons, 20 percent of the population would be killed outright by the blast, the heat wave, seismic effects, and exposure to neutrons and gamma rays. More would die later of fallout—not to mention building fires and collapses. Later still, lack of food, water, sanitation, and medical care would kill yet more. Most of the lethal radio nuclides produced by an atomic detonation decay quite rapidly, but such long-lived radioactive isotopes as strontium-90 and cesium-137 would accumulate in various "hot spots," rendering them uninhabitable for years, even decades. Food and water contamination dangers would also be significant for anywhere from one to five years.

This abandoned house near the nuclear power plant in Chernobyl, Ukraine, is grim testimony to the catastrophic reactor meltdown that occurred at the plant on April 26, 1986. The nineteen-mile "exclusion zone" around the plant remains uninhabitable as of 2009.

cellar or root cellar, albeit equipped with concrete-block walls and a heavy steel door. Inside, they were typically furnished with bunks, a table, a battery-powered radio, flashlights, a lot of canned food and bottled water, and the ubiquitous first-aid kit.

Home Sweet Shelter. This one was built in the basement of a family dwelling about 1957. Canned food, battery-operated radio, two-week supply of water, first aid kit—and don't forget the homey checkered tablecloth!

POP CULTURE

A New Routine

CONELRAD was augmented by the more traditional community air raid sirens, which, in most neighborhoods, were tested every week at a specific time. The punctual weekly wail of the siren became as familiar a fixture of American life as the sound of factory and locomotive whistles.

Shelters and evacuation plans offered doubtful protection from all-out nuclear war, but they would have been totally futile without a system in place to provide warning of attack. In 1951, President Truman issued an executive order creating CONELRAD (CONtrol of ELectromagnetic RADiation), a system by which federal authorities, in the event of an imminent attack, would alert a select network of "primary" CONELRAD radio stations, which, in turn, were constantly monitored by all commercial broadcast stations in the nation. In the event of an "emergency"—the word *attack* was judiciously avoided—all broadcast stations would monitor the warning then cease broadcasting in order to prevent enemy aircraft from homing in on their radio signals. Communications would be confined to two emergency AM frequencies, over which the CONELRAD stations would broadcast official information, news, and instructions. Between 1953 and 1963, federal law required all radio sets to mark the 640 kHz and 1240 kHz frequency points on their tuning dials with a triangle-in-circle symbol, known as a "CD Mark," to help listeners rapidly tune in to Civil Defense broadcasts.

By 1963, it was apparent that nuclear warfare would be conducted with intercontinental ballistic missiles (ICBMs) rather than bombers, so there was no longer any reason to restrict broadcasting to a pair of low-power AM frequencies, and CONELRAD was replaced by the Emergency Broadcast System (EBS), which used ordinary broadcast radio and television stations to carry official information. EBS, in turn, was replaced in 1997 by the current Emergency Alert System (EAS).

To provide early warning of an incoming attack, the United States and Canada cooperated in monitoring the World War II–era radar networks called the Pinetree and Mid-Canada Lines. On February 15, 1954, these were modernized by the addition of a third line of radar stations called the Distant Early Warning (DEW) Line. Financed by the United States, the DEW Line was built by more than twenty-five thousand Canadian workers and, when completed in 1957, consisted of sixty-three radar installations

This cheerful television logo used to accompany tests of the Emergency Broadcast System.

LINK

The Mountain

Today, NORAD is headquartered inside a giant cavity hollowed out of Cheyenne Mountain, near Colorado Springs, Colorado. Indeed, the informal nickname "Cheyenne Mountain" has largely replaced the official NORAD designation to describe the joint U.S.-Canadian defense operation. Although the personnel at Cheyenne Mountain still monitor the skies for incoming nuclear and thermonuclear attacks, since the terrorist attacks of September 11, 2001, the mission has expanded to monitoring all unscheduled, unexplained, and suspicious air traffic.

The North American Aerospace Command—NORAD—is headquartered in a massive cave hollowed out of Cheyenne Mountain near Colorado Springs, Colorado. The facility is intended to protect NORAD headquarters in the event of a nuclear attack—although even Cheyenne Mountain would not survive a direct thermonuclear hit.

from Alaska to Baffin Island, a span of about sixty-two hundred miles running more or less along the 69th parallel some two hundred miles north of the Arctic Circle. Although this vast project was deemed a miracle of modern electronic engineering, it was virtually obsolete by the time it was completed. It could provide useful early warning of incoming bombers, but it was incapable of tracking ground-launched ICBMs or submarine-launched missiles. Most of the DEW Line stations were decommissioned during the 1960s, but some were integrated into the thoroughly automated North Warning System as part of the North American Aerospace Defense Command (NORAD), a collaborative early warning and defense network maintained by the United States and Canada, which grew out of the North American Air Defense Command, created in 1958.

What brought the looming threat of thermonuclear annihilation home to most families were the government's efforts to "educate" schoolchildren in how to survive an attack. Throughout the 1950s and well into the 1960s, the nation's schools conducted air raid drills as routinely as they conducted fire drills. Students were instructed in the "duck and cover" method of personal protection. Children of all ages absorbed the lesson that a nuclear attack could come any day, at any

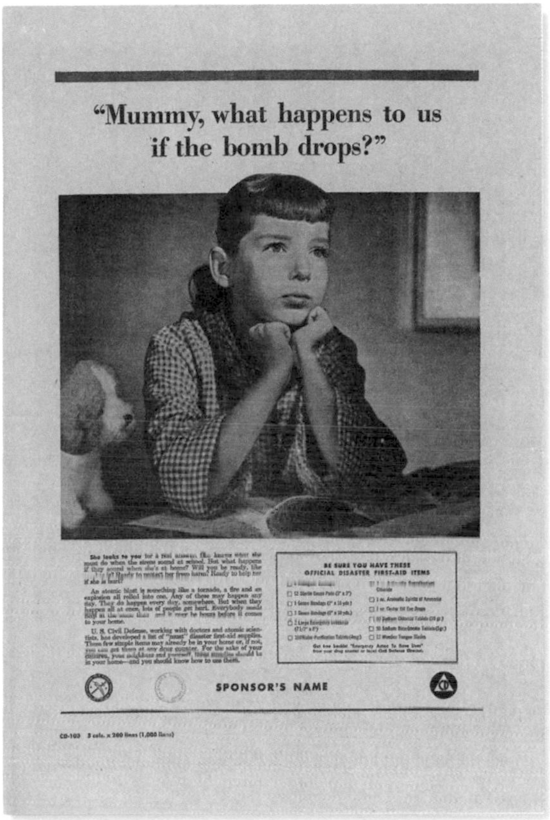
"Mummy, what happens to us if the bomb drops?"
SPONSOR'S NAME

Traditionally, parents fretted about how they would respond to "Where do babies come from?" Beginning in the 1950s, children's questions could get a lot harder, as this Civil Defense poster suggests.

time, and without warning. All that would precede the shockwave and the heat blast was a flash. If you saw this, you were to stop whatever you were doing and seek immediate cover—under a table, a classroom desk, a corner, any wall far from windows, or, if you were outdoors, even in a ditch. You were supposed to lie face down, pulling your legs up to your belly in a fetal position, and cover your head with your hands.

"Duck and cover" was widely mocked as soon as it was introduced. Even the youngest children did not believe the wooden desk into which they carved their initials would afford much protection against a thermonuclear fireball. In rural areas on the margins of a limited attack, duck and cover might possibly have provided some protection against flying glass and debris, but critics of the government's civil defense program, of which duck and cover seemed to be the absurd epitome, suggested that this routine was nothing more than an exercise in brainwashing, a federal effort to induce the American people to accept

POP CULTURE

A Turtle Named Bert

In an effort to drill the duck-and-cover procedure into the minds of the nation's youth, in 1952 the government issued an animated short film entitled *Duck and Cover*, in which Bert the Turtle strolls along (upright, on his hind legs) to the accompaniment of a jingle that jauntily repeats the refrain "duck and cover." Suddenly, a flash! "Duck and cover!" a voice-over announcer exclaims, and Bert immediately withdraws his head and limbs into his shell. Children, who have no shell, were instructed to do the next best thing: roll themselves into a ball and cower under a desk. Year after year, the film was shown in classrooms across the nation as well as on television.

TAKEAWAY

Racing to Armageddon

When the Soviet Union developed its own atomic bomb much sooner than most American experts expected, the United States escalated the nuclear arms race by creating the super, the hydrogen bomb, the destructive capacity of which dwarfed that of the atomic bomb. A frenetic nuclear arms race developed between the United States and the Soviet Union, the two nations stockpiling nuclear and thermonuclear arsenals sufficient to destroy all life on the planet many times over. Efforts at civil defense were widely perceived as not only impotent but also dangerous because they misled the people and their leaders into thinking an atomic war could be survived and was therefore a viable military option.

"If DUCK AND COVER is carefully integrated with a study of civil defense," this pamphlet produced to accompany the Civil Defense film Duck and Cover *advised teachers, "it can help your pupils acquire a quick and easy technique for self-protection from an atomic explosion . . ."*

nuclear war as a survivable political and military possibility rather than to reject it as nothing less than a self-inflicted apocalypse.

Many civil defense efforts, including a series of nationally orchestrated public air raid drills, triggered protests from a small but vocal cadre of antiwar groups during the 1950s. A number of individuals were arrested and prosecuted for publicly refusing to comply with the air raid exercises that were officially required in some communities. The point of the protests was that the notion of surviving a thermonuclear war was a lie—a particularly dangerous lie, because it promoted "thinking about the unthinkable," that is, seriously considering atomic warfare as a viable military option. Civil defense, as these protesters saw it, was an invitation to World War III, and they believed that the only thing preventing an all-out thermonuclear conflagration was the absolute conviction that it would mean the end of all life on earth. As it turned out, this calculus was not the exclusive property of an antiwar fringe, but became a cornerstone doctrine of international Cold War policy. It was called "mutual assured destruction," but was better known by its acronym: MAD.

CHAPTER 8

MAD WORLD

The Threat of Peace

STONE AGE, BRONZE AGE, IRON AGE—THE ANCIENT EPOCHS of humankind were named for the principal substance that built them. In August 1945, we stepped into the Atomic Age, the first era named for the force that threatened to destroy it. And as if a world in which two great hostile powers possessed staggering quantities of nuclear and thermonuclear weapons were not horrible enough, in October 1952, a third member, Great Britain, was added to what some had begun calling the "nuclear club." In counterpoint to the nuclear arms race between the two superpowers, the United States and the Soviet Union, a period of "nuclear weapons proliferation" began to unfold. France joined the nuclear club in February 1960, when it test-fired "Gerboise Bleue" (Blue Jerboa) in Algeria, at the time a French colony. More ominously—from the American point of view—the People's Republic of China (see Chapter 9) successfully tested a nuclear device on October 16, 1964.

Through the 1950s and into the 1970s, the American public was still hearing a lot about "defending" against a nuclear attack, but in political and military circles, the talk had long since turned from defense to deterrence, the doctrine that only by continually increasing our own nuclear stockpile could we discourage the other side from using theirs. It was what gunfighters in the Old West called a "Mexican standoff": If you shoot, then I shoot, and we both die. Only, in the "Atomic Age," it was called "mutual assured destruction": MAD.

STRATEGIC AIR COMMAND

THE AIRPLANE THAT DROPPED ATOMIC BOMBS on Hiroshima and Nagasaki, the B-29 Superfortress, was the most advanced bomber of its time, in 1945 outclassing everything else in the sky and the only bomber in any nation's air force capable of carrying atomic ordnance. No sooner had the Atomic Age dawned than U.S. military aviation planners realized that something even more advanced than the B-29 would be needed to create a credible nuclear strike force. Although it could carry a 20,000-pound bomb load, its 4,200-mile range, greater than any other wartime bomber, was barely intercontinental and, unless it flew from an advance European base, it was insufficient to make a round trip to most targets deep within the Soviet Union. Likewise, its 32,000-foot service ceiling was impressive for the time, but well within the range of Soviet radar, and, with a top speed of 364 miles per hour, the B-29 was highly vulnerable to attack from the emerging generation of jet fighters.

Colonel Paul Tibbets's B-29 Enola Gay *returns to the airfield at Tinian Island after dropping an atomic bomb on Hiroshima, August 6, 1945.*

EVEN MORE NUKES

Nuclear weapons proliferation took a decade-long recess after China exploded it's A-bomb in 1964, then resumed with the debut of India's bizarrely named "Smiling Buddha" device in 1974. This, in turn, spurred rival Pakistan to begin developing its own nuclear arsenal. More recently, India has claimed to have successfully tested a hydrogen bomb.

In the Middle East, the government of Israel has never confirmed or denied that it possesses nuclear weapons; however, it is generally assumed that the nation maintains a considerable stockpile. Assertions that Iran is close to developing nuclear weapons (something the Iranian government denies) drove bellicose threats from the administration of President George W. Bush. Back in Asia, North Korea in recent years has claimed to possess nuclear weapons, and reported a successful test on October 9, 2006. Sensors in the United States and Japan did detect seismic activity in the region at this time, and so it is generally assumed that a North Korean nuclear device was indeed tested. If the assumption is correct, the "Hermit Kingdom" is the latest member of the nuclear club; however, at the end of July 2008, the North Korean government agreed to dismantle its nuclear arsenal in exchange for the removal of trade and other sanctions imposed by the United States. Many Western officials have continued to speculate that North Korea still has a clandestine weapons program in operation.

Nuclear proliferation: These empty furnace pits were part of seven uranium metal production furnaces at a nuclear facility in Yongbyon, North Korea.

Even as new bombers were put on American drawing boards, the U.S. Army Air Forces created a unique organization to take exclusive responsibility for flying nuclear missions. Because these weapons were so destructive, intended to wipe out "strategic" targets, such as cities, rather than "tactical" targets, such as individual military installations or troop assemblies, the new outfit, established on March 21, 1946, was dubbed the *Strategic* Air Command (SAC). It was put under the leadership of the only top commander who had ever ordered the combat use of atomic weapons, Lieutenant General Curtis Emerson LeMay.

Born in Columbus, Ohio, in 1906, LeMay was a darkly intense presence, whose jaw appeared to be so hard set that it was impossible for him to crack a smile—were he ever so inclined. That was an unlikely prospect.

General Curtis E. LeMay, trademark cigar clamped firmly between his teeth, is shown here about the time that he was commanding officer of the Strategic Air Command. "Peace Is Our Profession" is the motto he chose for America's principal nuclear deterrent force. The men he commanded called LeMay "Iron Ass."

Since youth, only two things had interested him, the military and military flight. LeMay was one of the first army pilots to test fly the B-17, which became the most famous bomber of World War II. As commander of the 305th Bombardment Group in Europe during World War II, LeMay was instrumental in perfecting the tactics of precision bombing. In this mission, he revealed the two contrasting command traits that marked his approach to combat. On the one hand, he insisted that aircrews make meticulous target studies, using reconnaissance photographs, prior to each mission. On the other, he advocated improving accuracy by taking the extreme risk of abandoning evasive maneuvering over enemy targets. This got more bombs "on the pickle barrel," but it exposed the lumbering B-17s to deadly flak and Luftwaffe fighter planes. Aircrews were skeptical, but LeMay, whose confidence in himself and his ideas was unshakeable, stood fast. He wagered his career—and the lives of his men—on a tactic that most pilots considered suicidal. In the end, he succeeded in doubling the number of bombs placed on target.

"Everyone steps forward and expresses an idea. Once the decision is made, however—'This is the way we're going to do it.'" Bang. Everybody complies. If a man doesn't comply, his official head should roll."

General Curtis E. LeMay,
Mission with LeMay: My Story, *1965*

Promoted to the temporary rank of major general in March 1944, LeMay was transferred to China to lead the 20th Bomber Command in long-range missions against the Japanese. In January 1945, he took command of the 21st Bomber Group on Guam. Performance of the new B-29s had proved disappointing because bombing from the high altitudes for which the aircraft had been designed was often wildly inaccurate. LeMay was assigned to get better results at whatever cost he deemed necessary. He stripped his unit's B-29s of all their defensive guns (as well as gun crews and ammunition), so that each plane could carry more bombs. Next, he ordered the now defenseless giants to break formation and to attack targets singly. The one inviolable taboo of strategic bombing is that no aircraft should ever break formation. LeMay shattered the taboo, and many aircrews resigned themselves to embarking on suicide missions. But there was even worse to come. He designed those missions to be flown at low altitudes, typically below ten thousand feet. Common sense told LeMay that bombing low would greatly improve accuracy, but the B-29 had been designed for high-altitude flight specifically to evade ground-based flak and fighter planes. Flying low would bring the bombers well within the range of both.

From the very beginning, LeMay's bold tactics succeeded dramatically. What is more, his unconventional approach enabled the bombers to fly faster, maneuver more deftly, and spend less time over their targets. The result was a reduction rather than the expected increase in casualties. LeMay's reputation for daring and originality, coupled with his winning record and his unique experience with atomic weapons, made him the natural choice to create and lead SAC.

REALITY CHECK

War Plan for the Atomic Age

The first war plan Curtis LeMay drew up for the Strategic Air Command was promulgated in 1949. It proposed unloading the nation's "entire stockpile of atomic bombs in a single massive attack," dropping 133 atomic bombs on seventy cities in the space of a month. President Truman and the Joint Chiefs of Staff rejected the plan, but, under LeMay, SAC was maintained on a permanent war footing, prepared to execute an all-out nuclear attack when ordered.

Jet Fuel

The new SAC commander immediately lobbied for a new bomber to replace the obsolescent B-29. He wanted to transform SAC's complement of aircraft into an all-jet fleet, but large jet aircraft were still in development during the late 1940s, and he decided to settle for an interim solution, the ungainly looking B-36 Peacemaker, better known by its nickname, the "Flying Cigar." It was an enormous plane, with a 230-foot wingspan, a fuselage 162 feet long, and a staggering gross weight of 410,000 pounds. Rooted in the vanishing propeller age, the B-36 also reluctantly looked forward to the dawning era of the jet. Six pusher piston engines, the propellers mounted on the trailing edge of the wings rather than on the leading edge, were combined with four turbojets hung from the outboard ends of the wings. This arrangement gave the B-36 the ability to carry five tons of bombs more than 6,800 miles. It flew faster than the B-29, but not by much. Its top speed of 411 miles per hour and its service ceiling of 36,400 feet (modest by postwar standards) made it a sitting duck for Soviet fighters,

General Joseph W. "Vinegar Joe" Stilwell (in campaign hat, left) talks with General LeMay, then of the 20th Bomber Command, at a B-29 base somewhere in China, October 11, 1944.

Contrails stream from the six piston pusher engines of a reconnaissance version (RB-36H) of a B-36 nuclear-capable bomber. Note the dual radomes on the tail turret, which housed the most advanced radar system of the time. Also note the jet engines slung under the wings outboard of the piston engines. Two pods each contained two jet engines. The B-36 was an intermediate step on the way to the completely jet-powered B-47 Stratojet and B-52 Stratofortress.

as critics, including the navy admirals jealous over losing funding to the air force, were quick to point out. LeMay countered that the need for a credible nuclear deterrent was so pressing that the B-36 was an urgently needed stopgap. In the end, he prevailed, and 385 of the aircraft were delivered to the air force beginning in 1949.

LeMay made it clear that the more permanent answer to America's nuclear needs was an all-jet bomber fleet. The first of these aircraft was the B-47 Stratojet, which had its maiden flight in 1947 and was introduced into the air force fleet beginning in 1951. At 4,000 miles, its range was considerably more limited than that of the B-36; however, its six turbojets could carry 20,000 pounds of bombs at 606 miles per hour and at an altitude of 40,500 feet, making it far less vulnerable to attack. As to the matter of limited range, LeMay had a solution. Shortly after he had assumed command of SAC, he asked Boeing to design a midair refueling

As commander of SAC, General LeMay championed the development of midair refueling, which extended the range of bombers and fighters indefinitely. Here three Republic F-105D fighters wait their turn for refueling by a KC-135 tanker—a design modification of Boeing's epoch-making 707 passenger airliner.

system capable of transferring fuel from a tanker aircraft to a bomber (or other airplane) at a very high rate. Midair refueling had been used before this, but always with flexible hoses, which limited the speed of fuel transfer. For combat operations, speed was crucial, and Boeing developed a "flying boom" system, in which a rigid refueling boom, equipped with winglets near its nozzle end, was controlled remotely by a refueling operator, who actually flew it into a receptacle located on the aircraft being refueled. The rigid pipe allowed for fuel transfer at very high rates.

"Peace Is Our Profession."

Motto of the Strategic Air Command

Midair refueling gave any bomber a range limited only by the endurance of its aircrew. As SAC built up its fleet—2,040 B-47s were eventually produced—LeMay introduced the policy of maintaining a certain number of nuclear-armed bombers in the air at all times, day and night, "orbiting" at designated positions over international waters, but within quick striking distance of assigned targets in the Soviet Union. Even bombers on the ground, at their bases, stood loaded with their nuclear payloads, their crews prepared to take off—to "scramble"—at the wail of a klaxon. Each bomber crew carried sealed flight plans, fully outlining a mission against a specific Soviet target. On orders transmitted via a highly advanced single-sideband radio, the orders would be unsealed, and the aircraft flown to its assigned target. Improvisation and individual decision were replaced by programmatic preplanning, and LeMay maintained SAC on a hair trigger, a hair trigger capable of releasing Armageddon.

The point of all this was to create a credible defense by deterrence, pressing a thermonuclear revolver to the Soviet forehead twenty-four hours a day, seven days a week, 365 days a year. America's leaders reiterated time and again that the policy of the United States repudiated a "first strike." The nation would never start an atomic war, they said. But it was also the policy to respond to a first strike with all-out thermonuclear retaliation. *Retaliation*—that was the word LeMay wanted echoing in the consciousness of every Soviet political and military leader, and *retaliation*, inevitable, instantaneous, and massive, was the essence of the SAC mission.

LINK

Iron Ass

In the American military, tough commanders are called "hard asses." LeMay was referred to as an "iron ass." Promoted to four-star general in 1951, he was the youngest since Ulysses S. Grant. He became vice chief of staff of the air force in 1957 and chief of staff in 1961. During the 1960s, his right-wing bellicosity often brought him into conflict with the two commanders in chief he served, John F. Kennedy and Lyndon Johnson. His relations with Secretary of Defense Robert S. McNamara were bitterly contentious because he adamantly refused to reject a nuclear first strike as a strategic option. After retiring from the air force in 1965, an increasingly irascible LeMay became the running mate of segregationist former Alabama governor George Wallace in his failed third-party bid for the presidency in 1968. After the campaign, he withdrew into a reclusive private life until his death in 1990.

The B-52 was built to drop nuclear and thermonuclear bombs on targets in the Soviet Union, but it was used extensively in the Vietnam War (and has been used in subsequent conflicts) to drop massive loads of conventional ordnance, as seen here. First put into service in the 1950s, during the height of the Cold War, the B-52 is a key aircraft in the USAF fleet and is projected to remain in service well into the twenty-first century—even though manufacturing ended in 1962.

The mighty B-47 Stratojet was gradually replaced by the even more formidable B-52 Stratofortress, 159 feet long with a wingspan of 185 feet. Capable of a top speed of 650 miles per hour, it flies to a service ceiling of 50,000 feet carrying a bomb load of as much as 70,000 pounds. As with the B-47, midair refueling gives the B-52 a range limited only by crew endurance, but, even unrefueled, its combat range exceeds 8,800 miles.

THE MYTH OF THE "BOMBER GAP"

EACH B-47 COST UNITED STATES TAXPAYERS nearly two million 1947 dollars to build. The air force acquired more than two thousand of them. The price of a B-52 ran higher, each costing between $9.28 million and $14.43 million, depending on the model ordered. In production until 1962, a total of 744 B-52s, models B through H, were built. The Cold War was rife with very real dangers, but it was also riddled with the illusion of threats that had far less basis in reality. Indeed, as it turned out, reality alone was not sufficient to drive the acquisition of so many pieces of such costly aerial hardware.

LINK

Not Your Father's Air Force, but . . .

The remarkable B-52 first flew in 1954, and the first fully operational model, the B-52B, entered air force service in 1955. By 1964, the B-52 had supplanted the B-47 as *the* SAC bomber, and the enormous, brutish-looking plane became an icon of the Cold War.

Built as a strategic bomber, the B-52 was never actually used to carry out its strategic mission. It was flown extensively as a tactical bomber in the Vietnam War, the first Gulf War, the conflict in Bosnia, and the Iraq War. Updated with modern technology, the B-52H is still highly active in USAF operations and (as of 2009) is projected to continue service beyond 2045. This means that the air force will be flying a design nearly a century old in actual aircraft over eighty years old. Today's B-52 pilots tell new aircrews, "It's not your father's air force, but it may be your father's airplane."

What many politicians, the press, and the public came to call the "bomber gap" was born on February 15, 1954, when the authoritative journal *Aviation Week* published a frightening description of the Myasishchev M-4 Bison, a new long-range Soviet bomber capable of carrying nuclear weapons into the American heartland. In a climate increasingly thick with panicky rumor, LeMay and other air force brass pushed Congress for funding to buy more B-47 Stratojets and to speed up production of the B-52 Stratofortress. The tipping point in this acquisition campaign was reached in July 1955, when the Russian military celebrated "Aviation Day" north of Moscow, at Tushino Airfield, with a demonstration flight of the Bison.

Film of the event reached the West, where intelligence analysts studiously counted the aircraft. There were sixty. In view of the fact that a prototype had appeared just the year before, the rate of production staggered the imagination. If sixty operational bombers had been produced in about a year, it would not take the Soviets long to turn out ten times that number. As matters stood in 1955, six hundred nuclear-capable Soviet heavy bombers would dwarf the U.S. fleet. This was the bomber gap, and Congress rushed to write the necessary checks.

The flood of funds was not without some unwanted blowback. Unlike LeMay, Congress was unwilling to rely exclusively on *deterrence* to ward off nuclear attack. The air force was compelled also to accept the expansion of air *defense*, consisting of surface-to-air antiaircraft missile systems to defend American cities and an augmented fleet of interceptor aircraft, fighter jets designed to shoot down incoming bombers. LeMay and most other senior air force leaders were loath to divert funds from bomber acquisition to buy fighters. They were even less enthusiastic about funding antiaircraft missiles and missile installations, the most important of which, Project Nike, was run not by the U.S. Air Force but by the U.S. Army. LeMay and other members of what was called the air force's "bomber mafia" argued that money spent on air defense was money wasted. The experience of World War II had demonstrated, they said, that, in any attack, a high proportion of bombers always got through all defenses. Deterrence, not defense, was the only effective means of protecting America's cities. Despite these arguments, Nike installations were funded throughout the nation, deployed in rings around major cities, key industrial and utility plants, and military installations.

The Nike family of U.S. Army missiles became a familiar sight around many U.S. cities during the Cold War. The Nike's principal mission was as an antiaircraft weapon, intended to shoot down incoming nuclear-armed bombers, but, despite their relatively short range, later Nike models were armed with their own nuclear warheads. The photograph shows (from left) the Nike-Ajax, the Nike-Hercules, and the Nike-Zeus.

Fear of the bomber gap bought SAC a fleet of nearly three thousand planes. Dwight D. Eisenhower, who had succeeded Harry Truman as president in 1953, never succumbed to the bomber gap panic. It seemed to him more a product of rumor than hard intelligence, and his skepticism prompted him to authorize the development of yet another airplane. This was the revolutionary Lockheed U-2, a stealthy, ultra-high-altitude spy plane capable of flying over Soviet territory and taking pictures, lots and lots of pictures. We will have more to say about the U-2 in Chapter 11, but, for now, it is enough to know that the U-2 reconnaissance flights began in 1956. One mission, on July 4 of that year, photographed twenty Bisons parked at Engels Air Base near the city of Saratov. Intelligence analysts multiplied by 20 the number of known Soviet bomber bases and concluded that the Soviet air force was very far along in turning out hundreds of bombers. The bomber gap seemed to widen.

But the picture changed as more U-2 missions gathered more data. On no other Soviet air base could Bisons be detected. By late 1957, the conclusion was inescapable: that first U-2 had photographed the *entire* Bison inventory, twenty aircraft. As for the sixty originally calculated from the air show footage, it became apparent that the American analysts had fallen victim to Soviet sleight of hand. A formation of just ten Bison bombers flew past the reviewing stand, disappeared from sight, executed (out of camera range) a sharp turn and fly-around, then flew past the stand again, from the same direction. Repeat this six times, and you have the illusion of a sixty-plane flyby. The United States nuclear bomber fleet had been built in pursuit of a phantom.

The remarkable U-2 "spy plane" was developed by maverick Lockheed designer Clarence "Kelly" Johnson and his innovative design team known as the "Skunk Works." It was tested at the super-secret Area 51 site in southern Nevada, shown here, which test pilots familiarly called "The Ranch."

DETAILS, DETAILS

Just Do It?

The word "Nike" (the Greek goddess of victory), was first appropriated as a brand name by the U.S. Army for a series of ground-launched antiaircraft missiles, produced from 1945–74. The missiles were deployed in artillery batteries around cities, bomber bases, nuclear plants, and intercontinental ballistic missile (ICBM) facilities. Chicago had the largest concentration of emplacements, twenty-two, and those who lived in the city during the Cold War remember the sight of missiles, which were periodically raised from their mounded subterranean silos, silhouetted against the lakefront sky. Effective against bomber aircraft, the Nike system was not suited to intercept the much faster ICBMs and was phased out.

SPACE RACE

ON OCTOBER 5, 1957, THE *NEW YORK TIMES* hit the American people with this stunning headline:

> SOVIET FIRES EARTH SATELLITE INTO SPACE;
> IT IS CIRCLING THE GLOBE AT 18,000 M.P.H.;
> SPHERE TRACKED IN 4 CROSSINGS OVER U.S.

"The Soviet Union announced this morning that it successfully launched a man-made Earth satellite into space yesterday," the accompanying article began. ". . . The official Soviet news agency Tass said the artificial moon, with a diameter of twenty-two inches and a weight of 184 pounds, was circling the Earth once every hour and thirty-five minutes. This means more than fifteen times a day." America and the rest of the world soon learned that the satellite was named *Sputnik*, a word that simply meant "satellite." The *Times* went on to note that leaders of the United States' own "earth satellite program were astonished . . . to learn that the Soviet Union . . . satellite [was] eight times heavier than that contemplated by this country." Although the U.S. chief of naval research operations, Rear Admiral Rawson Bennett, tried to dismiss the achievement—*Sputnik*, he said, was a "hunk of iron almost anybody could launch"—two facts were undeniable. First, getting nearly two hundred pounds into Earth orbit meant that the Soviets had developed a rocket more powerful than anything in the U.S. inventory. Second, the Soviets had beaten the Americans into space. About this second fact, few U.S. military planners were as dismissive as Rear Admiral Bennett. Instead, they expressed high anxiety that the communists had seized the "high ground of outer space." If the Russians could lift 184 pounds into orbit and fly it high and fast over the United States—again and again—they were well on their way to lifting something a lot heavier, such as a space-launched thermonuclear bomb.

No sooner had the bomber gap faded from memory than U.S. political and military leaders began buzzing about the "*Sputnik* crisis." In response, the Eisenhower administration acted to create the National Aeronautics and Space Administration (NASA) and ushered through Congress the National Defense Education Act, which authorized a billion federal dollars to build new schools; to create science-education scholarships, fellowships, and loans; to establish a host of technical vocational education programs; and to institute general curriculum reform at all levels of schooling to emphasize mathematics and the sciences.

Its radio-broadcast antennas giving it the appearance of a metallic insect, Sputnik I *was history's first artificial earth satellite. Launched by the Soviets on October 4, 1957, it proved to be the starter's pistol in a frenzied U.S.-USSR "space race" that paralleled the "arms race" between the two Cold War superpowers.*

The U.S. Navy's Vanguard rocket was built as a launch vehicle to get the first U.S. satellite into orbit after the Soviets had beaten America into space with Sputnik I. *Trouble was it couldn't get very far off the ground—at least not at first. Vanguard was successfully test launched on October 23, 1957, but it exploded on the launch pad in a December 1957 attempt to loft a satellite into orbit. In the end, the U.S. Army's Juno rocket successfully carried* Explorer I, *the first U.S. satellite, into orbit on February 1, 1958.*

Even more immediately, the United States attempted to get its own satellite into orbit, but suffered a series of humiliating launch-pad failures, most notably that of the army's Vanguard rocket, which, after blowing itself to bits on the ground in a December 6, 1957, launch attempt, was variously dubbed "Kaputnik" and "Flopnik" by the press. It was not until January 1958 that the first American satellite, *Explorer I*, was successfully orbited.

Added now to the nuclear arms race between the United States and the Soviet Union was a "space race." In part, it was a contest to demonstrate whether a nation under democratic government was more than a technological match for one ruled by communist totalitarianism. At stake, many believed, was the validity of democratic capitalism. This symbolic aspect of the space race was important, but military planners saw it, in fact, as an extension of the arms race. Scientific exploration of space was all well and good, but the *real* goal, they believed, was to design, build, and launch the most powerful rocket boosters, spacecraft that could be used to loft a satellite into orbit or a thermonuclear weapon against an enemy living on another continent. The space race was in large measure a race to develop an arsenal of intercontinental ballistic missiles: ICBMs.

FINISH LINE? THE MOON

Students of American popular culture have often characterized the Eisenhower years—most of the 1950s—as prosperous but complacent. *Sputnik*, they say, helped kick the country out of its complacency and was one of the reasons why Americans chose, in 1960, the vigorous, charismatic young John F. Kennedy over Ike's vice president, Richard M. Nixon, as their president.

Yet on April 12, 1961, little more than three months after Kennedy took office, the Soviet Union scored another major triumph in the space race, launching the first human being, "cosmonaut" Yuri Gagarin, into space and orbiting him around the Earth. On May 5, 1961, less than a month after Gagarin's flight, Alan B. Shepard became the first American in space—though his flight was suborbital flight, no more than a fifteen-minute arc beyond the atmosphere and back. Still, Shepard received a well-deserved hero's acclaim, and before the month was over, on May 25, 1961, President Kennedy rode the momentum of Shepard's flight in a speech to Congress. "If we are to win the battle that is

The Soviet Union had beaten the United States into space with Sputnik I *in 1957, but, with the* Apollo 11 *mission, America was the first—and so far only—nation to put men on the moon. This photograph of astronaut Neil Armstrong—the first human being to set foot anywhere beyond planet Earth—was snapped on July 20, 1969, by fellow astronaut Edwin "Buzz" Aldrin.*

now going on around the world between freedom and tyranny, the dramatic achievements in space which occurred in recent weeks should have made clear to us all, as did the *Sputnik* in 1957, the impact of this adventure on the minds of men everywhere, who are attempting to make a determination of which road they should take." JFK continued: "I believe that this nation should commit itself to achieving the goal, before this decade is out, of landing a man on the Moon and returning him safely to the Earth. No single space project in this period will be more impressive to mankind, or more important for the long-range exploration of space; and none will be so difficult or expensive to accomplish."

It was one thing to pop a man into space for a quarter of an hour and quite another to get one from the Earth to the moon and back, but Congress heeded the president and voted the funds, and thus funded, NASA went to work. On July 20, 1969, American astronaut Neil Armstrong became the first human being to walk on the surface of the moon. It was a victory for science and for the human spirit. It was also a victory in the Cold War.

The missile programs of both the United States and the Soviet Union were initially outgrowths of the German V-2 rockets of World War II. Both the Americans and the Russians "acquired" (either by capture or by granting asylum requests) many key German rocket scientists during the final days of the war in Europe. The United States embraced the most famous of these men, Wernher von Braun, the father of the V-2, but the Russians already had a long history of experimental and theoretical work in rocketry, dating to the beginning of the century.

Rocketeer or Weaponeer?

Since youth, Wernher von Braun had been captivated by rocket science, and when Adolf Hitler's war against much of the rest of the world demanded rockets as weapons, von Braun saw an opportunity to obtain the funding to get into space. The V-2 he created in World War II was designed to strike London, but he set his sights on New York. He and his fellow rocket scientists set out to transform the V-2 into the A9/10, the world's first intercontinental ballistic missile (ICBM), whose two stages would give it sufficient range to reach across the Atlantic.

In the end, von Braun was daunted by two obstacles. The first was the relatively primitive state of remote guidance technology. No one could figure out a way to guide, by radio, a missile on such a long flight. This was overcome by redesigning the rocket to accommodate a pilot on what certainly would be a one-way trip. But a second problem remained. By the time von Braun was doing the first tests of the A9/10's vitally important second-stage booster during January and February of 1945, World War II in Europe was rapidly approaching its end and the project was never completed.

As World War II came to a close in Europe, Wernher von Braun, principal architect of Germany's V-2 rocket, surrendered to the U.S. Army, and was taken to the United States, where he became the prime mover of American space technology.

Operation Paperclip

Immediately after the war, von Braun and other German scientists were brought to the United States by the U.S. Army as part of Operation Paperclip, a program to keep the scientists and their families out of Soviet hands, to bring them to America, and to sanitize them of their Nazi affiliations. Under the aegis of the army, these scientists began work on IRBMs (intermediate range ballistic missiles) as well as ICBMs, which would also function as launchers for space exploration. It was the Soviets, however, who first succeeded in transforming the German V-2 into a missile powerful enough to lift a satellite into Earth orbit—the R-7, which carried *Sputnik I*. This was the first ICBM-class vehicle.

In the meantime, research and development in the United States were impeded by the very rivalries among the three armed services that the creation of the Department of Defense in 1947 was supposed to prevent. The army, navy, and air force each initiated its own independent ICBM program. The United States began its ICBM research in 1946, but the Atlas, developed by the air force beginning in 1951, was not successfully launched until December 17, 1957, four months behind the Soviet R-7. Within two years of launching the R-7 and the Atlas, both countries were hard at work building ICBM launch sites for the purpose of delivering atomic warheads. In 1958, the U.S. Army's Redstone rocket, an IRBM, was deployed at bases in the United States as well as in West Germany. Next, von Braun and his team developed the Jupiter-C from the Redstone, creating a three-stage rocket to provide greater thrust than the Redstone.

In 1957, in an effort to focus the national large missile effort, all ICBM projects were consolidated under the control of the air force. The army still fielded IRBM and shorter-range missiles, including several capable of carrying nuclear warheads, and the navy was tasked with developing nuclear-armed intermediate-range missiles capable of being launched from submarines. Thus, while the air force retained control of the ground-launched intercontinental-range thermonuclear weapons, it no longer held an atomic monopoly. The army "nukes" were tactical rather than strategic in nature, intended to be used on the battlefield—an inherently problematic proposition, since, presumably, American soldiers would be required to operate in combat environments contaminated by fallout. Indeed, both the United States and the Soviet Union conducted extremely hazardous exercises in which nuclear devices were detonated in the presence of troops in order to observe the effect of the initial blast and fallout and to determine how close to the blast soldiers could effectively operate.

Originally conceived as a strategic (population-killing) weapon and put into the hands of the U.S. Air Force, nuclear devices were also produced in smaller versions and tested by the U.S. Army as tactical (battlefield) weapons. Project Open Shot, a detonation in Nevada, April 1952, was intended to test a tactical "nuke"—and how it affected those who observed the blast at close range.

While the army fielded tactical weapons, the missiles the navy developed to be launched from a series of submarines—which not only carried the nuclear-tipped missiles but also were powered by nuclear reactors—became a major component of the U.S. nuclear deterrent. This led to the doctrine of the "nuclear triad," which, since the late 1950s and early 1960s, has served as the basis of the U.S. and Soviet (now Russian) nuclear and thermonuclear weapons strategy. The triad consists of three weapons systems: ground-launched ICBMs, submarine-launched ballistic missiles (SLBMs), and nuclear-armed bomber aircraft. The ICBMs would be used for long-range strikes launched from the United States or other "friendly" or "controlled" environments. The advantages of the ICBM include remoteness from its target, the difficulty of intercepting and destroying the missile once it is launched, and the capacity to carry very large warheads. Ballistic missiles are extremely high-trajectory weapons, which are launched into space, far above the atmosphere, before descending to their target at tremendous velocity. The disadvantage of the ICBM is that it typically must be launched from a fixed base, which is vulnerable to detection and attack—even when it consists of a hardened underground silo. The second leg of the triad, SLBMs, compensates for the vulnerability of the ICBM. Submarines have a much better chance of surviving an enemy first strike; however, because the range of an SLBM is shorter than that of an ICBM, the submarine must be positioned closer to its target, something that may consume valuable time and render the submarine increasingly vulnerable to detection and attack. Even more problematic was that, through most of the Cold War period, communication between submerged submarines and their home command authorities was constrained by available technology and therefore limited the control that central commanders could exercise over the use of the missiles. Orders to fire—and even more important, orders to "stand down"—were difficult to transmit and receive. A great degree of discretionary authority had to be entrusted to each submarine captain, a necessity that multiplied the chances of firing nuclear or thermonuclear weapons in error, an eventuality that would likely trigger massive retaliation.

The final leg of the triad, manned strategic bombers, introduced greater flexibility in the use of atomic weapons than either fixed ICBMs or ballistic missile submarines. Bombers can be used to carry out a first strike or to respond to the enemy's first strike. Critics argued that ICBMs made the slower and therefore more vulnerable strategic bomber obsolete, but LeMay and others countered that the flexibility of manned aircraft, including the capability of full and continuous communication between central command authorities and aircrews, was a key advantage. Not only could strikes be more thoroughly controlled, a bomber attack could be recalled in case of a false alert or the sudden resolution of a conflict.

U.S. defense policy gave the U.S. Air Force responsibility for air-dropped nuclear and thermonuclear weapons and ground-launched ICBMs, both strategic weapons systems. The U.S. Army controlled shorter-range ground-launched weapons—the tactical "nukes"—and the U.S. Navy launched strategic nuclear weapons from nuclear-powered submarines. Shown here is a navy Polaris A-3, test-fired from the submarine USS Robert E. Lee *on November 20, 1978.*

THE "MISSILE GAP" MYTH

AMERICAN PLANNERS had another compelling reason to retain and develop all three legs of the nuclear triad: the Soviets possessed them all. If U.S. Air Force brass was partial to manned bombers, politicians and the public called for more and bigger missiles.

The clamor was provoked by the *Sputnik* crisis and encouraged by Senator John F. Kennedy of Massachusetts, who warned that "the nation was losing the satellite-missile race with the Soviet Union because of . . . complacent miscalculations, penny-pinching, budget cutbacks, incredibly confused mismanagement, and wasteful rivalries and jealousies." Kennedy was either mistaken or deliberately misleading.

The Soviets were ahead in the number of ICBMs in their arsenal, but this was more a product of geographical necessity than technological or military superiority. Unlike the United States, which controlled bases in Europe and Turkey suitable for the shorter-range IRBMs, the Soviet Union had no overseas launch sites and was therefore compelled to concentrate on producing the bigger and more costly long-range ICBMs. In terms of military utility, the forward-based U.S. IRBMs were far more effective than the smaller number of Soviet ICBMs. The U.S. National Intelligence Estimate (NIE) issued in December 1957 projected that the Soviets would have ten operational ICBMs sometime between the middle of 1958 and the middle of the following year. Strangely enough, however, the intelligence experts responsible for compiling the NIE accepted at face value the claim of Soviet premier Nikita Khrushchev that his country was turning out ICBMs "like sausages." The NIE of August 1958 upped the estimate of Soviet operational ICBMs by a factor of 10, projecting that by 1960 there would be one hundred and by 1961 as many as five hundred. As far as anyone has been able to determine, the basis for this wildly inflated estimate was Khrushchev's sausage simile.

An American U-2 "spy plane" snapped this photo of a Tyuratam SS-6 ICBM launch site in the Soviet Union sometime during the late 1950s.

"Restraint? Why are you so concerned with saving their lives? The whole idea is to kill the bastards. At the end of the war if there are two Americans and one Russian left alive, we win."

General Thomas Power, Curtis LeMay's successor as SAC commander, in conversation with civilian government consultant William Kaufmann, who reportedly replied, "Then you had better make sure that they are a man and a woman."

President Eisenhower was one of very few Americans who knew the NIE estimate was false. Top-secret U-2 overflights of the Soviet Union consistently failed to reveal evidence of a significant number of ICBMs. The CIA pegged the number of Soviet ICBMs in 1958 at no more than a dozen, but could not make public the top-secret basis for its estimate. LeMay did know about the U-2 data, but argued that the spy plane had simply missed the missile sites.

In the tremulous atmosphere of the Cold War, and in the wake of Soviet strides in the space race, a majority of American political and military leaders believed the NIE estimate and dismissed the CIA numbers. They spoke now of a "missile gap" as they had earlier spoken of a "bomber gap," and while the bomber gap had been relatively easy to dismiss as an illusion (though not before it had stimulated production of a massive U.S. strategic bomber fleet), the missile gap was more difficult to disprove, in large part because the raw fear behind it was more intense. The idea of falling under attack by automated, pilotless, heartless missiles, hundreds of them, each carrying a cataclysmically destructive thermonuclear warhead, all launched from bases beyond American reach, was even more terrifying than visions of a bomber raid. Besides, the charismatic Senator Kennedy, already eyeing a run for the White House in 1960, was intent on making political hay from the missile gap theory and thus lent credibility to the perception of an urgent need to close the missile gap, which drove development and production of American ICBMs.

John F. Kennedy confers with Lyndon Johnson—at the time, both U.S. senators—during a break in the so-called Johnson Hearings (1957–58), convened in the wake of the Sputnik *launch. The hearings resulted in the creation of U.S. space program, inaugurated during the Eisenhower administration and given top priority during that of JFK. As vice president, LBJ was a passionate advocate of space exploration.*

ASSURING MUTUAL ASSURED DESTRUCTION

THE MULTIPLICATION OF WARHEADS fed the expansion of both the U.S. and Soviet triads, which, in turn, stimulated the production of more warheads. Both sides were very much aware that they were accumulating far more than enough weaponry to destroy each other many times over and probably render most, if not all, of the planet uninhabitable in the bargain. But that was precisely the point of MAD, mutual assured destruction. Since there was no adequate defense against a nuclear attack, and since neither side trusted the other to disarm, the only alternative was to make the consequences of a first strike unthinkable by ensuring that it would provoke massive retaliation. The triad was intended to create triple redundancy to discourage your adversary from thinking even for a moment that his first strike could knock out your strike or counterstrike capability. Manage somehow to destroy all my ICBM bases, and my submarine and bomber fleets will retaliate. Try to take out my subs, and my bombers and ICBMs will retaliate. And so on.

Once the air force took over command and control of the ICBMs, bigger and faster missiles were developed and produced in quantity, culminating in the Minuteman (produced in three variants beginning, respectively, in 1962, 1965, and 1970) and the Peacekeeper. If ever there was a doomsday weapon, the Peacekeeper was it. Capable of flying more than six thousand miles, it was fitted with MIRV (multiple independently targetable reentry vehicles) warheads, which enabled one Peacekeeper to deliver ten independently targeted thermonuclear warheads against an enemy. Each individual warhead had a yield of three hundred kilotons of TNT. By 2005, all of the Peacekeepers had been retired, the rockets modified for space exploration and the warheads retrofitted (as single warheads rather than MIRVs) to the Minuteman III fleet.

REALITY CHECK

JFK: Wild-Eyed Militarist?

Kennedy's trumpeting of the missile gap resonated in Moscow even more powerfully than it did in Washington. Premier Khrushchev came to regard JFK as a right-wing military extremist and believed that he was attempting to create in the American popular and political imagination the conviction that the Soviets were gearing up for a first strike, so that he, as president, could order a first strike against the Soviet Union. At the time of Kennedy's election, this was only a theory, but the Bay of Pigs invasion of Cuba suddenly made it seem much more real. Those who wonder what drove Khrushchev to commit the extraordinary provocation of sending missiles to Cuba in 1962 need look no further than the impression Kennedy had created (see Chapter 15).

The world's first nuclear-powered submarine, USS Nautilus, *enters New York Harbor in 1958.*

USS Francis Scott Key *(SSBN 657) is tied up alongside the submarine tender USS* Simon Lake*, which loads Trident C-4 missiles into the* Key's *launch tubes in November 1981. The Trident-class submarines were built as successors to the first-generation Polaris-class submarines. The Trident was a bigger missile with a longer range and a more destructive warhead than the Polaris.*

While the air force deployed more missiles, the navy began working toward the development of nuclear-powered submarines capable of launching nuclear-armed guided missiles. The world's first nuclear powered submarine, USS *Nautilus*, was launched in 1954. It could not launch ballistic missiles, but, just five years after *Nautilus* debuted, the navy commissioned the *George Washington*, the first of a class of three nuclear-powered submarines, each capable of launching sixteen Polaris missiles. Depending on the variant, the Polaris had a range of 1,000 to 1,500 miles and, again depending on the variant, carried either a single nuclear warhead or a MIRV. The final version of the W47 warhead was a thermonuclear device with a yield of 1.2 megatons. In 1961, the *Ethan Allen*, first of a five-ship class, was commissioned. Like the submarines of the *George Washington* class, it carried sixteen Polaris missiles. Between 1981 and 1984, eighteen *Ohio*-class ballistic missile submarines were launched, each of which carries twenty-four Trident I and Trident II missiles. The Trident I can be fitted with an eight-MIRV warhead, collectively yielding a blast of nearly 4 megatons. The Trident II can carry a dozen MIRVs. Thus, one *Ohio*-class submarine armed with a full complement of Trident IIs is capable of delivering the equivalent

TAKEAWAY

The Policy of Nuclear Paralysis

The era of the Cold War was defined by military and diplomatic policies built on deterrence, what the U.S. military called the doctrine of "mutual assured destruction" (MAD), by which the United States and the Soviet Union would refrain from embarking on World War III for fear of destroying one another and, quite possibly, the rest of the planet as well. MAD may have prevented the outbreak of thermonuclear war, but it encouraged—indeed, seemed to require—that the two superpowers build super-massive stockpiles of nuclear and thermonuclear warheads, together with the aircraft, missiles, and submarines to deliver them.

of 4 x 8 x 24 = 768 million tons of TNT. Throughout the development of the American ballistic missile submarines, the Soviets were developing a very large ballistic missile submarine fleet of their own.

Brinkmanship

MUTUAL ASSURED DESTRUCTION CREATED A STANDOFF, but not an absolute stalemate. There were some in the governments of both nations who believed that possession of a superior nuclear arsenal could be wielded as a threat to extort concessions from the other side—or even from what, in the 1950s and 1960s, was an up-and-coming third superpower wannabe, the People's Republic of China. Purposely threatening to bring the world to the brink of thermonuclear war was dubbed by Eisenhower's secretary of state, John Foster Dulles, "brinkmanship." It proved to be so unnerving and so genuinely dangerous a game that neither the Americans nor the Soviets indulged in it extensively—although the jockeying that characterized the Cuban Missile Crisis in 1962 came close (see Chapter 15). The wild cards in any game of brinkmanship were military commanders such as LeMay and General Douglas MacArthur, who expressed their willingness to employ nuclear weapons for tactical as well as strategic purposes. MacArthur fruitlessly lobbied for their use in the Korean War (Chapter 12), and LeMay unsuccessfully proposed them in the Vietnam War (Chapter 16).

A Lesson from Aristotle

The profusion and proliferation of thermonuclear weapons planted one universal fear in the back of the mind of virtually every American and every Soviet citizen—and although the weapons were new, the fear was very old. It was at least as old as the logic of Aristotle, who set down as one of his principles of reasoning that if a thing *can* be done, it *will* be done—eventually. The awful, haunting fear was that *because* these weapons existed (and they existed in massive quantities), they *could* be used, and if they *could* be used, the logic of human nature suggested—perhaps even dictated—that they *would* be used. Tying the survival of the human race to the certainty of MAD really did seem mad, and beginning in the 1960s, as we will see in the chapters of "Part Six, Détente," the members of the "atomic club" began, gingerly, mistrustfully, and with many misgivings, to grope for ways to step back from the brink.

CHAPTER 9

Red China

A Fourth of the World Goes Communist

The vast, troubled nation of China, invaded by Japan in 1937 at the start of the Sino-Japanese War, received remarkably little attention from the Allies during World War II. It was lumped together with Burma and India as the "C-B-I," the China-Burma-India Theater, the least adequately manned corner of the entire conflict. The West's attitude of neglect continued into the Cold War. While the United States, Great Britain, and other Western democracies focused on Soviet expansion in Europe, a civil war raged in China between Communist Chinese converts led by Mao Zedong and Nationalist followers of Chiang Kai-shek. Mao was unfamiliar to most Americans, but Chiang was well known as a "gallant ally" in the war, and President Harry Truman, along with most other Americans, initially assumed that he and his Nationalists would emerge victorious and maintain control over postwar China. As when assumptions concerning the U.S. monopoly on nuclear weapons were shattered, the actual outcome in China came as a hard jolt for the United States.

REALITY CHECK: Mao's Agenda

Mao Zedong made a great show of uniting with Chiang Kai-shek in gallant resistance against the Japanese invaders during World War II. But his only major action against the Japanese was the Hundred Regiments Offensive, a campaign that spanned August 20 to November 30, 1940, which had negligible effect. After this, Mao contributed little to the war effort. Although he did refrain from combat against KMT forces—and he resisted the temptation to collaborate with the Japanese to further the cause of the CCP—he exploited the chaos of the war to grow and consolidate the CCP in northern China and to solidify his own party leadership.

In Play: Half a Billion Human Beings

For two millennia, China had been ruled by emperors, but the imperial hegemony ended when the fatally weak and corrupt Qing (Manchu) Dynasty was brought down by revolution and replaced by a republic upon the abdication of Puyi, the "last emperor," on February 12, 1912. The new republic was torn by competing leaders, and from 1912 until the commencement of World War II, China was an ungovernable chaos of warlord-led feuding factions from which two major parties emerged, the Nationalists, also called the Kuomintang (KMT), and the Chinese Communist Party (CCP). The rival parties came together for a time after the 1911–12 revolution in a campaign to suppress the warlords, but by 1927, they fell into full-scale civil war, during which Chiang Kai-shek emerged as leader of the KMT, and Mao Zedong as leader of the CCP. The civil war was suspended after July 7, 1937, when the Japanese invaded China at the start of the Sino-Japanese War. Once again, the KMT and CCP united, resolved to resist the common enemy. This uneasy cooperation continued throughout the Sino-Japanese War and World War II, into which the earlier conflict dissolved. But even as the CCP collaborated with the KMT, Mao took his party from a 1937 membership of about forty thousand to a 1945 membership of 1.2 million, and the conclusion of World War II brought an almost instantaneous end to the protracted truce between the Nationalists and the Communists.

With the Japanese invaders expelled, Mao's followers descended from the north and Chiang's Nationalists advanced from the south, each scrambling to seize territory formerly occupied by the Japanese. Pursuant to the containment policy, Truman authorized U.S. transport aircraft to airlift thousands of Nationalist troops to hold Shanghai, Nanjing, and other major Chinese cities. Although the president expected Chiang to prevail in China, he recognized that the CCP was a major party and would therefore have to be accommodated in a unity government of some sort—a government under Chiang Kai-shek, of course, but one that included representatives of the CCP. Truman saw the unity government as a necessary compromise that would still foil any Soviet attempt to make the vast country a satel-

At the start of the Sino-Japanese War, 1937, Japanese marines and armored cars take the battle to the streets of Shanghai.

lite. The president dispatched to China General George Marshall, the U.S. Army's World War II chief of staff, to coax and goad the two sides into a negotiation that would result in a China the United States could at least live with.

Marshall was able to bring both sides to the negotiating table, but they spent the next two years in hot disputes that produced not a single significant agreement. Instead, both the KMT and CCP used the lull in the ongoing civil war—a truce enforced by U.S. Marines—to jockey for position and build their power bases. By February 1947, a profoundly frustrated Marshall threw in the towel and returned to the United States.

Chiang Kai-shek's archrival for control of the Chinese government was Mao Zedong, leader of the Chinese Communist Party and its military forces. Mao is shown here addressing followers on December 6, 1944, when he and Chiang suspended civil warfare to unite against Japanese invaders.

Generalissimo Chiang Kai-shek, leader of the Nationalist (KMT) Chinese forces, inspects high-ranking officers of the Officers Training Corps in Lushan, China. The photograph, difficult to date precisely, was taken between 1937 and 1943.

President Truman's envoy General George C. Marshall poses with Zhou Enlai, the future prime minister and minister of foreign affairs of Communist China, in 1946, during Marshall's doomed mission to broker a Chinese unity government incorporating both the Nationalist (KMT) faction and the communists.

Mao Triumphant

When Marshall left, freely admitting the failure of his mission, President Truman withdrew all American military personnel, and the Chinese Civil War resumed at full force. Truman funneled American economic aid—as well material military aid (but not troops)—to Chiang, but it did nothing to prevent KMT insiders from defecting to the Communists in droves. The KMT commanders were mostly political appointees—invariably corrupt, ineffectual combat leaders who devoted most of their time to squabbling with one another. In the meantime, inflation was rampant in China, and, coupled with corruption, brought the KMT into thorough disrepute. In the name of containment, the United States found itself propping up a rotten, despised, and moribund government. It would not be the last time.

In October 1948, three hundred thousand Nationalist troops threw down their guns in Manchuria and surrendered en masse to the Communists. In December, Maoist forces enveloped, then captured sixty-six Nationalist army divisions in north-central China. In April 1949, the Maoists crossed the Yangtze (Chang) River and swept through the south, taking Shanghai in May and Guangzhou in October. On the first of that month, Mao Zedong proclaimed the creation of the People's Republic of China, then captured Chongqing in November. The next month, Chiang Kai-shek and Nationalist diehards betook themselves to the small island of Formosa (present-day Taiwan), where Chiang proclaimed the Republic of China.

China "falls" to the communists, 1949. Members of the People's Liberation Army enter Beijing.

> "Not only in China but also in the world without exception, one either leans to the side of imperialism or the side of socialism. Neutrality is mere camouflage and a third road does not exist."
>
> *Mao Zedong, speech, July 1, 1949*

Butcher's Bill

In 1946, Chiang Kai-shek had an army of 5.7 million, about five times the number of Mao's CCP forces at the time. Little wonder that Truman was confident that Chiang and the pro-American KMT would retain control even of a unity government. But by the spring of 1949, Mao's army had grown to more than four million, and Chiang's forces had been drastically reduced. Nearly six hundred thousand were killed or wounded between June 1948 and December 1949, the period in which the Communists consolidated their victory. More than 4.5 million Nationalists were captured in the course of the entire war. Mao had also taken heavy losses—1.5 million killed or wounded—but prevailed.

制止美帝國主義的侵略行為，我們才能進行和平建設

The caption of this 1951 poster from the People's Republic of China reads: "Until we stop the American imperialist invasive actions, we cannot start peace reconstruction." A heroically proportioned Chinese factory worker seizes a dwarfish Yankee imperialist, who bears a bomb in one hand and blood-stained coins in the other.

The battle casualties, terrible as they were, represented only a fraction of the toll of civil war. Millions of Chinese civilians died of starvation and privation. Those suffering masses saw that one class continued to live very well—the military officers and party officials of the KMT, whose lavish lifestyles amid the general poverty and suffering were financed by aid from the United States. Communist Party members had political and philosophical reasons for opposing capitalist America, and, in view of America's support for Chiang, Mao Zedong assumed that Harry Truman intended to order an invasion. This assumption crystallized into a permanent perception of the United States as an enemy. That was bad enough, but even worse was how the highly visible linkage between the high-living and heartless KMT and the United States influenced Chinese public opinion. The Chinese masses, who had looked to America as a beacon of hope during World War II, now had real motives for hating the nation they believed—they *saw*—had betrayed them.

"Most of us saw Chiang Kai-shek's fall coming, but we were still disappointed when it happened. I saw it as a great tragedy, that the Chinese people, with their tremendous energy and potential, were now wedded to Communist ideology and allied with the Soviet Union."

Dean Rusk, undersecretary of state for the Far East, 1949

The View from Washington

War unquestionably brings death, destruction, and revolutions in power. These are facts. But war is also loaded down by perception of the facts, and perception is so compelling a force that it, too, becomes a fact of war. Mao Zedong perceived the material and financial aid the United States gave to the KMT as proof of President Truman's ultimate intention to overthrow the People's Republic. He failed to understand that the president of the United States wielded decidedly limited power, and Mao misinterpreted Truman's attitude toward the civil war in China. As early as the close of 1946, both President Truman and his envoy, General Marshall, had reached the conclusion that saving the Chiang government in China would require an extensive intervention by the United States, "a continuing commitment," Truman later wrote, "from which it would be practically impossible to withdraw." Even as Truman continued to fund Chiang, in November 1946 he ordered the U.S. Seventh Fleet to remove the detachment of U.S. Marines that had been stationed in China. Mao should have recognized that this was hardly the action of a president intending to invade. What he could probably not have understood, however, is the limitation of Truman's own autonomy. He was a head of state, but he was also a politician, and he was being pressed—hard—by the so-called China lobby in and around Congress. Consisting mostly of conservative Republicans, the China lobby favored maintaining Chiang Kai-shek and the Nationalists in power at practically any cost. Truman thought the cost of permanently propping up a corrupt and unpopular government too high, but neither could he simply turn his back on Chiang. For one thing, to do so would make a mockery of the "Truman Doctrine"; for another, the China lobby would not allow it. They would accuse the president of being "soft on communism" and of "giving China away." Hence Truman's somewhat schizophrenic response to the struggle between the KMT and CCP, supplying money even as he withdrew troops.

COULD AMERICA HAVE "SAVED" CHINA?

Many Americans, especially conservative Republicans, refused to believe that Mao Zedong had won China and instead embraced the notion that the Truman administration had lost the country because he refused to send a major military force to assist Chiang Kai-shek.

U.S. secretary of state Dean Acheson's claim on July 30, 1949, that "nothing that this country did or could have done within reasonable limits of its capabilities could have changed [the] result," seemed to many a hollow excuse. The administration's critics failed to appreciate Acheson's qualifying phrase, "within reasonable limits of its capabilities." Postwar demobilization had been so rapid—spurred by the very Republican legislators who now condemned Truman—that the U.S. military of 1948–49 was a shadow of what it had been during 1941–45. Still, a massive influx of U.S. troops may have turned the tide against Mao's immediate victory, but China was a vast country, and Mao and his followers were used to biding their time in methodical insurgency. Mao might have been blocked, but he would not have been decisively defeated.

Furthermore, as most Chinese saw the situation, America and the KMT were partners in corruption. Moreover, China had an age-old tradition of suspicion and hostility toward foreigners. Any substantial U.S. intervention in China would have been perceived not as an action to protect China against communism, but as a foreign invasion. To Americans, communism was a foreign invasion emanating from Moscow. To a growing number of Chinese, it was a philosophy of government fully domesticated by one of their own, the charismatic Mao Zedong. Far from defeating Mao, full-out U.S. intervention in China would probably have united more of the Chinese people under his banner and against both Chiang and America. Acheson was almost certainly right. No alternative outcome was possible in China.

Just as Mao Zedong's attitude and actions with regard to the United States were dictated by his perceptions, so was Washington's with regard to Mao and the People's Republic. That Mao proclaimed the establishment of the PRC on October 1, 1949, just one week after President Truman announced that the Soviet Union had detonated an atomic bomb, created a climate of confusion, depression, and panic across the country. There was a general impression, first and foremost, that communism radiated from Stalin and the Kremlin, that it was a monolithic force, and that the PRC would inevitably become, at half a billion people in 1949, the biggest Soviet satellite of all. Countervailing this majority sense was a theory—really, more of a hope—among some of Truman's advisers that Mao Zedong would emulate Marshal Tito of

馬克思列寧主義——毛澤東思想的光輝照耀着新中國

Typical of the heroic Chinese images of Mao Zedong from the early 1950s, this portrait shows the chairman in front of a flag decorated with busts of Stalin, Lenin, Engels, and Marx. Soon, Stalin would be dropped from the Maoist pantheon of communism's founders.

Yugoslavia and maintain autonomy from Stalin. The example of Tito, they claimed, was evidence that communism was not necessarily monolithic and that a country could have a communist government without bowing to Moscow, without automatically aligning itself against the United States, and without necessarily seeking to expand its ideology into neighboring nations.

Because the United States was only marginally involved in the Chinese civil war, there was no basis for the China lobby's claims that "*we* had lost China."; The statement was symptomatic of the widespread perception in government as well as among Americans in general that the United States was the principal guardian of the "democratic way of life" and "the free world." As the Cold War continued, this attitude appeared to many outside of the United States as so much evidence of "Yankee imperialism." Much as Americans feared that the Kremlin sought to pull the ideological strings of all nations everywhere, some in the rest of the world came to believe that Washington deemed itself the center of the planet as well as its ultimate arbiter and supreme authority. There is no doubt that Truman wanted to limit the spread of communism, but his ambition was not to make the United States the sole leader of the "free world." Thus, in contrast to the China lobby, Truman and his circle clung to the hope that Mao would go the way of Tito and defy Stalin in order to maintain the independence of the PRC. Even if China had been lost to us, the Truman administration could at least claim that it had also been lost to the Soviet Union. *Our* loss would not be *their* gain, and in this ideological Cold War, that was something of a victory.

To the demand from the China lobby that the Truman administration commit to the defense of the Chiang government on Taiwan, Secretary of State Dean Acheson replied that the president intended to "wait until the dust settles." But no sooner was this temporizing response made than Mao seemed to dash all of the administration's hopes that he intended to emulate Tito. In June 1949, Mao Zedong announced his intention of concluding an alliance with the Soviet Union "and with the proletariat and broad masses of the people in other countries" in order to "form an international united front." That certainly sounded like a willingness to become part of a communist monolith, and, in December 1949, he put his words into action. Mao boarded a train for Moscow, where he spent the next two months negotiating a Treaty of Friendship and Alliance and Mutual Help between the PRC and the Soviet Union. Reinforcing the perception of an evolving monolith was the proclamation—in January, while Mao was still in Moscow—by the Vietnamese communist leader Ho Chi Minh that the Vietminh, the Vietnamese Communist Party, was the only legitimate government of Vietnam, which the French still called French Indochina and considered their colony (see Chapter 16).

This Chinese postage stamp from 1950 depicts Stalin and Mao Zedong shaking hands. It was the vision of world communist unity that the United States feared.

DETAILS, DETAILS
The Tito Factor

In contrast to other rising communist leaders, the former Yugoslavian guerilla and partisan leader Josip Broz ("Tito") understood that fascists and capitalists were not his only enemies. Joseph Stalin posed perhaps an even more immediate threat. Rise too high too fast, and Stalin was apt to put you in front of a show trial and then a firing squad. Tito, who led the rebirth of Yugoslavia during the Cold War, repeatedly defied Stalin, maintaining independence from the "Soviet bloc" and productive (if not always cordial) relations with the West. Stalin tried to undermine Tito with a brutal economic blockade and by aiding several (failed) coups. He even ordered numerous assassination attempts. After Stalin's death in 1953, a letter from Tito was found among Stalin's papers: "Stop sending people to kill me. We've already captured five. . . . If you don't stop sending killers, I'll send one to Moscow and I won't have to send a second."

REALITY CHECK

A Hollow Alliance

Mao famously called "American imperialism" a "paper tiger," fierce looking but ultimately weak. The same might have been said about the ostensible military alliance between China and the USSR. Actual military assistance would be required only if Japan attacked either of the signatories. Both Stalin and Mao well knew that Japan had been totally disarmed by terms of its surrender to the Allies and, furthermore, had embraced a constitution that mandated renunciation of arms and war. If any state was likely to declare war on China, it was the breakaway Nationalist republic of Taiwan—presumably aided by the United States. Yet the treaty was silent on this realistic scenario.

After Mao's Kremlin visit, panic replaced hope in Washington. American politicians and diplomats failed to understand Mao just as they failed to understand Stalin. They saw both as committed Marxist ideologues and, therefore, as cut from identical—red—cloth. The fact was, as George Kennan had understood even before the end of World War II, Stalin was far more a pragmatist than an idealist. He embraced communist doctrine only insofar as it would serve to bring neighboring countries under Soviet control—more than anything as a first line of defense against future invasion—and, even more important, to keep him in power. Mao, in contrast to Stalin, was a truer Marxist, though he would modify Marxist theory extensively. He believed that the Bolshevik Revolution in Russia was the most successful political revolution of modern times, and he wanted to hitch the revolution in China to it. Yet, like Stalin, he had no intention of carrying the Marxist revolution through to what Marx had posited as its natural and desirable conclusion: the abolition of the state and its replacement by a stateless class consciousness. No. Like Stalin, Mao intended to create a dictatorship built upon a cult of personality. This was the best way of holding on to power.

Still, the differences between Stalin and Mao were significant, and they were destined to widen, beginning with Mao's inversion of Marxist process. Marx focused on radicalizing the proletariat—urban industrial workers—and deliberately overlooked the rural peasantry as incapable of revolutionary change. In contrast, Mao would focus on the peasants at the expense of the proletariat. More immediately, if anyone in the U.S. State Department had carefully analyzed the new Sino-Soviet treaty, they would have recognized that its terms were quite modest and moderate, hardly boding the subjugation of China to the Soviet Union. The two countries would come to one another's aid in time of war *only* if any other state (read: the United States) joined forces with Japan "directly or indirectly in acts of aggression"—a scenario so unlikely as to render the treaty nearly meaningless.

All these things—the differences between Mao and Stalin, the emptiness of the treaty between China and the Soviet Union—American analysts ignored. By 1949, all that was seen was that the most populous nation on the planet was now committed to communism, and a commitment to communism meant becoming a satellite of the Soviet Union. The great tragedy of the Cold War, the engine that kept

"The reddest red star in our hearts, Chairman Mao is together with us." The image was published in 1968.

it going for half a century, was the failure of the leaders of rival states to understand one another. Both sides operated from assumptions rather than knowledge.

Interlude: The Rebirth of Japan

In China, and, as we will see in Chapters 12 and 16, in Korea and Vietnam, the disruptions caused by World War II created power vacuums that the communists rushed to fill. China had been an ally of the United States and the other Western democracies during the war, yet it turned against all of its wartime allies except—initially, at least—the Soviet Union. Japan, of course, was an enemy during the war. Except for its emperor, Hirohito, its wartime government was shattered and its people were in dire want, yet, unlike China, Japan did not succumb to the expansion of communism. It was not that Japan lacked a communist party. The Japanese Communist Party (JCP) had been founded in 1922, but was immediately forced underground by Japan's Peace Preservation Law, which gave civil and military police unlimited authority to suppress it. As the only Japanese political party that opposed the nation's involvement in World War II, the JCP should have been ideally positioned for popularity in postwar Japan. What is more, under U.S. occupation, the JCP was fully legalized. Yet communism never became a powerful force in Japanese politics.

There were at least five reasons for this, all of them highly significant for the course of the Cold War in Asia and the Pacific. Let's begin by enumerating the first three.

POP CULTURE

Mao's "Little Red Book"

Throughout the 1950s, the mass of Americans kept their minds tightly closed to "Red China" and Chairman Mao, but in 1964, the Government of the PRC published *Quotations from Chairman Mao* and issued it in many languages, including a pocket-sized edition intended for distribution throughout the West. This became known as the "Little Red Book" and was very widely read throughout the United States (and other Western countries) during the flowering of "counterculture" thought in the second half of the 1960s. Worldwide, it is estimated that 5 to 6.5 billion copies of the book were published, making it more popular than the Holy Bible or, in fact, any other book in history. While it enjoyed a wide readership outside of China, within that nation, especially during the Cultural Revolution, it was nothing less than a popular icon. The Chinese government ceased publication of "The Little Red Book" in the late 1970s.

General of the Army Douglas MacArthur—in a characteristic pose, trademark corncob pipe clenched between his teeth, and familiar rumpled "scrambled eggs" cap perched on his head. The photograph was taken in Manila, Philippines, on August 2, 1945, as he prepared to invade the Japanese home islands. The atomic bombing of Hiroshima (August 6) and Nagasaki (August 9) would, much to the general's disappointment, make the invasion unnecessary.

Number one, the JCP had no leader around whom to develop the kind of personality cult that grew up around Stalin and Mao. Number two, the Communist Party never became a serious, militant contender for power in Japan, and, with the rise of a militarist, right-wing, even fascist government in the two decades leading up to World War II, it was effectively submerged and suppressed. Third, although World War II created power vacuums in Japan, much as it had in China, the United States intervened in the affairs of a defeated enemy in ways that were impossible with an ally. The U.S. military occupied Japan, the American government addressed the urgent physical needs of its devastated population, and it designed for the nation a brand new democratic government. What is more, all of this was administered by General Douglas MacArthur in his capacity as Supreme Commander, Allied Powers. The chief architect of the Allies' strategy in the Pacific war, MacArthur has been called (by biographer William Manchester) an "American Caesar." It is an appropriate appellation for a bold military leader who governed a defeated Japan with a wisdom, humanity, and insight that revived the devastated nation—the only country ever to suffer nuclear attack—and made it possible for it to enjoy a democratic prosperity.

When President Truman decided to bring the war with Japan to an end by accepting from that nation what was, in effect, a conditional unconditional surrender, which allowed Emperor Hirohito to remain on the throne, he did so on the condition that the emperor would be wholly subject to the authority of the Supreme Commander, Allied Powers. Truman knew MacArthur, and he did not much like him. Whatever his virtues as a military strategist, Truman rated his character as a compound of grandiose pomposity and outright megalomania. But now the president recognized that it was precisely this combination of traits Japan needed most in a provisional administrator. He knew that the Japanese people revered their emperor as a kind of divinity, and he sincerely believed that Douglas MacArthur revered himself in much the same way. If Hirohito, a divinity, was to be subject to anyone, what better candidate than another divinity?

"... discussed ... what to do with Mr. Prima Donna, Brass Hat, Five Star MacArthur. He's worse than the Cabots and the Lodges—they at least talked with one another before they told God what to do. Mac tells God right off. ... Don't see how a country can produce such men as Robert E. Lee, John J. Pershing, Eisenhower, & Bradley and at the same time produce Custers, Pattons, and MacArthurs."

Harry S. Truman, diary, June 17, 1945

President Truman's assessment of MacArthur was accurate as far as it went, but it did not go far enough. As it turned out, he proved to be a brilliant and enlightened administrator. Former secretary of the treasury Henry Morgenthau, whose harsh reconstruction plan for Germany Truman had rejected, formulated a similarly draconian plan for Japan, which would have reduced it to a nonindustrial "pastoral" state. Without consulting anyone, MacArthur scrapped the Morgenthau plan and imposed instead his own benevolent dictatorship for the next three years, until full sovereignty was returned to the Japanese. He used the time not merely to manage the country, but to reform and reshape it. He demanded that the Japanese government draft a new democratic constitution, and when, after reviewing it, he deemed it insufficiently democratic, MacArthur, like most American military leaders a conservative Republican, synthesized British and American models to personally write a constitution more liberally democratic than that of the United States. It established a complete government, with three branches—executive, legislative, and judicial, as in the United States—but with the legislature constructed on the parliamentary rather than the congressional model. Also included were social welfare provisions drawn right out of FDR's New Deal and—unique to the Japanese constitution—something called the "fundamental law," by which Japan "forever renounce[d] war as a sovereign right of the nation" and pledged to maintain no land, sea, or air forces. The United States would furnish the defense of the nation.

As military governor of occupied Japan, General of the Army Douglas MacArthur introduced a democratic regime so liberal that it allowed even the Japanese Communist Party to offer candidates for the diet (parliament). A Tokyo crowd scans JCP elections posters, April 16, 1946.

Acting counterintuitively to the implications of Truman's containment policy, MacArthur did not ban the Japanese Communist Party, but explicitly legalized it and also encouraged the proliferation of trade unions. In addition to imposing such democratic principles as total religious, political, and civil liberty, MacArthur introduced quasi-socialist (some said communist) land reform measures, splitting up the great Japanese rural estates and distributing the farmland to the peasants. This he considered essential to political and economic recovery and stability. At the same time, MacArthur purged the government and legislature of militarists and all members of militarist parties. Democracy would have to begin with a clean slate, even if it had to be forcibly erased.

To bring about these changes, MacArthur assumed extraordinary unilateral powers. At his insistence, the Soviets were entirely excluded from any governing role in Japan, but so were the British. As a sop to both the USSR and the United Kingdom, their representatives were given seats on a consultative council, which MacArthur mostly ignored.

MacArthur never allowed political and administrative reform to cloud his vision of the urgent physical needs of the Japanese. He became a very effective advocate for the welfare of his charges. One week after he assumed the reins of the occupation government, he shot a cablegram to Washington ordering the immediate shipment of three and a

Japan's Emperor Hirohito (in topcoat and fedora) tours the bomb-damaged factory of the Showa Electric Industry Company some time in 1946.

half million tons of food. When this was not instantly forthcoming, he transmitted a terse follow-up: "Give me bread or give me bullets."

Although Japan had suffered far fewer military and civilian casualties than Germany, the industrial infrastructure of the country had been savaged by intense strategic bombing. Like Marshall in Europe, MacArthur appreciated the urgency of restoring industrial capacity in order to promote economic recovery. Allied plans called for Japan to make war reparations that included the dismantling of eleven hundred intact Japanese factories and the removal of the equipment and machinery to Allied nations that had suffered at the hands of Japan. MacArthur intervened to halt the transfer. It was, he insisted, more important that Japan be given a chance to recover its industrial capacity as quickly as possible. In the meantime, however, MacArthur's liberal approach to resurrecting the Japanese government led to the rise of the now fully legal Japanese Communist Party, which, in an effort to raise industrial wages, called a general strike on February 1, 1947. At this, MacArthur finally bowed to American public opinion, which criticized his introduction of a socialist government to Japan. He consented to bring in Joseph M. Dodge, a retired American banking executive, to supervise reindustrialization on a more centralized model.

Despite the need for a course correction in Japanese industrial recovery, MacArthur's leadership in the recovery of Japan stood in stark contrast to the "loss" of China. The Chinese situation, however, prevented many Americans from recognizing that the revival of Japan—including its salvation from communist incursion—was on a par with the Marshall Plan in Europe as one of the great democratic victories in the Cold War. What is more, unlike some other American efforts to contain communism, the intervention in Japan did not require supporting a quasi-fascist right-wing government as an alternative to Soviet-inspired left-wing communist government. Japan developed a genuinely moderate democracy.

From Demon to Ally

We have just addressed three of the reasons for Japan's postwar recovery as a noncommunist nation, but we mentioned that there were at least five. The first three were in large part the work of Douglas MacArthur, but the last two were the result of developments outside of his control and outside of Japan itself.

REALITY CHECK
According to MacArthur

One of the things Harry Truman disliked about Douglas MacArthur was his complete absence of modesty. The general was more than willing to accept the lion's share of credit for winning World War II in the Pacific and, in assessing the postwar recovery of Japan, his praise for the Japanese people was just as much praise for himself. "The Japanese people since the war have undergone the greatest reformation recorded in modern history," he told Congress on April 19, 1952. "With a commendable will, eagerness to learn, and marked capacity to understand, they have from the ashes left in war's wake erected in Japan an edifice dedicated to the supremacy of individual liberty and personal dignity, and in the ensuing process there has been created a truly representative government committed to the advance of political morality, freedom of economic enterprise, and social justice." The thing is, this grandiose appraisal from the architect of Japan's postwar renaissance was quite accurate.

Despite a constitution—largely drafted by Douglas MacArthur—forbidding the creation of a Japanese military, the United States decided that the nation needed a "Self-Defense Force" to discourage communist aggression. Lieutenant General Arnold W. Braswell, commander of the U.S. Pacific Air Force, is shown reviewing airmen of the Japanese Self-Defense Air Force during a 1983 ceremony.

The establishment of the People's Republic of China and the outbreak of the Korean War made Japan vital to American interests as a bulwark against the spread of communism throughout all Asia and the Pacific. Japan was soon compelled to host an assortment of U.S. military installations, including air, naval, and army bases. Whether the Japanese liked it or not, they became the principal bastion fortress in the front line of the Asian theater of the Cold War. Then, in 1949, MacArthur as well as the Japanese people—who were overwhelmingly opposed to harboring in their bosom any new military establishment—were forced to accept a radical alteration of their year-old constitution, which had absolutely banned any Japanese armed forces. At the behest of the Truman administration, Japan was to be *obligated* to create a modest Self-Defense Force, financed and supplied by the United States. Thus America's most-hated enemy in World War II, the country that had brought war to America by attacking Pearl Harbor, was recruited as a key ally in the Cold War.

The Glass Half Empty

Despite the Japanese success story and hopeful developments in Europe, including the progress of the Marshall Plan and the success of the Berlin Airlift, a major victory in the United States' first toe-to-toe Cold War confrontation with the Soviet Union (see Chapter 10), the "fall" of China immersed the mass of Americans in deep gloom and intense anxiety. *Time* magazine gave voice to the prevailing sentiment that "the red tide . . . threatens to engulf the world." America's collective panic seemed fully justified when a "red tide" of communist soldiers flowed across the "demilitarized zone" separating Soviet-aligned North Korea from U.S.-aligned South Korea on June 25, 1950, igniting the Korean War (see Chapter 12), in which an American army would fight the Soviet-supported North Koreans and, later, the Chinese army itself.

Within months of the outbreak of the Korean War, on September 23, 1950, the Internal Security Act, better known as the McCarran Act, was passed over the veto of President Truman, who denounced it as "the greatest danger to freedom of speech, press, and assembly since the Alien and Sedition Laws of 1798." The new law required Communist organizations to register with the U.S. Attorney General and created a Subversive Activities Control Board authorized to investigate anyone suspected of engaging in subversive activities or otherwise "promoting" the establishment of a "totalitarian dictatorship." As we will see in Chapter 13, the McCarran Act was the platform from which an intense and widespread repressive response to a national "red scare" was launched. What is most significant about the act is what it reveals about the American psyche in the early stages of the Cold War. The preamble to the act declares that "World Communism has as its sole purpose the establishment of a totalitarian dictatorship in America, to be brought about by treachery, infiltration, sabotage and terrorism." As Chapter 11 will make clear, communist "treachery" and "infiltration" were undeniably at work in the United States, but defining the "sole purpose" of "World Communism" as the subjugation of America under a "totalitarian dictatorship" was a fantasy born of national egocentrism and projection. For if anyone had a "sole purpose," it was the United States, whose people and politicians wanted to erase communism from the world. The major communist powers, the Soviet Union and China, were by no means exclusively focused on the United States. Their leaders were concerned, first and foremost, with keeping themselves in power, with controlling their own populations, and then with extending their spheres of influence mainly to neighboring nations. Beyond these objectives, the goals of both the Soviets and the communist Chinese were—despite the absolute certainty expressed in the McCarran act—far more ambiguous. Many American politicians as well as members of the public knew just enough about communism to believe that its ultimate purpose was to engulf the world. As Karl Marx outlined the communist philosophy, this was true, but it was only a part of Marxist theory. The purpose of sowing communism across the planet was not totalitarian conquest, but liberation—not just liberation from this or that tyrannical regime, but liberation from the very concept of the state. The goal of communism, according to Marx, was the complete dissolution of nationalism in a global class consciousness.

It should have been manifestly apparent to any observer that neither Stalin nor Mao Zedong desired the annihilation of the state. On the contrary, their approach to rule required the elevation of the state and the submersion of the individual within it. This in itself was dangerous, but it also implied that, for Stalin and Mao, self-preservation was a motive that trumped all others, and this meant that pragmatic rationality would always tend to curb ideological zeal. Neither Stalin nor Mao was prepared to die for an idea.

We see this now. The fact to appreciate is that very few Americans, from national leaders to the man and woman in the street, saw it in the late 1940s and early 1950s. What they saw was communism, amorphous and undifferentiated like some monstrous amoeba, spreading across Europe and Asia. Every day, newspapers carried stories of "infiltration" and "treachery." The Soviets had atomic bombs. The communist Chinese had a half-billion people. War was simmering in Vietnam and had already burst upon Korea. The Marshall Plan, the Berlin Airlift, the rebirth of a democratic Japan notwithstanding, America was submerged in a "red tide" of defeatist sentiment and anxiety born of a primal instinct for self-preservation. These things were not conducive to the preservation of democracy.

A New Offensive

THE KOREAN WAR WAS A SOURCE OF GREAT FRUSTRATION to most Americans, especially since, by the spring of 1951, it had hardened into a bloody stalemate. It was on June 14, 1951, during the height of this frustration, that Senator Joseph McCarthy—a blustering, bibulous bully from Wisconsin—suddenly launched into an attack on George Marshall, at the time serving as President Truman's secretary of defense. McCarthy (whose anti-red crusade is discussed more fully in Chapter 13) laid the blame for the "loss of China" at Marshall's feet, then went on to declare that the United States fell from its position as "the most powerful Nation on earth" to one "of declared weakness by our leadership." The cause of this terrible decline, McCarthy asserted, was "a conspiracy so immense and an infamy so black as to dwarf any previous such

Senator Joseph McCarthy strikes a typically humorless pose in this photograph that also shows his chief legal counsel and attack dog, Roy Cohn.

venture in the history of man." McCarthy did not directly charge Marshall with treason, but he did allege that he was an incompetent who had been duped by those disloyal persons within the government who had successfully conspired to sabotage the wartime alliance between China and the United States. McCarthy then got down to specifics, which, though quite baseless, sounded highly persuasive. He claimed that when "Marshall was sent to China with secret State Department orders, the Communists . . . were bottled up in two areas and were fighting a losing battle." This had not been the case at all; no matter, McCarthy continued, asserting that Marshall's execution of his "secret" State Department orders "radically changed" the situation "in favor of the Communists." In this way, the junior senator from Wisconsin transformed Marshall's efforts to facilitate negotiations toward a Chinese unity government into the foolish denial of arms and ammunition to anticommunist forces and the even more foolish opening of "the Nationalist-held Kalgan Mountain pass into Manchuria, to the end that the Chinese Communists gained access to the mountains of captured Japanese equipment." Finally, McCarthy concluded: "No need to tell the country about how Marshall tried to force Chiang Kai-shek to form a partnership government with the Communists."

There were many in government and the public who thought McCarthy had gone too far in attacking a genuinely great man, but there were many as well who believed he was right.

In the climate created by McCarthy's accusations, opposition to China and to the Soviets hardened into something impenetrable and beyond questioning. To be sure, China and the Soviet Union posed very real dangers, but the mindset that motivated McCarthy's attack on Marshall transformed those two powers from real countries with real leaders into one-dimensional symbols of evil. While it is possible to negotiate and reason even with dangerous men, it is impossible to do so with demonic pasteboard figures better suited to frightening fairy tales than global politics. Every successful military commander, from Alexander the Great to George S. Patton Jr., has understood that victory depends on getting to know your adversary as intimately as possible. The politics of the early 1950s made this all but impossible, and, despite the existence of real enemies and real threats, the United States wasted much effort in shadow boxing and chasing phantoms, thereby endangering the very democracy McCarthy and his like claimed to be defending.

DETAILS, DETAILS

Ike Takes the Low Road

In 1952, no less a figure than the Republican presidential candidate Dwight D. Eisenhower publicly embraced McCarthy and his criticism of George C. Marshall, the very man who had put him forward in World War II as Supreme Allied Commander, Europe, and to whom, really, Eisenhower owed the major phase of his military career. That such a man as Eisenhower—universally respected for his integrity—could betray a mentor, former commander, and one of the architects of victory in World War II is testimony to the insidious power of McCarthy in a period dominated by panic instead of rational analysis.

President Eisenhower was widely criticized for not taking a stand against the reckless witch hunting of Joe McCarthy. "I will not get into a pissing contest with that skunk," he told his brother Milton, but he did work behind the scenes to force McCarthy's appearance at the 1954 Army-McCarthy Hearings, knowing that these would be the Wisconsin senator's undoing. This December 3, 1953, cartoon depicts McCarthy sharing a desk with the thoroughly intimidated Ike, about to hand him a pen for signing papers labeled "foreign policy," "national issues," and "GOP political plans."

THE MONOLITH CRACKS

IF A MAJORITY OF THE NATION'S LEADERS HAD BEEN CAPABLE OF SEEING beyond the phantoms of their own making, they would have noticed in Sino-Soviet relations fissures similar to those that had long existed in relations between Tito's Yugoslavia and Stalin's Soviet Union. Historically, relations between Russia and China had long been fraught with conflict, but, most immediately, during the 1930s, Mao Zedong had defied Stalin and the Soviet-controlled Comintern by pointedly focusing on the rural peasantry rather than the urban proletariat to bring about revolution. This signaled an important break between the two centers of communist power and thought—yet American leaders ignored it.

After World War II, just beneath the smooth surface of Sino-Soviet relations, a rift was widening. Mao harbored an ambition to shift the ideological center of world communism from the USSR to China and, without consulting Moscow, he initiated and supported communist movements throughout Asia. He also spoke out about the merits of China's agricultural peasant-based model of communist revolution versus Russia's industrial proletariat movement. Stalin reacted angrily, banning from the Soviet Union Mao's writings on this subject. In response, Mao pressed his approach even harder, asserting that it was the only "correct" path to communist revolution. The outbreak of the Korean War suspended incipient hostilities between the Soviets and the Chinese, once again giving America and the West the impression of complete ideological accord. Indeed, China did fall into line with the Soviets under Stalin as well as his successor, Nikita Khrushchev. In return, during the mid 1950s, Khrushchev offered China a variety of technical and financial support. Nevertheless, Mao and the Soviet leader drifted apart as Khrushchev began to talk about "peaceful coexistence" with the West. He had become fearful of the "Great Leap Forward," Mao's sweeping plan for rapidly transforming China from a primarily agricultural economy to an industrial one. He saw the Great Leap Forward as a maneuver to come into direct competition with the USSR as the ideological—and economic—center of world communism. Sensing that a rupture between his nation and China was in the offing, Khrushchev, unwilling to isolate the USSR, pursued the peaceful coexistence initiative. In 1959, he went so far as to host a summit with President

1956年到1967年全国农业发展纲要(草案

Details of a 1956 poster that promotes Chairman Mao's "10-year plan for the development of agriculture in China." His program of forced collectivization was an economic and human catastrophe of epic proportions.

Eisenhower in an earnest effort to reduce Cold War tensions. At the same time, he took back the Soviet offer to assist China to develop nuclear weapons, and, in 1962, when war broke out between China and India, the Soviet premier not only declined to support China but also made an effort to maintain civil, if not friendly, relations with China's rival.

Mao seemed not to appreciate that Khrushchev was in earnest about reducing the chances of thermonuclear war. All he saw was that the Soviets were betraying Marxism by these overtures to the capitalist West. Yet, as always, Mao did not act primarily from ideological motives, but from an urge to preserve himself in power. Even before the end of the 1950s, it was clear that the Great Leap Forward had been a complete disaster. Not only had it had failed to transform China into an industrial giant, but also the forced collectivization of Chinese agriculture, coupled with years of drought, had resulted in the starvation of millions. Mao's Communist Party rivals, Liu Shaoqi and Deng Xiaoping, prepared to seize on the catastrophe to force Mao to step down as chairman of the Communist Party. Mao recognized a plot in the making, and he saw a break with the Soviets as an opportunity to paint his rivals as Soviet agents. This, he believed, would rally the Chinese people behind him.

At first, instead of attacking one another directly, Mao criticized Yugoslavia's Tito, whom he regarded somewhat inaccurately as Khrushchev's boon ally, and Khrushchev, in turn, denounced Enver Hoxha, the leader of Albania, who had aligned his nation with China rather than the Soviets. Next, in June 1960, speaking at the congress of the Romanian Communist Party, Khrushchev publicly denounced Mao Zedong as "a nationalist, an adventurist, and a deviationist." China's Peng Zhen, who was also attending the congress, responded by condemning Khrushchev as "patriarchal, arbitrary, and tyrannical."

REALITY CHECK

A Motive for Mao

Mao Zedong typically moved in mysterious ways—or at least they seemed mysterious, because, while he preached a Marxist ideological purity, he acted in ways Marx would neither have approved nor understood. At the center of his desire to shift the center of world Marxism from the Soviet Union to China was a deep desire to reverse the long-standing European domination over Asia by asserting Asian dominance through translating Marxism from a European to an Asiatic form. What this meant was that, in ostensible furtherance of a political philosophy that aimed at annihilating nationalism, Mao worked toward a kind of super nationalism, the exultation of Asia over Europe.

President Eisenhower hosts Soviet premier Nikita Khrushchev at a 1959 White House state dinner. Nina Kukharchuk Khrushchev (the premier's wife) stands at left, beside Mamie Eisenhower. The president's white tie and tails make a capitalist contrast to the premier's plain business suit.

Khrushchev subsequently followed up this spasm of name-calling by reading out an eighty-page letter addressed to the congress, denouncing China itself.

From this point on, the clashes became chronic. In December 1961, the Soviet Union severed diplomatic relations with Albania, and in 1962, following the Cuban Missile Crisis (see Chapter 15), Mao unleashed a tirade against Khrushchev for "backing down" in the confrontation between the Soviet Union and the United States, accusing the Soviet premier of "capitulationism." Khrushchev responded candidly that Mao Zedong clung to policies that would inevitably lead to a nuclear war. By the end of 1963, the Soviet Union and the People's Republic of China had stopped communicating altogether and, the following year, Mao declared that the Soviet Union had clearly undergone a counterrevolution. The Chinese Communist Party severed all ties to the Communist Party of the Soviet and withdrew from the Warsaw Pact, the key military alliance of communist states.

THE CULTURAL REVOLUTION

THERE WAS WORSE TO COME. On May 16, 1966, Chairman Mao announced a campaign to purge elements of the "liberal bourgeoisie" from Chinese life and to mobilize in their place the "thoughts and actions" of China's youth, who had been organized nationwide into paramilitary units known as the Red Guards. The result was a violent upheaval, as Red Guards ravaged countryside and city alike, bringing China to the brink of civil war. Mao used the chaos of the Cultural Revolution to regain his grip on absolute power after the catastrophe of the Great Leap Forward. Once he felt firmly in control again, in 1969, he proclaimed the Cultural Revolution ended. By this time, China was isolated not only from the Soviet Union but also from much of the rest of the world. A year before Mao proclaimed the end of the Cultural Revolution, the Soviets deployed massive military forces along the Chinese border, and many in the West believed outright war between the two powers was imminent. Armed clashes did

In the Cultural Revolution of the 1960s, Mao turned the Red Guards on the nation in a deliberate effort to create violent chaos from which he hoped to emerge with a renewed grip on the government. The poster, from Canton, 1967, depicts Red Guard youths discarding the "four old traditions," religion, literature, capitalism, and imperialism.

break out, but a major war did not erupt, and the two countries restored minimal diplomatic relations. But, from this point forward, China and the Soviet Union were rivals, not allies.

PRELUDE TO A THAW

IN THE END, MAO ZEDONG AND A SUCCESSION OF SOVIET LEADERS did what the United States and its Western allies could not do and could probably never have done. They destroyed any prospect of a true "Soviet bloc" or "world communism." For both the Soviets and the Chinese, it was simultaneously an act of self-preservation and self-destruction. In order to preserve themselves from one another, the two nations had to break with one another, and that, in turn, drove both toward the West—a sacrifice of Marxist ideological union to national self-interest. As we will see in Part Six, this act of self-destruction and self-preservation facilitated U.S.-Soviet "détente" and U.S.-Chinese "normalization" during the 1970s, thereby beginning the great thaw that would finally end the Cold War.

TAKEAWAY

China—World Communism Rises, Then Begins to Fall

Many in the United States agonized over the "loss" of China to communism, believing that, united, China and the Soviet Union could well conquer the world with the ideology of Karl Marx. Panic at all levels of American government and society ushered in the period of repression known as the "red scare" or the "McCarthy era," which presented a greater danger to democracy than any threat posed by either the China or the Soviet Union. American leaders failed to recognize that the alliance between the world's two major communist powers was fatally flawed and that, given time, it would simply self-destruct. By the 1970s, China and the USSR had gone their separate ways—yet both were seeking better relations with the United States and the rest of the democratic West.

CHAPTER 10

Berlin Held Hostage

The Triumphant Airlift

THE GREAT PARADOX OF WORLD WAR II was that, for all its horror, many who lived through it—in the United States and even in Great Britain and France—looked back on it as "the good war," in which sacrifice gave intense meaning to life. The Cold War engendered no such feelings. Whereas World War II had meant sacrifice, action, and achievement, the Cold War brought only anxiety, dread, and frustration. Yet it did resemble World War II in one respect. It was global in scope.

National attention was riveted on Europe throughout most of the postwar 1940s. Then China exploded. But even as the forces of Mao Zedong overwhelmed those of Chiang Kai-shek, a new crisis, with the highest possible stakes, came to Europe.

The Plan That Would Not Die

PRESIDENT HARRY TRUMAN REJECTED THE MORGENTHAU PLAN, as explained in Chapter 6, which would have deindustrialized Germany, transforming it into an agricultural nation presumably incapable of ever again gearing up for war. Yet, at Potsdam during July 17 to August 2, 1945, the president did not explicitly renounce the Morgenthau Plan, and the Soviets therefore assumed that Germany would be "pastoralized." As late as 1946,

Soviet foreign minister Vyacheslav Molotov was still laboring under this misapprehension. He explained to his American counterpart, Secretary of State James F. Byrnes, that the USSR did want Germany put back together into a single country, but in the harmless form the Morgenthau Plan had specified and only after the Soviet Union had received the dismantled industrial machinery the plan promised as part of the war reparations Germany owed the Soviets.

Initially, the Truman administration did nothing either to stop the dismantling of German industrial plants or to inform the Soviets (or, for that matter, the British and French) that the Morgenthau Plan would not be carried through to completion. But it soon became clear that the stagnation of Germany's industrial economy was dragging down the economy of all Europe, and Truman's economic adviser William L. Clayton warned that millions of Germans were "slowly starving" in the absence of economic relief (see Chapter 6). Herbert Hoover, the former president popularly (and unjustly) blamed for the Great Depression, had served ably after World War I as head of American relief efforts. President Truman now sent him to Germany, and on March 18, 1947, Hoover reported acidly that the only way of reducing the nation to a "pastoral state" was to "exterminate or move 25,000,000 people out of it." That was all Truman needed to hear. Tearing down all vestiges of the Morgenthau Plan, he approved the sweeping relief and economic recovery program embodied in the Marshall Plan.

Every national leader committed to the stability of Europe as well as to basic humanity embraced the Marshall Plan. Joseph Stalin was committed to neither.

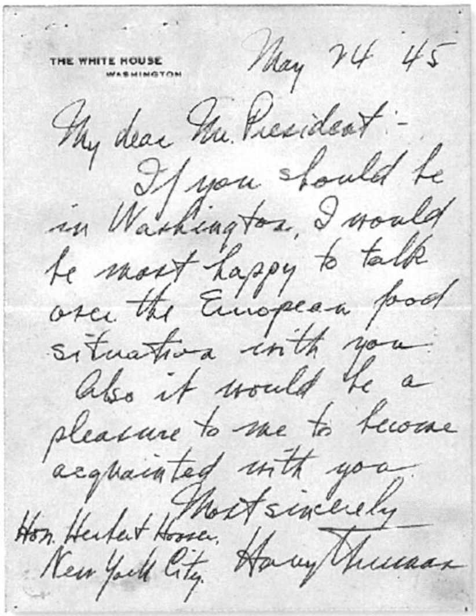
THE WHITE HOUSE
WASHINGTON

May 24 45

My dear Mr. President:-

If you should be in Washington, I would be most happy to talk over the European food situation with you. Also it would be a pleasure to me to become acquainted with you.

Most sincerely
Harry Truman

Hon. Herbert Hoover
New York City.

Before he was elected president of the United States in 1928, Herbert Hoover had directed massive relief efforts during and after World War I. On May 24, 1945, with characteristic informality, President Truman dashed off a note seeking the former president's advice on the humanitarian crisis in postwar Europe.

REALITY CHECK
What's the Deal?

American leaders criticized the Soviets for being uncooperative, duplicitous, and aggressive with regard to German reconstruction, but the Truman administration also failed to operate openly. The president allowed the Soviets to believe that the Morgenthau Plan was in force, and did nothing to countermand the occupation directive issued by the U.S. Joint Chiefs of Staff (JCS 1067), which embodied the Morgenthau goals as if the plan were still the blueprint for Germany. The directive specified that no steps were to be taken "to maintain or strengthen the German economy," and, in fact, many of the undamaged factories in the U.S. zone of control were dismantled, and officials began sending salvageable equipment to the Soviet Union. France also wanted Germany pastoralized, but ultimately accepted its industrial reconstruction as part of the Marshall Plan. The British government was never in favor of the Morgenthau Plan, believing, as Truman did, that a fully industrialized Germany was essential to the economic recovery of Europe.

Truman welcomes Herbert Hoover to the White House on May 28, 1945, where they discussed the problem of feeding the liberated peoples of Europe.

On the contrary, social and political instability coupled with human suffering were ideal conditions to facilitate the continued expansion of Soviet influence in Europe. Stalin also believed that the United States was less interested in humanitarian relief than in bribing the nations of Europe into a pro-U.S. and anti-Soviet alignment. Finally, Stalin also had a more urgent concern. To revive Germany as a fully industrialized economy would deprive him of the weak, neutral buffer state he hoped to place between the Soviet Union (including its Eastern European satellites) and the West. The perceived need for such a buffer flowed from a combination of bitter experience and personal paranoia. The Soviet Union had just lived through a catastrophic invasion and Stalin wanted to fashion a Europe in which that could never take place again. Stalin therefore barred any Soviet satellite nation—that is, any member of the Kremlin-controlled organization of international communism, the Cominform—from participating in the Marshall Plan.

"You are blind like young kittens; what will happen without me? The country will perish because you do not know how to recognize enemies."

Joseph Stalin to his entourage, as reported by Nikita Khrushchev in a speech to the 20th Party Congress, February 25, 1956

AT GERMANY'S THROAT

THE SUDDEN SHIFT IN U.S. POLICY TOWARD GERMANY drove a wedge between the Americans and the Soviets. Negotiations for the reunification of the nation fell apart, and in 1946, the Soviets cut off shipment of farm goods from the Russian zone to the western zones. The United States responded by halting delivery of industrial machinery from dismantled German factories. In retaliation, the Soviets commenced a propaganda blitz against the Marshall Plan and deliberately delayed the nuts-and-bolts inter-zone administrative operations necessary to keep Germany running.

If Stalin intended all this as a glimpse of the kind of stranglehold he could apply to Germany, the Truman administration was not intimidated. Perhaps it should have been. Remember that Berlin, the German capital, lay deep within the Soviet zone of occupation yet was itself divided into four zones among the French, British, Americans, and the Soviets. The western zones constituted an enclave surrounded by Soviet-controlled territory.

The Americans Make the Break

The Cold War has often been portrayed as a conflict between the generally cooperative and accommodating Western democracies, led by the United States, and a recalcitrant, combative Soviet Union. In the case of Germany, however, it was the United States that precipitated the final break-up of the wartime alliance between West and East. With reunification talks stalled, the Truman abandoned the idea of reunifying Germany in collaboration with the Soviet Union and decided instead unilaterally to begin openly stimulating industrial recovery in the Western-controlled portion of the nation. After Britain signed on to the program, the area under development was dubbed the "Bizone." When France joined, it was renamed the "Trizone." All three powers met in London beginning in February 1948 and on March 7 issued a stunning announcement—their intention to foster the unification of the three western zones into a sovereign nation under a U.S.-led economic recovery program.

Germany—under divided postwar occupation.

The Crisis Escalates

The Allied Control Council (ACC), the four-power administrative body for occupied Germany, had established a twenty-mile-wide air corridor from the western zones of Germany through the air space of the Soviet zone to Berlin. The corridor was to be open at all times to British and American aircraft. Additionally, the ACC calculated the volume of rail and highway traffic through the Soviet zone necessary to supply the western zones of Berlin. The Soviets agreed to allow unimpeded passage of this traffic.

On March 31, 1948, three weeks after the Western allies had announced their intention to create a West Germany, Soviet authorities began interfering with surface transport in and out of Berlin.

Red Army guards and other officials man the Soviet autobahn checkpoint on the East-West border at Helmstedt.

Special identification papers were required for travelers, and special permits for freight. All were subject to inspection at innumerable Soviet control points. At first, the restrictions were merely harassing, but, on April 3, they were tightened in response to a blunt Soviet order: "Free and unrestricted use of the established corridors," the directive said, would no longer be permitted to the United States.

Within a matter of weeks, the policy of control became a frank blockade. Surface traffic was greatly diminished, and military passenger traffic halted entirely. Modest supplies of food and other essential materials were transported by the only remaining avenue, the air corridor, using American as well as British aircraft and crews.

In defiance of the tightening blockade, the British, French, and Americans on June 7, 1948, reaffirmed their intention to create West Germany, which would include West Berlin. A few days later, on June 18, General Lucius Clay, military governor for the U.S. zone, informed the Soviet delegate to the ACC that the three Western powers would, on June 20, introduce currency reform throughout the western zones, but would refrain from applying the reform to the western sectors of Berlin. Presumably interpreting this as the first formal step toward actually establishing West Germany, the Soviets instantly responded by blockading all inter-zonal passenger traffic and all incoming traffic to Berlin. Two days later, the Soviets announced that *they* would carry out currency reform for the Soviet zone and Greater Berlin. Their plan was to make the Soviet-authorized currency the only currency for *all* of Berlin. Now it was the Americans' turn to protest what was clearly an attempt to undermine Western authority in the western sectors of Berlin. Still, the Americans suggested a compromise—a unique currency for all of Berlin, different from either the Western currency or the Soviet currency. When the Soviets rejected this, General Clay replied that the Western allies would begin the introduction into Berlin of the reformed currency of the western zones. On June 24, Soviet authorities suspended traffic on the Berlin-Helmstedt railway and stopped all barge traffic into and out of Berlin. West Berlin was now cut off from the rest of the world, save for what passed in and out by air.

Defiance—and Restraint

The Soviets downplayed the meaning of the blockade—explaining that it was intended to protect the economy of the eastern zone—but they knew very well that a blockade was an act of war. While denying hostile intention, the Soviets dared the United States to start World War III, confident that it was a dare from which America would retreat.

REALITY CHECK

Berlin: Stalin Plays His Hand

It is one thing for schoolyard boys to dare one another during recess, but superpower leader Stalin was daring the president of the world's only other superpower, a man whose finger was on the nuclear trigger. We can only surmise that Stalin felt secure in doing this because he had witnessed how the Western democracies had repeatedly backed down during the late 1930s when Hitler confronted them with the threat of war. He assumed they would do so again. Based on precedent, it was not an unreasonable assumption. But Harry Truman was not Neville Chamberlain. Stalin understood recent history, but he badly misunderstood the present.

This Soviet propaganda poster accuses the Western allies, the United States and Britain, of spoiling for war. "For a stable peace!" the caption shouts. "Against those who would ignite a new war." Russian men and women march forward as quaking caricatures of Winston Churchill and Uncle Sam—money bag in hand—look on.

The departments of State and Defense outlined three possible U.S. policies in Berlin at this point. The United States could withdraw from the city at some specified time, the United States could remain in Berlin at any and all costs, or the United States could stand firm, postponing a decision on withdrawal until it became absolutely necessary to make one. President Truman rejected the first alternative out of hand. Withdrawal would undercut what the press had dubbed the Truman Doctrine, the policy of acting to contain Soviet aggression wherever and whenever it occurred. To back down from Stalin was akin to British prime minister Neville Chamberlain's 1938 attempt to appease Adolf Hitler. By demonstrating an unwillingness to resist aggression, appeasement, instead of averting war, ensured its outbreak. Truman did not intend to repeat Chamberlain's tragic mistake.

Nor, however, was he prepared to stay in Berlin at the cost of a new world war, but he reasoned that the ultimate decision did not have to be made at the moment. The third alternative, stand firm and postpone any ultimate decision, was an acceptable compromise between capitulation and a declaration of World War III.

> "If we mean that we are to hold Europe against communism, we must not budge. I believe the future of democracy requires us to stay here until forced out."
>
> *Lieutenant General Lucius D. Clay, U.S. military governor of Germany, on the Berlin crisis, June 24, 1948*

While standing firm in Berlin, the United States would exploit the propaganda advantage of the position in which the Soviet Union had put the city. Holding a hostage, nobody looks like a hero. While standing firm, the United States would keep the situation in Berlin before the eyes of the world.

Yet more than propaganda and a piece of territory were at stake. The *people* of West Berlin needed food and, come winter, they would need both food and fuel. Some supplies were already being airlifted into the city, and, to Truman as well as General Clay, the notion of a massive airlift of supplies to the besieged city seemed to be the only way to "stand firm" without provoking all-out war.

General Hoyt Vandenberg, chief of staff of the newly independent United States Air Force, was not so sure. With the emphasis on the air force as *the* strategic arm of the U.S. military, Vandenberg felt a responsibility to be prepared to respond to a crisis anywhere in the world. He pointed out that a massive airlift would require the transfer of air force resources from other dangerous places and thus leave the United States and its allies vulnerable.

West Berliners anxiously watch a U.S. Air Force C-54 cargo transport come in for a landing at Tempelhof Airport in 1948, the height of the Berlin Airlift.

Truman did not begin talking immediately after Vandenberg stopped. After what must have seemed an interminable silence, he calmly asked the general "if he would prefer to have us attempt to supply Berlin by ground convoy. Then, if the Russians resisted that effort and plunged the world into war, would not the Air Force have to contribute its share to the defense of the nation?"

It was a question, Truman recalled in a memoir, that he had already answered for himself: "The airlift involved less risks than armed road convoys. Therefore, I directed the Air Force to furnish the fullest support possible to the problem of supplying Berlin."

"I don't think he should have tucked tail and gone to the air."

Senator Strom Thurmond (Rep., S.C.) on Truman's choice of an airlift instead of war, recorded in a 1984 BBC interview

Operation Vittles

At least one senior air force commander shared absolutely none of Vandenberg's doubts. On June 25, 1948, General Clay telephoned Lieutenant General Curtis E. LeMay, at the time commanding United States Air Forces-Europe (USAFE).

"Curt," Clay asked, "can you transport coal by air?"

"Sir, the Air Force can deliver anything."

DETAILS, DETAILS

Gooney Bird

Dwight D. Eisenhower observed that, without the bazooka, the Jeep, the atom bomb, *and* the C-47 Skytrain, the Allies could not have won World War II. The military version of the Douglas DC-3, a spectacularly successful commercial airliner first flown in 1935, more than ten thousand C-47s were built for the U.S. Army Air Corps and its successor, the U.S. Army Air Forces. Affectionately dubbed "Gooney Bird" by aircrews, the C-47 was used throughout World War II to carry personnel and cargo, to tow gliders, and to drop paratroops. The twin-engine aircraft flew at 230 miles per hour and could carry 10,000 pounds. It was modified during the Vietnam War as the AC-47 ground-attack gunship. The air force retired its last C-47 in 1975, but a surprising number of these veterans are still flown commercially today.

On the very next day, LeMay began collecting virtually the entire air force inventory of transport aircraft worldwide. He assigned Brigadier General Joseph Smith, commander of the Wiesbaden Military Post, as task force commander of what Clay had christened Operation Vittles and the world would call the Berlin Airlift.

The first thirty-two C-47 Skytrains took off for Berlin on June 26, carrying a total of eighty tons of cargo that included milk, flour, and vital medicines. Two days later, the Royal Air Force (RAF) made its first flight in the operation. It was anticipated that the airlift would have to be sustained no more than three weeks, and General Smith meant to have 65 percent of available aircraft in the air every day, regardless of the weather. The schedule allowed barely enough time for ground crews to fuel, let alone fully service the aircraft, virtually all of which were veterans of hard service during World War II. No matter; Smith ordered each plane to make three round trips to Berlin daily.

He established what he called a "block system," which grouped together into a kind of convoy system aircraft capable of the same cruising speeds. This would make air traffic control—in itself a major operation—and ground traffic control and cargo handling more efficient. Smith established an Air Traffic Control Center at Frankfurt am Main exclusively dedicated to scheduling and coordinating the flights—and keeping the aircraft from running into each other.

Days became weeks. With no sign of either side giving in, it was apparent that Operation Vittles would last much longer than three weeks; therefore, on July 23, 1948, it became the responsibility of the Military Air Transport Service (MATS), and Major General William H. Tunner replaced Smith as commander. He focused on transforming the airlift into a long-term yet unremittingly intensive operation. This meant orchestrating flight and ground operations according to what he described as a "steady rhythm, constant as the jungle drums." Tunner

Airlift cargo included fresh milk—delivered in glass bottles, no less.

calculated that there were 1,440 minutes in a day and set as his target the landing of an aircraft every minute. He achieved, on average, one landing every three minutes.

Brigadier General William H. Tunner, U.S. Air Force, directed the main phase of the Berlin Airlift, building it into a logistical machine of unprecedented efficiency.

Tunner studied every step of the airlift process, always looking for ways to maximize efficiency. He issued orders forbidding any air-crew member from leaving the site of his airplane at Tempelhof and Gatow airports. Each plane that touched down was met on the field by an operations officer and a weather officer, who drove up in separate jeeps to brief the pilot while another jeep rolled up with hot coffee, hot dogs, and doughnuts. Tunner hired industrial time-motion experts to analyze loading and unloading procedures with the objective of minimizing the number of steps and even movements. Soon, Tunner had twelve men loading ten tons of bagged coal into a C-54 Skymaster in six minutes flat. Unloading crews reduced what had been a seventeen-minute process to just five. Refueling crews cut refueling times from thirty-three minutes to eight. At the start of Operation Vittles, aircraft turnaround time—including unloading, loading, refueling, and maintenance check—had been an extraordinary sixty minutes. Tunner cut it to a phenomenal thirty.

An air force ground crew services the port engine of a venerable C-47 "Gooney Bird."

DETAILS, DETAILS
Skymaster

The four-engine C-54 was originally developed in the late 1930s as a commercial air transport, the DC-4, an early workhorse of the airline industry. The aircraft began production in 1941, and the U.S. Army Air Forces commandeered the entire first run off the Douglas assembly line. By the end of the war, the service had bought 1,163 C-54s.

During World War II, the long range of the C-54 made it the primary transoceanic airlifter. C-54s made 79,642 crossings of the North Atlantic with the loss of only three aircraft. A modified C-54, designated VC-54C and nicknamed the Sacred Cow, was the first airplane ever assigned to presidential airlift—the precursor of Air Force One. It carried President Franklin D. Roosevelt to the Yalta Conference in the Crimea.

With a top speed of 265 miles per hour, the C-54 had almost three times the payload capacity of the C-47. The aircraft remained in U.S. Air Force service until 1972.

The Berlin Airlift was the equivalent of a conveyor belt, continuous, unceasing. Four C-47s line up for loading at Tempelhof Airport in August 1948.

Triumph

Flying so many missions so close together day and night and in every kind of weather was every bit as hazardous as flying in combat. Aircrews, ground crews, cargo handlers, air traffic controllers, and ground controllers were pushed to the margins of endurance. Yet accidents were few, and Berliners neither starved nor froze. The machinelike precision of the Berlin airlift was sustained not for the projected three weeks, but for nearly a year. In the end, it was Soviet endurance that wore out. On May 12, 1949, the Soviets lifted the blockade. The airlift continued at a reduced volume for nearly five more months to make up the shortfall of food and fuel that had been created by the blockade. The last flight was completed on September 30, 1949.

A Tale of Two Countries

The Berlin Airlift was a triumph of containment—a battle won without bullets, a gallant people sustained, a propaganda harvest for the West, a humiliation for the Soviets, and a world brought back from the brink of a nuclear world war.

On May 24, 1949, the Federal Republic of Germany—familiarly known as West Germany—was established, including "West Berlin" deep in Soviet-controlled territory. The Soviets protested that a sovereign enclave within territory under their control was illegal, and on October 7, 1949, retaliated by establishing the German Democratic Republic: East Germany.

Now West Berlin was a fragment of a democratic country entirely surrounded by a hostile foreign country. In essence, the city was again a hostage, but the ransom was now much higher. West Berlin was no longer simply a Soviet bargaining chip, it was a captive of the Cold War itself. On the one hand, it was a democratic island in a red sea. Its presence served notice on the Soviets and their allies that the nations of the West had a claim on their territory. Unlike a politically divided Germany that was correspondingly divided geographically, the existence of the West Berlin enclave created an aberrant situation that could not be resolved until Germany was reunified. If West Berlin was a foot in the Soviet front door and therefore an American political asset, it was also an American military liability. It had to be defended if attacked, and such a defense meant invading East German territory, which the Soviets were bound to defend. West Berlin had become the tripwire that could detonate World War III. As we will see in Chapter 15, it figured in virtually every strategic decision the United States made during the Cold War.

NUMBERS

Frequent Fliers

U.S. Air Force (USAF) aircrews made 189,963 flights over Soviet-held territory into West Berlin during the whole of Operation Vittles. Royal Air Force (RAF) personnel made 87,606. USAF aircraft transported 1,783,572.7 tons of food, coal, and other cargo, and the RAF carried an additional 541,936.9 tons. American military transports also brought in 25,263 passengers and flew out 37,486. RAF transports handled even more, flying 34,815 passengers into Berlin and 164,906 out.

"Berlin is the testicles of the West. . . . Every time I want to make the West scream, I squeeze on Berlin."

Nikita Khrushchev, November 1958

If West Berlin was democracy's claim on the territory behind the "iron curtain," the divided city served the people of East Germany as a window on the West—and the United States was eager to keep this window open, wide. Although West Germany had been founded on May 23, 1949, it would not be declared "fully sovereign" until May 5, 1955. In the meantime, it remained divided into three zones of control. On November 14, 1953, the Western powers waived the *Interzonenpass*, the official passport that, since 1946, had been required to travel from one sector of Germany to another. After the West suspended the *Interzonenpass*, the Soviets made a

To reduce wear and tear on the aircraft continuously flown in the Berlin Airlift, General Tunner and his pilots developed the "Tempelhof landing," which USAF pilots practiced at such fields as Great Falls Air Force Base, Montana. The object was to come in at a very steep angle, touching down with the nose up until engine speed was reduced, so that the wings would serve as natural airbrakes, reducing the need to apply—and wear down—the plane's wheel brakes. Pictured here is a four-engine C-54 Skymaster, the largest aircraft used in the lift.

Before the border was closed, East Berlin refugees regularly flooded West Berlin, whose police are shown here distributing food to the newcomers in February 1953.

show of following suit. But although the *Interzonenpass* was no longer required, it was still necessary to secure special permission to travel to the West, the border between East and West having been closed by the East German government on May 26, 1952. To enforce the closure, a no-man's land was established behind the actual border and guard towers were erected at intervals. Anyone venturing into this frontier zone risked being shot. Yet many East Germans took the risk. Some wanted only to be reunited with family members who happened to live in the West, but more, far more, simply wanted to live under a democratic regime rather than a communist government. They could see, quite plainly, that the Western allies were financing a massive program of rebuilding, whereas recovery efforts in the Soviet-controlled East were sluggish. People lived much better and more comfortable lives in the West.

Remarkably, after closing and fortifying the border, the East German administration left one gaping corridor into the West. It was still easy to cross from East Berlin into West Berlin. All that was necessary was to purchase a ticket to ride the S-Bahn (suburban train) or the U-Bahn (subway), board at an East Berlin station, and get off at a station in West Berlin. This "Berlin gap" was not officially closed until December 11, 1957, when anyone who left East Germany without permission was subject to arrest, prosecution, and up to three years' imprisonment. Still, there were no physical barriers to prevent passage. That oversight was remedied on August 13, 1961, when, along the "sectorial border" separating East and West Berlin, barriers were erected at all street crossings. The next day, the majestic Brandenburg Gate, now marking the division between East and West Berlin at Unter den Linden—historically the city's principal boulevard—was closed. East German authorities began building what would become known across the globe as the Berlin Wall—to which we will return in Chapter 15.

Soviet and East German authorities close the border between East and West Berlin in 1961. The central Berlin landmark—the Brandenburg Gate—became the symbol of the divided city.

NEW ALLIANCES

FROM THE WESTERN POINT OF VIEW THE BERLIN CRISIS had been successfully resolved, but it signaled to the democracies that only a credible military response would discourage the Soviets from further acts of aggression in Europe. On March 17, 1948, Belgium, the Netherlands, Luxembourg, France, and the United Kingdom signed the Treaty of Brussels, a mutual defense agreement that spurred the creation of the Western European Union defense organization in September. The member nations did not believe that even their pooled military resources would be sufficient to counter aggression by the Soviet military and therefore invited the United States to participate in talks aimed at creating a military alliance that would include America. The result was the North Atlantic Treaty, signed in Washington, D.C. on April 4, 1949, and creating the North Atlantic Treaty Organization (NATO), whose charter members were the five Treaty of Brussels signatories in addition to the United States, Canada, Portugal, Italy, Norway, Denmark, and Iceland. Early in 1952, Greece and Turkey signed onto the alliance.

President Truman signs the North Atlantic Treaty, which created NATO on July 25, 1949.

"Do you know what the basis of our policy is? It is fear. Fear of you, fear of your government, fear of your policy."

Belgian prime minister Paul-Henri Spaak, speaking of Stalin's Soviet Union in an address to the United Nations General Assembly, September 28, 1948

In effect, NATO formalized and strengthened the Truman Doctrine. The language of the treaty proclaimed agreement among the

> Parties of NATO . . . that an armed attack against one or more of them in Europe or North America shall be considered an attack against them all. Consequently they agree that, if such an armed attack occurs, each of them, in exercise of the right of individual or collective self-defense will

LINK

From Deterrent Force to Active Force

Throughout the entire Cold War period, Article 5 of the NATO charter—an attack on any member is considered an attack on all members—was never invoked. But it was invoked, for the first time in the organization's history, after the September 11, 2001, terrorist attacks on New York and Washington. NATO undertook two major military operations, Operation Eagle Assist and Operation Active Endeavour, intended to interdict the movement of terrorists or weapons of mass destruction. On February 10, 2003, however, France and Belgium vetoed so-called silent approval of certain operations in Turkey related to the impending Iraq War. This notwithstanding, members approved, on April 16, 2003, NATO command of the International Security Assistance Force sent to combat terrorist insurgents in Afghanistan. This was the first time NATO assumed responsibility for a mission outside the North Atlantic region.

U.S. Army soldiers from Delta Company, 1st Battalion, 508th Parachute Infantry Regiment, provide security during a meeting with the district subgovernor in Sabara, Afghanistan, March 6, 2007. The American military operates in Afghanistan as part of a NATO force—the first time NATO has ever been employed outside of Europe.

assist the Party or Parties being attacked, individually and in concert with the other Parties, with such action as it deems necessary, including the use of armed force, to restore and maintain the security of the North Atlantic area.

The language of the treaty broadly reflected the Truman administration's containment policy in that it included a military response to aggression, but did not require one. "Such action" as any signatory "deems necessary" might range from economic boycott and other nonmilitary sanctions through various levels of military response. Moreover, although all of the members of NATO bound themselves to render assistance in the event of aggression against any member, each was absolutely free to determine just what kind of assistance was appropriate. In this way, the NATO agreement sought to create a unified defense against Soviet aggression without repeating the tragic mistake of the complex of binding military treaties that magnified a local dispute in the Balkans into World War I.

As the organization was originally conceived, member nations contributed only a modest standing military force to NATO, but in a conference convened in Lisbon, Portugal, in 1952, it was decided to create a major land force consisting of ninety-six divisions. Soon realizing that the cost of maintaining such a force would be prohibitive, in 1953 the requirement was reduced to thirty-five divisions. Much as the U.S. military establishment had done, NATO strategists decided to rely more heavily on nuclear weapons. This was a significant and perhaps ominous shift in NATO thinking. Originally, any conflict with the Soviets was envisioned as a conventional land war. Now, largely as a cost-control measure, the nuclear deterrent was emphasized. This policy decision further stimulated accelerated stockpiling of the nuclear arsenal, and because the weapons would be based in Europe rather than across the Atlantic in the United States, they could be carried by cheaper, more reliable, and more numerous intermediate range ballistic missiles (IRBMs) instead of the costly and more complex intercontinental ballistic missiles (ICBMs) the Soviets were obliged to rely on.

NUMBERS

How Big Is Big?

By the early 1950s, an army division varied in strength from about 8,500 men (in the case of an airborne division) to nearly 15,000 (for an infantry division). At the height of deployment in World War II, the United States Army had 89 active divisions—a total of about 8.5 million men. The force of 96 divisions contemplated for NATO's Long-Term Defense Plan would have been a very big force.

The Soviet Union observed the development and expansion of NATO with anxiety. In 1954, Premier Khrushchev suggested that the Soviet Union be granted membership in the organization—the better, he said, to preserve the peace in Europe. The suggestion was about as welcome to the NATO countries as the gift of a Trojan horse, and the members unanimously rejected it.

From Soviet Bloc to Warsaw Pact

In a move as momentous as NATO's shift from a conventional to a nuclear strategy, West Germany was admitted into the alliance on May 9, 1955. This meant rearming Germany, which had been without a standing army since the end of World War II. As was the case with Japan, rearmament required amending the postwar German constitution (called the "Basic Law"), which barred the creation of a military. France initially objected to German rearmament, but, in 1954, after the French National Assembly rejected a proposal for a pooled European military establishment called the European Defense Community, French legislators realized that they and their allies needed the military manpower of Germany and therefore agreed to rearmament and NATO membership.

While West Germany established the Bundeswehr, the Soviet Union authorized East Germany to create a military force of its own, the Nationale Volksarmee (NVA), although Soviet forces continued to be deployed in the country as well. More significant was the creation of the Warsaw Pact on May 14, 1955.

The Warsaw Pact created a joint military command, the Unified Command of Pact Armed Forces, which exercised control over all troops contributed by the member states, the Soviet Union, Hungary, Czechoslovakia, Poland, Bulgaria, Romania, Albania, and East Germany. The First Deputy Minister of Defense of the USSR was permanently designated as the supreme commander of the Unified Command, which insured that all military aspects of the Warsaw Pact would always be tightly controlled by the Soviet Union. In addition to its military component, the Warsaw Pact included a Soviet-dominated Political Consultative Committee, which exercised authority over the nonmilitary activities of member nations. Thus the pact allowed the Soviet Union to tighten its control of the Soviet-aligned nations.

The creation of NATO and the Warsaw Pact hardened the hostile division of sides in the Cold War. Until the Soviet Union entered the final phases of dissolution in 1990, these two organizations were the heavily armed camps sullenly facing off against one another and staking out all Europe as a potential battlefield.

DETAILS, DETAILS

NATO's Core

Financed and equipped largely by the United States, the Bundeswehr (as the new West German military was called) rapidly became the core of NATO's conventional—nonnuclear—forces. At its Cold War peak, the Bundeswehr consisted of nearly a half-million soldiers, airmen, and sailors in addition to a support staff of about 170,000 civilians. The army component of the Bundeswehr had a dozen divisions, the air force flew the most modern U.S.-made tactical aircraft, and the navy operated mainly to serve as a check on the Soviet surface fleet. Germany did not—and does not—possess nuclear weapons.

THE IDEA GOES GLOBAL

ALTHOUGH NATO CAPTURED THE LIMELIGHT, the United States simultaneously spearheaded creation of a NATO counterpart for Southeast Asia, the Southeast Asia Treaty Organization (SEATO), which was established by the Southeast Asia Collective Defense Treaty (Manila Pact), signed on September 8, 1954, by France, Great Britain, the United States, Australia, Thailand, the Philippines, and New Zealand. The SEATO nations contributed military forces to participate in joint training exercises, but the organization, in contrast to NATO, had neither a single joint command authority nor any permanent forces. Even more significantly, the underlying treaty did not proclaim that an attack on one member was to be considered an attack on all. Despite the fact that Pakistan, South Vietnam, and South Korea later joined SEATO, it was a fatally weak organization. Intended to contain communist aggression, SEATO failed both major tests put to it. France and the Philippines vetoed intervention early in the communist insurgencies in Cambodia, Laos, and Vietnam, and, later, when major SEATO intervention in the Vietnam War was again called for, France and Pakistan objected.

By the mid 1960s, it was clear that SEATO was little more than a phantom force. Pakistan withdrew in 1973 and France the following year. SEATO was officially dissolved on June 30, 1977. The Vietnam War and the conflicts in neighboring Cambodia and Laos associated with it are evidence that, in contrast to Europe, the Truman Doctrine failed to produce an effective deterrent in Asia, which consequently became the battlefield on which the major powers—the Soviet Union, the People's Republic of China, and the United States—fought "proxy wars," the hot conflicts of the Cold War era.

TAKEAWAY

The Democracies Take a Stand

The Soviet Union reacted to the creation of a democratic, capitalist West Germany by imposing a blockade of West Berlin, a West German enclave surrounded by the territory of East Germany. The United States and Great Britain responded with the epic year-long Berlin Airlift, an early Cold War victory for the West. As a result of the Berlin crisis, the Western democracies formed the North Atlantic Treaty Organization (NATO), a military alliance intended to deter and defend against any further Soviet aggression in Europe or North America. NATO's Asian counterpart, the Southeast Asia Treaty Organization (SEATO), was never effective in the containment of communism, but NATO became a fixture of the Cold War and continues to be active today.

The ministers of the Warsaw Pact convene in the conference room of the Council of Ministers Palace, Warsaw, Poland, in a 1965 meeting of the Political Committee.

CHAPTER 11

Spy Wars

In the Cold War's Shadows

SOVIET SOCIETY WAS VERY DIFFERENT FROM ITS COUNTERPART IN THE UNITED States, but as World War II segued into the Cold War, they had at least one trait in common. It was paranoia, and it pervaded every level of government, popular culture, and "ordinary" life. As a broken clock tells the right time at least twice a day, the suspicions of a paranoid can be accurate perceptions of reality—at least sometimes. During the Cold War, "sometimes" was pretty often.

The decision to betray one's country would seem momentous, even desperate; yet espionage in America on behalf of the Soviet Union was almost a casual occurrence during the closing years of World War II and the first years of the so-called peace that followed. Klaus Fuchs, the German-born British Manhattan Project physicist working in the United States (see Chapter 3), decided to give nuclear secrets to the Soviets because he believed it was wrong for the United States and Britain to withhold information from their ally. As a communist himself, Fuchs was sympathetic to the Soviet

REALITY CHECK

Espionage: Government and Grassroots

Today we think of spies as trained professionals, "secret agents" who swear oaths to their government. At the start of the Cold War, espionage in America was of two very different kinds: the professionals and the casual "grassroots" spies. In Britain and America, "professional" spies were often socially privileged dilettantes, for whom the OSS or CIA was something of an exclusive club. In the Soviet Union, spies were more carefully schooled, drawing on a long tradition of secret police forces dating back to the czars. But the *Americans* the Soviets recruited were neither country-club types nor secret agents, but left-leaning working stiffs (like Julius Rosenberg) or sympathetic diplomats and bureaucrats. Most of this chapter is devoted to the professionals and would-be professionals of institutionalized espionage. We'll meet the grassroots spies in Chapter 13.

society he idealized and, as a scientist, he believed that scientific advancement knew no national boundaries. Yet Fuchs was not a passionate Marxist, much less a Soviet patriot. Delivering to Stalin the secrets of the most destructive technology ever created by humankind just seemed to him the right thing to do. Fuchs's American contacts were similarly colorless. There was Los Alamos machinist David Greenglass, who—like many Americans during the Depression—was a casual communist, joining the Young Communist League as others might join the local Rotary Club (see "The Web Widens" in Chapter 3). Greenglass was recruited as a spy by his wife, Ruth, and her brother-in-law, Julius Rosenberg. These were certainly not sophisticated, trenchcoat-clad spooks, but ordinary people. Ruth Greenglass and her sister, Ethel Rosenberg, were Brooklyn housewives, and Julius Rosenberg an electrical engineer, who had enlisted in the U.S. Army Signal Corps before the war and owned a radio repair shop after it.

Paranoia? In America, spies lived just down the block, if not right next door.

This panel is from a story titled "The Sneak Attack" in the 1952 comic book Atomic War! *The message is as simple as the artwork: To trust the Russians means nuclear annihilation.*

Wild Bill Rides

The atomic secrets spy ring associated with the Manhattan Project was not uncovered until 1946, after it had done its damage, but communist spy paranoia had been triggered in America a year earlier when an Office of Strategic Services (OSS) agent discovered that *Amerasia*, a leftist magazine devoted to Asian affairs, had published an article about the rivalry between the British and Americans in Thailand. How could an obscure political journal with a microscopic circulation frighten anyone? The article, it turned out, quoted top-secret U.S. government documents, word for word and at length.

OSS agents followed up on the discovery of the article by breaking into the magazine's offices and found them "literally strewn with confidential government documents." Worst of all, *Amerasia*'s editor was a U.S. naval intelligence officer and one of his staff members was a State Department China expert. This was more than enough to ignite public fears that Washington was crawling with spies and traitors.

Americans were at least relieved that they had an organization sufficiently on its toes to break up the *Amerasia* spy ring. The OSS was new to the U.S. government. As Americans had historically opposed maintaining a large standing army, so they had resisted establishing a permanent federal intelligence agency. As a result, U.S. intelligence gathering was largely an improvised affair before World War II. The army, navy, and the Department of the Treasury each fielded its own independent intelligence and counterintelligence operations, which rarely communicated but often competed with one another. Following World War I, the State Department established its own cryptographic department, designated MI-8, but, in 1929, Secretary of State Henry Stimson shut it down, explaining that "gentlemen don't read each other's mail."

The revelations of whistleblower spy Elizabeth Bentley, shown here in 1948, helped trigger America's post-war red scare.

DETAILS, DETAILS

Red Tide

Even as the *Amerasia* affair played out, Elizabeth T. Bentley, vice president of a communist front called U.S. Service and Shipping, defected from the Communist Party USA and admitted to the FBI that she had been a Soviet spy. Turning informer, she exposed two Soviet espionage networks, involving more than eighty Americans, including twenty-seven employed by the U.S. government, among them Assistant Secretary of the Treasury Harry Dexter White and State Department diplomat Alger Hiss. As we will see in Chapter 13, Bentley's revelations, when they were made public in 1948, caused a national sensation, and, along with the trial of the Rosenbergs, the investigation and prosecution of Hiss was a cause célèbre of the McCarthy era, reinforcing the impression that American government was riddled with traitors.

After World War II erupted in Europe, President Roosevelt worried about the obvious inadequacy of the U.S. intelligence capability. William Stephenson, a Canadian who represented the British intelligence establishment in the Western hemisphere, met with FDR and recommended that he consult with a friend of his, William J. Donovan, better known as "Wild Bill" Donovan, a sobriquet earned playing football for Columbia University.

"The door for intelligence work opened for me when I undertook my first secret mission while on my honeymoon in Japan in 1919. The United States Government asked me to take a two-month trip to Siberia to report on the anti-Bolshevik movement. . . . Well, it wasn't your usual honeymoon, but Mrs. Donovan was very understanding. The mission was successful and opened doors to many more missions for the government. I was heading down the intelligence path and I was loving it."

Wild Bill Donovan

Born in Buffalo, New York, in 1883, Donovan began his career in the high-powered world of Wall Street law. In 1912, he took a sabbatical to organize his own New York State Militia cavalry troop, which participated in the 1916 "Punitive Expedition" in pursuit of the Mexican political leader and guerrilla Pancho Villa. During World War I, Donovan organized and commanded the 165th Regiment of the 69th New York Volunteers, which was federalized as the U.S. Army's 42nd Division. Near Landres-et-St. Georges, France, on October 14–15, 1918, Donovan led a nearly suicidal attack against a strong German position and continued in command even after machine gun bullets had torn through his leg. Awarded the Medal of Honor and three Purple Hearts, he suffered from his wounds for the rest of his life.

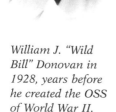

William J. "Wild Bill" Donovan in 1928, years before he created the OSS of World War II.

After the war, Donovan became U.S. attorney for the Western District of New York and earned a national reputation for his vigorous Prohibition-era prosecutions. President Calvin Coolidge tapped him to serve in the Antitrust Division of the Department of Justice, but he soon drifted into an informal intelligence role, traveling widely through Europe during the

Wild Bill Donovan reviews OSS Operational Groups assembled at Bethesda, Maryland, in 1945, preparing for assignment in China during World War II.

1930s and meeting most of the major leaders, including a rising dictator named Adolf Hitler. Donovan pursued his self-appointed intelligence-gathering mission with a passion driven by his growing conviction that a second world war was in the making.

By the time Stephenson mentioned Donovan to Roosevelt, the president was very familiar with Wild Bill's international experience, his intelligence, and his courage. FDR asked him to serve informally as his representative to Britain in 1940–41. He wanted Donovan's assessment of that nation's chances of successfully resisting Hitler, and he wanted Donovan to learn everything he could about the superb British intelligence community. Wild Bill returned to FDR brimming with admiration for Winston Churchill and was profoundly impressed with MI5 and MI6, the two principal British intelligence organizations. Early in 1941 he delivered to Roosevelt his "Memorandum of Establishment of Service of Strategic Information," a blueprint for the first central intelligence agency in U.S. history. In July, FDR appointed Donovan "Coordinator of Information," America's first official spymaster. On June 13, 1942, with the United States engaged in the new world war, Roosevelt created the OSS, with Donovan at its helm.

The original OSS mission was twofold. It was to collect and analyze *strategic*—militarily useful—information and to carry out "special operations" that were not assigned to the military or any

POP CULTURE
Celebrity Spies

By definition, spies are low-profile folk, but the OSS attracted a coterie of celebrities and future celebrities. Ralph Bunche, the African-American political scientist instrumental in the creation of the United Nations and who was awarded a Nobel Prize for his work as a Middle East mediator, served in the OSS, as did screen actor Sterling Hayden, film director John Ford, Boston Red Sox catcher Moe Berg, future Supreme Court associate justice Arthur Goldberg, historian Arthur Schlesinger Jr., and Julia ("The French Chef") Child. The OSS also recruited German-born screen actress Marlene Dietrich, an outspoken anti-Nazi, to record "Lili Marlene," a ubiquitous antiwar song in Germany during World War I, as well as German translations of popular American songs to be beamed in propaganda broadcasts to Germany. Her efforts were later recognized with the award of the Medal of Freedom, America's highest civilian honor.

other agency. The OSS gathered facts and made assessments, but it was by no means a central intelligence agency. Its work was confined to the war zone, whereas the FBI handled domestic counterespionage and all intelligence activities in Latin America. For their part, the army and navy continued to use their own poorly coordinated intelligence services.

More intriguing were the OSS "special operations," including training, arming, and supplying indigenous resistance movements—the most celebrated of which were Mao Zedong's Red Army and Ho Chi Minh's Viet Minh.

DETAILS, DETAILS

A Department Store of Espionage

The OSS was organized into ten divisions: Secret Intelligence (which acquired intelligence), Research and Analysis (which endeavored to make sense of the intelligence), Special Operations (which worked with indigenous partisan groups, planned and executed sabotage, and so on), X-2 (counterespionage), Research and Development (which created the technology of "tradecraft"—the art and science of espionage), Morale Operations (which created and disseminated propaganda), Maritime Units (which handled seaborne transportation in support of OSS operations), Operational Groups (formed to carry out specific missions), Communications, and Medical Services. Two specially created army units were seconded to OSS, the 2671st Special Reconnaissance Battalion and the 2677th Office of Strategic Services Regiment. During World War II, at least twenty-four thousand persons were employed by the OSS.

Venona

Far more controversial than intelligence or special ops was a third area of OSS activity not mentioned in FDR's order: planning the postwar world, especially with regard to the role the Soviet Union would play in it.

In 1944, Donovan authorized the covert purchase of Soviet code books through a Finnish army go-between. Discovering the transaction, Secretary of State Edward Stettinius Jr. objected to it as a direct violation of the president's solemn agreement to refrain from any interference with Soviet code transmissions from the United States. In January 1945, apparently bowing to the secretary, Donovan returned the Soviet cipher material—but not before secretly duplicating every bit of it. From the beginning, the government's keeper of secrets kept secrets from the government.

The material Donovan made a show of returning became an important source for one of the most secret of the Allies' espionage operations—not directed against Germany or Japan, but against an ally: the Soviet Union. Since 1942, American and British intelligence officers had been routinely intercepting Soviet cable traffic. In 1943, Carter W. Clarke, deputy chief of G-2 (military intelligence) for the U.S. Army, ordered the army's Signal Intelligence Service (known as "Arlington Hall") to begin systematic efforts to decrypt and analyze the intercepts, which were pouring in at high volume. Distrust of Stalin ran deep among many American and British military and civilian officials. After all, the Soviet leader had signed a pact with Hitler before the war, and many feared that he would make a separate peace with the Nazis. Thus, the very foundation of the wartime alliance between West and East was shot through with intense suspicion.

The Project Venona messages were intercepted between 1942 and 1945, when it was discovered that the program had been compromised. (The "mole," army cipher clerk and translator William "Bill" Weisband, employed by the Soviet secret police, the NKVD, was not identified until 1950.) Despite this setback, Project Venona had already intercepted a mountain of messages, which cryptographers began to decode in 1946 and were still working on when the project was officially terminated in 1980. Throughout the early Cold War period, the code breakers worked in deepest secrecy. Neither Roosevelt nor Truman was aware of Venona's existence.

DETAILS, DETAILS

What's in a Name?

A number of code words were attached to the project Carter Clarke authorized, the last of which was "Venona." Nobody knows what the word means. If it ever meant anything, the secret has been lost.

REALITY CHECK

The Last to Know

Although the Soviets knew about Venona as early as 1945, the project was not ended until 1980, by which time code breakers had completed decrypting the enormous stockpile of four-decade-old intercepts. The American public first learned of the project when retired FBI agent Robert Lamphere wrote about it in his 1986 book *The FBI-KGB War*.

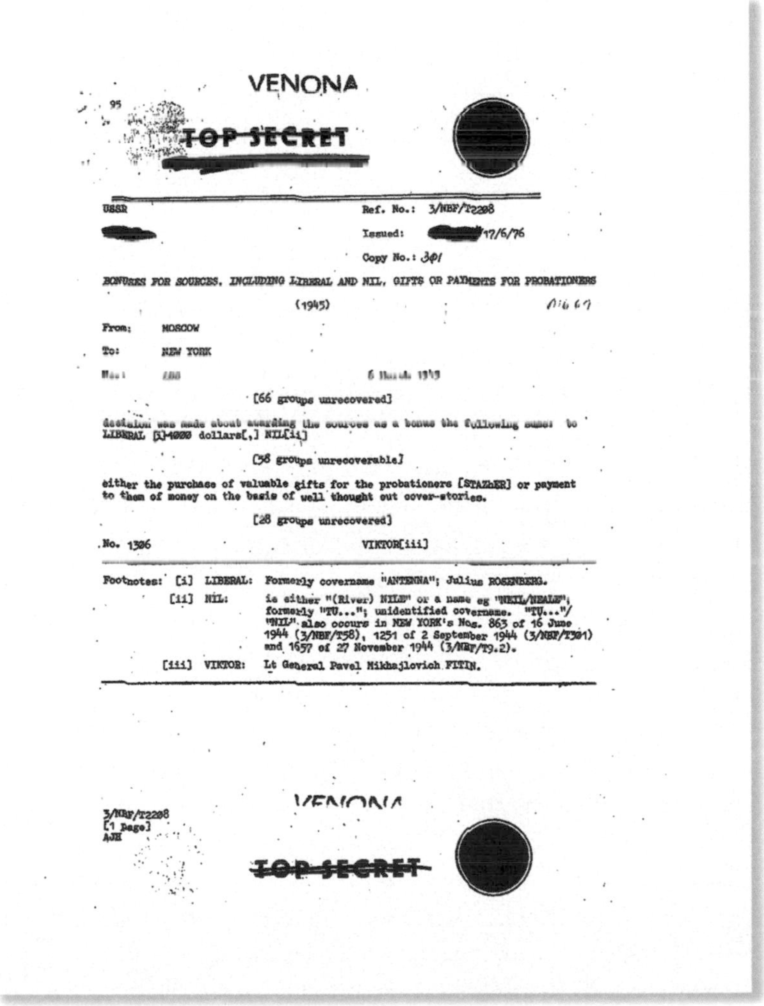

VENONA

95

TOP SECRET

[redacted]

[redacted]

USSR — Ref. No.: 3/NBF/T2208

[redacted] — Issued: [redacted] 17/6/76

Copy No.: 301

BONUSES FOR SOURCES, INCLUDING LIBERAL AND NIL, GIFTS OR PAYMENTS FOR PROBATIONERS

(1945)

From: MOSCOW

To: NEW YORK

[illegible]

[66 groups unrecovered]

decision was made about awarding the sources as a bonus the following sums: to LIBERAL [i] 4000 dollars[,] NIL[ii]

[58 groups unrecoverable]

either the purchase of valuable gifts for the probationers [STAZhER] or payment to them of money on the basis of well thought out cover-stories.

[28 groups unrecovered]

No. 1306 — VIKTOR[iii]

Footnotes: [i] LIBERAL: Formerly covername "ANTENNA"; Julius ROSENBERG.

[ii] NIL: is either "(River) NILE" or a name eg "NEIL/NEALE"; formerly "TU..."; unidentified covername. "TU..."/"NIL" also occurs in NEW YORK's Nos. 863 of 16 June 1944 (3/NBF/T58), 1251 of 2 September 1944 (3/NBF/T301) and 1657 of 27 November 1944 (3/NBF/T9.2).

[iii] VIKTOR: Lt General Pavel Mikhajlovich FITIN.

VENONA

3/NBF/T2208
[1 Page]
AJH

TOP SECRET

[redacted]

This top secret "Venona" document partially decrypts a cable message from Moscow to New York regarding payments to "sources," including one made to "LIBERAL," interpreted here as a code name for Julius Rosenberg. Note the gap between the date on which the message was transmitted and intercepted, March 6, 1945, and the date on which the decrypt was issued, June 17, 1976.

DETAILS, DETAILS

Get Out of Jail Free

The traditional penalty for treason is execution. Bill Weisband suffered nothing more than the loss of his job and security clearance. He did spend a year in prison for contempt of court when he failed to show up at a federal grand jury hearing on the activities of the Communist Party USA, but he escaped prosecution for espionage because the 1947 National Security Act barred the revelation of intelligence "sources and methods," including in a court of law. Without the presentation of evidence, he could neither be charged nor tried. Weisband never sought asylum in the Soviet Union, but spent the postwar years selling insurance in the Washington, D.C., area until he succumbed to a heart attack in 1967.

The Venona decrypts opened a window on Soviet espionage at Los Alamos as well as the presence of American, British, Canadian, and Australian moles at all levels of the federal government, including the OSS itself. Among those identified in the Venona decrypts were Julius and Ethel Rosenberg; Maurice Halperin, an OSS section head; and Lauchlin Currie, economic adviser to FDR, and, from 1949 to 1953, director of the World Bank's mission to Colombia.

During the McCarthy period (see Chapter 13), Venona served as a source for identifying targets for investigation and accusation, but the project was so secret that the evidence could not be presented openly or followed up conclusively.

The President Prods, Congress Acts

The CIA learned little of Venona until 1952, and Army Chief of Staff Omar Bradley declined to tell President Truman about it, partly to protect a project that violated FDR's word to Stalin (even though the Soviets had known about Venona since late 1945) and partly to preserve the president's "deniability." As long as he was ignorant of Venona, he could deny its existence without lying. All Venona material that wafted up to the White House found its way there via the FBI, the Justice Department, or CIA reports.

Unaware, then, of Venona and most other covert activities, President Truman dismantled the wartime OSS in 1946. Almost instantly regretting having done this, he issued an executive order on January 22, 1946, creating the National Intelligence Authority (NIA), responsible for establishing intelligence policy, and a Central Intelligence Group (CIG), responsible for executing that policy. These two agencies were conceived as stepping-stones toward a permanent intelligence establishment, which Truman proposed in February 1947 in his draft of the National Security Act. Congress held hearings on the proposed legislation in which a host of witnesses presented their fears that such an agency would become an "American Gestapo." Congress responded by ensuring that the new agency—the Central Intelligence Agency (CIA)—would have the authority to collect and evaluate intelligence from abroad, but would be barred from domestic espionage or surveillance, and would have no law enforcement authority. On July 26, 1947, the National Security Act was signed by the president, creating the Department of Defense, the U.S. Air Force, the National Security

President Truman (second from right) meets with his National Security Council (NSC), August 19, 1948. Seated at the table, clockwise from lower left: Secretary of Defense James Forrestal, National Security Resources Board chairman Arthur M. Hill (partly hidden), CIA director Roscoe Hillenkoetter, Marshall Plan administrator John W. Kenney, Secretary of State George C. Marshall, Secretary of the Army Kenneth C. Royall, NSC executive secretary Sidney W. Souers, Truman, and Assistant Secretary of the Air Force C. V. Whitney (looking toward Truman).

Council (NSC)—chaired by the president and including the secretaries of defense and state—and the CIA. Although it was modeled on the plan Wild Bill Donovan had submitted years earlier to FDR, the CIA would not be headed by Donovan—a blunt man who had earned powerful congressional enemies—but by Rear Admiral Roscoe H. Hillenkoetter, a solidly bland career naval officer.

Cold War World

The CIA emerged into a world permeated by fear of communism, talk of communism, and communism itself. The Soviets were in Iran; Soviet-backed communists had assumed power in Poland, Hungary, and Romania; Greece was torn by a Soviet-incited civil war; the Communist Party was on the rise in France; Spain seemed vulnerable; and even the government of the Philippines faced a challenge from communist-inspired guerrillas called the "Huks." Czechoslovakia had held out until February 1948, but then fell under communist domination.

REALITY CHECK

Nest of Spies?

If the Venona decrypts are to be fully believed, the OSS had been infiltrated by as many as twenty Soviet moles, and a host of other wartime agencies also harbored spies. Because the Venona documents use code names instead of given names, it is often impossible to identify individual spies. Typically, the documents offer few specifics concerning the extent of the relationship between those mentioned and the Soviet Union. Some may have been merely prospects perceived as sympathetic to the Soviet cause but never actually developed as spies. For these reasons, modern scholars are divided on the significance of Venona, some holding that the decrypts accurately suggest the vastness of the Soviet spy network in the United States, while others believe the documents paint a grossly inflated picture of the extent of Soviet infiltration.

No sooner had the "iron curtain" descended upon the Czechs than Italy seemed poised for a Communist Party sweep. It was at this point that Truman, via the National Security Council, assigned the CIA something more than an intelligence-gathering role. Ten million dollars in covert funds were released to the CIA's Office of Special Operations (OSO), which orchestrated a lightning propaganda campaign intended to scare the Italian people into resisting the rise of the Communist Party. In the United States, the OSO appealed to Italian-Americans to pressure relatives still living in the "old country" to vote for noncommunist candidates. CIA money was also used directly to bribe scores of influential Italian politicians. In a shameless application of dollar diplomacy, President Truman personally threatened to withhold U.S. economic aid from Italy if the government included Communist participation. Beyond this, OSO operatives hinted that the election of a Communist government would trigger a U.S.-financed military coup.

The CIA was highly successful in squelching Italy's Communist Party. This anti-Soviet, pro-American poster was issued in 1948 by the U.S.-backed Christian Democratic Party of Italy.

The Italian elections of 1948 ushered into office the pro-American Christian Democratic Party with a majority sufficient to keep the communists out of the government. It is impossible to say that the CIA's blitz was responsible for the victory, but, in the White House and Congress, the new agency was given all the credit.

And with that credit came calls for more of the same. This prompted George Kennan, now chief of the State Department's Policy Planning Staff, to propose creating a new agency to expand the OSO function. Funded by the CIA, but independent of it, the Office of Policy Coordination (OPC) was created to wage war against the Soviet threat in Europe and elsewhere using propaganda, sabotage, economic warfare, and paramilitary assistance. Although President Truman was aware of the OPC, he was purposely walled off from it, to preserve his deniability. By its very nature, the Cold War engendered a shadow government operating in parallel with but apart from the president and Congress. Under Director Frank Wisner, the OPC defined its own missions and executed them as it saw fit.

Who Was Frank Wisner?

Frank Wisner was the flamboyant but super-secretive chief of the CIA's Office for Policy Coordination and, later, CIA Plans Directorate. Under his leadership, the U.S. intelligence community recruited former Nazis and Nazi collaborators as spies and informants. Wisner is pictured here in naval uniform during World War II, when he served in the OSS.

He had been born in 1909 into a wealthy family in Laurel, Mississippi, and was sent to boarding school and then on to the University of Virginia, where he earned both undergraduate and law degrees. Like Donovan, Wisner rose to prominence as a Wall Street attorney, but six months before Pearl Harbor he joined the navy, was assigned to the naval censor's office, then transferred to OSS, where he headed operations in southeastern Europe. After this, he became a spymaster coordinating a small coterie of informants in Romania, and just before the end of the war in Europe, he was posted to Wiesbaden, Germany, as liaison between the OSS and one Reinhard Gehlen, a high-level Nazi who had served as Hitler's chief Soviet expert. To evade capture by the Red Army in 1945, Gehlen fled to the American lines and volunteered his services to the OSS, which, after the war, authorized him to create Organization Gehlen (ORG). Consisting entirely of former Wehrmacht (German military) and SS officers, ORG was the most important—and for a time the only—espionage unit the United States had in the Soviet Union and its satellites.

Late in 1946, Wisner returned to Wall Street with the white-shoe firm of Carter Ledyard, but within a year was recruited by Under Secretary of State Dean Acheson for service in the Office of Occupied Territories. In 1948, he became the OPC director and drew on his law firm and other Ivy League connections to build a staff. In this way, the U.S. intelligence service in the early years of the Cold War came largely to be a body of Eastern establishment dilettantes, well-heeled WASP defenders of American civilization against the godless Mongol proletarian hordes of Russia and Eastern Europe.

KEEPERS OF SECRETS

Skull and Bones, probably the most famous secret society in America, was founded at Yale University in 1832. Recent members have included Senator John Kerry and President George W. Bush.

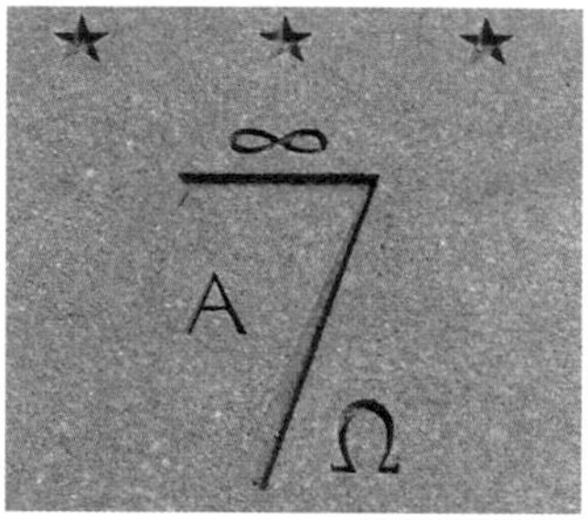

The Seven Society plaque, University of Virginia.

Like the Freemasons in eighteenth- and nineteenth-century America, Skull and Bones functioned for its members (exclusively Yale undergraduates) as an insiders' network on steroids.

Less well known is the Seven Society, founded at the University of Virginia in 1905. The organization is so secret that members carry their affiliation to their graves, their connection to the society revealed to the outside world only when they are buried. A black magnolia wreath shaped like a numeral seven is anonymously placed at the late member's grave site, and the UVA chapel bell tolls seven times at seven-second intervals on the seventh dissonant chord at seven past the hour. Less esoterically, notices are published in the university's alumni news and its newspaper, the *Cavalier Daily*.

Frank Wisner was a Seven Society member, as were Edward Stettinius Jr., who served as secretary of state under both Roosevelt and Truman, and Admiral William F. "Bull" Halsey, one of the architects of America's Pacific victory in World War II.

CLAWING AT THE IRON CURTAIN

RELYING HEAVILY ON REINHARD GEHLEN'S EXPERTISE, Wisner put together a parachute mission into the Carpathian Mountains, where anti-Soviet Ukrainian partisans were known to be active. On September 5, 1949, days after the Soviets had detonated "Joe One," two infiltrators took off from a West German airfield in a C-47 bearing neither insignia nor tail number, bailed out over the Carpathians, and linked up with the partisans. It was the first of many missions to infiltrate behind the iron curtain over the next five years. Recruits for this hazardous work were mostly gathered from among Eastern European refugees displaced by the war. Wisner's OPC established training camps staffed by a combination of U.S. military personnel and former German SS men, who taught recruits how to handle small arms, to work with plastic explosives, and to operate portable radio sets. Wisner also recruited émigrés to Western Europe and the United States, who claimed to have extensive contacts inside the Soviet Union and its Eastern European satellites. Virtually all of these émigrés had been wartime officials in the puppet regimes the Nazis had set up in the Eastern European territories they had occupied.

By 1952, Wisner had built the OPC into an espionage empire budgeted at $82 million (75 percent of the CIA operating budget at the time), with four thousand employees staffing forty-seven stations, mostly in bogus embassy offices, trade missions, and the like. Like most empire builders, Wisner created envy and suspicion and spawned turf battles. The OSO, relegated to working in the shadow of the OPC, criticized Wisner and his operatives as dilettantes and cowboys, and FBI director J. Edgar Hoover dismissed OPC as "Wisner's gang of weirdos." As he did with anyone in government who threatened to acquire more power than he wielded, Hoover launched a covert investigation of the "weirdos" and was gratified to uncover many connections between them and leftist politics during the 1930s. This information he passed on to the rising junior senator from Wisconsin, Joseph McCarthy, who, he knew, would make it very public (see Chapter 13). As always, Hoover was particularly interested in the sexual history of the targets of his investigations and soon uncovered evidence that Wisner had, during the war, carried on an affair with Princess Caradja of Romania. In itself that was not too damning, but Hoover was quick to label her as a Soviet agent.

FBI director J. Edgar Hoover in 1961.

However, the fact is that the OPC's efforts at espionage were remarkably ineffective. Almost everyone Wisner infiltrated behind the iron curtain was caught and killed. In one instance, a unit of U.S.-trained Ukrainians was parachuted into Soviet territory, equipped with nifty folding bicycles to help them get around. The first Soviet police officers who encountered them took note of the wonderful bicycles, which had never been seen in the Soviet Union, and arrested them on the spot. As for the intelligence produced by the émigré contacts, it was indeed voluminous—and entirely manufactured by Soviet counterespionage agents, who had thoroughly mastered the art of disinformation.

REALITY CHECK

Dancing with the Devils

Wisner and his ostensible boss, CIA director Allen Dulles—the wartime chief of the OSS office in Switzerland, who succeeded the CIA's first two directors, Rear Admiral Roscoe H. Hillenkoetter (1947–52) and General Walter Bedell ("Beetle") Smith (1952–53)—deflected criticism from Congress and other sources concerning their reliance on Nazis as informants. The most infamous was Klaus Barbie—the "Butcher of Lyons," who, as Gestapo chief in Lyons, had personally tortured hundreds of prisoners and was directly responsible for the deaths of at least four thousand civilians, mostly Jews—but the most publicly visible was Reinhard Gehlen. With regard to him, Dulles explained that there were "few archbishops in espionage. He's on our side and that's all that matters. Besides, one needn't ask him to one's club."

This five-kopek postage stamp from the twilight of the Soviet Union honors British double agent and defector Kim Philby.

THE TALENTED MR. PHILBY

MANY OF THE ÉMIGRÉ GROUPS WISNER "RECRUITED" had been referred to him by Kim Philby, a highly placed British intelligence operative, who explained to Wisner that the British government could not afford to fund the groups and he did not want these valuable assets to be lost. What Philby did not explain is that the groups in question had been thoroughly infiltrated by Soviet agents—a fact Philby well knew.

Born Harold Adrian Russell Philby in 1912 at Ambala, India, the son of a British Army officer, diplomat, explorer, and convert to Islam, he was nicknamed "Kim" after Kipling's celebrated fictional character. Like his U.S. counterparts, Philby acquired the upper-crust pedigree that comes with going to the right schools: Westminster School, then Trinity College, Cambridge. His university experience, however, drew him into the communist movement, and by the late 1920s he was well connected to the Comintern. Whereas the Americans were fairly new to espionage and generally regarded spying as un-American and ungentlemanly, Russians accepted secret police forces as a way of life. The Soviet intelligence service (then called the OGPU, the "All-Union State Political Administration") actively recruited all foreigners who expressed an interest in communist ideology. When OGPU reached out to Philby, he was highly receptive. In 1933, he went to Vienna to help refugees escape from Nazi Germany. Three years later, his Soviet handlers ordered him to infiltrate the fascist movement by pretending to have fascist sympathies. In 1937, *The Times* sent him to Spain as a stringer, and he solidified his fascist bona fides by reporting on the Spanish Civil War distinctly from Franco's point of view. In 1940, Guy Burgess, a British intelligence officer, recruited him for the British intelligence service, which soon became MI6. Philby was put in charge of counterespionage in Spain, Portugal, Gibraltar, and Africa, performing very effectively against German operations. His record of success brought him to the attention of his superiors, who, in 1944, appointed him to head counterespionage against the Soviet Union. It was just the kind of result toward which Soviet intelligence, with infinite patience, always worked: A longtime Soviet agent was head of the British effort to combat Soviet espionage.

After the war, Philby was assigned as head of the MI6 at Istanbul, working covertly at the British Embassy, but the high point of his Cold War career came in 1949, when he was sent to Washington as liaison between the British Embassy and the CIA. At this time, Venona decrypts revealed that nuclear secrets had been passed to the Soviet Union via the British Embassy in Washington during 1944–45 by an agent the Soviets called "Homer." In 1950, Philby was given the job of discovering the identity of Homer—something Philby already well knew. He was a friend (some historians believe he was a lover) from Cambridge days, Donald MacLean, second secretary of the British Embassy. While pretending to work on the assignment, Philby tipped MacLean off in 1951.

A HISTORY OF SECRECY

The Soviet Union had a long history of institutionalized espionage. The first organization, the Cheka, was founded by Felix Dzerzhinsky in 1917.

In 1922, the Cheka officially became GPU (State Political Directorate), a section of the NKVD (People's Commissariat for Internal Affairs), the Soviet secret police. GPU was restructured in 1923, as the OGPU (All-Union State Political Administration), which became GUGB in 1934. The GUGB (Main Directorate for State Security) operated as a division of the NKVD, which was taken over by its infamous chief, Lavrenty Beria, in 1938. Early in 1941, the GUGB was removed from the NKVD and put under the NKGB (People's Commissariat for State Security). After several reorganizations, in 1946 both the NKGB and NKVD were replaced by the MGB (Ministry for State Security), the KI (Committee of Information), which came to encompass the GRU (Main Intelligence Directorate), and part of the Foreign Ministry. Then on March 5, 1953, Beria merged the MGB with the MVD (Ministry of Internal Affairs). When Beria was purged early in 1954, the MVD became the wholly independent KGB: the Committee for State Security. It was this powerful and much-feared organization, always paramilitary in character, that functioned as the heart of Soviet intelligence and counterintelligence until the dissolution of the Soviet Union in 1991.

Post-Soviet Russia has retained a version of the KGB in the form of two agencies, the SVR (Foreign Intelligence Service) and the FSB (Federal Security Service of the Russian Federation). A revived GRU also continues to function as an intelligence-gathering organization.

Lavrenti Beria, longtime head of the Stalin-era secret police and espionage apparatus, relaxes at Stalin's dacha (summer house), Stalin's daughter, Svetlana, on his knee. Stalin himself is in the background at left. Beria was notorious in Kremlin inner circles as a sadist who personally tortured prisoners, a serial rapist with a preference for teenagers, and a man who relished threatening his political enemies with the words, "We'll grind you into dust." Svetlana Stalin called him "Uncle Lara."

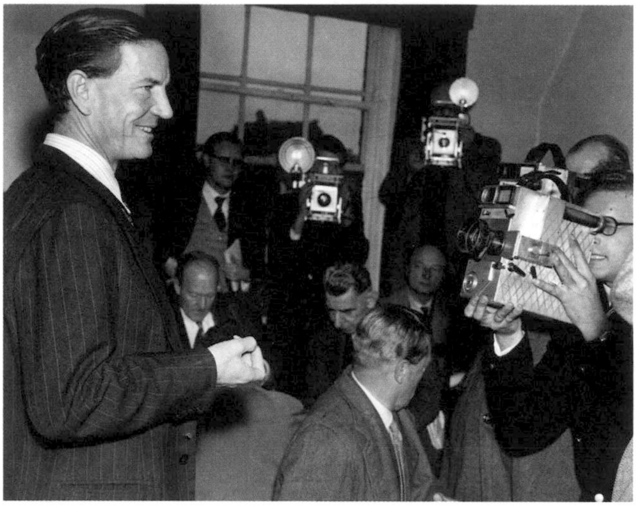

Kim Philby, at a 1955 London press conference, smilingly denies accusations that he was the infamous "third man" who tipped off British spies Guy Burgess and Donald MacLean as they were about to be arrested.

In the meantime, Philby shared a house with another Cambridge chum (and possibly lover), Guy Burgess, a British intelligence officer who was also a double agent in the service of the Soviets. All during this period, Philby was given all the important Venona decrypts, which he selectively transmitted to his Soviet handlers. Even more important, Philby sabotaged repeated CIA-MI6 joint operations to instigate anticommunist uprisings in Albania and Ukraine, by tipping off the Soviets. Philby also provided key intelligence concerning the true size of the U.S. nuclear arsenal, disabusing Soviet intelligence of the impression that the stockpile was inordinately large. Some Cold War historians have concluded that, based on Philby's reports, Stalin discounted the U.S. nuclear deterrent and proceeded with the Berlin blockade. It is also true that, at this time, the Soviet Union began large-scale arms shipments to communist insurgents in northern Korea, apparently without fear of nuclear retaliation.

Exposed—Sort Of

With double agents like Philby, MacLean, and Burgess in high places, Soviet espionage was far more effective than anything the British or Americans fielded. Both MacLean and Burgess were unmasked in the spring of 1951, but they defected to Moscow before they were apprehended. Philby was suspected of being what British counterintelligence identified as "the third man," the man who facilitated their defection. He resigned from MI6, his pension withheld pending investigation. Astoundingly, on October 25, 1955, British Foreign Secretary (later prime minister) Harold Macmillan announced that he had "no reason to conclude that Mr. Philby has at any time betrayed the interests of his country, or to identify him with the so-called 'Third Man,' if indeed there was one." Even more incredibly, Philby was rehired by MI6 the following year and sent to the Middle East. By the early 1960s, suspicions about him again developed, and in January 1963, Philby finally defected to Moscow, where he died in 1988 at the age of seventy-six.

The CIA Soldiers On

While Wisner and the OPC repeatedly tried and failed to duplicate elsewhere the earlier intelligence triumph against Italian communism, the CIA dutifully plodded along in its principal mission of intelligence gathering and analysis. Lacking reliable informants inside the iron curtain, the CIA produced little hard information. Nevertheless, the agency expanded throughout the 1950s, especially during the Korean War (1950–53, see Chapter 12) and sometimes competed with both the FBI and the National Security Agency (NSA), established in 1952 as the nation's central cryptological intelligence service. The CIA's first director, Roscoe H. Hillenkoetter, had done little to advance the agency, prompting Truman to replace him with Beetle Smith, under whom the CIA's first important expansion occurred. When Dwight D. Eisenhower entered the White House, he replaced Smith with Allen Dulles, brother of Ike's secretary of state, John Foster Dulles, and a proven OSS spymaster who combined the élan of Frank Wisner and the intellect of Beetle Smith with an ingratiatingly urbane charm all his own.

Harvey's Hole

Dulles, eager for the CIA to make its mark, enthusiastically embraced a joint endeavor of British, West German, and American intelligence services officially called "Operation Gold." Unofficially, it was known as "Harvey's Hole."

William K. Harvey was Dulles's chief of CIA operations in Berlin, who, having learned that the principal telephone cables for East Berlin ran very close to the sectorial border separating West from East, hit on the bold idea of digging a tunnel to the cables, tapping them, and monitoring East German and Soviet communications at will. Dulles approved, and U.S. Army engineers, working under the cover story that they were building a "secret" radar station, stealthily excavated into East Germany. Berlin's soft, sandy soil made for dangerous digging, but the tunnel was completed on February 22, 1955, and, in a special listening room excavated at its end, 150 sound-activated tape recorders were tapped into the lines. The resulting tapes were shipped on a continuous basis to a nondescript building on the National

Secretary of State John Foster Dulles (left) and Charles Bohlen, newly nominated as ambassador to the Soviet Union, flank President Dwight D. Eisenhower, 1953.

LINK

A Very Big Secret

Far lower in profile than the CIA, the NSA is much bigger (though nobody is saying just how big). Authorized by a presidential letter in June 1952 only recently declassified, the organization remains so obscure that Washington wags insist the letters NSA stand for "No Such Agency." Headquartered at Fort Meade, Maryland, it is a complex of huge and featureless rectangles surrounded by approximately eighteen thousand parking spaces. The NSA monitors, collects, decrypts, and analyzes foreign communications and recently has begun monitoring all federally operated computer networks to protect them against attacks. U.S. law limits its mission to monitoring foreign communications only, but, after 9/11, President George W. Bush issued a secret executive order authorizing the agency to wiretap—without warrant—the communication of certain individuals calling from the United States to foreign countries. In 2006, U.S. District Court Judge Anna Diggs Taylor, in *ACLU v. NSA*, found such wiretaps unconstitutional, but her ruling was overturned in 2007 by the Sixth Circuit Court of Appeals.

"Harvey's Hole"—the CIA's tunnel that tapped Soviet and East German telephone and cable communications. Note the sandbags, which provided insulation and deadened outgoing noise. The rails on the floor accommodated a forklift.

Mall in Washington, where transcribers and translators plowed through them twenty-four seven.

Dulles loved it. Operation Gold yielded no political information of note, but there was a ceaseless flow of data concerning the position of Soviet troops and their order of battle (the number and make-up of each unit), which certainly seemed valuable. For nearly a year, Harvey's Hole churned—until Soviet authorities shut it down early in 1956. Far from attempting to hide any embarrassment created by the presence of the CIA listening post under East German soil, the acting commandant of the East Berlin Soviet garrison, Colonel Ivan A. Kotsyuba, invited every reporter stationed in *West* Berlin to accompany him on a tour of the facility on April 25, 1956.

To Dulles the exposure of the Operation Gold hardly mattered. So much data had been collected that analysts would be translating and poring over it well into 1958. Besides, it showed the initiative, daring, and guts of the CIA. Only later was it discovered that Harvey's Hole had never really been a secret from the Soviets. George Blake—born George Behar in Holland—one of the British intelligence agents who had worked on Operation Gold, was yet another Soviet mole. Unwilling to blow Blake's cover by simply shutting down the eavesdroppers before they began, the KGB made sure that nothing very important flowed through the tapped lines. While the CIA listened and analyzed, the KGB kept working its mole.

Puzzle Palace Triumphant

Thanks equally to Allan Dulles's high-energy approach to intelligence and to the fact that his brother was secretary of state, the CIA rose to prominence during the Eisenhower years. It geared up for major espionage operations as well as for covert paramilitary projects. Most visibly, the CIA created a massive propaganda machine, which infiltrated foreign political parties, trade unions, and other organizations. It established Radio Free Europe and Radio Liberation, which broadcast Western propaganda through an iron curtain that—as RFE literature proclaimed—"wasn't sound proof."

In 1962, the CIA moved into elaborate new headquarters in McLean, Virginia, across the Potomac from Washington, D.C. Outsiders called it the "Puzzle Palace," a name Dulles did not mind at all. For him, the CIA was where all the strings of all the little nations, the "Third World," came together, awaiting just the right manipulation to keep them out of the clutches of communism and win them to the American fold. China had been "lost," and the Korean War had ended in a bloody draw. But the rest of that Third World was still in play, and Allen Dulles meant to ensure that the outcome of future contests would be far more satisfactory.

"It is now clear that we are facing an implacable enemy whose avowed objective is world domination by whatever means and at whatever cost. . . . If the United States is to survive, long-standing American concepts of 'fair play' must be reconsidered. We must develop effective espionage and counterespionage services and must learn to subvert, sabotage and destroy our enemies by more clever, more sophisticated and more effective methods than those used against us."

General James H. Doolittle, USAF, report to Dwight D. Eisenhower, 1953

The "Puzzle Palace": President John F. Kennedy dedicated the headquarters of the CIA on November 28, 1961.

TAKEAWAY

Spy vs. Spy

The Anglo-American alliance with the Soviet Union during World War II was undermined from the beginning by mutual distrust, which gave rise to programs of espionage on both sides. These developed into a full-blown spy war waged throughout the Cold War period. While the Soviet Union had long-established intelligence and espionage agencies, the United States struggled to invent them, transforming the wartime OSS into the CIA, NSA, and other agencies. Whereas the Soviets exploited left-leaning Brits and Americans, turning them into KGB agents and double agents, the fledgling CIA rarely infiltrated behind the iron curtain, but was more successful in large-scale propaganda efforts. By the beginning of the Eisenhower years, the CIA was a powerful agency with strong links to the State Department and was poised for covert warfare in the as-yet "non-aligned" (favoring neither the United States nor the Soviet Union) nations of the Third World.

Part Four

Crossing the Line

CHAPTER 12

HOT WAR IN A COLD PLACE

The Korean War, 1950–53

LIKE MOST OTHER WARS, THE COLD WAR was a struggle for dominance and was marked by distrust, hostility, even hatred. But, in contrast to other wars, both sides usually held their fire. Usually? More accurately, they got—or tried to get—somebody else to do the shooting for them. The Cold War spawned a new kind of armed conflict, the "proxy war," in which the superpowers, which dared not fight one another directly for fear of triggering World War III, fought through third-party, usually Third World, combatants. The "hot wars" of the Cold War—the Korean War, the Vietnam War, and so-called brushfire wars in other parts of the world—all began as wars by proxy.

A WAR OF THEIR OWN

AT LEAST THAT IS THE WAY AMERICAN, SOVIET, AND CHINESE LEADERS looked at things. For them, the whole world was a potential battlefield on which the great contest between capitalism and communism would be decided. This view disregarded the sentiments and motives of those who actually lived on that battlefield. The war we call the Korean War—the fighting spanned 1950 to 1953, but a permanent peace has yet to be concluded—had its origin in 1910, when the empire of Japan, in the first throes of imperial expansion following its triumph over czarist Russia in the Russo-Japanese War of 1904–5, annexed Korea, a nation so little known to the West that it was dubbed the "Hermit kingdom." The annexation of the country failed to create so much as a diplomatic ripple outside of Asia.

Only after the Japanese attacked Pearl Harbor on December 7, 1941, were U.S. leaders moved to espouse the cause of Korean independence. In declaring war on Japan, the

American government belatedly acknowledged, among a litany of Japanese transgressions, that the empire had made Korea one of its first victims of imperialist aggression. Thus, at the 1943 Cairo Conference among wartime allies China, Great Britain, and the United States, it was agreed to include securing the independence of Korea among the objectives of their joint prosecution of the war against Japan. At Cairo, in the midst of war, the Allied leaders decided that the postwar occupation should be controlled by a joint international commission consisting of the United States, Great Britain, China, and the Soviet Union. At the Yalta Conference in February 1945, President Roosevelt attempted to go a step further by persuading Stalin to agree to an international trusteeship to prepare Korea for independence following the defeat of Japan. Stalin raised no objection, but neither did he give his approval, and the matter was allowed to rest until the Potsdam Conference during July 27–August 2, 1945, when President Truman reintroduced FDR's proposal. It was not until August 8, however, when the Soviets finally declared war on Japan, that Stalin announced agreement to a Korean trusteeship.

The Japanese surrender on August 14, 1945, made the military occupation of Korea unnecessary, but the Allies still had to be present to accept and oversee the surrender of those Japanese military forces occupying the country. The U.S. proposed that the Soviets receive Japan's surrender north of the 38th parallel while the United States would accept surrender south of this line. It was strictly a practical arrangement; Red Army forces had easy access to the north, whereas U.S. forces were poised to occupy the south.

U.S. forces accepted the Japanese surrender in Korea below the 38th parallel, while Red Army forces accepted it north of that line. The lowering of the Japanese flag was the culmination of the surrender ceremony.

DETAILS, DETAILS

National Geographic

In July 1945, U.S. Army colonels Dean Rusk and Charles Bonesteel were assigned to figure out how the Korean peninsula should be divided for temporary military occupation. It seemed to them that the U.S. forces needed access to at least two major seaports, so, grabbing the only map they had available, one published by National Geographic, the colonels determined, after a half-hour of discussion, that the 38th parallel made the most convenient demarcation. Rusk, who would become secretary of state in Kennedy's administration, later explained that U.S. forces in the region were scarce, and it was not practical for them to push farther north than the 38th parallel. Neither Rusk nor Bonesteel dreamed that the line they hastily penciled in would harden into the no-man's land of a bitter and bloody war.

Previous spread: *During South Korean evacuation of Suwon Airfield, a 37-mm antitank gun is hauled out of the area by a weapons carrier for repairs.*

REALITY CHECK

A Modest Force

Stalin outfitted about one hundred thousand North Korean People's Army troops with small arms, some artillery, and a few tanks. He contributed a little more than a hundred outmoded aircraft, manned by Korean pilots trained in the Soviet Union or at Soviet facilities in China. The modest scope of the Soviet contribution invited Kim Il Sung to act against the South while leaving open the possibility of a Soviet occupation on the pretext of defending the North. Stalin gave Kim just enough to furnish a saber for him to rattle, but not enough to allow him to face an American-backed South Korea alone.

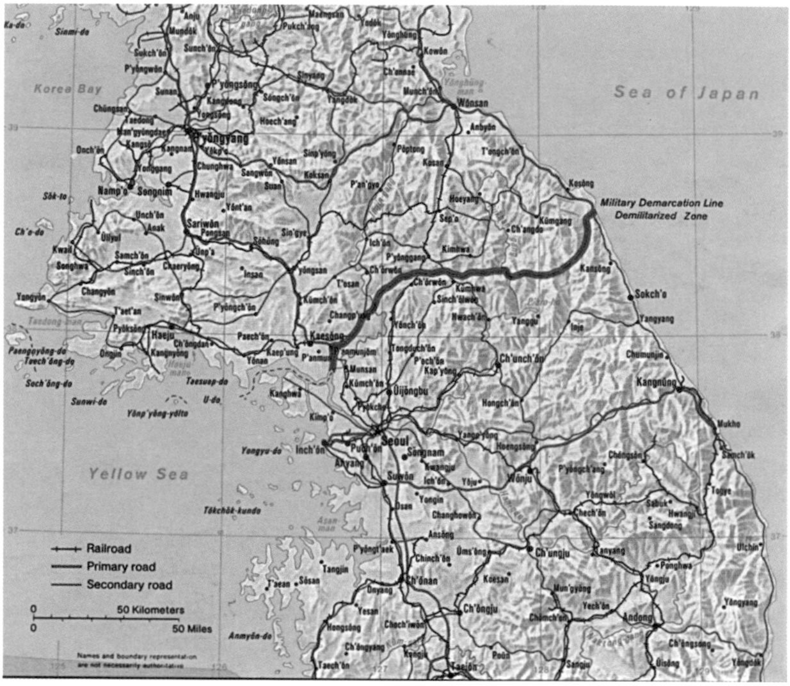

Drawn roughly across the 38th parallel, the demilitarized zone (DMZ) separated North and South Korea.

The Soviets Latch On

What no map showed in 1945 was that the territory north of Korea's 38th parallel had long harbored a significant communist presence.

At the end of World War II, the figure most closely associated with Korean communism was Kim Il Sung. He had been born Kim Sŏng-ju in 1912 near Pyongyang (today the North Korean capital) and was raised in a Protestant family that fled to Manchuria either to avoid arrest by Japanese authorities—Kim's official biography describes his family as anti-Japanese activists—or to escape the famine gripping the region. In either case, it was in Manchuria that young Kim joined an underground Marxist group and then, in the 1930s, became active in anti-Japanese guerrilla units operating in northern China, including a force led by the Chinese Communist Party. Kim steadily developed as a communist, adopting in 1935 the nom de guerre Kim Il Sung ("become the sun"). He also ascended in military rank among the guerrillas, but by the close of 1940, he was hotly pursued by Japanese troops. Leading the survivors of the army he commanded,

Kim crossed the Amur River into the Soviet Union, where party officials embraced him, sending him to a camp where refugee Korean guerrillas like himself were given special training. He emerged with the rank of captain in the Red Army and served the Soviet Union in this capacity to the end of World War II.

Kim Il Sung returned to Korea in September 1945 as part of a Red Army unit, and was named to head the Provisional People's Committee, which the Soviet occupiers set up to govern the north. While the U.S. occupiers focused their attention on Korea's feeble official Communist Party headquartered in Seoul, Kim, up north, created the North Korean People's Army (NKPA), trained and equipped by the Soviets.

Kim Il Sung, "Great Leader" and "Eternal President" of the Democratic People's Republic of Korea.

While occupying the North and arming Kim Il Sung, the Soviets fortified the 38th parallel. They also agreed to the creation of a joint commission to help the Koreans establish a provisional government, but persistently declined to move forward with the commission's work. At last, in September 1947, the United States appealed to the United Nations to intervene, and, over a Soviet objection, the UN decided that a unified government should be established for Korea following a general election and that this government would be protected by a UN security force. Supported by the Soviets, Kim's communists prevented the UN commission from holding elections north of the 38th parallel. South of the parallel, the elections went off as scheduled on May 10, 1948, creating the Republic of Korea (ROK) under President Syngman Rhee.

In 1948, a divided Korea held the first democratic elections in the nation's history. Mandated by the United Nations, the elections were nevertheless suppressed by the Soviet-backed government of the North.

Twice, the United Nations affirmed that, as the only government established by democratic election, the ROK was the lawful government of Korea. In response, the Soviets, on May 25, 1948, sponsored elections in the North, which created the Supreme People's Assembly. Claiming to represent all of Korea, the assembly proclaimed the People's Democratic Republic of Korea (DRK), under the leadership of Kim Il Sung. The United Nations refused to recognize the DRK, but it nevertheless controlled the territory and people north of the 38th parallel, while the ROK held sway south of this line.

THE AMERICAN CANDIDATE

Syngman Rhee, the Republic of Korea's first president, was born in Whanghae, Korea, in 1875. Rhee received a classical Confucian elementary education, but then enrolled in a Methodist school and became both a Christian and an ardent nationalist, helping to found the Independence Club in 1896. Two years later, pro-Japanese right-wing forces destroyed the club, and Rhee was arrested.**Syngman Rhee, the Republic of Korea's first president, was born in Whanghae, Korea, in 1875. Rhee received a classical Confucian elementary education, but then enrolled in a Methodist school and became both a Christian and an ardent nationalist, helping to found the Independence Club in 1896. Two years later, pro-Japanese right-wing forces destroyed the club, and Rhee was arrested.**

He was imprisoned until 1904 and, on his release, came to the United States, where he earned a PhD from Princeton University in 1910. That year he returned to Korea, which had just been formally annexed to Japan. Menaced in his native land, he returned to the United States in 1912.

Following the brief Korean independence uprising of March 1, 1919, Rhee was elected president of the Korean Provisional Government in Exile, based in Shanghai, China. Ousted in 1925, he nevertheless continued to work toward Korean independence and in 1940 moved to Washington, D.C., where he spent World War II lobbying for U.S. recognition of an independent Korea. This proved an uphill struggle until Rhee persuaded key members of Congress and the Roosevelt administration that the Soviet Union opposed the provisional government. By presenting himself as an anticommunist, Rhee obtained the backing of conservative American politicians as well as U.S. military occupation authorities. He returned to Korea on October 16, 1945, having amassed great political influence, and began recruiting from the police the muscle to enforce his clout. His strong-arm squads intimidated all opposition. Those who would not give in were disposed of, generally by assassination. When negotiations between the United States and the Soviet Union over reunification failed, Rhee, the only viable candidate for president of the Republic of Korea (South Korea), was elected in 1948, and reelected in 1952, 1956, and 1960.

Rhee ruled postwar Korea with an iron hand, outlawing the opposition Progressive Party and, for good measure, executing the party's leader. He assumed personal control of every government department, down to the local level. Because he was anticommunist, the United States backed him despite his dictatorial policies. However, by 1960, South Koreans decided that they could no longer tolerate a leader who had sacrificed their freedom in a long campaign that was supposed to secure both unification and liberty. Amid charges of election fraud, student uprisings, and protests by the National Assembly, and recognizing that he could no longer rely on toleration from the Eisenhower administration, Rhee stepped down as president of the ROK on April 27, 1960. He took refuge in Honolulu, Hawaii, and lived in quiet exile there until his death on July 19, 1965.

Syngman Rhee, who became the first president of South Korea in 1948, greets General Douglas MacArthur at Kimpo Airfield on August 15, 1945, the official day of liberation from Japanese occupation.

What Now?

Even as it fortified the 38th parallel and backed a government in defiance of the United Nations, the Soviets announced the withdrawal of Red Army troops from the country by January 1, 1949. Eager to withdraw U.S. troops from the South, the Truman administration welcome the Soviet pledge, but also resolved to train and equip an ROK security force and to provide economic aid. The United States also continued to pressure the UN to force the reunification of the country.

The Soviets' simultaneous aggression and conciliation put the United States in a delicate diplomatic position. Truman wanted to arm South Korea for defense, yet without giving the appearance of sponsoring South Korean aggression, which might lead to war involving the North Koreans *and* the Soviets. The American objective was to contain the communists north of the 38th parallel while continuing to push for ultimate unification under a noncommunist government. Truman proposed to train an ROK army of 65,000, a coast guard of 4,000, and a police force of 35,000. The U.S. would supply small arms (defensive weapons), but no tanks or artillery (offensive weapons).

Rhee protested that he needed a regular army of at least 100,000 in addition to a militia force of 50,000, a police force of 50,000, and a 10,000-man navy, not just a coast guard. He also called for an air force of 3,000 pilots and support personnel. Without waiting for official U.S. response, he hired Claire L. Chennault—the retired U.S. Army Air Forces major general who had commanded the famed "Flying Tigers" that had defended China against Japan early in World War II—to create a plan for a South Korean air force. Over U.S. objections, Rhee built his air force while American troops withdrew from Korea by June 29, 1949, leaving behind only a 500-man U.S. Korean Military Advisory Group (KMAG).

Crossing the Line

For some time, Kim Il Sung engaged in sporadic low-intensity guerrilla combat against South Korean forces. Early in 1950, however, he sought Stalin's blessing for a full-scale invasion, and by May 1950, U.S. KMAG members reported a North Korean military buildup along the 38th parallel, which, however, created little stir, either at the Pentagon or in the Tokyo headquarters of General Douglas MacArthur, commander of U.S. forces in Asia. Thus the invasion of South Korea, which began at four o'clock on the morning of June 25, 1950, caught ROK forces unprepared.

POP CULTURE

Cable from United Press Correspondent Jack James

URGENT PRESS
UNIPRESS NEW YORK
25095 JAMES
FRAGMENTARY REPORTS EXTHIRTY EIGHT PARALLEL INDICATED NORTH KOREANS LAUNCHED SUNDAY MORNING ATTACKS GENERALLY ALONG ENTIRE BORDER PARA REPORTS AT ZERO NINE THIRTY LOCAL TIME INDICATED KAESONG FORTY MILES NORTHWEST SEOUL AND HEADQUARTERS OF KOREAN ARMYS FIRST DIVISION FELL NINE AYEM STOP ENEMY FORCES REPORTED THREE TO FOUR KILOMETERS SOUTH OF BORDER ON ONGJIN PENINSULA STOP / TANKS SUPPOSED BROUGHT INTO USE CHUNCHON FIFTY MILES NORTHEAST SEOUL STOP / LANDING EXSEA ALSO REPORTED FROM TWENTY SMALL BOATS BELOW KANGNUNG ON EASTERN COAST WHERE REPORTEDLY OFFCUT HIGHWAY ENDITEM NOTE SHOULD STRESS THIS STILL FRAGMENTARY AND PICTURE VAGUE / SYET JAMES.

The NKPA surged across the 38th parallel, brushing aside resistance. A main invasion force drove directly toward Seoul, the South Korean capital, about thirty-five miles below the parallel. Simultaneously, smaller forces advanced down the center of the Korean peninsula and along the east coast.

America Responds

As the NKPA captured Seoul, Truman ordered MacArthur to rush equipment and ammunition to the ROK army, which, in its headlong retreat, had abandoned most of what it had.

Yet again, Truman faced a crisis created by the inherently contradictory aims of his Soviet policy: to contain the aggressive expansion of communism *and* to avoid igniting a third world war. His next move was to order the U.S. Seventh Fleet to steam toward Korea, but, as the ships approached the peninsula, Truman decided to redeploy most of the fleet to Taiwan, to forestall what he and his advisers believed was an imminent communist Chinese assault on the Nationalist stronghold.

Truman did order immediate air and naval strikes against North Korean positions below the 38th parallel and expanded MacArthur's directive to allow him to use *all* available U.S. forces to aid the ROK, but he ordered the response confined to South Korean territory rather than risk provoking Soviet or Chinese intervention.

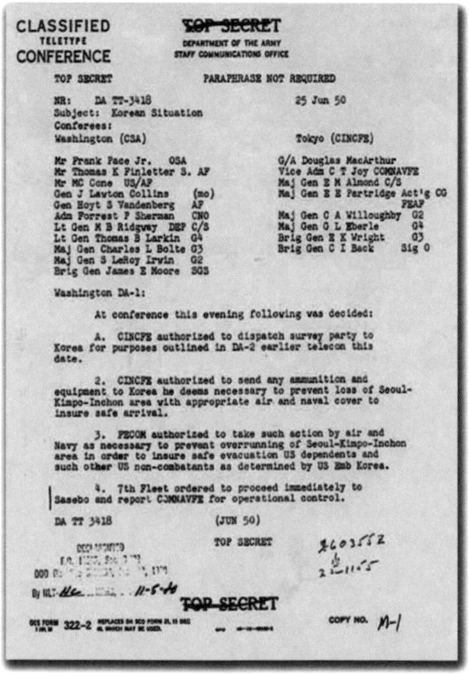

CLASSIFIED TELETYPE CONFERENCE

~~TOP SECRET~~

DEPARTMENT OF THE ARMY
STAFF COMMUNICATIONS OFFICE

TOP SECRET PARAPHRASE NOT REQUIRED

NR: DA TT-3418 25 Jun 50
Subject: Korean Situation
Conferees:

Washington (CSA)	Tokyo (CINCFE)
Mr Frank Pace Jr. OSA	G/A Douglas MacArthur
Mr Thomas K Finletter S. AF	Vice Adm C T Joy COMNAVFE
Mr MC Cone US/AF	Maj Gen E M Almond C/S
Gen J Lawton Collins (mo)	Maj Gen E E Partridge Act'g CG FEAF
Gen Hoyt S Vandenberg AF	Maj Gen C A Willoughby G2
Adm Forrest P Sherman CNO	Maj Gen O L Eberle G4
Lt Gen M B Ridgway DEP C/S	Brig Gen E K Wright G3
Lt Gen Thomas B Larkin G4	Brig Gen C I Back Sig O
Maj Gen Charles L Bolte G3	
Maj Gen S LeRoy Irvin G2	
Brig Gen James E Moore SGS	

Washington DA-1:

At conference this evening following was decided:

A. CINCFE authorized to dispatch survey party to Korea for purposes outlined in DA-2 earlier telecon this date.

2. CINCFE authorized to send any ammunition and equipment to Korea he deems necessary to prevent loss of Seoul-Kimpo-Inchon area with appropriate air and naval cover to insure safe arrival.

3. FECOM authorized to take such action by air and Navy as necessary to prevent overrunning of Seoul-Kimpo-Inchon area in order to insure safe evacuation US dependents and such other US non-combatants as determined by US Emb Korea.

4. 7th Fleet ordered to proceed immediately to Sasebo and report COMNAVFE for operational control.

DA TT 3418 (JUN 50)

TOP SECRET

~~TOP SECRET~~

322-2 COPY NO. M-1

This fateful teletype from June 25, 1950, summarized the decisions of an emergency conference between Army Department headquarters in Washington and Douglas MacArthur's Far Eastern command in Tokyo concerning the "Korean Situation."

REALITY CHECK
Proxy Mindset

Truman and his military planners operated under the assumption that in the climate of the Cold War there could be no such thing as a merely "local" war. They interpreted the invasion of South Korea as a grand communist ploy to draw U.S. military resources away from the "real" communist objective—in this case, the conquest of Taiwan. The kneejerk tendency to view local conflicts through a global ideological lens, to see them for everything *except* what they most immediately were, distorted the initial response to the invasion of Korea and, with even graver consequences, would later warp U.S. military policy in Vietnam. To be sure, the Korean War and the Vietnam War did involve Soviet and Chinese interests and support, but they were first and foremost local civil wars, not the products of monolithic communist aggression. The failure of American policy makers to understand and accept this fact created unrealistic expectations for victory as well as an inflated assessment of the consequences of defeat.

At this time, "all available forces" included some units of the Japanese-based Eighth U.S. Army and the 29th Regimental Combat Team, both significantly under strength because of postwar demobilization, as was the Far East Air Force, the U.S. Air Force unit in the region. U.S. naval assets in the area were also modest. In short, the United States was in no shape to fight a major war.

United Nations Resolution

In a show of the kind of global communist solidarity America most feared, the Soviet Union signed a treaty of friendship, alliance, and mutual assistance with Communist China, but then followed this with a blustering strategic error by announcing a boycott of all United Nations organizations and committees on which Nationalist China participated. This protest meant that the Soviet delegate was not present to exercise his veto of the June 27 UN Security Council resolution authorizing military action against North Korea. Thus President Truman obtained the military and moral backing of the world organization, which thereby diplomatically isolated the Soviets, Chinese, and North Koreans.

Because the United States would contribute the major portion of the UN military forces, Truman named Douglas MacArthur as commander of all UN troops. Yet even as the UN entered the war, it was still undecided whether UN forces would be permitted to operate north of the 38th parallel.

REALITY CHECK

Cold War Constraints

Postwar demobilization had reduced the United States Army to a force of 1,460,000 soldiers, most of them serving in undermanned and underequipped divisions. Pinched postwar military budgeting was a problem, but not the only problem. Truman believed that if he devoted large numbers of troops, aircraft, and warships to fight in Korea, the rest of the world—especially Europe—would be left vulnerable to Soviet aggression. Moreover, he also feared that a sudden U.S. military buildup would send a provocative signal to the Soviet Union, goading a massive buildup on that side. Rearmament, Truman believed, provokes rather than prevents war.

The undermanned, under-equipped post–World War II U.S. Army scrambled to defend South Korea against invasion from the North. Here an Eighth U.S. Army 105-mm howitzer crew readies its equipment near the Kum River in July 1950.

NKPA VICTORIES AND DEFEATS

AMERICAN GROUND UNITS BEGAN ARRIVING IN SOUTH KOREA just six days after the June 25 invasion. By this time, the NKPA had crossed the Han River *south* of Seoul and was still advancing down the peninsula. By July 3, Kimpo Airfield and the strategically vital port of Inchon were in communist hands. Ideally, MacArthur would have waited to launch a counterstrike until his forces were consolidated, but he believed South Korea would have to surrender by the time all of his forces were ready. He decided, therefore, to make a stand with what he had. Reasoning that the North Koreans intended to capture the port of Pusan, the last major sea link between South Korea and the rest of the world, he deployed on July 5 "Task Force Smith" just above Pusan. Initially successful against the advancing NKPA, the task force was soon outgunned and broke into a disorganized retreat. Hoping to stem the tide, MacArthur sent in three more units, but by July 13, the NKPA had pushed ROK and UN forces as far south as Taejon, in south central South Korea.

MacArthur continued costly delaying actions to buy time for a buildup of forces in Japan, and by July 18 he was able to send two more divisions to help defend Taejon. Despite this, the city was lost to the NKPA on July 20.

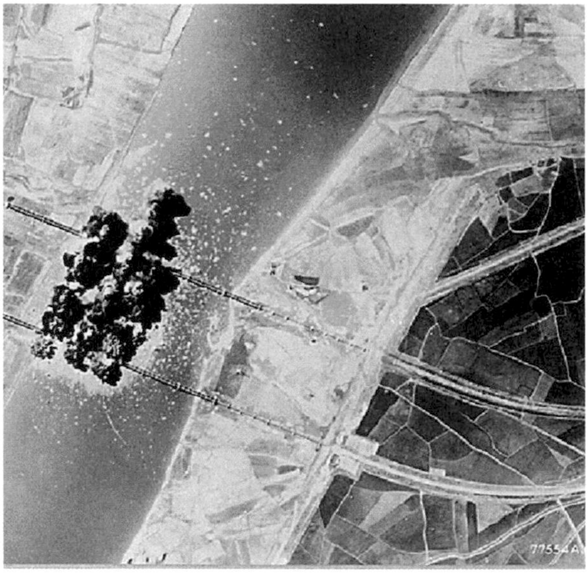

Aerial reconnaissance records a B-29 strike against railroad bridges in South Korea on July 27, 1950. U.S. airpower was used to disrupt the lines supplying North Korean invading forces.

To the American public, these defeats came as a profound humiliation, but MacArthur did not despair. He saw that the NKPA was paying a high price for its rapid advance, its lines of communication and supply stretched dangerously thin; and, although U.S. ground forces were outmanned and outgunned, the U.S. Air Force quickly established air superiority. This achieved, attack aircraft hit the vulnerable lines supplying the NKPA. Simultaneously, the U.S. Navy set up a highly effective blockade to prevent resupply from the sea.

Walker's Pusan Stand

Despite the defeat of Task Force Smith and the fall of Taejon, Pusan held, and Lieutenant General Walton H. Walker, commander of the Eighth U.S. Army, principal ground force in Korea, took a stand along what he called the "Pusan perimeter," a 140-mile-long arc north of the port city, from the Korea Strait to the Sea of Japan.

Walker had to spread his forces thinly, but he established excellent lines of communication among his units, which gave him the flexibility to shift troop strength wherever and whenever necessary. The NKPA threw thirteen infantry divisions and one armored division against the Pusan perimeter during August and September 1950, but many of the troops were raw recruits commanded by freshly minted officers, who made inept piecemeal attacks instead of massing at a single point. This was a fatal error, and Walker's defense of Pusan not only dealt the NKPA its first serious defeat, it gained for MacArthur the one commodity he most urgently needed: *time* to build up forces for an offensive counterthrust.

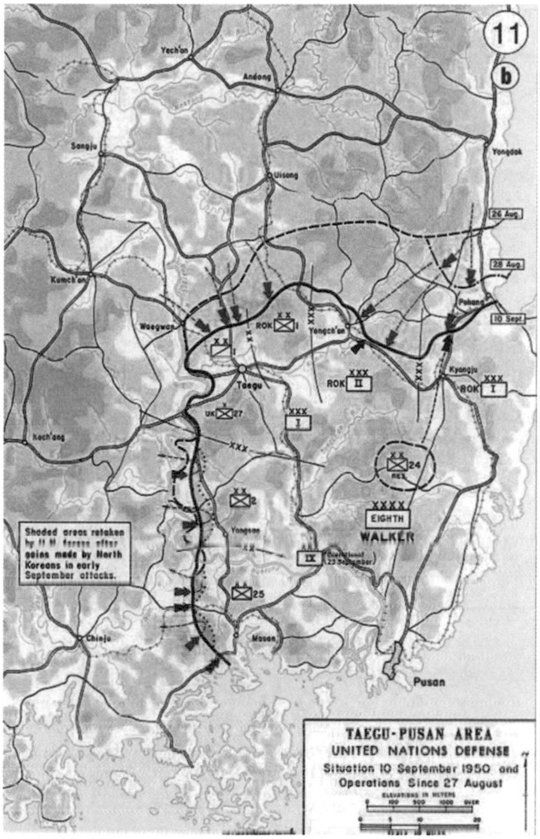

General Walker's Eighth U.S. Army struggled to hold the "Pusan perimeter" against a massive attack by North Korean invaders. Note the shrinkage of UN-controlled territory from August 26, 1950, to September 10.

Wagering All at Inchon

While others fretted over the magnitude of the NKPA advance, MacArthur believed the North Koreans had made themselves vulnerable. Their supply lines, fiercely harried by U.S. air attacks, were near the breaking point, and Walker had tied down major enemy forces at the Pusan perimeter. Attack the invaders from behind, sever their supply lines completely, and the leading NKPA units would be trapped between the force attacking from the north—from behind them—and the Eighth U.S. Army at the Pusan perimeter.

The problem was how to get a force north of the present NKPA position. Drawing on his World War II experience, MacArthur decided to make an amphibious assault at Inchon. Studied on a map, Inchon looked ideal from a strategic and tactical point of view. But no map could reveal the reality of the waters and the topography of Inchon. Tides there were variable, creating extreme hazards for landing craft, and the approach to Inchon lay through a very narrow channel, yet

General of the Army Douglas MacArthur anxiously observes the shelling of Inchon from the bridge of the USS Mt. McKinley, *September 15, 1950. Brigadier General Courtney Whitney (left), Major General Edward Almond (right), and an unidentified U.S. Navy officer (behind MacArthur) also look on.*

another opportunity for disaster. Assuming the landing craft survived the approach, once ashore, troops would have to scale a high seawall, exposing themselves to opposing fire. Then, assuming they got over the seawall, they would find themselves not on a beach, but in a city, through which they would have to fight.

For the very reason that Inchon presented such formidable obstacles to invasion, MacArthur guessed that the North Korean commanders would fail to anticipate and to defend against an assault there. He decided to gamble everything he had, leaving nothing in reserve. If the landing fell afoul of tides, weather, and topography, or came under heavy attack, there would be no reinforcements to bail it out. Catastrophic losses would leave Eighth Army vulnerable, without the possibility of reinforcement.

On September 15, 1950, the general rolled the dice. A commander legendary for his supernatural calm under fire, he was uncharacteristically anxious as he observed the landings from the bridge of one of the warships supporting the assault. But the reports, as they came in, were all good. The treacherous tides had been predicted with absolute accuracy, the ships steered safely through the perilous straits, and the troops encountered only light resistance. As MacArthur had assumed, no one expected a landing here.

The Inchon landing was the most innovative and brilliant operation in the remarkable career of Douglas MacArthur, the kind of battle military historians call a "masterpiece." It undid everything the NKPA had gained. Within two weeks after the landing, Seoul was once again in ROK hands, and all the NKPA lines were blocked. From September 16 to 23, Walker's Eighth Army fought its way out of the Pusan perimeter, meeting very heavy resistance until the NKPA commanders realized to their horror that they were caught between the Inchon landing force and the Eighth Army. The stomach for the fight left them, and the NKPA melted away, rapidly withdrawing. Walker gave chase, crushing as much of the enemy between his army and the landing forces as he could. On September 26, the Eighth Army linked up with the landing force.

"Inchon blazed against the darkening sky, and the air over the city was choked with fumes and cinders. But in the far west the brightness of the setting sun painted one last patch of sky a peaceful, soothing yellow. A Marine chaplain standing on the ridge with me looked first at the sunlit sky in the west, then back at the smoke and fire around us. 'Heaven on one side,' he said slowly, 'and hell on the other.' "

Frank Gibney, reporting in Time *magazine, September 25, 1950*

Four LSTs ("landing ships, tank") disgorge men and equipment on the beach at Inchon during the high-stakes September 15, 1950, amphibious invasion.

The NKPA had not been wiped out, but the Inchon landing and the breakout from Pusan neutralized it as a fighting force in South Korea. The sovereign integrity of South Korea had been established below the 38th parallel.

Counterinvasion?

Like most American military men, Douglas MacArthur believed that victory should be regarded as an investment to be capitalized on. After Inchon, he advocated crossing the 38th parallel to invade North Korea. There were compelling reasons to do so: At least thirty thousand NKPA troops had withdrawn across the parallel, and there were at least another thirty thousand NKPA in the North, making for an effective North Korean force of sixty thousand, which could reenter the South at will. MacArthur added another argument for invasion. Taking the battle to the enemy would advance the cause of reunification by giving the South a foothold in the rival's territory. On the other hand, as Truman well knew, invading North Korea could bring the Chinese and Soviets into the fight.

Truman decided it worth the risk. On September 27, 1950, he ordered MacArthur to pursue the NKPA across the 38th parallel, specifying, however, that the advance was to proceed only in the absence of Chinese or Soviet intervention, and only South Korean forces were to be used near the Yalu River (the border separating North Korea from Manchuria, Communist China) and the Tumen River (the Soviet border). Truman wanted no American soldiers fighting Chinese or Soviet troops.

Across the Parallel

On October 1, two ROK corps crossed the 38th parallel. On October 9, General Walker led I Corps, Eighth Army, across as well. By October 19, I Corps had cleared Pyongyang, the North Korean capital and, by October 24, the unit was just fifty miles outside of Manchuria. ROK forces were positioned even closer to the Chinese border.

Predictably, China threatened to intervene. In response, Truman flew to Wake Island in the Pacific for a one-on-one with MacArthur. He wanted to look his general in the eye and ask him if he thought China would intervene. MacArthur voiced absolute confidence that the Chinese threats were hollow. Truman authorized the advance to continue.

The Chinese Intervene

After a triumphant counteroffensive, UN forces faced growing resistance everywhere except along the coasts of the Korean peninsula. Even worse were the increasingly frigid temperatures that came with the onset of an early winter. For many veterans of the war, it was the weather even more than the enemy that made the fiercest impression.

On October 26, General MacArthur reluctantly admitted the obvious: the stunningly strong resistance was being stiffened by Chinese troops—though he persisted in believing their numbers were small. By the next month, however, it was all too apparent that the Chinese commitment was significant, some five divisions. Even so, MacArthur continued to insist that Chinese operations were strictly defensive and no large number of Chinese troops had crossed into North Korea. Accordingly, he ordered the advance to continue, and, on November 24, part of the 7th Division, Eighth U.S. Army, reached North Korea's border with China.

On the following night, Chinese forces hit the 7th Division hard on its center and right. Two days later, even more powerful Chinese attacks overran units of X Corps on its left flank, and by November 28, United Nations positions were crumbling. That some three hundred thousand

ALTERNATE TAKE

Fatal Underestimation

At Wake Island, Truman asked MacArthur pointblank: "What are the chances for Chinese or Soviet interference?" The general responded that there "was very little chance" of the Chinese entering North Korea; at most, they could get fifty or sixty thousand men across the Yalu, but because they had no air force, "if the Chinese tried to get down to Pyongyang, there would be the greatest slaughter." As for the Soviets, MacArthur assured the president that the Russian aircraft and pilots were no match for the U.S. Air Force, and with winter imminent, the Soviets would never commit a large number of ground troops.

If MacArthur had assessed the situation more realistically, he would have concluded that Chinese intervention was inevitable. Yet, given the general's character, it is unlikely that this would have altered his aggressive strategy. He might have pushed hard for the use of nuclear weapons as a back-up, and this might have prompted President Truman to relieve MacArthur sooner than he did.

Chinese—thirty infantry divisions plus artillery and cavalry—had crossed into North Korea struck MacArthur, Truman, and the American public like a thunderbolt.

Faced with massively superior numbers, Walker had no choice but to withdraw or suffer envelopment. Even more stunningly, U.S. air superiority evaporated as Soviet-built Chinese MiG-15 jet fighters entered Korean air space. The U.S. Air Force had concentrated on building up the SAC nuclear bomber fleet at the expense of the tactical air force and had few jet fighters. The MiGs outperformed the propeller-driven U.S. aircraft, and only the superior skill of the American pilots avoided catastrophic losses. By December 15, battered UN forces had withdrawn to the 38th parallel, hunkered down, and established a defensive line across the breadth of the Korean peninsula.

"'It took them 30 minutes to get my boots off,' he said. 'They were froze stuck to my feet.' Back in Japan they operated on his leg and told him that he would lose most of both feet. But lying in his bed at Percy Jones [Military Hospital], holding up his black, shriveled fingers, Pvt. Baldridge was able to smile. 'They'll cut off my toes,' he said, 'but they'll save the balls of my feet. I'm glad of that.'"

Time *magazine article (February 5, 1951) on a U.S. Marine suffering from frostbite during the retreat from the Yalu*

The bitter Korean cold was especially hard on U.S. soldiers, most of whom lacked battle gear appropriate to the harsh weather. Frostbite and exposure were often greater dangers than enemy fire.

A Korean Dunkirk

The U.S. Navy and U.S. Air Force mounted a massive effort to evacuate beleaguered X Corps from North Korea. In a magnificently orchestrated operation by sea and airlift, which called to mind the "miracle at Dunkirk"—the rescue of British and French forces pushed to the English Channel by the Nazis at the end of the Battle of France in World War II—105,000 troops, almost 100,000 Korean civilians, 17,500 vehicles, and 350,000 tons of cargo were transported to Pusan, out of enemy reach. In the course of the evacuation, General Walker was killed in a car crash, and Lieutenant General Matthew B. Ridgway was rushed from Washington to replace him as commander of the Eighth Army.

DETAILS, DETAILS

Under New Command

After an impressive tour of duty in the Mediterranean and European theaters during World War II, Matthew Ridgway worked in high-level State-side posts until he took over command of the Eighth Army in Korea. After leading the "Meatgrinder" counter-offensive (see page 269), he replaced MacArthur as UN commander and commander in chief, Far East, on April 11, 1951. He left Korea in May 1952 to succeed General Eisenhower as NATO supreme commander. In 1953, he returned to the United States as army chief of staff and was embroiled in Senator Joseph McCarthy's reckless charges that the army was riddled with communists. Ridgway proved as successful against McCarthy as he had been against the North Koreans.

Ridgway championed the development of tactical (conventional) forces, which, he argued, had been sacrificed to create the strategic (nuclear) deterrent. This brought him into sharp conflict with the Department of Defense, and in June 1955 he retired from the army and entered business. Ridgway died in 1993.

Lieutenant General Matthew B. Ridgway assumed command of the Eighth U.S. Army in Korea after the death of General Walton H. Walker in December 1950, and then replaced MacArthur as commander of United Nations forces in April 1951.

MacArthur Roars

MACARTHUR'S MISREADING OF CHINESE INTENTIONS had been breathtaking, and his response to his own error of judgment was anything but humble. He lobbied for authority to attack the Chinese airfields in Manchuria. Truman and his advisers, including Secretary of Defense George C. Marshall, believed that attacking China would risk a new world war, and that the Korean conflict itself was a Soviet gambit to force a troop reduction in Europe, which would leave NATO vulnerable to Soviet attack. Unwilling to save Korea at the expense of losing Europe, Truman ordered MacArthur to contain operations within Korea. If necessary, he was authorized to evacuate the peninsula altogether.

Permission to run from a fight did not sit well with Douglas MacArthur, who responded to Truman's instructions by calling for a naval blockade of the Chinese mainland, combined with aerial and naval bombardment of industrial targets within China. Even more provocatively, he proposed reinforcing the UN and ROK armies with troops from Nationalist China and also to use Nationalist Chinese forces to launch diversionary attacks against the Chinese mainland.

Seoul Falls—Again

MacArthur's counterproposal triggered a debate in the highest military circles, during which Ridgway, the new Eighth Army commander, reached the melancholy conclusion that his troops had been so thoroughly demoralized by overwhelming attacks that the army believed itself defeated. Moreover, intelligence reports indicated that combined Chinese and North Korean forces were preparing to hit Seoul and the center of the Korean peninsula. If there was any hope of holding at the 38th parallel, Ridgway argued, it was to commit every last reserve to the immediate reinforcement of the Eighth Army and to prepare a separate defensive position just above Seoul.

Ridgway's preparations came too late. An attack launched on New Year's Eve 1951 hammered the Eighth Army. Thanks to Ridgway's steady hand, however, the retreat toward Seoul was orderly, but the capital could not be held. On January 4, 1951, Seoul fell for the second time.

A U.S. Army engineer battalion blows up the Han River Bridge out of Seoul in an effort to slow the advance of invading North Korean and Chinese forces, January 4, 1951.

"Meatgrinder"

The Eighth Army withdrew south of Seoul—and, to Ridgway's great relief, the communists did not pursue. Ridgway recognized the enemy's familiar problem: overextended supply lines. He decided to exploit the enemy's logistical shortcomings by pounding away at the stalled troops, inflicting as many casualties as possible in what would no longer be a war of rapid maneuver but one of relentless attrition. That, Ridgway argued, was the best alternative to defeat he could offer. MacArthur disagreed and pushed again for permission to attack China. The Joint Chiefs of Staff intervened, advising MacArthur to follow Ridgway's recommendation. Truman made this advice an order.

Thus, on January 25, Ridgway began an excruciating offensive aptly dubbed by front-line GIs "Operation Meatgrinder." It produced results. By mid March, the Eighth Army retook Seoul, and by March 21, UN forces returned to the 38th parallel.

Lowered Expectations

And it was at the 38th parallel that those forces halted. The United Nations agreed on a new war aim. Instead of achieving unification of Korea under a democratic government, securing the Republic of Korea below the 38th parallel was an acceptable outcome. When MacArthur was officially informed that President Truman would announce his willingness to commence negotiations with the Chinese and North Koreans on the basis of current positions, he responded by preempting Truman's announcement with one of his own. He declared that, if the United Nations would expand the conflict to North Korea's coastal areas and interior strongholds, the Chinese would realize that they were at serious risk of suffering total military defeat.

Truman seethed. MacArthur had sabotaged the peace overture, leaving him no choice but to withhold the peace initiative and await military developments. He could not afford to further demoralize American soldiers and simultaneously embolden the Chinese by publicly arguing with his top military leader.

> "I fired him because he wouldn't respect the authority of the President. . . . I didn't fire him because he was a dumb son-of-a-bitch, although he was."
>
> *President Harry S. Truman, on his relief of Douglas MacArthur, 1951*

Old Soldiers Never Die

But MacArthur forced his hand.

Ignoring the Constitution, which makes the president commander in chief, above any uniformed commander, MacArthur sent Republican representative Joseph W. Martin—a virulent critic of Truman—a letter proclaiming the urgency of opening up a second front against China with Nationalist troops. On April 5, 1951, Martin read the entire letter into *Congressional Record*. It closed with the ringing phrase: "There is no substitute for victory."

No military figure was more popular than Douglas MacArthur. To fire him would be to court political suicide. Truman did not hesitate. On April 11, 1951, he relieved MacArthur of command. Although the Joint Chiefs endorsed the action, the American public was outraged. Frustration and disgust over the war swelled.

THE COMMUNISTS RENEW THE OFFENSIVE

TRUMAN APPOINTED RIDGWAY TO REPLACE MACARTHUR as supreme commander of UN forces, and Ridgway in turn, entrusted command of the Eighth Army to Lieutenant General James A. Van Fleet. No sooner did these changes take place than, on April 22, a new communist offensive consisting of twenty-one Chinese and nine North Korean divisions

Relieved of command by President Truman, MacArthur returned to the United States and a hero's welcome. He is shown here in April 1951, addressing a crowd of fifty thousand at Chicago's lakefront Soldier Field stadium.

"Old soldiers never die. They just fade away."

Douglas MacArthur, farewell address to Congress, April 19, 1951

descended upon the UN forces. The first phase of this "Spring Offensive" exacted a heavy toll on UN troops, but it burned itself out by April 30. Seven thousand Eighth Army soldiers had been killed or wounded, but Communist casualties were ten times those.

Despite their losses, on May 14, the communists unleashed a second phase of the Spring Offensive, hurling twenty divisions into the right flank of X Corps. Van Fleet had anticipated an attack precisely here and had positioned ample reserves to bolster his front lines. The result stunned the attackers, who lost nearly ninety thousand killed or wounded in the space of a single week. Having failed to gain victory with massive assaults, the communists shifted their approach. For big attacks, they substituted stealthy hit-and-run raids using small units. Van Fleet, however, intended to take the offensive, commencing an advance on May 22, 1951. He made headway all along the front, only to be ordered to hold his position.

Once again, the UN allies feared the consequences of provocation. With the Chinese in the war, they did not want to draw the Soviets in as well. Following orders, Van Fleet consolidated all positions just north of the 38th parallel. The communists used the lull in the fighting to construct strong defenses in the North as a safeguard against invasion. Yet even as they did this, small-unit guerrilla actions continued to nibble away at UN positions. The Korean War was devolving into a series of skirmishes, a war of wills in a desolate, cold, and miserable place.

"Red China is not the powerful nation seeking to dominate the world. . . . This strategy [of all-out war in Korea and the surrounding area] would involve us in the wrong war, at the wrong place, at the wrong time, with the wrong enemy."

General of the Army Omar Bradley, chairman, Joint Chiefs of Staff, May 15, 1951

WAR WITHOUT END

INSTEAD OF THREATENING TO JOIN THE WAR as expected, the Soviets offered a proposal for a cease-fire. The United States and its allies greeted the overture warmly, but it soon became obvious that the North Korean and Chinese negotiators meeting with the Americans at the 38th parallel town of Panmunjom intended to drag out peace talks as long as possible, buying time to refit their troops, reinforce their defensive positions, and generally exploit propaganda opportunities.

Lieutenant General Matthew Ridgway (right), as commander-in-chief of United Nations forces in Korea, poses with (left to right) U.S. Fifth Air Force commander Lieutenant General Earle E. Partridge, Eighth U.S. Army commander Lieutenant General James A. Van Fleet, and President Syngman Rhee of the Republic of Korea.

The talks began at the end of June 1951, but it was July 26 before even a simple agenda was agreed to. After this, the talks ground on, frequently breaking down, then reconvening over the next two years, during which grim but strangely purposeless combat continued. At length, both sides agreed that an armistice would require accord on a demarcation line and demilitarized zone (DMZ) separating North and South, impartial international supervision of the truce, and arrangements for return of prisoners of war (POWs).

The POW issue proved the toughest. United Nations negotiators wanted released POWs to decide for themselves whether they would return home, whereas the communists, fearful of mass defection to the South, held out for mandatory repatriation. In a bid to break the negotiation stalemate, General Mark Clark, who succeeded Ridgway as UN commander in May 1952, ordered stepped-up bombing raids on North Korean cities. Yet it was not until April 1953 that a compromise permitted freed prisoners to choose sides, albeit under supervision of a neutral commission.

UNHAPPY ALLY

IF THE COMMUNISTS WERE DIFFICULT TO DEAL WITH, America's ally, South Korean president Syngman Rhee, proved nearly impossible. He wanted no armistice unless Korea was unified under his presidency. Seeing that this was not about to happen, he insisted that, at the very least, the repatriation of POWs be wholly voluntary, and, refusing to accede to a neutral commission, he sabotaged the peace process by unilaterally ordering the release of twenty-five thousand North Korean prisoners who had announced their desire to live in the South.

Seeking to placate Rhee, the United States signed a mutual security pact with South Korea and promised long-term economic aid. Still, Rhee rejected the armistice, which was therefore concluded without the participation of South Korea on July 27, 1953. Because the ROK was incapable of fighting the war without U.S. aid, the armistice held, and while the Korean War has yet to end—there is no treaty between North and South or between the North and the United States—the shooting stopped.

POP CULTURE

Brainwashing

During the Cold War, the concept of propaganda became pervasive and took on especially sinister implications as a kind of mass mind control practiced by "godless" communists. This view culminated during the Korean War in the concept of "brainwashing," a theme later dramatized in the 1959 novel and 1962 film *The Manchurian Candidate*. The belief was that adept practitioners of military psychological operations ("PSYOPS") could seize absolute control over the human mind and will, regardless of existing beliefs and loyalties. In *The Manchurian Candidate*, communist Chinese behaviorists manufacture a war hero whom they have brainwashed to operate on command as a political assassin.

October 11, 1951: With pens to paper, Colonel Chang Chun San, North Korean army, and Colonel James Murray Jr., U.S. Army, initial the DMZ ceasefire boundaries agreed to at the Panmunjom conference.

NUMBERS
Butcher's Bill

The numbers of Chinese and North Korean troops killed in the war is unknown, but estimates range between 1.5 and 2 million, in addition to at least a million civilians. The UN command lost 88,000 killed, of whom 23,300 were American. Many more were wounded. South Korean civilian casualties probably equaled those of North Korea.

TAKEAWAY
Fighting a "Limited War"

The Korean War, the first major "hot war" of the Cold War era, put the Truman Doctrine and the policy of containment to the ultimate test. The outcome of this, America's first "limited" war, was itself limited. That Korea remained divided persuaded some Americans that U.S. political leaders had allowed the nation to lose its first war ever, whereas others deemed the outcome a successful demonstration of the Truman Doctrine because U.S. intervention contained communist aggression above the 38th parallel without provoking a third world war with the Soviets and Chinese.

Twilight

The outcome of the Korean War was profoundly unsatisfactory to most Americans. Some accepted it as a draw, a standoff, while others decried it as the first military defeat in U.S. history. President Dwight D. Eisenhower, who had succeeded Truman at the start of 1953, announced his belief that the outcome had met United Nations' objectives by ending communist aggression. As of 2009, nearly thirty thousand American military personnel were still stationed in South Korea, and great fears persist that the North will develop an arsenal of nuclear weapons. More immediately, the Korean War provided a grim precedent for intervention in another Asian war, this time in a divided Vietnam—a war even longer, even harder, and even more bitter.

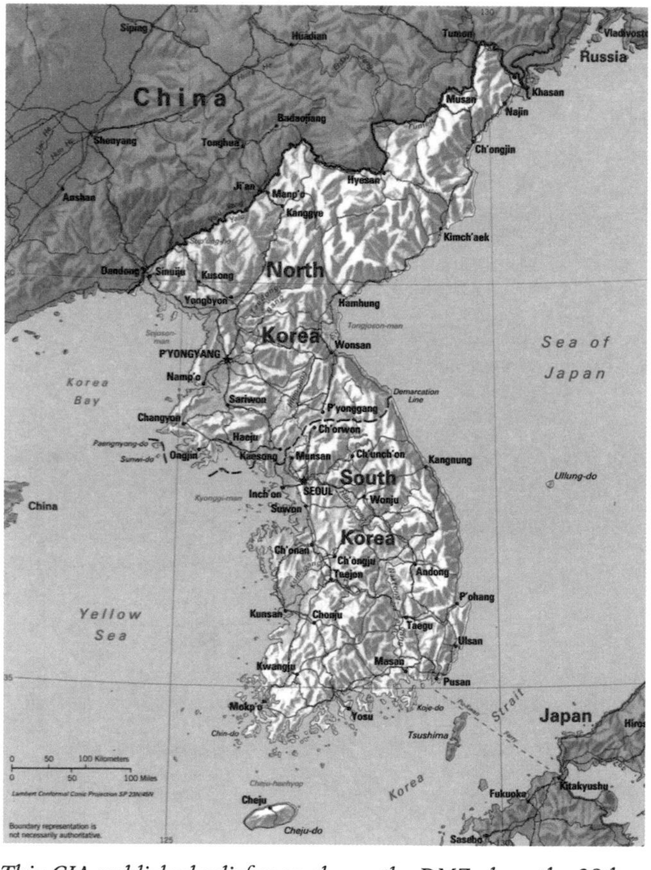

This CIA-published relief map shows the DMZ along the 38th parallel, which has divided North and South Korea since the armistice of July 27, 1953.

CHAPTER 13

RED SCARE NATION

ON THE ONE HAND, IT WAS ALMOST ACCIDENTAL; on the other, it was inevitable: an American Red Scare had come two years after the 1917 Bolshevik Revolution in Russia, and, little more than two decades later, the aftermath of World War II set the stage for another. The spread of Soviet communism, the emergence of a Russian atomic bomb in 1949, Mao Zedong's victory in China, the Korean War, Alger Hiss, atomic spy Klaus Fuchs, and the arrest of homegrown spies Julius and Ethel Rosenberg raised the curtain on a new episode of panic.

The actor who made the opening entrance in the drama was a most unlikely star and, far from having rehearsed his role, ad libbed shamelessly. Yet the clamor his performance created was deafening—for a time.

AN ACCIDENTAL DEMAGOGUE

JOSEPH RAYMOND MCCARTHY WAS BORN IN 1908 near Appleton, Wisconsin. His parents were poor, and he dropped out of junior high at fourteen to help out on the farm. He saw a bigger future for himself, however, returned to high school at twenty, finished in a single year, then worked his way through Marquette University, taking a law degree in 1935. He supplemented his meager income as a neophyte attorney by gambling and, in 1939 at the age of thirty-one, became the youngest circuit judge in Wisconsin history.

LINK
The Palmer Raids

The first American Red Scare began on the evening of January 2, 1919, when U.S. Attorney General A. Mitchell Palmer launched simultaneous raids on the headquarters of radical organizations in thirty-three cities, indiscriminately rounding up six thousand persons, U.S. citizens and noncitizens alike, believed to be "sympathetic to communism." Palmer and others lumped communists, radicals, and "free thinkers" together with out-and-out anarchists, who, in the wake of the Russian revolutions, were indeed committing acts of terrorism in the United States. Anarchists mailed bombs to Rockefeller, J. P. Morgan, Palmer himself, and more than thirty other prominent establishment luminaries. Most of the bombs failed to reach their destinations, the anarchists having mailed them with insufficient postage.

The Washington, D.C., home of U.S. Attorney General A. Mitchell Palmer was damaged by an anarchist bomb in 1919, prompting him to launch the infamous Palmer Raids during America's first major Red Scare.

McCarthy left the bench in 1942 to serve in the U.S. Marine Corps, entering as a second lieutenant—though he later claimed to have enlisted as a buck private and risen through the ranks. He was an intelligence briefing officer for a Marine dive bomber squadron and even flew a dozen combat missions as a gunner-observer—an admirable war record that earned him the nickname "Tail-Gunner Joe." But, preparing to enter politics, he claimed thirty-two missions—qualifying him for the Distinguished Flying Cross. In addition to this deviously acquired medal, he possessed a letter of commendation signed by Fleet Admiral Chester W. Nimitz—a forgery confected by a talented intelligence officer named Joe McCarthy.

Building on this hybrid of fact and fiction, McCarthy made a premature run for the Republican Senate nomination in 1944 while still a marine. After the war, however, he defeated incumbent Wisconsin senator Robert M. La Follette Jr. Yet McCarthy couldn't get any traction during his first three years in the Senate. Colleagues in both parties judged him a lightweight—and an ill-tempered lightweight at that. Barred from the important committees, he nevertheless found an early issue in the fight to end wartime price controls, but even this drew

"Tail-Gunner Joe" McCarthy plies his favorite tool, the microphone, c. 1954.

contempt from fellow senators when he accepted a $20,000 loan from Pepsi Cola in return for promoting the removal of price controls from sugar. The senators dubbed him the "Pepsi Cola Kid."

Mediocre, inept, despised by his colleagues, McCarthy appeared to be a nonstarter when, on February 9, 1950, it fell to him to deliver a Lincoln Day speech in a dismally obscure venue, the Republican Women's Club of Wheeling, West Virginia. Nobody knows for certain what the senator said since no manuscript exists and nobody thought of recording the speech, but the consensus is that, at one point, McCarthy drew from his coat pocket a paper and declaimed: "I have here in my hand a list of 205—a list of names that were made known to the Secretary of State as being members of the Communist Party and who nevertheless are still working and shaping policy in the State Department." No one ever actually saw the document the senator held aloft, and, apparently, no one ever asked to see it. It may have been nothing more than a random scrap McCarthy happened to have in his pocket, which came to hand as an impromptu prop.

None of the ladies in attendance had the sense that they were listening to history, and it is not likely that even McCarthy believed that

REALITY CHECK

Man in Search of a Cause

In addition to fighting price controls, McCarthy latched on to the controversial Malmedy Massacre case, in which Nazi SS officers were tried and convicted for having murdered on December 17, 1944, U.S. POWs captured during the Battle of the Bulge. McCarthy called for the commutation of death sentences handed down in July 1946 on the grounds that confessions had been extorted through torture. On the surface, it was a noble cause, which might have garnered the kind of positive public notice McCarthy craved, but instead of carefully gathering and analyzing evidence, he loudly and recklessly charged that the U.S. Army Judge Advocate Corps was covering up the torture. In the end, unable to produce a shred of evidence, he emerged not as a champion of justice, but a defender of Nazis convicted of murdering GIs. The Senate press corps unanimously voted Joseph McCarthy the worst senator holding office.

LINK
Class Warfare

McCarthy's appeal was not just against communism, but against what many identified as cultural and economic elitism. He called the communists who had purportedly been detected in the State Department "the bright young men who were born with silver spoons in their mouth." Crude populism—the pandering appeal to the "salt of the earth" in American society, the men and women not born to privilege and lacking an Ivy League education—was not new in U.S. politics when McCarthy used it, and it continues to serve as a staple of political and campaign rhetoric, in which even a presidential candidate possessed of great wealth and too many homes to keep accurate count of may deride his opponent for "elitism."

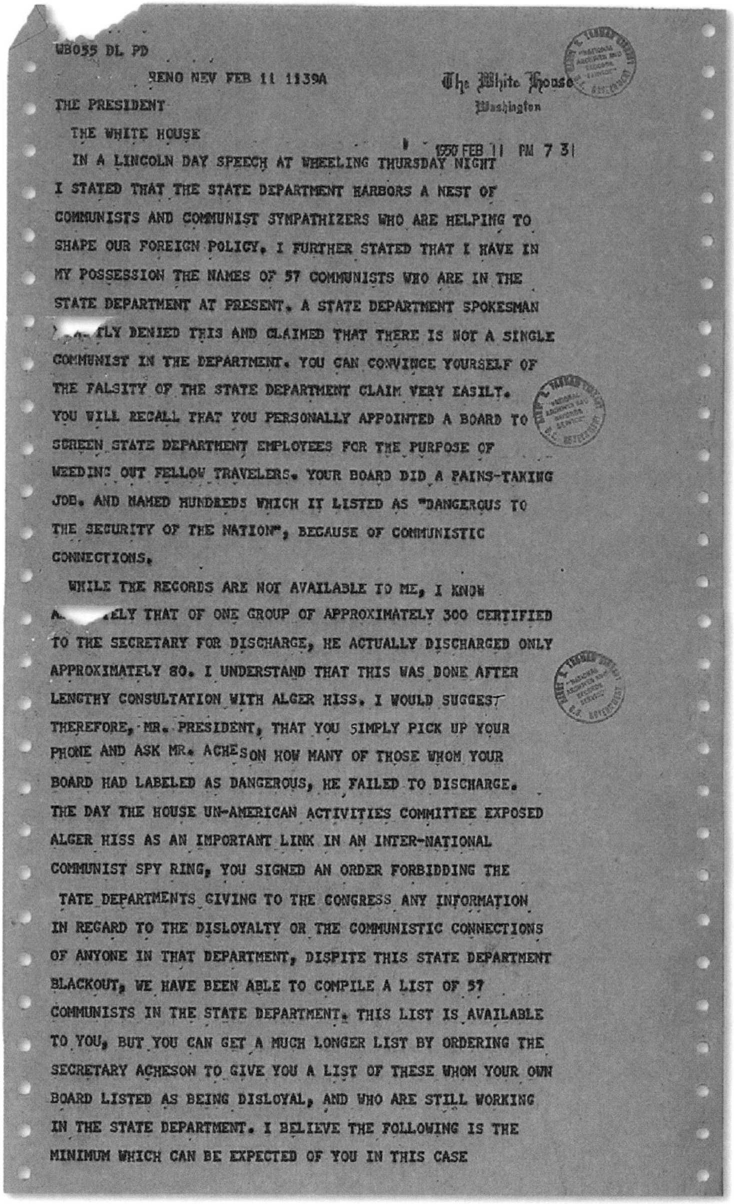

WB035 DL PD

RENO NEV FEB 11 1139A

The White House
Washington

THE PRESIDENT

THE WHITE HOUSE

1950 FEB 11 PM 7 31

IN A LINCOLN DAY SPEECH AT WHEELING THURSDAY NIGHT I STATED THAT THE STATE DEPARTMENT HARBORS A NEST OF COMMUNISTS AND COMMUNIST SYMPATHIZERS WHO ARE HELPING TO SHAPE OUR FOREIGN POLICY. I FURTHER STATED THAT I HAVE IN MY POSSESSION THE NAMES OF 57 COMMUNISTS WHO ARE IN THE STATE DEPARTMENT AT PRESENT. A STATE DEPARTMENT SPOKESMAN [illegible]TLY DENIED THIS AND CLAIMED THAT THERE IS NOT A SINGLE COMMUNIST IN THE DEPARTMENT. YOU CAN CONVINCE YOURSELF OF THE FALSITY OF THE STATE DEPARTMENT CLAIM VERY EASILY. YOU WILL RECALL THAT YOU PERSONALLY APPOINTED A BOARD TO SCREEN STATE DEPARTMENT EMPLOYEES FOR THE PURPOSE OF WEEDING OUT FELLOW TRAVELERS. YOUR BOARD DID A PAINS-TAKING JOB. AND NAMED HUNDREDS WHICH IT LISTED AS "DANGEROUS TO THE SECURITY OF THE NATION", BECAUSE OF COMMUNISTIC CONNECTIONS.

WHILE THE RECORDS ARE NOT AVAILABLE TO ME, I KNOW A[illegible]ELY THAT OF ONE GROUP OF APPROXIMATELY 300 CERTIFIED TO THE SECRETARY FOR DISCHARGE, HE ACTUALLY DISCHARGED ONLY APPROXIMATELY 80. I UNDERSTAND THAT THIS WAS DONE AFTER LENGTHY CONSULTATION WITH ALGER HISS. I WOULD SUGGEST THEREFORE, MR. PRESIDENT, THAT YOU SIMPLY PICK UP YOUR PHONE AND ASK MR. ACHESON HOW MANY OF THOSE WHOM YOUR BOARD HAD LABELED AS DANGEROUS, HE FAILED TO DISCHARGE. THE DAY THE HOUSE UN-AMERICAN ACTIVITIES COMMITTEE EXPOSED ALGER HISS AS AN IMPORTANT LINK IN AN INTER-NATIONAL COMMUNIST SPY RING, YOU SIGNED AN ORDER FORBIDDING THE TATE DEPARTMENTS GIVING TO THE CONGRESS ANY INFORMATION IN REGARD TO THE DISLOYALTY OR THE COMMUNISTIC CONNECTIONS OF ANYONE IN THAT DEPARTMENT, DISPITE THIS STATE DEPARTMENT BLACKOUT, WE HAVE BEEN ABLE TO COMPILE A LIST OF 57 COMMUNISTS IN THE STATE DEPARTMENT. THIS LIST IS AVAILABLE TO YOU, BUT YOU CAN GET A MUCH LONGER LIST BY ORDERING THE SECRETARY ACHESON TO GIVE YOU A LIST OF THESE WHOM YOUR OWN BOARD LISTED AS BEING DISLOYAL, AND WHO ARE STILL WORKING IN THE STATE DEPARTMENT. I BELIEVE THE FOLLOWING IS THE MINIMUM WHICH CAN BE EXPECTED OF YOU IN THIS CASE

Senator Joseph McCarthy sent this telegram to Harry S. Truman from Reno, Nevada, on February 11, 1950, challenging the president to look into the "nest of communists" lodged in the State Department. The document refers to McCarthy's famous speech in Wheeling, West Virginia, where he claimed to have a list of 205 State Department communists. In the telegram, the number became 57 and would prove to be a wildly moving target in the days and weeks to come.

anyone outside of the room would take notice of what he said that evening. But Frank Desmond, reporting for the *Wheeling Intelligencer*, was present and quoted the declaration in the story he wrote. His editor, Norman Yost, thought it of more than local interest and phoned the opening paragraphs to the Associated Press (AP) branch office in Charleston. The Charleston AP man phoned Yost back to ask him for confirmation about the 205 figure. Yost, in turn, called Desmond, who replied that it was the figure he'd heard, and Yost therefore confirmed it to AP, which put the story out on the national wire.

Propelled by Wheeling, McCarthy shot from nonentity to hot item. He flew to Denver, where an impromptu press conference was convened in the airport. Unlike Wheeling's Desmond, the Denver reporters were intensely curious to see the list the senator had mentioned. McCarthy responded that he would be only too happy to show it to them, but he had left it in his other suit, which was on the plane. "Left Commie List In Other Bag" was how the *Denver Post* captioned its page-one photo of McCarthy.

Tail-Gunner Joe did not look back. From Denver, he flew to Salt Lake City and leveled new charges, then continued on to Reno, where he was scheduled to speak as the guest of right-wing Nevada Republican senator George W. "Molly" Malone. Before the speech, McCarthy set himself up in Malone's office, phone to ear, frantically collecting names from one of his staffers on the other end of the line. Frank McCulloch, reporting for the *Reno Gazette*, was there and observed as the senator scribbled names, pausing greedily to ask for more. McCulloch looked at McCarthy's scratchpad and saw the name "Howard Shipley" beside the notation "HARVARD ASTR." He asked the senator what the annotation meant. "A Harvard astrologer," McCarthy replied and invited McCulloch and another reporter to the meeting scheduled for that night, where, he promised, they would get an earful. To pique their curiosity, he showed them the text of a telegram he was about to send to Harry Truman. It listed fifty-seven "card-carrying Communists" or Communist Party "loyalists," all in the government. When McCulloch pressed for more details, he was again admonished just to come to the meeting.

Before the meeting, McCulloch phoned Harvard University to ask for "Professor Howard Shipley," who, he understood, was "a scientist of some kind there."

REALITY CHECK

Take a Number

To this day, there is a dispute over whether McCarthy gave the number of names on the list as 205 or 57. Both in a subsequent telegram to President Truman and when he entered an account of the speech into the *Congressional Record*, McCarthy used the number 57. In subsequent Senate debates, however, McCarthy referred to a 1946 letter from James Byrnes (at the time secretary of state) to Congressman Adolph J. Sabath in which Byrnes reported that State Department security investigations recommended against the "permanent employment" of 284 persons, of whom 79 had been removed from their job. Subtract 79 from 284 and the remainder is 205 supposedly remaining on the department payroll. The fact was that, by the time of the Wheeling speech, only 65 of the employees alluded to in Byrnes's letter were still in the State Department. All of these had passed additional security checks.

McCarthyism as vandalism: in this piece from 1950, political cartoonist Daniel R. Fitzpatrick portrays the reckless allegations of the junior senator from Wisconsin as just so much malicious mischief.

The person who answered the phone replied that there was no Howard Shipley on the Harvard faculty, but when McCulloch insisted that there had to be, the helpful voice on the other end of the line suggested that maybe he was thinking of Harlow Shapley, a Harvard *astronomer*. Had McCulloch found a few extra moments to go to the public library, he would have discovered that Shapley was not just any astronomer, but was director of the Harvard College Observatory and the foremost authority on the Milky Way. Still, it was clear enough: McCarthy was shooting from the hip, collecting names without regard for the actual identity of those to whom the names were attached.

The reporter's misgivings were amply borne out by the speech that night in Reno. McCarthy named four names, including "Howard Shipley" of Harvard, identifying them not as communists or fellow travelers or even communist sympathizers—not really identifying them as anyone or anything, but nevertheless linking them to "people who furthered the purpose of Communism." Not only were the Reno accusations murky and indirect but they also apparently suffered from severe deflation. In Wheeling, it was 205 communists, in Malone's office, 57, and here: just 4.

"McCarthyism is Americanism with its sleeves rolled."

Senator Joseph McCarthy

After the speech, McCulloch and AP reporter Edward Olsen accompanied McCarthy to the bar at the Mapes Hotel, where the senator drank deep and drank fast. The reporters tried to pin him down. McCarthy fended them off. The audience had understood him, he said, why couldn't *they*? Undeterred, the reporters replied that he just wasn't being clear. At one point, the senator remarked that he was "not saying they're Communists," but he stood by his speech. A frustrated Olsen asked to see the list McCarthy had told the reporters back in Denver that he had left in his other suit. Obligingly, the senator first patted his pockets, then dug right into them. He stopped, turned on the reporters, and accused them of having stolen it. With this, the three men, by now all quite drunk, began an argument so loud that bar owner Charlie Mapes asked them either to hold it down or leave.

And so the shouting stopped. After one for the road, the reporters parted company with McCarthy, convinced that he was a con artist whose substantiated accusations would have negligible impact on the nation.

SEASON OF FEAR

MCCULLOCH AND OLSEN ASSUMED WRONG. McCarthy the former lawyer and judge knew his accusations would hardly stand up in a court of law, but he also realized that they were more than sufficient to make thunderous echoes in the court of public opinion. By 1950, communism had come to seem a force of nature, and most Americans were ready to hear the message of Joe McCarthy, which, though garbled and vague, was plenty loud and, given recent and current events, all too plausible.

On February 20, 1950, McCarthy brought his accusations from the popular platform back to the Senate with a marathon five-hour speech in which he claimed to have identified eighty-one "loyalty risks" in the State Department. For those keeping count, it was 205, 57, 4, and now 81. Although McCarthy substituted what he called "case numbers" for the names of those he identified as communists, he enumerated key details about each. He refused to disclose his sources, however, saying

From March 8 to July 17, 1950, Senator Millard Tydings chaired the Subcommittee on the Investigation of Loyalty of State Department Employees. He thought it would be an easy matter to show up McCarthy as a demagogue and fraud. He was mistaken.

REALITY CHECK
McCarthy's Source

Modern scholars who studied the "revelations" of February 20, 1950, have concluded that McCarthy distilled his eighty-one names from a list assembled three years earlier by investigators under the leadership of ex-FBI special agent Robert E. Lee at the request of the House Appropriations Committee. Lee's operatives sifted through State Department security documents and found that the clearances for 108 employees were deficient. This did not mean that they *were* communists, let alone spies, but that there was insufficient information to assure that they were *not*. McCarthy grossly exaggerated Lee's conclusions relating to 81 of the 108 employees, asserting that they *were* communists.

DETAILS, DETAILS

Dirty Tricks

McCarthy set his sights squarely on Tydings. When the Democrat ran for reelection in 1950, McCarthy's staff distributed a picture of Tydings with Earl Browder, former head of the American Communist Party, even though Tydings had never met Browder before July 1950, when he testified before the Tydings Committee. Retouchers had combined a 1938 photo of Tydings listening to the radio and a 1940 photo of Browder delivering a speech. McCarthy staffers included a caption pointing out that, after Browder testified before Tydings Committee, Senator Tydings replied, "Thank you, sir." It was an accurate quote, but quite out of context. As committee chair, Tydings was merely thanking the witness for his testimony. Tydings was defeated by his Republican opponent John Marshall Butler.

only that he had penetrated the "iron curtain" of secrecy enveloping the State Department.

Senator Millard Tydings, Democrat from Maryland, convened a Subcommittee on the Investigation of Loyalty of State Department Employees (the "Tydings Committee") to investigate McCarthy's allegations. Tydings was confident that he would discredit the junior senator from Wisconsin once and for all. "Let me have him for three days in public hearings, and he'll never show his face in the Senate again."

Hearings ran from March 8 to July 17, 1950. Far from being intimidated, McCarthy used the hearings as a platform from which he augmented his eighty-one "case numbers" with nine *named* individuals, implying that they were active in the State Department, even though some no longer worked there or, like Harlow Shapley (whose name McCarthy finally got right), never had. As usual, pressed for evidence, McCarthy could furnish none, but insisted that his allegations were valid nevertheless. Predictably, the Republicans fought the Democrats on the committee, generating, as the old saying goes, much heat but no light. Because Tydings was a Democrat, as was the majority of members, the Tydings Committee concluded that McCarthy had failed to prove his allegations. Tydings personally denounced McCarthy's accusations as a "fraud and a hoax," which provoked McCarthy ally Senator William Jenner, Republican from Indiana, to charge Tydings with having committed "the most brazen whitewash of treasonable conspiracy in our history." Thus the Tydings Committee concluded in a partisan standoff, which McCarthy took as a victory. For far from driving Tail-Gunner Joe out of the Senate, the Tydings Hearings ushered in the main phase of the "McCarthy Era."

SCOUNDREL TIME

McCARTHY PUT A DISTINCTIVE FACE ON ANTISUBVERSIVE CONGRESSIONAL ACTIVITY that had been ongoing since 1938. In that year, on the House side of the Capitol, a Special Investigation Committee, called the House Committee on Un-American Activities (HUAAC), was spun off of the Special Committee on Un-American Activities Authorized to Investigate Nazi Propaganda and Certain Other Propaganda Activities, created four years earlier. The new group's brief was to look into the involvement of German Americans in domestic Nazi agitation and Ku

Klux Klan activity. Almost immediately, HUAAC backed off of the KKK investigation and turned instead to probing rumors that the American Communist Party had penetrated the Depression-era Works Progress Administration (WPA).

HUAAC's activities were largely suspended during the war, when the Soviet Union was officially regarded as an ally. In 1945, however, HUAAC became a permanent House committee assigned to investigate subversion.

Target: Hollywood

HUAAC burst upon the public scene in a big way in October 1947, when forty-three members of the Hollywood film industry were subpoenaed to answer charges that they had planted communist propaganda in American movies. Those summoned included known members of the American Communist Party as well others believed to be "sympathetic to" the party—not surprising, since many in the Hollywood community were political liberals who, before and during World War II, had sided with the communist left against the fascist right. Nineteen of the forty-three declared their intention not to give evidence. Eleven of these were called before the committee. Bertolt Brecht, the famed German-born playwright and screenwriter (librettist of Kurt Weill's *The Three Penny Opera*), reversed his decision and testified, but the other ten stood firm, citing the First Amendment's guarantee of free speech and the right to assemble.

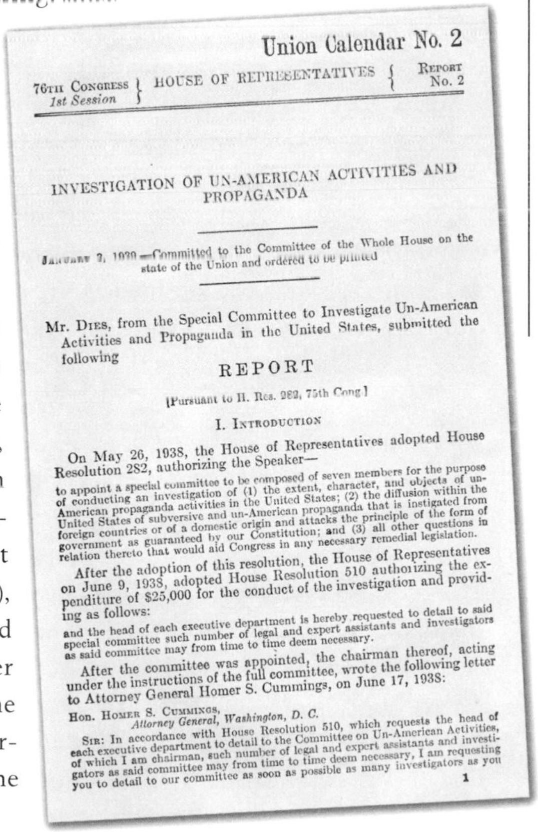

Union Calendar No. 2

76TH CONGRESS, 1st Session | HOUSE OF REPRESENTATIVES | REPORT No. 2

INVESTIGATION OF UN-AMERICAN ACTIVITIES AND PROPAGANDA

JANUARY 3, 1939.—Committed to the Committee of the Whole House on the state of the Union and ordered to be printed

Mr. DIES, from the Special Committee to Investigate Un-American Activities and Propaganda in the United States, submitted the following

REPORT

[Pursuant to H. Res. 282, 75th Cong.]

I. INTRODUCTION

On May 26, 1938, the House of Representatives adopted House Resolution 282, authorizing the Speaker—

to appoint a special committee to be composed of seven members for the purpose of conducting an investigation of (1) the extent, character, and objects of un-American propaganda activities in the United States; (2) the diffusion within the United States of subversive and un-American propaganda that is instigated from foreign countries or of a domestic origin and attacks the principle of the form of government as guaranteed by our Constitution; and (3) all other questions in relation thereto that would aid Congress in any necessary remedial legislation.

After the adoption of this resolution, the House of Representatives on June 9, 1938, adopted House Resolution 510 authorizing the expenditure of $25,000 for the conduct of the investigation and providing as follows:

and the head of each executive department is hereby requested to detail to said special committee such number of legal and expert assistants and investigators as said committee may from time to time deem necessary.

After the committee was appointed, the chairman thereof, acting under the instructions of the full committee, wrote the following letter to Attorney General Homer S. Cummings, on June 17, 1938:

HON. HOMER S. CUMMINGS,
Attorney General, Washington, D. C.

SIR: In accordance with House Resolution 510, which requests the head of each executive department to detail to the Committee on Un-American Activities, of which I am chairman, such number of legal and expert assistants and investigators as said committee may from time to time deem necessary, I am requesting you to detail to our committee as soon as possible as many investigators as you

1

HUAAC, an institution of the Cold War Red Scare, had been founded before American entry into World War II to keep tabs on pro-Nazi propaganda and other "un-American" activities in the United States.

POP CULTURE
The HUAAC IQ

In a famous early HUAAC exchange, committee member Joe Starnes (Democrat from Alabama) asked Hallie Flanagan, director of the WPA's Federal Theatre Project (FTP), if one of the playwrights that the FTP had produced, Christopher Marlowe, was a member of the Communist Party. The author of *Doctor Faustus*, Marlowe, a contemporary of Shakespeare, was murdered in Deptford, England, on May 30, 1593. In the same exchange, Starnes also observed that another playwright on the FTP roster, a "Mr. Euripides," had apparently agitated for class warfare.

On October 27, 1947, a galaxy of Hollywood celebrities converged on Washington to show their support for the "Hollywood Ten." Prominent in the front row are Humphrey Bogart and Lauren Bacall.

The most infamous question the ten refused to answer was "Are you now or have you ever been a member of the Communist Party?" It had never been illegal to be a Communist Party member, but for their failure to answer, each of the "Hollywood Ten" was indicted for contempt of Congress. As contempt proceedings got under way, the Hollywood establishment, including the president of the Motion Picture Association of America (MPAA) and many studio heads, made a show of siding with HUAAC. Such luminaries as Walt Disney, Ronald Reagan, and suave character actor Adolphe Menjou freely testified that communists were active in Hollywood and did pose a danger to America. On November 17, 1947, the Screen Actors Guild voted to compel its officers to swear an oath affirming they were not communists, and, on November 25, a day after the House voted overwhelmingly (346 to 17) to approve the contempt citations, MPAA President Eric Johnston announced that the "Hollywood Ten" would be suspended or fired and not reemployed until they were cleared of contempt charges and had sworn that they were not communists. This was the beginning of the "Hollywood blacklist."

POP CULTURE

Movie Martyrs

All of the Hollywood Ten were convicted of contempt in 1948. All received year-long prison sentences in 1950; director Edward Dmytryk (*Murder, My Sweet*; *The Caine Mutiny*) won early release by admitting to having been a Communist Party member and subsequently "named names" (identified other communists). Most of the others suffered irreversible damage to their careers. Two hundred four members of the Hollywood community courageously affirmed their support of the Ten by signing an amicus curiae (friend of the court) brief protesting the convictions.

Naming Names

The blacklist grew like a cancer. In 1949, the "Americanism Division" of the American Legion veterans' organization issued a blacklist of its own, identifying 128 individuals as members of a "Communist Conspiracy." The most famous of these was playwright and screenwriter Lillian Hellman (*The Children's Hour*, *The Little Foxes*, *Toys in the Attic*), who was effectively exiled from her profession until 1966; her 1976 memoir, *Scoundrel Time*, is an account of the blacklist period.

On June 22, 1950, another list appeared in a pamphlet titled *Red Channels*, which "outed" 151 Hollywood professionals as communists. Like Hellman and the others, they were barred from employment in the entertainment field. Throughout all of this, HUAAC was unable to unearth actual evidence of communist propaganda in American film, but a new round of investigations was launched in 1951. This time, those subpoenaed generally pleaded the Fifth Amendment—protection from self-incrimination—rather than the First. In this way, witnesses avoided "naming names" without suffering indictment for contempt, but the price was enrollment in the blacklist and loss of livelihood.

By no means was it only studio heads and financiers who threw the accused to the wolves, sacrificing the Constitution to avoid offending ticket buyers. Many directors, writers, and actors, hoping to preserve their careers, testified as "friendly witnesses" and named names. In 1952, the growing blacklist was institutionalized by the Screen Writers Guild, which gave movie studios permission to delete writing credit to anyone who failed to clear himself after being called before Congress.

Red Channels *was published in 1950 by the right-wing journal* Counterattack *in an effort to expose "Communist Influence in Radio and Television." The names it named formed a basis for the Hollywood blacklist that blighted or ended many careers in the entertainment industry for some fifteen years.*

"I do not like subversion or disloyalty in any form and if I had ever seen any I would have considered it my duty to have reported it to the proper authorities. But to hurt innocent people whom I knew many years ago in order to save myself is, to me, inhuman and indecent and dishonorable. I cannot and will not cut my conscience to fit this year's fashions."

Lillian Hellman, testimony to HUAAC, May 19, 1952

Fighting Back

Having for the most part abjectly surrendered to a Red-baiting Congress, Hollywood began to fight back only after the tide of public opinion turned against Joseph McCarthy. A senator, McCarthy was not a member of HUAAC—a House committee—but he was the spearhead of what by the mid 1950s had become a communist "witch hunt." In

DETAILS, DETAILS
Blacklist Population
The blacklist eventually came to contain the names of more than three hundred directors, radio commentators, actors, and screenwriters. Perhaps only thirty of those blacklisted were ever able to resume their professional careers openly.

1958, radio personality John Henry Faulk sued AWARE, one of many private consulting firms companies hired to vet employees for evidence of communist affiliations, after he was fired by CBS Radio. The suit encouraged various movie, radio, and television employers to defy the blacklist by hiring actors, writers, directors, and others who had been proscribed. On January 20, 1960, high-profile director Otto Preminger announced that Dalton Trumbo, one of the Hollywood Ten, had written the screenplay for his forthcoming blockbuster *Exodus*. Later in the year, Kirk Douglas, producer and star of *Spartacus*, saw to it that Trumbo was given screen credit for having written that film. By the mid 1960s, the blacklist was a thing of the past, having blighted the entertainment world for more than a decade and a half.

"I was a rat, a stoolie, and the names I named of those close friends were blacklisted and deprived of their livelihood."

Actor Sterling Hayden, 1963, concerning his HUAAC testimony

Alger Hiss testifies at his trial for perjury, 1949.

The Ordeal of Alger Hiss

Baltimore-born Alger Hiss was one of the "bright young men" of FDR's New Deal era. Graduate of Johns Hopkins and Harvard Law, protégé of Felix Frankfurter, he clerked for Supreme Court Justice Oliver Wendell Holmes Jr., practiced law, then entered government service shortly after the inauguration of Franklin D. Roosevelt. His distinguished government career was capped by a prominent role in the creation of the United Nations. He left the State Department in 1946 to become president of the Carnegie Endowment for International Peace, but as early as 1939, Whittaker Chambers, a self-admitted Soviet courier, warned Assistant Secretary of State Adolf Berle that Hiss, then Berle's assistant, was a communist. Berle wrote off Chambers as a crank, but, French intelligence had also identified Hiss as well as his brother Donald as Soviet agents. State Department official Stanley Hornbeck summoned Hiss to his office, asked if he was a communist, received a denial in response, and dropped the matter. It was not raised again until 1945, when Elizabeth Bentley, confessing to having been a courier for a Soviet spy ring, supplied the FBI with the name of Alger Hiss. That put him on the radar.

But it was not until August 3, 1948, when Chambers was subpoenaed before HUAAC, that Hiss was publicly accused of having been a Communist Party member and a spy while serving at State. Hiss's refutation before HUAAC on August 5 was so persuasive that a number of committee members urged dropping the case. Member Richard M. Nixon, an up-and-coming Republican representative from California, was not among them. Based on information he had received indirectly from the FBI, he insisted on pressing the case; however, it was Hiss himself who brought the matter to a crisis by challenging Chambers to repeat his allegations in public, outside of the slander protection afforded by a congressional hearing. Chambers called Hiss's bluff, repeating the charges on radio's *Meet the Press*. Taking the bait, Hiss brought suit, which prompted Chambers to produce in pretrial discovery documents he claimed that Hiss had copied from secret State Department files.

Both Chambers and Hiss had denied to HUAAC having committed espionage. The new evidence—if legitimate—revealed both as perjurers. The difference was that Chambers, as state's witness, was immune from prosecution, whereas Hiss was not.

More bizarrely, on December 2, 1948, Chambers revealed what came to be called the "pumpkin papers," five rolls of uncut 35-mm film—two of which consisted of images of State Department documents—which Chambers claimed to have hidden in a hollowed-out pumpkin on his Maryland farm. Following the revelation of the pumpkin papers, Nixon called for a grand jury.

The federal grand jury indicted Hiss on two counts of perjury. (He was safe from the more serious espionage charge because the statute of limitations had run out on the crimes to which Chambers pointed.) The first trial resulted in a hung jury on July 7, 1949, but Hiss was retried and found guilty on both counts of perjury on January 21, 1950, and sentenced to two concurrent five-year prison terms. Released after forty-four months, he spent the rest of his long life—he died in 1996 at the age of ninety-two—trying to prove his innocence.

A Couple from Brooklyn

BETWEEN THE LATE 1940S AND THE MID 1950S, AMERICANS WERE ASSAULTED by a political fugue, in which the strident themes of the Soviet threat, espionage, HUAAC, Hiss, Korea, McCarthy, and the Hollywood blacklist played against each other, creating a brutal cacophony. For many, the volume and tempo of this unholy music became unbearable when an unassuming, even mousy, couple from Brooklyn, Julius and Ethel Rosenberg, were put on trial beginning on March 6, 1951. The charge: conspiracy to commit espionage; the penalty: death. We met them briefly in Chapter 3, as peripheral figures in the Los Alamos espionage of Klaus

REALITY CHECK

In re Hiss

On July 31, 1975, Alger Hiss successfully sued the U.S. Department of Justice under the Freedom of Information Act to secure copies of the "pumpkin papers," the only physical evidence used to convict him of perjury. Of the five rolls of film, one was overexposed and therefore blank and two contained images of nonclassified U.S. Navy Department documents. The remaining two rolls contained photographs of documents already in evidence at the Hiss trials. With the deflation of the pumpkin papers evidence, Hiss, who had been disbarred, was readmitted to the Massachusetts bar on August 5, 1975. Despite this, Richard Nixon—who, under the weight of Watergate, had recently become the first president in U.S. history to resign—continued to assert his belief in Hiss's guilt. Historians remain divided on the subject, but most believe that Hiss had been active in the Communist Party USA and may well have furnished sensitive State Department documents to the Soviets during World War II.

Fuchs. Born in 1912, Julius Rosenberg was the son of Jewish immigrants who eked out a living in a Lower East Side sweat shop. It was a life experience that drove young Julius, as it did many others in similar situations, into the camp of communist philosophy. He joined the Young Communist League, a common institution in 1930s urban America but one with a direct pipeline to Moscow. At the league, he met Ethel Greenglass in 1936, and married her in 1939, the year he took his degree in electrical engineering from the City College of New York. In 1940, Rosenberg left the small Brooklyn apartment he shared with his wife to enlist in the army and was assigned to the Signal Corps, where he repaired radar equipment—at the time an emerging technology.

Ethel Greenglass Rosenberg was three years older than her husband. Her early aspiration was to be an actress or singer, but like many young women with similar dreams, she settled for secretarial work. At the office—she worked for a shipping company—Ethel gravitated toward union activism and, through this, the Young Communist League and the fellowship of other left-wing idealists.

The collapse of the Soviet Union in the early 1990s opened a window on information unavailable at the time of the Rosenberg trial. It became known that Julius Rosenberg had been recruited by the KGB as a spy on Labor Day 1942 through a member of the Communist Party USA. Rosenberg furnished his Soviet handlers with technical information on a variety of advanced electronic devices, including radios, radar components, and a proximity fuse that made antiaircraft ordnance more accurate. His principal KGB contact revealed that Rosenberg supplied production drawings of the Lockheed P-80 Shooting Star, America's first jet fighter. Soviet information suggests that Rosenberg also recruited other spies, including fellow electrical engineer Morton Sobell, who, at the age of ninety-one in September 2008, admitted for the first time that he and Rosenberg had given secrets to the Soviets—though he specified that he personally furnished only information on radar equipment and antiaircraft artillery devices, not atomic weapons.

According to sources from the former Soviet Union, the most important intelligence asset Rosenberg recruited was his brother-in-law David Greenglass, a GI assigned to Los Alamos as a skilled machinist. Arrested in June 1950, Greenglass confessed to having passed secrets to the Soviets. At first he denied that his sister, Ethel Rosenberg, was involved, but he later testified that it had been Julius

REALITY CHECK

Junk Secrets

While few historians continue to dispute Julius Rosenberg's guilt, there is a great deal of disagreement among scholars as to the value of the secrets he transmitted. It is now widely believed that the information Rosenberg furnished relating to nuclear weapons (including a crude cross-section diagram by his brother in law, David Greenglass) was so vague as to be of no use to Soviet scientists. It is believed, however, that Soviet munitions experts were able to exploit material Rosenberg supplied concerning the proximity fuse. The S-75 Dvina (SA-2 surface to air missile) that brought down Gary Powers's U-2 spy plane on May 1, 1960, over Sverdlovsk, USSR, was equipped with a proximity fuse that functioned like that of the American design (see Chapter 15). Sobell's information on the advanced SCR 584 radar was also probably used to target U.S. aircraft during the Korean and Vietnam wars.

who persuaded her to recruit him during a 1944 visit to him in Albuquerque. Based on Greenglass's confession, the FBI arrested Julius Rosenberg on July 17, 1950, and Ethel on August 11.

The government tried the Rosenbergs and Sobell on March 6, 1951, with David Greenglass serving as the principal prosecution witness. His most damning testimony was that Julius obtained nuclear and other military secrets and brought them to the Brooklyn apartment, where Ethel typed them for delivery to the Soviets. He also testified that he gave Julius a cross-section sketch he had made of the kind of atomic bomb dropped on Nagasaki, which Rosenberg intended to deliver to his Soviet handler.

Tried with the Rosenbergs in 1951, Morton Sobell steadfastly protested his innocence of espionage—until 2008, when, at age ninety-one, he admitted that he and Julius Rosenberg had given military secrets to the Soviets.

Cause Célèbre

The trial ended on March 29, 1951, with guilty verdicts for all three defendants; on April 5, the Rosenbergs were each sentenced to death, and Sobell to thirty years' imprisonment (he would serve eighteen). The trial itself commanded the attention of the media but created little controversy. The death sentences, however, passed upon the parents of two boys, ages four and eight, provoked national and international protests of anti-Semitism and witch hunting. Luminaries ranging from the French Nobel Laureate Jean-Paul Sartre to Albert Einstein to Pablo Picasso to Pope Pius XII appealed for clemency, as did hundreds of thousands of ordinary Americans. President Eisenhower, persuaded that the trial had been fair, announced on February 11, 1953, his decision to withhold clemency.

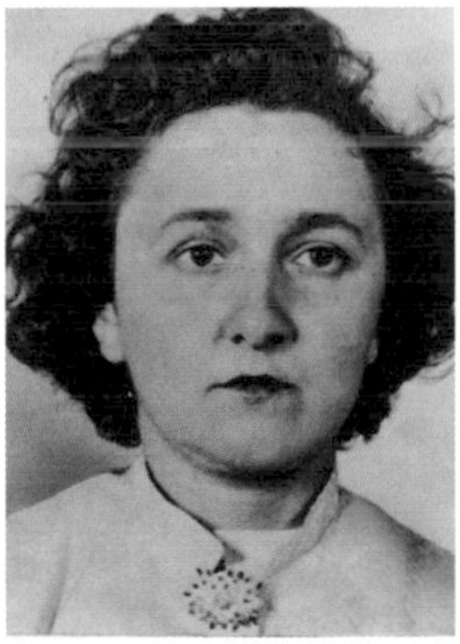

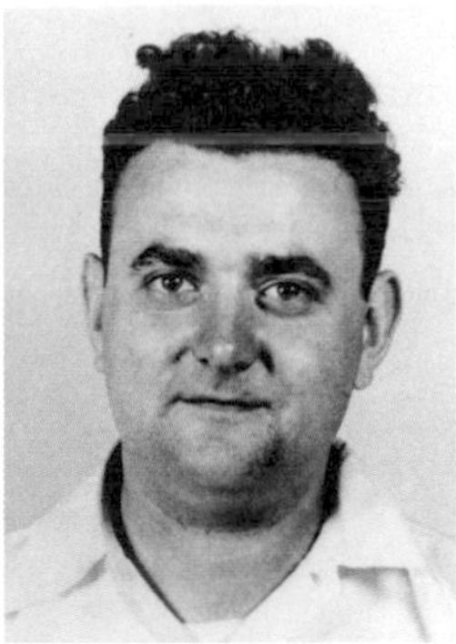

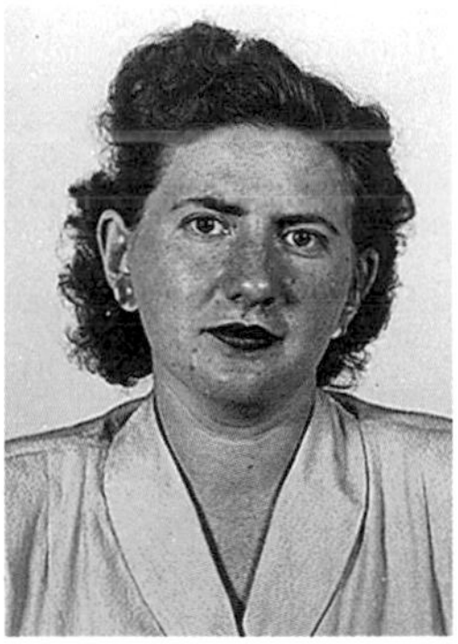

Julius and Ethel Rosenberg, the unlikely faces of Soviet espionage in America; FBI mug shot of David Greenglass, atomic spy—and government witness against his sister Ethel Rosenberg and brother-in-law Julius; Ruth Greenglass persuaded her husband, David Greenglass, to pass Los Alamos secrets to their brother-in-law, Julius Rosenberg. In return for immunity from prosecution, she testified at the Rosenberg trial, implicating Ethel Rosenberg in the espionage conspiracy.

LINK

Extraordinary Rendition, Old School

Morton Sobell was vacationing in Mexico City at the time of the arrest of the Rosenbergs, and he later claimed that Mexican police illegally abducted him on August 16, 1950, and drove him across the U.S. border, where FBI agents arrested him. The U.S. Department of Justice maintained that he was formally extradited by Mexico, but the Mexican government admitted in 1956 that there had been no formal extradition.

A fundamental principle of international law designed to protect individual rights, extradition was almost certainly violated in the Sobell case, much as U.S. law enforcement authorities, in prosecuting the so-called war on terror after September 11, 2001, have abducted or authorized the abduction of individuals in foreign countries for the purpose of interrogating them. Often, the interrogation has been carried out in yet other friendly foreign countries unconstrained by U.S. laws against torture. The practice is called "extraordinary rendition."

"I consider your crime worse than murder . . . millions more of innocent people may pay the price of your treason. Indeed, by your betrayal you undoubtedly have altered the course of history to the disadvantage of our country."

Judge Irving Kaufman in his sentence of the Rosenbergs on April 5, 1951

After all appeals failed, the Rosenbergs were scheduled to be executed in the electric chair at Sing Sing, in Ossining, New York, on June 18, 1953. The day before, Supreme Court Associate Justice William O. Douglas granted a stay, which, however, was vacated at noon on Friday, June 19. This put the hour of the executions after sundown and the commencement of the Jewish Sabbath. Rosenberg attorney Emanuel Hirsch Bloch accordingly filed a complaint based on freedom of religion, but if he had hoped to put off the execution, he failed. The objection was satisfied by advancing the execution before the sun set.

Julius Rosenberg was seated in the electric chair first. Eyewitnesses reported that it was a textbook operation, and that he died quietly as soon as the current was applied. His wife did not pass so gently. Sing Sing's electric chair had been built to accommodate a man. Ethel Rosenberg was a small woman, and the electrodes at all points fit her loosely, making imperfect contact. As a result, she had to be electrocuted three times before the presiding physician pronounced her dead. Witnesses were haunted by her convulsive struggle and by the eerie plume of smoke rising from her hooded head.

THE "MCCARTHY ERA"

A FEW PERIODS OF AMERICAN HISTORY HAVE BEEN IDENTIFIED with influential figures—the Age of Jefferson, the Jacksonian Era, the Roosevelt Years—but only one is remembered as infamous: the McCarthy Era.

From 1950 onward, "McCarthyism" gathered an awful momentum. The senator's accusations, innuendoes, and Senate hearings generated limitless publicity and were greeted with approval from a public grateful for a selfless tribune unafraid to lift every rock under which communist snakes lurked.

McCarthy's rise was the product of the senator's hunger for celebrity and his willingness to exploit a nation's fear to climb above his own mediocrity, but it was also symptomatic of the collective egocentrism of postwar America. Most Americans emerged from World War II persuaded that the United States was the most powerful nation on earth and could therefore control the course of world events. Instead of seeing the Soviet European expansion as a function of Soviet power, and instead of seeing the triumph of communism in China as the end stage of centuries of Chinese feudalism and the corruption of the rival KMT, Americans interpreted both events as a failure of the U.S. government to use its power to defeat the march of communism. McCarthy's message was not directed against Stalin or Mao, but against Harry Truman and the Democratic Party for having tolerated communist subversion of American government. McCarthy was never able to bring about the actual prosecution of anyone he identified as a subversive, but he soon discovered that mere accusation was sufficient, and it was on a pile of accusations that McCarthy climbed to power.

The Rosenbergs are transported to prison after having been found guilty on March 29, 1951, of conspiracy to commit espionage. Their death sentences were handed down the following month.

"The issue between Republicans and Democrats is clearly drawn . . . by those that have been in charge of twenty years of treason."

Joseph McCarthy, Republican National Convention, July 9, 1952

McCarthy was known to drink Scotch by the tumbler and to chase it with bicarbonate of soda and a quarter-pound stick of butter, which, he believed, coated his stomach the better to hold his liquor. He admitted to assaulting liberal columnist Drew Pearson in the Senate cloakroom—but claimed only to have slapped him, whereas Pearson reported that he had been painfully kneed in the groin. For this,

POP CULTURE

Enduring Coinage

The term "McCarthyism" was first used in print by the political cartoonist Herbert Block—whose nom de plume was Herblock—in a March 29, 1950, *Washington Post* cartoon. Herblock did not intend it as a compliment, but as shorthand for demagoguery; however, McCarthy himself was quick to preempt the term. He used it in speeches and the title of his 1952 memoir-manifesto, *McCarthyism: The Fight for America.*

Pearson sought revenge by collecting evidence that McCarthy was a closet homosexual—a career-destroying accusation in the 1950s—but no newspaper would publish it anymore than they dared publish stories about McCarthy's drinking. Anyone who crossed McCarthy exposed himself to an accusation of disloyalty, of being "soft on communism," or even of being a communist.

McCarthy treated Senate witnesses with the verbal equivalent of a knee to the groin. He was a bully, and like any bully, he recruited a gang—consisting of friendly or at least compliant reporters. "If you want to be against McCarthy, boys," he told a group of them at an impromptu press conference, "you've got to be a Communist or a cocksucker."

Decline

The truth was that McCarthy needed more than a willing audience and a complicit corps of journalists: he needed people to accuse. As long as Truman was in office, he had the Democrats, but when Republican

A Catholic lay organization called the Catechism Guild published this anticommunist comic book in 1947. The "What if?" approach was typical of popular American propaganda during the early Cold War period.

Dwight D. Eisenhower won the White House in 1952, carrying on his coattails a Republican majority in both houses of Congress, Tail-Gunner Joe found himself without targets.

McCarthy was also reelected in 1952—but by a narrower margin than other Republicans. He did not heed this warning to mend his bullying ways. In a November 1953 speech, he criticized the new president for retaining communists in key government positions and for failing to secure the release of American pilots shot down over China during the Korean War. Worse, before the year was out, McCarthy altered the slogan he had coined at the 1952 Republican National Convention to describe the FDR-Truman era—"twenty years of treason"—to "*twenty-one* years of treason," thereby including Ike's first year in office.

Even as he bit the Republican hand that fed him, McCarthy, in 1953, was named chairman of the Senate Committee on Government Operations, which included the Senate Permanent Subcommittee on Investigations. From this platform he continued his witch hunting, recruiting an oily young attorney, Roy Cohn, as his chief counsel and another young lawyer on the make, Robert F. Kennedy, as assistant counsel. Both served as hatchet men in a series of breathtakingly reckless investigations. The subcommittee looked into purported subversion of the Voice of America, an operation of the State Department's U.S. Information Agency, tasked with beaming anti-Soviet propaganda to the iron curtain countries. McCarthy next sent Cohn to purge the library program of the International Information Agency of books by "pro-Communist" authors. As a result, some embassy libraries burned the banned books. McCarthy also appointed as staff director of the subcommittee J. B. Matthews, who had recently asserted that the "largest single group supporting the Communist apparatus in the United States is composed of Protestant Clergymen." When fellow senators denounced the appointment, McCarthy at first stood firm, but finally yielded to pressure and accepted Matthews's resignation. It was the first chink in the McCarthy armor.

Fall

Despite the Matthews debacle, McCarthy pushed the envelope in the autumn of 1953 by steering his subcommittee into an investigation of the U.S. Army Signal Corps laboratory at Fort Monmouth, New Jersey.

REALITY CHECK

Ike's Shame

In a 1952 campaign speech delivered in Green Bay, Wisconsin, candidate Eisenhower sought to distance himself—slightly—from McCarthy by explaining that he agreed with the senator's goal of purging disloyalty from U.S. government, but that he objected to his methods. Originally, Ike had included in his speech a vigorous defense of George Marshall, Truman's envoy to China, secretary of state, and secretary of defense—and, as U.S. Army chief of staff during World War II, Eisenhower's commanding officer, mentor, and champion. In perhaps his most outrageous accusation, McCarthy had blamed Marshall for the "loss" of China and the "subversion" of the State Department. Ike's handlers, however, persuaded him to drop the defense from his Green Bay speech—and from subsequent versions of the speech delivered elsewhere. Although a *New York Times* reporter learned of the deletion and the news was published on page one, Ike easily triumphed over his Democratic opponent, Adlai Stevenson.

Attorney Roy M. Cohn was McCarthy's Machiavellian cheerleader and hatchet man.

He hoped to expose a spy ring there, but when that effort came to nothing, he turned instead against Irving Peress, an army major who had refused to answer questions about his political affiliations on a loyalty-review questionnaire. Subpoenaed before McCarthy's subcommittee on January 30, 1954, Peress pleaded the Fifth Amendment, whereupon McCarthy demanded that Secretary of the Army Robert Stevens court-martial him. To get Stevens off the hook, Peress requested of his commanding officer that his discharge from the army—mandated within ninety days because of his refusal to respond fully to the loyalty questionnaire—be made effective immediately. Brigadier General Ralph W. Zwicker complied, prompting a frustrated McCarthy to subpoena him. When Zwicker refused to answer some of McCarthy's questions, the senator pronounced him unfit "to wear that uniform." Abuse of a decorated World War II combat officer turned the military squarely against Joseph McCarthy. Seeking to head off a rebellion by uniformed officers, McCarthy and his allies met with Army secretary Stevens and persuaded him to sign a "memorandum of understanding" acknowledging the authority of McCarthy's subcommittee to obtain answers from army personnel. McCarthy then crowed to reporters that Stevens "could not have given in more abjectly if he had got down on his knees."

That did it.

President Eisenhower, former supreme allied commander in World War II, a career army officer, secretly authorized a counterattack. With his blessing, the army leveled a charge of its own, accusing McCarthy and Cohn of exerting illegal influence on the army to secure special treatment for a draftee, Private G. David Schine, an aide to McCarthy and a friend (many believed a lover) of Cohn. McCarthy's own subcommittee was charged with investigating the allegations, Republican Senator Karl Mundt appointed to chair the proceedings in place of McCarthy.

The "Army-McCarthy hearings" were convened on April 22, 1954, and, in a history-making innovation, were televised live—for the next thirty-six days. An estimated twenty million viewers (at a time when relatively few families even owned television sets) were riveted. McCarthy behaved as he had always behaved—a reckless, slanderous bully—but now Americans saw the behavior, close up and in real time.

The climax of the hearings came on June 9, when the army's civilian lawyer, Joseph N. Welch, called on Roy Cohn to produce, "before the sun goes down," the list McCarthy claimed to have of 130 communists currently employed in defense plants. At this, McCarthy interrupted, seeking to deflect Welch's attack by calling on *him* to look into his own Boston law offices, which (he said) harbored one young attorney, Fred Fisher by name, who had once belonged to the National Lawyers Guild, which McCarthy called "the legal mouthpiece of the Communist Party."

Before the TV cameras, Welch turned from Cohn to McCarthy: "Senator McCarthy, I think until this moment . . ." McCarthy interrupted: "Just a minute. Let me ask, Jim—will you get the news story to the effect that this man belongs to this Communist front organization." Welch cut him off: "I will tell you that he belonged to it. Senator, you won't need anything in the record when I finish telling you this. Until this moment, Senator, I think I never really gauged your cruelty or your recklessness." He went on to explain that Fisher had volunteered to accompany him to the hearings, but admitted to having been a

REALITY CHECK

Unpopularity Contest

Gallup polls in January 1954 indicated that 50 percent of the American public had a positive opinion of Joe McCarthy. By June, the number had plummeted to 34 percent, and those expressing a negative opinion of the senator rose from 29 to 45 percent.

Testifying at the Army-McCarthy Hearings, 1954, Senator Joseph McCarthy uses a chart in an effort to disprove allegations that he and Roy Cohn (behind the senator's hand and pointer) had improperly exerted influence to obtain special treatment for Private G. David Schine.

SEE IT NOW

Edward R. Murrow, a broadcast journalist who first rose to national fame for his CBS Radio eyewitness reports of the London Blitz, devoted the March 9, 1954, episode of his pioneering TV news show, *See It Now*, to "A Report on Senator Joseph R. McCarthy."

Murrow condemned McCarthy with clips of his own diatribes, concluding the program by observing that "His primary achievement has been in confusing the public mind, as between the internal and the external threats of Communism. We must not confuse dissent with disloyalty." Murrow continued: "We will not walk in fear, one of another. We will not be driven by fear into an age of unreason, if we dig deep in our history and our doctrine, and remember that we are not descended from fearful men. . . . We proclaim ourselves, as indeed we are, the defenders of freedom, wherever it continues to exist in the world, but we cannot defend freedom abroad by deserting it at home."

Murrow devoted another *See It Now* episode to McCarthy and invited him to respond. He did, on the April 9 broadcast, delivering a cascade of countercharges against the newsman. They only further undermined McCarthy. Coupled with the debacle of the Army-McCarthy Hearings, Murrow's *See It Now* rung down the curtain on the McCarthy Era.

The demagogue McCarthy met his match in the newsman Edward R. Murrow, who used his television program See It Now *to undo the Wisconsin senator's shoddy crusade.*

member of the National Lawyers Guild. "And I said," Welch continued, "'Fred, I just don't think I'm going to ask you to work on the case. If I do, one of these days that will come out and go over national television and it will hurt like the dickens.' So, Senator, I asked him to go back to Boston. Little did I dream you could be so reckless and so cruel as to do an injury to that lad. It is true he is still with Hale & Dorr. It is true that he will continue to be with Hale & Dorr. It is, I regret to say, equally true that I fear he shall always bear a scar, needlessly inflicted by you. If it were in my power to forgive you for your reckless cruelty, I would do so. I like to think I'm a gentle man, but your forgiveness will have to come from someone other than me."

McCarthy interrupted again: "Now, I just give this man's record, and I want to say, Mr. Welch, that it has been labeled long before he became a member as early as 1944."

Welch shot back: "Senator, may we not drop this? We know he belonged to the Lawyer's Guild."

Again, McCarthy tried to drown Welch out. But the army counsel would have none of it and proceeded to deliver the most memorable lines in the entire thirty-six days of hearings: "Let us not assassinate this lad further, Senator. You've done enough. Have you no sense of decency, sir? At long last, have you left no sense of decency?"

The packed gallery burst into applause, and the Republican Party cut McCarthy loose. Before the year was out, the Senate voted censure of McCarthy, and although he continued to serve, his speeches on the Senate floor were delivered to a conspicuously empty chamber. He retreated more deeply into the bottle, and died on May 2, 1957, of inflammation of the liver. He was forty-eight.

TAKEAWAY

A Reign of Fear

The Cold War advances by the Soviet Union, the victory of the communists in China, and the outbreak of the Korean War combined with revelations of Soviet espionage in various levels of American government to create a climate of fear, outrage, and frustration that made fertile ground for a national Red Scare. The most visible manifestations were the reckless demagoguery of Senator Joseph McCarthy, the partisan-driven work of HUAAC, and the trials of Alger Hiss and the Rosenbergs. Americans were faced with an all-too familiar political paradox: the prospect of defending democracy with actions that destroyed it. It was the most chilling aspect of the Cold War.

A LEGACY

THE MCCARTHY ERA LEFT THE NATION MORE DEEPLY AND BITTERLY DIVIDED along partisan lines than ever before. Republicans never relinquished their claim to being the party most committed and best able to "fight communism." For their part, the Democrats were put perpetually on the defensive, always feeling constrained to prove they were not "soft on communism." This burden would influence Democrats John F. Kennedy in his response to the Cuban Missile Crisis (see Chapter 15) and Lyndon B. Johnson in his prosecution of the Vietnam War (see Chapter 16).

PART FIVE

COMBAT BY PROXY

CHAPTER 14

HIGH NOON IN HUNGARY

Freedom Thwarted in the Soviet Bloc

FRANK JAMES COOPER OF HELENA, MONTANA, flopped as a salesman and then as a front man for a photographer before he moved to Hollywood and landed an uncredited bit in a 1925 Tom Mix silent western. Four years later, in his first talking picture—an adaptation of the classic Owen Wister western novel *The Virginian*—Gary Cooper became a star and was on his way to becoming an American icon. So pervasive was Cooper's "strong, silent type" image that World War I hero Sergeant Alvin York refused to approve any movie about his life that did not star Gary Cooper, and the actor won his first Oscar for his 1942 performance as the title character in *Sergeant York.*

Five years later, on October 23, 1947, Cooper disappointed some and pleased others when he voluntarily appeared before the House Un-American Activities Committee (HUAAC). He didn't "name names," but did testify that he had turned down many scripts because "they were tinged with communistic ideas" and, in Hollywood circles, had certainly heard his fair share of "statements . . . to the effect that the communistic system had a great many features that were desirable."

A month after Cooper testified, the blacklist gripped Tinsel Town, and five years after that, Cooper starred in the film with which he is now most thoroughly identified. It was a western called *High Noon.*

AMERICAN ALLEGORY

EVERYONE—INCLUDING THE MEMBERS of the Academy of Motion Picture Arts and Sciences, who awarded him the 1952 Best Actor Oscar—agreed that "Coop" had been *the* man to play Will Kane, the marshal of Hadleyville, Kansas, whose conscience compels him to face down the vengeance of murderer Frank Miller and his gang on the town streets at "high noon," even after everyone else runs away, leaving him to confront four killers alone.

Gary Cooper as Marshal Will Kane in High Noon, *1952.*

It was a quintessentially American story, a story of righteousness and courage. At least that's the way the studio billed it. But screenwriter Carl Foreman later explained that he all along intended *High Noon* as an allegory of how "good men" failed to speak out against McCarthyism and of how, in particular, the Hollywood community (Hadleyville = Hollywood) had cravenly surrendered scores of their members to the blacklist.

If *High Noon* was intended as a gripping allegory of betrayal in Hollywood, the 1952 film can also be seen, in retrospect, as a symbolic foreshadowing of another Cold War betrayal, this one on an international scale, which took place four years later.

HUNGARY HELD CAPTIVE

HUNGARY WAS AMONG THE NATIONS the Red Army "liberated" and then occupied at the end of World War II. The Soviet-controlled Hungarian Communist Party systematically replaced the democratically elected postwar government, and the once-vigorous economy of Hungary was nationalized on the Soviet model, resulting in economic blight and spiritual malaise. The Soviets forced the Hungarian government to turn the Interior Ministry over to a Kremlin-approved communist, László Rajk. Rajk created the Hungarian State Security Police (Államvédelmi Hatóság, or AVH), the terroristic muscle by which the communists took over completely, proclaiming the People's Republic of Hungary

POP CULTURE

An Angry Duke

John Wayne, another American screen icon, did not need screenwriter Carl Foreman to tell him that *High Noon* was a McCarthy-era allegory. He caught on to the blacklisting theme right away, and it made him furious—a fact he did not reveal until May 1971 when, in a *Playboy* interview, he condemned the celebrated classic as "the most un-American thing I've ever seen in my whole life." As it turned out, *High Noon* was the last film Foreman wrote before *he* was blacklisted. With some others who shared his fate, Foreman moved to England and wrote for American studios under pseudonyms. As for "Duke" Wayne, he eagerly took credit for having helped put Foreman on the blacklist.

PREVIOUS SPREAD: *A "Huey" helicopter prepares to land during a resupply mission during Operation MacArthur in South Vietnam, December 1967.*

A c. 1949 propaganda print depicts Hungary's communist dictator Mátyás Rákosi as a benevolent ruler thoughtfully examining stalks of wheat. Rákosi had prints such as this posted publicly all over Hungary.

in 1949 and transforming the country into a Soviet satellite. Under the dictatorship of Mátyás Rákosi, the People's Republic used the AVH to purge dissidents; thousands were exiled to concentration camps in eastern Hungary, remote from the political hotbed of Budapest. Hundreds of others were executed.

The Winds of Democracy

Even as Hungarian government and society became increasingly repressive, Soviet society experienced the first intimations of liberalization. Joseph Stalin died suddenly on March 5, 1953, prompting the communist parties of the Soviet Union and many satellite countries to propose liberal reforms. In this spirit, the hard-line Stalinist Mátyás Rákosi was replaced by the moderate reformer Imre Nagy as Hungary's prime minister. Two years later, however, in April 1955, Rákosi managed to discredit and remove Nagy. A month later, Hungary joined other Soviet satellites in the Warsaw Pact, signed on May 14.

From the point of view of the Western democracies, the creation of the Warsaw Pact, a Soviet response to NATO (see Chapter 10), wedded Hungary to the Soviet Union. But as many Hungarians saw it, the Warsaw Pact promised greater independence. After all, the pact bound Soviet leaders to "respect [the] . . . independence and sovereignty" of members and to refrain from interfering in their internal affairs. In effect, therefore, Rákosi, the communist reactionary, found that he had returned to power at a moment of unexpectedly forward-looking reform and liberalization.

The Hungarian intelligentsia believed the noninterference pledge provided an opening for Hungary to *leave* the pact altogether and to declare neutrality. Liberals began agitating for withdrawal from the Warsaw Pact, a movement that both Rákosi and Nikita Khrushchev, who had assumed the reins of Soviet government after the death of Stalin, opposed. Yet even as he sought to block any defection, Khrushchev delivered in a February 24, 1956, speech to the delegates of the Communist Party's Twentieth Congress, a stunning repudiation of Joseph Stalin for the catastrophic excesses of his long regime. This denunciation extended to the disciples of Stalin and thus signaled to the reformers in Hungary that the Kremlin might not oppose their removing Rákosi. Accordingly,

PLIGHT OF THE MIDDLE TIER

Hungary, like many other Central and Eastern European countries, had the geographical misfortune of being located between great empires, the Germans and Austrians to the west, and the Ottoman Turks and Russians to the east. As a result, since the sixteenth century, its history was one of domination by one side or the other.

In the eighteenth century, Hungary was swallowed up by the Hapsburgs and was dominated by Austria. The dismemberment of the Austro-Hungarian Empire after World War I gave Hungary independence, but also made it ripe for the opposing influences of Soviet communism and German fascism. In the 1930s, the Hungarian government was dominated by German-aligned fascists, and the country entered World War II on the side of Germany, but in 1943, after Hungarian forces had suffered horrific reverses on the Russian front, the government sought a separate peace with the Allies.

Hitler responded by invading its erstwhile ally early in 1944, and when Hungarian regent Miklós Horthy, fascist though he was, attempted to disengage the nation from the war in October, Hitler authorized a daring commando operation that forced Horthy from power and replaced him with a Nazi puppet, Ferenc Szálasi. This sharply divided the nation between the pro-Nazi Arrow Cross Party and the antifascist resistance aligned with the Soviet Union; however, when the Red Army occupied Hungary at the end of the war, it did so brutally, as if it were occupying an enemy nation. Nevertheless, a significant pro Soviet faction was willing to subordinate Hungarian autonomy to the needs of the evolving Soviet bloc. So Hungary entered the Cold War period, still deeply divided, though no longer between fascists and communists, but among three major factions: communists willing to accept Soviet domination, communists who desired a high degree of autonomy, and non communists, who wanted a democratic future.

Hitler lieutenant Hermann Göring, dagger in scabbard, confers with Admiral Horthy at Carinhall, Göring's luxurious country estate northeast of Berlin.

the hard liner was replaced as general secretary of the Hungarian Communist Party by moderate Ernő Gerő on July 18, 1956.

In the meantime, another crack appeared in the presumed monolith of the Soviet bloc as Polish workers in Poznań rose up in violent anti-Soviet protest in June 1956. Although the uprising was quickly crushed, the Polish government sought to mollify the people by appointing a liberal reformer, Władisław Gomułka, as first secretary of the Polish Communist Party. In October, Gomułka obtained from the Soviets valuable trade concessions as well as a reduction in the Red

These anti-Soviet protestors in Poznań, Poland, 1956, carry a banner proclaiming "We Demand Bread!"

Army occupation force. Soon, word of this "Polish October" spread throughout the communist world.

Since the resignation of Rákosi in July, Hungary's intelligentsia, mostly university students, had been forming groups to discuss reforms. As it evolved, Polish October became the catalyst that promoted the transition from political discussion to a full-fledged political movement, and on October 16, university students in Szeged publicly resigned from the officially sanctioned communist student union (DISZ) to resurrect the banned Union of Hungarian University and Academy Students (MEFESZ), a democratic organization. Soon, students at other Hungarian universities did the same, and on October 22, students at Budapest's Technical University drew up a formal list of demands for the reform of Hungarian government.

Uprising

On the next day, October 23, 1956, the students joined members of the Hungarian Writers' Union to proclaim solidarity with the Polish reformers by ceremonially laying a wreath at the base of a statue of General Józef Bem, Polish-born hero of the Hungarian War of Independence of 1848–49. By the afternoon, some twenty thousand young men and women had gathered at the statue. The president of the Writers' Union read out a manifesto; the students declaimed their proclamation of demands; then everyone joined in singing the Hungarian National Anthem. Throughout the crowd, people seized Hungarian flags, cut out the communist insignia from them, and waved the banners, holes and all.

"What is immutable in socialism can be reduced to the abolition of the exploitation of man by man. The roads of achieving the goal can be and are different. . . . The model of socialism can also vary. It can be shaped in a manner as we see it in Yugoslavia; it can be different still."

Władysław Gomułka, speech of October 20, 1956

The crowd then crossed the Danube to join another group of protestors outside of the Parliament. By early evening, nearly a quarter million had gathered at the heart of Hungarian government.

Moderate though he was, Ernő Gerő broadcast a speech condemning the demonstrations as "reactionary." This served only to incite the protestors further, moving them to attack a massive bronze statue of Stalin on the site of a church that had been demolished to make room for the monument. In the meantime, another crowd attempted to break through the AVH guards surrounding the studios

Budapest revolutionaries take out their rage against a statue of Stalin.

of Radio Budapest. The guards fired on the protestors, who responded by swarming the outnumbered AVH. Hungarian army troops arrived to reinforce the police, but suddenly removed their caps, ripped the red star insignias from them, and joined the protestors. It was now a full-scale insurrection, as soldiers helped the protestors seize guns from the local armory.

Before the night of October 23 ended, Gerő called on the Soviet military for help, and, early on the morning of October 24, Red Army tanks rolled into Budapest. They deployed outside of the Parliament building and at bridges and roads. In response to this, the armed demonstrators—now more properly called revolutionaries—erected street barricades of their own and even commandeered a few of the Soviet tanks. Amid the growing chaos of October 24, the original reformer, Imre Nagy, returned to assume the post of prime minister. He broadcast a plea for an end to the violence and pledged political reforms. But by this time, the revolution had a momentum of its own, and the insurrectionists seized the radio building as fighting erupted against AVH units. Mostly, the Soviet troops did nothing but observe.

Imre Nagy, doomed prime minister of Hungary during its short-lived 1956 independence.

On the next day, October 25, the revolutionaries attacked the Parliament building itself, forcing Gerő and András Hegedüs, unseated as prime minister by Nagy, to flee for their lives. The collapse of the Soviet-backed government emboldened the revolutionaries to turn their attacks against the Soviet troops as a general strike was called and workers poured into the streets, joining the students and other revolutionaries.

Throughout the day, various leaders struggled to get their arms around the revolution and to bring it under a central authority. But combat remained localized, fragmented, and often brutal. In many places, the fighting was nothing less than out-and-out riot, in which mobs attacked the symbols of Soviet authority and burned communist books. Elsewhere, neighborhoods organized themselves into ad hoc militias to bring rough justice to anyone identified as a member of the AVH or a pro-Soviet sympathizer.

The disorganized revolution burned on until October 28, when a general ceasefire was proclaimed. Two days later, all Soviet forces withdrew from Budapest and holed up quietly in rural garrisons.

REALITY CHECK
Communist Front

Even as they witnessed signs of rebellion in Poland and outright revolution in Hungary, most Americans persisted in the belief that "world communism" was essentially unified, even monolithic. In fact, by the mid 1950s, relations between the two biggest communist states, the Soviet Union and the People's Republic of China, were in sharp decline; nevertheless, it is believed that Mao Zedong, through Chinese Communist Party deputy chairman Liu Shaoqi, pressured Khrushchev to crush the Hungarian uprising. No one suggests that the Soviet leader simply yielded to Chinese pressure, but, at the very least, it must have confirmed him in his decision to intervene.

Victory?

Unwilling to provoke the Soviets, Imre Nagy, on October 27, formed a government that included both communist and non-communist ministers. It abolished the AVH and ended the single-party system. Formerly outlawed parties were authorized to reconstitute; by November 4, many of the revolutionaries were confident that Red Army units were withdrawing from Hungary. In another hopeful sign, high-profile political prisoners held by the pro-Soviet government were released.

The events of the Hungarian Revolution were observed from both sides of the iron curtain. Yet while the Eisenhower administration made few public statements concerning it, the broadcast propaganda arm of the CIA, Radio Free Europe, beamed a continuous stream of encouraging messages, promising the revolutionaries the full support of the United States. For his part, Khrushchev tried at first to steer a minimally interventionist course. He and his top military adviser, war hero Marshal Georgi Zhukov, resisted calls from hard-line Stalinist holdovers, especially Vyacheslav Molotov, to put a swift end to the revolution. Khrushchev shared one important trait with the leader he had so recently denounced. Like Stalin, he was first and last a pragmatist, who both distrusted and downplayed idealism as a motive for political action. He believed that the uprising in Hungary was not so much an ideological revolt as it was an expression of anger over the way Hungary's communists had mismanaged the economy. The people did not want democracy, he thought. They wanted refrigerators. Thus, on October 30, 1956, the Soviet Presidium voted not to act against the new Hungarian National Government, and on October 31 even promulgated "Principles of Development and Further Strengthening of Friendship and Cooperation between the Soviet Union and other Socialist States," which hinted at the peaceful withdrawal of Soviet troops from Hungary.

"THE IRON CURTAIN ISN'T SOUNDPROOF"

Radio Free Europe (RFE) was founded in 1949 in New York by the National Committee for a Free Europe. Ostensibly a private organization—funded through a combination of private and community initiatives as well as a congressional endowment—the committee and RFE were actually CIA operations. Transmission facilities were based in Munich, Germany, and the debut broadcast was made on July 4, 1950, beamed to Czechoslovakia.

Despite the CIA connection, RFE broadcasts were never crude propaganda. Instead, RFE sought to establish popular credibility as a source offering a factual alternative to the Communist Party–controlled press and radio. RFE's supporters regarded it as a practical manifestation of the biblical injunction that the "truth shall set you free."

Until the Hungarian Revolution, RFE balanced policy directives from the CIA and the State Department. The embarrassing—not to say tragic—mixed message conveyed to the Hungarian freedom fighters, implying imminent U.S. support even as the Eisenhower administration distanced itself from unfolding events, prompted RFE after 1956 to return to its role of providing a factual Western perspective on world events rather than attempting to incite or direct any action.

In 1976, RFE merged with another federally funded broadcast project, Radio Liberty (which had been founded in 1951 as a private initiative by the American Committee for the Liberation of the Peoples of Russia) and became Radio Free Europe/Radio Liberty (RFE/RL). During the Soviet occupation of Afghanistan, RFE/RL spun off a new entity, Radio Free Afghanistan, which broadcast from 1985 to 1993. RFE/RL continues to operate.

Although mostly funded by the CIA, Radio Free Europe presented itself as private organization that relied on private donations. This 1970 poster appeals for contributions.

HOW A CRISIS IN EGYPT CRUSHED A REVOLUTION IN HUNGARY

IF KHRUSHCHEV HAD PRAGMATISM in common with Stalin, he shared another quality with an even more unlikely counterpart: the political leaders of the United States. Like former president Harry Truman and current president Dwight Eisenhower, Nikita Khrushchev possessed an acute awareness that, in the power contest between communism and democratic capitalism, what happened in one part of the world profoundly affected what happened in another.

The newsreels of the Republic Square violence and the prospect of the National Government's unraveling the Warsaw Pact were powerful motives for the Soviets to put a stop to the revolution in Hungary, but perhaps even more compelling was the fact that, at this very time—on October 29, 1956—a combination of Israeli, British, and French forces had invaded Egypt, whose leader, Gamal Abdel Nasser, was very friendly to the Soviet Union and looked to it for support. Khrushchev felt that his hand had been pushed, that the invasion of Egypt made it necessary to intervene in Hungary to "restore order"—which meant to restore Soviet-controlled communism as the exclusive political authority.

The Soviet premier reportedly put it this way to the Presidium: withdrawing from Hungary would encourage the West to seize control of Egypt. Khrushchev's position in October 1956 thus became a mirror image of President Truman's position in the late 1940s. As Truman had proposed "containing" communism, now Khrushchev proposed intervening in Hungary to "contain" democratic capitalism. Besides, if Hungary declared itself neutral and withdrew from the Warsaw Pact, the buffer zone of Eastern European satellites would erode, leaving the Soviet Union as vulnerable as it had been when Hitler invaded in June 1941. At Khrushchev's urging, the Presidium voted to end the ceasefire, crush the Hungarian revolution, and replace the National Government with a "Provisional Revolutionary Government" under Soviet loyalist János Kádár.

The Suez Crisis

Like Khrushchev, we, too, must turn our attention from the waters of the Danube to those of the Suez Canal. That waterway, critical to commerce and global military strategy, had opened in 1869, linking the Mediterranean with the Red Sea via the Gulf of Suez, providing a shortcut between European and American ports as well as between those ports and the ports of southern Asia and eastern Africa. When the canal was first opened, Great Britain used it extensively as an avenue to its far-flung colonies in India, the Far East, Australia, and New Zealand. In 1875, the British government purchased the Egyptian share of the company that operated the canal, then in 1882, after invading and occupying Egypt, the British seized control of the canal outright. Six years later, by the 1888 Convention of Constantinople, the Suez Canal was proclaimed a neutral zone under British protection, and the Ottoman Empire, to which Egypt was then subject, agreed to allow all shipping to pass freely through it, whether in peace or war. The neutrality of the Suez Canal became a universally recognized article of international law.

Following World War I, the League of Nations put Palestine under a British mandate, which endured until 1948, when British forces withdrew and Israel proclaimed independence on territory that the United Nations had partitioned for the creation of a Jewish state. The Arab League (at the time consisting of Egypt, Iraq, Jordan, Lebanon, Saudi Arabia, Syria, and Yemen), refusing to recognize either the UN partition or the state of Israel, went to war against the new country—only to suffer the first of several defeats, which created an enduring enmity between the Arab nations and Israel and also between those countries and Israel's Western supporters. By the early 1950s, Great Britain, which maintained a large garrison at Suez, became the target of increasing Arab hostility, and in October 1951, Egypt denounced the Anglo-Egyptian Treaty of 1936, which gave Britain a twenty-year lease on its Suez bases. When Britain refused to withdraw from Suez, anti-Western riots broke out in Cairo, contributing to the instability of the Egyptian government under King Farouk. In a 1952 coup d'état, Nasser became the country's president, and Egypt began interfering with the passage of ships through the Suez Canal, targeting in particular those with cargoes bound for Israel.

After the coup, the British government sought to improve relations with Egypt by agreeing to a phased withdrawal of British troops from Suez. For his part, however, Nasser continued to focus on bringing about the total defeat of Britain in the region, which he believed would allow him to consolidate his own tenuous hold on Egypt by establishing the nation as the principal power in the Arab world. Nasser's intransigence locked Egypt and Britain in a struggle to establish spheres of influence in the Middle East, a contest that mirrored what was happening between the Soviets and the West in Europe. In September 1955, Nasser also established a relationship between Egypt and the Soviet bloc by concluding an arms deal with Czechoslovakia for tanks, aircraft, artillery, and small arms and with Bulgaria for four destroyers, two submarines, and one frigate.

Clearly, Egypt was entering the Soviet orbit and was scarcely a step away from becoming a Middle Eastern Warsaw Pact power. It was therefore only natural that Britain's prime minister, Anthony Eden, would take for granted the support of the United States in any move Britain made against the growing menace of Nasser.

The Suez Canal—strategic, commercial, cultural, and political prize—on a 1906 map.

That assumption, as it turned out, was a grave diplomatic error and a symptom of single-minded Cold War thinking. Whereas Eden believed that the United States would automatically align itself with Britain against an emerging communist threat, the Eisenhower administration was more interested in strengthening its alliance with Saudi Arabia, which joined Egypt in opposition to the influence of the so-called Baghdad Pact, the British alliance with Iraq and Jordan. As unpalatable as Nasser was making himself by reaching out to the Warsaw Pact, Eisenhower had no desire to diminish U.S. influence in the Middle East by alienating its own strongest ally, the Saudis.

If President Eisenhower was a moderate with regard to the Soviet-leaning Nasser, his secretary of state, John Foster Dulles, a hard-line anticommunist, was not, and, after Nasser proclaimed Egypt's recognition of the People's Republic of China on May 16, 1956, Dulles, standing up for the rival Nationalist government in Taiwan, withdrew U.S. financial aid for the Aswan Dam project, which was essential to controlling Nile floods, generating vast amounts of electricity, and transforming large desert tracts into arable land. A week after Dulles announced the end of aid, Nasser issued an announcement of his own on July 26: the nationalization of the Suez Canal.

"At this moment as I talk to you, some of your Egyptian brethren are proceeding to administer the canal company and to run its affairs. They are taking over the canal company at this very moment—the Egyptian canal company, not the foreign canal company."

Gamal Abdel Nasser, speech of July 26, 1956

The Western Bloc Breaks

Rebellion in Poland and, even more, in Hungary suggested to many in the West that the Soviet bloc was not the seamless monolith it had been assumed to be; however, it was still popularly believed that the "Western bloc," though not monolithic in the Soviet sense, was flawlessly unified when it came to opposing communist aggression. The growing Suez crisis gave the lie to this perception.

Britain could not tolerate the nationalization of the Suez Canal, and Prime Minister Eden was eager to topple Nasser; however, he could afford to alienate neither the other Arab states nor the United States—whose president was making it increasingly clear that he had no interest in moving against Nasser. In effect acknowledging that the traditional Anglo-American alliance had cracked, the Eden government turned from the United States to make a secret military alliance with France and Israel, the object of which was to recover control of the Suez Canal.

Egyptian Prime Minister Gamal Abdel Nasser is cheered in Cairo after announcing the creation of the Egyptian Suez Canal Company, August 1, 1956.

"There is no doubt in our minds that Nasser, whether he likes it or not, is now effectively in Russian hands, just as Mussolini was in Hitler's. It would be as ineffective to show weakness to Nasser now in order to placate him as it was to show weakness to Mussolini."

British prime minister Anthony Eden to U.S. president Dwight D. Eisenhower, October 1, 1956

On October 22, 1956, Israeli prime minister David Ben-Gurion, Israeli defense minister Shimon Peres, and Israel Defense Forces chief of staff Moshe Dayan converged on a secluded house in Sèvres, France, where they met with French officials and British foreign secretary Selwyn Lloyd, who was accompanied by his aide, Sir Patrick Dean. There they agreed that Israel would launch an invasion of the Sinai, whereupon Britain and France would intervene to bring about an ostensible cease-fire, under which the armies of Israel and Egypt would be obliged to withdraw sixteen kilometers from the Suez Canal. The invasion would provide a pretext for Britain and France, supposedly enforcing the cease-fire, to argue before the United Nations that, given the volatility of the region, Egypt was incapable of controlling the Suez Canal and that it must therefore be placed under Anglo-French authority and management. As for Ike, his administration would be presented with a fait accompli and, given Nasser's

Moshe Dayan (with eye patch) and Avraham Yoffe, commanding officers of the 9th Brigade, Israel Defense Force, at Sharm el-Sheikh, Egypt, on the southern tip of the Sinai Peninsula, following the Sinai campaign of 1956.

alignment with the Soviet bloc, would have no choice but to accept both the Anglo-French intervention and proposal for control.

The Israeli invasion of the Sinai stepped off on October 29, 1956, and on October 30, the British and French governments issued a joint ultimatum to Egypt, calling for a cease-fire. When no answer came, an Anglo-French bombing campaign began on October 31, culminating on November 3, with a carrier-launched French air attack on the Cairo airport. By way of response, Nasser ordered the forty ships currently passing through the Suez Canal to be sunk in place, thereby closing the canal.

Now the British began landing parachutists and commandos, supported by a heavy naval bombardment, which devastated much of Port Said. French paratroopers also landed at key points and control of the Suez Canal was soon in Anglo-French hands—though the canal had been rendered useless by the sunken ships and would not be reopened until the following year. Despite the success of the military operation, the United States did not fall into line with its Western allies or with Israel. Although Dulles favored a hard line against Egypt, Eisenhower was still unwilling to alienate the Saudis. Even more urgently, he did not want to fan the flames of a Middle Eastern crisis when the crisis in Hungary was already ablaze. Ike did not want to undermine the message Radio Free Europe was broadcasting to Hungary, that the United States abhorred invasion by a foreign power. He also feared that U.S. support for the invasion would draw the Soviet Union and possibly the other Warsaw Pact nations either into Egypt itself or prompt Soviet bombers to target London, Paris, and Tel Aviv. The result in either case would be regional or even world war. Faced with this prospect, Eisenhower demanded that Britain, France, and Israel cease fire and end the invasion. A UN Security Council resolution to this effect was vetoed by France and Britain—an unprecedented action against a U.S.-sponsored resolution—whereupon the United States brought the matter before the entire General Assembly, which voted to form a United Nations Emergency Force (UNEF) to intervene. More critically, NATO members Portugal and Iceland called for ousting both Britain and France from NATO if they failed to withdraw from Egypt.

President Eisenhower confers with Secretary of State John Foster Dulles, October 30, 1956. Dulles urged Ike to back the revolution in Hungary, but the president demurred.

Britain's Sir Anthony Eden made a bad situation worse by precipitously announcing a cease-fire on November 6—but without securing agreement from France or Israel. Humiliated and broken in health, Eden then resigned as prime minister. The entire Anglo-French invasion force completed its withdrawal before the end of December, but Israeli units remained in the Sinai until March 1957. As the invaders withdrew, the UNEF entered to keep the peace.

The Consequences of Crisis

Eisenhower's response to the Suez Crisis arguably prevented a catastrophic war involving the Middle East and Europe; however, it ensured the diminishment of France and Britain, the two most important Western allies of the United States, as world powers. Worse, not only did the Suez Crisis increase Nasser's standing among his fellow Arabs but the U.S. withdrawal of aid for the Aswan Dam project also propelled him that much more deeply into the Soviet camp. In 1958 the Egyptian leader accepted Soviet funding as well as the participation of Soviet technicians in the building of the dam.

Of even more enduring consequence was the catalytic effect the Suez Crisis had on global decolonization. The postwar era saw the gradual dismemberment of the old European empires in India, Africa, and Asia, a process that rapidly accelerated after the Suez affair. But, more immediately, the Suez Crisis muted Eisenhower's response to the Hungarian revolution. Secretary Dulles had taken it upon himself to describe the Hungarian uprising as evidence of "irresistible" forces of "liberation," which had been "unleashed in Eastern Europe." President Eisenhower, on the eve of his bid for election to a second term, was at pains to tone down what he considered the provocative nature of his secretary of state's rhetoric. He wanted neither the American electorate nor the leaders of the Soviet Union to believe that he was taking the United States to the verge of a military alliance with a newly independent Hungary. He did not want the Soviets to think that the United States deliberately planned to use the defection to establish a beachhead on the border of the Soviet Union. As the president remarked to his speechwriter Emmet John Hughes, "Those boys [that is, the Soviets] are both furious and scared. Just as with Hitler, that makes for the most dangerous possible state of mind." Clearly, the president was concerned that if the United States acted in any way to suggest that it had a

REALITY CHECK

With Friends Like This . . .

New Jersey born (1920) Emmett John Hughes was a journalist who became a close aide and speechwriter for President Dwight D. Eisenhower and is credited with helping to propel him to easy victory over his Democratic presidential challenger, Adlai E. Stevenson, in 1952. Yet Hughes became increasingly distressed by what he saw as Eisenhower's uncertain handling of Cold War strategy, and, by the late 1950s, was an outspoken critic of the president. In 1962, he wrote the best-selling memoir *The Ordeal of Power*, in which he portrayed Ike as a dullard who should never have ascended to the White House.

A SPUR TO PROLIFERATION

Critics of the Eisenhower administration claim that had the United States either cooperated with or simply refrained from interfering in the invasion of Egypt, a Western democratic presence would have been established in the Middle East, thereby making the rise of dictators such as Iraq's Saddam Hussein and Islamic extremist regimes such as that of Iran's Ayatollah Ruhollah Khomeini far less likely. Those who approve of Eisenhower's restraint, however, point out that U.S. involvement or acquiescence in the invasion might have touched off a major war.

These are the most obvious "what ifs": less obvious is the effect unified Western action might have had on curbing nuclear proliferation. Because the Suez Crisis revealed the limit of the effectiveness of the NATO alliance, French president Charles de Gaulle quickly drew the conclusion that France could place little reliance on either of its long-time allies, Great Britain and the United States. Accordingly, in 1958, France launched the *Force de frappe* (Strike Force) program, to develop a nuclear deterrent it could wield on its own. De Gaulle further underscored French military autonomy by withdrawing the nation from the integrated NATO military command in 1966. Had NATO unity prevailed at Suez, it is unlikely that de Gaulle would have contributed to nuclear proliferation in this manner.

military stake in the independence of Hungary, the Soviets might launch a preemptive war. "If these fellows start something," he said to Hughes, "we may have to hit 'em," adding "and if necessary, with everything in the bucket," by which the president meant nuclear weapons.

Eisenhower delayed acting on Dulles's recommendation, made on October 24, that the United States introduce a Security Council resolution to forestall Soviet intervention. Khrushchev delayed in nothing, however. During the first three days of November, he visited individually with the communist leaders of Poland, Romania, Czechoslovakia, Bulgaria, and even with Yugoslavia's maverick communist leader, Tito, to secure their buy-in for Soviet action to end the Hungarian uprising. He also heeded Tito's advice to tap János Kádár to lead the new Hungarian communist government.

Having ensured that the key leaders of the Soviet bloc were with him, Khrushchev ordered Soviet tanks to reenter Budapest at three o'clock on the morning of November 4, 1956. These were the spearhead of an invasion by no fewer than seventeen Soviet divisions under World War II commander Marshal Ivan Konev. Soon, tank, infantry, artillery, and air strikes were brought to bear against the revolutionaries and the Hungarian Army, which, although mostly loyal to the revolution, was outnumbered, outgunned, and ineffectively led.

Final Broadcast

Throughout the entire uprising, Radio Free Europe had broadcast a message of American solidarity with Hungary. To the very end, RFE cranked out appeals to Hungarians to fight the Soviet invaders and even gave specific tactical pointers for effective resistance. Those who heard and heeded the broadcasts assumed they meant that the United States intended to support—militarily—the fight for independence. The assumption was wrong.

On November 4, at 5:20 A.M., Imre Nagy made a broadcast of his own, beaming it to the United States, beaming it to the world. He explained that Soviet forces were attacking Budapest, that help was desperately needed, and that "the Government" remained in place. Then, at 8:07 A.M., all broadcasts stopped.

Having retreated to the Parliament building, Nagy convened an emergency meeting of the cabinet, but only three of his ministers were present. Soviet troops entered the building and made arrests. In the meantime, at six in the morning, in the town of Szolnok, János Kádár proclaimed the Hungarian Revolutionary Worker-Peasant Government. The Hungarian Revolution was effectively at an end, although sporadic fighting continued until November 10, when a final cease-fire was concluded.

NUMBERS

The Toll of Revolution

During some two weeks of intermittent fighting, more than twenty-five hundred Hungarians and 722 Red Army troops were killed in the Hungarian Revolution.

Soviet tanks take up positions on a Budapest street, November 5, 1956.

TAKEAWAY

The Consequences of Inaction

The Hungarian Revolution of 1956 revealed both the fissures in the Soviet bloc and those in the solidarity of the Western democracies. The perceived strategic relationship between events in Hungary and the Suez Crisis demonstrated the high-stakes global interrelatedness of events in the Cold War. In its response, the Eisenhower administration signaled a retreat from the Truman Doctrine and a willingness to maintain the status quo between the free world and the iron curtain countries. Finally, the U.S. failure to give military aid to the Hungarian revolutionaries was widely regarded as a dishonorable lapse in America's stated resolve to promote and protect democracy. But the spectacle of the Soviet military crushing freedom in Hungary had much greater international impact on the image of the Soviet Union and the prospects for the enduring viability of communism and the Soviet system.

American Silence

In response to Nagy's final broadcast, a resolution was finally proposed in the United Nations Security Council condemning the Soviet intervention. It was not only too late but also was, naturally, vetoed by the Soviet delegate. By the time the General Assembly voted overwhelmingly to call on the Soviet Union to withdraw from Hungary, the Kádár government was already in place and was turning back all United Nations observers.

The United States supported the UN resolutions, but Ike had already decided that there was no advantage and very great risk in U.S. military intervention in Hungary—or, for that matter, in any Soviet satellite that happened to express discontent with Soviet hegemony. Eisenhower was willing to use political rhetoric and economic aid to encourage defection from the Soviet bloc, and, as the Radio Free Europe broadcasts tragically demonstrated, he was also willing to use propaganda. But military confrontation with the Soviet Union was, as he saw it, out of the question.

Much as the Korean War had ended in stalemate, so the muted American response to the Hungarian Revolution marked the commencement of stalemate in the European phase of the Cold War. A divided Korea was at least a Korea in which the shooting had stopped. Likewise, a divided Europe garrisoned on one side by NATO troops and on the other by those of the Warsaw Pact was hardly a comfortable place, but at least no one was shooting—or dropping atomic bombs. Nevertheless, many Americans were disgusted by what they regarded as the government's failure to stand behind a valiant people fighting for democracy. Yet nothing in the Cold War was ever a simple matter of absolute defeat or absolute victory. The free world—together with those parts of the world that wanted to be free—may have been disappointed by the inaction of the United States, but their response to the spectacle of Soviet tanks and aircraft destroying freedom to enforce communism was far stronger. The suppression of the Hungarian Revolution was a tactical victory for the Soviet Union, but, in the fullness of time, it would prove a terrible ideological and strategic defeat. The truth was clear to everyone with eyes to see it: people fought *for* democracy. They fought *against* the totalitarianism of Soviet-imposed, single-party communism.

CHAPTER 15

FROM THE BAY OF PIGS TO THE CUBAN MISSILE CRISIS

On the Brink of Armageddon

MOST AMERICANS THINK OF THE COLD WAR AS A CONTEST between democratic capitalism and communism. And so it was. Yet the period was also defined by another social, economic, and political process: the end of colonialism. World War II provided the final push required to topple an already creaky Europe-centered imperialism. At the beginning of the Cold War, Britain relinquished India, from which an independent Pakistan was partitioned. It also loosed its grip on the Middle East, even as French power in North Africa rapidly eroded. Korea, long dominated by Japan, achieved a tumultuous and fractured independence after 1945, and Vietnam broke free of France, though, like Korea, it was torn between communism and Western-aligned capitalism. By the late 1950s and early 1960s, the former colonial provinces throughout central and southern Africa won their independence as well.

Americans and Europeans accustomed to thinking in terms of two political worlds, one democratic and capitalist, the other totalitarian and communist, were now compelled to accept what independent India's first prime minister, Jawaharlal Nehru, called the Third World, consisting of nations—many of them newly independent—aligned with neither the "First World" (the democratic powers) nor the "Second World" (the communist powers). Yet it was over the alignment of a number of these states that the powers of the First and Second Worlds fought in a bid to extend their respective spheres of influence.

DETAILS, DETAILS

Out of Alignment

The Non-Aligned Movement (NAM) was founded at the Bandung (Indonesia) Conference in April 1955 by Jawaharlal Nehru of India, Sukarno of Indonesia, Tito of Yugoslavia, Gamal Abdel Nasser of Egypt, and Kwame Nkrumah of Ghana. Today, NAM has 118 member states, which pledged to adhere to five founding principles:

1. Mutual respect for each other's territorial integrity and sovereignty
2. Mutual non-aggression
3. Mutual non-interference in domestic affairs
4. Equality and mutual benefit
5. Peaceful coexistence

Equally important was a shared desire not to become involved in the Cold War and to promote instead "world peace and cooperation." By the 1960s, the Western powers, including the United States, concluded that a majority of NAM members (for example, Castro's Cuba) were actually aligned with the Soviet Union and questioned the relevance of the organization.

Crisis in Lebanon

The United States was itself the product of a successful struggle against colonialism, and it was therefore only natural that most Americans approved of the independence movements sweeping the emerging nations of the Third World—especially when they perceived that the issues of national liberation were remote from the United States.

President Eisenhower did not see the issues as remote. In 1957, he promulgated what the press called the "Eisenhower Doctrine," holding that the "independence" of nations in the Middle East was vital to the interests of the United States. This linkage was in part due to the oil resources of the region, but was more immediately the result of the Soviet backing of the United Arab Republic (UAR), a union between Egypt and Syria just then in the process of forming. Egypt's Soviet-leaning Gamal Abdel Nasser saw the UAR as the first step toward a pan-Arab state, to be dominated by his country. Eisenhower saw it as a Soviet satellite threatening the security of Jordan, Turkey, Iraq, and Lebanon, states friendly to the United States.

In 1952, five years before Eisenhower put forth his Middle East policy, Camille Chamoun, candidate of the Christian (Maronite) Party, was elected president of Lebanon. He quickly developed close ties with the United States, thereby alienating Lebanese Muslims, about 50 percent of the population, who favored alignment with neighboring Arab nations, many of which were hostile to the West. Alienation mushroomed into riots during May 9–13, 1958, in Tripoli and Beirut, probably incited by the UAR, which endorsed Kamal Jumblatt, leader of the Druse, a quasi-Islamic sect concentrated in Lebanon, Syria, and Israel. Jumblatt-led forces defeated Lebanese government forces in several encounters.

As civil war developed in Lebanon, Chamoun appealed to Eisenhower for military aid, and on July 15, 1958, marines began amphibious landings at Khalde Beach. A stunned American public suddenly realized that the struggles of the Third World were not nearly as remote as they had thought. American leaders called it a "proxy war," a "brushfire" (that is, relatively limited) conflict between opposed indigenous elements supported by the United States on one side and the Soviet Union on the other. If the American proxy won, Lebanon would emerge as a pro-West, capitalist democracy. If the Soviet proxy was victorious, the nation would align itself with the Soviet Union, perhaps eventually joining the UAR and thereby delivering most of the Middle East into the Soviet sphere of influence. To the Lebanese themselves, this was no "proxy war," but a civil war.

Egyptian president Gamal Abdel Nasser (left) and Indian prime minister Jawaharlal Nehru (center) are pictured with their jovial host, Tito, at a 1956 summit of the Non-Aligned Movement convened on the Yugoslav island of Brioni.

More marines were airlifted into Lebanon on July 16 and were joined on July 19 by U.S. Army troops. Hoping to avoid the appearance of Yankee imperialism, Eisenhower also called for a United Nations peacekeeping force. After the Soviets vetoed this, Eisenhower sent Deputy Undersecretary of State Robert D. Murphy to Lebanon to mediate between the warring factions, and while this diplomatic initiative was under way, the Lebanese government forces, stiffened by the U.S. military, enforced a shaky cease-fire. American and Lebanese forces established a defensive perimeter around Beirut, mainly to prevent Syrian and Syrian-backed guerrillas from pulling off a coup to topple Chamoun. Murphy negotiated an agreement to hold a new election, which resulted in the elevation of another Maronite Christian, General Faud Chehab, to the presidency. Following his inauguration on September 23, 1958, U.S. forces—about fourteen thousand men—withdrew.

Closer to Home

Americans were relieved by the nearly bloodless (for U.S. forces) intervention, which seemed a clean victory against Soviet-backed troublemakers. Closer to home, however, the Cold War was seriously heating up.

Cuba, just ninety miles off the Florida coast, had been a rambunctious American neighbor for more than a century. In the Spanish-American War of 1898, the United States intervened to help Cuba achieve independence from Spain. Congress and President William McKinley had been motivated by a popular imperative to both overcome repressive Spanish imperial policies and to share the blessings of democratic liberty with all nations in the hemisphere. Moreover, in the spirit of the Monroe Doctrine of 1823, there was a desire to rid the hemisphere of the taint of European colonialism, and—not least of all—a drive to protect extensive U.S. business interests in Cuba. The war brought quick victory, and Congress voted to guarantee Cuban independence, albeit under tight U.S. supervision. American fruit and sugar companies continued to exploit cheap Cuban labor and carved out a partnership with the new Cuban government to ensure favored treatment. This meant that the Cuban government took steps, often harsh, to ensure a compliant workforce.

In 1930, the brutality of the U.S.-backed regime of Gerardo Machado y Morales prompted a new liberation movement led by Fulgencio Batista y Zaldívar and Carlos Manuel de Céspedes y Quesada, ending with the ouster of Machado by Céspedes. In 1933, Batista led a coup d'état against Céspedes and assumed control of Cuba as a military chief who manipulated a series of civilian puppet presidents. For U.S. lawmakers, this arrangement created an acceptable illusion of democracy, but the FDR administration was nevertheless relieved when Batista put away his uniform and officially became president. He served a single term, then left Cuba for a comfortable retirement in Florida. It did not last long. In 1952, he flew back to Cuba, where a bloodless coup returned him to office.

Although friendly to American interests, Cuban president Fulgencio Batista—shown here speaking in the 1950s—grew too corrupt even for the United States to stomach. Many Americans cheered when Castro sent him packing.

Batista's second regime was far more repressive and corrupt than his first. He made deals not only with big U.S. business interests but also with U.S.-based organized crime, which sought in Cuba—a playground for middle-class vacationers—a partnership with a pliant government. As opposition to Batista mounted within Cuba, a young attorney, Fidel Castro Ruz, emerged as a leader of a revolutionary movement.

He had been born in 1926 (some sources report 1927) on a farm in rural Oriente Province, took a law degree from the University of Havana in 1950, and earned a reputation as a fiery orator against Batista. On July 26, 1953, Castro turned words into deeds when he led an assault on the Moncada army barracks, a government armory. Arrested, he was sentenced to fifteen years' imprisonment but was granted amnesty in 1955 after serving only two. Upon his release, he went into self-exile in Mexico, where he prepared to carry out full-scale revolution in a Cuba already simmering with insurrection.

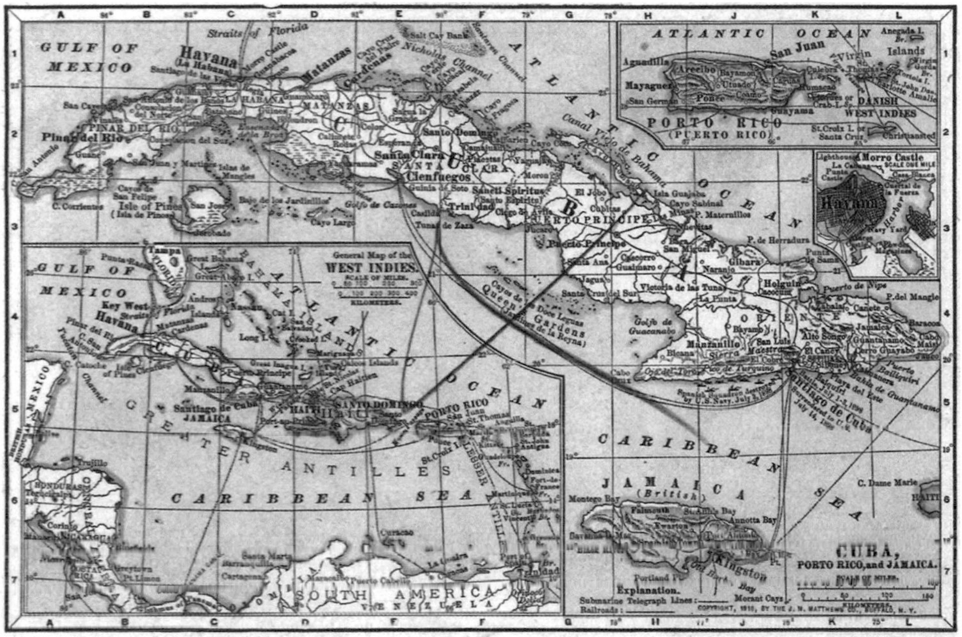

A 1916 map of Cuba—scene of revolution, failed counterrevolution, and, very nearly, the end of the world. The Bay of Pigs (Bahia de Cochinos) is on the south side of the island, to the left of Santa Clara. Guantánamo Bay is in the far southeast.

On November 30, 1956, Castro and just eighty-one others, including the charismatic guerrilla leader Ernesto "Che" Guevara, returned to Cuba. Batista's forces intercepted them and reported wiping them out, but Castro and the others had fled into the remote Sierra Maestra and set up a secret camp from which they conducted a guerrilla war throughout 1957 and into the fall of 1958. During this period, Batista's tyranny became increasingly brutal, generating sympathetic coverage of Castro in the international press, including among American papers. By the time the guerrilla leader emerged from his mountain headquarters in October 1958 to call for "total war" against Batista, events unfolded with such stunning speed that on December 31, 1958, Batista realized he was without support. He fled the country, with a fortune in looted government treasure. It was not so much that Fidel Castro had won as that Batista had decided to cut his losses. On January 8, 1959, Castro marched at the head of his motley revolutionary army, the ranks of which were swelled by jubilant crowds feeling the joy of liberation, and led it into Havana.

"History will absolve me."

Fidel Castro, October 16, 1953, at his trial for the Moncada barracks raid

Fidel Castro,with trademark beard and military fatigues, upon arrival in Washington, D.C., April 1959.

Ike and Fidel

The day before Castro entered Havana, the Eisenhower administration declared U.S. recognition of a Castro government. Taking its cue from this declaration, the Cuban army made no attempt to stop the guerrilla heroes. A provisional government was rapidly formed, with Castro taking the title of "premier."

Eisenhower could no longer bring himself to prop up Batista's criminal regime. Besides, unlike such leaders as China's Mao Zedong, North Korea's Kim Il Sung, and North Vietnam's Ho Chi Minh, Castro had conducted his revolution not in the name of Marxism, but in the cause of anti-imperialism, nationalism, and general reform—all values sufficiently palatable to Washington. If America could do business with a thief like Batista, it could deal with an idealist like Castro, scruffy beard and all.

But then Castro began to talk—and talk—earning a reputation for marathon speeches filled with bellicose condemnations of American imperialism. Castro nationalized all industry, including U.S. firms. The Cuban masses approved of the new direction, and the minority that objected either followed Batista into exile—Florida was the destination of choice—or suffered imprisonment, exile, and even execution by the new regime.

President Eisenhower looked on with increasing alarm. On May 7, 1960, Premier Castro announced the resumption of diplomatic relations with the Soviet Union—broken off by Batista—and by the middle of the year had explicitly aligned Cuba with the Soviets, prompting Nikita Khrushchev to warn the world—and especially the United States—that he would defend Cuba against all aggression, even to the point of thermonuclear war. Soviet expansion was no longer a phenomenon of faraway places.

As a result of the Spanish-American War of 1898, an independent Cuba gave the United States anirrevocable lease on Guantánamo Bay, where the U.S. Navy established a base that remains a capitalist toehold in the heart of Marxism. This panorama from 1911 shows the encampments of 1st, 2nd, and 3rd U.S. Marine Regiments at Deer Point Camp.

Castro wasted little time in counterpointing to his anti-American rhetoric the rattle of a saber. He threatened to shut down and take over the U.S. naval base at Guantánamo Bay—which had been established on the basis of an irrevocable lease after the Spanish-American War. In effect, Guantánamo Bay was now like West Berlin, simultaneously a toehold in and a hostage to the communist world. On November 1, 1960, Eisenhower announced that the United States would take "whatever steps are necessary to defend" the base, and on January 3, 1961, he severed diplomatic relations with Cuba.

NEW FRONTIER, OLD LEGACY

JANUARY 3, 1961, was just seventeen days before the inauguration of a new American president, John F. Kennedy. Rarely has an outgoing chief executive dropped onto the plate of the incoming president an act of such consequence. In his speech accepting the Democratic Party's presidential nomination, Kennedy spoke of facing a "New Frontier," but the fact was that he and the nation were also weighed down by the bitter *old* legacy of "Yankee" exploitation of Latin America, to which was now added the breakdown of relations between the United States and its Soviet-aligned neighbor. The new president was also aware that he had inherited something else from the Eisenhower administration: a secret plan to invade Cuba and win back the island for the West.

"The torch is passed to a new generation"—John F. Kennedy is sworn in as the thirty-fifth president of the United States, January 20, 1961.

ALTERNATE TAKE

Mutual Misjudgment

Relations between revolutionary Cuba and the United States had every hope of being cordial until Castro chose to align his nation with the Soviet Union. President Eisenhower responded by severing diplomatic relations, thrusting Castro more firmly into the Soviet embrace. Had both leaders followed pragmatic rather than ideologically doctrinaire courses, the costly tension between the United States and Cuba would probably not have hardened into the changeless tradition that it still is. Castro would have been wiser to use the *threat*—rather than the *fact*—of communist alignment to extract good behavior and a profitable trade relationship with the United States. The island would have been wealthier for it.

The CIA's director for plans, Richard Bissell, was the author of A Program of Covert Action against the Castro Regime, *code-named JMARC, the blueprint for the Bay of Pigs invasion.*

Prelude to a Fiasco

As early as 1959, despite the Eisenhower administration's official recognition of the Castro government, the CIA started planning an invasion of Cuba. At first, it was only a contingency plan, in case Castro should prove a threat, but before Eisenhower left office, the contingency plan became an action plan.

At Palm Beach, Florida, on November 18, 1960, President-elect Kennedy was briefed by CIA director Allen W. Dulles and his director for plans, Richard Bissell, on an operation to overthrow Castro. Bissell presented a paper drafted in March, *A Program of Covert Action against the Castro Regime*, code-named JMARC, which argued that the way to overthrow Castro was to create an exile government, launch a propaganda offensive, then form a resistance group within Cuba as well as a military invasion force outside of the country. When Bissell had originally presented JMARC to outgoing President Eisenhower, he had insisted on the necessity of eliminating Castro immediately *before* the invasion, pointing out that this sequence was essential to the success of the plan. Ike authorized $13 million to fund JMARC.

The CIA was tasked with devising a means of removing Castro. Initially, Sidney Gottlieb—an agent in the CIA's Technical Services Division assigned to devise a way to undermine the premier's popularity that could not be traced back to the United States—proposed spraying a television studio from which Castro was going to broadcast with a hallucinogenic drug. Cuban viewers would then see and hear a babbling madman. Gottlieb also proposed contaminating Castro's shoes with radioactive thallium, which would cause the hair of his trademark beard to fall out, thereby humiliating him. Ike's advisers rejected these ludicrous schemes, and Bissell decided that the only alternative was assassination. In September 1960, he and Dulles approached two American Mafia bosses, Johnny Roselli and Sam Giancana (who later brought in Carlos Marcello, Santos Trafficante, Meyer Lansky, and lesser Mafia figures) to execute a "hit" against Castro. The CIA was willing to pony up $150,000 for the job.

After Castro had been "whacked," Bissell's plan called for landing a force of 750 men near the port of Trinidad, on Cuba's southern coast, a region (the CIA believed) rife with anti-Castro partisans. Bissell

REALITY CHECK

Castro's Support

Americans like to think that the world wants to emulate the government of the United States, but, overwhelmingly, the Cuban people supported Castro and the Cuban Revolution. Of six million Cubans, no more than 250,000 left the country after the fall of Batista. Of those who stayed (the CIA knew by the late 1950s) at least 90 percent proclaimed their full support for Fidel Castro. However, Castro's failure to honor his pledge of holding elections persuaded the CIA that the Cuban people, regardless of what they proclaimed, were ready to rebel. This proved more wishful thinking than reasonable assumption.

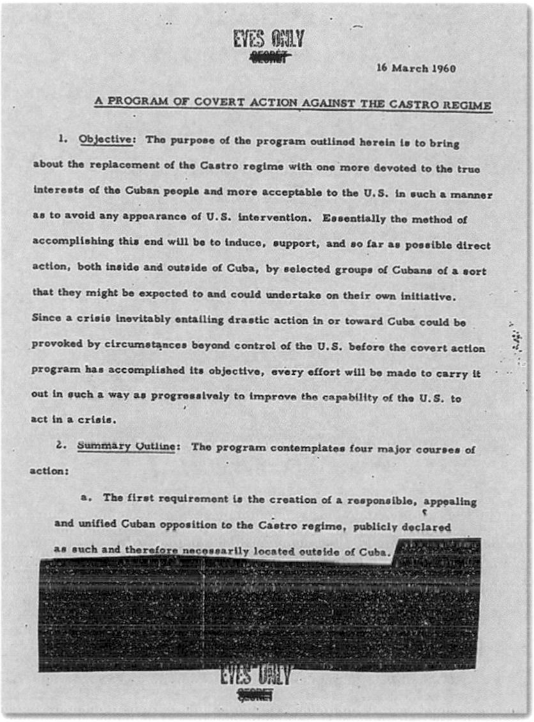

EYES ONLY
~~SECRET~~

16 March 1960

A PROGRAM OF COVERT ACTION AGAINST THE CASTRO REGIME

1. Objective: The purpose of the program outlined herein is to bring about the replacement of the Castro regime with one more devoted to the true interests of the Cuban people and more acceptable to the U.S. in such a manner as to avoid any appearance of U.S. intervention. Essentially the method of accomplishing this end will be to induce, support, and so far as possible direct action, both inside and outside of Cuba, by selected groups of Cubans of a sort that they might be expected to and could undertake on their own initiative. Since a crisis inevitably entailing drastic action in or toward Cuba could be provoked by circumstances beyond control of the U.S. before the covert action program has accomplished its objective, every effort will be made to carry it out in such a way as progressively to improve the capability of the U.S. to act in a crisis.

2. Summary Outline: The program contemplates four major courses of action:

a. The first requirement is the creation of a responsible, appealing and unified Cuban opposition to the Castro regime, publicly declared as such and therefore necessarily located outside of Cuba. [redacted]

EYES ONLY
~~SECRET~~

JMARC, the top-secret CIA plan to overthrow Fidel Castro, was drawn up at the end of the Eisenhower administration and presented to President Kennedy. Note the portion at the bottom of page 1 of the plan report that has been blacked out: it remains classified.

predicted that within four days after landing, the invaders would have recruited at least another 750 indigenous rebels. In the meantime, paratroops would have seized the roads leading to Trinidad, and the combined forces would link up with anti-Castro guerrillas believed to be occupying the nearby Escambray Mountains.

Kennedy listened to Bissell noncommittally, but in March 1961 took JMARC to the Joint Chiefs of Staff for evaluation. They were not optimistic. *If* the invaders had four days of effective air cover, *if* the locals joined the rebellion, and *if* the combined force successfully linked up with the Escambray guerrillas, they gave the plan a 30 percent chance of success. The chiefs recommended against JMARC.

Kennedy summoned Bissell to a meeting on March 11 and instructed him to come up with a new plan. In a bizarre misinterpretation of the Joint Chiefs' report, Kennedy reduced the military experts' criticism of JMARC to a single point: Trinidad was too conspicuous a landing site. He therefore directed Bissell to propose a more remote site. Bissell redrafted the plan with a landing site at Bahia de Cochinos—

REALITY CHECK

Contract on Castro

As the CIA saw it, Mafiosi were ideal assassins, since no one would dream that the U.S. government would hire the Mob to do its "wet work." Besides, the Mafia had a motive for "clipping" Castro, who had shut down their network of Havana brothels and casinos. Apparently, the Mafia bosses showed better judgment than the CIA by concluding early on that killing Castro would not undo the Cuban Revolution. Nevertheless, Roselli and Giancana continued to humor the agency in the hope of avoiding federal prosecutions against organized crime operations.

the Bay of Pigs. Located eighty swampy miles from the Escambray Mountains, it put the landing too far from the guerrillas to include them in the early stages of the operation. Bissell pointed this out to the president, but pushed the plan nevertheless, claiming a two-in-three chance of success. Recent historians believe that Bissell and Dulles actually expected the invasion to fail, but believed that when it did, Kennedy, unwilling to let the operation end in humiliating disaster, would order a major U.S. invasion.

> "We consider that the Monroe Doctrine has outlived its time, has outlived itself, has died, so to say, a natural death. Now the remains of this doctrine should best be buried as every dead body is, so that it should not poison the air with its decay."
>
> *Nikita Khrushchev, July 13, 1960*

At the Bay of Pigs

On April 12, 1961, President Kennedy told a press conference that he had no intention of intervening in Cuban affairs. Even as he spoke, fifteen hundred Cuban exiles prepared to depart from its assembly point in Guatemala for a Nicaraguan port, from which six ships left for Cuba on April 14. On April 15, Cuban-exile aircrews flew obsolescent B-26B bombers in attacks against three Cuban military bases, the airfields at Camp Libertad and San Antonio de los Baños, and the civilian Antonio Maceo Airport at Santiago de Cuba. In a crude attempt to make it look as if the attacks were being carried out by defectors from the Cuban air force, the U.S. World War II bombers were painted with Cuban insignia, and a single bona fide defector, Mario Zúñiga, was presented to the press along with his airplane. His cover story was riddled with holes, and the press quickly revealed the truth—that the operation was backed by the U.S. government.

The landings were supposed to follow the air attacks, beginning shortly after midnight on April 16, but coral reefs offshore had been misidentified by U-2 spy planes as seaweed, and these unanticipated obstacles delayed the landings until after two o'clock on the morning of the seventeenth, thereby sacrificing the element of surprise. Worse, due to another failure of pre-operation intelligence, the landing force found itself bogged down in a swampy marsh.

Castro's military was quick to react. The Cuban air force bombed and strafed the bogged-down invaders onshore and attacked their ships offshore. The command vessel *Mariposa* was sunk, and the supply ship *Houston* had to be beached, cutting off the beleaguered invaders. The popular support the CIA had counted on failed to materialize; within the first few hours of the landings, it was clear that the invasion was doomed.

On April 18 Castro's air force turned its attention to the dozen aircraft the invaders had deployed, shooting down ten. Bissell, General Lyman Lemnitzer, chairman of the Joint Chiefs of Staff, and Chief of Naval Operations Admiral Arleigh Burke told Kennedy that the invasion might still be saved if U.S. combat aircraft were scrambled to provide air support. But the president decided it was time to cut losses and declined to send in more planes. With air supremacy unchallenged, Castro's infantry advanced to surround the landing force. Some invaders fled into the hills, but most surrendered on April 19.

Defeat Is an Orphan

Publicly, Kennedy accepted responsibility for the failure of the Bay of Pigs, repeating to the White House press corps what he identified as "an old saying": "Victory has a thousand fathers, but defeat is an orphan." Privately, he met with Bissell and told him, "In a parliamentary government, I'd have to resign. But in this government I can't, so you and Allen [Dulles] have to go." Bissell was actually offered a different CIA position, but turned it down; Dulles, under pressure, resigned as head of the CIA in November 1961.

A group of Bay of Pigs invaders, members of Assault Brigade 2506, await confinement as prisoners of war, April 1961.

On April 20, the president addressed the American Association of Newspaper Editors to explain what had happened at the Bay of Pigs: "While we could not be expected to hide our sympathies, we made it repeatedly clear that the armed forces of this country would not intervene in any way. Any unilateral American intervention, in the absence of an external attack upon ourselves or an ally, would have been contrary to our traditions and to our international obligations." Having defended his decision not to support the operation with a full-scale military invasion, Kennedy went on the offensive:

NUMBERS

The Cost of Failure

Of about 1,500 invaders, 114 were killed in action and 36 died as prisoners of war. Losses to Castro's forces were 54 killed. One thousand two hundred nine members of the invasion force were captured and tried for treason. A small number were executed, and the remainder sentenced to thirty years in prison. After twenty months of negotiations with the United States, the prisoners were exchanged for $53 million in food and medicine.

> But let the record show that our restraint is not inexhaustible. Should it ever appear that the inter-American doctrine of non-interference merely conceals or excuses a policy of non-action if the nations of this Hemisphere should fail to meet their commitments against outside Communist penetration—then I want it clearly understood that this Government will not hesitate in meeting its primary obligations which are to the security of our Nation! . . . it is clearer than ever that we face a relentless struggle in every corner of the globe that goes far beyond the clash of armies or even nuclear armaments.

New Frontier?

Kennedy now revealed that he shared the vision of his predecessors Eisenhower and Truman, that the spread of communism was relentless and had to be contained. He was prepared to fight brushfire wars anywhere in the world. The Bay of Pigs would not be in vain. "We intend to profit from this lesson. We intend to re-examine and reorient our forces of all kinds—our tactics and our institutions here in this community. We intend to intensify our efforts for a struggle in many ways more difficult than war, where disappointment will often accompany us. . . . Let me then make clear as the President of the United States that I am determined upon our system's survival and success, regardless of the cost and regardless of the peril!"

A New Crisis in Berlin

IT WAS NOT A CHEERFUL PROSPECT President Kennedy outlined in the wake of the Bay of Pigs. Almost immediately, Soviet premier Khrushchev seized upon the fiasco as evidence of the new president's weakness and decided to challenge him elsewhere—for even higher stakes.

The American triumph over the blockade of West Berlin in 1948–49 (Chapter 10) had hardly settled the issue of that democratic city's right to exist in communist East Germany.

In November 1958, Khrushchev challenged the Western democracies to leave Berlin within six months, guaranteeing that it would be made a free and demilitarized city, neither a part of East nor West Germany. The Soviet premier warned that if the Western powers failed to leave the city, access would be strictly by permission of the East German government. The United States, Great Britain, and France rejected the ultimatum, and in 1959, the Soviets backed down and engaged in talks with the West, which led to a historic visit by Khrushchev to the United States in the fall of 1959 and an agreement to a summit in Paris in 1960. That event never came to pass, however. On May 1, 1960, CIA contract pilot Francis Gary Powers, flying a U-2 spy plane, was shot down over the Soviet Union, precipitating an embarrassing propaganda crisis for the Eisenhower administration, which torpedoed the scheduled summit.

Thus the Bay of Pigs came at a low point in U.S.-Soviet relations, and on June 4, 1961, Khrushchev issued a new ultimatum, calling for the West to withdraw from West Berlin by December 31, 1961. Kennedy and the leaders of Britain and France again refused. The president delivered a televised speech on July 25, declaring his willingness to reopen talks with the Soviets but also announcing his intention to ask Congress for $3.25 billion to finance conventional weapons—in other words, nonnuclear weapons suitable to a land war in Europe—and specifying that he would add six divisions to the army and two to the marines. He would call up the reserves and triple the draft. That very day, he asked Congress to authorize an increase in the size of the army from 875,000 to 1,000,000 men and to fund a major civil defense initiative, including a fallout shelter program. Clearly, he was putting the nation on a war footing. Khrushchev denounced the speech as the equivalent of a declaration of war, and he warned that he was prepared to give the United States just that.

Instead of war, however, Khrushchev authorized a wall separating the sectors of Berlin. The order to close the border and begin construction of the wall was signed on August 12, 1961, by East German premier Walter Ulbricht. At midnight of that day, East German troops were deployed to block passage between the sectors, and, beginning at daybreak on Sunday, August 13, soldiers and civilian workers erected barriers and tore up streets to stop traffic. Barbed wire was immediately uncoiled along the twenty-seven-mile sectorial border, then some thirty thousand East German troops labored to replace the barbed wire barriers with a permanent concrete and brick wall. East German border police were then deployed to patrol as well as to improve the wall. In response, on August 30, JFK activated 148,000 National Guard and Reserve troops, including twenty-eight fighter, reconnaissance, and transport squadrons of the Air National Guard (ANG). In November, the U.S. Air Force mobilized three more ANG fighter-interceptor squadrons. By late fall, nearly three hundred fighters were stationed in Europe.

DETAILS, DETAILS

Most Famous Spy Plane in History

By the early 1950s, the USAF inventory of conventional bombers converted for reconnaissance work was judged inadequate to meet the demands of modern aerial surveillance. Lockheed assigned legendary aircraft designer Clarence "Kelly" Johnson and his team to create a spy plane capable of flying silently at seventy thousand feet or higher. What emerged was a radical craft with long, slender glider-style wings mated to the fuselage of the advanced Johnson-designed F-104 Starfighter. It was too unconventional for the USAF, but the CIA liked it and bought it after its first top-secret test flight on August 1, 1955 (see "The Myth of the 'Bomber Gap'" in Chapter 8).

The aircraft was designated "U" standing for "utility"—a purposely deceptive moniker. The "2" that followed was entirely arbitrary.

The U-2 became an icon of the Cold War. It was capable of a relatively slow top speed of 528 miles per hour, but it had a range of 4,600 miles and could climb to 85,000 feet to glide silently over its targets.

ALTERNATE TAKE

Nuclear Flashpoint

Most of the fighter aircraft sent to Europe were obsolescent Korean War–vintage planes. Worse, because the air force under Curtis LeMay had focused almost exclusively on preparing for strategic (nuclear) warfare, few pilots and crews had been trained in tactical (nonnuclear) warfare. They would have to learn—fast. The Soviets had far more planes and trained crews available. The same was true of ground forces. Troops and tanks immediately available to the Soviets substantially outnumbered those fielded by the United States. Had the Soviets chosen to attack, U.S. conventional forces would have been quickly defeated, and the Kennedy government would have had little choice other than to launch a retaliatory strike with nuclear weapons.

East German soldiers do the grunt work of building the Berlin Wall, 1961.

Showdown

The Berlin Wall rapidly evolved into a shameful symbol of Soviet communist repression, a self-inflicted propaganda defeat. More immediately, it marked the brink of thermonuclear war. The terms of the Potsdam Conference at the end of World War II specified that neither side would interfere with the passage of official personnel in any sector of Berlin. When East German police at Checkpoint Charlie, the portal between West and East Berlin, began interfering even with the free passage of U.S. and British diplomats, retired U.S. Army general Lucius D. Clay, the president's special adviser in West Berlin, directed U.S. tanks and infantry to stand by at Tempelhof Airport. In response, on October 27, 1961, thirty-three Soviet tanks rolled up to the Brandenburg Gate, which now marked the division between West and East sectors. Ten of these tanks rolled all the way up to the Soviet checkpoint. American tanks responded by taking positions just behind Checkpoint Charlie, and from about five o'clock in the afternoon to eleven o'clock the next morning, U.S. and Soviet tanks and troops faced off at the iron curtain.

It was an iconic moment in the Cold War. It was also a moment in which both sides had their fingers on the nuclear trigger. Soviet and American commanders issued orders to fire if fired upon, and the Strategic Air Command, the principal nuclear arm of the United States, was put on heightened alert. The standoff prompted direct communication between Kennedy and Khrushchev, Kennedy agreeing to make no provocative pronouncements on Berlin if the Soviets would be the first to pull back their tanks. The Soviet premier agreed, and, immediately, one Soviet tank withdrew five yards from the checkpoint. A U.S. tank matched its move. One by one thereafter, in alternating fashion, the tanks withdrew. The Berlin Crisis was defused.

Soviet and U.S. tanks face off at Checkpoint Charlie, the portal between East Berlin and West Berlin, between the iron curtain and the free world, October 27, 1961.

"It's not a very nice solution, but a wall is a hell of a lot better than war."

John F. Kennedy reacting to the construction of the Berlin Wall, August 13, 1961

The Missiles of October

As the highly combustible interface between West and East, Berlin was still very much on JFK's mind the following autumn, when, on October 16, 1962, he was shown U-2 reconnaissance photographs taken two days earlier revealing construction of an SS-4 medium-range ballistic missile (MRBM) launch site at San Cristóbal, in western Cuba. The SS-4 was capable of delivering a nuclear warhead to any number of U.S. East Coast and even Midwestern cities. Without a plan in place to deal with the presence of Soviet nuclear weapons on the doorstep of the United States, the president assembled under his brother Robert a fourteen-member "Executive Committee" (EXCOMM) of the National Security Council and put them to work formulating a response that would remove the threat without igniting Armageddon.

EXCOMM formulated five alternative responses to the missiles:

1. No response.
2. Rally and apply international diplomatic pressure to compel the Soviets to remove the missiles.
3. Bomb the missile installations and destroy them.
4. Invade Cuba.
5. Set up a naval blockade of Cuba to interdict, board, and inspect ships suspected of carrying missiles or personnel and turn them back. Since a blockade was technically an act of war, it could be more innocuously described as a "quarantine."

This map, showing the range of the Soviet MRBMs based in Cuba, was shown to President Kennedy during briefings on the Cuban Missile Crisis.

To a man, the Joint Chiefs of Staff recommended combining options 3 and 4, a massive air assault immediately followed by an invasion. The military advisers believed that the Soviet Union would never go to war to save Cuba. President Kennedy was critical of this course of action for two reasons. First, even in the best-case scenario, if the air attack destroyed every single missile before any could be launched, and if the invasion was also an overwhelming success, the Soviets could still retaliate against Berlin or directly against the United States. The latter meant nuclear war. Even if the Soviets responded only against Berlin, that might leave the United States no option but to respond against the Soviets and thereby trigger a nuclear exchange. And what if the air force failed to destroy all of the missiles? What if some were fired? Even a limited nuclear attack against American cities would require an all-out nuclear response against Soviet targets. Again, the result would be World War III.

As for launching an air attack without a follow-up invasion, Kennedy believed that this, too, would goad the Soviets into overrunning Berlin. Worse, if a move against Berlin took place because the United States initiated an air attack against Cuba, JFK thought it highly likely that even the NATO allies would condemn the United States as a collection of "trigger-happy cowboys" who threw away Berlin because they were unwilling to peacefully resolve the crisis in Cuba. NATO might dissolve.

President Kennedy signs Proclamation 3504, ordering the "naval quarantine" of Cuba, October 23, 1962.

Because the president rejected the option of doing nothing, only the naval quarantine remained. It would be a positive military action that was, of all the available military options, least likely to provoke a major war.

In the meantime, additional U-2 reconnaissance revealed more missiles deployed in four separate sites. Although Kennedy had decided on the quarantine, he also ordered preparations for air attack and invasion. The entire 1st Armored Division and five infantry divisions were sent to Georgia for quick deployment, and SAC positioned its nuclear-armed B-47 Stratojet bombers at civilian airports within striking range of Cuba. The nuclear-armed B-52 Stratofortresses were sent aloft, poised to attack Cuba as well as the Soviet Union.

At seven o'clock on the evening of October 22, the president delivered a televised address in which he announced the discovery of the missiles as well as the nation's intention to take all steps necessary for defense. His speech left no doubt in the minds of the American people. The world was on the brink of all-out thermonuclear war.

As the world awaited the first contact between Soviet vessels and the ships of the quarantine, EXCOMM member George Ball sent a cable to the U.S. ambassadors to Turkey and NATO informing them that the president was considering offering to withdraw U.S. missiles from Turkey in exchange for the withdrawal of Soviet missiles from Cuba. The message was sent "in the clear"—uncoded—in the expectation that the Soviets would intercept it. The idea was to add credibility to a back-channel offer the Kennedy administration intended to make to remove the Jupiter missiles, which were, in any case, obsolete and already scheduled for removal. By making them part of an exchange deal, Kennedy would give the Soviet premier a way to save face at home. The withdrawal of missiles from Cuba would look like a bargain, not a defeat. At last, on October 24, the first Soviet cargo ships approached the quarantine line. At sea and in Washington, tensions mounted. But the freighters turned back. Secretary of State Dean Rusk sighed gratefully: "We're eyeball to eyeball, and I think the other fellow just blinked."

There was no armed exchange and no war—but day by day, the missiles that had already been delivered were still being erected, and Kennedy was forced to seriously contemplate an invasion. EXCOMM persuaded him to wait for the premier's response to the back-channel offer. In the end, Kennedy agreed to remove missiles from the Turkish-Soviet border in exchange for Khrushchev's removal of all missiles in Cuba.

At nine o'clock on the morning of October 28, Khrushchev communicated with Kennedy via a Radio Moscow broadcast: "the Soviet government, in addition to previously issued instructions on the cessation of further work at the building sites for the weapons, has issued a new order on the dismantling of the weapons which you describe as

REALITY CHECK

Hidden in Plain Sight

The first consignment of SS-4 "Sandal" MRBMs (medium range ballistic missiles) arrived in Cuba on the night of September 8, 1962, followed by a second shipment on September 16. This nuclear-capable missile could travel 1,400 miles, putting it in range of most of the eastern seaboard. A shipment of SS-5 "Skean" MRBMs arrived later. With a 2,400-mile range, they endangered more than half of the United States. The Soviets planned to install forty launchers in Cuba, a move that would have increased the Soviet nuclear first-strike capability by 70 percent. Construction of the launchers was so poorly concealed that many Cubans saw it and talked about it. More than a thousand reports poured into the Cuban exile community in Miami *before* the U-2 reconnaissance. Oblivious, the CIA dismissed the reports as hysterical rumors.

POP CULTURE

Hot Line

The Cuban Missile Crisis revealed the need for a means of direct contact between Washington and the Kremlin that could be activated in times of crisis. The result was the "Hot Line," established pursuant to a memorandum signed June 20, 1963, in Geneva by Soviet Union and U.S. representatives.

The Hot Line made headlines and immediately entered into pop culture as the fabled "red telephones"—one set in the Kremlin, the other in the Oval Office. Actually, the Hot Line was not a telephone but a dedicated duplex (capable of simultaneously receiving and transmitting) telegraph circuit routed between Washington and Moscow via relays. The available technology permitted direct voice communication, but Hot Line designers purposely avoided this option in the belief that off-the-cuff verbal exchanges, especially in time of crisis, were too vulnerable to misunderstanding. The Hot Line was upgraded in 1971 with voice capabilities and continues to be modernized as technology evolves. A U.S.-China hotline was first used in 2008.

AN UNLIKELY HERO

Twice defeated for president by Eisenhower, mild-mannered, balding Adlai Stevenson emerged as an unlikely popular hero with the American people at the height of the Cuban Missile Crisis (see below). As U.S. ambassador to the United Nations, on October 25, 1962, he confronted Soviet ambassador Valerian Zorin with incontrovertible evidence of Soviet missiles in Cuba:

"Do you, Ambassador Zorin, deny that the U.S.S.R. has placed and is placing medium-and intermediate-range missiles and sites in Cuba? Yes or no—don't wait for the translation—yes or no?" Taken aback, Zorin replied, "I am not in an American courtroom, and therefore I do not wish to answer. In due course, sir, you will have your reply." Stevenson was relentless: "You are in the courtroom of world opinion right now, and you can answer yes or no." Again Zorin played for time: "You will have your answer in due course." Stevenson glared at him: "I am prepared to wait for my answer until hell freezes over."

This exchange is the image of Stevenson that endures in American popular culture; however, the year before, it had been Ambassador Stevenson who was abashed in the face of evidence. Before the General Assembly, he struggled to sell to the world the lie that the American government was uninvolved in the Bay of Pigs. When flatly contradictory evidence surfaced within hours of his U.N. appearance, he was humiliated. Nor was his sense of honor assuaged when he learned that President Kennedy had cynically referred to him in private as his "official liar." Stevenson came close to resigning his post as ambassador.

On October 23, 1962, Adlai Stevenson, U.S. ambassador to the United Nations (right), dramatically confronted Soviet deputy foreign minister Valerian Zorin (left) with photographs of Soviet missiles in Cuba. Mario Garcîa-Incháustegui (center) was Cuba's permanent representative to the UN.

'offensive' and their crating and return to the Soviet Union." The president responded that he considered this "an important and constructive contribution to peace," and he added that the United States would make a statement to the United Nations declaring that it would "respect the inviolability of Cuban borders, its sovereignty" and never attempt to invade.

Bottom Line

The bottom line? The people of the planet were given the privilege of continuing to enjoy the rising and the setting of the sun.

The cost to the Soviet premier had been a substantial amount of prestige. However the negotiation had been framed, it was Khrushchev, not Kennedy, who backed down. Cuba's Castro emerged from the crisis a winner because Kennedy's pledge to respect Cuban sovereignty reinforced his hold on power. He would continue to rule Cuba until old age and illness compelled him to relinquish the reins of government to his brother Raoul in 2008. But Khrushchev would last just two more years before the Communist Party forced him into an unwilling retirement, replacing him with a pair of communist hard liners, Leonid Brezhnev (as Communist Party first secretary) and Alexey Kosygin (as Soviet premier). Although implacable "cold war rior" Curtis LeMay grumbled to Kennedy that he considered the resolution of the Cuban Missile Crisis the "greatest defeat in our history," his was distinctly a minority opinion. Most Americans and virtually all modern historians view it as a high point of the Kennedy years and a Cold War victory for the United States.

Return to sender: U.S. aerial reconnaissance shows Soviet personnel and six missile transporters loaded on a Soviet freighter after removal from launch sites on Cuba. Note the vivid black shadow (lower right) of the U.S. Navy RF-101 reconnaissance aircraft that took the photograph.

TAKEAWAY

Cuba, Berlin, and Armageddon

Castro's communist revolution in Cuba brought the Cold War close to home. The pressure to "do something" about Castro and Cuba prompted President Kennedy into a reckless invasion, the failure of which helped trigger a potentially cataclysmic crisis in Berlin, followed by the Cuban Missile Crisis, which brought the world to the brink of thermonuclear war. Kennedy's handling of the Missile Crisis proved masterful, averted World War III, removed an unacceptable threat to U.S. security, and fatally weakened the Khrushchev regime. None of this came without cost. Khrushchev, moderate as Soviet leaders went, was replaced by hard liners, Leonid Brezhnev and Alexey Kosygin, whose policies prolonged the Cold War. The resolution of the Missile Crisis also strengthened Castro, helping to ensure the continuation of a Cuban government hostile to the United States.

CHAPTER 16

VIETNAM

The Longest War

IN THE SPEECH HE MADE TO THE AMERICAN ASSOCIATION OF NEWSPAPER EDITORS on April 20, 1961, concerning the fiasco at the Bay of Pigs, President John F. Kennedy spoke about more than just Cuba. "The message of Cuba, of Laos [Vietnam's neighbor], of the rising din of Communist voices in Asia and Latin America—these messages are all the same. . . . The complacent, the self-indulgent, the soft societies are about to be swept away with the debris of history. Only the strong, only the industrious, only the determined, only the courageous, only the visionary who determine the real nature of our struggle can possibly survive."

Having promised in his inaugural speech a "New Frontier," Kennedy took up from Truman and Eisenhower the old burden of "containment." He told the newspaper editors "that our security may be lost piece by piece, country by country, without the firing of a single missile or the crossing of a single border," and he therefore intended "to re-examine and reorient our forces of all kinds—our tactics and our institutions . . . to intensify our efforts for a struggle in many ways more difficult than war, where disappointment will often accompany us."

VIETNAM LOOKS LIKE THE PLACE

IN JANUARY 1961 AS KENNEDY CAME INTO OFFICE heavily mindful of Nikita Khrushchev's recent pledge to support what the Soviet premier called "wars of national liberation." Five months later, consistent with his remarks to the newspaper editors, the president sent four hundred Green Berets—U.S. Special Forces soldiers—as "Special Advisers" to train members of the South Vietnamese army, the Army of the Republic of Vietnam (ARVN). In June, he met with Khrushchev at a summit in Vienna, a contentious meeting, in which Kennedy protested North Vietnam's aggression in Laos and warned Khrushchev that the United States would take steps to support the neutrality of that nation. Khrushchev responded by agreeing to endorse Laotian neutrality, but JFK left the summit convinced that the Soviets intended to install a communist government in Laos and, ultimately, to sow communism throughout Southeast Asia. He believed that the purpose of this was to challenge, in a far-off place, the will of the United States to maintain its containment policy. Kennedy was dogged, moreover, by the Bay of Pigs fiasco, and he feared for the prestige of his administration. Even more, he feared that the United States was losing credibility as a deterrent force in the eyes of the Soviets and the rest of the world. To James Reston of the *New York Times*, the president remarked shortly after the Vienna Summit: "Now we have a problem in making our power credible, and Vietnam looks like the place."

Khrushchev and Kennedy meet in Vienna. The photograph was taken on June 3, 1961, in the U.S. Embassy residence.

VIETNAM: A LONG BACK STORY

AFTER THE VIENNA SUMMIT, KENNEDY TOOK A STEP across the threshold of war in Vietnam. That was the prospect that lay ahead of him and the nation. At his back, however, was a history of conflict typical of the Cold War.

Laos, Cambodia, and Vietnam came under French colonial control in the nineteenth century. After France caved in to Germany during World War II, in 1940, Germany's ally Japan permitted French colonial

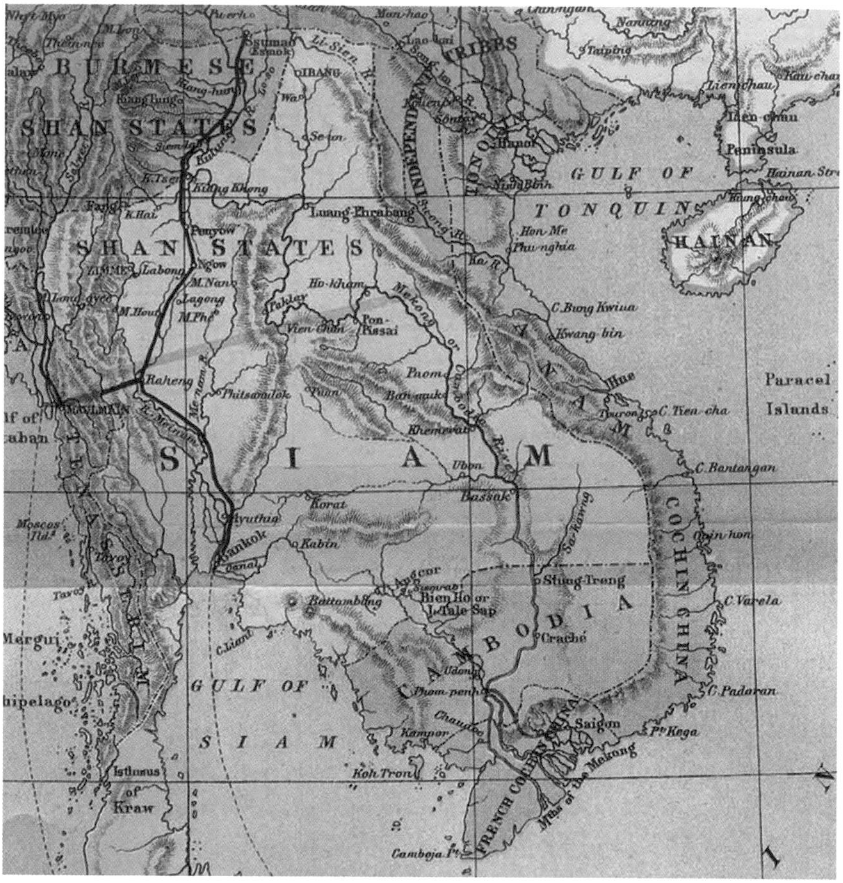

French Indochina—at the height of imperial France, 1886.

officials to continue administering Indochina under Japanese supervision until after the liberation of France. In March 1945, the Japanese seized complete control in the region. With the French colonial police gone, a host of independence groups became active. In Vietnam, the most powerful of these was the Viet Minh, led by Soviet-trained Ho Chi Minh. Aided by the U.S. Office of Strategic Services (OSS), Ho launched a guerrilla war against Japanese occupation forces. Even before World War II was over, the Viet Minh had wrested control of Vietnam's northern territory.

After the war in Europe had ended—but before the surrender of Japan—Allied forces turned their attention to Southeast Asia, which they had neglected during most of the war. Chiang Kai-shek's anticommunist Nationalist Chinese forces moved into the Tonkin provinces of northern Vietnam, while the British secured southern Vietnam for the reentry of the French. In 1946, the Nationalist Chinese withdrew from northern Vietnam and were replaced by the French military. In November of that year, Viet Minh militia fired on a French patrol boat in Haiphong harbor. The French retaliated, bombarding Haiphong in a raid that took the lives some six thousand civilians. Ho Chi Minh retreated with his provisional government into the hill country of Tonkin and commenced an all-out guerrilla war against the French.

Ho Chi Minh signed an agreement with France on March 6, 1946, which gave the Republic of Vietnam recognition as an autonomous state within the Indochinese Federation and the French Union. It was but one step removed from empire, and the agreement quickly broke down. He is pictured here speaking at City Hall, Paris, during negotiations with the French in July 1946.

"The French are foreigners. They are weak. Colonialism is dying out. Nothing will be able to withstand world pressure for independence."

Ho Chi Minh, March 1946, quoted in The Pentagon Papers *(1971)*

An anti-imperialist, President Truman sympathized with Ho Chi Minh's cause, but he feared that an independent Vietnam would be a communist Vietnam. At first he barred direct export of U.S. war matériel to French forces in the country, but did not prevent shipments to France itself. It was a symptom of America's ambivalence, which faded after the fall of China to communism in 1949 and the intensification of the Cold War in Europe. At that point, Truman deemed maintaining French authority in Vietnam the only alternative to a communist takeover. He also recognized that the newly formed NATO would succeed only if France supported it, and he did not want the French to waste their military on a guerrilla war in Vietnam. Therefore, on February 7, 1950, the Truman administration recognized Vietnam as constituted by the French under their puppet, former emperor Bao Dai.

Congress immediately voted $75 million in military aid to France, and, on June 25, 1950, when North Korean forces invaded South Korea, starting the Korean War (Chapter 12), Truman, anxious to avoid a collapse throughout Asia, secured additional aid.

On August 3, 1950, the president sent the first contingent of U.S. military advisers—the U.S. Military Assistance Advisory Group (MAAG)—to Saigon. By 1952, the United States was financing a third of the French military effort in Vietnam. Nevertheless, the French lost both ground and heart.

Dien Bien Phu

In April 1953, the Viet Minh made a major push in the western Tonkin region, advanced into Laos, and even menaced Thailand. The French asked for the loan of large American C-119 transports to airlift heavy equipment into Laos. President Eisenhower, in office just four months, allowed USAF ground personnel to work in Vietnam, but did not want air crews flying combat missions. Accordingly, he ordered military crews to fly the transports to Nha Trang, where civilian pilots, flying under covert U.S. government contracts, took over for the flight to Cat Bi Airfield near Haiphong.

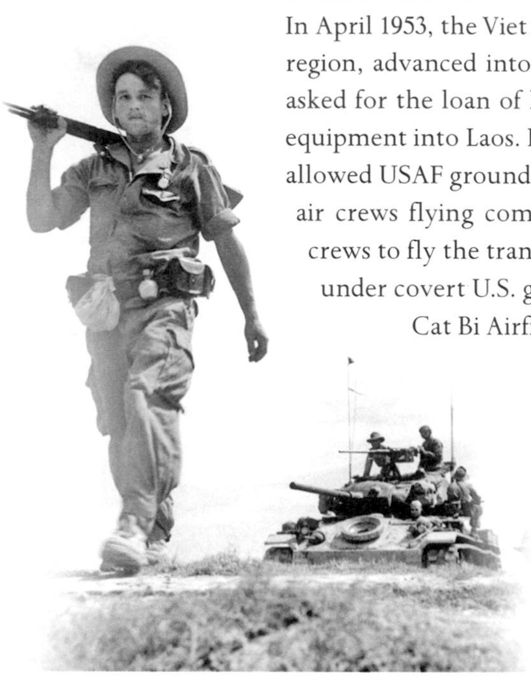

The year is 1954, the place is the Red River Delta between Haiphong and Hanoi, the soldier is a French Foreign Legionnaire, and the tank is a gift from the United States of America.

Under General Henri Eugene Navarre, French forces planned to lure the Viet Minh into open battle and render them incapable of conducting anything other than a low level of guerrilla warfare, which, Navarre believed, could be contained by Vietnamese government troops. In the fall of 1953, Navarre began operations on the plain of Dien Bien Phu in northwest Tonkin, near Laos.

The Eisenhower administration was becoming increasingly nervous about Viet Minh attacks against Hanoi and Haiphong, from which Navarre had withdrawn forces to bolster Dien Bien Phu. Worse, despite the build-up, Ho Chi Minh was massing forces around Dien Bien Phu. Eisenhower authorized additional military aid, including three hundred USAF ground personnel, whom he described in a speech to an anxious American public as "some airplane mechanics . . . who would not get touched by combat."

U.S. logistical support notwithstanding, the French defensive perimeter at Dien Bien Phu steadily contracted. President Eisenhower contemplated sending combat forces, but held back because the British were not on board and the French would not pledge ultimately to grant Vietnam its independence. Eisenhower believed that, once the Viet Minh had been defeated, independence, not continued colonial status, would be a bulwark against any renewed communist incursion. Nevertheless, on April 7, 1954, the president sought to prepare the nation for deeper involvement in Vietnam, offering to reporters a metaphor: "You have a row of dominoes set up, you knock over the first one, and what will happen to the last one is the certainty it will go over very quickly." Thus was born the "domino theory," destined to overshadow U.S. policy for some twenty years as a rationale for ever-deepening involvement in the Vietnam War.

The following month, on May 7, 1954, the first domino seemed to topple. Dien Bien Phu fell to the forces of Ho Chi Minh, a stunning loss followed by additional Viet Minh victories that persuaded the French government, in July, to agree with the Viet Minh to divide Vietnam along the 17th parallel and conclude an armistice.

North Vietnamese general Vo Nguyen Giap (dressed in black) confers with his aides in planning the decisive Battle of Dien Bien Phu. Little known in the West, Giap was a commander of brilliance and daring.

THE ADVISERS

HO CHI MINH WAS CONFIDENT that a plebiscite on reunification, mandated by the armistice and scheduled for July 1956, would unify Vietnam under a communist government. Unwilling to accept this, the U.S. and French governments worked with South Vietnamese leaders to install a stable government below the 17th parallel and try to build up a credible South Vietnamese military. The United States sponsored the creation of the Southeast Asia Treaty Organization (SEATO) as a NATO-style coalition against communist aggression. Eisenhower also expanded MAAG in defiance of the international armistice commission. This "advisory" force was the nucleus from which U.S. involvement in Vietnam would expand.

When the appointed time for the reunification plebiscite arrived in July 1956, the South Vietnamese government refused to hold the promised vote, and Eisenhower committed the United States to a long-term advisory role, hoping to build an effective South

An American military adviser demonstrates self-defense tactics to South Vietnamese combat police.

South Vietnamese president Ngo Dinh Diem dedicates Vinh Long Airfield on October 10, 1961. The president's brother, the Roman Catholic archbishop of Hue, looks on.

Vietnamese military. In the meantime, North Vietnamese insurgents waged guerrilla warfare south of the 17th parallel, and in September 1959, the Vietcong (a communist guerrilla group that succeeded and absorbed elements of the Viet Minh, communist-oriented nationalists) ambushed two ARVN companies in the Plain of Reeds southwest of Saigon. The United States responded early in 1960 by further expanding MAAG to 685 men, but there was nothing the U.S. military could do to reverse the unpopularity of the South Vietnamese government under President Ngo Dinh Diem, who narrowly survived an attempted coup d'état on November 11, 1960. Compounding this crisis was the disintegrating situation in Laos, the government of which was being challenged by military forces of the Pathet Lao.

By the time Kennedy took office in January 1961, an intense insurgent war was under way. In October, the new president sent additional advisers, the Green Berets, and a USAF contingent that not only trained South Vietnamese fliers but also surreptitiously flew combat missions in Operation Farm Gate.

From Advice to Combat

Also in October, Kennedy sent his adviser Walt Rostow and General Maxwell Taylor to Vietnam to report on whether to commit to a full combat mission. The pair recommended giving Farm Gate more combat assignments. JFK's acceptance of the recommendation on November 3 marked a shift from advice to combat, and by June 30, 1962, there were 6,419 American soldiers and airmen in South Vietnam.

FRUSTRATION AND THE FALL OF DIEM

THE PACE OF VIETCONG ATTACKS INCREASED throughout 1963, despite the growing U.S. presence. Worse, whereas U.S.-ARVN progress against the NVA seemed only to increase Vietcong aggression, North Vietnamese attacks against ARVN forces undermined popular support for

General Maxwell Taylor, military adviser to John F. Kennedy, peers at the enemy through the sights of an ARVN field gun while on a fact-finding tour of the front lines in October 1961.

the corrupt Diem government. Determined to keep the Vietnamese domino from falling, Kennedy turned a blind eye to the problems of the Diem regime. But soon the whole world had its eyes opened.

A devout Catholic, Diem supported his nation's Catholic minority while persecuting the Buddhist majority. To protest this, a succession of Buddhist monks doused themselves in gasoline and set themselves ablaze in the streets of Saigon—the horrific images captured by television news crews and broadcast worldwide. Secretly, Kennedy acquiesced to a CIA-backed military coup that overthrew Diem on November 1, 1963. What the president did not expect was that the deposed leader would be assassinated on the following day, along with his brother, inside an armored personnel carrier.

Buddhist monk Quang Duc immolates himself on a Saigon street, June 11, 1963, to protest the Diem government's persecution of Buddhists. Images such as these shocked the world and revealed the brutality and corruption of the unpopular Diem regime.

A military junta set up a provisional government, which the United States recognized on November 8. For their part the Vietcong exploited the disarray and stepped up their attacks. It was clear that the situation in Vietnam was rapidly deteriorating—and in the midst of this, on November 22, 1963, twenty days after the assassination of Diem, President John F. Kennedy was gunned down during a visit to Dallas.

Vice President Lyndon Johnson took office within hours of the president's murder. Initially, he and the secretary of defense he carried over from JFK, former Ford Motor Company president Robert McNamara, opted to confine operations to South Vietnam.

TONKIN GULF

ALTHOUGH JOHNSON AND MCNAMARA WERE CAUTIOUS about expanding the war, in June 1964, the president appointed an outspoken advocate of expansion, General William Westmoreland, to take command in Vietnam. On July 27, five thousand more "advisers" were ordered to the country, bringing the total ground forces there to twenty-one thousand. Four days after this, the destroyer USS *Maddox* set out on a reconnaissance mission in the Gulf of Tonkin, off the coast of North

NUMBERS

Vietnam: America's War Begins to Escalate

By the end of 1962 and beginning of 1963, American assistance and the buildup of ARVN forces was having an impact on the insurgents, especially on Vietcong guerrilla units, which were seen as a bigger threat than the regular North Vietnamese Army (NVA). The price of this progress? At the start of 1961, some 900 U.S. military personnel were stationed in Vietnam. By the end of 1962, there were more than 11,000, a number that would rise by midyear to 16,652. As of the end of 1962, 27 of these servicemen had been killed and 65 wounded. Five were prisoners of the Vietcong. Throughout Viet Nam, the war claimed about 2,000 lives—mostly North Vietnamese—each week.

This photograph, taken from the bridge of USS Maddox *on August 2, 1964, shows three North Vietnamese motor torpedo boats (similar to U.S. PT boats) in the Tonkin Gulf. The original Defense Department caption ran: "North Vietnamese torpedo boats attacking USS* Maddox*, 2 Aug, 1964." The current caption refers only to the destroyer's "engagement" with the boats and does not use the word* attacking.

Vietnam. On August 2, the ship reported itself in international waters and under attack by five North Vietnamese patrol boats. *Maddox* withdrew to South Vietnamese territorial waters, where it was joined by the destroyer USS *C. Turner Joy*. Damage incurred during the exchange consisted of an inconsequential ding by a single .50-caliber machine gun bullet.

Two days later, on August 4, U.S. patrol craft detected what its crew interpreted as signals indicating another attack by the North Vietnamese. In response, *Maddox* and *C. Turner Joy* fired their guns for some two hours against what were believed were hostile radar contacts. No enemy vessels were ever actually sighted.

In response to the reported attacks, President Johnson cast aside his former doubts and ordered immediate retaliatory strikes against North Vietnam. On the evening of August 4, he made a television address describing the attacks and the retaliation. In the meantime, Secretary McNamara testified to Congress that the North Vietnamese attacks had been unprovoked—although he knew that the mission of *Maddox* had been to provide intelligence to support South Vietnamese strikes against the North. The secretary also testified to "unequivocal proof" of the "unprovoked" August 4 attack, about which there was actually considerable doubt.

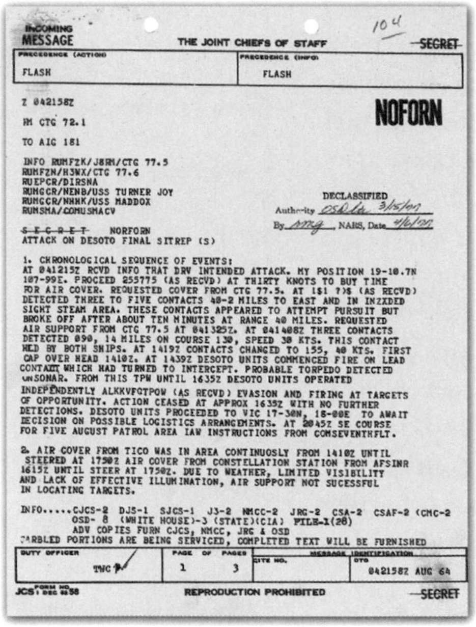

INCOMING MESSAGE
THE JOINT CHIEFS OF STAFF
SECRET
104

PRECEDENCE (ACTION)	PRECEDENCE (INFO)
FLASH	FLASH

Z 042158Z
NOFORN
FM CTG 72.1
TO AIG 181
INFO RUMFZK/J8RM/CTG 77.5
RUMFZN/H3WX/CTG 77.6
RUEPCR/DIRSNA
RUMGCR/NENB/USS TURNER JOY
RUMGCR/NHHK/USS MADDOX
RUMSMA/COMUSMACV

DECLASSIFIED
Authority OSD ltr 3/15/77
By mg, NARS, Date 4/6/77

~~SECRET~~ NORFORN
ATTACK ON DESOTO FINAL SITREP (S)

1. CHRONOLOGICAL SEQUENCE OF EVENTS:
AT 041215Z RCVD INFO THAT DRV INTENDED ATTACK. MY POSITION 19-10.7N 107-99E. PROCEED 255775 (AS RECVD) AT THIRTY KNOTS TO BUY TIME FOR AIR COVER. REQUESTED COVER FROM CTG 77.5. AT 1$1 7)$ (AS RECVD) DETECTED THREE TO FIVE CONTACTS 40-2 MILES TO EAST AND IN INZXDED SIGHT STEAM AREA. THESE CONTACTS APPEARED TO ATTEMPT PURSUIT BUT BROKE OFF AFTER ABOUT TEN MINUTES AT RANGE 40 MILES. REQUESTED AIR SUPPORT FROM CTG 77.5 AT 041325Z. AT 041408Z THREE CONTACTS DETECTED 090, 14 MILES ON COURSE 130, SPEED 30 KTS. THIS CONTACT HED BY BOTH SHIPS. AT 1419Z CONTACTS CHANGED TO 155, 40 KTS. FIRST CAP OVER HEAD 1410Z. AT 1439Z DESOTO UNITS COMMENCED FIRE ON LEAD CONTACT WHICH HAD TURNED TO INTERCEPT. PROBABLE TORPEDO DETECTED ON SONAR. FROM THIS TPW UNTIL 1635Z DESOTO UNITS OPERATED INDEPENDENTLY ALKKVFGTPOW (AS RECVD) EVASION AND FIRING AT TARGETS OF OPPORTUNITY. ACTION CEASED AT APPROX 1635Z WITH NO FURTHER DETECTIONS. DESOTO UNITS PROCEEDED TO VIC 17-30N, 18-00E TO AWAIT DECISION ON POSSIBLE LOGISTICS ARRANGEMENTS. AT 2045Z SE COURSE FOR FIVE AUGUST PATROL AREA IAW INSTRUCTIONS FROM COMSEVENTHFLT.

2. AIR COVER FROM TICO WAS IN AREA CONTINUOSLY FROM 1410Z UNTIL STEERED AT 1750Z AIR COVER FROM CONSTELLATION STATION FROM AFSINR 1615Z UNTIL STEER AT 1750Z. DUE TO WEATHER, LIMITED VISIBILITY AND LACK OF EFFECTIVE ILLUMINATION, AIR SUPPORT NOT SUCESSFUL IN LOCATING TARGETS.

INFO.....CJCS-2 DJS-1 SJCS-1 J3-2 NMCC-2 JRG-2 CSA-2 CSAF-2 (CMC-2
OSD- 8 (WHITE HOUSE)-3 (STATE)(CIA) FILE-1(28)
ADV COPIES FURN CJCS, NMCC, JRG & OSD
GARBLED PORTIONS ARE BEING SERVICED, COMPLETED TEXT WILL BE FURNISHED

DUTY OFFICER	PAGE OF PAGES	CITE NO.	DTG
TWC	1 3		042158Z AUG 64

JCS FORM NO. 1 DEC 58
REPRODUCTION PROHIBITED
SECRET

This flash cable from the destroyers Maddox *and* C. Turner Joy *to the Joint Chiefs of Staff, dated August 4, 1964, tells the story of the events in Tonkin Gulf that launched a war. The "DESOTO UNITS" referred to are the two destroyers.*

"All Vietnam is not worth the life of a single American boy."

Senator Ernest Gruening (Dem., Alaska), August 6, 1964, during debate on the Tonkin Gulf Resolution

After Senate debate following McNamara's testimony and a message to Congress delivered by President Johnson on August 5, the Tonkin Gulf Resolution was passed by both houses. It authorized the president "to take all necessary steps, including the use of armed force, to assist any member or protocol state of the Southeast Asia Collective Defense Treaty requesting assistance in defense of its freedom." It was a blank check that gave LBJ permission to conduct the war as he wished, without seeking congressional approval.

LBJ Holds the "Check" . . .

Given a blank check, the temptation is always great to cash it immediately, but Johnson bided his time. Even as Vietcong attacks on South Vietnamese hamlets and military outposts doubled and, on November 1, 1964, the Vietcong briefly overran Bien Hoa air base, killing four USAF personnel, wounding seventy-two, and wrecking aircraft and buildings, LBJ refused to yield to the recommendation of the Joint Chiefs for severe reprisals. It was, after all, election eve, and Johnson was running against a Republican conservative, Barry Goldwater, whose unabashed hawkishness on the war frightened voters. LBJ did not want to suddenly "outhawk" his opponent.

No sooner did Johnson defeat Goldwater—and by a landslide—than he authorized air strikes on Laos, through which the Vietcong infiltrated into South Vietnam. Instead of disheartening the VC, the air strikes triggered more aggression. In December, a VC explosive charge destroyed U.S. bachelor officer quarters at Saigon's Brink Hotel, killing two Americans and injuring sixty-four others in addition to forty-three Vietnamese. Again, the Joint Chiefs pushed for reprisals, but, discouraged by the ineffectiveness of the air strikes, LBJ again demurred. A few days later, on December 27–31, Vietcong raided the hamlet of Binh Gia and ambushed the marines who marched to its aid. Maxwell Taylor, the U.S. ambassador to Vietnam who had been arguing for restraint, now joined the Joint Chiefs in calling for the bombing of North Vietnam.

Despite the tremendous pressure on him, President Johnson continued to hesitate because the government that had replaced the Diem regime was unstable (so unstable that, from 1963 to early 1965, it would be succeeded by eleven more governments, all incapable of standing without U.S. support). LBJ agonized over whether to commit U.S. forces directly against North Vietnam or to disengage from a losing proposition

REALITY CHECK

Fighting from False Premises

Although the crews of the *Maddox* and *C. Turner Joy* sincerely believed they were under attack, current military historians and even some of those former crew members have concluded that the radar signals interpreted as enemy attack craft were "false echoes"—electronic artifacts—and that the August 4, 1964, attack never actually occurred. In 1995, former Secretary of Defense Robert McNamara admitted that his testimony to Congress, that the August 2 attack was "unprovoked" and that evidence for the August 4 attack was "incontrovertible," was not merely mistaken, but false—a lie.

Evidence discrediting the Tonkin Gulf Incident culminated on November 30, 2005, when the National Security Agency (NSA) declassified and released documents that included a 2001 article in which NSA historian Robert J. Hanyok asserted that NSA intelligence officers had "deliberately skewed" the evidence NSA delivered to policy makers and the public to suggest that North Vietnamese ships had attacked the U.S. destroyers on August 4, 1964.

and let the Vietnam domino fall. Johnson sent adviser McGeorge Bundy on a fact-finding mission to Saigon in February 1965. While he was there, on February 7, VC teams attacked U.S. advisery forces near Pleiku, killing 9 Americans and wounding 108. Jointly with Taylor and Westmoreland, Bundy sent President Johnson an unequivocal recommendation to strike North Vietnam. Operation Flaming Dart, an air strike against a major NVA barracks, brought a counterstrike on the U.S.-ARVN barracks at Qui Nhon, killing twenty-three U.S. airmen and seven Vietnamese troops. This triggered a U.S. reprisal the next day.

> "My solution to the problem [of North Vietnamese aggression] would be to tell them . . . we're going to bomb them back into the Stone Age."
>
> *General Curtis E. LeMay,*
> Mission with LeMay: My Story, *1965*

. . . Then Cashes It

The year 1965 saw steady escalation, beginning with air strikes against North Vietnam code-named Rolling Thunder and continuing through 1968. While the war expanded, LBJ and his advisers struggled to define their war aims. The goal of reunifying Vietnam was rejected, and the new, lesser objective was to protect the independence of South Vietnam. Johnson believed this could be achieved primarily through an air war, but Westmoreland argued that bombing alone would have little effect on North Vietnamese aggression. He wanted to introduce a blocking force along the major artery by which the North Vietnamese infiltrated the South. Johnson opposed this, but approved creating an "air cavalry," the 1st Cavalry Division (Airmobile), equipped with more than four hundred helicopters, to be used in a campaign for the Central Highlands during late 1965 and early 1966. And although Westmoreland was denied his blocking force, he was authorized to launch the first major U.S. ground operation on June 28, 1965, in Bien Hoa Province, just twenty miles northeast of Saigon. The results were mixed, but during August 18–21, 1965, Operation

General William Westmoreland, commanding general of U.S. forces in Vietnam, confers with U.S. ambassador to Vietnam Maxwell Taylor at Tan Son Nhut Airport (later Air Base), Saigon (now Ho Chi Minh City), February 11, 1965.

Starlight scored major victories against the Vietcong in Quang Ngai Province.

During October 23–November 20, the Central Highlands campaign culminated in the Battle of Ia Drang, the first major battle of the war, in which the 1st Cavalry Division (Airmobile) defeated VC and NVA forces in western Pleiku Province. Both sides suffered heavy casualties, but American forces foiled a North Vietnamese bid to seize this region and thereby cut South Vietnam in half.

Marines with their Vietcong POWs during Operation Starlight, south of Chu Lai, South Vietnam, August 1, 1965. The helicopter in the background is a UH-34D Seahorse, mainstay of the USMC rotary fleet in the Vietnam War era.

SEARCH AND DESTROY

THE YEAR 1966 BEGAN with Operation Marauder, the first foray of an American unit, the 173d Airborne Brigade, into the Mekong Delta. Subsequently, Operation Van Buren (January 19–February 21) secured Phu Yen Province in the central coastal region, setting the pattern for the "search and destroy" actions that would become the principal tactic of the war as U.S. and ARVN forces took the battle to the enemy.

By 1966, combined U.S.-ARVN forces were winning battles and securing territory. But it was one thing to take territory and quite another to hold it. Captured areas were reoccupied by the enemy almost as soon as U.S. and ARVN forces moved on. Moreover, although North Vietnamese losses were far greater than those of the United States, the North Vietnamese were willing to absorb the losses in a strategy of fight, die, but outlast.

Operation Oregon was one of many "search and destroy" missions that brought the battle to the enemy. Here, soldiers of the 1st Cavalry Division (Airmobile) probe a Vietcong tunnel during a recon mission, Quang Ngai Province, April 24, 1967. In many places, the VC operated through a network of tunnels. It was the job of intrepid reconnaissance troops—"tunnel rats"—to flush out the enemy. Tunnel rat volunteers had to be fearless, small, and wiry.

This map, created in 1966, depicts a portion of a typical VC tunnel. The immense tunnel system was like a complex multilevel subterranean city, with command centers, living centers, food and arms storage, hospitals, and kitchens. The Cu Chi tunnel system, twenty miles outside of Saigon, was one of the largest Vietcong bases, a labyrinth spread out over an estimated two hundred miles.

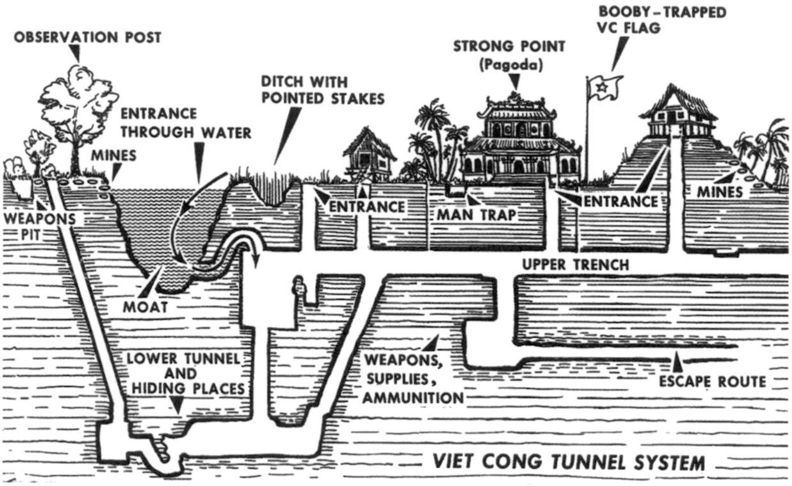

"If the tiger ever stands still the elephant will crush him with his mighty tusks. But the tiger does not stand still. He lurks in the jungle by day and emerges by night. He will leap upon the back of the elephant, tearing huge chunks from his hide. And slowly the elephant will bleed to death."

Ho Chi Minh, quoted in Jean Lacouture,
Ho Chi Minh, *1968*

B-52s and the Doctrine of Main Force

In April 1966, the U.S. Air Force began flying B-52 bombers from bases in Guam to attack North Vietnamese infiltration routes near the border of North Vietnam and Laos. Using giant, unwieldy bombers designed—and crews trained—to execute a global *strategic* mission in *tactical* warfare revealed the shortcomings of the Cold War policy of preparing almost exclusively to fight a thermonuclear war against the Soviet Union while neglecting preparation for combating a guerrilla insurgency.

Another outmoded doctrine was "main force," the strategy of attempting to overwhelm enemy insurgents wherever they surfaced. This meant mounting operation after operation with no objective other than to meet force with overwhelming force. Typical of a "main force" encounter was Operation Attleboro, at the end of 1966, which was conducted just north of Saigon. About one hundred ARVN and U.S. troops died in this operation, while the communists lost eleven hundred or more men. Yet, apart from inflicting higher casualties, no strategic goal was achieved by Attleboro—or any other main force operation.

Hearts, Minds, and Bombs

While the United States waged the "main force" war during 1966–67, ARVN pursued a "pacification" policy, which was intended—in the catchphrase popularized by LBJ—to win the "hearts and minds" of the South Vietnamese peasantry, turning them against the insurgents. There was a military component to pacification, but the campaign emphasized education, land reform, communications, agriculture, and other civil programs. Recognizing that the VC repeatedly withdrew from contested territory only to return after U.S. and ARVN forces left, the architects of pacification sought to destroy, village by village, the infrastructure that supported the VC. U.S. forces took over supervision of pacification from ARVN before the end of 1967, and it produced measurable results, including increased desertion rates among South Vietnamese communist units.

U.S. bombing of North Vietnamese targets intensified during 1966–67 over the Laos panhandle, where the Ho Chi Minh Trail served as the principal supply and infiltration route into South Vietnam. The North Vietnamese responded with improved anti-aircraft guns and SAMs (surface-to-air missiles), shooting down many U.S. aircraft, capturing the pilots, and subjecting them to brutal torture in such POW facilities as the infamous "Hanoi Hilton."

The air force estimated that its attacks on the Ho Chi Minh Trail destroyed about 18 percent of enemy vehicular traffic into South Vietnam, but the ever-resourceful North Vietnamese continued bringing in supplies on foot and by bicycle—with skilled riders learning to balance loads of many hundreds of pounds. Still, LBJ believed the bombing was useful as a tool of negotiation. Eight times in 1967 alone, he halted bombing in an effort to facilitate talks. Repeatedly, the talks failed to develop, and leaders outside of the Johnson administration argued that the bombing served only to harden Hanoi's resolve.

Captured from a Vietcong POW, this rare photograph of the Ho Chi Minh Trail in use reveals the VC's principal supply vehicle: the human being. The main line of supply and communication, the trail allowed the Vietcong to operate deep in South Vietnamese territory.

HOME FRONT: THE TURN AGAINST THE WAR

BY 1967, AN ANTIWAR MOVEMENT was gathering momentum throughout the United States and especially on college campuses. To counter it, the Johnson administration launched a "media offensive" fronted by General Westmoreland, who argued to the American public that the United States was inflicting losses that outpaced enemy recruitment and reinforcement. In 1965, Westmoreland pointed out, communist insurgents had closed 70 percent of South Vietnam's roadways and waterways; by the beginning of 1967, he said, 60 percent were open. That few challenged the accuracy of Westmoreland's data is telling. The data did not matter. Despite statistics, the lack of progress toward peace persuaded a growing number of Americans that the war was stalemated. In the face of this sentiment, LBJ did his best to assure television viewers that there was "light at the end of the tunnel." The phrase, often repeated, became the subject of mocking skepticism, and the press came up with a catchphrase of its own, "credibility gap," to describe the gulf between what the administration claimed and what the public believed.

"Declare the United States the winner and begin de-escalation."

Senator George Aiken (Rep., Vermont), October 19, 1966

American POWs, mostly pilots captured from downed aircraft, were often exhibited to the press. Subject to torture and deprivation, many publicly "confessed" to the "war crime" of bombing civilian targets. This photograph, taken in Hanoi, is from June 1972.

REALITY CHECK

Keeping Score, Counting Corpses

Because control of territory shifted continually in Vietnam, U.S. commanders did not report their progress by exhibiting maps with regions captured, but by submitting a "body count"—the phrase would become a sickening Vietnam-era mantra—to prove that more of the enemy had died than friendly forces. As the war ground on, American reporters and critics of the war argued that body counts were often inflated and even fabricated; nevertheless, it is incontrovertible that the North Vietnamese suffered far greater losses than the United States—though not always greater than the ARVN. Yet the unconventional enemy in this so-called unconventional war refused to give up. The Vietcong showed themselves willing to accept terrible casualties without accepting defeat.

By the end of 1967, the Vietnam War had polarized the public and politicians alike, pitting those who opposed the war (in Congress called doves) against those who continued to support it (hawks). In response to its growing "dove" membership, Congress called on the administration to mount a peace initiative in the autumn of 1967. Secretary of State Dean Rusk dismissed such initiatives as futile, and Westmoreland, on November 21, declared to reporters: "I am absolutely certain that whereas in 1965 the enemy was winning, today he is certainly losing."

Tet

Just as Americans turned against the war in increasing numbers, the North Vietnamese launched a series of massive offensives, first along the border, and then, beginning on January 30, 1968, deeper into South Vietnam. Corresponding with Tet, a Vietnamese lunar holiday, the attacks on major cities and military bases were collectively dubbed the Tet Offensive. The Tet Offensive was costly to U.S. and ARVN forces, but it took a far heavier toll on the NVA and VC. Of an estimated eighty-four thousand attackers, some forty-five thousand were killed. By any military standard, the U.S.-ARVN response to Tet was a spectacular triumph, but on the American home front, the three-week offensive was a devastating psychological victory for the communists. Tet persuaded many Americans that the Vietnam War was simply unwinnable, and 1968 marked the height of the U.S. commitment to the war, the number of American military personnel in Vietnam topping off at 536,000.

The monolithic U.S. Embassy in Saigon was a target of the 1968 Tet Offensive. Although U.S. and ARVN forces defeated the offensive, inflicting catastrophic casualties on the Vietcong, the campaign was a stunning psychological victory for North Vietnam, a watershed event that turned many Americans solidly against the war.

DETAILS, DETAILS

Talking Hearts and Minds

LBJ used some version of the phrase "hearts and minds" a total of twenty-eight times in speeches, in ten instances inverting the phrase as "minds and hearts." The first use was on January 16, 1964, and the last on August 19, 1968. The most famous usage was in a speech of May 4, 1965, in which he said that "ultimate victory [in Vietnam] will depend upon the hearts and the minds of the people who actually live out there."

LBJ may have drawn the phrase from John Adams, who, in an 1818 letter, recalled that the American Revolution "was effected before the War commenced. The Revolution was in the minds and hearts of the people" and that the "radical change in the principles, opinions, sentiments, and affections of the people, was the real American Revolution."

An icon of the antiwar movement: a young female protestor offers a flower to a military policeman during a 1967 protest.

Protest Turns to Resistance

Increasingly during 1968, protest turned to resistance as many young men defied federal Selective Service law by refusing to register for the draft, burned their Selective Service registration identification cards (draft cards), and even fled the country to avoid service.

THE PRESIDENT BOWS OUT

LYNDON BAINES JOHNSON is one of the modern presidency's genuinely tragic figures. Catapulted into office by the murder of a young president, he entered the White House determined to use the memory of JFK to promote a legacy of social welfare and justice legislation even more ambitious than the New Deal of his political hero, Franklin Roosevelt. Medicare, Medicaid, the Civil Rights Act of 1964, and the Voting Rights Act of 1965 were highlights of the policy program Johnson called the "Great Society." But as Johnson became ever more desperately entangled in the war he had escalated, funding for these programs melted away, and a president who might have been hailed as the architect of magnificent social reform instead heard protestors outside his Oval Office window condemn him as a "War Monger" and "Baby Killer."

After Tet, LBJ understood that he personally had become a divisive force in American politics, and he also had come to believe that peace negotiations would never succeed as long as he occupied the White House. Thus, on March 31, 1968, he appeared on television, acknowledged the "divisiveness among us all tonight," and announced "I shall not seek, and I will not accept, the nomination of my party for another term as your President." The speech contained another stunner: a decision to restrict bombing above the 20th parallel, a move intended to open the

February 9, 1968: Dean Rusk, President Johnson, and Robert McNamara at a cabinet meeting; fifty-two days later Johnson would announce bombing restrictions and his intention not to run for reelection.

REALITY CHECK

War Crimes

The U.S.-directed pacification campaign included the Phoenix Program, in which ARVN "intelligence-action teams" captured or killed South Vietnamese civilians identified as part of a network that supplied, housed, and fed Vietcong infiltrators. Waging war in this manner against civilians was a violation of international conventions of "civilized" warfare, including those to which the United States subscribed.

door to a negotiated settlement of the war. Cease-fire negotiations began in May, only to bog down over Hanoi's demands for a *complete* bombing halt and the presence of the Vietcong's political parent organization, the NLF (National Liberation Front), at the peace table.

"Hey, Hey, LBJ, how many kids did you kill today?"

Antiwar chant, 1968

The War Comes Home

Johnson's withdrawal left open the possibility that the Democrats might nominate an antiwar candidate. Senator Eugene McCarthy of Minnesota filled the bill, and his strong showing in the New Hampshire primary encouraged another antiwar candidate, Massachusetts senator Robert F. Kennedy, to offer himself. RFK handily won the Indiana and Nebraska primaries, then went to California, where, after declaring victory in that primary on June 6, 1968, he met the same fate as his brother, gunned down by an assassin. This tragedy gave the "mainstream" Democratic candidate, Vice President Hubert H. Humphrey, the lead for the nomination, and he defeated McCarthy at the Democratic National Convention held in Chicago during August 26–29, 1968.

Although McCarthy garnered just 23 percent of the delegate vote, the party was hardly unified around Humphrey, who announced his intention to fight the war to its conclusion. Rioting broke out in Chicago's lakefront Grant and Lincoln parks during the convention, suggesting to many a foretaste of the violence that would sweep the country if the war were not ended.

U.S. Attorney General Robert F. Kennedy speaks to demonstrators at a 1963 civil rights rally outside of the Justice Department, Washington, D.C. Five years later, Kennedy would bid for the Democratic presidential nomination as an antiwar candidate, only to be assassinated on June 6, 1968, after winning the California primary.

POP CULTURE

The Television War

The Vietnam War exploded during the first great heyday of televised news. By the middle of 1965, all of the major networks opened Saigon bureaus, which grew into the third largest they maintained, behind only New York and Washington, D.C. Coverage of Vietnam did much to create the antiwar movement by bringing into the nation's living rooms graphic images of the conflict's horrors. In August 1965, CBS aired a report showing U.S. Marines igniting the thatched roofs of the village of Cam Ne with Zippo lighters. During the 1968 Tet Offensive, NBC viewers saw Colonel Nguyen Ngoc Loan blow out the brains of his captive in a Saigon street. After the Tet Offensive, TV coverage exhibited increasing skepticism concerning government claims of progress. While this reflected changing American public opinion at least as much as it shaped that opinion, TV reinforced antiwar sentiment, validating antiwar activism not only as a legitimate political stance but also as a mainstream movement.

REALITY CHECK
Credibility Gap

With American casualties having risen from 780 per month during 1967 to 2,000 a month in February 1968, it was very difficult for the public to believe official military pronouncements that Tet was an American victory. Although the public focused on losses among U.S. ground forces, the performance of the U.S. Air Force was even worse. The kill ratio—North Vietnamese aircraft shot down versus U.S. aircraft lost—was even by 1968: for every MiG shot down, a U.S. plane was lost. It was and remains the worst performance in the history of American aerial combat.

NIXON'S WAR

IN CONTRAST TO THE CHAOS surrounding the Democrats, the Republicans rallied behind their nominee, Richard M. Nixon. Like Humphrey, Nixon intended to continue the war, but claimed he had a "secret plan" to achieve "peace with honor." This helped him edge out Humphrey with 43.4 percent of the popular vote to the Democrat's 42.7 percent. (Third-party segregationist candidate George Wallace captured 13.5 percent of the popular vote.)

The "secret plan" for victory Nixon had promised during the campaign failed to materialize, but Nixon did have a plan. Working closely with his foreign policy adviser, former Harvard political scientist Henry Kissinger, the new president—known as an uncompromising "cold warrior"—developed a conciliatory approach to the Cold War, which was also intended to maneuver the Vietnam War to a successful conclusion.

Nixon called for achieving "détente" with the Soviets through expanded trade and an arms-limitation agreement, intended partly to ease Cold War tensions and to disengage Moscow from Hanoi, thereby isolating North Vietnam. Coupled with this, an effort to normalize relations with the People's Republic of China would (Nixon hoped) help bring the Cold War to an end while also neutralizing another source of support for North Vietnam. Cut loose from its communist sponsors, North Vietnam would have no choice but to negotiate a peace the United States could call honorable.

That was the long term. In the short term, the Vietnam War still had to be fought.

The My Lai Massacre, March 16, 1968, was wanton slaughter of South Vietnamese civilians—suspected VC supporters—by U.S. army soldiers under Second Lieutenant William Calley. The atrocity was officially covered up until investigative journalist Seymour Hersh broke the story on November 12, 1969, giving fresh impetus to the antiwar movement in the streets of America as well as in the halls of Congress. The photograph shows Vietnamese homes ablaze in My Lai village, where over three hundred were killed, including woman, children, and the elderly. Soldiers routinely razed villages suspected of harboring Vietcong. Most American soldiers carried a Zippo lighter in addition to their standard-issue M-16 rifles.

With Kissinger, Nixon formulated what he called a two-track approach, one track consisting of uninterrupted military operations, the other holding out to the North Vietnamese the benefits of a negotiated resolution. In reality, there was a third track in the Nixon approach to the war. The new president emphasized the "Vietnamization" of the war—a rapid reduction of U.S. ground forces enabled by stepped up training and equipping of ARVN troops. Through Vietnamization, the United States would disengage from the war, and restless Americans would be placated. As the North Vietnamese saw it, however, Vietnamization proved that the United States had lost its stomach for the fight. This prompted them to take an intractable stand in peace talks.

To accelerate negotiations, Nixon stepped up bombing in North Vietnam and expanded the war into Laos and Cambodia—the routes of communist infiltration. Yet simultaneously, Nixon pursued Vietnamization, beginning in May 1969 to withdraw army ground units.

"The conventional army loses if it does not win.
The guerrilla wins if he does not lose."

Henry Kissinger, January 1969

Decline . . .

As the Paris Peace Talks crawled, the Nixon-Kissinger bid to isolate North Vietnam from Soviet support failed when the Kremlin announced its recognition of the Provisional Revolutionary Government (PRG) formed by North Vietnam's National Liberation Front (NLF) in June 1969. Frustrated, Nixon pressed ahead with Vietnamization, but the performance of increasingly demoralized ARVN troops was disappointing. Worse, as U.S. ground forces dwindled, those left behind came to believe that the war was a lost cause. Amid critically deteriorating morale, drug and alcohol abuse became epidemic in the ranks, and instead of speaking of embarking on search and

HOW MANY MORE MUST DIE?
MARCH AGAINST DEATH—A VIETNAM MEMORIAL
Washington, D.C.
November 13-15, 1969
MASS MARCH AND RALLY — SATURDAY, NOVEMBER 15

The New Mobilization Committee to End the War in Vietnam was one of myriad antiwar organizations that came into being all across the United States. This handbill announces a protest rally set for Washington, D.C., November 13–15, 1969.

ALTERNATE TAKE

RFK's Unfulfilled Promise

The closeness of the race left people to wonder how Robert Kennedy would have fared, had he achieved his party's nomination. Pitting an antiwar candidate against a prowar candidate would have transformed the 1968 election into a referendum on the war. Very likely, Kennedy would have prevailed, and the course of history would have changed. Assuming the United States would have withdrawn from Vietnam sooner, it is conceivable that much of LBJ's "Great Society" would have been restored, thereby marking out a new social and cultural landscape on the home front.

"HELL, NO! WE WON'T GO!"

A main driver of the antiwar movement was the military draft. Young men were liable to fight, kill, and quite possibly die in a war that fewer and fewer Americans supported. Added to this was a perception of social injustice in the draft.

The antiwar movement was also an antidraft movement, as this handbill from 1971 suggests.

The Selective Service law provided various "draft deferments," including a deferment for college students. To many, this seemed the equivalent of a pass for children of the white middle class—since, at the time, far fewer African American and Hispanic young men attended college. Therefore, antiwar activists commonly asserted that the Vietnam War was being fought disproportionately by members of racial and ethnic minorities.

Popular perceptions aside, the army preferred to send volunteers to Vietnam because it was believed that they made better combat soldiers than draftees. Two-thirds of the army personnel who fought in Vietnam had voluntarily enlisted. Most draftees remained in the United States or Europe or were assigned to noncombat roles in Vietnam. Moreover, minorities did not bear a disproportionate burden in the war. Of those killed in the conflict, 86 percent were white, 12.5 percent were black, and 1.2 percent were members of other races—percentages that accurately reflected the racial makeup of the nation at the time.

destroy missions, soldiers now called their patrols "search and avoid" missions. Peace with honor? As most soldiers saw it, the only objective was to get through the war alive.

While Nixon continued "phased withdrawal" from Vietnam, the Paris Peace Talks faltered. The president responded with a ground invasion of communist supply and staging areas in Cambodia in April 1970. Attacking a neutral Buddhist country ignited violent protests across college campuses in the United States, including a demonstration at Kent State University in Ohio on May 4, 1970, which resulted in the killing of four unarmed students and the wounding of nine more by panicky National Guardsmen. In the wake of Kent State, one hundred thousand antiwar protestors descended on Washington, and, perhaps even more dramatically, Congress registered its own protest by rescinding the Tonkin Gulf Resolution, thereby signaling to the president that his continued authority to make war was coming to an end.

President Nixon held a press conference on April 30, 1970, in an effort to justify the U.S. invasion of Cambodia.

Pressured, Nixon withdrew ground forces from Cambodia, but intensified bombing raids of that country. When this failed to stem communist infiltration, the air force supported an ARVN invasion of Laos in February 1971.

As ground troops continued to leave the country—by the end of 1971, U.S. troop strength in Vietnam stood at 175,000—antiwar protests subsided. But in March 1972, exploiting the reduced U.S. presence, NLF forces seized an entire South Vietnamese province in what U.S. officials called the "Easter Offensive." In response, Nixon redoubled air attacks, ordered the mining of Haiphong harbor, and set up a naval blockade of North Vietnam. This military resurgence kick-started the stalled peace talks, inducing North Vietnamese negotiator Le Duc Tho to conclude with U.S. negotiator Henry Kissinger an agreement governing the withdrawal of U.S. troops, the return of POWs, and establishing a special council of reconciliation to oversee a political settlement.

DETAILS, DETAILS

Christmas Bombs

In the 1972 Christmas bombing, 155 B-52s flew continuously for 11 days, flying 729 sorties against 34 targets in North Vietnam above the 20th parallel. Fifteen thousand tons of ordnance destroyed or damaged some 1,600 military structures, 500 rail targets, 3 million gallons of fuel (a quarter of North Vietnam's reserves), and 10 airfields. It knocked out 80 percent of electrical power production capacity. Fifteen B-52s were lost, killing between 14 and 28 crew members and resulting in the capture of 33 others.

. . . and Fall

Nguyen Van Thieu, president of South Vietnam, rejected the terms Kissinger and Le Duc Tho had negotiated because they permitted VC forces to remain in place in the South. The objection, however, came after the U.S. general election of 1972, and because Kissinger had been able to announce that "peace is at hand," Nixon sailed to reelection by a comfortable margin. No sooner was he reelected, however, than the president repudiated the terms Kissinger had negotiated. When the North Vietnamese delegation angrily withdrew from the peace talks, Nixon ordered eleven days of intensive bombing of North Vietnamese cities during Christmas 1972.

The Paris Accords are signed in Paris, January 27, 1973. The fighting continued for another two years.

The Christmas bombing brought the North Vietnamese back to Paris on January 8, 1973, and the Paris Peace Accords—an agreement that barely differed from what Kissinger had earlier concluded—were signed nineteen days later, on January 27. Thieu again objected, but this time President Nixon ignored him. The agreement did not end the fighting, but did accelerate U.S. withdrawal, and on the same day as the signing of the treaty, Secretary of Defense Melvin Laird

NUMBERS
The Cost of War

The Vietnam War had cost more than $150 billion and had resulted in the deaths of 58,178 Americans from 1959 to 1975. The total number of U.S. wounded was 303,678. ARVN casualties were 220,357 killed and 502,383 wounded. Combined NVA-VC deaths have been estimated at 927,124 between 1961 and 1975. Estimates of civilian casualties include 1.7 million South Vietnamese civilians killed or wounded. In the South, the war produced 83,000 amputees, 8,000 paraplegics, 30,000 cases of permanent blindness, 10,000 cases of permanent deafness, and some 50,000 additional types of permanent disability. Six and a half million South Vietnamese became refugees, as did 2 million Cambodians, and 1 million Laotians. Some sources claim that 65,000 South Vietnamese soldiers and civilians were executed by the communists after the war and a quarter million more died in communist "reeducation camps." The civilian toll in North Vietnam is unknown.

Operation Ranch Hand, which spanned 1962–71, was a defoliation offensive in which more than twelve million gallons of defoliating agents were sprayed from aircraft over the South Vietnamese jungle in an effort to deprive the Vietcong of both cover and food. The operation created both an ecological and health crisis—as many U.S. soldiers (and untold numbers of Vietnamese civilians) suffered long-term effects from the principal defoliant, Agent Orange, including a variety of cancers and other chronic illnesses induced by the highly toxic dioxin component of the herbicide.

announced an end to the military draft. On March 29, the last U.S. combat troops departed Vietnam, leaving behind some eighty-five hundred U.S. nationals, described as "civilian technicians."

In an effort to end innumerable cease-fire violations, a new cease-fire agreement was signed on June 13, 1973, but fighting nevertheless continued between ARVN and communist forces. The Nixon administration continued to funnel massive military and financial aid to the Thieu government and bombed Cambodian infiltration routes. While the North Vietnamese communists showed no signs of war weariness, the U.S. Congress had had enough. It turned solidly against the war as a lost cause, and, even more, it turned against Richard Milhous Nixon, who was by now wallowing in the unprecedented Watergate Scandal, from which fresh revelations of illegal executive subterfuge and subversion of the Constitution emerged almost daily. In November 1973, Congress passed the War Powers Act, requiring the president to inform Congress within forty-eight hours of deployment of U.S. military forces abroad and mandating their withdrawal within sixty days if Congress failed to approve. In 1974, U.S. aid to South Vietnam was reduced from $2.56 billion to $907 million, and on August 9 of that year, Nixon, facing certain impeachment, became the first president in U.S. history to resign office.

His successor, Gerald Ford, asked Congress for $300 million to supplement the paltry $700 million appropriated for 1975. Congress turned him down flat.

From the beginning of 1975, the thoroughly dispirited ARVN suffered defeat after defeat. On April 21, 1975, President Nguyen Van Thieu resigned and was briefly replaced by Tran Van Huong, with whom the communists refused to negotiate. Huong was succeeded by Lieutenant General Duong Van Minh, whose one official act as president of South Vietnam was to surrender to the North. On the day of surrender, April 30, 1975, Saigon fell.

North and South Vietnam would not be officially unified under a communist regime until July 2, 1976, but for most Americans, the spectacle—beamed by television to the world—of a frenzied evacuation on April 29–30, 1975, including the helicopter airlift of American personnel and certain Vietnamese from the roof of the American Embassy, marked the final defeat of the United States in Vietnam.

TAKEAWAY
A Cold War Tragedy

Most recent historians—and no less a figure than former Secretary of Defense Robert McNamara—have concluded that the Vietnam War was a tragic misapprehension. The rigorous mindset of the Cold War era had compelled five U.S. presidents to perceive the Vietnam War as a struggle between the forces of democratic capitalism and those of communism, whereas, for the people of Vietnam, it was neither more nor less than a civil war to achieve both unification and sovereign independence. As such, it was, for the interloping United States, inherently unwinnable—from the very start.

As Saigon fell to the victorious communist forces, South Vietnamese refugees were evacuated by U.S. Marine helicopters in Operation Frequent Wind and flown to waiting U.S. Navy vessels.

In an ignominious end to the Nixon-Ford dream of "peace with honor" in Vietnam, a U.S. "Huey" helicopter perches on top of a downtown Saigon apartment building roof to evacuate civilians and CIA staffers who had been staying there. This iconic April 29, 1975, photograph was taken by UPI photographer Hubert Van Es. Similar helicopter-borne evacuations were conducted from the roof of the U.S. Embassy.

Part Six

DÉTENTE

CHAPTER 17

The President, the Chairman, and the Premier

The First Thaw

On September 26, 1960, seventy million Americans turned on their Dumonts, Philcos, and Admirals to watch the first-ever televised presidential debate. Those who were not near a television tuned in on radio. After the debate—it was the first of four—the majority of the radio audience believed that Richard M. Nixon, just coming off eight years as vice president under Dwight Eisenhower, was the winner. But a majority of those who viewed the debate on TV gave the nod to John F. Kennedy, the youthful junior senator from Massachusetts.

The disparity between the radio listeners and the television audience is today regarded as a classic lesson in the impact of television and the importance of cultivating a savvy approach to the medium. Some have pointed out that JFK was younger, better looking, and sexier than Nixon. Others have observed that, less than a month before the debates, Nixon had injured his knee and was laid up for two weeks in a hospital bed. He emerged twenty pounds underweight and sickly pale. His shirt fit his reduced frame poorly, and, at the TV studio, he indignantly refused makeup to camouflage his pallor and hide his trademark five o' clock shadow. Next to Kennedy, freshly tanned from campaigning in the Southern California, Nixon looked all used up.

So much is obvious. But if you look carefully at the primitive black-and-white videotapes of that broadcast, something more is apparent. Kennedy comes off as a man without art or artifice, whereas Nixon, his upper lip beaded with sweat, his smile fleeting and forced, looks like someone acutely uncomfortable—not just before a TV camera, but in his own skin.

THE OUTSIDER

RICHARD MILHOUS NIXON was born in Yorba Linda, California, in 1913. His mother was a devoutly observant Quaker, whose presence suffused the family with an asceticism that barred (among other things) alcohol and cursing. Much as he worshipped the memory of his mother, the adult Nixon was a heavy drinker who (as recorded on his secret White House tape-recording system) swore with enthusiasm. In childhood and youth, however, the Quaker lifestyle isolated Nixon and his four brothers. He grew up feeling himself an outsider, a self-image hardened by the inability of his hard-working father to achieve financial success. Francis Nixon struggled to make his Yorba Linda lemon grove pay, but, throughout Dick Nixon's early childhood, it was on the edge of collapse, finally failing altogether in 1922, when the boy was nine, prompting the family to move to Whittier, where Francis Nixon opened a grocery store and filling station.

The Kennedy-Nixon debates, 1960.

PREVIOUS SPREAD: *President Richard Nixon and first Lady Pat Nixon visit the Great Wall of China, February 1972.*

"Many people who knew my mother in Whittier referred to her, even during her lifetime, as a Quaker saint."

Richard M. Nixon, RN: The Memoirs of Richard Nixon, *1978*

Richard Nixon threw himself into his schoolwork, graduating from Whittier High School in 1930 second in his class and winning scholarship offers from both Harvard and Yale. Even with tuition paid for, however, the family could not afford to send him so far away, and he declined both offers, enrolling instead in a local Quaker institution, Whittier College, which he could attend while living at home and helping out in the family store.

In college, Nixon struggled mightily to overcome his outsider status, cofounding a fraternity, joining the debate and drama societies, and even winning election as student-body president. More than anything, he wanted to be recognized as an athlete. He repeatedly tried out for the varsity football team and was repeatedly rejected because of his conspicuous lack of talent in the sport. Ultimately, however, his persistence moved the coach to include him on the team, primarily as a tackling dummy for the other players to practice on.

Richard Milhous Nixon, cold warrior and family man, poses in 1947 with his wife, Pat, their baby daughter Patricia, and the family dog—predecessor to the famous Checkers.

As in high school, Nixon graduated from Whittier second in his class. He won a full scholarship to Duke University School of Law in North Carolina. A Duke law degree was certainly held in high esteem, and Nixon managed to graduate third in the class of 1937; nevertheless, he was unable to shake the sense of having missed out on the Ivy League, the exclusive club populated by the "bright young men" demagogue Joseph McCarthy would condemn years later as communist traitors at the highest levels of government. It was the preserve of John Fitzgerald Kennedy.

Nixon's first thought fresh out of law school was to become an FBI agent, but he returned instead to Whittier to practice corporate law, hoping to earn credentials for a political career. In the meantime, he diverted himself by joining the Whittier Community Players, where, in January 1938, he was cast opposite a local high school teacher, Thelma Ryan—whom everyone called Pat—in Alexander Woollcott's *The Dark Tower*.

At first, and for a long time, she was unreceptive to Nixon's overtures, but eventually yielded to his persistence. They married in 1940 and moved to Washington, D.C., where, in 1942, Nixon joined the wartime Office of Price Administration. In August, he was commissioned in the U.S. Navy and served as a supply and aviation ground officer in the South Pacific until 1946. No sooner did he return to California that year than the Whittier Republican organization invited him to run for Congress against the formidable five-term incumbent, liberal Democrat Jerry Voorhis.

The perpetual outsider who always managed to get himself inside, Nixon understood it would not be easy to unseat the popular Voorhis, but he soon identified his opponent's weakness—an early association with a left-leaning political action committee (PAC) from the 1930s—and he dedicated his campaign to branding his opponent a communist sympathizer. The result was an ugly contest that defeated Voorhis and gave Nixon an identity—a *dual* identity, actually. To those who had voted for him, he was a gloves-off anticommunist. To those who had voted against him, he was a red baiting opportunist.

BIRTH OF A COLD WARRIOR

INCURABLY UNCOMFORTABLE WITH HIMSELF, Richard Nixon had nevertheless found a perfect fit in politics. When he ran for reelection to the House of Representatives in 1948, he entered both the Democratic and Republican primaries and, running on his anticommunist platform, won both, which meant that there was no need for him even to compete in the general election.

His spectacular reelection victory, coupled with his growing reputation as an anticommunist crusader, marked Nixon as a rising star in the Republican firmament, and he was installed on the increasingly powerful House Un-American Activities Committee (HUAAC). As discussed in Chapter 13, Nixon was especially zealous in his investigation of Alger Hiss, the Ivy League alumnus accused of being a Soviet mole in the State Department.

POP CULTURE
Checkers

In 1952, Nixon was plucked from the Senate as running mate to presidential candidate Dwight D. Eisenhower, the GOP eager to pair the genial Ike with a cold warrior. Soon, however, Tricky Dick was accused of accepting funding for a secret campaign slush fund. On the verge of being dumped, Nixon appeared on television on September 23, 1952, to deliver what is now known as the "Checkers speech." He admitted to the fund's existence, but calmly denied that it was improper or secret. Explaining to viewers that he was by no means wealthy, he listed his family's modest assets—noting that his wife, Pat, owned no mink, but did have a "respectable Republican cloth coat." Nixon admitted accepting one political gift, a cocker spaniel puppy his six-year-old daughter Tricia named Checkers. He looked affably into the camera and vowed, "Regardless of what they say about it, we are going to keep it."

Maudlin as a 1950s sitcom, the "Checkers speech" saved Nixon's career and actually boosted his popularity.

Dick Nixon thus became a certified "cold warrior." Armed with this credential, he ran for the Senate in 1950, opposing Democratic Representative Helen Gahagan Douglas, a one-time musical comedy star who was now the wife of screen actor Melvyn Douglas. Whereas his campaign against Voorhis had been built on innuendo, his run against Douglas consisted of vulgar invective. Nixon called Douglas a "Pink Lady," proclaiming her "pink right down to her underwear."

Helen Gahagan Douglas—"Pink," Nixon proclaimed when he ran against her for the U.S. Senate in 1950, "pink right down to her underwear."

Nixon defeated Douglas, who nevertheless exacted a vengeance more enduring than she could have known at the time. During the campaign she branded her opponent "Tricky Dick," an epithet the *Independent Review*, a California paper, picked up and popularized. Nixon would never shake the "Tricky Dick" tag—to the very day that scandal would force him to step down from the presidency of the United States.

Reinventing Himself

Nixon served two terms as Ike's vice president and ran for president in 1960 in the full expectation of victory. That his loss to Kennedy came by a razor-thin margin was bitter, the bitterness intensified by JFK's Ivy League pedigree. Nixon ran next in 1962 for California governor and took defeat in that bid very hard, sarcastically congratulating a press corps he believed hated him with this valediction: "You won't have Dick Nixon to kick around anymore."

Nixon moved from the California that had spurned him to New York City, where he joined a law practice and, out of the public view, remodeled himself into a centrist conservative. He ran for president again in 1968 and, against a Democratic Party in disarray, won the White House in part on a vague promise that he had a "secret plan" for extricating the nation from the Vietnam War.

At first blush, Nixon approached that war as anything but a centrist conservative. He came on like a hawk, but soon blurred that

On the campaign trail in 1968, Nixon flashes the double V-for-victory that became his trademark. In contrast to Winston Churchill's exuberantly easygoing wartime V gesture—made with one hand only—Nixon's looked stiff and forced, typical of a man chronically uncomfortable in his own skin.

image by reducing the number of U.S. ground forces in Vietnam at the very same time as he intensified bombing operations and even pushed the war into neighboring Cambodia and Laos. The "secret plan" to end the war did not materialize, but it was clear that Nixon had figured out that the objection most Americans had to the war was the prospect of their sons getting killed or wounded fighting it. By substituting an air war for a ground war, fewer Americans would get killed, the antiwar protest would be blunted, but the pressure would nevertheless continue against the North Vietnamese.

The new Nixon was less a cold warrior than a pragmatist. He still wanted to defeat the communists, but he was willing to do so in a way that created the least dissension.

The Next Move

The problem was that, while Nixon had become a pragmatist, the leaders of North Vietnam were as committed as ever to unifying the country under their communist rule. Just as they had been willing to absorb massive infantry losses year in and year out, they were now willing to endure Nixon's bombing—something Americans were less and less willing to endure. At first, the home front welcomed his phased withdrawal of ground troops and showed their appreciation with a reduction in antiwar protest activity. But as the airstrikes against Cambodia and Laos intensified, Nixon began to discover that it was not just an objection to the military draft that moved antiwar

REALITY CHECK
Nixon's Rebirth

Lyndon Johnson's landslide victory over conservative Arizona Republican Barry Goldwater in 1964 persuaded the mainstream of the Republican Party that the American electorate would no longer send a right-wing hawk to the White House. Nixon always claimed that his move toward the center of the political spectrum represented a genuine intellectual journey, whereas his critics looked on it as a matter of political expediency. Whatever his imperative for change, the party bought it and nominated Nixon in 1968. The president's subsequent epoch-making overtures both to the Soviet Union and China tend to suggest that Nixon's political metamorphosis had been genuine—or at least more genuine than not.

REALITY CHECK
Nixon and McCarthy

There has long been a perception among Nixon's many detractors that he hopped on the McCarthy red-baiting bandwagon to further his career. However, Nixon's exploitation of the fear of communism predated the 1950 Wheeling speech that launched McCarthy's anticommunist crusade. At McCarthy's request, Nixon even opened his own files on communists in government for the senator to comb through in his never-ending quest for targets. In his remarkable 1978 memoir, *RN*, Nixon portrays himself as embarrassed, even appalled by McCarthy. This was certainly the case after Nixon became vice president in 1953, when McCarthy was a thorn in Eisenhower's side and dared to mount an attack on the loyalty of U.S. Army officers, including George C. Marshall. This said, it is apparent that, between 1950 and 1952, Nixon allowed himself to rise on the red-baiting tide created by McCarthy. Even more, he consciously used McCarthy, whose accusations were crude and careless, as a foil to his own anti-communist activities, which, by comparison, appeared rational and thoroughly sober.

protest, it was also genuine moral outrage over the war. Once again, antiwar protests increased in volume and stridency. Nixon had to find a definitive path to what he called "peace with honor" in Vietnam—a way to satisfy the swelling ranks of antiwar Americans without allowing the triumph of communism in Vietnam. The urgent necessity of attaining these apparently mutually exclusive objectives drove the president and Henry Kissinger to the boldest of all reinventions of Richard Nixon.

As briefly discussed in Chapter 16, North Vietnam received material and moral support from the world's two major communist parties, the Soviet Union and China. Knock these two props out from under North Vietnam, Nixon believed, and its leaders would become highly motivated to negotiate a favorable peace.

This, however, was the Cold War. It was only *natural* that the Chinese and the Soviets should be aligned with North Vietnam and opposed to the United States. Conversely, it was also only *natural* that Nixon the cold warrior should also be opposed to all three. But the Nixon of the late 1960s and early 1970s was not the Nixon of 1946–60. Uneasy under the best of circumstances, nothing ever really seemed "natural" to Richard Nixon, and perhaps for that reason he was able to contemplate and execute not one, but two, *unnatural* acts—instigating a thaw in the Cold War by negotiating détente with the Soviet Union and, even more daringly, beginning the process of normalizing relations with the People's Republic of China. He made both these moves during the election year of 1972 and was reelected by a landslide.

The task, Nixon and Kissinger saw, was twofold. It would require persuading the Soviets and the Chinese that they had more to gain from nonhostile—if not exactly cordial—relations with the United States than they did from continuing to help North Vietnam fight the United States. It would also require maintaining the support of all those Republican cold warriors who thought they knew Dick Nixon. That *he* of all leaders should make overtures to the great communist powers would, to put it mildly, come to them as a shock. But Nixon boldly counted on his very reputation to give him the required license to carry out his plan. If a liberal Democratic president made overtures of conciliation to either Russia or China, he would doubtless be denounced as a traitor, but, Nixon believed, *he* had the credentials to carry it off.

The poster was published in 1972 to protest the expansion of bombing in and around North Vietnam.

New Realities

After the death of Joseph Stalin in 1953, political leaders in the United States as well as the Soviet Union began slowly to relinquish the fiction of a planet divided into two uniform camps, the "Soviet bloc" and the "Free World." To be sure, the leaders often acted as if they still believed in this absolute bifurcation, but the most intelligent of them began to look toward a new geopolitical vision. By the time he entered the White House in 1969, perhaps no American leader saw this new vision more clearly than Nixon.

The first solid breakthroughs had come before his presidency. During the Kennedy years, the peaceful resolutions of the Berlin and Cuban Missile crises (Chapter 15) were hopeful signs, as was the August 1963 Nuclear Test Ban Treaty. Signed by the United States, Great Britain, and the Soviet Union (and later by other nations as well), the treaty banned all above-ground atomic weapons tests in a first step toward what would later be called Strategic Arms Limitation Talks (SALT) and also in affirmation of Kennedy's and Khrushchev's genuine desire for peaceful coexistence.

Unfortunately, it was for precisely these breakthroughs that Kremlin conservatives succeeded in forcing Nikita Khrushchev into premature retirement in 1964 and splitting his offices between a pair of

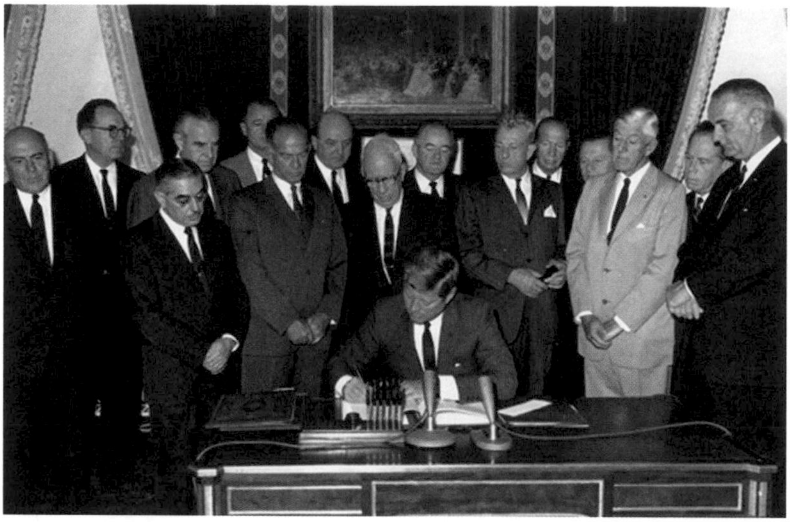

President Kennedy signs the Nuclear Test Ban Treaty, October 7, 1963—a first tentative step toward nuclear disarmament.

hardliners, Leonid Brezhnev (who was named first secretary of the Communist Party) and Alexey Kosygin (Soviet premier). On the American side, the expansion of the Vietnam War under Lyndon Johnson also acted to refreeze the old Cold War enmities.

Prague Spring

But the so-called Soviet bloc was undergoing a thaw of its own. In the Czechoslovak Socialist Republic (ČSSR), growing outrage over how Soviet-style industrial policy had damaged the Czech economy brought economic reforms in 1965, which, in turn, spurred demand for broader social and political reform. This led to the replacement of hard-line Czech party leader and president Antonín Novotný with the more progressive Alexander Dubček (as party first secretary) and Ludvík Svoboda (as president) early in 1968. In April, Dubček introduced a remarkable package of liberalizations, which even opened the door to the future introduction of a multiparty government. In the pattern of Yugoslavia's Tito, Dubček called for improving relations with the West while still "cooperating" with the Soviet Union.

"In the service of the people we followed such a policy that socialism would not lose its human face."

Alexander Dubček, speech, June 19, 1968

The reform package, called an "Action Program," was bold, but Dubček approached it cautiously, building into it a decade-long period of transition and always avoiding criticism of the Soviet-imposed policies it was created to replace. The proposed reforms were so appealing, however, that a vocal segment of the Czech nation refused to wait and demanded immediate action. And while Dubček avoided criticizing the Soviets, those who agitated for rapid reform did not hesitate for a moment. Intellectuals, students, members of the professional class (lawyers, physicians, and so on), political leaders, and even many ordinary citizens engaged in open protest on the one hand and lavish praise of Western-style democracy on the other. Dubček and other leaders anticipated a Kremlin crackdown at any moment, but when this failed to materialize, even Czech political leaders began speaking of a "Prague Spring," a time of political rebirth and exhilaration of hope.

Alexander Dubček, liberal-leaning secretary of the Czechoslovak Communist Party, attends the Bratislava Conference in August 1968. With him are Soviet premier Alexei Kosygin (center) and Communist Party General Secretary Leonid Brezhnev. Note that only two of the three men appear to be having a good time.

Leonid Brezhnev was indeed fearful of Dubček's reforms, as were leaders of some of the other Soviet bloc nations, who worried that a second "Hungarian counterrevolution" (see Chapter 14) was brewing. On August 3, 1968, leaders from the Soviet Union, East Germany, Poland, Hungary, Bulgaria, and Czechoslovakia convened in Bratislava, where they signed the Bratislava Declaration, pledging absolute faith in "Marxism Leninism" and affirming their commitment to fighting against capitalism and other "anti-socialist forces." Set against the "Prague Spring," it was a dismaying assertion of retro-communist orthodoxy restating belief in the unbridgeable divide between West and East. Worse, Brezhnev asserted the right and intention of the Soviet Union to intervene in (i.e., to invade) any Warsaw Pact nation that introduced a multiparty system in which capitalism was represented. Brezhnev made a show of good faith by withdrawing all Soviet troops from Czechoslovakia after the Bratislava Conference, but then redeployed them along all of the country's borders.

From Spring to Winter

No sooner did the Bratislava talks end than Brezhnev amplified his declaration concerning intervention, declaring that all Soviet satellite nations were obliged to subordinate nationalism to the collective interests of the "Eastern Bloc." This statement was dubbed by the Western world the "Brezhnev Doctrine," and it did not take long for it to swing into action.

In Prague, Czech students and others protest the Soviet-Warsaw Pact invasion of Czechoslovakia, August 21, 1968.

On the night of August 20/21, 1968, 200,000 troops (and some two thousand tanks) from the Soviet Union and three other Warsaw Pact nations, Bulgaria, Poland, and Hungary, invaded Czechoslovakia. The vastly outnumbered Czech military was quickly neutralized and confined to barracks. Dubček broadcast to the nation his instruction that the people should offer no resistance. For its part, the Brezhnev government publicly disclaimed responsibility for the "intervention," saying that it had been initiated by the three Warsaw Pact participants, which were alarmed and outraged by Czechoslovakia's moves toward capitalism. No one believed him, and he probably did not expect to be believed. But the disclaimer had to be made nevertheless.

NUMBERS

Invasion: The Immediate Cost

In the lightning invasion of Czechoslovakia by the Soviet Union and the three other Warsaw Pact armies, 72 Czech and Slovak civilians were killed, including 19 in Slovakia; 266 were severely wounded, and 436 received minor injuries. By the end of 1968, a total of 108 had been killed. Another cost of the invasion was the tidal wave of emigration that followed as some 70,000 Czechs and Slovaks fled immediately. The outpouring continued over several months, the total reaching about 300,000.

Although Western governments bemoaned a resurgence of the Cold War, even in its suppression, the Prague Spring was evidence of growing weakness in the Soviet bloc. Moreover, unwilling to make a martyr of Dubček, the Kremlin, having first arrested him, returned him to Prague and even authorized what was described as a program of "moderate reform." It was a hopeful sign.

Even more hopeful was the reaction from communist parties outside of the Warsaw Pact nations. Romania's dictator Nicolae Ceauşescu publicly condemned the invasion, as did the communist parties of Italy, France, and Finland. To East and West alike, the handwriting was now on the wall. The Soviet Union could no longer maintain the fiction of one "communist world."

Strange New World

When Richard Nixon entered the White House in 1969, in the aftermath of the Prague Spring and the Soviet response to it, perhaps only one other world leader possessed as keen an awareness as he that global politics had become a strange new world. That man was Leonid Brezhnev. Like Nixon, he had come of political age as the consummate

FROM THE *GOOD SHIP LOLLIPOP* TO PRAGUE

Among the handful of Americans who witnessed the Warsaw Pact invasion was Shirley Temple Black, who had been sent to Prague by the Johnson administration to prepare to become U.S. ambassador to a "free" Czechoslovakia. The invasion delayed that appointment twenty-one years; President George H. W. Bush officially appointed her ambassador to Czechoslovakia in 1989.

In August 1968, however, she sat in the lead vehicle of a convoy assembled to evacuate hundreds of Westerners from Prague. Officials were confident that her presence would smooth the way for the evacuation—because *everybody*, knew Shirley Temple.

By any measure, Temple had been the most famous child star in Hollywood history. She made her feature debut in 1934 at age five in the musical *Stand Up and Cheer*, followed by *Little Miss Marker*, *Baby Take a Bow*, and *Bright Eyes*, the film in which she sang what became her signature song, "On the Good Ship Lollipop." In 1935, she danced onscreen with the great African-American hoofer Bill "Bojangles" Robinson in *The Little Colonel*, the first time white and black dancers appeared on film together. Between 1936 and 1938, Temple out-earned every other Hollywood star; with the onset of puberty, Shirley Temple's film career ended.

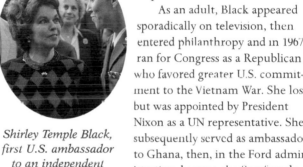

Shirley Temple Black, first U.S. ambassador to an independent Czechoslovakia.

As an adult, Black appeared sporadically on television, then entered philanthropy and in 1967 ran for Congress as a Republican who favored greater U.S. commitment to the Vietnam War. She lost, but was appointed by President Nixon as a UN representative. She subsequently served as ambassador to Ghana, then, in the Ford administration, became the first female White House chief of protocol. Her last government post was as ambassador to Czechoslovakia (1989–92), where she bore witness to the "Velvet Revolution," the nonviolent overthrow of the communist government in November–December 1989.

cold warrior. Born into a working-class Ukraine family in 1916, Brezhnev worked as a land surveyor before joining the Communist Party in 1931. He graduated from engineering school in 1935 and became deputy chairman of the provincial Soviet Committee in Dnipropetrovsk. With the outbreak of World War II, he joined the Red Army in 1941. Thanks to Stalin's prewar purges of the officer corps, he made a meteoric rise to major general by 1943. After the war, Brezhnev rose in the party hierarchy as well, in large measure due to his friendship with Nikita Khrushchev, whose chief adviser he became in 1964—the very year Brezhnev joined the coalition that forced Khrushchev out of office and put himself in his place.

Leonid Brezhnev, 1974.

Brezhnev wanted to return the Soviet Union to the more ideologically committed, harder communist line, which (he and others felt) Khrushchev had softened; however, like Nixon, Brezhnev recognized that, by the mid 1960s, the world was becoming less bipolar—less defined by the Western democracies on the one hand and Soviet- and Chinese-dominated communism on the other—and increasingly multipolar, as Third World nations assumed greater importance and as more Eastern Bloc nations sought to exercise autonomy from the Soviet Union. Moreover, relations between the USSR and the People's Republic of China were so strained that they verged on border warfare. Finally, in 1973, the mostly Middle Eastern members of the Organization of the Petroleum Exporting Countries (OPEC) revealed themselves collectively as a potent force in the world because they controlled a disproportionate amount of the planet's petroleum energy resources. Also like Nixon, Brezhnev found himself having to deal with discontent at home as the Soviet command economy creaked and buckled under pressures intensified by the relentless necessity of Cold War military spending.

Détente

Thus Brezhnev the hard-liner, like Nixon the cold warrior, was primed for détente—not friendship, but an easing of tensions through increased diplomacy as well as economic contact.

All of this took place against a background of Cold War proxy conflicts. In South America, the United States assisted a number of right-wing dictatorships in suppressing left-wing dissent—at least some of which was backed by Soviet or Cuban military and financial aid. In the Middle East, the United States was committed to aiding Israel in its ongoing struggle against Arab nations, including Egypt, long a Soviet client. At times, the Soviets also supported Syria and Iraq in their actions against Israel. The Yom Kippur War of 1973, which pitted Egypt, Syria, and Iraq against Israel, seemed at one point on the brink of becoming a direct confrontation between the Soviets and the

A NEW PROXY WAR?

Since its founding in 1948, Israel had been under continual threat from its Arab neighbors, who vowed to annihilate the nation. A combination of Israeli determination and military prowess—and the backing of the United States—repeatedly thwarted every effort to destroy Israel, but on October 6, 1973, on Yom Kippur, the holiest day of the Jewish calendar, Egyptian and Syrian forces made a two-front surprise attack, which appeared to have every chance of finally defeating Israel.

However, after the costly failure of repeated counterattacks in the first few days of what was now being called the "Yom Kippur War," Israeli forces began to push back the Syrians on October 10 and invaded Syria itself. The Soviets responded by airlifting matériel into both Syria and Egypt, which prompted an American airlift to Israel during October 12–13. Freshly supplied, the Israelis now broke out against the Egyptian front, crossing the Suez Canal, and enveloping the entire Egyptian Third Army. Fearing the loss of a major force, Egyptian president Anwar al-Sadat appealed to the Soviets not merely for military equipment but for air support and boots on the ground. The Soviets responded not with troops but with the threat of troops.

It was potentially the most dangerous U.S.-Soviet situation since the Cuban Missile Crisis of 1962 (Chapter 15). Had the Soviets actually introduced military forces, the United States would have honored its treaty obligations and delivered large numbers of troops and aircraft, supported by the Mediterranean Fleet. Although a U.S.-Soviet military confrontation in the Middle East was less likely than the Cuban Missile Crisis to spark an immediate nuclear exchange, the possibility certainly existed, especially if one side or the other suffered serious conventional (nonnuclear) losses. Even if a U.S.-Soviet war in this region had been confined to the use of conventional weapons, it would have been a massively destabilizing event, which, at the very least, would have wrecked détente.

It turned out that neither the Americans nor the Soviets were interested in exploiting the Yom Kippur War as yet another Cold War proxy war, however. Secretary of State Henry Kissinger flew to Moscow to negotiate a cease-fire. An Israeli violation of the cease-fire brought renewed threats from the Soviets, but this time the United States applied diplomatic pressure to Israel, which yielded to a second cease-fire on October 25, whereupon both sides declared victory and departed the field.

The end of détente (or worse) had been avoided, and Israel survived. Although Egypt, Syria, and Israel had suffered serious losses (eighty-five hundred Egyptian and Syrian soldiers killed; six thousand Israeli soldiers killed), the United States hardly emerged unscathed. On behalf of the Arab nations, OPEC retaliated by doubling the price of export oil, triggering crippling gasoline shortages in the United States and contributing to the recession of 1974–75.

A U.S. Air Force C-5A Galaxy cargo aircraft unloads equipment sent to aid Israel during the Yom Kippur War in October 1973.

Americans, but, in the end, both sides retreated from that abyss, and détente resumed.

The Chinese Connection

President Nixon hoped that expanded trade and an arms-limitation agreement would disengage Moscow from Hanoi, thereby giving the United States the upper hand in the ongoing Paris Peace Talks (see Chapter 16). This failed to happen, as the Soviet Union did not retract its recognition (announced back in 1969) of the Provisional Revolutionary Government (PRG) created by North Vietnam's National Liberation Front (NLF). Although continued Soviet recognition of the PRG was disappointing, Nixon was not discouraged. While negotiating détente with the Soviets, he also increasingly contemplated normalization of relations with the People's Republic of China. He had three motives for this. As with his policy toward improving U.S.-Soviet relations, the most immediate motive was isolating North Vietnam—in this case, by disengaging China from it. His second motive was to drive a wedge to widen the already considerable gulf between the Soviet Union and China. He hoped to put them in a position in which they were obliged to compete with one another for more favorable relations with the United States. In this way, Nixon intended to promote what he saw as the ongoing dissolution of the communist world.

Nixon's third reason for seeking to open productive relations between the United States and China was more far reaching. As early as 1967, before he became president, he had written in the journal *Foreign Affairs* of the desirability of creating an "open world." He drew on this concept two years later in his inaugural address, speaking of his aspiration toward "a world in which no people, great or small, will live in angry isolation," and within two weeks of taking office, he instructed his national security adviser, Henry Kissinger, to begin exploring the "possibilities of rapprochement with the Chinese." The new president dared not rush into the project. The way had to be prepared carefully, because there would be tremendous opposition among leaders both in the United States and in China, and a rejection from either side could worsen relations. Instead of approaching the Chinese government, therefore, he began by approaching his own, raising the possibility of improving "practical relations" with China in his February 1970 *Foreign Policy Report to Congress*. Because the *Report* was a public document, he knew that China's leaders would read it. They did. At the time, there were no official diplomatic relations between the United States and China, but diplomacy was conducted nevertheless. U.S. diplomat Walter Stoessel periodically met with his Chinese counterpart in Warsaw. Two days after the *Report* appeared, the Chinese diplomat suggested to Stoessel that U.S.-Chinese meetings should be moved to Beijing, and he indicated that the government would welcome "a high-ranking American official" to lead the delegation. President Nixon responded in March 1970 by lifting most restrictions on travel to China. In April, he ordered the easing of many restrictions on trade as well.

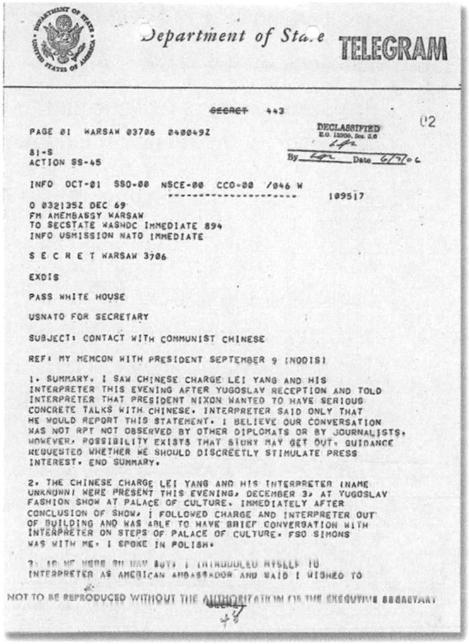
Department of State TELEGRAM

~~SECRET~~ 443

02

PAGE 01 WARSAW 03706 040049Z

DECLASSIFIED
E.O. 12958, Sec. 3.6

By ___ Date ___

81-S
ACTION SS-45

INFO OCT-01 SSO-00 NSCE-00 CCO-00 /046 W

109517

O 032135Z DEC 69
FM AMEMBASSY WARSAW
TO SECSTATE WASHDC IMMEDIATE 894
INFO USMISSION NATO IMMEDIATE

S E C R E T WARSAW 3706

EXDIS

PASS WHITE HOUSE

USNATO FOR SECRETARY

SUBJECT: CONTACT WITH COMMUNIST CHINESE

REF: MY MEMCON WITH PRESIDENT SEPTEMBER 9 (NODIS)

1. SUMMARY. I SAW CHINESE CHARGE LEI YANG AND HIS INTERPRETER THIS EVENING AFTER YUGOSLAV RECEPTION AND TOLD INTERPRETER THAT PRESIDENT NIXON WANTED TO HAVE SERIOUS CONCRETE TALKS WITH CHINESE. INTERPRETER SAID ONLY THAT HE WOULD REPORT THIS STATEMENT. I BELIEVE OUR CONVERSATION WAS NOT RPT NOT OBSERVED BY OTHER DIPLOMATS OR BY JOURNALISTS. HOWEVER, POSSIBILITY EXISTS THAT STORY MAY GET OUT. GUIDANCE REQUESTED WHETHER WE SHOULD DISCREETLY STIMULATE PRESS INTEREST. END SUMMARY.

2. THE CHINESE CHARGE LEI YANG AND HIS INTERPRETER (NAME UNKNOWN) WERE PRESENT THIS EVENING, DECEMBER 3, AT YUGOSLAV FASHION SHOW AT PALACE OF CULTURE. IMMEDIATELY AFTER CONCLUSION OF SHOW, I FOLLOWED CHARGE AND INTERPRETER OUT OF BUILDING AND WAS ABLE TO HAVE BRIEF CONVERSATION WITH INTERPRETER ON STEPS OF PALACE OF CULTURE. FSO SIMONS WAS WITH ME. I SPOKE IN POLISH.

3. [illegible] I INTRODUCED MYSELF TO INTERPRETER AS AMERICAN AMBASSADOR AND SAID I WISHED TO

NOT TO BE REPRODUCED WITHOUT THE AUTHORIZATION OF THE EXECUTIVE SECRETARY

Walter Stoessel, U.S. ambassador to Poland, sent this telegram on December 3, 1969, to Secretary of State William Rogers describing his early efforts, at the behest of the Nixon administration, to establish diplomatic relations with the People's Republic of China.

The road to a meeting between the American president and Chairman Mao Zedong—a figure considered unapproachable and quite probably mad—was not smooth. When Nixon invaded Cambodia, the invitation to move U.S.-Chinese meetings to Beijing was withdrawn, but there really was no turning back. After an interval of several months, the Chinese government released from imprisonment Roman Catholic Bishop James E. Walsh, who had been arrested in 1958 on phony charges that he was a spy for the Vatican and United States.

Ping-Pong Diplomacy

Secretly, Nixon sent Kissinger to China early in July 1971. Kissinger's talks with Chinese officials did not lead directly to a presidential visit, but did garner an invitation for the U.S. table tennis team to compete in China against the Chinese team. The American team went in 1971, and the Chinese team came to the United States the following year. It was called "ping-pong diplomacy," and the occasions were used to hammer out the details of the visit.

President Nixon welcomes members of the Chinese table tennis team to the White House, April 18, 1972.

Three and a Half Minutes

The White House booked air time on all the major TV networks for 7:30 P.M. (Eastern time) on

GETTING THE BALL ROLLING

Two apparently casual encounters in March 1971 sparked the "ping-pong diplomacy" that opened the door to the normalization of U.S.-Chinese relations.

Roy Evans, president of the International Table Tennis Federation, was summoned to a meeting with Chinese premier Zhou Enlai, who asked Evans to exclude South Vietnam from the upcoming 31st World Table Tennis Championship in Nagoya, Japan. Evans responded that he could not do this, but, on the spur of the moment, he suggested that China invite several Western teams to visit China on their way home from Japan. Apparently, Zhou warmed to the suggestion, although it is unclear if what happened just days later in Japan was directly related to the meeting between Evans and the premier or was coincidental.

At the games, after practice one afternoon, U.S. player Glenn Cowan missed his team bus. A Chinese player motioned for him to climb aboard the Chinese team bus. Cowan began talking (through an interpreter) to the Chinese players, including Zhuang Zedong, who gave him a silk-screen portrait of Huangshan Mountains. Cowan later reciprocated by giving Zhung a T-shirt decorated with a peace-emblem flag above the words—from a Beatles song—"Let It Be."

This encounter also developed into talk about the U.S. team visiting China. Reportedly, the Chinese Department of Foreign Affairs was prepared to decline any request for such a visit, but Mao Zedong joined Zhou EnLai in calling it a very good idea, and on April 10, 1971, nine American players (plus four officials and two spouses) crossed a bridge from Hong Kong to mainland China and played a week of exhibition matches. Dubbed "ping-pong diplomacy," it proved to be the overture to the Nixon visit.

July 15, 1971. All that was needed was three and a half minutes. President Nixon announced that he had accepted an invitation from Zhou Enlai, premier of the People's Republic of China, to meet in Beijing in an effort "to seek the normalization of relations between the two countries and also to exchange views on questions of concern to the two sides."

As Nixon had predicted, the Republican right was shocked, but, as he had also banked on, his credentials as a cold warrior gave him the credibility necessary to overcome all objections. Besides, the PRC was being recognized by one nation after another. If the United States failed to establish relations, it would find itself isolated, confined to a global minority. Since 1949, the United States had blocked the PRC's admission to the United Nations, insisting that the government Chiang Kai-shek had established on Taiwan was the official government of all China. Nixon ordered the objection lifted, and the PRC took the Chinese seat at the United Nations on October 25, 1971.

West Meets East

The president was in China from February 21 to February 28, 1972. Almost immediately after Air Force One touched down in Beijing, Nixon was asked to meet directly with Mao Zedong at his home. Although this meeting with Mao was the symbolic core of the visit, the substantive discussions were held with Zhou Enlai and produced the "Shanghai Communiqué," in which the United States and China pledged jointly to work toward the full normalization of diplomatic relations.

The American commitment to Taiwan had long been the great obstacle to normalization. In the Shanghai Communiqué, Nixon took the one step many U.S. cold warriors could not stomach. He acknowledged that there was only one China, and Taiwan was part of it. On their side, the leaders of the PRC agreed to work toward an entirely peaceful settlement of the Taiwan question.

"We have been here a week. This was the week that changed the world."

Toast offered by Richard Nixon at the banquet closing his visit to China, February 28, 1972

REALITY CHECK

Taiwan: A Half Step Out

Many were shocked by Nixon's unilateral retreat from America's long-held position that the Republic of China—Taiwan—and not the People's Republic of China was the legitimate government of all China. Had Nixon been more of an ideologue, doubtless he could never have made this concession. He was, however, willing to compromise an ideological stance in what he saw as the interests of world peace and prosperity and to prevent the United States from becoming the odd man out in a world that was beginning to turn toward China. Even so, Nixon did not sever all ties to Taiwan. Despite the Shanghai Communiqué, the U.S. government maintained official relations with the government of the Republic of China in Taiwan until 1979, when the Carter administration broke them off to establish full diplomatic relations with the PRC.

President Nixon and Chinese premier Zhou Enlai toast better times during the president's epoch-making visit to China.

REALITY CHECK

Why Limit Defensive Weapons?

The ABM Treaty was the first arms treaty to limit defensive weapons. The purpose of the treaty was to ensure the continuation of MAD—mutual assured destruction—under which both the United States and Soviet Union acknowledged that a nuclear attack would bring nuclear retaliation. The existence of a viable ABM system threatened MAD by suggesting that nuclear warfare was survivable, even winnable. For that reason, in 1972, both the United States and the Soviet Union disavowed ABMs.

In 1983, President Ronald Reagan attempted to deflect Soviet protests that the proposed Strategic Defense Initiative (SDI), familiarly called "Star Wars" (see Chapter 18), violated the ABM Treaty. Reagan proposed sharing SDI technology with the Soviets, but he knew that the USSR was in no financial position to implement the technology—even if it were actually available. SDI faded after Reagan left office, but the issue reemerged when President George W. Bush pursued nuclear defense vigorously. In 2002, the Bush administration unilaterally withdrew from the ABM Treaty.

The president meets the chairman—Nixon and Mao Zedong shake hands on February 29, 1972, during President Nixon's historic trip to China.

The Triangular Proposition

KISSINGER AND NIXON OFTEN SPOKE of "triangular diplomacy," by which they meant using U.S. relations with one nation to influence the behavior of another. Nixon had hoped that détente with the Soviet Union would influence the behavior of China, and, in fact, the Chinese receptivity to normalization was partly motivated by Chinese fears that U.S.-Soviet détente would put China at a disadvantage. However, the U.S.-Chinese breakthrough was even more powerful in moving Leonid Brezhnev to negotiate favorably with the United States. Brezhnev did not want to contend with the hostility of both China and the United States. On May 26, 1972, the United States concluded the first SALT (Strategic Arms Limitation Talks) agreement, which limited the development of costly antiballistic missiles and offensive nuclear missiles. A major leap beyond the 1963 Nuclear Test Ban Treaty, SALT I (as it was called) sought to begin an end to the nuclear arms race that had been the insistent, apparently endless drumbeat of the Cold War. SALT I set limits not only on offensive nuclear weapons but, with the Anti-Ballistic Missile (ABM) Treaty that was part of the SALT I package, also on development of purely defensive antiballistic missiles (ABMs), which were intended to shoot down incoming intercontinental ballistic missiles (ICBMs).

SALT I was only the beginning. Between 1972 and 1974, the United States and the Soviet Union also agreed to expand trade relations, and although, as we will see in the next chapter, there would be a fateful swing back to something resembling the old cold warrior mentality during at least part of the administration of Ronald Reagan (1981–89), détente and normalization were the beginning of the end of the Cold War.

The great irony was that Richard Nixon would not preside over what President George H. W. Bush called the "new world order," a world without a Soviet Union and with a China friendly to capitalism. Nixon would not share in what the first President Bush declared as America's victory in the Cold War. On August 9, 1974, he resigned the presidency, having fallen victim in the Watergate debacle to his insatiable hunger for secrecy and an apparently boundless willingness to break the rules—two of the very traits that had both emboldened and enabled him to shake the hand of Leonid Brezhnev as well as that of Mao Zedong.

TAKEAWAY

The Unlikeliest Peacemaker

Richard Milhous Nixon laid his political foundation as a hard-line conservative Republican anticommunist only to evolve into a moderate political leader determined to make the compromises necessary to end the Cold War. He used his reputation as a "cold warrior" to assuage conservative Republican fears that compromise with communist leaders meant surrender to them, and, as president, with his national security adviser Henry Kissinger, he initiated détente with the Soviet Union and normalization of relations with the People's Republic of China. Together, these two steps constituted the beginning of the end of the Cold War that had come to seem a permanent fixture of modern existence.

The new president and first lady, Gerald Ford and Betty Ford, bid the former president and first lady, Richard Nixon and Pat Nixon, farewell after Nixon resigned the presidency on August 9, 1974.

CHAPTER 18

ASYMMETRIC DAWN AND SOVIET SUNSET

The Cold War Thaws, Refreezes, and Thaws Again

THE PERIOD FROM AUGUST 9, 1974, the day Richard Nixon resigned, to January 20, 1981, when Ronald Reagan was inaugurated as the fortieth president, was sown with prominent Cold War landmarks. In July 1975, the first joint flight of the U.S. and Soviet space programs, the Apollo-Soyuz Test Project, took place. To anyone who had been following the space race that had begun with Sputnik I in 1957, its significance was unmistakable: the former rivals were now teammates. The very next month, on August 1, the Helsinki Accords were signed by thirty-five communist and non-communist states in an effort to achieve peaceful cooperation across the ideological divide. On September 9, 1976, Mao Zedong died. On June 2, 1979, Pope John Paul II, a son of Poland and a champion of human rights, made his first pastoral visit to his native land. "We want God, we want God!" shouted the millions of Poles who greeted him at his various stops in the country. In return, he enjoined the Polish people: "Be not afraid." Ten years later, when Solidarity, a Polish trade union became a full-fledged political party and triumphed over the Communist Party in parliamentary elections, Poles looked back at the pope's visit as the beginning of their liberation.

THE HELSINKI HOPE

The Final Act of the Conference on Security and Cooperation in Europe—the "Helsinki Accords"—was the product of the Conference on Security and Co-operation in Europe held in the Finnish capital during July and August, 1975. Thirty-five states, including the United States and the Soviet Union, signed the accords, which represented agreement on ten broad principles:

1. Sovereign equality, respect for the rights inherent in sovereignty
2. Refraining from the threat or use of force
3. Inviolability of frontiers
4. Territorial integrity of states
5. Peaceful settlement of disputes
6. Non-intervention in internal affairs
7. Respect for human rights and fundamental freedoms, including the freedom of thought, conscience, religion, or belief
8. Equal rights and self-determination of peoples
9. Cooperation among states
10. Fulfillment in good faith of obligations under international law

As the Soviet Union interpreted them, the Helsinki Accords ratified the territorial gains it had made immediately after World War II.

Gerald R. Ford signs the Helsinki Agreements, August 1, 1975.

More importantly, however, the accords became the basis for monitoring and enforcing international human rights and resulted in pressure on the Soviet Union and its Warsaw Pact satellites and allies to liberalize political policies that resulted in the imprisonment, torture, and even deaths of dissidents.

Little more than two weeks after the pope's visit, Leonid Brezhnev and Jimmy Carter performed a less spiritually freighted act but one with more immediate effect on the Cold War. On June 18, 1979, they signed the SALT II Treaty, which limited the number of strategic (nuclear) missile launchers in the Soviet Union and the United States.

Cineplex

Consider for a moment another event of this period, an event unrelated to the Cold War yet nevertheless instructive. In 1978, in the city of Toronto, Canada, Nat Taylor joined the words *cinema* and *multiplex* to create *Cineplex* as the brand name for the chain of multiscreen theaters he was about to open. The multiscreen theater was a cost-efficient solution to movie exhibiting during an era in which the traditional neighborhood movie house was dying out, unable to generate a profit from showing a single feature on a single screen. The Cineplex idea caught on quickly. Audiences like having choices.

But there was one big problem, especially with the first multiscreen theaters. You would watch your tender love story in theater number 10, only to be bombarded by gunfire from the war movie playing on the other side of the thin wall in theater number 11 and assaulted by the screams issuing from the slasher film in theater number 9. You wanted to concentrate on the movie in front of you, but the noise on either side was a continual distraction. Of course, what was a distraction to you was the *movie* for those in 9 or 11. It was all a matter of location and perspective.

The Cold War had always been a kind of Cineplex experience. In the United States, politicians as well as ordinary people, tried to focus on some main event, while a multiplicity of other events registered—if at all—only as distractions. In the period defined by the administrations of Gerald Ford, Jimmy Carter, and Ronald Reagan, this Cineplex effect intensified. Americans wanted to watch Apollo-Soyuz, Helsinki, and the Pope. They wanted to celebrate Brezhnev's handshake with Carter. They wanted to read in the progression of these events a story of triumph in the Cold War, a narrative rolling to a happy ending.

But other movies were incessantly running in the adjacent theaters, and the noise, the discordant babble of multiple soundtracks playing simultaneously, kept coming through the paper-thin walls. They were running in Africa, in Southeast Asia, in South America, in Iran, and in a place called Afghanistan.

Marxists and Maoists

On September 12, 1974, a month after President Nixon resigned, news came that Emperor Haile Selassie I, the long-reigning pro-Western autocrat who ruled Ethiopia, had been overthrown by a military junta known as the Derg (or Dergue). Most Americans had heard of Haile Selassie in a historical context, as the heroic figure who, in 1936 appealed in vain to the League of Nations for aid in resisting Benito Mussolini's savage invasion of Ethiopia. The emperor was restored to his throne in the course of World War II, and, by and large, Americans heard little of his repressive reign thereafter. This lack of information and interest suited one U.S. presidential administration after another, because it was

Emperor Haile Selassie of Ethiopia, about 1942.

the policy of the American government to bolster the regime. Hardly a democratic ruler, Haile Selassie nevertheless possessed the most important qualification for receiving U.S. aid and support during the Cold War era: he was not a communist.

As first promulgated by President Truman in the early years after World War II, the policy of containment was intended to protect the free peoples of the world against Soviet interference in their governments. In practice, containment became a war against the expansion of the Soviet—and, later, the Chinese—sphere of influence. This often meant giving financial and military aid to regimes that, though resolutely anticommunist, were certainly not democratic, but sufficiently repressive to call to mind the adjective *fascist*. In Greece, in South Korea, in South Vietnam—and in many other, far more obscure places, including Ethiopia—the United States found itself devoting substantial resources to propping up unpopular, autocratic, even brutal regimes for the sole reason that they were anticommunist.

By the 1970s and 1980s, American support often proved finally incapable of preventing the overthrow of unpopular pro Western governments. Yet—and this is especially important—it was not the forces of Soviet-controlled, Soviet-supported communism that took over in Ethiopia. The members of the Derg called themselves "Marxists," not communists. This was typical of another feature of Third World government at this stage in the Cold War. Insurgent or revolutionary leaders and juntas of the 1970s and 1980s rarely identified themselves with the Soviet Union, but with "pure" communism, a kind of Marxist fundamentalism. In the hands of Stalin, Khrushchev, and the Soviet leaders who followed them, ideology was always more or less subordinated to pragmatic politics. The Derg, in contrast, was of the new breed, which adhered rigorously, even fanatically, to ideology. In Ethiopia, the result of this orientation was a reign of terror in a civil war that spanned 1975 to 1987, during which the Derg rounded up and executed hundreds of thousands of its opponents—as many as a half-million, according to Amnesty International. This, too, was emblematic of the course the Cold War took through much of the Third World. It seemed that the poorest nations had a grim choice between anticommunist oppression or communist oppression.

The next year, 1975, while Americans focused on the collapse of South Vietnam, the Khmer Rouge—Cambodian communists—seized power in Cambodia on April 17, ousting Premier Lon Nol, whom the United States supported. The Khmer Rouge described itself as "Maoist," not Marxist; but this did not mean that it was a puppet of or even allied with Communist China. As with the Derg in Ethiopia, the Communist Party of Kampuchea (CPK), better known as the Khmer Rouge, was driven by a "fundamentalist" communist ideology—Marxism as interpreted by Mao Zedong—rather than by any allegiance to an established communist power. Even more than in the case of the Derg, the Khmer Rouge, under its leader Pol Pot, put a fanatical adherence to ideology before any consideration of humanity. Between 1975 and 1979, Pol Pot converted Cambodia—which he renamed Democratic Kampuchea—into what the rest of the world dubbed the "Killing Fields."

Pol Pot, radical Marxist and mass murderer, photographed in 1979.

ALTERNATE TAKE

Was Pol Pot Made in the USA?

Some historians have argued that President Nixon's policy of carpet bombing Cambodia in an effort to interdict Vietcong supply and infiltration routes during the Vietnam War greatly stimulated Khmer Rouge recruitment and thereby enabled Pol Pot's victory over Lon Nol and that, therefore, the United States bears significant responsibility for the dictator's reign of genocidal terror.

Would Pol Pot and the Khmer Rouge have risen to power if the United States had not brought such suffering to the Cambodian people? The verdict of the historians is mixed. For every argument that Pol Pot was, to some extent, a product of American policy in Vietnam, there is a counterargument that the Khmer Rouge, a powerful movement, would have prevailed with or without the bombings. Without definitive evidence to support one conclusion over the other, we might resort to common sense, which suggests that bombing a nation endears the people neither to the bomber nor to whatever ideology the bomber represents.

"To keep you is no benefit. To destroy you is no loss."

Khmer Rouge slogan, referring to the people of Cambodia

Executing a program of agrarian reform modeled on what Mao had attempted in China, Pol Pot forced the entire Cambodian population to work on collective farms or on collective projects of forced labor. In the process, an estimated 1.5 million human beings were killed—about 20 percent of the nation's population. Many who escaped death languished in forced labor or other forms of imprisonment and were subject to starvation and torture.

Some eight thousand skulls of Khmer Rouge victims are today exhibited at Choeung Ek, one of the "killing fields" outside of the capital city of Phnom Penh, as a reminder of Pol Pot's reign of terror.

Africa Erupts

The news out of Cambodia overshadowed that coming out of Africa, where Portugal ended its long war, begun in 1961, to hold on to Portuguese West Africa, consisting of modern Angola, Mozambique, and Guinea-Bissau. After Portuguese forces withdrew on June 25, 1975, Marxist governments were immediately installed in all three newly independent countries, which received Cuban financial aid; the Mozambique government was also directly backed by troops from Cuba. Civil war broke out immediately in Angola and a year later in Mozambique. The Angolan civil war pitted the Marxist Popular Movement for the Liberation of Angola (MPLA) against an anticommunist alliance between Total Independence of Angola (UNITA) and the National Front for the Liberation of Angola (FNLA). Cuba backed the MPLA, and South Africa backed the opposition, both nations contributing soldiers to the fight. The war would not end until early in the twenty-first century. Despite South Africa's abominable human rights record—associated with its

Poster rallying support for the Movimento Popular de Libertação de Angola (Popular Movement for the Liberation of Angola), the revolutionary party that came to power in Angola when the country achieved independence from Portuguese rule in 1975.

REALITY CHECK

Pol Pot as a Mass Murderer

Pol Pot has frequently been ranked with Adolf Hitler, Joseph Stalin, and Mao Zedong as a mass murderer. While it is true that these three were responsible for far more deaths than Pol Pot, in proportion to the Cambodian population of about 7.5 million, he may well be counted as the most bloodthirsty of the four.

policy of apartheid, absolute racial segregation—the Reagan administration sent financial and military aid to UNITA, not only to help it continue guerrilla warfare against the MPLA but also to expand and strengthen its hold on the north, center, and southern portions of Angola.

Both South Africa and the United States—the former with troops, the latter with material aid—also intervened in the Mozambican civil war, in which the ruling Marxist party, the Front for the Liberation of Mozambique (FELIMO), fought a number of anti-Marxist factions, chief among which was the Mozambican National Resistance Organization (RENAMO). War ravaged the country from 1976 to 1996, ending more through mutual exhaustion than because of the RENAMO victory that installed a nominally democratic government to preside over a ruined nation.

CHILEAN COUP: THE CIA CONNECTION

THE UNITED STATES ENTERED the Cold War carrying the heavy historical baggage of troubled relations with many of its Latin American neighbors—from Cuba and Mexico, through Central America, and into South America. On September 11, 1973, right-wing leader General Augusto Pinochet led a military coup against Chile's democratically elected Marxist president Salvador Allende Gossens, who died in the event. Pinochet succeeded Allende and instituted a brutally repressive military dictatorship in which political opponents were simply made to "disappear."

Allende's fall and Pinochet's rise followed a pattern already familiar. Although democratically elected, Allende embraced both Fidel Castro in particular and Marxism generally. Although he was a brutal military dictator, Pinochet offered a pro-American alternative to Allende. For this reason, in the autumn of 1972, the Nixon administration used the CIA to support and fund a series of crippling strikes that undermined the Allende government. The CIA also funneled funds to a growing anti-Allende movement within the Chilean

This "not wanted" poster from 1977 protests the visit of U.S.-backed Chilean dictator Augusto Pinochet to the United States.

military, led by Pinochet. In effect, therefore, the September coup d'état was sponsored by the United States.

Flight of the Condor

General Robert W. Porter Jr., commanding officer of United States Southern Command, remarked in 1968 that, "to facilitate the coordinated employment of internal security forces within and among Latin American countries, we are . . . endeavoring to foster interservice and regional cooperation by assisting in the organization of integrated command and control centers; the establishment of common operating procedures; and the conduct of joint and combined training exercises." In short, the U.S. military was working with various Latin American governments to oppose communist political movements and insurgencies. The Chilean coup d'état was one result of this program of cooperation, but it was only a prelude to a much more organized and ambitious campaign.

On November 25, 1975, the chiefs of military intelligence for Argentina, Bolivia, Chile, Paraguay, and Uruguay gathered in the Santiago de Chile headquarters of Manuel Contreras, chief of the Chilean secret police, to lay out Operation Condor, a coordinated campaign of political control and repression that included intelligence operations and assassinations, all directed against left-wing activists. The object of Operation Condor was to eradicate actual as well as potential political opposition movements. Ultimately, the right wing governments of Argentina, Chile, Uruguay, Paraguay, Ecuador, Peru, Bolivia, and Brazil participated—with the covert knowledge, approval, and support of the United States. American officials justified supporting Condor on the grounds that its principal targets were Marxist insurgents and guerrillas and that, therefore, support conformed to the long-held containment policy. That in reality Condor indiscriminately targeted *any* political opposition—or potential opposition—was winked at. What is not certain is the degree to which U.S. officials were aware that Condor was targeting not only political opponents but also their families, friends, and other associates. Because the actions under Condor were secret, it is impossible to know just how many people fell victim to it. But throughout the right-wing Latin American dictatorships during the 1970s and 1980s, thousands of persons disappeared. Such disappearances were so commonplace that the victims were simply referred to as *los desaparecidos*, literally "the disappeared."

REALITY CHECK

Allende: Suicide or Homicide?

The official announcement from Pinochet's forces was that Salvador Allende had committed suicide with an AK-47 assault rifle that had been the gift of Fidel Castro and that was inscribed by the Cuban president, "To my good friend Salvador from Fidel, who by different means tries to achieve the same goals."

Allende's supporters rejected the suicide theory, asserting that Allende had been murdered by the troops who stormed and captured La Moneda (the Presidential Palace). As the battle for the palace was nearing its end, Allende made a radio broadcast to the nation, in which he seemed to announce his intention to fight it out to the end. Today, even most of Allende's partisans believe he did take his own life—although probably with a handgun and not the assault rifle presented to him by Castro.

NUMBERS

Desaparecidos

As of 2008, a total of 1,198 Chilean *desaparecidos*—"disappeareds"—have been identified by name; however, no one knows for certain how many political opponents the Pinochet regime caused to disappear.

Carter Preaches a New Policy

When he succeeded Richard Nixon on August 9, 1974, Gerald Ford entered the White House as the first nonelected president in American history; he had been appointed to the vice presidency by President Nixon in December 6, 1973, to replace Spiro T. Agnew, who had resigned in disgrace after pleading no contest to charges of bribery and income tax evasion. For many, Ford's avuncular personality had been a pleasant change after Nixon's polarizing presence, but the electorate never shook the suspicion that his appointment as vice president had been contingent on an understanding that, if Nixon resigned, he would pardon him in order to bar criminal prosecution relating to the Watergate scandal. In 1976, Ford failed in his bid to gain election in his own right, losing by a narrow margin to a dark horse candidate from Georgia, Democrat Jimmy Carter.

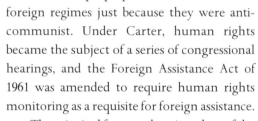

On March 17, 1977, shortly after his inauguration, President Carter addressed the UN General Assembly and announced that, during his administration, the promotion and protection of human rights would occupy the forefront of American foreign policy. Although he did not say so directly, this was a repudiation of containment policies that had moved one American president after another to prop up distasteful, even brutal foreign regimes just because they were anticommunist. Under Carter, human rights became the subject of a series of congressional hearings, and the Foreign Assistance Act of 1961 was amended to require human rights monitoring as a requisite for foreign assistance.

Presidential candidate Jimmy Carter disembarks from his campaign plane, Peanut One, *for a stop in Pittsburgh during his 1976 presidential bid.*

The principal focus and testing place of the Carter administration's commitment to human rights was Central and South America, especially Nicaragua, Guatemala, and El Salvador. Under Carter, the State Department officer responsible for human rights was upgraded to the rank of Assistant Secretary for Human Rights and Humanitarian Affairs. In addition, the Department of State created in 1977 an independent Bureau of Human Rights and Humanitarian Affairs. The president required the appointment of human rights officers in each U.S. overseas mission and made significant efforts to require greater accountability on the part of the CIA, specifying that all intelligence operations were to be conducted within constitutional limits.

HENRY KISSINGER AND THE "DIRTY WAR" IN ARGENTINA

When right-wing Argentine president Juan Perón died in 1974, his second wife and vice president, Isabel Perón, assumed power, only to be ousted by military junta, which waged a vicious war against individuals and groups perceived as political rivals, concentrating on leftist guerrillas. The junta used terror and abduction extensively, targeting leftists and their families. It is estimated that between eighteen thousand and thirty thousand "disappeared" during this long "Dirty War."

As the international community became increasingly aware of the junta's war crimes, diplomatic pressure mounted against the right-wing government. As the U.S. Congress was about to begin debating sanctions against Argentina, Secretary of State Henry Kissinger met with Argentina's visiting foreign minister, Admiral César Augusto Guzzetti on October 7, 1976. "Look," Kissinger said to Guzzetti, "our basic attitude is that we would like you to succeed. I have an old-fashioned view that friends ought to be supported. What is not understood in the United States is that you have a civil war. We read about human rights problems but not the context. The quicker you succeed the better. . . . The human rights problem is a growing one. Your Ambassador can apprise you. We want a stable situation. We won't cause you unnecessary difficulties. If you can finish before Congress gets back, the better. Whatever freedoms you could restore would help." The shocking ambivalence of the U.S. response to the "Dirty War"—approaching official approval of the junta's policies—is typical of America's Cold War posture under presidents Nixon and Ford.

In the end, the Argentine junta defeated the leftists militarily, but, in a bid to suppress growing domestic criticism by rallying patriotism, the junta suddenly launched a military campaign to retake Las Islas Malvinas—the Falkland Islands—from Great Britain. The resulting Falkland Islands War of 1982 ended on June 14, 1982, in a humiliating defeat for Argentina, discrediting the junta, which immediately yielded to popular pressure to restore basic civil liberties and retract its ban on political parties. Elections held the following year ousted the military government entirely.

The Asociación Madres de Plaza de Mayo *(Mothers of the Plaza de Mayo), an association of Argentine mothers whose children "disappeared" during Argentina's "Dirty War," issued this poster commemorating the* desaparecidos.

"You may rest assured that the American people and our government will continue our firm commitment to promote respect for human rights not only in our own country but also abroad."

President Jimmy Carter, February 1977, replying to a letter from the celebrated Soviet dissident and human rights advocate Andrei Sakharov

Cold War Comes to Afghanistan

Jimmy Carter's high-road approach to human rights was gratifying, especially to the growing number of Americans who were appalled by the brutality of U.S.-supported right-wing Latin American regimes, but jarring events in another part of the world soon drew the national focus away from the western hemisphere.

On December 25, 1978, the People's Democratic Party of Afghanistan (PDPA) overthrew the ruling regime of Mohammad Daoud Khan, who was killed (along with his wife, brother, three sons, and several grandchildren), and proclaimed the Democratic Republic of Afghanistan (DRA) under Nur Mohammed Taraki, leader of the Marxist-Leninist Khalq Party, also known as the People's Faction Party. In contrast to most of the "Marxist" and "Maoist" regimes that had been established in various Third World countries, the DRA was supported militarily by the Soviet Union—an unwelcome reprise of the "classic" Cold War scenario.

No sooner had the Taraki government been installed than opposition arose against it, primarily among the Muslim mountain tribes, who formed loose armies of rebellion, collectively called the Mujahideen. During one shootout between rebel and government forces, on February 14, 1979, in Kabul, U.S. ambassador Adolph Dubs was abducted and killed.

The Soviet Union responded by sending more military aid, but the DRA was suffering internal upheaval, and in March 1979, Hafizullah Amin replaced Taraki as prime minister—although Taraki remained president, with nominal control of the army. Amid the DRA infighting, in April 1979, the city of Herat fell to the Mujahideen rebels. As a very bloody guerrilla war developed, President Carter, on July 3, secretly authorized U.S. aid to opponents of the pro-Soviet regime. It was not that Carter believed he was promoting a democratic regime in Afghanistan—he understood that those fighting the Soviets were Islamic

Supporters of the Soviet-backed Afghan communist regime march in Kabul to mark the first anniversary, April 28, 1979, of the communist April Revolution.

fundamentalists—or even that, as in the early days of the Cold War, he wanted to "contain" communism; his real objective was to fan the flames of a conflict he believed would contribute to the weakening of a Soviet Union already struggling to prop up its creaking command economy.

Helpless Giants?

Even as he exploited the situation in Afghanistan to weaken the Soviet Union, President Carter was confronted with a heartbreaking crisis in Afghanistan's neighbor to the west. On January 16, 1979, the Ayatollah Ruhollah Khomeini led an Islamic nationalist revolution that toppled longtime U.S. ally Mohammad Reza Pahlavi, the Shah of Iran. Losing a reliable ally was a blow to the United States, but, seen through the lens of the Cold War, it came at first as some relief that the new government was Islamic rather than Marxist. Nevertheless, the new regime was hostile to the United States because of its alliance with the hated Shah, and, in October, when the deposed monarch fell desperately ill with cancer, President Carter invited him to the United States for medical treatment. In an expression of outrage over this gesture, some five hundred Iranians stormed the U.S. Embassy in Tehran on November 4, 1979, and took ninety hostages, including sixty-six

LINK

Unintended Consequences

Americans liked to think that the Cold War was a contest between democracy and communism. In Afghanistan, it was a civil war between a Soviet-supported secular government and those who supported a fundamentalist Islamic government. The Soviet-backed government introduced a number of reforms that any Western democracy would approve of, among them freedom of religion, land reform, and rights for women—including education and employment. In Afghanistan's cities, most people welcomed the reforms. In rural areas, dominated by Islamic conservatives, the reforms were despised and rejected.

In supporting the Mujahideen, the United States—in the name of Afghani sovereignty and self-determination—actually fostered a less tolerant government than that backed by the Soviets. The unintended consequence was the establishment of an ultimately anti-Western fundamentalist Islamic movement, including the Taliban. The Taliban, which ruled most of the country from 1996–2001, supported religiously motivated militants, including the terrorist organization al-Qaeda, responsible for the devastating attacks on New York and Washington, D.C., September 11, 2001.

A Sea Stallion helicopter lifts off the deck of the nuclear aircraft carrier USS Nimitz *in Operation Evening Light, the ill-fated attempt to rescue the Iran hostages, April 1980.*

U.S. nationals. The non-Americans and thirteen American women and African-American hostages were released during November 19–20, leaving fifty-three U.S. nationals in captivity. As ransom, their captors demanded the return of the Shah. Carter refused, but the Shah, in the hope of ending the crisis, voluntarily left the United States in early December. The hostages remained in captivity.

On April 24, 1980, Carter authorized an elite army Delta Force unit to mount a daring—indeed, desperate rescue operation, but a combination of mechanical and human errors caused the mission to be aborted. Fortunately, the failure did not result in harm to the hostages, but it came as the culminating defeat for the United States, making the nation appear, in this situation, as a helpless giant.

"What happened in Tehran was the diplomatic equivalent of Pearl Harbor. It was bad. We totally missed the significance of the Revolution. We supported the Shah much too long. We couldn't cut loose from him. . . . It was laziness, sheer intellectual laziness."

Moorhead Kennedy, U.S. diplomat taken hostage in Iran

For its part, in Afghanistan, the Soviet Union was acquiring a similar aura of muscle-bound impotence. By the autumn of 1979 rebel forces controlled twenty-two of the country's twenty-eight provinces. In September, Taraki was killed by Hafizullah Amin, who assumed total control of the government. To the great consternation of the Soviets, Amin embraced the kind of extreme Marxism seen in many other Third World radical regimes, and his rhetoric became increasingly anti-Soviet. It was at this point, as much to suppress Amin as to defeat the Mujahideen, that the Kremlin ordered the 105th Guards Airborne Division into the Bagram Air Base in Kabul. On December 20, a Soviet armored division seized the Salang Tunnel, the major overland route between the Soviet Union and Afghanistan, and on Christmas

Eve, a massive airlift into Kabul International Airport began. In the space of seventy-two hours, an airborne division and more than five thousand Soviet special forces troops were in the Kabul area and had seized major strategic points. Simultaneously, four mechanized rifle divisions rolled across the country's northern border. Early in the morning of December 28, Soviet forces announced that Amin had been sentenced to death by a "revolutionary tribunal." (He may actually have been killed in combat.)

With Amin disposed of, the Soviets replaced him with a puppet, Babrak Karmal, and supported the new president with an invasion of more than a hundred thousand troops. The Soviet objective was to crush Mujahideen resistance with a single blow.

It did not work out that way.

Throughout the Cold War, the Soviet military had been built up to fight the military of the United States, even as the U.S. military was designed to fight the Soviets. Like the United States, the Soviets were capable of deploying enormous forces and fierce weaponry, including thermonuclear devices, but in Afghanistan the Soviets were discovering what the Americans had found in Vietnam and were also discovering in the Iran Hostage Crisis. The military instrument fashioned to fight a similarly armed opponent was frustratingly ineffective against a truly determined insurgency. In Iran, a handful of religious zealots held hostage an embassy and, through it, the United States itself. In Afghanistan, the Soviet war machine came under relentless attack from a national resistance spearheaded by the Mujahideen, who received aid from the United States as well as Pakistan.

The two Cold War superpowers were each feeling the bitterly corrosive effects of what military theorists call asymmetric warfare, combat between a power wielding a large traditionally constituted military force and a much smaller power operating unconventionally, by means of insurgent, guerrilla, and terrorist tactics. Because asymmetric wars are not fought in a series of traditional "set" battles, one army against another, winner take all, but are a process of attrition in which resistance—often consisting primarily of opportunistic, catch-as-catch-can hit-and-run attacks—the enemy is never decisively eradicated. Asymmetric conflicts become a test of each side's will to continue the fight. Whereas the larger force is an invading army, the resisting force is indigenous and enjoys a substantial advantage fighting on home ground.

Afghan resistance fighters—mujahideen—return to a village that has been destroyed by Soviet forces, March 25, 1986.

Merely fielding and maintaining a large force in a foreign theater of war requires a potentially exhausting expenditure of resources, and this, in turn, drains the will of the invading nation to maintain the invasion.

DÉTENTE DIES

THE SOVIET INVASION OF AFGHAN-ISTAN failed to deal a fatal blow to Mujahideen resistance, but it did kill détente. On December 29, 1979, President Carter sent a memorandum to his national security adviser, Zbigniew Brzezinski. The president wrote that the Soviets might well suffer in Afghanistan what the United States suffered in Vietnam, but he expressed the fear that if "the Soviets succeed in Afghanistan, . . . the age-long dream of Moscow to have direct access to the Indian Ocean will have been fulfilled." More immediately, Carter was concerned that the Soviet invasion might stimulate calls for U.S. military action in Iran. Critics of his administration, Carter believed, would be quick to contrast "Soviet 'decisiveness' . . . with our restraint, which will no longer be labeled as prudent but increasingly as timid." He also worried that "regional instability may make a resolution of the Iranian problem more difficult for us, and it could bring us into a head-to-head confrontation with the Soviets." As for détente, "SALT is likely to be damaged, perhaps irreparably, because Soviet military aggressiveness will have been so naked."

To confront these issues, Carter informed Brzezinski that it "is essential that Afghanistani resistance continues. This means more money as well as arms shipments to the rebels, and some technical advice." He understood that to "make the above possible we must both reassure Pakistan and encourage it to help the rebels. This will require a review of our policy toward Pakistan, more guarantees to it, more arms aid." Carter wanted to "concert with Islamic countries both a propaganda campaign and in a covert action campaign to help the rebels." To the Soviets, he decided to issue a warning that the invasion was putting SALT and other aspects of détente in jeopardy. Indeed, on January 3, 1980, President Carter formally requested that the U.S. Senate delay consideration of ratification of the SALT II Treaty—which he and Brezhnev had signed on June 18, 1979—in view of the Soviet invasion of Afghanistan. The treaty never entered into force.

Carter campaigned for reelection in 1980 with the nation's economy at low ebb—mostly a hangover from the so-called Nixon-Ford recession, but compounded by an energy crisis largely brought on by stringent OPEC limits on oil production. Depending on how one looked at it, the return of Cold War hostilities was alarming and depressing or actually hopeful. The war in Afghanistan was straining the Soviet economy and, even more important, it was reducing the Soviet capacity as well as its will to suppress calls for reform among the Warsaw Pact nations. Fault lines were becoming increasingly apparent throughout the Soviet bloc, and nowhere more so than in Poland, where Lech Wałesa, a labor activist in the Lenin Shipyard at Gdańsk, led the Solidarity trade union in a local strike that triggered a strike nation wide. This, in turn, prompted the Polish government to sign the Gdańsk Agreement on August 31, 1980, which not only guaranteed greater civil rights but also permitted the establishment of Solidarity as a trade union independent of Communist Party control—a first major step toward multiparty government in a Soviet satellite nation.

For the U.S. electorate, however, the specter of the captives still languishing in Iran overshadowed everything else. Not until November 1980 did the Iranian parliament propose definitive conditions for the

Miracle on Ice—members of the U.S. hockey team pile on goalie Jim Craig after their 4–3 victory against the Soviet team in the 1980 Winter Olympics, Lake Placid, New York.

POP CULTURE

Miracle on Ice

The 1980 Olympic Winter Games were played in Lake Placid, New York, amid the collapse of détente and at the height of renewed Cold War tensions. On February 22, the U.S. ice hockey team squared off against the Soviet team, universally considered the best in the world. In a stunning upset, the U.S. team defeated the Soviets 4 to 3. American fans were ecstatic over what they deemed the "miracle on ice," which seemed to many a Cold War victory. After subsequently defeating the Finnish team, the United States took home a gold medal.

By the summer, relations between the Soviets and the United States had so deteriorated that President Carter ordered a U.S. boycott of the Moscow summer games. In 1984, the Soviets retaliated by boycotting the Summer Olympics held in Los Angeles.

liberation of the hostages, including a U.S. pledge not to interfere in Iranian affairs, the release of Iranian financial assets in the United States that President Carter had frozen, the lifting of all U.S. sanctions against Iran, and the return of the Shah's property to Iran.

A NEW COLD WARRIOR

JIMMY CARTER'S BID FOR A SECOND TERM was opposed by a smiling and radiantly optimistic Ronald Reagan, who confronted the anxiety and malaise that beset the Carter presidency with the promise of a vision of what his memorable campaign advertising called "morning in America."

Ronald Reagan's own life had certainly been suffused with sunlight. Born above a grocery store in the central Illinois town of Tampico in 1911, he worked his way through college and quickly realized his first ambition, to become a radio sportscaster. He left this career for Hollywood, where he may have been a less than brilliant actor, but he was undeniably a successful journeyman performer, compiling fifty-three films and many TV appearances to his credit. A Democrat during his years on screen, Reagan left acting to enter Republican politics, offering constituents two messages: crush communism abroad and end "big government" at home. He defeated the overconfident incumbent governor of California, Pat Brown, in 1966 and served two terms in Sacramento, during which he made a national reputation as a tax cutter. When it came time for him to run against the unpopular Carter, he delivered with charm and eloquence a straightforward "feel-good" message to an electorate tired of feeling bad. He promised large tax cuts, a radical reduction in the size of government ("It's time to get government off our backs!"), and, most important of all, the return of a sense of pride and greatness to the people of the United States. The "Great Communicator," as he was later called, defeated Carter 42,797,153 to 34,434,100. What Ronald Reagan had to communicate obviously resonated with the electorate.

Ronald and Nancy Reagan campaign in Columbia, South Carolina, in October 1980.

The agreement hammered out with Iran to gain the release of the hostages was signed in the waning days of the Carter presidency, but the Ayatollah Khomeini delayed the release of the hostages until

January 20, 1981, the very day Jimmy Carter left office and Ronald Reagan was inaugurated. In a moving act of humble grace, the new president sent Carter as his personal envoy to welcome the returning hostages when they landed at a U.S. Air Force base in West Germany. But the Ayatollah had had his vengeance on Jimmy Carter; many Americans regarded the Iran Hostage Crisis as the crowning failure of his administration and, conversely, the release of the hostages as a kind of inaugural miracle performed by the incoming president.

Free at last—released Iran hostages (left to right) Bruce German, Bruce Laingen, and Robert C. Ode arrive at the Rhein-Main U.S. Air Force Base on their way home to the United States.

"With our eyes fixed on the future, but recognizing the realities of today . . . we will achieve our destiny to be as a shining city on a hill for all mankind to see."

Ronald Reagan, speech, March 17, 1978

Almost exuberantly, President Reagan plunged back into the Cold War, sending to Congress budgets in which welfare and other domestic programs were slashed whereas defense spending was set at record-breaking levels. He continually excoriated Soviet oppression in Eastern Europe, pointing to the struggle of Solidarity against attempts by the Polish government to suppress it as a sign that the people of the iron curtain countries would surely win their freedom. He goaded the Soviets repeatedly, most notably in a speech he made on March 8, 1983, to the National Association of Evangelicals in Orlando, Florida. Commenting on the Strategic Arms Reduction Talks (START), which had gotten under way in Geneva, Switzerland, the year before, Reagan declared:

> In your discussions of the nuclear freeze proposals, I urge you to beware the temptation of pride, the temptation of blithely declaring yourselves above it all and label both sides equally at fault, to ignore the facts of history and the aggressive impulses of an evil empire, to simply call the arms race a giant misunderstanding and thereby remove yourself from the struggle between right and wrong and good and evil.

Speaking to the audience of evangelicals, the president transformed the Cold War from a political to a spiritual struggle—and one on a biblical scale, a contest of good versus evil, a crusade against an "evil empire."

Arms reduction talks were all well and good, but Reagan seemed to preclude even the possibility of compromise.

Eager to demonstrate his willingness to intervene militarily in the world, the president, against the counsel of military advisers, sent U.S. Marines in the summer of 1982 to Lebanon as a peacekeeping force. On October 23, 1983, 241 marines were killed in their sleep, and another 70 wounded, when a truck loaded with 25,000 pounds of TNT was driven by an Islamic suicide bomber into the marines' Beirut headquarters building. Chastened, the president responded by ordering the immediate withdrawal of all the marines from Lebanon; however, in a bizarre act of global sleight of hand, a mere two days after the bombing, he ordered an invasion of the Caribbean island nation of Grenada.

In contrast to peacekeeping in Lebanon, the Grenada invasion was a classic Cold War operation, a direct assault—as Reagan saw it—against communist aggression in the Americas. Cuban troops had come to the tiny country—its population at the time was 110,100—at the invitation of its anti-American dictatorship, which had also secured Soviet funding to build an airstrip. Ostensibly to be used for commercial aviation, the runway was excessively long, long enough to accommodate large military jet aircraft, such as Soviet heavy bombers. Learning that some eleven hundred U.S. citizens lived in Grenada, most of them students at a local medical school, President Reagan declared his determination to protect them. Clearly, the mission also had an ulterior purpose. "Liberating" Grenada from "communist oppression" by means of a triumphant hit-and-run invasion would serve as a collective national "feel-good" antidote to the effect of the death of the marines in Beirut.

The Grenada operation was a success—the medical students and other U.S. nationals were safely evacuated, and the Cubans were sent packing—but Ronald Reagan's saber-rattling was alarming to many American and foreign leaders, who were distressed by the deadlock in the START talks even as, during November 1983, the United States added to the nuclear missiles already deployed in Europe.

An Assault on MAD

It was in 1983 that the president also announced the most ambitious and costly military project ever undertaken by any nation up to that time. It was the Strategic Defense Initiative (SDI) mentioned in Chapter 17, a project the popular press christened "Star Wars," after the popular George Lucas movie of 1977. The reason for the nickname? To many, the proposed system seemed pure science fiction.

As conceived, SDI would employ an orbiting weapons system to create a shield against Soviet ICBM attack by detecting and destroying incoming missiles before they began their descent. The problem was that the technology required for every major component of Star Wars was far beyond even the foreseeable cutting edge. Even if SDI could somehow be made to work, critics—both in the United States and the Soviet Union—objected that it was a violation of the 1972 SALT I (Strategic Arms Limitation Talks) Treaty. Those who were alarmed by Reagan's often bellicose rhetoric feared that he proposed to give the nation a defensive system that overturned the long-standing MAD—mutual assured destruction—deterrent to a nuclear first strike by making thermonuclear war survivable. Even as a concept, SDI was seen as a massively destabilizing move in the Cold War.

The larger controversy was whether SDI could ever be made to work, and the even more heated debate was over the cost of the program. Estimated at $100 to $200 billion or more, it was staggering for the time. Some argued that it would create a deficit from which the United States could never recover. No matter, President Reagan and his successor, George H. W. Bush, pursued Star Wars to the tune of $30 billion, producing for that money precious few demonstrable results.

Soldiers of the 82nd Airborne Division walk toward the aircraft that will take them to Grenada in Operation Urgent Fury, October 25, 1983.

REALITY CHECK

Star Wars: Blunder or Brilliance?

In 1993, Secretary of Defense Caspar Weinberger corroborated speculations that SDI had been nothing more than a huge deception: a ploy to defeat the Soviet Union economically. When anonymous SDI researchers revealed that at least one major space test of SDI had been "rigged" to yield apparently successful results, Weinberger eventually claimed that the entire program had been designed to dupe the Soviet Union into spending huge sums on its own SDI program—a program that U.S. scientists already knew was unworkable.

Under President George W. Bush, a reduced Star Wars reemerged as the National Missile Defense (NMD). In 2001, Bush called for accelerated development of NMD and formally withdrew from the ABM Treaty. In February 2007, the United States opened negotiations with Poland and the Czech Republic to build missile defense bases in those countries, and on February 23, 2008, an NMD missile successfully shot down an errant U.S. spy satellite.

To President Reagan's detractors, SDI was a monument to the tragic waste of renewing the Cold War. Yet there were those who countered with the speculation that SDI *had* worked in that the entire missile shield function was an elaborate ruse, that the *real* purpose of SDI had all along been a ploy to force the Soviet Union to match its defense spending to that of the United States. Instead of dropping a bomb on Russia, America's pursuit of SDI induced the Soviets to spend themselves to death. Critics of the Reagan administration deemed such speculation an attempt to excuse a $30 billion failure.

SANDINISTAS AND CONTRAS

AS PART OF HIS STAND ON HUMAN RIGHTS, President Carter, in 1978, had sharply curtailed U.S. "security" assistance to the Somoza family, the brutal, repressive, and self-serving Nicaraguan ruling dynasty that had been resisting leftist incursions into Nicaraguan government since the 1920s and that now was fighting to suppress the quasi-Marxist Sandinistas. The Sandinistas enjoyed the support of a majority of the Nicaraguan people as well as certain elements of the Catholic Church and, in July 1979, with Cuban military assistance, overthrew the Somoza government and assumed power. President Carter's critics saw the "fall" of Nicaragua to communism as yet another instance of how, on his watch, the United States had been reduced from superpower to helpless giant.

When President Reagan assumed office in January 1981, he did not repudiate the human rights stance of the Carter administration, but he did remove the emphasis from the protection of human rights to the application of old-school Cold War policies. Accordingly, the Reagan administration supported efforts to unseat the Sandinista government in Nicaragua and to prevent Sandinistas from exporting their Marxist revolution to neighboring Central American states. Most of Reagan's fellow Republicans enthusiastically greeted the economic sanctions the president imposed against the Sandinista regime and the economic aid he persuaded Congress to authorize in support of the "Contras," the right-wing movement opposed to the Sandinista regime. President Reagan dubbed the Contras "freedom fighters"—though they were closely tied to the discredited Somoza regime.

Beginning in the very first year of the Reagan administration, the CIA, whose activities had been suppressed during the Carter presidency, reemerged and instituted training programs for the Contras. A pair of

REALITY CHECK

Did Carter Wink?

Some historians have questioned just how thoroughly Jimmy Carter cut the United States loose from the Somoza regime. The fact was that as the United States reduced its assistance to the Somoza government, Israel and Argentina stepped in to fill the gap with military advisers as well as shipments of weapons and aircraft. There remains significant disagreement over the degree to which the Carter administration was aware of this flow of arms, but a majority of scholars believe that it could not have taken place without approval from the Pentagon and the CIA. The bigger question concerns the awareness of the president himself and whether or not he, in effect, winked at the continuation of support for Somoza.

CIA training manuals from this time, *Freedom Fighter's Manual* and *Psychological Operations in Guerrilla Warfare*, drew unwanted public attention in the United States and prompted Congress to pass in December 1982 the Boland Amendment to the War Powers Act of 1973, which barred the CIA and the Department of Defense from covertly funding the overthrow of the Nicaraguan government. Two years later, a second and a third Boland Amendment were passed after the CIA mined harbors on Nicaragua's Atlantic and Pacific coasts; however, when the 1986 midterm elections sent a Republican majority to Congress, $70 million was immediately voted for overt—and therefore perfectly legal—aid to the Contras.

Economic Warfare

In November 1984, elections in Nicaragua installed Sandinista candidate Daniel Ortega Saavedra as president. An international commission of observers, including former president Carter, certified the election and its results. Unmoved by international acceptance of the legitimacy of new government, President Reagan—who himself was re-elected in a landslide that November—denounced it as fraudulent and intensified the economic warfare he had commenced against the Sandinistas in 1982, when he had used U.S. leverage in the World Bank and the Inter-American Development Bank to block loans to Nicaragua. In 1985, Reagan imposed a total embargo against Nicaragua, an action that pushed the impoverished nation's depleted economy into complete collapse. By 1988, inflation in Nicaragua stood at 30,000 percent, forcing Ortega to end all of the health, education, housing, and nutrition programs his party had introduced. Reagan's economic war undermined the Sandinista government and eroded Ortega's popular support.

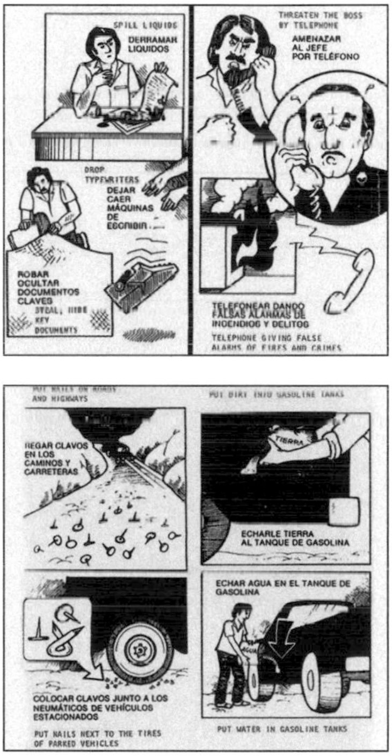

The CIA's Freedom Fighter's Manual, *distributed to the anti-Sandinista "Contras" of Nicaragua, was full of ideas for those who wanted to overthrow a government.*

Soviet Senescence

While the Reagan administration was fighting a containment battle in Central America, the original Cold War adversary was enduring a series of convulsions that we now know were the death throes of the Soviet Union. Leonid Brezhnev died on November 10, 1982, and was succeeded as general secretary of the Communist Party by the chief of the KGB, Yuri Andropov. During his KGB tenure, Andropov had presided over the suppression of the dissident movement in the Soviet Union, and so it was expected that he would be a reactionary and repressive leader. Surprisingly, however, he introduced significant reforms throughout the Communist Party and the government bureaucracy and, for the first time in Soviet history, invited the Soviet people to criticize the government's management—or mismanagement—of the economy. On the international front, however, Andropov continued the war in Afghanistan, refused to negotiate controls on the presence of nuclear missile deployment in Europe, and generally responded in kind to President Reagan's hard line.

The administration of the aged Andropov (he was sixty-eight when he took office) was destined to be brief—just fifteen months, from November 1982 until his death on February 9, 1984—but his tenure was marked by two incidents that revealed just how dangerous the Cold War still was.

On September 1, 1983, a Korean 747 jetliner, Flight KAL 007 out of New York and bound for Seoul, strayed into Soviet airspace over Sakhalin Island and, without warning, was shot down by a Sukhoi Su-15 interceptor. Two hundred sixty-nine passengers, including eighty-one Americans, were killed. The Soviets claimed that the crew of the 747 refused to identify themselves, and Soviet air defense therefore had no alternative but to assume the aircraft was hostile. President Reagan was quick to condemn the attack in the most inflammatory terms, calling it the "Korean airline massacre," a "crime against humanity," an "act of barbarism" and "inhuman brutality." Two weeks after the incident, he ordered the revocation of the license of Aeroflot Soviet Airlines to fly in and out of the United States (the ban was not lifted until April 29, 1986).

The KAL 007 tragedy was headline news. Two months later, another, potentially far more catastrophic incident occurred with barely any public awareness. On November 2, a ten-day NATO exercise, code-named Able Archer 83, got underway. It was a simulation of a conflict that escalated over a period of days and resulted in a nuclear launch. The centerpiece of the exercise was an extended test of a new type of coded radio communication, which included prolonged radio silences as well as participation by simulated and actual heads of state as NATO instantly transitioned from DEFCON 5—peacetime status—to simulated DEFCON 1: nuclear war. Although the original plan, which included the participation of Reagan, Vice President George H. W. Bush, and Secretary of Defense Caspar Weinberger, was rejected before the exercise began, British prime minister Margaret Thatcher and West

This Soviet "Crate" aircraft was photographed from the USAF HC-130 operating near Soviet airspace in the search-and-rescue operations that followed the Soviet shoot-down of Korean Airlines Flight 007. The Crate intercepted and shadowed the Hercules.

German chancellor Helmut Kohl did participate. The result was a level of realism so intense that Soviet air defense mistook it as either preparation for an actual NATO attack or a decoy to hide one. In response, Soviet forces were put on the highest alert. Taking place as it did during a period of marked U.S.-Soviet hostility, Able Archer 83 was the nearest approach to thermonuclear war since the Cuban Missile Crisis of 1962.

Gorbachev Rising

The world survived KAL 007, Able Archer 83, and the administration of Yuri Andropov. He was succeeded by Konstantin Chernenko, an ailing seventy-three year old, who died on March 10, 1985, a year and twenty-five days after taking office. He was succeeded not by yet another sick old man, but by Mikhail Gorbachev, who, at fifty-four, was a youngster by Kremlin standards. Gorbachev immediately broke with the hard line that had been enforced by Brezhnev, Andropov, and Chernenko with a series of breathtaking reforms. In 1987, these initiatives would be grouped under the twin banners of *perestroika* and *glasnost*, the names by which they were identified to the world; however, the reforms began as soon as Gorbachev took office.

Perestroika was a radical *restructuring*—that is the sense of the Russian word—of the bureaucratically ossified central government and included multiple-candidate elections intended to end the Communist Party's monopoly on governance. *Perestroika* extended to the arena of economics by introducing limited private enterprise as well as a liberalization of the Soviet command economy, with more flexible price structures that were determined at least in some measure by the marketplace rather than government fiat. In foreign policy, Gorbachev exhibited a genuinely cheerful willingness to improve U.S.-Soviet relations, and on November 21, 1985, he met President Reagan in Geneva, Switzerland, for what would be the first of four summits.

Soviet premier Mikhail Gorbachev at the Berlin Wall, 1986.

Along with *perestroika* came *glasnost*, a word meaning "openness" or "transparency." The door to *glasnost* had been opened ever so slightly by the short-lived Andropov, only to be slammed shut by the even shorter-lived Chernenko. Gorbachev threw it wide open—at least by Soviet standards. Censorship was significantly lifted, and freedom of speech not merely permitted, but invited, as was criticism of government and a reexamination of Soviet history. The new leader's reforms were intended not only to revitalize a moribund Soviet society but also to end tensions with the West.

Iran-Contra vs. *Glasnost*

The era of change heralded by Gorbachev proved irresistible, even making a deep impression on the likes of Ronald Reagan, who, in a meeting with the Soviet leader in Reykjavík, Iceland, during October 11–12, 1986, fell just short of achieving a long-delayed breakthrough in nuclear arms control.

Yet even as Soviet government was undergoing a revolution of *glasnost*—"transparency"—the Reagan White House had been conducting a major Cold War campaign in deepest secrecy. It began to come to light on November 15, 1986, when President Reagan held a press conference at which he confirmed new reports that the government had covertly sold arms to Iran, the implacable enemy that had held America hostage. At the November 15 press conference President Reagan denied that the arms sale was intended to coax Iran to use its influence to facilitate the release of U.S. hostages who were being held by terrorists in Lebanon. Before long, however, the president backpedaled, admitting the arms-for-hostages swap.

And then the plot took another, even wilder turn, as Attorney General Edwin Meese announced that he had learned that a portion of the revenue raised by the arms sales had been diverted to aid the Contras in their efforts to topple the Sandinista government of Nicaragua. This covert financing was in blatant violation of the Boland Amendment, far beyond what Congress had officially authorized, and, since only Congress can appropriate funds for war, an assault on the Constitution itself.

Meese's revelation triggered an extensive investigation, which revealed that, in 1985, a cabal of Israelis had approached National Security Adviser Robert MacFarlane with a scheme in which Iran, in exchange for U.S. arms, was to use its influence to free the American hostages held in Lebanon. Secretary of State George Schultz and

Secretary of Defense Caspar Weinberger had objected to the plan, but (MacFarlane later testified) President Reagan agreed to it. In another singularly bizarre twist, U.S. Marine lieutenant colonel Oliver ("Ollie") North proposed a modification to the scheme that would funnel revenue from the arms sales to the Contras. In this way, the president could free the hostages *and* finance a Nicaraguan counterrevolution—all without the interference or even the knowledge of Congress.

In a pattern that recalled the Watergate era of a decade earlier, additional investigation and testimony implicated officials on successively higher rungs of the White House ladder, including national security advisers John Poindexter and MacFarlane, CIA director William J. Casey (who died of a stroke in May 1987), and Defense Secretary Weinberger. It was becoming difficult for Americans to believe that President Reagan had been ignorant of the scheme, and an increasing number thought it likely that he had been an enthusiastic advocate for it. Ultimately, the president did admit publicly to wrongdoing in his administration, and he announced that he accepted responsibility for what had happened "on my watch"—though he never admitted to having authorized, let alone advocated, the scheme.

Despite predictions that the Iran-Contra Scandal would be "Iran-Gate," Ronald Reagan's Watergate, and would lead to impeachment or forced resignation, this president was simply too popular to suffer that fate. He was criticized by many in the press, but no official action was taken against him.

DETAILS, DETAILS

Some of the President's Men

Unlike the president, others implicated in the Iran-Contra affair did not escape prosecution. Oliver North was convicted on three of twelve criminal counts charged against him, but the convictions were subsequently set aside on appeal. Poindexter was convicted on five counts of deceiving Congress, but his convictions were also set aside. CIA administrator Clair E. George was indicted for perjury, but his trial ended in mistrial. Caspar Weinberger was indicted on five counts of lying to Congress. All of those charged were pardoned by President Reagan's successor, former vice president George H. W. Bush. A 1994 report by special prosecutor Lawrence E. Walsh was unsparing in its criticism of both Reagan and Bush, but neither was ever charged with criminal wrongdoing.

THE TEFLON PRESIDENT

"I WAS COOKING BREAKFAST THIS MORNING FOR MY KIDS," said Colorado congresswoman Patricia Schroeder, quoted in the October 24, 1984, edition of the *Boston Globe*, "and I thought, 'He's just like a Teflon frying pan. Nothing sticks to him.'" What *did* stick to Ronald Reagan was the very label Schroeder had just minted. He became the "Teflon president."

President Reagan meets with Contra leader Adolfo Calero in the White House office of National Security Adviser Robert McFarlane in April 1985. Lieutenant Colonel Oliver North is in the background.

It wasn't that Ronald Reagan could do no wrong, it was that nothing stuck to him. Everyone agreed that the Iran-Contra affair was a bad business, but there was no

President Reagan motions toward Attorney General Edwin Meese during a press briefing on the Iran-Contra affair, November 25, 1986.

outcry for impeachment. To this day, President Reagan's admirers—and their numbers are legion—credit him with bringing the Cold War to a triumphant end. Others take a more balanced view, arguing that the victory really began with Harry Truman and those who followed. Still others point out that Reagan, always a lucky man, progressing cheerfully through a career as a sportscaster, actor, politician, and president, served in the White House at a singularly propitious moment in history, when history turned against the Soviet Union and the political ideology it embodied.

Mikhail Gorbachev's reforms were intended to revive a dying state. Instead, they only weakened it further. The Soviet leader was plagued by a series of cataclysms, including the horrific explosion at the Chernobyl nuclear power plant in Ukraine on April 26, 1986—the worst nuclear accident in history—a devastating earthquake in Armenia two years later, and the urgent nationalist fervor of most of the "republics" that made up the Union of Soviet Socialist Republics. *Perestroika*—"restructuring"—turned into a process of *deconstruction* as Gorbachev's economic reforms, implemented hesitantly, faltered, triggering strikes and severe national shortages of practically everything needful.

What manmade, natural, and administrative catastrophe did not undermine, the interminable war in Afghanistan did. In 1986, the demoralized Soviets withdrew support from the puppet Karmal, who resigned as Afghanistan's president and was replaced by the former chief of the country's much-feared, much-hated secret police, Sayid Mohammed Najibullah. He called for a ceasefire, which seven Mujahideen groups flatly rejected, defiantly demanding to negotiate directly with the Soviet Union and not a leader they denigrated as a mere henchman. As the Soviet military position in Afghanistan become less and less tenable—the Soviet Union was so broke that it could no longer adequately support and supply the troops—Najibullah in November 1987 convened a summit of tribal leaders, who approved a new constitution and elected him president. In April 1988, an international agreement was negotiated for the withdrawal of Soviet troops, half of whom left by August 15, 1988, and the remainder by

Defeat in Afghanistan—Soviet troops withdraw from the country in 1988.

February 15, 1989. As the United States had lost the war in Vietnam in 1975, the Soviet Union was defeated in Afghanistan in 1989. The difference was that the United States healed, recovered, and went on, whereas the Soviet Union had suffered a mortal wound. Americans were thrilled.

And there was more good news, this in the form of a surprise ending in Nicaragua. The 1990 elections held in the wake of Ortega's draconian program of economic austerity made necessary by Ronald Reagan's embargo unseated the Sandinista government and replaced it with the National Opposition Union Party, which was backed by the United States. The party's presidential candidate, Violeta Barrios de Chamorro, the widow of a crusading newspaper publisher slain by Somoza's National Guard, possessed bona-fide anti-Somoza credentials yet was by no means hostile to the United States. The civil war in Nicaragua ended, a new regime was installed—friendly to the United States, but no puppet—and the conclusion was as inescapable as it was gratifying: democracy had worked!

All of these encouraging events unfolded by the end of the Reagan presidency or during the single term of his successor, George H. W. Bush. But the iconic moment, the single event that ensured the salvation of the Reagan legacy—despite Iran-Contra—came on June 12, 1987. Like President John F. Kennedy a quarter-century earlier, Ronald Wilson Reagan came to West Berlin, that symbolic no-man's land in the struggle between Soviet communism and Western democracy, to deliver a speech. From a platform beside the brick, stone, concrete, and razor-wire of the Berlin Wall, the American president spoke directly to the leader of the Soviet Union: "Mr. Gorbachev," he called out above the cheers of the crowd, "open this gate! Mr. Gorbachev, tear down this wall!"

"Mr. Gorbachev, tear down this wall!" President Reagan speaks at Berlin Wall, Brandenburg Gate, West Berlin, June 12, 1987.

TAKEAWAY

Prelude to a New World Order

President Jimmy Carter begin his administration in 1977 determined to reform America's record on human rights, which had been compromised in pursuit of a Cold War containment policy that often put the United States in the distasteful position of supporting repressive right-wing regimes. Despite his good intentions, however, relations with the Soviet Union deteriorated, détente died, and the stage was set for his successor, Ronald Reagan, to renew the Cold War at a sometimes dangerously high level of intensity. Even as Reagan applied pressure to leftist regimes in Latin America, the Soviet Union began to disintegrate in the face of liberation movements in Poland and elsewhere in the old Soviet bloc and under the strain of a ruinous war to prop up a pro-Soviet regime in Afghanistan. When Mikahail Gorbachev took the helm of the Soviet Union, he introduced sweeping reforms on the domestic and international front, which reduced Cold War tensions, but also hastened the decline of the USSR and Soviet communism.

CHAPTER 19

"A New World Order"

The Cold War Ends, a New World Order Begins

For Americans—and perhaps for just about everybody who heard it—President Reagan's call to Mikhail Gorbachev on June 12, 1987, to tear down the Berlin Wall marked the end of the Cold War. However, the British historian Eric Hobsbawm pushes the date a few months later, to December 8, 1987, when Reagan and Gorbachev signed the Intermediate-Range Nuclear Forces Treaty (INF Treaty), which eliminated both nuclear and conventional missiles with a range of three hundred to thirty-four hundred miles. This ban meant that the missiles both sides had maintained for decades in Europe would be scrapped, and the figurative tents of the two great armed camps that had occupied the continent since the end of World War II would finally be struck.

History as Victory

After Reagan's Berlin Wall speech and the signing of the INF Treaty six months later, momentous events occurred in accelerating succession.

On May 15, 1988, Soviet troops began withdrawing from Afghanistan, a process that would be completed by early February of the following year (see Chapter 18). On April 15,

1989, Hu Yaobang, the former general secretary of the Communist Party of China whose advocacy of quasi-capitalist reforms had brought about his ouster in 1987, died of a heart attack. The next day, a modest number of supporters of liberalization gathered at Tiananmen Square in Beijing to call for democratic reform of the Chinese government. Over the next few weeks, the protests escalated massively, culminating on May 4 in a protest march of some one hundred thousand students in the Chinese capital. Simultaneously, throughout China, other protests were launched—but it was on Beijing's Tiananmen Square that the attention of the world, via television broadcast, focused. That the Chinese government seemingly allowed the protest gave many in the West hope that a profound democratic reform was in the offing; this vision was shattered, however, when tanks rolled through the square on June 4, and the military cracked down, killing or injuring two to three thousand civilians (according to a Chinese Red Cross estimate; the official government toll was one-tenth this number).

A round of arrests and other repressive measures followed the assault on Tiananmen Square, and foreign press correspondents were shooed out of the country. But these actions brought down on the regime the condemnation of the world, which was itself a turning

This iconic image of the end of the Cold War shows the defiance of a single man as the Chinese government brings its might to bear against the pro-democracy movement at Beijing's Tiananmen Square, June 5, 1989.

LINK

INF under Siege

In response to an announcement early in February 2007 by President George W. Bush that the United States planned to deploy in Poland and the Czech Republic a portion of its proposed Ground-Based Midcourse Defense system—an antimissile defense system intended to counter threats against Europe primarily from Iran—Russian Federation President Vladimir Putin declared on February 10, 2007, that the INF Treaty no longer served Russia's interests. Four days later, on February 14, Russian military chief of the general staff, General Yuri Baluyevsky, announced that Russia's decision to withdraw from the INF would depend on whether the United States installed missiles in the two former Warsaw Pact nations. Fears mounted over the prospect of "Cold War II," but then Putin suggested in June 2007 that Moscow "would drop its objections if the radar-based system were installed in [the former Soviet republic of] Azerbaijan"—geographically a very good place to intercept Iranian missiles.

POP CULTURE

Ol' Blue Eyes Is Back

On October 25, 1989, Gennadi Gerasimov, a spokesman for the Soviet Foreign Ministry, wryly commented that Mikhail Gorbachev had repudiated the Brezhnev Doctrine and replaced it with the "Sinatra Doctrine," explaining that allowing the Warsaw Pact countries to exercise complete control of their internal affairs expressed the spirit of "My Way," a trademark Frank Sinatra song. Gorbachev did not receive a Grammy for his version of the Sinatra favorite, but it was a big hit with the Nobel committee, who awarded him the Nobel Peace Prize for 1990.

point. Whether it liked it or not, the Chinese government was on the road to reform. Democracy might have been far off, but capitalism was a growing force and would not be stopped.

"Armoured personnel carriers formed the spearhead while soldiers on foot shot to kill from both sides. Meanwhile, the first of the night's armoured cars and tanks smashed its way through the citizens' barricades to the east. . . . Several cyclists who could not get out of the way in time were crushed or tossed aside."

Journalist John Gittings's eyewitness account of the assault on Tiananmen Square, the Guardian, *June 5, 1989*

In Poland, the Solidarity movement fielded a slate of non-communist candidates who swept the 1989 elections in August. These victories, in turn, inspired the so-called Revolutions of 1989, peaceful anticommunist revolts throughout the Soviet bloc. As if to ratify the revolts, Mikhail Gorbachev formally renounced the "Brezhnev Doctrine" (see Chapter 17), by which the Soviet Union had asserted its right to intervene militarily in Warsaw Pact countries. Those in the West who watched and those in the East whose lives were changing were giddy with the enthusiasm of imminent liberation, and the Soviet Union, due to a combination of Gorbachev's reforms and near bankruptcy, was both unwilling and powerless to intervene.

While Solidarity candidates were winning office in Poland, Hungary opened its border with Austria on August 23, 1989, and early the next month more than thirteen thousand East German tourists in Hungary crossed into Austria. In October, East Germany erupted in antigovernment demonstrations, prompting Erich Honecker, the country's hard-line chancellor, to resign on October 18, 1989. By November, mass protests were practically routine in East Berlin. The Berlin Wall had been rendered useless as a practical barrier, since thousands of East German refugees had begun passing through a liberalized Czechoslovakia and thence to the West. On November 9, the new East German leader Egon Krenz decided to permit refugees to leave the country directly, via any number of crossing points between East and West Germany, including through the checkpoints separating East and West Berlin. Radio broadcast of this new regulation unleashed a torrent of East Berliners clamoring for entry into West Berlin. The East

German border guards, having received no official orders, were overwhelmed and stood aside, slack jawed, as people streamed westward.

November 9, 1989, is remembered as the day the Berlin Wall—which Erich Honecker had only recently predicted would last a hundred years or more—fell. Soon, spontaneously, people on both sides of the wall began chipping away at it with everything from sledgehammers to pocketknives. Less than a year later, on October 3, 1990, East and West Germany would be reunified as a single democratic nation, and one of the Cold War's most volatile flashpoints was extinguished.

> "We are witnessing sad things in other socialist countries, very sad things."
>
> *Fidel Castro, on the fall of the Berlin Wall, November 1989*

REALITY CHECK

Revolutions (Almost) without Blood

The sweeping transformation of the former Soviet satellites in 1989, although on a revolutionary scale, was almost totally peaceful. Only Romania experienced significant rioting during December 16–25, 1989, as the brutal regime of Nicolae Ceauşescu was toppled and he and his wife, Elena, were executed for crimes against the state, genocide, and "undermining the national economy." Some foreign statesmen condemned the tribunal as a kangaroo court, but the couple's passing was generally unmourned by the world.

Speaking June 12, 1987, at the Brandenburg Gate, which separated East from West Berlin, President Ronald Reagan called on Soviet premier Mikhail Gorbachev to "tear down" the Berlin Wall. This photograph was taken on December 1, 1989, twenty-one days before the East-West crossing was officially opened.

Between the fall of the wall and the official reunification of Germany, Mikhail Gorbachev and Ronald Reagan's successor, President George H. W. Bush, emerged from a summit in Malta on December 3, 1989, to jointly declare to the world that a new era of peace had begun.

DESERT FLAMES

PEACE? ON AUGUST 2, 1990, the despotic president of Iraq, Saddam Hussein, invaded its small oil-rich neighbor, Kuwait. The dictator was driven not by ideology, but by a desire to extend power and to add to the oil wealth of Iraq. In part because Kuwait was a U.S. ally and in part because the government of another, more powerful ally, Saudi Arabia, had expressed fear that Hussein would invade it next, President George H. W. Bush worked through the United Nations to assemble a coalition of thirty-one nations to oppose the invasion.

Run up to the Persian Gulf War: President George H. W. Bush hosts Saudi foreign minister Prince Saud al-Faisal at the Bush family's vacation residence in Kennebunkport, Maine, to discuss the menacing situation in the Gulf, August 6, 1990.

For half a century, Americans had become accustomed to their leaders intervening throughout the world to block communist expansion. Now the motive was different. The United States led the coalition not against an ideology, but against the avarice of a tyrant—and, of course, to safeguard strategic sources of petroleum energy. The brief Persian Gulf War, in which this intervention culminated, was the first American war since the end of World War II that had nothing to do with the Cold War. Moreover, the successful eviction of Saddam Hussein from Kuwait, seemed to cleanse the United States of the humiliation it had suffered in the last major hot conflict of the Cold War, Vietnam. On March 6, 1991, several days after the coalition's victory in the Persian Gulf, President Bush addressed Congress concerning the American "commitment to peace in the Middle East":

> The consequences of the conflict in the Gulf reach far beyond the confines of the Middle East. Twice before in this century, an entire world was convulsed by war. Twice this century, out of the horrors of war hope emerged for enduring peace. Twice before, those hopes proved to be a distant dream, beyond the grasp of man.

Until now, the world we've known has been a world divided—a world of barbed wire and concrete block, conflict and cold war.

Now, we can see a new world coming into view. A world in which there is the very real prospect of a new world order. In the words of Winston Churchill, a "world order" in which "the principles of justice and fair play . . . protect the weak against the strong . . . " A world where the United Nations, freed from cold war stalemate, is poised to fulfill the historic vision of its founders."

A smiling President George H. W. Bush addresses a joint session of Congress, March 6, 1991, on the successful end of the Persian Gulf War.

With the Cold War over and won, the president argued, the United States was at the epicenter of "a new world order," and, the implication was, because the United States, and not the Soviet Union, was at the center, that new world order would be beneficent.

"By the grace of God, America won the Cold War."

President George H. W. Bush, State of the Union address, January 28, 1992

"I do not regard the end of the Cold War as a victory for one side . . . The end of the Cold War is our common victory."

Mikhail Gorbachev, remark, January 1992

Collapse

At a meeting in Prague, the Warsaw Pact, established in 1955 to counter NATO, was formally dissolved on July 1, 1991, and, the very next month, the nation that had instigated the Warsaw Pact was convulsed by a dramatic but abortive coup d'état.

In the darkness that preceded the dawn of August 19, 1991, a clique of old-school Communist Party conservatives, including members of the KGB, sent Soviet army units to the dacha (vacation house) of Mikhail Gorbachev and placed Gorbachev and his family under house arrest. Simultaneously, another army unit rolled up to the dacha of Gorbachev's more radical rival, Boris Yeltsin, president of the Russian Republic, the largest republic of the USSR. The coup plotters had intended on arresting Yeltsin, as they had Gorbachev, but they held back, fearful of provoking an uprising in defense of the highly popular and charismatic leader.

REALITY CHECK

Mitterrand Throws in *la Serviette*

Of all the world's leaders, France's Socialist president François Mitterrand seemed almost eager to see the overturn of the Gorbachev era. Early in the coup, he appeared before television cameras to acknowledge Gennady Yanayev, one of the coup plotters, as the "new leader" of the Soviet Union. Almost jauntily, he assured the people of France that the nation could surely "do business" with the new regime. The premature announcement would prove a profound embarrassment.

Looking at the soldiers and tanks outside his dacha window, Yeltsin was not intimidated. He recognized that a successful coup d'état had to be decisive and swift. This one was neither. Looking out his window, Yeltsin saw (as he recalled in a memoir) "People with real assault rifles . . . rushing around with worried expressions on their faces."

While the operations against Gorbachev and Yeltsin were unfolding, tanks and armored personnel carriers rumbled into central Moscow.

The world, as the cliché goes, held its breath. Would Gorbachev's reforms, his democratic revolution, go the way of the Tiananmen Square protest, perhaps to be crushed in a similar "massacre"?

Boisterous and hard-drinking, Boris Yeltsin nevertheless possessed profound insight into the soul of leadership under the old Soviet system. He understood that the coup plotters would not be content with overthrowing Gorbachev by force alone. As rock-ribbed Soviet apparatchiks—bureaucrats—they craved the appearance of law as the basis of their coup. This desire introduced a fatal hesitancy to act, and Yeltsin resolved to exploit it.

In tactical terms, the biggest mistake the coup leaders had made was failing to cut Yeltsin off from the world. From his dacha, he was able to galvanize his supporters and coordinate action via telephone and fax. He composed an appeal to the people of the Soviet Union, faxed it to supporters, and within an hour of its transmission it was being broadcast on television and radio in Moscow and elsewhere.

Muscovites demonstrate against the August 1991 attempted coup by old-style communist hard-liners. The building to the left is the so-called White House, seat of the Russian government and headquarters of pro-democracy Russian president Boris Yeltsin.

Yeltsin believed that military support for the hesitant coup was soft. Accordingly, just before nine o'clock on the morning of the nineteenth, he decided to leave his dacha and drive through the lines of troops that ringed his compound. He intended to go to the "White House," as the Russian parliament building in Moscow is called, and, from the very center of power, lead the opposition to the coup. "Where are you going? There are tanks out there. They won't let you through," his wife protested.

Yeltsin replied: "We have a little Russian flag on our car. They won't stop us when they see that."

On the face of it, the statement must have seemed absurd. But Yeltsin had faith that, in the climate of dawning democracy, the flag "was now a symbol of hope," a symbol of "faith in . . . a decent and benevolent future."

As he had predicted, the troops did nothing to stop him. Yeltsin drove into Moscow, entered the White House, and set about transforming the building into another symbol of the new democratic Russia. Looking down from his office window, he saw the people of Moscow unafraid of the soldiers and their tanks. Turning from the window, he left his office and walked outside. According to his account, he "clambered onto a tank, and straightened myself up tall. . . . Next I greeted the commander of the tank upon which I was standing and talked with the soldiers. From their faces, from the expression in their eyes, I could see they would not shoot us." He then spoke to crowd and returned to his office.

Muscovites erected barricades to impede the tanks and formed a human chain around the White House. To attack the building, the troops would have to kill a great many of their unarmed countrymen and countrywomen. The result was a standoff through the night of August 19 and the next day, and as the hours of August 20 ticked by, many soldiers made an open show of joining the ranks of the civilians surrounding the White House. After daybreak on the twenty-first, the soldiers were ordered out of Moscow. Late that same night, Mikhail Gorbachev and his wife, Raisa, were released. The coup had collapsed. Soon after, the Communist Party itself

REALITY CHECK

The Technology of Liberation

Boris Yeltsin understood that the social and cultural revolution Gorbachev began had already had a powerful effect on technology. Fax machines and photocopiers, rarities under the old Soviet regime, now abounded, as did portable video cameras in the hands of foreign and domestic journalists. Isolating dissent and hiding acts of repression were almost impossible in a world bound together electronically. Yeltsin also understood that the backward-looking leaders of the coup had little awareness that Soviet society had entered into the information age. They had hoped for a stealthy removal of the reformers. Instead, they had what Yeltsin characterized as "a totally public fight on their hands." Totalitarian oppression could not stand the bright light of day.

Russian president Boris Yeltsin addresses anti-coup demonstrators from atop a Soviet tank parked in front of the Russian parliament building (the "White House"), August 19, 1991.

simply deflated—there is no better word for it—and the Union of Soviet Socialist Republics disintegrated. Russia and most of the other republics reconstituted themselves as the Commonwealth of Independent States. Mikhail Gorbachev was a free man, but without a party or a nation. On Christmas Day 1991, he resigned as premier. On this same day, the USSR officially ceased to exist, and President George H. W. Bush delivered a speech in which he acknowledged—not proclaimed, but acknowledged as a simple fact—that the Cold War was over.

"Gorbachev was the best thing the Communist Party had to offer. He played the central role in a remarkable chapter of world history but was forced in the end to go, because in the historical play there was no longer any room for a man who still wanted to be a communist."

Boris Yeltsin, quoted in the Wall Street Journal, *December 27, 1991*

THE NEW WORLD ORDER

THE UNITED STATES OF AMERICA was now the sole superpower on planet earth. Some, President Bush among them, believed that the end of the Cold War really had put America at the controlling core of a "new world order."

What the president and many others hadn't bargained on was the newest feature of this "new world order." It had no core at all.

The Cold War embodied a world vision in which global power emanated from two poles, the West (dominated by the United States) and the East (dominated by the Soviet Union and, to a lesser extent, China). This vision made such conflicts as the Korean War and the Vietnam War seem like contests between the Western and the Eastern poles rather than the local civil wars they were. The American quagmire that was Vietnam and the Soviet quagmire that was Afghanistan should have signaled to both Washington and the Kremlin that the bipolar vision had lost its validity and its utility. As the unaligned or marginally aligned nations of the Third World rose to prominence, the balance of power became less bipolar and increasingly multipolar.

From this perspective, America's role in the "new world order" seemed far less certain and, in some cases, certainly less powerful. Shortly before Bill Clinton succeeded George H. W. Bush as president of the United States in 1993, U.S. soldiers arrived in Somalia, on the east

As its name implied, Operation Restore Hope was a mission to provide humanitarian relief to the people of Somalia, who were suffering in the anarchical chaos of a country torn by competing warlords. Somali men carry sacks of wheat delivered by UN forces. In the background, a U.S. Marine CH-53 Sea Stallion helicopter hovers just fifty feet over the scene, its mission to protect the wheat from being hijacked by the forces of one of the warlords contending for dominance.

coast of Africa, pursuant to Bush's pledge of military and humanitarian aid. The Somali government had crumbled, and the people, languishing in famine and civil war, were at the mercy of competing warlords. The Americans were to serve as UN-sanctioned peacekeepers and as police, charged with preventing the relief supplies from being stolen by the warring factions.

President Clinton soon discovered the futility of trying to be a cop in a country without law, and he authorized an operation he hoped would bring quick and decisive results. Of Somalia's welter of warlords, Mohamed Farah Aideed was the most powerful and ruthless. Neutralize him, and there was hope of bringing order and aid to the country. Accordingly, at 3:40 P.M. on October 3, 1993, elite U.S. Army Delta Force commandos in Black Hawk helicopters swooped down on Somalia's capital, Mogadishu, disembarked, then swept through the Olympic Hotel in search of Aideed and his top officers. Although the warlord himself eluded the soldiers, they grabbed a number of his lieutenants—only to be ambushed by Aideed's militia in a vicious street battle that lasted fifteen hours. In the end, eighteen U.S. soldiers were killed, and American television screens beamed scenes of the aftermath, including one indelible image of the body of an American soldier being dragged triumphantly through the streets. For the American public, that was enough. On March 31, 1994, all U.S. forces were withdrawn from Somalia by order of the president.

Meanwhile, in Europe . . .

Vicious warfare arising from a morass of clan and tribal agendas was not peculiar to impoverished Africa. The death of Yugoslavia's strongman, Tito, in 1980 revealed that the "nation" thrown together after World War I had been held together largely by the benevolent despot who governed it. In Tito's absence and with the collapse of the Soviet Union and the Soviet bloc, the Balkans in southeastern Europe erupted as the constituents of what had been communist Yugoslavia broke apart and began to fight one another.

The Communist Party gave up its monopoly on power in January 1990. Despite this, the Slovenes and Croats remained intent on breaking free from the old nation. Later in the year, the two groups proclaimed independence and proposed that constituents of Yugoslavia create a federal government in the form of a loose union. The union was opposed by Slobodan Milošević , communist leader of Serbia, another of the Yugoslav republics. At his instigation, Croatia's Serbian minority rose up against the Croatian government, and Milošević ordered the Yugoslav army, whose top commanders were all Serbs, to invade Croatia in support of the Serbs there. Now civil war morphed from a political contest into a bloody clash of ancient ethnic allegiances. The new world order? Twentieth-century Europe was convulsed in medieval tribal warfare among the Serbs, the Croats, and the Muslims of what had been Yugoslavia.

The United Nations enforced a truce in the region in January 1992, but fighting began anew when Bosnia seceded from Yugoslavia in March. Bosnia's Serb population now revolted, and the newly independent republic was convulsed by a civil war waged with modern weapons to fight age-old ethnic feuds. In August 1995, the Clinton administration began brokering a peace settlement among the warring factions, and on November 21, 1995, after lengthy negotiations at the Wright-Patterson Air Force Base near Dayton, Ohio, the Dayton Peace Accord was formally signed in Paris. But the region erupted again, this time in Kosovo, which had been accorded the ambiguous status of "autonomous province" within Serbia. Ninety percent of Kosovo's population was ethnic Albanians, mostly Muslims, while Serbs accounted for 10 percent. The ethnic Albanians objected to Serbia's seizure of the Kosovar administration, and, in 1992, the majority population voted to secede not only from Serbia but from Yugoslavia as well. The plan was to join Kosovo with Albania, a majority Muslim nation. Milošević cracked down on Kosovo, and when this failed to crush the independence movement, he waged all-out war against the Kosovar Albanians. Europe was swept by fear that this latest Balkan war would ignite a wider conflict, as was the case in 1914, when Balkan violence triggered World War I.

December 14, 1995: The Bosnian peace agreement, brokered by the United Nations, NATO, and the United States, is signed in Paris. Serbia's Slobodan Milošević is seated at the left, President Bill Clinton stands second to left in the back row.

ETHNIC CLEANSING IN A DIRTY WAR

Ethnic cleansing was an especially horrific aspect of the Bosnian war. Practiced by Serb and Croat forces, but most notoriously and specifically identified with Serbian leader Slobodan Milošević, ethnic cleansing was a systematic program of forced expulsion or killing of members of the targeted ethnic group in a region. In addition, efforts were made to expunge everything associated with them, such as churches or mosques, cemeteries, and cultural monuments.

Ethnic cleansing often became outright genocide in the Bosnian conflict. Of the 140,000 Bosnians, 97,300 Serbs, and 28,400 Croats killed between 1992 and 1995, most were civilians. The war produced a total of 1.37 million refugees, the majority victims of ethnic cleansing. In May 1993, the United Nations created the International Criminal Tribunal for the Former Yugoslavia (ICTY), which investigated ethnic cleansing and other war crimes in Bosnia, issued indictments, and conducted trials. As of 2009, the ICTY had convicted more than sixty persons and was in the process of trying more than forty others. The highest-profile figure to be tried was Milošević himself. Indicted in May 1999 for crimes against humanity in the Kosovo War, he was also charged on January 30, 2002, with genocide in Bosnia and war crimes in Croatia. His trial began at The Hague on February 12, 2002, and was still in process on March 11, 2006, when Milošević was found dead, of an apparent heart attack, in his cell.

President Clinton intervened with a compromise by which Kosovo would be granted greater autonomy, but not full independence. The Kosovar Albanians agreed, but Milošević rejected the compromise, and, starting in February 1998, waged war against the Kosovo Liberation Army (KLA). Some two thousand, almost all of them civilian noncombatants, were killed, and the violence unleashed a tsunami of refugees. At the behest of the Clinton administration, and with the United States in the lead, NATO staged major airstrikes against the Serbian army, even as the organization worked with the United Nations in an effort to bring about a ceasefire. Only after weeks of punishing attacks did Milošević give in, agreeing on June 10, 1999, to evacuate his troops from the province.

Stateless Threats

The actions of the Clinton administration in Africa and the Balkans produced controversy and criticism. In the Balkans, they also produced measurable positive results. Yet the American people could not identify with U.S. intervention in this region as they—and their parents and grandparents—had in the execution of containment against Soviet aggression during the Cold War. In the Balkans, there was no opposing ideology to confront. There was no nuclear-armed military presenting an existential threat to the United States. Americans could bring themselves to understand the U.S. mission in the Balkans intellectually, but the gut-level engagement that had characterized the long struggle against Soviet communism was missing.

The post–Cold War world was at once harder to understand, yet—it seemed—safer, at least for Americans.

Then came a beautiful autumn morning in New York City, 8:45, September 11, 2001. A Boeing 767 passenger jetliner—later identified as American Airlines Flight 11 out of Boston—roared low, much too low, across the acetylene-blue sky, banked sharply, and exploded into the gleaming silver skin of the North Tower of the World Trade Center in lower Manhattan. All the television networks broke into their usual morning fare, cameras focused on the thick black smoke billowing from the tower's gaping wound. Video crews had begun covering the catastrophe within three minutes after the impact. And so they bore witness and broadcast to the nation the horrific crash of a second 767, United Airlines Flight 175, at 9:03, this time into the World Trade Center's South Tower.

It was 9:30 before President Clinton's successor, George W. Bush, appeared on television to announce that the nation had suffered "an apparent terrorist attack." Thirteen minutes later, at 9:43, American Airlines Flight 77, a Boeing 757, sliced into the Pentagon, headquarters of the U.S. military, ten thousand pounds of Jet A fuel igniting a massive

Asymmetric warfare comes to America, September 11, 2001. Smoke billows from the North Tower of the World Trade Center after it was hit by a hijacked Boeing 767 airliner at 8:45 in the morning. Eighteen minutes later, a second hijacked plane exploded into the South Tower.

The Pentagon blazes after being hit by a hijacked airliner on September 11, 2001.

explosion and fire. Back in New York, at 10:05, the South Tower of the World Trade Center collapsed, swallowing up 110 stories of steel, concrete, and humanity. At 10:10, the peace of rural Somerset County, Pennsylvania, was shattered when another 757, United Airlines Flight 93, cratered the dark loam. Eighteen minutes after this, the North Tower of the World Trade Center collapsed.

Television viewers were soon told that the aircraft downed in Pennsylvania had almost certainly targeted the White House or the United States Capitol. It and the other three planes had been hijacked by terrorists acting as suicide pilots of airliners that had become guided missiles. By the late afternoon of September 11, David Ensor of CNN was reporting that U.S. intelligence officers believed that a multimillionaire backer of terrorism, Osama bin Laden—a Saudi national living in Afghanistan under the protection of the country's radical Islamic Taliban regime—had organized and instigated the attacks. He was the chief of al-Qaeda (Arabic for "The Base"), an Islamic guerrilla group sworn to jihad (holy war) against Israel and the West, including the United States. Although it was believed that al-Qaeda consisted of about ten thousand adherents in 2001, it was later learned that the attacks themselves had been carried out by just nineteen young men from the Middle East—most of them (like bin Laden) from Saudi Arabia. For months before the attacks, they had lived in American motels and apartment complexes, some of them paying cash to train in small American flight schools while banking at American banks and hardening their bodies in American gyms.

Nineteen suicides, supported by a Saudi-born millionaire, had accomplished in fact what the Soviet Union, for a half century, had threatened to do—but never actually did. Nineteen young men had attacked the United States with improvised guided missiles, destroying a monument to American commerce and finance, and damaging the headquarters of the most powerful military in the world. The nation's vaunted air defense network, which had been built up during the Cold

War to monitor and intercept incoming Soviet ICBMs and Soviet bombers, had failed—or, worse, proved irrelevant. For half a century, Americans had been assured that any air attack would be instantly met with overwhelming force, countered by flights of hundreds of interceptor aircraft ready to scramble at a moment's notice. On September 11, 2001, just two F-15s were ordered into the air in response to word from FAA flight controllers that Flight 11 had been hijacked. By the time a few more fighters got into the air, the attacks were under way or finished. None of the four hijacked aircraft were intercepted. On September 11, 2001, the United States might have had no air defense of any kind, and the results would have been exactly the same.

"The First War of the Twenty-first Century"

It was the most extreme instance of asymmetric warfare. Nineteen men had successfully attacked the U.S. mainland, defeating—for all practical purposes—the entire air defense establishment of the nation's military.

President Bush, who had been reading *The Pet Goat* to children at the Emma E. Booker Elementary School in Sarasota, Florida, during the attacks (continuing to do so for approximately ten minutes after Andrew Card, his chief of staff, whispered in his ear the news of the first impact), was flown in Air Force One on a meandering course from one air force base to another before returning to the White House at 6:44 P.M., nearly ten hours after the first impact. On the next day, he remarked in a speech, "We have just seen the first war of the twenty-first century," without mentioning that, so far, the "war" had been waged by no more than nineteen men.

U.S. Navy Seals discovered this propaganda poster featuring Osama bin Laden in an al-Qaeda stronghold at Zhawar Kili, Afghanistan.

On September 20, eight days after 9/11, President Bush delivered an address to a special joint session of Congress. By this time, U.S. intelligence had determined definitively that Osama bin Laden and al-Qaeda were behind the attacks and that both the leader and his organization were being hosted and protected by the Taliban government of Afghanistan. The great problem with waging war against a stateless power, such as terrorists, is the absence of a country to retaliate against. Fighting terrorists is primarily a law-enforcement issue, not a military mission, but in identifying Afghanistan as bin Laden's base, the Bush administration was able to threaten war against

WAS FLIGHT 93 SHOT DOWN?

Based on cell phone calls passengers made from Flight 93 on September 11, 2001, and fragments of radio transmissions from the aircraft's cockpit, it is apparent that a group of passengers decided to storm the cockpit in an attempt to wrest control of the airplane from the hijackers.

It has been assumed that, in the struggle, the aircraft crashed, perhaps deliberately forced down by one of the hijackers. Despite persuasive evidence of such a scenario, several eyewitnesses in the Shanksville, Pennsylvania, area reported having seen a *second* plane, white, without markings, but "unmistakably" military (they said), roar low overhead at the time of the crash.

The government has vigorously denied a shoot-down, although, as Vice President Dick Cheney explained on the September 16, 2001, edition of NBC's *Meet the Press*, this was indeed an option. "Well, the—I suppose the toughest decision was this question of whether or not we would intercept incoming commercial aircraft," Cheney told host Tim Russert, who replied: "And you decided?" Cheney answered: "We decided to do it. We'd, in effect, put a flying combat air patrol up over the city; F-16s with an AWACS, which is an airborne radar system, and tanker support so they could stay up a long time . . ." Russert probed deeper: "So if the United States government became aware that a hijacked commercial airliner was destined for the White House or the Capitol, we would take the plane down?" Cheney: "Yes. The president made the decision . . . that if the plane would not divert . . . as a last resort, our pilots were authorized to take them out." The eyewitness reports have never been satisfactorily explained.

The Shanksville, Pennsylvania, crash site of United Flight 93 on September 11, 2001, has been memorialized. Each of the benches from which the site can be viewed is engraved with names of the passengers and crew killed on that day.

the Taliban to force them to surrender "all the leaders of al-Qaeda who hide in your land." When the Taliban replied with defiance, the United States unleashed an air war followed by a limited ground war—which made extensive use of indigenous warlords opposed to the Taliban—and the Taliban was quickly toppled. A new, democratic government was installed in Afghanistan, although the war continued, at first at a low level, and then with increasing intensity as a resurgent Taliban managed to regain control of much of the country. Osama bin Laden remained at large.

NUMBERS

The Toll of 9/11

While the U.S. military fought the war in Afghanistan, stateside crews labored through months of hazardous and heartbreaking operations to recover fragmentary human remains and to remove a twisted mountain of debris. After the completion of recovery work, the death toll at "ground zero" was reported as close to 3,000—to which had to be added 189 killed at the Pentagon, including the 64 passengers and crew of Flight 77, and the 44 persons killed (including the hijackers) in the Pennsylvania crash.

Among those who died in the fiery collapse of the World Trade Center were 23 New York City police officers, 37 New York–New Jersey Port Authority police officers, and 343 New York City firefighters.

Most Americans understood and supported the war in Afghanistan, which harbored those who had trained and supported the 9/11 attackers. But the Bush administration set its sights on a second target, Iraq. Many in and out of government questioned the wisdom, justice, and feasibility of invading that country, which had not been implicated in the 9/11 attacks. Nevertheless, on September 12, 2002, one year after 9/11, President Bush declared to the United Nations General Assembly that Iraq presented a global threat and that Saddam Hussein—who had not been unseated in the war Bush's father had waged against him in 1990–91—was a threat to the authority of the United Nations itself. A month later, the president secured resolutions from Congress authorizing the use of military force against Iraq. On November 8, the UN approved the U.S.-sponsored Resolution 1441, which ordered Iraq to provide proof that it had divested itself of all weapons of mass destruction (WMDs). UN weapons inspectors were dispatched to Iraq but found nothing of significance. Citing its own intelligence, however, the Bush administration asserted that Iraq possessed WMDs, which the UN inspectors had simply missed. On February 5, 2003, U.S. secretary of state Colin Powell took the administration's case to the UN Security Council.

The evidence Powell presented was provocative, but hardly definitive, and most of the international community continued to withhold support for a war against Iraq. Yet while debate raged, President Bush suddenly changed his definition of what constituted an appropriate cause for war. Leaping beyond the issue of WMDs, he broadcast in a speech of March 17, 2003 an ultimatum directly to Saddam Hussein, demanding that he, his inner circle—including his sons, Uday and Qusay—permanently leave Iraq within forty-eight hours, declaring that:

> Intelligence gathered by this and other governments leaves no doubt that the Iraq regime continues to possess and conceal some of the most lethal weapons ever devised. . . . The danger is clear: using chemical, biological or, one day, nuclear weapons, obtained with the help of Iraq, the terrorists could fulfill their stated ambitions and kill thousands or hundreds of thousands of innocent people in our country, or any other. . . . Many Iraqis can hear me tonight in a translated radio broadcast, and I have a message for them. If we must begin a military campaign, it will be directed against the lawless men who rule your country and not against you. As our coalition takes away their power,

> we will deliver the food and medicine you need. We will tear down the apparatus of terror and we will help you to build a new Iraq that is prosperous and free. . . . The day of your liberation is near.

When this deadline passed, on March 19, the president authorized a "decapitation" attack on the Iraqi leadership, an aerial bombardment of a bunker in Baghdad believed to shelter Hussein. This strike, from which the dictator emerged uninjured, was the commencement of the undeclared war called Operation Iraqi Freedom.

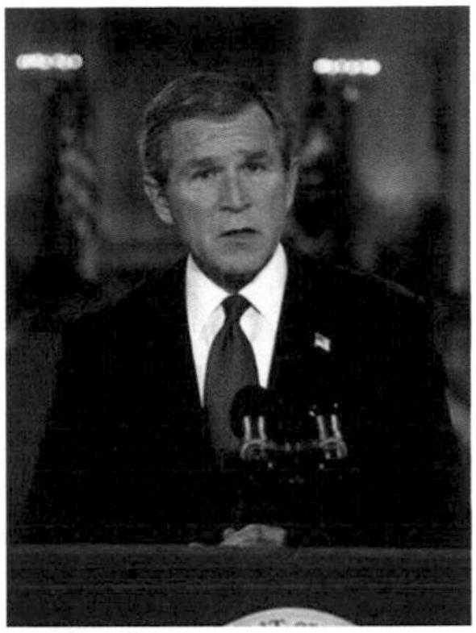

On March 17, 2003, in a televised address from the Cross Hall of the White House, President George W. Bush issued his stunning ultimatum to Saddam Hussein and his inner circle: leave Iraq within forty-eight hours or suffer attack. Two days later, Operation Iraqi Freedom—the Iraq War—began.

As in the 1990–91 war, victory seemed to come quickly. On April 6, U.S. and British troops began the encirclement of the Iraqi capital, and on the following day, U.S. forces advanced into the city itself. On April 9, international television broadcast memorable images of massive statues of Saddam Hussein being pulled down in Baghdad and other cities, apparently by jubilant Iraqis aided by U.S. soldiers. On April 11, 2003, Pentagon officials announced that the "major combat phase" of Operation Iraqi Freedom "appeared" to have ended, and six days later, on April 20, a full scale occupation of Iraq began. On May 2, President Bush landed in an S-3 Viking aircraft on the deck of the aircraft carrier *Abraham Lincoln*, anchored off the coast of San Diego, and emerged from the jet, attired in a full flight suit. A few hours later, he reappeared on deck, in business suit and tie, and delivered a congratulatory message to the crew while standing before a banner emblazoned with the phrase "MISSION ACCOMPLISHED."

LESSON FROM AN UNNECESSARY WAR

IT WAS SOON APPARENT THAT THE MISSION had not been accomplished. Invading Iraq was not the same as holding Iraq, let alone governing Iraq. Civil war between opposing religious factions and violence from al-Qaeda and Iranian-backed insurgents raged daily. As of 2009, the war continues, having cost some forty-three hundred American and uncounted Iraqi lives. It was being financed by the United States—during the autumn of 2008 wallowing under an economic meltdown that recalled the prelude to the Great Depression—to the tune of $12 billion *per month.*

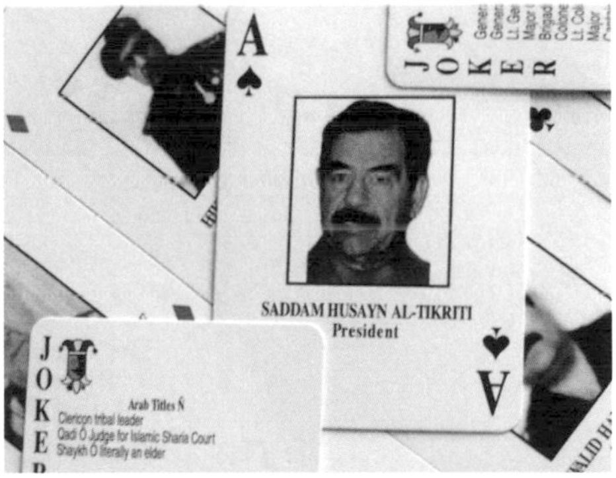

In one of the more bizarre American acts of the Iraq War, the Pentagon issued a standard poker deck, each card emblazoned with a photograph, with identifying information, of a key Iraqi figure marked by the U.S. for capture or death. Saddam Hussein had the honor of being designated the ace of spades.

The "Mission Accomplished" banner festooning the aircraft carrier USS Abraham Lincoln *became infamous as the backdrop of President Bush's declaration on that "In the Battle of Iraq, the United States and our allies have prevailed." As of this writing, in March 2009, the Iraq War is still being fought, although President Barack Obama has announced draw-down and unilateral withdrawal of "combat" troops over a nineteen-month period.*

The Bush administration had developed no firm exit strategy. The WMDs were never found for the simple reason that they had never existed.

Beware of what you wish for, the old saw goes, because you may get it.

For half a century, America and its allies had wished for the Cold War to end in the defeat of the Soviet Union. And so it did. But the world's sole remaining superpower found that, in the loss of its enemy, it had also lost what it had prepared for so long to fight. In place of a giant to oppose, the new adversaries were numerous, small, elusive, very nearly invisible, and certainly hard to understand. When just nineteen men killed thousands on the soil of the United States, the first impulse was to declare a war and fight a nation, then declare another and fight another. The "mission accomplished," however, accomplished nothing. The enemy, after all, was not a nation or even an individual. It was a complex of ideas, attitudes, emotions, and beliefs sufficient to drive men and women to exchange their lives for those of others. These things were difficult to understand, bound up as they were in a people and a religion practically unknown to most Americans. Added to a spiritual feud between Muslims and Christians founded in the early Middle Ages were more recent issues of resentment over the exploitation of the Third World by the nations of the first—of which the United States, having defeated the Soviet Union, was now the most prominent—and the extraordinary fact that, buried beneath the earth of this most spiritually and emotionally volatile region, near the very heart of Islam, was an abundance of oil, the life's blood of a world whose demand for energy was rapidly exceeding its supply.

U.S. Navy engineman 2nd class Russell Osbun of Riverine Squadron 3, Detachment 2, Regimental Combat Team 5, scans a moonlit Lake Quadsiyah, Iraq, on the night of July 11, 2008. River and lake patrols use night vision devices such as the one attached to Osbun's helmet to detect insurgent operations on Iraq's rivers and lakes.

After the end of World War II, the leaders of the United States understood that they had beaten one set of enemies only to be confronted by another. They also understood, however, that this new enemy could not be defeated by the same means that had brought victory over Germany and Japan. A third world war would mean almost certain universal annihilation. Therefore, a new way of fighting had to be developed. The result was the Cold War. It was costly and grim, but the strategies and tactics the United States and its allies employed over half a century brought the defeat of the enemy and did so without destruction on the scale of World War II, let alone on the scale of Armageddon.

After the end of the Cold War, the United States and its allies were presented with new enemies. This time, however, the leaders of our nation and those of our allies reached for the very same weapons, tactics, and strategies that had served before. They were no longer effective. As a generation of cold warriors learned to prevail in the new order of their world, so a post–Cold War generation of warriors, diplomats, and leaders will have to learn or invent the means by which all of us who cherish democracy, liberty, and human rights may prevail in yet another new world order.

TAKEAWAY

Surviving Victory in the Cold War

President Truman embraced Cold War policies designed to "contain" communism not only to counter immediate threats but also to buy the time in which, he believed, democratic capitalism would inevitably triumph over communism. The rapidly unfolding events of the late 1980s and early 1990s proved the validity of Truman's assumptions and policy. But the "new world order" brought into being by the end of the Cold War presented new challenges for which the United States and its allies have yet to create sufficiently new tactics, strategies, and solutions.

January 28, 2009: Eight days after his inauguration as the forty-fourth president of the United States, Barack Obama, having inherited wars in Iraq and Afghanistan from the forty-third president, addresses members of the media during his first visit to the Pentagon. With him, from left, are USAF chief of staff General Norton Schwartz, USA chief of staff General George W. Casey, Joint Chiefs of Staff vice chairman General James E. Cartwright (USMC), and chairman Admiral Mike Mullen (USN).

COLD WAR TIMELINE

1939

AUGUST 23: The Hitler-Stalin Pact, also known as the German-Soviet Non-Aggression Pact, stuns the world by uniting ideological enemies.

SEPTEMBER 1: Germany invades Poland, starting World War II.

1941

JUNE 22: Germany unilaterally abrogates the Hitler-Stalin Pact by invading the Soviet Union in Operation Barbarossa; the Soviet Union therefore becomes an ally of the West.

DECEMBER 7: Japan's attack on Pearl Harbor brings the United States into World War II.

1944

AUGUST 29: The Red Army pushes all Axis invaders out of the Soviet Union and enters Poland.

1945

FEBRUARY 4: At the Yalta Conference, the United States, Soviet Union, and Great Britain divide Germany into three occupation zones (a fourth is later assigned to France). It is also agreed that the United Nations will replace the defunct League of Nations.

APRIL 12: Franklin D. Roosevelt dies of a cerebral hemorrhage; Vice President Harry S. Truman becomes U.S. president.

JULY 24: At the Potsdam Conference, Truman informs Stalin that the United States has an atomic bomb. Stalin barely reacts.

AUGUST 2: The Potsdam Agreement includes new boundaries for Poland, divides Berlin as well as Germany among the Allies, and authorizes the Nuremberg Tribunal to try Nazi war criminals.

AUGUST 6: A U.S. B-29 drops an atomic bomb on Hiroshima, Japan.

AUGUST 8: The Soviet Union declares war on Japan, invading Japanese-held Manchuria as well as Sakhalin and the Kuril Islands.

AUGUST 9: A B-29 drops an atomic bomb on Nagasaki, Japan.

SEPTEMBER 2: The unconditional surrender of Japan ends World War II.

1946

JANUARY: Suspended during World War II, the Chinese civil war resumes between Communist and Nationalist factions.

FEBRUARY 22: The State Department's George F. Kennan sends his "Long Telegram."

MARCH: Civil war breaks out in Greece between Soviet-supported communists and the right-wing Greek government.

MARCH 2: The Red Army continues to occupy Iran even after British troops withdraw.

MARCH 5: Winston Churchill delivers his "iron curtain" speech at Westminster College, Fulton, Missouri.

APRIL 5: Soviet forces withdraw from Iran.

SEPTEMBER 6: Secretary of State James F. Byrnes formally repudiates the Morgenthau Plan, and announces that the United States will maintain a military presence in Europe indefinitely.

DECEMBER 19: French attempts to reclaim control of French Indochina meet resistance from communist Viet Minh nationalists.

1947

MARCH 12: Truman promulgates what the press calls the "Truman Doctrine," the policy of "containing" communist expansion.

MAY 22: At Truman's behest, Congress votes $400 million in military aid to Greece and Turkey to help these nations defend against communist incursions.

JUNE 5: Secretary of State George Marshall outlines the European recovery program the press dubs the "Marshall Plan."

AUGUST 14: Great Britain grants India and Pakistan independence.

NOVEMBER 14: The United Nations calls for the withdrawal of foreign soldiers from Korea, free elections in the divided nation, and UN commission to engineer Korean unification.

1948

FEBRUARY 26: The Communist Party takes control in Czechoslovakia.

APRIL 3: The Marshall Plan goes into effect.

JUNE 21: In Germany, the United States, United Kingdom, and France establish the deutsche mark as a common currency.

JUNE 24: Stalin initiates a blockade of West Berlin. Truman responds by ordering the Berlin Airlift.

JUNE 28: Yugoslavia's Tito defies Stalin by taking his country out of the Soviet sphere of influence.

JULY 17: The Republic of Korea (South Korea) promulgates a constitution.

SEPTEMBER 9: The Soviet Union unilaterally proclaims the Democratic People's Republic of Korea (North Korea) the only legitimate government of all of Korea.

1949

APRIL 4: NATO is founded.

MAY 11: Foiled by the Berlin Airlift, the Soviets lift the blockade of Berlin.

MAY 23: The Federal Republic of Germany (West Germany) is established.

JUNE 8: The House Un-American Activities Committee (HUAAC) hears testimony about communist infiltration of Hollywood.

AUGUST 29: The Soviet Union successfully tests its first atomic bomb, "Joe 1".

OCTOBER 1: Mao Zedong proclaims the People's Republic of China (PRC), instantly adding 25 percent of the world's population to the communist fold.

OCTOBER 7: The Soviets proclaim the German Democratic Republic (East Germany).

OCTOBER 16: The Greek civil war ends in defeat for the communists.

1950

FEBRUARY 14: The USSR and the People's Republic of China conclude a mutual defense treaty.

MARCH 1: Nationalist Chinese leader Chiang Kai-shek establishes a government on Taiwan.

JUNE 25: North Korea invades South Korea, igniting the Korean War.

JUNE 27: The United Nations votes to aid South Korea.

SEPTEMBER 15: After a string of defeats, U.S.-led UN forces land at Inchon, defeat North Korean forces, and advance northward.

OCTOBER 7: UN forces invade North Korea.

OCTOBER 25: China invades Korea with 300,000 soldiers, then withdraws.

NOVEMBER 26: China invades Korea again, pushing UN forces into South Korea.

1951

MARCH 14: UN forces regain South Korea to the 38th parallel, along which the Korean War reaches a bloody stalemate.

APRIL 11: Truman relieves General of the Army Douglas MacArthur as UN commander in Korea.

1952

JUNE 21: The U.S. Navy launches Nautilus, the world's first nuclear-powered submarine.

JULY 26: Gamal Abdel Nasser leads a successful coup d'état against Egypt's King Farouk.

NOVEMBER 1: The United States successfully tests the world's first hydrogen (thermonuclear) bomb.

1953

JANUARY 20: Dwight D. Eisenhower becomes president.

MARCH 5: Stalin dies.

JULY 27: The Korean War ends in a ceasefire.

AUGUST 19: The CIA helps to overthrow pro-Soviet Iranian Prime Minister Mohammad Mosaddeq.

September 7: Nikita Khrushchev becomes first secretary of the Soviet Communist Party.

1954

May 7: Ho Chi Minh's Viet Minh defeat the French at Dien Bien Phu, Vietnam.

July 23: Nasser aligns Egypt with the Soviet Union.

September 8: The Southeast Asia Treaty Organization (SEATO) is founded.

1955

March: The Soviet Union extends military and other aid to Syria.

April: The Non-Aligned Movement is launched by Jawaharlal Nehru of India, Sukarno of Indonesia, Tito of Yugoslavia, Nasser of Egypt, and Kwame Nkrumah of Ghana.

May 14: The Warsaw Pact is created.

July: Eisenhower and Khrushchev meet in Geneva, Switzerland.

1956

February 25: Khrushchev denounces Stalin and Stalinism in a speech to the Twentieth Party Congress of the Soviet Communist Party.

July 26: Nasser nationalizes the Suez Canal.

October 23–November 10: The Hungarian Revolution unfolds.

October 29: The Suez Crisis develops as France, Israel, and the United Kingdom attempt to remove Nasser by attacking Egypt. The United States repudiates the action, forcing the attackers to withdraw.

1957

January 5: President Eisenhower commits the United States to defending Iran, Pakistan, and Afghanistan against communist incursion.

October 1: The Strategic Air Command (SAC) begins a policy of continuous nuclear alert.

October 4: The Soviets launch *Sputnik I*.

1958

July 14: Iraqis overthrow their pro-Western monarch and install a pro-Soviet (though not communist) government.

1959

January 1: The Cuban Revolution brings Fidel Castro to power; he soon declares opposition to the United States and creates a pro-Soviet Marxist government.

September: Khrushchev visits the United States.

1960

May 1: U-2 pilot Francis Gary Powers is shot down over the Soviet Union.

June: China and the Soviet Union split over differing concepts of communist ideology; they become increasingly hostile to one another.

1961

January 20: John F. Kennedy is inaugurated as president of the United States.

February 4: In Angola, a communist/nationalist insurgency begins against Portuguese rule.

April 15: The CIA-instigated Bay of Pigs invasion ends in fiasco.

May 25: President Kennedy announces the goal of putting a man on the moon by 1969.

June 4: Kennedy and Khrushchev meet in Vienna.

June: The United States deploys IRBMs in Turkey; they join missiles already deployed in Great Britain and Italy.

August 13: Construction of the Berlin Wall begins.

October 31: The Soviet Union detonates "Tsar Bomba," at 50 megatons, the most powerful thermonuclear weapon ever tested.

1962

July 20: Laos is officially neutralized, but North Vietnam refuses to withdraw forces from there.

October 16–28: The Cuban Missile Crisis unfolds.

1963

JUNE 20: The United States and Soviet Union create the "hotline" between Washington and the Kremlin.

AUGUST 5: The United States, Britain, and the Soviet Union conclude the Partial Test Ban Treaty, JFK ratifies it two days later.

NOVEMBER 22: Upon the assassination of John F. Kennedy, Lyndon B. Johnson becomes president of the United States.

1964

AUGUST 4: The Gulf of Tonkin Incident moves Congress to pass the Gulf of Tonkin Resolution, giving LBJ wide latitude to escalate U.S. involvement in the Vietnam War.

OCTOBER 14: Leonid Brezhnev succeeds Khrushchev as general secretary of the Communist Party of the Soviet Union.

OCTOBER 16: The People's Republic of China successfully tests its first atomic bomb.

1965

MARCH 8: As U.S. forces build up in South Vietnam, the USAF begins sustained bombing of North Vietnam.

1966

MARCH 10: France withdraws from the NATO command structure.

1968

JANUARY 30–JULY 8: The Tet Offensive is waged in South Vietnam.

MARCH 31: LBJ announces that he will not seek reelection and suspends bombings of North Vietnam.

AUGUST 20–21: Warsaw Pact forces invade Czechoslovakia to crush the "Prague Spring" reform movement.

1969

JANUARY 20: Richard Nixon is inaugurated as president of the United States.

MARCH 2: Armed border clashes break out between the Soviet Union and China.

MARCH 17: Nixon authorizes bombing of Viet Cong infiltration routes and sanctuaries in Cambodia.

JULY 20: The Apollo 11 mission lands two U.S. astronauts on the moon.

JULY 25: Nixon's "Vietnamization" program begins with phased U.S. ground-troop withdrawals.

1970

MARCH 5: The Nuclear Non-Proliferation Treaty enters into force.

MARCH 18: After Lon Nol takes power in Cambodia, Khmer Rouge communists wage civil war.

MAY 4: The Kent State massacre is the tragic high-water mark of U.S. home-front protest against the Vietnam War.

NOVEMBER 18: The United States begins program to aid the Lon Nol regime

1971

OCTOBER 25: The United Nations General Assembly recognizes the People's Republic of China as the legitimate government of China.

1972

FEBRUARY 21: Nixon visits China.

MAY 26: The SALT I agreement initiates U.S.-Soviet détente.

1973

JANUARY 27: The Paris Peace Accords formally end U.S. involvement in the Vietnam War.

SEPTEMBER 11: U.S.-backed right-wing general Augusto Pinochet leads a military coup d'état against the democratically elected Marxist government of Chile. President Salvador Allende dies during the coup.

OCTOBER 6–26: The Yom Kippur War is fought between U.S.-supported Israel and Soviet-backed Egypt and Syria.

1974

SEPTEMBER 12: The Marxist Derg junta overthrows Haile Selassie, pro-Western monarch of Ethiopia.

JUNE: SEATO is dissolved.

AUGUST 9: Nixon resigns and is succeeded as president of the United States by Gerald Ford.

1975

APRIL 17: The Khmer Rouge seizes power in Cambodia; its leader Pol Pot unleashes a reign of genocide, transforming the country into the "Killing Fields."

APRIL 30: South Vietnam surrenders to North Vietnam; The United States evacuates its embassy in the "Fall of Saigon."

JUNE 25: Portugal withdraws from Angola and Mozambique; Marxist governments are installed, and civil war erupts in both nations.

JULY: Apollo-Soyuz, the first U.S.-Soviet joint space project, effectively ends the space race and becomes a symbol of détente.

AUGUST 1: The Helsinki Accords are signed by the United States, Canada, the Soviet Union, and the countries of Europe.

NOVEMBER 29: The Marxist Pathet Lao takes power in Laos.

1976

MARCH 24: A U.S-supported right-wing coup d'état in Argentina ignites the "Dirty War" against leftist politicians and guerrillas.

SEPTEMBER 9: Mao Zedong dies.

1977

JANUARY 20: Jimmy Carter is inaugurated as president of the United States, promising renewed U.S. commitment to international human rights.

1978

DECEMBER 25: A communist regime is installed in Afghanistan.

1979

JUNE 18: SALT II is signed by Brezhnev and Carter.

JANUARY 16: The pro-U.S. shah of Iran, Mohammad Reza Pahlavi, is deposed in the Iranian Revolution, which installs an Islamic theocracy under the Ayatollah Khomeini.

MAY 9: Civil war erupts in El Salvador between Marxist insurgents and the U.S.-supported right-wing government.

JUNE 2: Pope John Paul II makes his first pastoral visit to his native Poland.

JULY 3: President Carter authorizes covert U.S. aid to opponents of the pro-Soviet regime in Afghanistan.

JULY 17: The Marxist Sandinistas overthrow the U.S.-supported Somoza regime in Nicaragua.

NOVEMBER 4–JANUARY 20, 1981: The Iran Hostage Crisis takes place.

DECEMBER 24: In an effort to prop up the pro-Soviet government, the Soviet Union invades Afghanistan. This brings a sudden end to détente.

1980

FEBRUARY 22: The U.S. Olympic Hockey Team defeats the Soviet team in the "Miracle on Ice" of the Winter Olympics.

MARCH 21: In response to the Soviet invasion of Afghanistan, Carter orders a boycott of the 1980 Summer Olympics in Moscow.

AUGUST 31: With the conclusion of the Gdansk Agreement, Solidarity becomes Poland's first trade union independent of communist party control.

1981

JANUARY 20: Ronald Reagan is inaugurated as president of the United States. The U.S. hostages are released from Iranian captivity.

NOVEMBER 23: The CIA begins covert support of the anti-Sandinista Contras in Nicaragua.

1982

APRIL 2: Argentina invades the Falkland Islands starting the Falklands War.

1983

SEPTEMBER 1: Soviet air defense shoots down KAL Flight 007, a 747 jetliner that had strayed into Soviet airspace.

October 25: The United States invades Grenada.

November 2: NATO's Exercise Able Archer 83 begins and is mistaken by Soviet air defense for the prelude to a NATO nuclear first strike.

1985

March 11: Mikhail Gorbachev assumes leadership of the Soviet Union and announces a program of sweeping reforms.

November 21: Reagan and Gorbachev hold their first summit in Geneva.

1986

April 26: The Chernobyl disaster rocks the Soviet Union.

October 11–12: At the Reykjavík Summit, Reagan and Gorbachev come close to a major nuclear arms control breakthrough.

November 3: The Iran-Contra scandal begins to unfold.

1987

June: Gorbachev formally announces glasnost and perestroika.

June 12: Reagan dramatically calls on Gorbachev to "tear down" the Berlin Wall.

December 8: Reagan and Gorbachev sign the Intermediate-Range Nuclear Forces Treaty.

1988

May 15–February 2, 1989: Soviet forces withdraw from Afghanistan.

1989

January 20: George H. W. Bush is inaugurated as president of the United States.

April 15–June 4: The Tiananmen Square protests unfold—and are ultimately crushed by the PRC government.

August: Thanks to the Solidarity Movement, a noncommunist government is installed in Poland.

August 23: Hungary opens its borders to the West.

November: The so-called Revolutions in Eastern Europe begin, one satellite nation after another peacefully leaves Soviet orbit.

November 9: The Berlin Wall falls.

December 3: At the conclusion of the Malta Conference, Gorbachev and Bush announce the start of an era of peace between the United States and the Soviet Union.

December 16–25: The Romanian Revolution overthrows and executes the communist dictator Nicolae Ceauflescu and his wife, Elena, in the only violent anticommunist revolution of the period.

1990

February 26: Democratic elections oust the Sandinista government of Nicaragua, replacing it with a U.S. friendly regime.

August 2, 1990–February 28, 1991: The Persian Gulf War is fought.

October 3: Germany is formally reunified under a democratic government.

1991

July: The Warsaw Pact is dissolved.

August 19–21: Hard-line communists and KGB leaders stage an abortive coup d'état against the Gorbachev government.

December 25: President George H. W. Bush formally announces the end of the Cold War, and Mikhail Gorbachev resigns as president of the Soviet Union.

December 26: The Union of Soviet Socialist Republics is officially dissolved.

LIVE AND IN PERSON

BRADBURY SCIENCE MUSEUM
Community Programs Office
1350 Central, MS C330
Los Alamos, NM 87545
(505) 667-4444
http://www.lanl.gov/museum/
Come here for the story of the Manhattan Project—and more.

THE CIA MUSEUM
No reservations necessary, you can't go there—except online:
https://www.cia.gov/about-cia/cia-museum/cia-museum-tour/index.html

THE COLD WAR HERITAGE PARK AND CULTURAL MUSEUM
A physical museum, to be located at the former Lorton Nike Missile Base in Fairfax County, Virginia, is in the early planning stages. In the meantime, visit www.coldwar.org for an online museum experience.

THE GREENBRIER BUNKER TOURS
The Greenbrier
300 W. Main Street
White Sulphur Springs, WV 24986
(800) 624-6070
http://www.greenbrier.com/site/bunker-tourguidelines.aspx
Tour the ultimate fallout shelter: the government's World War III getaway.

MINUTEMAN MISSILE NATIONAL HISTORIC SITE
21280 SD Hwy 240
Philip, SD 57567
(605) 433-5552
http://www.nps.gov/mimi/
A tour of the land-based leg of America's Cold War strategic deterrent triad.

NIKE MISSILE SITE
Everglades National Park
40001 State Road 9336
Homestead, FL 33034-6733
(305) 242-7700
Take a tour of what was for many Americans the most visible piece of the Cold War in the late 1950s and 1960s.

READ MORE, SEE MORE

Acheson, Dean. *Present at the Creation: My Years in the State Department.* London: Hamish Hamilton, 1969.

Andrew, Christopher, and Vasily Mitrokhin. *The Sword and the Shield: The Mitrokhin Archive and the Secret History of the KGB.* New York: Basic Books, 1999.

Axelrod, Alan. *Benito Mussolini (Critical Lives).* Indianapolis, IN: Alpha Books, 2001.

———. *The Real History of World War II: A New Look at the Past.* New York: Sterling Publishing Co. Inc., 2008.

Beschloss, Michael. *The Conquerors: Roosevelt, Truman and the Destruction of Hitler's Germany, 1941–1945.* New York: Simon & Schuster, 2002.

Brands, H. W. *The Devil We Knew: Americans and the Cold War.* New York: Oxford University Press, 1993.

Breuer, William B. *Race to the Moon: America's Duel with the Soviets.* New York: Praeger, 1993.

Bullock, Alan. *Hitler and Stalin: Parallel Lives.* New York: Knopf, 1992.

Bundy, McGeorge. *Danger and Survival: Choices about the Bomb in the First Fifty Years.* New York: Random House, 1988.

Burrows, William E. *Deep Black: Space Espionage and National Security.* New York: Random House, 1986.

Ceplair, Larry, and Steven Englund. *The Inquisition in Hollywood: Politics in the Film Community, 1930–60.* Champagne-Urbana: University of Illinois Press, 2003.

Clodfelter, Micheal. *Warfare and Armed Conflicts, 2d ed. Jefferson,* NC: McFarland & Company, 2002.

Cohen, M. J., and John Major, eds. *Cassell's History in Quotations.* London: Cassell, 2004.

Cray, Ed. *General of the Army: George C. Marshall, Soldier and Statesman.* New York: Norton, 1990.

Divine, Robert A. *Blowing on the Wind: The Nuclear Test Ban Debate, 1954–1960.* New York: Oxford University Press, 1978.

———. *The Sputnik Challenge.* New York: Oxford University Press, 1993.

The Effects of Nuclear War in America. Washington, DC: Office of Technology Assessment, May 1979.

Ellsberg, Daniel. Secrets: *A Memoir of Vietnam and the Pentagon Papers.* New York: Viking, 2002.

Ferrell, Robert H., ed. *Off the Record: The Private Papers of Harry S. Truman.* 1980. Reprint ed., Columbia: University of Missouri Press, 1997.

Frankel, Benjamin, ed. *The Cold War, 1945–1991.* Detroit, MI: Gale Research, 1992.

Frankel, Max. *High Noon in the Cold War: Kennedy, Khrushchev, and the Cuban Missile Crisis.* Novato, CA: Presidio Press, 2004.

Freedman, Lawrence. *The Evolution of Nuclear Strategy*, 2d ed. London: Macmillan Press, 1989.

Gaddis, John Lewis. *The Cold War: A New History*. New York: Penguin, 2005.

Gerber, Michelle S. *On the Home Front: The Cold War Legacy of the Hanford Nuclear Site*. Lincoln: University of Nebraska Press, 1992.

Glasstone, Samuel, and Philip J. Dolan. *The Effects of Nuclear Weapons, 3rd ed. Washington*, DC: U.S. Government Printing Office, 1977.

Halberstam, David. *The Fifties*. New York: Ballantine, 1994.

Harrison, Hope Millard. *Driving the Soviets Up the Wall: Soviet-East German Relations, 1953–1961*, footnote p. 240. Princeton, NJ: Princeton University Press, 2003.

Haynes, John Earl, and Harvey Klehr. *Venona: Decoding Soviet Espionage in America*. New Haven, CT: Yale University Press, 2000.

Herken, Gregg. *Cardinal Choices: Presidential Science Advising from the Atomic Bomb to SDI*. New York: Oxford University Press, 1992.

———. *Counsels of War*. New York: Alfred A. Knopf, 1985.

———. *The Winning Weapon: The Atomic Bomb in the Cold War, 1945–1950*. Princeton, NJ: Princeton University Press, 1988.

Hill, Kenneth L., ed. *Cold War Chronology: Soviet-American Relations, 1945–1991*. Washington, DC: CQ Press, 1993.

Hillman, William. *Mr. President: The First Publication from the Personal Diaries, Private Letters*. New York: Farrar, Straus and Young 1952.

Hogan, Michael J. *The Marshall Plan: America, Britain and the Reconstruction of Western Europe, 1947–1952*. New York: Cambridge University Press, 1989.

Holloway, David. *Stalin and the Bomb*. New Haven, CT: Yale University Press, 1994.

Kaplan, Fred. *The Wizards of Armageddon*. New York: Simon and Schuster, 1983.

Kennan, George F. *Memoirs*. New York: Pantheon, 1983.

Kennedy, Robert F. *Thirteen Days: A Memoir of the Cuban Missile Crisis*. New York: W. W. Norton, 1999.

Klehr, Harvey, John Earl Haynes, and Fridrikh Igorevich Firso. *The Secret World of American Communism*. New Haven, CT: Yale University Press, 1995.

Leslie, Stuart W. *The Cold War and American Science: The Military-Industrial-Academic Complex at M.I.T. and Stanford*. New York: Columbia University Press, 1993.

Lippmann, Walter. *The Cold War: A Study in U.S. Foreign Policy*. New York: Harper Torch Books, 1972.

MacKenzie, Donald. *Inventing Accuracy: A Historical Sociology of Nuclear Missile Guidance*. Cambridge, MA: MIT Press, 1990.

Mann, James. *About Face: A History of America's Curious Relationship with China, from Nixon to Clinton*. New York: Knopf, 1998.

Matlock, Jack F. *Autopsy on an Empire: The American Ambassador's Account of the Collapse of the Soviet Union*. New York: Random House, 1995.

May, Elaine Tyler. *Homeward Bound: American Families in the Cold War Era*. New York: Basic Books, 1988.

May, Ernest R., and Philip D. Zelikow, eds. *The Kennedy Tapes: Inside the White House during the Cuban Missile Crisis*. New York: W. W. Norton, 2002.

May, Ernest R., ed. *American Cold War Strategy: Interpreting NSC-68*. New York: St. Martin's, 1993.

McCullough, David. *Truman*. New York: Simon & Schuster, 1992.

McDougall, Walter A. *The Heavens and the Earth: A Political History of the Space Age*. New York: Basic Books, 1985.

Miller, Nathan. *Spying for America: The Hidden History of U.S. Intelligence*. New York: Paragon House, 1989.

Miller, Roger G. *To Save a City: The Berlin Airlift, 1948–1949*. College Station: Texas A&M University Press, 2000.

National Commission on Terrorist Attacks. The 9/11 Commission Report: Final Report of the National Commission on Terrorist Attacks upon the United States. New York: Norton, 2004.

Nixon, Richard M. *RN: The Memoirs of Richard Nixon*. New York: Simon & Schuster, 1990.

Overy, R. J. *Russia's War*. New York: Penguin Books, 1998.

Radosh, Ronald, and Joyce Milton. *The Rosenberg File*, 2d ed. New Haven, CT: Yale University Press, 1997.

Rhodes, Richard. *Dark Sun: The Making of the Hydrogen Bomb*. New York: Simon & Schuster, 1996.

———. *The Making of the Atomic Bomb*. New York: Simon and Schuster, 1986.

Rudenstine, David. *The Day the Presses Stopped: A History of the Pentagon Papers Case.* Berkeley: University of California Press, 1998.

Sandler, Stanley. *The Korean War: An Encyclopedia.* New York: Garland Publishing, 1995.

Schain, Martin, ed. *The Marshall Plan: Fifty Years After.* New York: Palgrave Macmillan, 2001.

Scott, David, and Alexei Leonov. *Two Sides of the Moon: Our Story of the Cold War Space Race.* New York: St. Martin's Griffin, 2006.

Spector, Ronald H. *Eagle against the Sun: The American War with Japan.* New York: Free Press, 1985.

Stein, Kenneth W. *Heroic Diplomacy: Sadat, Kissinger, Carter, Begin, and the Quest for Arab-Israeli Peace.* New York and London: Routledge, 1999.

Stern, Sheldon M. *The Week the World Stood Still: Inside the Secret Cuban Missile Crisis.* Palo Alto, CA: Stanford University Press, 2005.

Stoler, Mark A. *George C. Marshall: Soldier-Statesman of the American Century.* New York: Twayne, 1989.

Truman, Harry S. *Memoirs, Volume 1: Year of Decisions.* Garden City, NY: Doubleday, 1955.

_______. *Memoirs, Volume 2: Years of Trial and Hope.* Garden City, NY: Doubleday, 1956.

Tusa, Ann, and John Tusa. *The Berlin Airlift.* New York: Sarpedon Publishers, 1998.

U.S. Department of Defense. *The Pentagon Papers: The Defense Department History of United States Decision Making on Vietnam.* Boston: Beacon Press, 1971.

Unger, Irwin, and Debi Unger. *LBJ: A Life.* New York: Wiley, 1999.

Walker, Martin. *The Cold War: A History.* New York: Owl Books, 1993.

Weigley, Russell F. *The American Way of War: A History of United States Military Strategy and Policy.* Indianapolis: Indiana University Press, 1977.

Wicker, Tom. *Shooting Star: The Brief Arc of Joe McCarthy.* New York: Harcourt, 2006.

Yeltsin, Boris. *Against the Grain: An Autobiography.* New York: Summit, 1990.

———. *Putsch—The Diary: Three Days That Collapsed the Empire, August 19–21, 1991.* New York: Mosaic Press, 1992.

———. *The Struggle for Russia.* New York: Times Books, 1995.

Ziemke, Earl F. *The U.S. Army in the Occupation of Germany, 1944–1946.* U.S. Army Historical Series. Washington, DC: U.S. Government Printing Office, 1975.

WEB SITES

Atomic bomb history
www.atomicarchive.com

The Bunker (U.S. Government Relocation Facility under the Greenbrier Hotel)
www.greenbrier.com/site/bunker.aspx

Cold War International History Project
www.wilsoncenter.org/index.cfm?fuseaction=topics.home&topic_id=1409

Cold War Museum
www.coldwar.org/

The Communist Chronicles
www.communist-chronicles.com/

Cuban Missile Crisis
http://www.cubacrisis.net/

Los Alamos National Laboratory
www.lanl.gov/history/index.shtml

The Manhattan Project
www.cfo.doe.gov/me70/manhattan/index.htm

The Marshall Plan
www.loc.gov/exhibits/marshall/marsintr.html

National Security Archive (from George Washington University)
www.gwu.edu/~nsarchiv/

Revelations from the Russian Archives
www.loc.gov/exhibits/archives/

Selected Venona Messages
www.cia.gov/library/center-for-the-study-of-intelligence/csi-publications/books-and-monographs/venona-soviet-espionage-and-the-american-response-1939-1957/part2.htm

World Wars: The Cold War (from BBC)
http://www.bbc.co.uk/history/worldwars/coldwar/

RECOMMENDED FILMS

Features

The Day the Earth Stood Still.
Dir. Robert Wise, 1951. *Science fiction meets the Cold War. A visitor from another planet (Michael Rennie) comes to earth with a tough love proposal for peace in the nuclear age.*

Dr. No.
Dir. Terence Young, 1962. *This, the first James Bond film, follows 007 (Sean Connery) as he stalks a rogue scientist who concocts Cold War doomsday technologies.*

Dr. Strangelove, or How I Learned to Stop Worrying and Love the Bomb.
Dir. Stanley Kubrick, 1964. *Brilliant, hilarious, terrifying satire of the MAD (mutual assured destruction) doctrine. In a tour de force, Peter Sellers plays multiple roles.*

Fail-Safe.
Dir. Sidney Lumet, 1964. *Another look at MAD—this one brilliant and terrifying, but not satirical and far from hilarious. Henry Fonda stars as the U.S. president called on to make an unthinkable sacrifice to save the world.*

Godzilla, King of the Monsters.
Dir. Terry Morse, 1956. *Cold War-era atomic testing makes an oversized mutant lizard—and, boy, is he angry.*

High Noon.
Dir. Fred Zinnemann, 1952. *Gary Cooper stars in this allegory of the Red Scare, HUAAC, and the Hollywood blacklist disguised as a western*

Invasion of the Body Snatchers.
Dir. Don Siegel. 1956.*The earth is invaded by pod people from outer space, who take over the bodies of earthlings, transforming them into soulless but very well-behaved citizens—exactly what Soviet communists want to do to the people of the free world.*

The Manchurian Candidate.
Dir. John Frankenheimer, 1962. *Frank Sinatra gives a bravura performance in this classic view of "brainwashing" as a means of communist infiltration of American politics.*

On the Beach.
Dir. Stanley Kramer, 1959. *This film version of Neville Shute's novel depicting the aftermath of a thermonuclear war—with the people of Australia as the last survivors, awaiting inevitable death by radiation poisoning—remains as terrifying and depressing as when it was first released. Gregory Peck, Ava Gardner, Fred Astaire, and Anthony Perkins star.*

On the Waterfront.
Dir. Elia Kazan, 1954. *At first glance, this Marlon Brando classic seems to have little to do with the Cold War. Look closer. It is the story of one man who stands up to the thuggish tyranny of mob mentality (read McCarthyism).*

Red Dawn.
Dir. John Milius, 1984. *Patrick Swayze and Jennifer Grey unite to resist Soviet invaders just after the start of World War III and three years before Dirty Dancing.*

Seven Days in May.
Dir. John Frankenheimer, 1964. *A dazzling cast—Burt Lancaster, Kirk Douglas, Fredric March, Ava Gardner, Edmond O'Brien, Martin Balsam, and George Macready—star in this dark narrative of a would-be military coup intended to seize the U.S. government and confront the Soviets once and for all.*

WarGames.
Dir. John Badham, 1983. *A precocious computer hacker (Matthew Broderick) stumbles into a Defense Department supercomputer (via his 300 baud dial-up modem!) and nearly starts World War III.*

Documentaries

Atomic Cafe.
Dirs. Kevin Rafferty, Jayne Loader, Pierce Rafferty, 1982. *A marvelous window into 1950s civil defense culture.*

The Fog of War.
Dir. Errol Morris, 2003. *Robert S. McNamara, secretary of defense in the JFK and LBJ cabinets, narrates a riveting documentary about Cold War decisions at the highest level; the Oscar-winning film focuses most intensively on the Vietnam War in a Cold War context.*

The McCarthy Years.
Drawn from the Edward R. Murrow Television Collection. 1991. An anthology of Edward R. Murrow's landmark exposé broadcasts on Senator Joseph McCarthy.

The War Game.
Dir. Peter Watkins, 1966. *This fictional documentary about the impact of a thermonuclear war on an ordinary English city won an Academy Award.*

INDEX

PICTURE CREDITS

Associated Press: 284, 339, 342 (bottom), 343, 348–49, 350, 396, 411

CIA Library/Center for the Study of Intelligence: 239, 243, 250–51, 324, 403 (Scribd.com)

Getty Images
Getty Images: 105, 305 (top), 315, 330, 364, 371
AFP/Getty Images: 319, 327, 341 (top), 372, 393
National Geographic/Getty Images: 342 (top)
Popperfoto/Getty Images: 248, 359 (bottom)
Time & Life Pictures/Getty Images: 42, 72, 76, 95, 100, 189, 196 (top), 228 (top), 281, 295, 386, 407

The Granger Collection, New York: 5 (bottom), 30; 71, 82, 90, 112, 127, 144, 280, 301, 417
a
Courtesy of The Greenbrier: 163

Internet Archive/American Libraries: 283: http://www.archive.org/details/investigationofu1939unit

© iStockphoto.com/DNY59: vi–viii

Courtesy Library of Congress
Prints & Photographs Division:
xii–1: LC-DIG-ppmsca-19261; 4: LC-USZ62-16530; 6: LC-DIG-cwpbh-03301; 9: LC-USZ62-45074; 10 (top): LC-USZ62-42897; 10 (bottom): LC-USZ62-79597; 11: LC-USZ62-47639; 13: LC-DIG-ggbain-33302; 14: LC-USZC4-3624; 15: LC-USZ62-123350; 16: LC-USZ62-15478; 17: LC-USZC4-6441; 18: LC-USZC4-7353; 19: LC-USZC4-7529; 21: LC-USZ62-101607; 24: LC-USZC4-3626; 27: LC-USZ62-75078; 28: LC-USZ62-121825; 29: LC-USZ62-80532; 35: LC-USZ62-71313; LC-USZ62-104519; 41: LC-USZ62-96489; 45: LC-USZ62-57665; 63: LC-USZ62-134192; 64: LC-USZ62-39852; 66: LC-USZ62-111645; 66: LC-USZ62-121807; 73: LC-USZ62-49043; 81: LC-USZ62-111883; 88: LC-USZ62-80757; 92: LC-USZ62-97132; 93 (bottom) LC-USZ62-104297; 94: LC-USZ62-104520; 101 (bottom): LC-USZ62-92146; 114: LC-USZ62-114938; 117: LC-USZ62-113153; 119: LC-USZ62-104727; 120: LC-USZ62-43468; 121: LC-USZ62-53003; 134: LC-USZC4-2767; 138–39: LC-DIG-ppmsca-13353; 143 (bottom): LC-USZ62-133851; 173: LC-USZ62-132808; 194: LC-USZ62-35226; 195 (bottom): LC-USZ62-112372; 197: LC-USZC4-3375; 200: LC-USZC4-3345; 203: POS 6 – China, no. 77; 205: LC-USZ62-95422; 206: LC-USZ62-111646; 210: LC-USZ62-84978; 212: LC-USZ62-108203; 213: LC-USZC4-4536; 215: LC-USZC4-3346; 221: LC-USZC4-3342; 224: LC-USZ62-108143; 232: LC-USZ62-110993; 235: LC-USZ62-109688; 236: LC-USZ62-109385; 242: LC-USZ62-99607; 245: LC-DIG-ppmscc-03262; 249: LC-USZ62-91783; 257 (bottom): LC-USZ62-66033; 268: LC-USZ62-130863; 276: LC-USZ62-41499; 277: LC-USZ62-94487; 286: LC-USZ62-130365; 289 (top): LC-USZ62-118217; 290 (bottom left two images): LC-USZ62-127228; 291: LC-USZ62-117772; 294: LC-USZ62-117816; 302: LC-USZ62-110986; 303: LC-USZ62-31820; 305 (bottom): LC-USZ62-111269; 307: POS 6 - U.S, no. 98; 322 (top): LC-DIG-ppmsc-03256; 322–23 (bottom): LC-USZ62-122243; 334: LC-USZ62-132434; 353: LC-DIG-ppmsca-04295; 355: POS 6 - U.S., no 1446; 356 (top): POS 6 - U.S., no 212; 360–61: LC-U9-25538-35; 366: LC-USZ62-116058; 369: LC-USZC4-8202; 385: LC-USW33-019078-C; 387 (bottom): LC-USZC4-13344; 388: LC-USZ62-130898; 390: LC-DIG-ppmsca-09741; 422: LC-DIG-ppmsca-02137
Averell Harriman Papers, Manuscript Division: 128–29, 135–37
Revelations from the Russian Archives: 247
Geography and Map Division: 274: g7900 ct000970; 321: g420 ct000857b

W. Keith Luse/http://iis-db.stanford.edu/evnts/5220/gallery/images/IMG_2037.jpg: 171

George C. Marshall Foundation: 124

Courtesy NASA: 180–84

National Security Archive/Dino A. Brugioni Collection: 335

Courtesy North American Aerospace Defense Command (NORAD): 166

nuclearweaponarchive.org: 160

Courtesy Oregon Historical Society: 168

Courtesy Organisation for Economic Co-Operation and Development (©OECD Photo): 68–69

Courtesy Perry-Castañeda Library Map Collection, University of Texas at Austin: 93 (top), 256, 338

Courtesy Presidential Libraries
George Bush Library: 414–15
Gerald R. Ford Library: 374, 383,
John F. Kennedy Presidential Library & Museum: 332, 337, 370
Nixon Presidential Library & Museum: 377, 379, 381
Ronald Reagan Presidential Library: 398, 408 (top), 409
Harry S. Truman Library & Museum: 54, 58, 65 (right), 77, 87, 103, 105, 116, 122, 131, 143 (top), 150, 218, 220, 226, 229, 241, 255, 260

www.sakharov-archive.ru: 141

Courtesy the U.S. Armed Forces
Department of Defense Imagery: 187, 191, 208, 252–53, 258, 269, 272–73, 340, 347 (top), 373, 394, 395, 399, 401, 405, 419, 423, 424, 428 (bottom), 429
U.S. Air Force: 170, 223, 225, 227, 375
National Museum of the U.S. Air Force: 172, 174, 176, 179, 188
U.S. Army, Redstone Arsenal Garrison: 178
U.S. Department of the Army/U.S. Army Center for Military History: 261, 298–99, 351,
Maps courtesy of the Department of History, U.S. Military Academy: 23; 263,
Navy.mil: 428 (top)
Naval Historical Center: 55, 99, 147, 204, 341 (bottom), 344 (top),
U.S. Navy Arctic Submarine Laboratory: 190

U.S. Department of Energy, National Nuclear Security Administration/Office of History and Heritage: iii, v, 50–52, 60–61, 154, 156, 158

Courtesy the U.S. National Archives and Records Administration, Washington, D.C.: 3; 32, 33, 37 (www.ourdocuments.gov), 43, 46, 57, 62 (top); 65 (left), 97, 142, 162, 164 (bottom), 167, 185–86, 195 (top), 214, 217, 262, 264–67, 271, 278, 289 (bottom right and second from right), 312, 323 (top), 325, 344 (bottom), 347 (bottom), 352, 356 (bottom), 357, 358, 367, 380

http://faculty.umf.maine.edu/~walters/web%20104/50s-cold-war-map.jpg: 80

Courtesy Wikimedia Commons: 5 (top): Lenin CL Colour; March on rome 1; 12: Stalin's Mug Shot/Author: Ldingley; 44: V-E-Day Stars and Stripes No 285 Paris 8 May 1945/US Army; 49: Tokyo kushu 1945-4; 62 (bottom): Greenglass bomb diagram; 72: Soviet flag on the Reichstag roof unaltered; 84: Kennan/http://moscow.usembassy.gov/images/Kennan.jpg; 85: Tukhachevsky trial/http://www.prometej.info/solnce/foto/st09-9.jpg; 96 Ahmad ghavam; 101 (top): Marshal Tito/Yugoslav's Peoples Army - JNA; 132 (top): Klement gottwald; 145: Convair XB-36 050620-F-1234P-010; 149: Joe one//http://nuclearweaponarchive.org; 152: EdwardTeller1958/Lawrence Livermore National Laboratory; 153: AtomicWar0101; 161: SurvivalUnderAtomicAttack/Author: Bolesjohnb; 164 (top) Deadzone/Author: Elena Filatova; 165: Ebs logo; 196 (bottom): Communists enter Beijing (1949)/ http://image.muzi.com/pfm_image/202905848959296.jpg; 201: Chinese stamp in 1950/Author: Mila Zinkova; 219: Besatzungszonen2/ http://www.deutschlanddokumente.de/; 228 (bottom): 13.8 scharf/Author: Steffen Rehm; 230: Afghan village/U.S. Army Photo/Author: Justin Holley (Staff Sgt.); 234: AtomicWar0103; 237: Donovan reviews OGs/www.ossog.org/pics_pages/donovan_01.html; 243: Sevensociety/Author: Queerbubbles; 246: 1990 CPA 6266/Author: Mariluna; 257 (top): Kim Il Sung/Federal Research Division of Library of Congress Edited by Andrea Matles Savada; 285: RedChannelsCover/Authentic History Center/Author: Ted Wilkes; 292: Is this tomorrow/Catechetical Guild; 296: Edward r murrow challenge of ideas screenshot 2/http://www.archive.org/details/Challeng1961; 304: Poznan 1956/Author: Piotrus; 310: Atlantik Suez Panama; 311 (top): Nasser cheered by supporters in 1956; 311 (bottom): Dayan 9th Brigade 1956/http://lccn.loc.gov/58050503/Mivtsa' Sinai/Author: Golf Bravo; 320: Fulgencio Batista/http://www.cubanology.com/Articles/Batista_the_Mafioso_and_Castro_the_Pimp.htm; 331: Checkpoint Charlie 1961-10-27/Author: National Archives; 349: HoChiMinhTrial1001/Stanley Karnow, Vietnam, A History, ISBN 0-670-74604-5; 354: MyLai Haeberle P33 BodiesNearBurningHouse/Author: Ronald Haeberle; 359 (top): Vietnamese refugees on US carrier, Operation Frequent Wind/http://www.okinawa.usmc.mil/; 363: Kennedy Nixon Debat/Images of American Political History/http://bill.ballpaul.net/iaph/main.php/Credit: National Park Service; 387 (top): Choeungek2 (square)/Author: Adam Carr; 391: Que digan dónde estan/Author: Pepe Robles; 406: Bundesarchiv Bild 183-1986-0416-418, Berlin, Michail Gorbatschow an der Mauer/Deutsches Bundesarchiv (German Federal Archive)/Author: Reiche, Hartmut; 408 (bottom): Evstafiev-afghan-apc-passes-russian/Author: Mikhail Evstafiev; 413: BrandenburgerTorDezember1989/Author: SSGT F. Lee Corkran; 416: 1991coup2 ST/Author: ST; 420: BosniaPeaceSigning/Author: BIGZ; 425: United93CrashSite May 06/Author: JoeyBLS; 427 (bottom) Poker Saddam Ace

Courtesy George W. Bush/White House Archives: 427 (top)

ADK 125-2
IRGENDWANN fallt jede